THE RISE OF BUCKNELL UNIVERSITY

The Rise of Bucknell University

J. ORIN OLIPHANT

APPLETON-CENTURY-CROFTS
Division of Meredith Publishing Company, New York

For information address the publisher,
Appleton-Century-Crofts,
Division of Meredith Publishing Company,
440 Park Avenue South, New York, N.Y. 10016
635-1

Library of Congress Card Number: 65-17600

PRINTED IN THE UNITED STATES OF AMERICA

TO

BUCKNELLIANS OF ALL TIMES

Those of Long Ago: *in memoriam*
Those of My Time: *ave atque vale*
Those in Years to Come: *ad astra per aspera*

Contents

Illustrations

Foreword

This is not the first effort to write what is called, in language as common as it is imprecise, a complete history of Bucknell University. The first general history of this institution, entitled the *Centennial History of Bucknell University,* was written by a former colleague of mine, the late Lewis Edwin Theiss, B. U. '02, and was published in 1946. For the breaking of ground that Dr. Theiss did for those who would follow him in such an endeavor, I wish here to express my gratitude.

In this book I have endeavored to tell in brief compass the story of the rise of an educational institution which was founded, hopefully, to become a university, but which, at least until 1961, remained a college miscalled a university. Yet it has risen—risen remarkably high in recent times; and the end thereof, presumably, is not yet. The nature and extent of this rise it is the purpose of this book to reveal.

The way of Bucknell University has not been easy. In times gone by Bucknell has kept the long years through a continuing rendezvous with poverty; more than once it has been compelled to grope, fearfully and painfully, in the valley of dark shadows. Yet it has never been without faithful friends; in times of its greatest crises, it has been saved by friends as able as they were generous, as courageous as they were self-sacrificing. From its experience with frugality and adversity, Bucknell has acquired considerable institutional vitality. Accordingly, to those whose moments of despondency might give rise to doubts about its future, I would say, clearly and in good conscience: *sursum corda.* This, I think, is the lesson which this book should teach.

In writing this book I have incurred numerous debts—some to institutions and others to individuals. Most of these debts I can never hope to repay, but my obligations to a few institutions and to a few persons I am unwilling to pass by with a general acknowledgment of my gratitude. I am especially thankful for courtesies shown me by Colgate University, by the American Baptist Historical Society, by the Crozer Theological Seminary, and by the Library of Congress; and I am grateful beyond measure to those members of the administrative staff and of the staff of the Ellen Clarke Bertrand Library who have put at my disposal all the records of Bucknell University. To a few persons my debt is extraordinarily great: to Dr. Arnaud C. Marts, a former president of Bucknell, for sharing with me information which otherwise I might not have obtained; to Miss Trennie

E. Eisley, director of public relations for Bucknell, for getting together the illustrations used in this book; to Mrs. Arthur Lewis, secretary to the president of Bucknell, for lending me materials in the files of recent presidents of the University; and to Mrs. Harold W. Hayden, the librarian in charge of the Archives of the University, for quickly "finding" many things that I needed. Lastly, to my good friends, Dr. Floyd G. Ballentine and Dr. Robert R. Gross, I owe much for their kindness in reading and criticizing the entire manuscript of this book.

J. Orin Oliphant

Lewisburg, Pennsylvania
Summer, 1964

THE RISE OF BUCKNELL UNIVERSITY

Part One

This Great Enterprise

1

Thy Kingdom Come

A quorum of members being present Mr. Wattson the Chairman then suggested . . . that . . . we . . . now devote some time in Prayer to divine Providence for the unparalleled success we have met with in this great enterprise, which suggestion was unanimously responded to.—*University at Lewisburg, Minutes of the Trustees, January 18, 1849.*

To the foregoing suggestion, made by a faithful Baptist, nine other equally faithful Baptists had responded. These ten men were trustees of a recently authorized Baptist University, and Thomas Wattson, of Philadelphia, was their chairman. Pursuant to a call for a special meeting, they had assembled at eleven o'clock, on the very cold morning of January 18, 1849, in the house of one of their group in Lewisburg, Pennsylvania. So momentous was the occasion, however, that, after a season of prayer, they adjourned their meeting until two in the afternoon.

The institution which these men had been selected to govern, chartered as the University at Lewisburg by the Commonwealth of Pennsylvania on February 5, 1846, is today called Bucknell University. No doubt to test the good faith and endurance of the Baptists of Pennsylvania, the charter granted to this institution required that, before its Board of Trustees could assume full corporate responsibility, there should be subscribed for the support of this enterprise the sum of $100,000. Consequently, for nearly three years Baptists in Pennsylvania had expended much labor and had offered many prayers in behalf of a state-wide campaign to obtain the needed subscriptions. This work was now completed; the test of fidelity had been passed; the Baptists of Pennsylvania had not been found wanting. The required sum of money being now subscribed, the Trustees were meeting, thankfully, to transact important business. What heretofore had been tentative and hesitant would now become permanent and legal, and thus the way would be more fully opened to the Baptists of Pennsylvania to participate effectively in the wondrous work of Christian benevolence that had become one of the glories of America. It was truly a great enterprise that had now been set on foot, an enterprise that seemingly enjoyed the favor of Divine Providence; but, as presently a good businessman, Thomas Wattson, would affirm, tactfully but pointedly, the continued prosperity of this enterprise would depend upon the "promptitude" of its "patrons and friends" in redeeming the pledges that they had made in its behalf.[1]

The University at Lewisburg was the product of various forces released in an expansive era of our national history. The immediate impetus to its founding, however, was the concern of some enterprising Baptists of Pennsylvania about the needs of their growing denomination in this state. These needs were as numerous as they were varied. Foremost among them was that of obtaining more educated Baptist ministers. The need was great for such ministers in Pennsylvania; the need was even greater for such ministers in the expanding American West; and the need, as many would have affirmed, was both great and urgent for such ministers in the ever-widening fields of Christian endeavor in far-distant lands. Everywhere, it seemed, fields were whitening to the harvest, but qualified Baptist workers to enter therein were wanting. Nor was this all. Besides the additional need for educated Baptist laymen for Christian work within and without the Baptist denomination, there was urgent need, as good Baptists could not help believing, for means to educate the children of Baptists not only under Christian influence, but also under Baptist auspices. Accordingly, the great enterprise that was beginning in Lewisburg was intended to be a great Baptist enterprise—of the Baptists, by the Baptists, but, happily, not exclusively for the Baptists. Others of good will and of good behavior would, in the spirit of Christian charity, be permitted to share the benefits of this new enterprise.

More remotely, the beginning of the University at Lewisburg will be found in the currents of thought and of emotion which, since the later years of the eighteenth century, had been giving form, especially in the Anglo-American community, to what may well be called a system of Christian benevolence. Like nearly all other Protestants of this community, American Baptists, in general, had accepted the thought which sustained this movement. Its central idea—an idea that was becoming widely diffused as early as the middle 1820's—was that, within a comparatively short time, the world by human means would, under God, be fully evangelized; [2] and widely accepted also by Protestant Americans at this time was another idea, equally significant to them—namely, that America, as successor to Great Britain, presently would be playing the leading part in the magnificent drama of universal conversion of the world to Christ. These ideas were accommodations of thought and feeling resulting from the interaction, during a generation or more, of rational and emotional forces which the eighteenth century had bequeathed to the nineteenth. From the eighteenth century had come not only the sentiment of humanitarianism which the Enlightenment had fostered, but also the sentiment of evangelicalism which, with the passing years, was intensified by revivals of religion in both Great Britain and the United States. From the interaction of these forces there emerged in the Anglo-American Protestant community a movement of Christian benevolence which, from the middle 1820's onward, rapidly rose to its zenith. This movement was, of course, a single but an important expression of a *weltanschauung*—co-extensive with Western Civilization—that had set enlightened men striving in a variety of ways to bring about the emancipation of mankind and the amelioration of the lot of the human race. In the United States, however, this *weltanschauung* was profoundly affected, especially during the second decade of the nineteenth century and after, by the upsurge of American cultural nationalism, which, thanks to one of its religious manifestations, presently joined the idea of universal evangelization to the American conception of an American national mission. As thus enlarged and exalted, the conception of their national mission unfolded to the view of Protestant Americans as a twofold conception—that is, on the one hand, of the mission of America to be an example of freedom and of democracy to the world, and, on the other hand, of the mission of America to assume, when American wealth and power should become greater than British wealth and power, the major responsibility for promoting the evangelization of peoples the world over.[3]

Thus conceived, the American mission was to Protestant Americans both a call and an opportunity—a call to them to help prepare America for the fulfillment of her divine mission, and an opportunity for them to share in the glory of being co-workers with God in ushering in the latter-day glory. As they looked about them and saw that the church was "waking from her slumbers," that benevolent enterprises were multiplying in their own country, and that America was growing in wealth and in power, they became impressed not only by the "peculiar favorableness of the present age for the success of Christian enterprise," but also by the certainty that their country was "destined . . . to outstrip all other nations, and to take [the] lead in the career of Christian philanthropy."[4] To prepare America for this mission was, of course, to make America completely Christian, a task of enormous magnitude when the Great Valley of the West was being rapidly peopled. Thus it fell out that, in the early decades of the nineteenth century, Protestant Americans were becoming as much concerned with home missions as with foreign missions. But all thoughtful Americans of that era perceived that the ultimate object of both home and foreign missions was the same: the conversion of the world to Protestant Christianity. America, they perceived, must be fully Christianized, not only for the sake of America, but also for the sake of the world. Here was work in plenty for a generation of men who were proud to be called Christians, patriots, and philanthropists.[5]

For Christians on the Atlantic coast of the United States during forty or more years immediately preceding the Civil War, the problem of Christianizing America was largely the problem of Christianizing the Great Valley of the Mississippi. It was this valley, destined as they firmly believed at no distant day to give law to their country, to which much of the home-missionary effort of that era was directed. Fearful of what would happen to the East, as well as to the political experiment to which the American people were committed, if a rising tide of barbarism compounded of ignorance, infidelity, insobriety, and Romanism were to rise so high as to flood the Atlantic seaboard, religious leaders in the East sounded loudly a call to action—a call which was repeated again and again—for Christians in the East to make over the West in the image of the East. Accordingly, in response to this call, there was effort in the East to send into the West preachers and teachers, to provide for distribution in the West of Bibles and religious tracts, and to support the founding throughout the West of Sunday Schools and churches, of primary schools and academies, of libraries and colleges. To carry out this program there was urgent need of educated men and women.[6]

By the opening of the 1830's the call to save the West had become sharp, shrill, and insistent. Of its many expressions, the one which follows is, perhaps, fairly representative:

> Let good and intelligent men at the East know, before the statement falls upon their ears, in a thunder-clap, that they are approaching a fearful crisis in the history of their country. They might now hope under God, could they be persuaded to put forth the mighty effort, to impress their own image on the forming mass of intelligence, which is filling the great western basin. . . . What they intend to do, must be quickly done. The mass on which they are to operate, now soft and impressible, is fast becoming hard and rigid. If they now choose indolently or selfishly to neglect the task, which demands their attention and their efforts, they may rest assured, that their children will heap curses on their memory, so weighty and so withering, as well nigh to break the slumbers of the grave. If the West is neglected, the East must perish. The destinies of the one and the other are intertwined together, and can be separated by no hand less powerful than Jehovah's.[7]

Those who responded to this call by supporting the societies for promoting the education of preachers and teachers for the West, as well as other agencies for diffusing the light of truth in the Great Valley and beyond, were not merely Christian philanthropists; they also were Christian patriots working for the salvation of their country, and thus for the speedy evangelization of the world. To them an unevangelized West meant an unevangelized America; to them an unevangelized America meant an unevangelized world. The matter was as simple as that.

Protestant Americans of that period were encouraged not only by the belief that God was inspiring them to prepare America for the fulfillment of her divine mission, but also by the belief that God was opening the way for America to fulfill this mission. To them there appeared to be good reason for their so thinking, for, wherever they looked abroad, they seemed to see a world in turmoil—proof to them that at last the prophecies were being fulfilled, proof beyond doubt that these were

> the times foretold by the prophets of old, when many shall run to and fro, and knowledge shall be increased; when wars shall cease unto the ends of the earth; when nation shall not lift up sword against nation, neither shall they learn war any more. And the times are at hand, when the knowledge of the Lord shall cover the earth as the waters cover the sea.[8]

Such "shaking" of the nations, they also believed, was God's way of preparing them to receive his pure gospel. As one of their spokesman, summing up their thought on this subject, remarked:

> The world is tired of paganism, tired of infidelity, tired of the multiform corruptions of Christianity,—nothing will avail to alleviate its uneasiness, but the pure religion of Jesus Christ. The field of Christian enterprise is the world, and that world is literally white for the harvest.[9]

Or, if we turn to the Presbyterian interpretation of the "signs of the times" as recorded in the "Narrative of the State of Religion within the Bounds of the Presbyterian Church in the United States" in May, 1831, we read that

> The revolutions taking place upon the Eastern Continent and the power of God there manifested in overthrowing the thrones of kings, wresting the sceptre from the hands of princes, causing the long oppressed to breathe the air of freedom, humbling the crescent of the false Prophet, entering the encroachments of the man of sin and scattering his devoted hosts, give encouragement that the day of the world's redemption is rapidly

approaching. The Lord is shaking terribly the earth and overturning the nations to prepare the way for Him whose right it is to reign.[10]

Stirred by so grand a vision of the destiny of their nation, and impelled to act by a sense of great urgency, Protestant Americans during the later years of the 1820's acquired the zeal of crusaders for righteousness. The faith that produced and sustained this zeal was briefly but effectively summed up in Philadelphia, in June, 1830, by a group of distinguished American clergymen, who spoke as follows:

> That it is God's purpose to convert the world; that the church is his chosen instrument for accomplishing this purpose; that the church must accomplish it by missionary operations; and that the period of its accomplishment is fast approaching—[these] are things most surely believed among us. If our nation should be completely evangelized, the conversion of the world would follow, perhaps speedily, and no nation under heaven presents a field so white to the harvest; or that with equal ease may, by the divine blessing, be entirely subjected to Christ's dominion.[11]

This affirmation, although it was made as a part of an appeal for the enlargement of home-missionary effort in the United States, is significant not only because it reveals the relation of such effort to the ultimate purpose of foreign-missionary effort, but also because it affirms the conviction of Protestant Americans of that era that the way of world-wide conversion passed through the United States of America. It was the conviction that the fulfillment of God's purposes depended, in large part, upon the efforts of Protestant Americans—a conviction expressed again and again as the 1820's were yielding to the 1830's—which provided the principal emotional springs of action for the many-sided religious-humanitarian crusade for the reformation of America during the three decades immediately preceding our Civil War—a crusade which, in more than one of its aspects, profoundly affected the course of American history. In part as agencies to help promote this crusade for righteousness, numerous church-related colleges were founded in the United States between 1830 and 1860, one of them being the University at Lewisburg, Pennsylvania.[11a]

The means by which the grand object of Protestant Christian benevolence was to be achieved were the labor, the wealth, and the prayers of Christians united principally in voluntary associations. The idea of voluntary association, like many other ideas that have shaped our culture, had come to us from Great Britain, the country in which, broadly speaking, the modern Protestant missionary movement had its beginning with the formation in 1792 of the English Baptist Missionary Society.

Between 1792 and 1804 other important British benevolent societies—missionary, tract, and Bible—were formed, and these societies not only laid substantially the structural foundation of the modern missionary movement in Great Britain; they also served as models for similar societies or associations on the continent of Europe and, more importantly, in the United States of America. Before the end of the 1790's, small missionary societies had begun to appear in the United States, and in 1808 the first Bible society in the United States was formed in Philadelphia. Presently also there appeared in the United States tract and Sunday School societies—in fact, there arose an American counterpart of virtually every British benevolent society; and many of the early American benevolent societies received generous subsidies from British Protestant Christians.[12]

Through the organizations that constituted the American part of the system of Christian benevolence, American Protestant Christians were, in the period under consideration, applying all the enginery of Protestantism for the diffusion of Christian knowledge. By their efforts Bibles were being distributed, Sunday Schools were being established, church-related colleges were being founded, a Christian literature was being created and diffused, and, ordinarily as beneficiaries of Education Societies, Christian ministers were being educated and then sent into service at home or abroad. Through many long years, as presently we shall see, not a few preministerial students in the University at Lewisburg were beneficiaries of the Pennsylvania Baptist Education Society.[13]

From 1810 forward, thanks to the pervasive influence of American nationalism, the process of integrating American local benevolent societies into national societies proceeded rapidly. In 1810 there appeared the American Board of Commissioners for Foreign Missions, in 1815 the American Education Society, in 1816 the American Bible Society and the American Colonization Society, in 1824 the American Sunday School Union, and in 1825 the American Tract Society—to mention only the most important ones. Paralleling these societies, which were interdenominational, were American denominational missionary societies formed on a nationwide basis, such as that of the Baptists in 1814, that of the Methodists in 1819, and that of the Episcopalians in 1820.[14] By the middle 1820's national benevolent societies had become so significant for American life that a patriotic American writer in that year could affirm that they were "the glory of the land." Our national societies, he averred, "designed to promote the general diffusion of virtue, . . . claim the attention of the patriot and the Christian. . . . They are a stronger bond of union than any other. Our beloved and revered Constitution, that stands forth the unrivalled monument of wisdom, does not bind together the inhabitants of this extended country, like her benevolent institutions." [15]

All these societies, of course, needed money to carry on their operations, and to maintain a fairly steady flow of money into their respective treasuries they resorted, early in the history of their activities, to a practice called agency. Presently the agent became an important officer in the administrative organization of each of them. His was the task of traveling far and wide to explain the objects of the society that he represented, to help form auxiliary societies, to fill pulpits on special occasions, to attend concerts of prayer, to address anniversary meetings, and to propose resolutions for adoption by such organizations as could influence people to contribute labor, money, and prayers for the cause that he was serving. The agents of benevolent societies were, in brief, forerunners of later publicity agents and of present-day directors of development. As soon we shall learn, agents played in the history of the University at Lewisburg a role as significant as they played in the history of any other benevolent or eleemosynary institution.

The American system of Christian benevolence that was thus taking form was, of course, a part of an international system—largely but not wholly Anglo-American—that was vitally concerned with the task of winning the world for Protestant Christianity. Between British Protestant Christians and American Protestant Christians, as between British Protestant Christians and European Protestant Christians, there had been before 1826 (to use an arbitrary date), as there would be during many years thereafter, effective co-operation for the extension of Christian truth. Before 1826 Americans helped to support in India a missionary enterprise of English Baptists; before 1826 missionaries trained in Basle or in Berlin had served British as well as Dutch missionary societies; before 1826 missionary writings had moved freely across the English Channel and across the Atlantic Ocean; and before 1826 British money had helped to sustain Christian benevolence in both Europe and America. Wherever it spread, the movement of Christian benevolence had a truly popular appeal. It enlisted, besides the efforts of men, the efforts of both women and children; it derived support from the pounds and the dollars of the wealthy and from the pence and the pennies of the poor.[16]

As the use of voluntary association was a principal physical means, so also was the use of voluntary association for the offering of prayer a principal spiritual means, of promoting Christian benevolent enterprises. For the success of Christian benevolence Protestant Christians, in Europe as in America, established the monthly concert of prayer. In the United States, moreover, the general concert of prayer came in time to be supplemented by specialized monthly concerts in which prayers were offered for the success of particular objects of Christian endeavor. Moreover, an annual day of prayer for colleges had been established in the United States long years before the founding of the University at Lewisburg in 1846, and after that year it was widely observed in American churches and in American colleges through at least the remaining years of the nineteenth century. But wherever they were offered, whether in America, in Great Britain, or in Europe, such concerts of prayer, whether for a general or for a specific object, were offered not merely for the success of American, or British, or European efforts; such prayers, wherever offered, were offered for the success of all efforts that would promote the triumph of the great cause. American Protestant Christians did not permit even their exuberant nationalism to submerge in their thought the international character of the movement of Christian benevolence. They believed that, even after American leadership had supplanted British leadership, American Protestant Christians and British Protestant Christians would continue to co-operate with each other, and with other Protestant Christians, in the movement to convert the world.[17]

Baptists, both British and American, had helped to create the various agencies that were promoting the varied objects of Christian beneficence. Baptists had been deep in the modern missionary movement from its beginning. To them the principle of voluntary association was no novelty; for them, indeed, it was a necessity. In Baptist polity the central principle is that a church, which is complete in itself, is a voluntary association of baptized believers. A Baptist congregation recognizes no ecclesiastical authority higher than itself. Relatively early, however, Baptist churches had adopted the practice of forming regional organizations of churches called associations. But such associations had never been given, and such associations do not now possess, ecclesiastical authority. Their purpose has been otherwise. They have been used for the encouragement of church fellowship, for the interchange of religious views, and for the furtherance of missionary endeavors. The desire of Baptists for denominational coherence and their determination to participate effectively in an expanding system of Christian benevolence, however, persuaded them eventually to bring into being larger associations as agencies for collecting money and for dispensing Christian charity. By means of a loosely integrated system of such voluntary organizations, the American Baptists presently acquired a remarkable semblance of denominational coherence. In addition to their traditional regional associations, they formed state conventions for missionary purposes, and, even before their state conventions had begun to appear, they had set on foot, as we have seen, a movement of national organization that grew stronger with the passing years. Their national convention for foreign missions dated from 1814, their national publication society from 1824, and their national home missionary society from 1832. As late as the decade of the 1840's, however, the American Baptists had no national educational society; but much earlier than this decade they had begun the forming of state or regional educational societies that used their means for the furtherance of ministerial education.

Baptists in Pennsylvania, those of the Philadelphia Association perhaps excepted, had been somewhat backward in the matter of joining and supporting the various agencies that were promoting Christian benevolence. Baptists of neighboring states had by their generosity put Baptists of Pennsylvania to shame. As late as 1845, for example, there was no Baptist institution of higher learning in Pennsylvania for the education of ministers. In New York, as early as 1819, the Baptist Education Society of the State of New York had founded the Hamilton Literary and Theological Institution (now Colgate University). Two years later the Congress of the United States had chartered in the District of Columbia a Baptist Institution, Columbian College (now George Washington University), which had for its first president Dr. William Staughton, a Philadelphia Baptist minister who had been giving instruction in Philadelphia to a few candidates for the Baptist ministry. Dr. Staughton's incipient seminary, recognized in 1817 by the Baptist Triennial Convention as its theological department, was transferred in 1821 to the District of Columbia to become the Department of Theology in Columbian College. Ten years later the Ohio Baptist Education Society had founded, in 1831, in Granville, in the state of Ohio, a literary and theological institution (now Denison University).[18] But as late as the middle 1840's there was no similar institution in Pennsylvania. Why should young Baptists of Pennsylvania be required to leave their state in order to prepare themselves for the Christian ministry? Why should the money of Pennsylvania Baptists be expended in support of Baptist institutions in other states? More to the point, what was wrong with the Baptists of Pennsylvania? To some Baptists in Pennsylvania, these were questions as disturbing as they were pertinent.

From whatever position the problem may have been viewed, it should have seemed obvious then, as it seems obvious now, that the first Baptist institution of higher learning in Pennsylvania should be established within the bounds of the Philadelphia Baptist Association. Not only was there a concentration of Baptist strength in Philadelphia and its vicinity; there was also in this area a concentration of Baptist prestige derived from a record of long and creditable achievement. The Philadelphia Baptist Association, founded in the year 1707, was the mother of American Baptist associations. With matriarchal complacency, therefore, if not always with maternal pride, the Philadelphia Association could look out upon a numerous and widely dispersed brood. By no forced thinking or forced construction of language were such associations to be thought of as her offspring, for the bounds of the Philadelphia Association had once extended from Connecticut to Virginia, and from this association there had gone forth in past years zealous ministers to gather on our remote frontiers Baptist churches which subsequently united to form new associations. Moreover, it was in this venerable association that the "design of founding" the Baptist College of Rhode Island (now Brown University) had originated.[19] Directly or indirectly, Baptist churches everywhere in America owed much to the Philadelphia Baptist Association. Here, then, if anywhere in Pennsylvania, there should have arisen an institution that would have as one of its major concerns the education of Baptist ministers, and here indeed, during the decade of the 1830's, a serious effort was made to establish such an institution.

In 1832, the Philadelphia Association referred to its board of trustees a proposal that it establish a manual-labor school on a farm recently bequeathed to it.[20] A year later the board reported that, having decided that the farm was an unsuitable place for such an institution, it had purchased an estate at Haddington, four miles west of Philadelphia, and had made arrangements for the opening of a school thereon during the month of October, 1833. The association approved the action that its board had taken, appointed a board of trustees for the Haddington Institution, and directed its clerk to invite each association in Pennsylvania that was in correspondence with the Philadelphia Association to appoint one of its "judicious" members to serve as a trustee of this institution; and it made known the fact that young men who were not candidates for the ministry could receive either an English or a classical education at the Haddington Institution.[21] In October, 1834, the directors of the Haddington Institution reported to the Philadelphia Association that their institution was flourishing, having between forty and fifty students, a president and three other professors, and a principal of the English department.[22] This institution completed its first academic year on July 30, 1834, with an examination and a public exhibition.[23]

As a further means of broadening the support for this enterprise, the Philadelphia Association, responding to a suggestion from a committee of Baptists in New Jersey, issued a call on October 9, 1834, to the Baptist Churches in the Middle States to send two delegates from each church to a convention which would meet on the first Wednesday in December, 1834, in the Sansom Street Church in Philadelphia. The purpose of this convention would be to consider the "general system of Education."[24]

The convention met pursuant to the call. After it had been organized, and a season of prayer had been held, the chairman told the delegates that the important matter of ministerial education was the "subject before the Convention." Accordingly, the minister of the Great Valley Church of the Philadelphia Association proposed that the convention "organize a Baptist Education Society for the Central States, for the purpose of establishing a Baptist Theological Seminary, and providing means for its support." This proposal raised a troublesome and controversial issue, for, whereas there was unanimous agreement that a Central Baptist Education Society should be formed, there was no such agreement about *establishing* either a "theological seminary" or a "literary and theological seminary." On this issue hung the question of adopting or of by-passing the Haddington Institution. A motion that the convention adopt a literary and theological institution was defeated. Thereupon the president of the Haddington Institution proposed that the convention vote to "sustain a suitable Institution" for providing an adequate education for "pious young men of the Baptist denomination" who wished to enter the gospel ministry. Immediately this motion was amended to read "establish and sustain," but action on the amended motion was deferred. Subsequently a proposed constitution for a society was reported, but, in stating the purposes of the society, it made no provision for recognizing "a literary department, distinct from the theological course." But an amendment proposing that a theological institution should be the "prominent" object of the society—but that one having a distinct literary department would be acceptable—received "a very unexpected and unanimous concurrence." [25]

The main difficulty had now been resolved; the motion to "establish and sustain a suitable Institution" was voted down, and, in the spirit of good neighborhood, the convention made a concession to the brethren of New Jersey by voting unanimously to recommend "to the confidence and support of the Baptist public" a Classical Institution then in progress in Plainfield, New Jersey. The constitution of the Central Baptist Education Society was then approved, and, before adjourning, the convention voted unanimously "That the Board of Directors, when appointed, be instructed to enter into negociation with the Trustees of the Philadelphia Association for the transfer to this Society of the Haddington Institution, upon such terms as shall secure purity of doctrine, the interests of the Philadelphia Association, and the objects of the Society now constituted." The convention appeared to have been highly successful not only for the Haddington Institution, but also for the Baptist denomination in the Middle Atlantic States. It elected officers and a board of directors, it made arrangements to distribute two thousand copies of its minutes and of the constitution that it had adopted, and it agreed that the Central Baptist Education Society should hold its first meeting on the second Tuesday of June, 1835, in the New Market Street Baptist Church in Philadelphia. In a note appended to the minutes, the clerk expressed the view that the "whole Session of the Convention was characterized by unusual Christian unanimity and affection; and [that] the result was such as had long been prayed for, and most ardently desired." [26]

But soon something went wrong. The educational efforts of Baptists in the Middle Atlantic States did not become unified in the Haddington Institution, perhaps because "the interests of the Philadelphia Association" could not be harmonized with the interests and ambitions of other Baptist associations. Before May 27, 1835, the Central Baptist Education Society was giving its support to a new institution in Burlington, New Jersey.[27] By 1836, according to the *Triennial Baptist Register,* this institution was housed in buildings formerly occupied by an academy on a campus of about six acres. It had an enrollment of about forty in its literary department and of about twelve in its theological department. Also, it had a library of about eight hundred volumes, and it had an extensive philosophical apparatus. The program of studies that it was offering consisted, besides lectures on chemistry and on natural philosophy, of the "various branches of English Literature, Mathematics, Latin, Greek, Hebrew, French and Spanish languages, together with the studies which usually form a Theological course in the other Theological Institutions of the denomination." To those who were working and praying for its prosperity, it may well have appeared, as one writer hoped, that from it would soon issue "streams which will make glad the city of God." [28]

Nor did the Philadelphia Baptist Association receive much support for the Haddington Institution from other Baptist associations in Pennsylvania. More especially did it fail to receive the support of the strong and neighboring Central Union Association of Independent Baptist Churches. This last-named association, meeting in its second session in May, 1834, was told by its committee on education that it was "high time that something effectual should be done to give encouragement and ensure success to those worthy though indigent young brethren" who were desirous of studying for the ministry. Hopefully, the committee called attention to the cherished belief that the Haddington Institution might become not only a "rallying point" for the Baptists of Pennsylvania, but also a fountain from which would flow waters of "Biblical theology" that would irrigate "the dry and barren soil of Pennsylvania, and make glad the churches of the living God." Despite its fear that, because of financial embarrassment, this institution might be delayed in achieving its purpose, the committee, affirming that in union there would be strength, recommended, and the association adopted, resolutions directing the executive committee of the association to make to the directors of the Haddington Institution proposals of co-operation "on just and equitable principles," and, if such proposals were rejected, directing this committee "to adopt immediate and efficient measures" to obtain for their young brethren the privileges that they were seeking.[29]

A year later this committee reported that, having failed to obtain "equal participation" in the "privileges and direction" of the Haddington Institution, it had acquired a site at Holmesburg, and there for several months had maintained a school. It recommended, however, the new seminary at Burlington, New Jersey, "as one likely to afford . . . candidates for the ministry the best preparations, in the shortest time." Having voted to accept this report, the Central Union Association, in 1835, passed a resolution recommending the Burlington Institution "to the patronage and liberality of the churches." [30] Thus ended the incipient school at Holmesburg. On May 31, 1836, the managers of this institution, calling attention to the establishment of a Baptist Literary and Theological Institution in Burlington, resolved that thenceforth their attention should be given exclusively "to the great concern of promoting the spread of the Gospel, the growth and support of weak Churches, and the missionary cause in general, at home and abroad." [31]

The Burlington Institution had what appears to have been a very short career. In September, 1835, a committee of the New Jersey Baptist Association, after visiting the Burlington Institution, had recommended "most cordially" this institution "to the Baptist community and to their fellow citizens of the middle states generally." [32] More than a year later the New Jersey Baptist State Convention, on November 2, 1836, "earnestly" recommended this institution to the Baptists of New Jersey.[33] In 1837, however, this same convention, expressing a deep interest in the important subject of ministerial education, called a convention for the purpose of adopting "measures for the promotion of that object." The result was the formation of the New Jersey Baptist Education Society.[34] On November 7, 1839, this society warmly endorsed the Hamilton Literary and Theological Institution "as admirably adapted to the wants of the rising ministry," and the next day the New Jersey Baptist State Convention resolved that the Hamilton Literary and Theological Institution was "worthy of the confidence and patronage of the Churches" of New Jersey.[35] Two months earlier the New Jersey Baptist Association, affirming that no means existed within the bounds of the New Jersey Baptist Education Society of giving the instruction needed by Baptist young men called to the ministry, urged that advantage be taken of "the liberal proposition of the brethren of Hamilton" for receiving beneficiaries of the New Jersey Baptist Education Society.[36] Consequently, it appears that the Burlington Institution had gone the way that the Haddington College would later take, and that the interstate Central Baptist Education Society had been overwhelmed by the force of separatism that had given rise, on the one hand, to the New Jersey Baptist Education Society, and, on the other hand, to the Pennsylvania Baptist Education Society, which had been formed in 1839.

Despite lack of support from the Central Baptist Education Society and from the Union Central Association, the Haddington Institution, chartered as a college on March 31, 1836, was reported during the middle years of the 1830's to be in a prosperous condition.[37] Its charter created "a college for the purpose of educating youth in the English, learned and foreign languages, the liberal arts, sciences and literature, the style and the title of which shall be 'The Haddington College, in the county of Philadelphia.' " It designated temporary trustees, declared them and their successors to be "one body corporate and politic," to have "perpetual succession," and to be vested with authority needed to govern a college. It provided for a faculty consisting of a president, masters, and tutors, and it authorized the faculty, with the approval of the trustees, to grant degrees in the liberal arts and sciences.[38] Later in the year 1836 it was advertised as an institution designed by its founders to inculcate principles of morality and religion and to afford an opportunity "to pious young men to obtain such an education as would prepare them for future usefulness." Its course of instruction was divided into four departments—Primary, Academical (consisting of a classical division and a scientific division), Collegiate, and Theological. Its faculty consisted of a president and two other professors, with one professorship vacant. The cost of tuition per annum was forty dollars. The number of students in the Collegiate Department was *about* sixty, and in the Theological Department, *about* fifteen.[39]

Here, then, was a not untypical American college of that era, and, with adequate support, it might have grown and prospered. But it was poorly supported, and by the autumn of 1836 there was serious talk of its being removed to the "interesting village of Germantown." [40] By October, 1837, it had been removed to Germantown, and the Philadelphia Association was enthusiastically commending the "Germantown Collegiate Institution" to the churches of this association and to other Baptists of the Middle Atlantic States.[41] A year later it gave this institution a similar endorsement, but, in October, 1839, making no mention of the Germantown College, it commended to its member churches the Hamilton Literary and Theological Institution, urging them to foster this institution by contributing liberally for the support of ministerial students therein, and recommending that they use the recently formed Philadelphia Baptist Education Society (soon to become the Pennsylvania Baptist Education Society) as the "medium through which their contributions shall pass." [42] In these recommendations we can all but hear the crash of the collapsing Haddington College.

Thus by 1839 the Baptists of the Philadelphia Association and of the Central Union Association, as well as the Baptists of New Jersey, were obliged to derive what comfort they could from the fact that, thanks to their unwillingness to co-operate with one another, they had raised up, and then ruined, two potential Baptist colleges, not to mention the temporary school at Holmesburg. In respect to an institution for educating Baptist ministers, the Philadelphia Baptist Association and the New Jersey State Baptist Convention were apparently agreed, in that year of remorseful reflection, on only one point—namely, that the Baptist churches in their respective jurisdictions should be liberal in their support of the Hamilton Literary and Theological Institution; and in that year, understandably, the Baptists of the Central Union Association were saying nothing about an institution for the education of ministers. Ironically, the consequence of the internal dissensions and associational rivalries of Baptists in Pennsylvania and New Jersey was revealed, perhaps inadvertently, in 1842 by a Baptist of New York, who, presumably not with tongue in cheek, wrote of this situation as follows: "A much larger territory than our own state, is at present dependent on this institution [the Hamilton Literary and Theological Institution] for the means of ministerial education. Since the discontinuance of the schools at Haddington, Holmesburgh and Burlington, the Education Societies of New Jersey and Pennsylvania have sent hither their young brethren preparing for the sacred work." [43] By this time it may well have appeared to Baptists in the Middle Atlantic States that there was rising in Hamilton, New York, an institution of higher learning which, in good time, would serve them as well as Brown University had served through long years the Baptists of New England.

The Hamilton Literary and Theological Institution, founded by the Baptist Education Society of the State of New York pursuant to its charter of March 5, 1819, was formally opened in the spring of 1820. Its program of instruction was enlarged as the years passed by, but it was not until the academic year 1837–38 that its three departments—Theological, Collegiate, and Academic—were fully developed. Two years later it opened its doors to lay students, its sole concern theretofore having been the education of men for the gospel ministry. For this purpose it drew numerous students from other states as well as from the state of New York.[44] As early as 1823 it received the undivided support of what might have become a rival institution in the city of New York—the New York Baptist Theological Seminary. This institution was begun in 1813 by the formation of a group to assist the work of instruction in theology that the Reverend Dr. William Staughton was giving in Philadelphia. Subsequently it was incorporated and acquired a board of trustees and a faculty of its own, but, after its agreement in 1823 to aid the institution in Hamilton, it functioned only as a society to aid ministerial students.[45] Regardless of the service that it was rendering, the institution in Hamilton, as long as it operated under the charter of the Baptist Education Society of the State of New York, was not empowered to grant degrees. By an arrangement made near the middle of the 1830's, the Columbian College in the District of Columbia agreed to award degrees to such students at Hamilton as completed a full collegiate course.[46] The power to grant degrees the Hamilton Literary and Theological Institution acquired when it was chartered as Madison University on March 26, 1846.[47] As we soon shall see, the influence of this institution on the founding and early development of the University at Lewisburg was considerable.

In a renewed effort to establish an educational institution within its own bounds, the Philadelphia Baptist Association, in 1841, had appointed a committee and had authorized it not only to inquire into the expediency of establishing within the jurisdiction of this association "a primary School for ministerial education," but also, if it seemed advisable so to do, to take appropriate measures to establish such an institution.[48] A year later this committee, in a report wherein feelings of remorse mingled with a sense of injured pride, asserted the need for such an institution, reviewed the honorable record of the Philadelphia Baptist Association, and declared that the committee had taken no steps toward the establishment of such an institution. Its recommendation that a "primary School for ministerial education" be established under the care of the association "as soon as practicable" was a pathetic confession of helplessness in the face of a situation that seemingly had become an impossible one.[49] Whatever the reasons therefor may have been, the Philadelphia Baptist Association had not succeeded in uniting the Baptists of New Jersey and the Baptists of Pennsylvania in support of a Baptist institution of higher learning in either New Jersey or Pennsylvania. On the contrary, it appears to have succeeded in uniting many Baptists of both these states in support of such an institution in the state of New York.

The second failure of the Philadelphia Association to establish an educational institution in the neighborhood of Philadelphia opened wide the way to courageous men of other Baptist associations of Pennsylvania to attempt to establish elsewhere in this state a college under the auspices of Baptists. Soon such an attempt was made by dedicated Baptists in the interior of Pennsylvania, near the point where the West Branch and the North Branch of the Susquehanna River come together. This territory lay within the bounds of the Northumberland Baptist Association. Here there were no large cities; here there was no great accumulation of wealth; and here the number of Baptists was not large. For the Baptists, indeed, much of this territory was missionary ground, and here, of course, the need for Baptist ministers was as great as it was urgent.

As early as 1832, the Northumberland Baptist Association had approved a proposal to establish, "in the interior of this Commonwealth," an educational institution, the purpose of which would be not only to provide educational opportunity for the sons of Baptists generally, but also to make available literary and theological facilities to those who should be called to preach. What was specifically proposed was the establishment of a manual-labor academy.[50] But nothing came of this proposal, for the Northumberland Association gave right of way to a more ambitious educational program that was soon to get under way within the bounds of the Philadelphia Association. It may well be, however, that the idea of establishing an educational institution within the bounds of the Northumberland Association was not forgotten. However that may be, the Northumberland Association gave its support to the Haddington Institution as long as it was feasible for it to do so, and then, like other Baptist associations in Pennsylvania and New Jersey, began giving its support to the Literary and Theological Institution in Hamilton, New York.[51]

During the years that Baptists in the Northumberland Association seemed obligated to support Haddington, and even after those years, some of them, conscious of their own need, carried on a campaign in behalf of ministerial education. As early as 1836 this association appointed an associational committee on ministerial education, and before long it was supporting two young men who, as students in the Hamilton Literary and Theological Institution, were preparing themselves for the gospel ministry.[52] In 1841 this association became an auxiliary of the Pennsylvania Baptist Education Society.[53] But because the Baptist denomination was growing in Pennsylvania, in the Northumberland Association as elsewhere, at least some of the leaders in the Northumberland Association became keenly aware of the need for educating Baptist ministers for service in Pennsylvania. From year to year the subject of ministerial education was before the association, in reports of the committee on education and in resolutions commending the Hamilton Literary and Theological Institution. On August 17, 1843, the committee on education reported that two young brethren in the association were desirous of studying for the ministry but could not do so because of lack of money, and it urged the churches of this association to adopt the Pennsylvania Baptist Education Society "as one of the great objects of their benevolent action." [54] One year later this committee complained that, whereas Baptists in New Jersey were generous in their support of ministerial education, Baptists in the Northumberland Association were manifesting little interest in that cause, and it called attention to the fact that there were within the association persons who were eager but who were unable, because of lack of money, to begin a course of study leading to the ministry.[55]

The agitation in the Northumberland Association for better support of ministerial education reached a climax in the summer of 1845 when, during the annual session of that year, the Reverend Joel E. Bradley, minister of the Baptist Churches in Milton and in Lewisburg, reported on August 14 as chairman of the associational committee on education. After saying that Pennsylvania presented "a large field" for ministerial labor, and that young men were waiting to enter upon preparation for labor in that field, provided that means were available for them to do so, he concluded his report with these words:

> Your committee have endeavored to discover the cause of the lamentable lethargy on this subject which seems to pervade the Pennsylvania Churches, and are inclined to ascribe it, in great part, to the facts, that our literary institutions are in other States, and that young men educated elsewhere cannot act as efficiently upon the population of our State as could those educated among us. The establishment of an Institution in our midst is absolutely necessary, in order to bring out the strength of our denomination in Pennsylvania. Your Committee therefore earnestly recommend to this Association the adoption of measures for the establishment of a Literary and Theological Institution in this State.[56]

Moved to action by this appeal, the Northumberland Association thereupon resolved that a committee of five be appointed to report in the afternoon of that day "on the propriety of forming a Literary and Theological Seminary in central Pennsylvania," and that this committee consist of Charles Tucker, Dr. William H. Ludwig, Joel E. Bradley, J. Green Miles, and James Moore, Sr. Pursuant to instructions, this committee, by its chairman, Dr. Ludwig, duly reported, and the association at once accepted, a series of resolutions, one of which affirmed the desirability of establishing in central Pennsylvania a literary institution of high order, "embracing a high school for male pupils, another for females, a college, and also a theological Institution, to be under the influence of the Baptist denomination." The other resolutions provided for the continuance of this committee for the purpose of bringing this object to the attention of the appropriate Baptist organizations in Pennsylvania, and, if it seemed feasible to do so, of adopting and presenting at the next annual meeting of the Northumberland Association such other measures as the committee might think appropriate to accomplish this object.[57]

Thus, once again, a group of Baptists in Pennsylvania had proposed to set on foot a project for a Baptist institution of higher learning in their state. What came of this effort the following chapters are intended to tell. Here it remains to say that, a year later, Dr. Ludwig, serving as moderator of the session of the Northumberland Baptist Association in 1846, signed the "Corresponding Letter" of this association for that year, and in this letter, addressed to the different bodies with which the Northumberland Association corresponded, is expressed the wish to commend "the University at Lewisburg, for which a Charter has been granted by the Legislature of this State, to take effect when $100,000 shall have been secured," and through which they hoped that God would do much for them as "a denomination of Christians." Accompanying this wish, and no doubt expected to be realized in part by the newly chartered University, was the further wish "to see the cause of God, the honour and glory of the Redeemer's Kingdom promoted in all our bounds, and spreading far and wide until the Kingdoms of this world shall become the Kingdoms of our Lord and his Christ." [58]

2

The First Years

Unite; and in the wisdom and strength which God has given you, rise and build.—*Stephen W. Taylor, in the Philadelphia Christian Chronicle, December 9, 1846.*

The past history of the University is associated at every step with that of Professor Taylor. Faithfully and efficiently has he laboured in its service, and to him, under God, it owes in no small degree, its present prosperity.—*University at Lewisburg, Minutes of the Trustees, August 21, 1851.*

Pursuant to instructions, Dr. William H. Ludwig, speaking for the committee on a literary and theological institution, made a report to the Northumberland Baptist Association on August 13, 1846. It was a report of progress beyond his "most sanguine expectations," but the progress, which he did not describe, had been made, not by his committee, but by a State Association that had done what his committee had been appointed to do.[1] More enlightening on this matter is the report of the associational committee on ministerial education that the Reverend Joel E. Bradley had presented earlier that day, a report which reaffirmed and lamented the backwardness of the Baptists of Pennsylvania in respect to ministerial education in past years, but which also expressed the belief that some recent happenings seemed to indicate that something "worthy of the state" was on the "eve of accomplishment"; and the report concluded by asking for a resolution declaring it to be the duty of every Baptist in the association to do what he could to put "upon a solid and permanent basis" the recently chartered University at Lewisburg. This resolution the association adopted.[2]

Of the Association that had taken over the work of the above-named committee, we have no precise knowledge, for its records, if it kept any, are not now available. We do know, however, that Joel E. Bradley was its corresponding secretary, and that Eugenio Kincaid,[2a] a Baptist missionary to Burma then on leave in the United States, was a member of it, as were also a few well-to-do Baptist laymen within the bounds of the Northumberland Association. Among these were Dr. Ludwig, James Moore, Joseph Meixell, Samuel Wolfe, George F. Miller, and James Moore, Jr.[3] Moreover, we are fairly certain that this organization was named the Baptist Literary Association of Pennsylvania; that the number of its members was small, consisting, at least for the most part, of men residing in or near the borough of Lewisburg; and that these men, earnest in their desire to promote the work of God through an educational institution of the highest order, were uncertain, because of their inexperience and lack of prominence, about what they should do. By avoiding mistakes which theretofore had kept the Baptists of Pennsylvania divided, they hoped now to unite these people in support of an educational institution in a part of Pennsylvania which, as they firmly believed, the Baptists should lose no time in occupying.[4]

While the members of this association were still pondering such matters, word came to them that Professor Stephen William Taylor, who had long been a member of the faculty of the Literary and Theological Institution in Hamilton, New York, had recently resigned his professorship in that institution, and would probably seek a position somewhere in the West.[5] Through Eugenio Kincaid and Joel E. Bradley, they got in touch with Taylor and told him that their object was to found in central Pennsylvania an educational institution of the highest quality, that they wished to get started right away, and that they so much desired Taylor's advice that they were willing to pay the cost of his journey to Lewisburg in the hope that they could persuade him to join them in this enterprise. Taylor visited Lewisburg, and on December 8, 1845, he was appointed general agent of this association, a position which was to continue until the association should be superseded by an incorporated body. The men who had thus employed him Taylor found to be highly optimistic, believing that a university could be started *de novo* and be ready for the reception of students by the autumn of 1846. One of his undeclared duties would be that of disillusioning them on this subject.[6]

Stephen W. Taylor, now fifty-three years old, had acquired a long experience in educational work before he came to Lewisburg. He had been the valedictorian of his class in Hamilton College, Clinton, New York, in 1817. Thereafter he became principal of the academy in Lowville, New York, a position which he held until, in 1834, he became principal of the Academic Department in the Hamilton Literary and Theological Institution. Four years later he was made professor of mathematics and natural philosophy in this institution, and this position he held until he resigned it in 1845.[7] He brought to his new work in Lewisburg a broad experience, a deep piety, considerable learning, a vast deal of energy, and a stubborn determination that few men could match. What he did for the University at Lewisburg the sequel should show. It is not without interest to observe, however, that one of his perceptive colleagues in Lewisburg, who wrote in 1870, expressed the opinion that "without him it is almost certain that our University would never have existed." [8]

Taylor began his duties in Lewisburg on December 27, 1845. After he had pointed out to them the major difficulties that confronted them, his employers told him that they wished to proceed. Accordingly, Taylor soon discovered that, as general agent, he was expected to do many things. The general character of the proposed institution he must define, and he must draft a charter for it; for this institution he must prescribe a course of studies, select a list of textbooks, and prepare a code of by-laws; for it he must select the articles of a philosophical apparatus; and for it he must make up a list of books that its library would need.[9] Like Caesar in ancient Gaul, Professor Taylor must do all things, and, it seemed, he must do them all at once.

The place to which Taylor had come was not ideal as the site for a university, for, in the days before the coming of the railroads brought it relatively close to the large towns and cities of the East, Lewisburg, Pennsylvania, despite the fact of its being close to the geographical center of the state, was much more isolated than its inhabitants liked to believe. But by 1846 it had become an attractive and a prosperous little borough of some two thousand inhabitants.[10] It was situated at the mouth of Buffalo Creek in a thriving agricultural community, but it was not then a county seat. What is now Snyder County, Pennsylvania, was then a part of Union County, which had its seat of government in New Berlin, in the valley of Penn's Creek, beyond the ridge that separates this valley from Buffalo Valley. For transportation to the world beyond it, Lewisburg then depended upon the Susquehanna River, upon roads, and upon the canal which passed from Northumberland up the valley of the West Branch. But this canal, unfortunately for Lewisburg, lay east of this river, in Northumberland County. Nevertheless, Lewisburg had contrived, more than a decade before 1846, to become a canal port as well as a river port.[11] Its connection with the canal was achieved by a cross-cut, constructed by the state at considerable expense, that ran eastwardly from the river to the canal. But this cross-cut, valuable though it was, left something to be desired. That something the Catalogue of the University at Lewisburg for 1853–54 explained as follows: "Freight comes directly to the wharf [in Lewisburg] through a crosscut, but the Packet

Boats pass straight on through Milton, Williamsport, etc. Strangers, therefore, coming to the University by canal, should apprise some of the Faculty of the day, so that a carriage may be in waiting for them at the packet landing" [east of the river].[12] This handicap of isolation Lewisburg did not overcome, even relatively, until the coming of railroads into the valley of the West Branch in the later 1850's.

After it had been definitely decided by the Literary Association that Lewisburg should be the site of the proposed University, Taylor proceeded to draft a charter. This draft was publicly read and explained and was unanimously approved. Taylor was then sent to Harrisburg for the purpose of presenting it to the Legislature. There, as he tells us, he succeeded, after more than two weeks of labor, in getting it passed by the legislature and approved by the governor.[13] From a letter that he wrote on January 24, 1846, to one of his sponsors in Lewisburg we learn something of the difficulties that confronted him. On January 20 he had presented to Senator James L. Gillis a letter of introduction from Eugenio Kincaid. Gillis, becoming immediately interested in the project, had introduced on that day a bill for the enactment of the charter, and this bill was referred to the senate committee on education. In this committee objections to it were raised. Here it was affirmed that the Baptists already had a "literary institution" at Haddington, that the request that all the trustees of the proposed university be Baptists was unprecedented, that the amount of income specified for the institution was "dangerously great," and that the request for exemption from taxation was inadmissible. To meet these objections Taylor labored for several days, and with considerable success;[14] but on January 24 the bill (No. 78) was reported from the committee with amendments. Five days later, in committee of the whole, the senators discussed the measure and then reported it with amendments to the senate. Forthwith it was read a second time, amended in both text and title, and, under a suspension of a rule, read a third time, passed, and sent to the house of representatives. The house passed the bill without amendment and returned it to the senate on February 4. The next day Governor Francis R. Shunk reported to both the senate and the house of representatives that he had "approved and signed" an "Act to establish the University at Lewisburg." [15] Accordingly, Taylor's subsequent statement that, "after a lapse of seventeen days under the guidance and blessing of Divine Providence a charter was unanimously granted of the identical form in which it had been asked," [16] must mean, if this statement was intended to be precise rather than rhetorical, that later amendments repealed earlier amendments while the bill was passing through the senate.

However that may be, Stephen W. Taylor now returned to Lewisburg with a charter for a proposed university.[17] This charter provided that, in or near Lewisburg, there should be established a university, consisting of a primary school and academy, a college, "and such other departments appropriate to a university as the patrons and managers" thereof should find themselves able to maintain. This institution, to be designated the University at Lewisburg, was to be governed by a board of not more than twenty trustees and by a board of not more than forty curators. All the trustees and a majority of the curators must be "regular members" of the Baptist denomination. A quorum of the trustees should consist of five or more, and a quorum of the curators should consist of seven or more.

The original trustees, named in the charter, were declared to be a body "politic and corporate, with perpetual succession," and were invested with such powers and such authority as were appropriate to a corporate body and were "customary in other universities, or in colleges" within the Commonwealth of Pennsylvania. Such powers included, *inter alia,* those of electing members of their board and of choosing their officers; of acquiring, managing, and disposing of property; of transacting the business of the university and of enacting ordinances and bylaws for its governance; of electing or appointing the president, professors, tutors, and other teachers; of agreeing with them for their "salaries and stipends," and of "removing them for misconduct, breaches of the ordinances of the institution, or other sufficient causes." Moreover, the trustees were required, after having obtained in "valid" subscriptions the sum of $100,000, to purchase "a lot or farm" and to erect thereon suitable buildings and to procure the "requisite library[,] apparatus, and specimens in natural history." They were required, furthermore, to see to it that one-fourth of the above-mentioned $100,000 and at least twenty-five per cent of all other moneys and property capable of producing revenue should be safely invested, and that the revenue accruing therefrom be appropriated for the support of the university; and they were forbidden either to mortgage the real estate or other property of the university or to incur indebtedness beyond their means of paying "consistently with the restrictions" imposed upon them. Finally, they were obliged to publish annually an abstract of the minutes of their meetings.

The original curators, also named in the charter, were empowered to choose their own officers, to fill vacancies in their board, and, in general, to carry on their affairs pursuant to the rules prescribed by the trustees. The governor and the secretary of the commonwealth, the judges of the supreme court, and the president of the university were made members *ex officio* of this board. The curators were charged with the general oversight of the academic work of the university, were required to be represented at the principal examinations and at the commencements of the university, and were authorized to consent or not to consent to every promotion of a student, and to the awarding of every degree, whether *pro merito* or *honoris causa*. They were to have access to the minutes of the faculty and to the business transactions of the trustees, and they were required to audit the accounts of the treasurer of the university. Finally, they were required to publish annually, in at least three papers of "extensive circulation" in different parts of the commonwealth, such summary of their observations on the operation of the university as would benefit this institution and enlighten its friends and patrons concerning it.

To the faculty, consisting of the president, the professors, the tutors, and the other teachers, was granted power to enforce the rules and regulations adopted by the trustees for the government and instruction of the students; to grant, with the counsel and consent of the curators, to students and to others deemed worthy, "such degrees in the liberal arts and sciences, or in certain branches thereof, as have been usually granted in other universities"; to grant to graduates under the seal of the corporation diplomas to "perpetuate the memory of such graduation"; and also to grant certificates to such students as have completed the prescribed course of studies "in any subordinate department of the university" (such, for example, as courses in the Academy, and, presently, in the Female Institute).

Finally, the charter prescribed that no religious sentiments should be considered a barrier to the election of any person "to any office among the teachers of the institution, or to debar persons from admittance as pupils, or in any manner to abridge their privileges or immunities as students, in any department of the university." [18]

This charter was printed in full in the *Lewisburg Chronicle* of February 14, 1846, and on that day the Board of Trustees of the newly chartered University met for the first time and elected a chairman, a secretary, a treasurer, and an assistant treasurer. These four men and one other were chosen as an executive committee "to transact such business as may be necessary" before the next meeting of the Board. Dr. William H. Ludwig was elected chairman, the Reverend Joel E. Bradley was elected secretary, and James Moore, Sr., was elected treasurer of the Board. Also at this meeting the Board appointed Stephen W. Taylor as its general agent, his term to begin with January 1, 1846; and it ordered that five hundred copies of the charter be printed for distribution.[19]

For the time being, there was little business for the Board to do, for, as we have already learned, the charter prescribed that, until the sum of $100,000 should be subscribed for the support of the University, the Board could not exercise fully its corporate authority. Hence the immediate task that confronted the Trustees and all other friends of the University was that of advertising and solicitation. Until the prescribed sum should be pledged, whatever was done for and in the name of the University would be anticipatory and preparatory.

Naturally, the burden of subscribing to the $100,000 fund fell, first of all, upon the people of Lewisburg, who were expected to profit materially from this enterprise; and as early as February 14, 1846, the editor of the *Lewisburg Chronicle* had affirmed that the citizens of "this region" had already subscribed $20,000 to this fund. Consequently, the promoters of "the great enterprise" within the bounds of the Northumberland Association now turned their eyes toward Philadelphia, rightly presuming that the success of their undertaking would depend upon their forming a solid Lewisburg-Philadelphia axis. This, of course, would be a combination of unequal partners, for the resources of the Baptists within the relatively new Northumberland Association, even when united with non-Baptist interests in Lewisburg, could not hope to match the wealth within the old and venerated Philadelphia Association and in other Baptist associations contiguous thereto. But it was fervently hoped by many, and perhaps actually believed by a few, that the co-operation of Baptists and others in the Northumberland Association with Baptists in Philadelphia and its vicinity might induce Baptists generally in Pennsylvania to rally to the support of a much-needed educational institution for their denomination in Lewisburg, a borough not far from the geographical center of the state.

On this subject, as early as January 24, 1846, Taylor had written from Harrisburg as follows: "Br. Kincaid would do well to inform the brethren in Philadelphia that our enterprise merits their approbation & we must & shall have it. Our hope is in God; may he speed the enterprise." [20] No informed person in Lewisburg would have questioned this assertion, just as no informed person there would have doubted the advisability of Taylor's undertaking a mission to the brethren in the City of Brotherly Love. Accordingly, armed with pledges of a large subscription in Lewisburg and with printed copies of the charter, Taylor set out for Philadelphia. There, for about three months, he labored as the representative of a "noble enterprise" that had been set on foot in Lewisburg. The task was arduous, fatiguing, and nerve-racking. On March 9 he wrote from Philadelphia, saying that patience and "great strength of perseverance" would be required. He believed that, on the whole, the cause was gaining ground, and he was cheered by the knowledge that the renowned Baptist missionary to Burma, Dr. Adoniram Judson, approved the undertaking.[21] Time did prove to be on the side of this enterprise, for when Taylor left Philadelphia, his work of explanation and of persuasion completed, he left with the knowledge that measures had been taken to employ an agent to collect subscriptions throughout the Philadelphia and the Central Union Associations, and that, after assurance had been given that subscriptions in the Northumberland Association would be increased to one-third of the $100,000 required by the charter, a promise had been made by a meeting in the Fifth Baptist Church of Philadelphia to endeavor to raise immediately among the Baptists of Philadelphia and its neighborhood "one third of the sum required to found and endow the proposed university." Nor was this all that he took home with him. Although soliciting subscriptions in Philadelphia was only incidental to his principal duty there—that of creating permanent and active friends to the enterprise that he represented—he did take back to Lewisburg subscriptions amounting to more than $8,000.[22]

Upon his return to Lewisburg, the executive committee of the Board extended Taylor's term of service as general agent for a year, or for so long as would be required to complete the arrangements for the opening of the University, and it also promised him a professorship in the University, the appointment to date from the opening of this institution.[23] While the work of collecting subscriptions was in progress, Taylor was assigned new duties preparatory to the opening of the University. One of these was that of preparing for publication a series of articles explaining the nature and the scope of the proposed University at Lewisburg and the reasons for its being started. Pursuant to his instructions, he prepared and published in the Philadelphia *Christian Chronicle,* between August 26 and December 9, 1846, sixteen articles in which, *inter alia,* he pointed out the need for such a Baptist institution in Pennsylvania, described the measures taken by those who were setting the project on foot, gave reasons for its location in Lewisburg, and explained various and sundry of the provisions of the charter that had been granted. He made much of the fact that provision had been made in this charter for expanding the institution beyond what was specifically required, and that authority had been granted to establish therein "any professorship of medicine, theology, law, or of the arts elegant or useful, which benevolent individuals may please to found. . . ." Indeed, he continued, "a great school is planned, and it requires a *united* effort of Pennsylvania Baptists to carry the plan into execution." [24]

Besides explaining and defending the charter, Taylor took pains to justify the inclusion in the proposed University of a Female Academy, an institution in the plans of the founders but one not specifically mentioned in the charter. Such an institution, Taylor affirmed, was necessary in order that the daughters as well as the sons of the patrons of this institution might be rightly educated. Not only did he point out the economic and the educational advantages of having a ladies' seminary as an appendage to the College; he also, on the one hand, gave assurance that the building occupied by the young women would "not be much less than one-fourth of a mile from that of the young gentlemen," and, on the other hand, that the young ladies would not recite in the same classes with the young gentlemen.[25]

Then, after relating what had been done in Lewisburg and in Philadelphia, and what was intended to be done elsewhere, to raise the sum of $100,000 required by the charter of the University, he told of the opening of a school in Lewisburg in the interest of the University, pointed out the great advantages that would accrue to Baptists by educating their children in Pennsylvania rather than outside Pennsylvania, and concluded by calling to the attention of the Baptists of Pennsylvania the general usefulness which the University at Lewisburg would have once it got fully under way. It would, he affirmed, train both men and women as teachers, and it would give education "in its very best form, not only to youth, destined to the learned professions, but to those likewise, who engage in the various branches of industry." [26] Accordingly, the conclusion of his appeal in these articles to the Baptists of Pennsylvania was

> Unite; and in the wisdom and strength which God has given you, rise and build. One noble effort will bring into existence a University which will remain to supply the subordinate schools with well qualified educator's [*sic*]; the missionary field with able laborers, and Bible Societies with correct translators—to minister the benefits of sound learning to all the learned professions, and to all the great departments of honest industry, and to every benevolent institution, during all coming time.[27]

The second new duty assigned to Taylor, a duty mentioned incidentally in a preceding paragraph, was that of opening in Lewisburg a school preparatory to the University. Such a school, it was believed, would not only prepare students for collegiate studies; it would also, as an actual beginning of the enterprise of a university, make easier the way of those agents who, in behalf of the University, would traverse the state of Pennsylvania in quest of subscriptions to complete the fund of $100,000. Accordingly, on October 5, 1846, Taylor, with the assistance of his son Alfred, opened what he called a high school for both boys and girls in the basement of the meeting-house of the Baptist Church in Lewisburg.[28] This was an important event, and it was not lost on a thirteen-year-old diarist, J. Merrill Linn, who presently would be attending this school.[29]

The building in which this school was held was not entirely finished.

The First Baptist Church in Lewisburg had been formed on January 3, 1844, and a day later it had been recognized by a council of delegates from other churches in the Northumberland Association. At the meeting of this council, Eugenio Kincaid had served as moderator.[30] During 1845 this church had begun to construct a building, described by a visitor as a "very neat and substantial brick building," and in September of the next year, a few days before Taylor began his school, the basement of this building was opened for preaching and for use as a Sunday School. The completed building was dedicated on November 15, 1846.[31] Here this school would have its quarters until the spring of 1849.

From its beginning the new school was well patronized, and as early as December 26, 1846, the Board of Trustees had voted to protract the session for five and a quarter weeks, and then, after a spring vacation of a little more than a month, to open a summer session that would extend into August. At this time, also, the Board authorized the employment of an additional male teacher for the school.[32] The third teacher, however, did not appear until the opening of the fall term in 1847.[33]

Of the progress of this school during its first year, we catch, now and again, fleeting glances. Its growth was steady and rapid. Taylor tells us that it began with an enrollment of twenty-two, and that during the course of the year seventy-six enrolled.[34] Before the end of October, 1846, when George W. Anderson visited it, the school had "about thirty pupils, each at a separate desk and all busily yet quietly engaged in their studies." [35] On October 26, young J. Merrill Linn, as he tells us in his diary, "began to go to Professor Taylor," and he remarked that he liked him "very well." From time to time he noted the enrollment of more students. Also from his diary we learn that, on January 19, 1847, he began the Greek Reader, and that, on February 2, 1847, he began to read Cicero. By June 21, 1847, he had got "through the seven orations of Cicero," and the next day he began the "Eneaid [*sic*] of Virgil," of which he "recited 80 lines." Also from young Linn we learn that the winter term ended at noon on April 6, 1847, and that the summer term, which began on May 6 with the house "crowded ram yam full," ended, after examinations were finished, in the afternoon of August 24, 1847. On this occasion the Reverend Mr. Bradley and the Reverend Mr. Kincaid spoke, and Taylor, in the opinion of our young diarist, gave "a very affecting speech." [36]

The second year brought important changes in this school. In the fall of 1847 the third teacher, Isaac N. Loomis, a graduate of what now had become Madison University in Hamilton, New York, joined the teaching staff. To him was given the subject of Greek, and, as he wrote on October 9, 1847, soon after his arrival in Lewisburg, if he could only "sustain the reputation" he then had, he would be accomplishing as much as he could expect. Presently he was also teaching vocal music. He was "pleasantly" situated, he wrote, "perfectly" contented, and resolved to attend to business.[37] There was business enough for all three teachers during that year, for perhaps as many as one hundred students were present for the opening of the fall term in 1847. So crowded were the quarters in the Baptist Church that, by October 20, the Trustees had rented on Market Street a room in which some of the students could study.[38] As the days went by, more students came, and by December 14 young Linn believed that they numbered "about 108." [39] Meanwhile, this young man had been making progress in his studies, for on November 9, a "middling warm" day, he read his first lesson in Livy, and three days later he bought for 87½ cents "an annabasis" and "harpers aids to composition." By May 19, 1848, he was reciting in the third book of Livy and in the fourth book of Xenophon. At the end of that month he noted that there were twelve in his class.[40] Presumably they were all prepared by this time to spell correctly the word *Anabasis.*

After two years of being crowded in the basement of the Baptist Church, both teachers and students could look forward to the day, not many months distant, when they would be housed in better quarters. A new building was then under construction. At the end of the first year of this school, the Trustees were so favorably impressed by its progress that, at their meeting on August 23, 1847, they requested their Executive Committee "to procure a plan of University buildings to lay before the Board at their next meeting." Although as late as January 1, 1848, they expressed a willingness to purchase for $750 the Lewisburg Academy Building, they considered at their January meeting of that year a plan for University buildings that Taylor presented, as well as a plan presented by Joel E. Bradley. They approved the "oblong plan of Academical buildings . . . as a general basis," and agreed to refer this plan to a competent architect for such improvements in it as he might recommend. In the construction of a proposed Male Academic Building, the Trustees authorized their Executive Committee to act for them. The climax of this matter came during the first two days in February, 1848. On February 1, the Trustees approved a "draft" of a building submitted by Thomas U. Walter, architect for Girard College, as a guide for their Executive Committee in the erection of an Academic Building, and on February 2, after "viewing the ground" on College Hill that was being held in trust for the University, they approved the site for their first building.[41]

On February 25, 1848, in an editorial entitled "Ground Broke," the *Lewisburg Chronicle* announced that the first building of the University was under contract, and that the ground for it had been broken. This building, it said, would be of brick, three stories in height, and 51 by 75 feet.[42] Although intended for the Male Primary and Academic Department, it would, for the time being, accommodate all the students. "We understand," the editorial continues, "that no installment of the subscription is required at present, the estimated expense of $6,500 being voluntarily met by some of the earnest and liberal friends of the Institution." The word "subscription" in this editorial referred to the project, then under way, of collecting subscriptions for the required $100,000 Fund. Subscriptions to this fund, however, would not be due until the full sum of $100,000 had been subscribed, and then they could be paid in four annual installments. The new building was completed by January, 1849, and was occupied in April of that year, before the close of the winter term.[43]

While the Academy Building was in course of construction, and while efforts were being made to raise enough money to pay for it, other measures preparatory to the University were being adopted. On May 3, 1848, the Trustees appointed a committee to get from Taylor such information as he might have gathered in relation to a plan of government, a course of study, and textbooks for use in the high school. At the meeting of the Trustees on August 28–30, 1848, Taylor, on request, presented an elaborate report, which was referred to a special committee of the Board. After studying this report, the committee recommended, and the Board approved, a code of laws, as revised by the committee, for the governance of the high school; the purchase, when money should become available therefor, of a philosophical apparatus; and a list of textbooks for the high school. The Board appointed Taylor professor of mathematics and natural philosophy, Isaac N. Loomis tutor in the University, and Alfred Taylor assistant teacher in the Academic Department; and it also appointed a committee of four on the library and charged it with the duty of assembling a library as soon as money therefor should become available. Taylor's "scheme of University Buildings" the Board referred to a committee in Philadelphia, the members of which, in co-operation with a competent architect, were instructed to prepare a plan of such buildings and an estimate of the cost thereof, which, however, should not be greater than $50,000. Before it adjourned, the Board, in order to dispel some annoying rumors, affirmed not only that the high school taught by Taylor and his assistants had arisen and had been operated under the authority of the Board, but also that thenceforth this school should be known as the Academical and Primary Department of the University at Lewisburg.[44]

Meanwhile, by the efforts of soliciting agents, the state was being canvassed for subscriptions to the $100,000 Fund. This work was being done under the direction of Eugenio Kincaid, who had accepted the appointment of soliciting agent on January 17, 1846,[45] and of William Shadrach, who had given up the pastorate of the Fifth Baptist Church of Philadelphia to engage in this work. On August 30, 1848, the Board had been informed that, thanks to the arduous labors of its dedicated agents, about $81,000 of the required sum had been subscribed. The work of soliciting was not inspiring, and the fatigue of traveling in bad weather could be depressing. Of the hardships endured by these men while they were visiting churches and associations throughout Pennsylvania, we get some understanding from the final report that Shadrach submitted to the Board on January 19, 1849. Nevertheless, between May 4, 1848, and the closing of the subscriptions on January 9, 1849, he had collected in central and western Pennsylvania, and in Philadelphia and its vicinity, subscriptions amounting to $14,065.[46] But of the hardships of soliciting we learn even more from a surviving letter that Eugenio Kincaid wrote from southwestern Pennsylvania on March 25, 1848. After telling of an illness that hardships and exposure had brought upon Shadrach, he continued as follows:

> The roads in Western Pennsylvania have been nearly impassable since the middle of November. Ten churches more are to be visited, and then all the work is done south and west of Pittsburgh.
>
> So far, we have nothing to complain of the churches west of the mountains. George's Creek has come up to *eleven hundred* dollars, and many who have subscribed liberally would double their subscriptions, rather than have the enterprise fail.[47]

All told, the effort for this fund had yielded, in subscriptions, the sum of $101,236.50. Shadrach, having submitted his report, now resigned his agency, and Kincaid, his work as soliciting agent being also completed, was appointed general agent of the Board.[48]

The first meeting of the Board after the completion of the campaign for subscriptions lasted from January 18 through January 20. It was, as we have learned, a meeting for rejoicing; but it was more than that. It was also a meeting for the transaction of business which, theretofore, could not have been done. Now the Board, in full possession of its corporate authority, was eager to get started. There was much for it to do. There was need for it to take possession of the land that was being held in trust for it; there was need for it to get started with a program of building; there was need for it to enlarge the faculty; and there was need for it to inform the public of what had been done and of what yet remained to do.

The importance of this meeting, which had been duly advertised,[49] was a subject of gossip on the streets of Lewisburg, where it was common knowledge that the campaign to obtain the required subscriptions had been successfully concluded. In his diary for January 17, 1849, J. Merrill Linn wrote not only that most of the Trustees had arrived for the meeting, but also, erroneously, that he had seen his "future Greek teacher," whose name was Anderson.[50] In his entry for the next day he wrote that the Trustees had held a meeting, but that he did not know what they had done. Nevertheless, he affirmed that they were going to put up a new building next summer, assuming perhaps that such must be the case because Thomas U. Walter, architect for Girard College, was in town.

Of most immediate concern to the Trustees at this meeting, judging by their actions, was the matter of buildings. Accordingly, Thomas Wattson, who had been elected chairman of the Board on August 28, 1848, to succeed the late Dr. Ludwig, submitted a report for the committee on the plan of buildings. This report recommended a plan that Walter had drawn, "with dormitories and study rooms," although the committee was uncertain whether the Board intended to let the students get rooms and meals in the village, a practice which the committee favored, not only because it thought that experience had justified it, but also because it believed that, if the students were lodged and boarded in the town, the citizens thereof would be bound to the University by a strong tie of self-interest. Accordingly, the committee recommended that the Board erect the center building first, and then later, if it seemed desirable to do so, add dormitories to this building. It recommended also that the Observatory be "disconnected from the College buildings, even if it should involve the Board in some additional expense." The Board was well pleased with this report. It voted unanimously to put under contract for completion on July 1, 1850, "the whole of the buildings" according to Walter's plan, and to let Walter choose the site of the University Building; it appointed Walter architect to the University, his services to be gratuitous; and it chose a committee of seven to carry out the plan in conjunction with Walter. One of the seven was Stephen W. Taylor.

From the matter of buildings the Board turned to the subject of additional professors. As professor of Greek it elected the Reverend George R. Bliss, pastor of a church in New Brunswick, New Jersey, and as professor of Latin it elected George W. Anderson, editor of the Philadelphia *Christian Chronicle*. Professor Bliss would begin his service to the University in May, 1849, and Professor Anderson would join the faculty in the autumn of that year. Both these men were graduates of the Literary and Theological Institution in Hamilton, New York, now become Madison University.[51]

Still other matters claimed the attention of the Board. It approved the "form and devise" of a corporate seal for its use, adopted a set of bylaws, and ordered that one hundred and fifty copies of these bylaws and of the charter be printed. Also, it appointed a committee to get a press and another committee to see to it that the Academic Building would be adequately insured. It elected Shadrach a member of the Board to succeed the late Dr. Ludwig, appointed Eugenio Kincaid its general agent, and by unanimous vote chose Shadrach a collecting agent "for west of the mountains so far as consistent with his other duties." It approved a paper that Shadrach had written, at the request of the Board, on the progress of the University, and ordered that it be published in the *Christian Chronicle,* the *Pittsburgh Gazette,* the *Lewisburg Chronicle,* "and in such other papers as are willing to publish it without charge." [52]

When the Board met again, John P. Crozer of the building committee, on April 18, 1849, presented bids on the University Building ranging from $38,000 to $58,500. The lowest of these was submitted by the architect, Thomas U. Walter. His bid the Board accepted on April 19, provided that one wing[53] could be completed by August 1, 1850, and that the central part of the building and the other wing be constructed when money for them should become available. It authorized the building committee to ascertain whether economies in construction might be made without affecting "the size and general plan of the building," and, if such could be done, to agree thereto; and, finally, it affirmed that the total cost of the building should not exceed $38,000. The Board also agreed that, should Walter refuse such a contract, the building committee should be empowered to obtain a contract "on the best terms possible from any other responsible contractor." Before adjourning, the Board appointed a committee to "obtain reliable pledges of advances on loan to the amount of $7,000 for the purpose of erecting the northwest angle of the University buildings." [54]

On May 15 Walter accepted in principle the conditions of the Board and proposed a schedule of payments to himself, but, at an adjourned meeting of the Board on May 19, he refused to accept a contract pursuant to a resolution of the Board authorizing the construction of one wing of the building, provided that a subscription of $7,000 for the payment thereof "be first made." On August 23 Shadrach reported that pledges obtained for erecting a wing of the University Building now amounted to $7,690. On the following day, when the building committee reported its inability to put under contract the work of constructing this wing, the Board clothed this committee with discretionary bargaining power, restricted, however, by a provision that the total cost thereof be not greater than $12,000. Thereafter the project proceeded more effectively,[55] and about a year later the Curators could report that the west wing of the University Building was under roof, and that the building would be ready for occupancy when the winter term opened in October of that year.[56]

Part of the pressing business that the Board did not deal with at its meeting in January, 1849, was that of acquiring title to land which, pursuant to the charter, it was obligated to do when the $100,000 Fund had been subscribed. This business, however, was one of the major concerns of the Board during its session in April of that year. On April 19, 1849, it acquired from Samuel Wolfe, James Moore, Jr., and the estate of Dr. William H. Ludwig title to a tract in the south part of the borough of Lewisburg, including the Hill on which the Academy Building had been erected, consisting of seventy-three acres and seventy perches, "neat measure," that Wolfe, Moore, and Ludwig had earlier acquired and had held for the University until the Trustees thereof should become fully vested with their corporate powers.[56a] To each of these three parties the Board paid the sum of $2,337.44. The Board also agreed to accept on this property an encumbrance of $2,443.73 "and three mills," the interest on which ($146.62) the Board agreed to pay annually to Hannah Brown, widow of John Brown, during her lifetime, and at her death to pay the aforesaid sum to the "person entitled to the same." The Board also acquired several other small parcels of land for the purpose of straightening lines and for providing roads. All this land was presently surveyed, and a considerable part of it was laid off in lots which were offered for sale, either privately or by auction. Some large lots along what is now University Avenue were laid off as "Professors' Lots," the price of which, after April 19, 1850, would be $500 each. On August 26, 1850, the Board adopted a regulation, thereafter to be inserted in deeds of conveyance of University lots, that on the lots thus conveyed there be forever prohibited the sale, except for "medical purposes," of "spirituous or vinous liquors." On the professors' lots there was imposed a further restriction—namely, that, in case such lots were offered for sale, the Board would have preference in repurchasing them.[57]

Within this tract now acquired by the University was an elevation, which from the beginning had been chosen as the site of the University Building. This elevation, commonly called "the Hill," the Curators, in their annual report at the end of the year 1849–50, described somewhat rapturously, saying:

> The site of the buildings is on the west bank of the West Branch of the Susquehanna river, about one fourth of a mile south of the Borough of Lewisburg, in a beautiful grove of 20 acres, on an eminence about 90 feet above the level of the river, and some 200 yards from its margin

> —very happily adapted by nature to the object to which it is now devoted. This height commands an extensive view of the beautiful and picturesque scenery for which this part of the State is remarkable—looking, westwardly, over the fertile and highly cultivated Buffalo Valley, to the bold mountains which, at a distance of from 8 to 20 miles, mark its limits; northwardly, over the flourishing towns of Lewisburg and Milton, along the windings of the river, 18 miles, to the Muncy Hills, and beyond them, 18 or 20 miles further to the dim blue mountains of Sullivan county; eastwardly, over the rich valley of the Chillisquaque, bounded on the right by Montour's Ridge, and reaching 20 miles to the iron hills of Columbia county; and southwardly, along the West Branch to the cliffs of the Blue Hills, opposite the town of Northumberland, and the lofty promontory of Mahonoy mountain.[58]

By the end of the academic year 1848–49, the Trustees, although much concerned with such matters as buildings and grounds, the collection of money subscribed, the getting of new subscriptions, the management of the land recently acquired, and the sale of lots, found themselves also confronted with problems of collegiate organization and of collegiate teaching. They were paying close attention to the details of their job. The next year there would be a junior class of collegiate rank, and, partly in anticipation of this fact, the faculty had recently been enlarged. With the University now removed from its crowded quarters in what Professor Taylor called the "damp, dark and unhealthy rooms in the basement of the Baptist Church" [59] into more commodious and more attractive quarters in the new Academic Building, there was both the opportunity as well as an increasing need to make improvements in the work of the institution. The need of more equipment had now become obvious. For Professor Taylor's work in teaching what we now call physics there was need of a philosophical apparatus; for anticipated lectures in chemistry there was need of other equipment; for the benefit of the students there was need of flourishing literary societies; and for everyone in the University, teachers as well as students, there was need for a library. Finally, as the collegiate work was extended from year to year, it would be necessary to enlarge the scope of the curriculum.

Upon Professor Taylor fell much of the burden of academic planning. Unfortunately, we know little in detail about the reports that he made from time to time to the Board, for the loose papers of the Trustees have not been preserved. We do know, however, that in August, 1849, he made a report accompanied by several "schedules"; that this report was studied by a committee of the Trustees; and that, upon the recommendation of this committee, the Board voted unanimously a resolution of thanks to the members of the faculty for "their efficiency, zeal, and laborious industry in promoting the interests of the institution placed under their charge." Three days later the Board, still in session, requested Professors Bliss and Anderson to serve during the vacation as agents of the University to procure money pledged for the purpose of purchasing for the University books and a philosophical apparatus.[60] Whether they consented to serve as such agents we do not know.

When the Board met in April, 1850, Professor Taylor was ready with a report as pleasing to the Trustees as it was to himself. In this report he told how, pursuant to authorization, he had, by a generous advance of money by the chairman of the Board and by gifts from others, been able to procure in New York and to bring to Lewisburg not only an adequate philosophical apparatus, but also a chemical apparatus and enough chemicals to last for two or three years. The total value of this equipment, he reported, was $2,213.02; but, thanks to some gifts and to the seller's reduction of twenty per cent on the price, he was able to get the material laid down in Lewisburg for a cost to the University, apart from $14.15 that he had paid for freight, of only $1,664.15. The Board paid Taylor's bill for freight and thanked him and others involved in this transaction for their contributions to the well-being of the University.[61]

At its annual meeting in August of 1850, the Board took more than one action of significance for the Collegiate Department of the University. First of all, by what was probably the final step needed to legalize fully this department, it affirmed that, since by the formation of four regular collegiate classes the Collegiate Department had been put into full operation, the Board now recognized this department as being in "full existence" and thus invested with "all the rights, powers and privileges" that usually pertain to collegiate institutions.[62]

The second action of importance taken by the Trustees at this meeting is comprised in the disposal that they made of a report submitted to them by Professors Taylor and Bliss. Pursuant to the recommendations in this report, the Board not only made an appropriation to provide for a course of lectures in chemistry, but also authorized the reduction in length of the school year from forty-two to forty weeks, which was "the usual length in other institutions." On the recommendation touching the subject of bylaws, the Board appointed Taylor, Bliss, and Anderson a committee to revise the existing bylaws of the Collegiate Department and to submit their work at the earliest practicable date so that their revision, if approved, could be printed for the guidance of the students. Also, in compliance with a recommendation of the faculty, the Board appointed a committee to report on the state of the Primary Department. But the most important of the recommendations of the faculty, the one touching the matter of the presidency of the University, required the Board to decide whether, at that time, to choose a president or to defer action until a later day. By the formation of a senior class at the close of the year 1849–50, there would be created a need, the faculty pointed out, that commonly was filled by the president of a college or university. Consequently, the choice lay between that of appointing at once a president and that of asking the present members of the faculty to assume, in addition to their usual work, the added burden of instructing a senior class. The faculty had expressed a desire for the appointment of a president, but, in case the Board should think it inadvisable to make such an appointment, the faculty would be willing to assume an added burden of instruction. Apologetically, the Board resolved this problem by choosing the way of less effort and of no additional expense to the University. Hard pressed for money to meet obligations already assumed, the Trustees decided that, since the immediate choice of a president was impracticable from the pecuniary standpoint, they would "respectfully request the Professors, in addition to their present important duties, to take charge of the senior class to be raised the coming term." [63]

The third significant action taken by the Board at this meeting was its approval of a new Circular, which proved to be the immediate precursor of the first Catalogue of the University that appeared a few months later. The Circular of 1850, effective from the beginning of the academic year 1850–51, described the two-year program of the Academy, and, for the first time, the four-year collegiate program. Nothing, however, was said about women in the institution, although from the beginning of the institution instruction had been given to both girls and boys in classes below those of collegiate rank.[64] Other pertinent information in this Circular made it, except that the names of members of the governing bodies and the names of the students were omitted, equivalent to the catalogue of an American college of that era. It mentioned the subjects taught in the Primary and in the English Department of the Academy, and it described with some fullness the two-year classical program of the Academy, the purpose of which was to prepare young men for the four-year classical program of the College, the only collegiate program described in the first Catalogue of the University at Lewisburg. This program, which emphasized Latin, Greek, and mathematics, and which gave some attention to such other subjects as natural philosophy, natural theology, intellectual philosophy, and moral philosophy, led to the degree of Bachelor of Arts. Essentially, it did not differ, except perhaps in a few minor details, from the programs offered for the degree of Bachelor of Arts in other American colleges in the middle of the nineteenth century. It was the aim of the University at Lewisburg to be equal to, not to be different from, other American colleges.

In still other ways this Circular tells us that the University at Lewisburg was following the course laid down by tradition in American higher education. Here students were required to attend regularly some religious service; here they were required to study textbooks that were much used in other American colleges; here they were taught by professors or tutors who had each received the degree of Master of Arts; here they were required to pay for tuition, annually, the sum of thirty dollars; here they were required to stay in school during a forty-week academic year divided into three terms; and here they were allowed a spring vacation of four weeks and an autumnal vacation of eight weeks.[65]

While the program of the Collegiate Department of the University was being expanded, and while equipment for instruction in scientific subjects was being obtained, steps also were being taken to acquire a library that would meet the needs of both the faculty and the students. To provide a library was one of the specific duties that the charter imposed upon the Trustees after the sum of $100,000 had been subscribed for the support of the University. Measures toward meeting this need had been anticipated, for in August, 1848, several months before the close of the first campaign for subscriptions had closed, Professor Taylor presented to the Trustees a comprehensive report on the University, and, as we have seen, the Trustees, before adjourning, appointed a committee of four on the library, referred to it Taylor's observations on this subject, and instructed it to make arrangements "for the collection of a Library as soon as the necessary funds" could be obtained. Of this committee Taylor was a member.

The first librarian of the University, Professor George R. Bliss, did not begin his service to the University until May, 1849. By this time the University had been moved from the Baptist Church to the new Academic Building. Here the collegiate library of the University was organized, and here it remained during the next ten years. In his first report as librarian, presented in August, 1849, Professor Bliss said that 438 books had been put into his hands. Most of these books, perhaps all, had been acquired as gifts.

At least some of the founding fathers of the University at Lewisburg were as much interested in acquiring a library for their University as they were in procuring for it materials for teaching scientific subjects. One such person was Stephen W. Taylor; another was George W. Anderson, editor of the Philadelphia *Christian Chronicle* since its founding in 1845. Mr. Anderson was a member of the first committee on the library and, as we have learned, was chosen to be the first professor of Latin. No doubt his being elected a member of the faculty stimulated his interest in the library. However that may be, less than three months after his election, there appeared in the issue of the *Christian Chronicle* for April 11, 1849, under the title of "The University at Lewisburg," a moving appeal for the adoption of a generous policy in respect to the library of this institution. Perhaps in part as a consequence of this appeal, the spirit of liberalism did inform for several years the efforts made in behalf of this library. During those years it was only the lack of money that prevented the acquisition for it of a large number of books.

In August, 1850, the Board authorized the committee on the library to spend, during the ensuing year, $300 on the library; and it requested its agents to solicit contributions to the library whenever it might be expedient for them to do so. The Board agreed also that any profit which might accrue from the graduation fee should be paid into a fund for the library. By this time the library contained 698 volumes. A year later the librarian announced that the total had been increased to 1,077. Most of the 379 volumes acquired during the year had been purchased, but there were some gifts of value, including publications of the Smithsonian Institution; and in concluding his report for the year 1850–51 Professor Bliss expressed the hope that gradual appropriations might be made for further increasing the holdings of the library as the means of the Board would permit. By pursuing a policy of constant enlargement, he concluded, there should be eventually in the library of the University a collection that would meet the demands not only of instructors and students, but also those of the denomination at large.[66] Thus early this library aspired to both adequacy and excellence.

Also something else in the American collegiate way of life in mid-nineteenth century America—something unnoticed in the earliest official records of the University at Lewisburg—was not overlooked by Stephen W. Taylor in his early efforts to found a university. At that time an American college would have been considered lacking something essential if there had not been connected with it student societies commonly called literary, but sometimes debating, societies. Such societies, which dated from the latter half of the eighteenth century, were in the colleges, but they were not quite a part of the curricula thereof. Technically, they belonged in the extracurriculum. Nevertheless, because they supplemented some of the instruction of the colleges and promoted objectives that the colleges desired to see achieved, they were fostered by college faculties and college presidents. They came to be taken for granted, as much as Livy and Horace, or as much as paternal government and compulsory chapel. Commonly they were given exclusive use of rooms in buildings owned by collegiate corporations, and now and again there could be found such societies that enjoyed the full use of buildings. Ordinarily two literary societies were formed in a college, and perhaps more often than not their rivalries were more evident than their co-operation was helpful. Many such societies accumulated and administered libraries of their own—libraries which, on some collegiate campuses, were more useful than the collegiate libraries, and, at least to their own members, more accessible.[67]

Such societies arose early in the history of the incipient University at Lewisburg. In the first issue of the Catalogue thereof we read that "Three Literary Societies have been formed in the University—two in the Collegiate and one in the Academical Department; and a Society of Moral and Religious Inquiry, in which students of both Departments [*i.e.*, Collegiate and Academic] participate." [68] As subsequently explained in an official notice of this institution, the literary societies "attached to the University" were not "secret societies," for they admitted visitors to their meetings. They were intended to be educational, for in them the students would learn to "meet objections, detect sophistry, influence emotion, and elucidate truth"; and, at the same time, they would become familiar with the "forms and usages of a deliberative assembly." [69] Of a different character were the societies of moral and religious inquiry, and of them more will be said in a subsequent paragraph.

The literary societies mentioned in the first issue of the Catalogue of the University at Lewisburg were all formed during the first session of the academic year 1850–51; but behind that year lies a tenuous, an intriguing, and a short history of one or more such societies. From the diary that he was then keeping, we learn that George Good, a member of the senior academic class of 1847–48, attended between December 25, 1847, and February 19, 1848, three meetings of what he called "our Debating Society." It may well be that he attended a debating society, of which we have no record, that had been formed for preparatory students.[69a] However that may be, we read in the diary of J. Merrill Linn, a sophomore in the Collegiate Department in 1847–48, that on October 31, 1848, a "debating society" was formed "in the school." Three days later this society adopted a constitution and bylaws and elected officers, one of whom was Mr. Linn. This was no doubt the collegiate society called Philomathian, a society which, although its own records have disappeared, has left slight traces of its existence. We know that it was operating as late as the summer of 1849.[70] By October 18, 1849, it seems to have been virtually defunct, for on that day J. Merrill Linn spoke to Professor Taylor about forming a new society, and from Linn's diary we learn that Professor Taylor said that he intended to form two new societies, "desolving the old" and dividing the students between the new ones.

However soon the old society, or societies, may have been "desolved," no new literary societies appear to have come into being until the autumn of 1850. Then two such societies, named, respectively, Theta Alpha and Euepia, were formed, and they endured, at least nominally, into the early years of the twentieth century. As we shall see hereafter, the role that they played in the history of the University was considerable. In organization, in procedure, and in purpose, they differed in no significant way from similar societies in other American colleges of that era. Their proceedings in their weekly meetings—their questions argued and their orations delivered, their essays read, and their business transacted—all this can today be traced in their old books of records. Both these societies gathered libraries of their own, and forty years later, in the era of their decline, they gave their collections of books to the collegiate library. From the beginning of 1851 to the summer of 1859, each of these societies occupied a room of its own in the West Wing of the University Building, and thereafter each of them had a room on the second floor of the central part of this building.[71]

Theta Alpha and Euepia were successors and, by default, heirs to the Philomathian Society, which had expired intestate and poverty-stricken. Consequently, representatives of these successor societies met at an appointed time, in December, 1850, and divided between them the property of "the late Philomathian Society." [72] What each of them received would have excited the envy of few persons.

Between November 16 and December 7, 1850, there was formed by the senior academic class for its own members a society, probably also a successor society, called Phirhoan. Its purpose was to do for these students what Theta Alpha and Euepia were expected to do for the collegiate students, except that the Phirhoan Society made no effort to gather a library. The influence of this society was not so pronounced as that of the collegiate societies, nor was its life so long.[73] It presently gave way to other academic societies of like character.

So much, then, for the literary societies formed during the Taylor era. We turn now to the subject of a society of a different sort—the Society for Moral and Religious Inquiry—an organization formed in the University at Lewisburg during the autumn of 1849 and modeled specifically on the plan of a similar society in Madison University (now Colgate University) in Hamilton, New York.[74] Societies of this sort had become well known on American collegiate campuses before the middle of the nineteenth century, but they were of more recent origin and were perhaps less widely dispersed than were the literary societies. Being a product of the modern missionary movement, they had their beginning when students in the Andover Theological Seminary united on January 8, 1811, to form what they called the Society for Inquiry, on the Subject of Missions.[75] The idea spread rapidly, and the societies that arose in theological seminaries and in some American denominational colleges in imitation of the society in Andover were much alike in name, in purpose, and in procedure. Their main concern was the furtherance of the missionary movement at home and abroad, and their method of so doing was to arouse interest in the cause of world-wide evangelization by disseminating knowledge about the need for missions at home and abroad and about the accomplishments of missionaries in their respective fields of endeavor.[76] Such was the nature of the Society for Moral and Religious Inquiry in the University at Lewisburg. Being in no sense a rival of the literary societies, its membership was open to all interested students, whether they were in the Academy or in the College. It held monthly meetings, and also, like the literary societies, it acquired, partly by purchases and partly by gifts, a library for the use of its members. Eventually this library, like the libraries of the two literary societies, was merged with the collegiate library. This society, which functioned pursuant to one of the major purposes of the University, was officially described, concisely and accurately, for the patrons and the friends of the University in these words:

> The Society for Inquiry is a religious body, comprising students from both departments [*i.e.,* the Collegiate and the Academic]. It receives religious periodicals, corresponds with kindred societies and with Missionaries in various parts of the world. At its monthly meetings there is always an essay read in public, touching upon some subject connected with the evangelization of the world. It has a valuable library connected with missions, and a museum of ethnological articles.[77]

The academic year 1850–51, which saw the University at Lewisburg operating for the first time under a full collegiate program, was for Stephen W. Taylor not so much a time for triumphant rejoicing, as it was a time for soul-searching. The Trustees, in deciding at their August meeting in 1850 not to appoint a president because of their pecuniary embarrassment, did not affirm that they would not eventually select for this position a person already in their employ; but when, during the same session, they instructed a committee on nominations that they had appointed in 1848 to nominate a president for the University at the "earliest day practicable," [78] they at least implied that their choice of a president would not be made until they had looked about for a while. If any one of the faculty of the University at Lewisburg were to be considered for such position, that person would be Stephen W. Taylor; and, in view of his long educational experience, and more especially of his remarkable services in setting this institution in motion, he would have been an excessively modest man had he not thought of himself as being qualified for and entitled to the position now open. In a sense that no one could deny, the University at Lewisburg was a child of his brain. As if to make the problem more complex for him, the trustees of Madison University, on August 22 of that year, invited him to resume in that institution the professorship that he had resigned in 1845.[79] What should he do?

Madison University was then in a somewhat precarious condition. For three years it had been shaken to its foundation by a spirited controversy as to whether it should be removed to Rochester, New York; and, although the movement to "remove" it had failed, Madison University had lost one of its most distinguished professors to the newly created University of Rochester.[80] It had need of an able, faithful, and mature man like Taylor, and the opportunity to help rebuild the institution in which he had long labored would have a strong appeal for a man of Taylor's temperament and energy; and there can be no doubt that influential friends of his who were associated with Madison University were eager for his return to Hamilton.

On September 7, 1850, while he was visiting in Hamilton, he wrote to Philetus B. Spear, professor of Hebrew in Madison University, saying that he must decline the professorship offered him in Hamilton because of obligations that he had assumed in Lewisburg for the ensuing year. Such obligations he could not conscientiously disregard, even though private interest and his own convenience might argue strongly for his return to Hamilton. Moreover, although he did not say so in this letter, he had no reason to think that he could not retain indefinitely his position as senior professor in the University at Lewisburg. But for several months thereafter his attitude as to the course that he might take was cautious, somewhat secretive, and therefore difficult to understand—in part, no doubt, because not all his correspondence on this subject is available. That he did not wish to lose contact entirely with Madison University seems to be evident from what he said, as early as September 14, 1850, in another letter to Professor Spear. He then and there affirmed that, although he must remain in Lewisburg for the ensuing year, if at some future time it should become evident to him and to the Trustees of the University at Lewisburg that he "could better promote the interest of religion and learning in Madison University than in the one at Lewisburg," he could no doubt obtain a release from his position in Lewisburg. But, he continued, were it to become practicable for him to return to Hamilton to work, he would like to have an answer to this question: "What arrangements are to be made for the government and discipline of the University?" Was this a hint that he would like to be offered the presidency of Madison University?[81]

By the latter part of December, 1850, Taylor was willing to say, "in confidence," that there was a probability of his leaving Lewisburg at the end of the academic year 1850–51, and on December 20 he expressed to his friend, Professor Spear, his willingness to consider seriously a very definite offer "unanimously" made by the trustees of Madison University and "unanimously" approved by the faculty of that institution.[82] Three days later he wrote, but did not then send, a letter of resignation to the chairman of the Board of Trustees of the University at Lewisburg.[83]

On February 5, 1851, Taylor was officially invited to take the position of president of Madison University and to occupy in this institution the chair of mathematics and natural philosophy. This offer was mailed to him by Professor Spear on February 7.[84] A week later Taylor promised Spear that he would give a definite answer to this invitation before the next commencement at Madison. He waited to see what action the Trustees of the University at Lewisburg would take at their next meeting, which would be held in April. To that body its committee on nominating a president reported on April 16, 1851, that, in its opinion, the time had not yet come to elect a president of the University; and it proposed, and the Board approved the proposal, that Taylor be made acting president of the University from the beginning of the next term "until a Professor of Mental and Moral Science be elected." [85] Also the Board approved the appointment of a committee of three of its members—James P. Crozer, William Bucknell, and Thomas Wattson—and charged this committee to correspond with "the most prominent persons in the United States of the Baptist denomination" about the choice of a president. On the same day Taylor, who no doubt had heard of the action that the Board had taken in respect to this matter, appeared before the Board and submitted to its chairman the letter of resignation that he had written several weeks before. Recalling in this letter his services for this University, and his promise to remain with the institution until the first collegiate class therein should be graduated, he remarked that, "after prayerful and long deliberation," he was persuaded that it was now "the will of Divine Providence" that his services in the University at Lewisburg should end on August 20, 1851.[86] He accepted, for the ensuing term, the title of acting president, and on May 14 he wrote his acceptance of the offer to him to become president of Madison University; but, seemingly still hopeful that he might be offered the presidency of the University at Lewisburg, he did not mail this letter until May 31.[87] The die was now cast.

Taylor's resignation made it necessary for the Board to enlarge its quest for a president to a quest for both a president and a professor of mathematics and natural philosophy. Accordingly, it at once replaced its committee of three to look for a president with a committee of five—William Bucknell, George B. Ide, William Shadrach, Adie K. Bell, and James P. Crozer—and instructed these men to correspond with such persons they might think it expedient to consult about filling all positions that then were, or that might presently become, vacant in the University, and to report their findings to the Board on the first day of its session in August, 1851.[88]

Our knowledge of the unwillingness of the Board of Trustees to offer Taylor the presidency of the University at Lewisburg raises an intriguing, but at this late day an unanswerable, question. There is little doubt, I think, that he would gladly have accepted such an offer. It is true that Taylor was not a minister of the gospel, and thus, in the opinion of most persons of that era, not qualified for the presidency of a college or a university. But such deficiency did not prevent Taylor's being elected president of Madison University. We must look elsewhere. It may well be that, for reasons of prestige, the Board hoped, now that the institution was founded, to get for a president a Baptist minister of national repute, a man whose prominence in the denomination might help to unite effectively all the Baptists of Pennsylvania in support of their university; and also it may be true that Taylor had made himself objectionable to some persons of importance, in the faculty as well as in the Board of Trustees. Taylor was a deeply pious man—no one questioned that fact; but he frequently gave the impression of being unctuous and self-righteous, and he was as determined as he was self-confident. He could, and perhaps he did, set the teeth of some persons on edge. Whether there was general discontent among the professors with his conduct as an administrator, we do not know; but we do know that at least one of the professors had a low opinion of him as a collegiate disciplinarian.[89] Accordingly, it may well be that the perception by the Board, by members of the faculty, and by others of defects of personality in Taylor combined with reasons of broad policy entertained by the Board to keep Taylor from being chosen president of the University at Lewisburg. Whatever the reasons may have been for such decision, neither faithlessness to the University nor incompetency in his professorship was among them. He was a good teacher, and he deserved well of those whom he had served, as they unquestionably recognized. There was much truth, as also there was much pathos, in the reply, unanimously approved, of the Board to Taylor's letter of resignation. "The past history of the University," we here read, "is associated at every step with that of Professor Taylor. Faithfully and efficiently has he laboured in its service, and to him, under God, it owes in no small degree, its present prosperity." Accordingly, in regretting his departure, the Board assured him of its "undiminished confidence in him as an Instructor, Gentleman and Christian." [90]

For Stephen W. Taylor the summer term of the University at Lewisburg in 1851 was a time of preoccupation with the completion of one task and with emotional preparation to leave that task for another. The time was approaching when he must prepare for the graduation of the first collegiate class of this University, and, at the same time, his mind was revolving the thought that, as he wrote to a friend in Hamilton on May 31, 1851, he was "destined to hard work" in Madison University.[91] Even after he had made his decision, once for all, he continued to labor under an emotional strain which revealed the fact, as we shall see, that, even on the last day of his service to the University at Lewisburg, it was not easy for him to break loose from the institution which he had labored hard to establish in Lewisburg.

While the work of the summer term was progressing, and the seniors were making preparations for their final examinations and for their commencement, the readers of the *Lewisburg Chronicle* were learning (if they did not already know) that a big change was impending in their community. On July 2 the *Chronicle* carried an announcement of Taylor's acceptance of the presidency of Madison University, and two weeks later it printed a story saying that the Reverend Dr. Howard Malcom had been elected president of the University at Lewisburg. On August 6 this newspaper printed another story saying that Malcom had accepted the position to which he had been elected. Actually, Malcom was not formally elected by the Board of Trustees until August 19, but, as he said a day later when he formally accepted the position, this appointment had "long been expected." [92]

Whether by special invitation or as a matter of his own convenience, Malcom arrived in Lewisburg a few days before the summer session ended. George Good, a junior in the University at that time, tells us in his journal that he passed the night of August 10 at the home of Professor Bliss "so as to bring Doct. Malcom across from the cross-cut," which was on the east side of the Susquehanna River. There, at three-thirty the next morning, he met the canal boat which had brought Dr. Malcom up the river, and from the place of landing he took him to the home of Professor Bliss in Lewisburg. Incidentally, perhaps as a record for posterity, he noted that Dr. Malcom was "to be elected President of our institution." [93] The next day he observed that two other men of distinction, Dr. George B. Ide and the Reverend J. Lansing Burrows, had arrived in anticipation of the commencement exercises for which, on July 22, the senior class had met and made "all the arrangements." [94]

The activities of the first Commencement Week of the University began on Thursday, August 14, the first day of a three-day public examination of the senior class. Although he reported it to be thorough and difficult, J. Merrill Linn was pleased with the outcome of this examination, saying of his class, "we came off splendidly." [95] At ten o'clock in the morning of Sunday, August 17, Dr. Malcom preached in the Baptist Church, and of this performance Linn remarked that Malcom was "rather a comical man," but one who, as his writings showed, had a powerful mind. The afternoon of that day had been reserved for the annual sermon before the Society for Moral and Religious Inquiry, and for this occasion, as we learn from the diary of George Good, the Reverend Mr. Burrows preached a sermon in two parts, each of which lasted about forty-five minutes. Nor was the day yet ended. At seven-thirty that night the Reverend Dr. Ide preached another sermon, taking as his text Revelation 5:7. George Good, who enjoyed days like this one somewhat more than did Merrill Linn, and who has given us most of what we know about the afternoon and evening of August 17, 1851, in Lewisburg, did not forget to conclude the entry in his diary for that day with these words: "quite a heavy shower of rain overtook us coming from meeting this evening." Even the weather was co-operating with the Baptists on this occasion.

On Monday and Tuesday, August 18 and 19, the remaining classes of the College and the classes of the Academy were examined, and in the evening of August 19 the senior class of the Academy and the freshman and the sophomore classes of the College gave a public exhibition in the Baptist Church. On Monday evening there had been held in the Baptist Church an educational meeting, at which one of the speakers was the Honorable James Buchanan, of Lancaster, Pennsylvania, who, as one of the Curators of the University, was present for the session of that body on August 18 and 19.[96]

All the preliminaries having been completed, the first collegiate commencement in the upper Susquehanna Valley was held on Wednesday, August 20, 1851. It began with a procession which formed at the Baptist Church and marched to the Academy on the hill. There, at ten o'clock in the chapel, the exercises began before a crowd so large that not everyone who came could be seated in a very large room. The acting president, Stephen W. Taylor, presided. There were seven candidates for graduation, each of whom delivered an oration. J. Merrill Linn was the salutatorian, and J. Harvard Castle was the valedictorian. Pursuant to a provision in the charter of the University, the young men had previously been recommended to the Board of Curators for graduation, and this body, on the motion of the Honorable James Buchanan, had approved this recommendation.[97] After the orations had been delivered, Professor

Taylor, speaking in Latin, conferred upon each of the candidates the degree of Bachelor of Arts. Also, upon the recommendation of the faculty and approval of the Board of Curators, previously given, he conferred upon the Reverend Horatio Gates Jones, of Roxboro, Pennsylvania, the honorary degree of Doctor of Divinity.[98]

Three other events remained to be heard or seen. One of these was the delivery of an inaugural address by Professor George R. Bliss on the importance of the study of the classical languages. After this performance there came the one event of sadness, the leave-taking of Professor Taylor, whose farewell remarks, in the words of one reporter thereof, "brought tears to the eyes of nearly all present, and evinced the existence of a warm attachment, both on the part of the Dr. and his auditors." To these remarks the chairman of the Board of Trustees, Thomas Wattson, made an appropriate reply, and then he installed the Reverend Howard Malcom as the first president of the University at Lewisburg. The ceremonies closed with a benediction by Dr. Ide.[99]

It had been a day of triumph for the graduating class, some of whom had been in the University from its beginning in the Baptist Church. It had been a day of more than ordinary triumph for the salutatorian of the class who, although he had barely missed the first honors, was proud of what had happened to him. On this day he wrote in his diary as follows: "To day I graduated & have my diploma & degree of A.B. . . . The class have done well & we have only to complete what is begun. I am elected Alumni speaker for next year & [George B.] Ide Poet." [100] Nor had he yet said everything, for two days later, in an expansive letter in which he told his mother about the commencement exercises, he observed casually, but nevertheless with a feeling of satisfaction, that "papa was so much pleased that he did not say a word against the expense." [101]

3

Completing the Foundation

Go into the world not to be mere farmers, lawyers, or divines, but *men*, and let whatever concerns men, concern you.—*Howard Malcom, Baccalaureate Address, August 17, 1853.*

The work of founding a University is not the work of a day. —*Adie K. Bell, Report, 1858.*

When Howard Malcom was chosen to be its first president in 1851, the University was not resting on a foundation that was solid and complete. Its endowment was negligible, its proposed Institute for women had not been established, its Department of Theology had not been instituted, and its buildings had not been completed. Nor, at least from the standpoint of "progressive educators" of that era, was its program of collegiate instruction complete, for as yet it was offering no program leading to a degree other than the traditional degree of Bachelor of Arts. When he retired, six years later, the foundation of this University was all but complete. The University at Lewisburg had acquired some endowment; it had in operation two collegiate programs: one leading to the degree of Bachelor of Arts and the other leading to the degree of Bachelor of Philosophy; it had established the Female Institute and the Department of Theology; it had acquired equipment for the teaching of scientific subjects; it had laid the foundation for a substantial collegiate library; and, finally, it was in the way of completing its building program. It had made remarkable progress; it could claim, and it was claiming, a bright future for itself. In his final report to his Trustees, in July, 1857, President Malcom could say that the University, despite urgent needs, had "passed through its trying period of youth," and that it was "now ready to expand & flourish to the full amount of the hopes and intention of its founders." [1] His role in bringing about this transition we shall now endeavor to determine.

Howard Malcom was no novice when he came to Lewisburg. On the contrary, he was a man past fifty years of age, of broad education, and of wide and varied experiences as a minister, a philanthropist, an educator, and an author. He was born in Philadelphia on January 19, 1799; was prepared for college in Burlington, New Jersey; and was admitted to Dickinson College in 1813. But he left Dickinson College in his junior year, studied theology with Dr. William Staughton in Philadelphia, and subsequently, for about two years, attended the Princeton Theological Seminary. He was licensed to preach by the Sansom Street Church in Philadelphia on June 8, 1818, and was ordained in the same church on April 23, 1820. During the next twenty years he held two important pastorates, one of five years in Hudson, New York, and one of eight years in the Federal Street Baptist Church in Boston; and, moreover, he had written several works, of which the most extensively used or read were, perhaps, his *Dictionary of the Bible* (1828) and his *Travels in South-Eastern Asia* (1839). As early as 1827 he was awarded by Brown University the honorary degree of Master of Arts.[2]

In 1840 Malcom became president of the Baptist college in Georgetown, Kentucky, and this position he held with remarkable success until the summer of 1849, when he resigned this office and left Kentucky because his views on the subject of slavery had become inharmonious with those of his constituency.[3] Soon after leaving Georgetown College he was called to the pulpit of the Fifth Baptist Church in Philadelphia, and this call he accepted on October 7, 1849. Here he remained until, after accepting the presidency of the University at Lewisburg, his resignation of his pastorate was accepted by this church on October 27, 1851.[4] Meanwhile, besides traveling in Asia and serving in one way or another several benevolent societies, he had received the degree of Doctor of Divinity from Union College and also from the University of Vermont.[5] Accordingly, he had become a widely known and a highly accomplished man before he took charge of the incipient university in Lewisburg, Pennsylvania.

To his second presidency of an institution of higher learning Malcom brought, besides distinction and experience, the gentleness of polished urbanity, the serenity of a philosophical temperament, the patience of intellectual maturity, and an earnestness of purpose that was tempered by a quiet humor. He had need of such qualities, for he had undertaken to serve a newly born university that was suffering from poverty, that was then and would continue to be plagued by increasing debts, and that was situated, as he rather dryly observed in 1854, "in a location reached only with a measure of difficulties and expenses to which in these days few will submit."[6] Such an observation, because it was true, was perhaps not amusing to a community which, as late as 1856, was making much of the affirmation that the location of its university was "about in the centre of Pennsylvania." [7] Be that as it may, it was against a background of the hardships of educational pioneering, of frustrations at having recommendations ignored by superiors because the acceptance of such recommendations would require increased expenditures, and of other "backdraws" (to use one of his words), that Malcom counted, in report after report, his institutional blessings. Of the University at Lewisburg, as early as July, 1856, he could boast as follows: "Our grade of scholarship is high, our instruction thorough, our students remarkably orderly, our name extending & our alumni warmly attached." [8] This was an accomplishment worthy of a boast, for it had been achieved despite such "backdraws" as persisting poverty, disturbing agitation for removing the University from Lewisburg to Delaware County, the "prevalence of fever and ague," the inadequacy of buildings, the "unpopularity of one of the professors," and the handicap of "sustained hostility." "Backdraws" such as these would have discouraged a lesser man than Malcom.

To Lewisburg Malcom brought also a view of education which, at that time, was considered highly progressive, if not somewhat leftish; and, interestingly enough, his first significant educational service to the University was one that affected the curriculum. On August 19, 1851, while he was still president-elect, Malcom, on invitation, appeared before the Board of Trustees and made some suggestions about instruction. Thereupon the Board appointed a committee of its members to consult with the faculty on the subject of instruction. After consultation that night, this committee authorized President Malcom and Professors Bliss, Anderson, and James to submit a plan of English studies [*i.e.*, one free of the classical languages]. The plan these men prepared the committee accepted and submitted as its report to the Board, which approved it by unanimous vote. This plan provided, in addition to the Classical Program leading to the degree of Bachelor of Arts, that there should be instituted another program, one of three years, which would lead to the degree of Bachelor of Philosophy. Except for the omission of both Latin and Greek, and the inclusion of six new courses offered in the English language, the new three-year program would be identical with the four-year Classical Program. To put the new program into operation would require no enlargement of the faculty.[9]

Here we see the first gesture—a friendly one—that the University at Lewisburg made to the New Education which some American progressive educators were then advocating. Foremost, perhaps, among these progressives was a distinguished Baptist, Francis Wayland, widely known as the president of Brown University. With Wayland's famous *Report* of 1850 Malcom appeared to be familiar, but, whether he had or had not read this document, he shared with Wayland the belief that in America collegiate education should not be restricted to aristocrats and to the few who were preparing themselves for the learned professions, but that, on the contrary, it should be made beneficial to all classes of young men. "The demand for general education in our country," Wayland wrote, "is pressing and universal." To make such education available to the many, he continued, it must be so arranged that, "so far as it is practicable, every student might study what he chose, all that he chose, and nothing but what he chose." The objection that his program would, if put into effect, diminish the study of the classics bothered him not at all. He replied that Latin and Greek, if unable "upon their own merits" to retain their preëminence "in the education of civilized and Christianized men," should "give place to something better." "They have," he continued, "by right, no preëminence over other studies, and it is absurd to claim it for them." [10]

Whether Malcom would have gone the whole way with Wayland is doubtful; and speculation thereon is fruitless, for, even if he had desired to do all that Wayland wished to do, he would not have been permitted to do so—first, because he was working for conservative people, and, secondly, because no money was available for him to use in making unconventional educational experiments. No doubt it was the prospect of getting more students without increasing the cost of instruction that led the Trustees of the University at Lewisburg to put alongside their regular Classical Program a three-year Scientific Program leading to a degree that most persons would have considered inferior to the degree of Bachelor of Arts. Nevertheless, the step thus taken was a relatively bold one, and by September, 1852, the Trustees to the University at Lewisburg were boasting that their institution was "modeled on the new plan adopted in Brown, Harvard and other Universities: thus opening the advantages of the higher studies, in whole or in part, as the student may elect." [11] Perhaps they assumed that their new program was roughly equivalent to the Lawrence Scientific School recently established by Harvard.

On two formal occasions, and in language that Wayland and some other educational progressives would have applauded, Malcom made clear to his Trustees his progressive views on collegiate education. In August, 1852, in recommending the establishment soon of a professorship of the natural sciences, "with special reference to agriculture and the mechanic arts," he disclosed his familiarity with, and his approval of, the rising sentiment which eventually compelled the enactment of the Morrill Act in 1862. If subjects such as agriculture and the mechanic arts were not soon introduced and well taught in the higher seminaries, he affirmed, special institutions lacking solid learning in the ancient branches that should never be abandoned would arise to teach these subjects. By establishing a professorship such as he had recommended, he argued, the University at Lewisburg would be "as effectually an agricultural college as if . . . [it] were exclusively such," for, in addition to what it already offered, everything needed to make it "truly equal to any contemplated agricultural college is comprized under analytical Chemistry, with special reference to the analysis of plants, soils and manures, Botany and comparative phisiology [*sic*] with special reference to the laws of hereditary influences." Such addition, he concluded, would entitle the University to more generous patronage than it then received, and, moreover, as he affirmed, there were good reasons for educating "the youth of this country . . . together, and not parted off into schools for each class separately." [12] The new professorship was established in 1853, but it did not, as Malcom had predicted, make the University the equivalent of an agricultural college. Presently, the land-grant colleges came, one of them in Pennsylvania. Interestingly enough, the man called to the new professorship in the University at Lewisburg, Justin R. Loomis, was elected to the presidency of this institution soon after Malcom resigned this office.

Two years after recommending the appointment of a new professor, on the occasion of his announcing to the Trustees that twenty-three students were enrolled in the Scientific Program of the University and that three of them would be graduated at the next commencement, Malcom made a rather full confession of his faith in democratic education. "It has been my earnest wish in taking charge of this Institution," he said, "to see it assume & maintain that position which the present condition of the human family demands. . . . Higher education as given in a University can never be made general till it is so shaped as to suit the generality, & only by such adaptation can the state gain the fullest advantage in the cultivation of every class of citizens." There was a time, he admitted, when higher education, being aristocratic and exclusive, and sciences that are now important being non-existent, Greek, Latin, and mathematics were perhaps the only subjects worthy of a scholar's attention. Accordingly, some few "learned what Greeks & Romans knew or said two thousand years ago, but none were taught what to say and do themselves, or how they might bring out the riches of earth, air & sea." But now, he continued, the "range of philosophy" covered everything that would promote the well-being of humanity—so much so that any man with a fair common-school education and an active mind could, without laborious study of "dry and difficult studies," pursue "various branches of natural science with mental & moral philosophy, political economy &c. and qualify himself not only to acquire fame and fortune, but to bless his country by his skill and labor." [13]

Such views Stephen W. Taylor would most likely not have endorsed.

Nor would probably most other American collegiate professors and administrators of that era. Educational reformers, or at least the prominent spokesmen of such reformers, were neither numerous nor popular in pre-Civil War America, for they were opposing both tradition and vested interest. Philip Lindsley at Nashville, Francis Wayland at Brown, Howard Malcom at Lewisburg, and reformers at Amherst, at Oberlin, and elsewhere were pretty much as voices crying in a wilderness of emotion and of vested interest in the long-established program of collegiate education.[14] That program was the Classical Program leading to the coveted degree of Bachelor of Arts. As it stood at the middle of the nineteenth century, that program, if carefully scrutinized by a critic hostile to it and flippant in his expression of such hostility, might have been characterized as a hoary structure having a large and solid foundation of Greek, Latin, and mathematics, upon which rested a shaky superstructure of superficial scientific studies that were lightly embellished by introductions to political economy, mental philosophy, and moral philosophy, and that were topped off by Butler's *Analogy*. But such characterization would have been less than fair to those of conservative temperament, defenders of something that had been tried and found not wanting, who had rallied round the standard raised by the authors of the *Yale Report* of 1828. This document, an expression of learned opinion from the faculty of Yale, solemnly affirmed that "the two great points to be gained in intellectual culture are the *discipline* and the *furniture* of the mind: expanding its powers and storing it with knowledge." Accordingly, a liberal education could be acquired only by "such a course of discipline in the arts and sciences as is best calculated, at the same time, both to strengthen and enlarge the faculties of the mind, and to familiarize it with the leading principles of the great objects of human investigation and knowledge." Such course could be in no sense either professional or vocational, and in achieving its objects there could be no substitute for the classical languages and no room for electives. Accordingly, Yale had no need of "new-modelling"; [15] and the influence of Yale on this subject was through many years highly persuasive and widely pervasive. For the acceptance of the views of reformers of American collegiate education the fullness of time was not yet.

A vision of the New Education was not all that Malcolm brought to Lewisburg. He brought also enthusiasm for orderly procedure; enthusiasm for making the campus a place of ravishing beauty; enthusiasm for the acquisition of adequate equipment for teaching the sciences; enthusiasm for acquiring a collegiate library that would be both useful and distinguished; enthusiasm for teaching by hearing recitations and by giving lectures; enthusiasm for promoting through its newly established University the objects of the Baptist denomination in Pennsylvania; and, equally significant, he brought an abiding respect for the traditional system of paternalism in the governance of colleges. In respect to most things his enthusiasm ran in conservative channels, and in respect to everything that he undertook his energy was equal to his enthusiasm.

Characteristically, the first paragraph of his first annual report, submitted in August, 1852, dealt with the subject of arrangements and procedures. The year then ending had begun, he said, with various new arrangements that had proved to be beneficial. Moreover, in respect to order and procedure, two things of special significance had been done. One of these was the preparation of a complete code of laws for the governance of both the faculty and the students, the approval of this code by the Trustees, and the printing and distribution of it among the people concerned. The other important thing that had been done was the establishment of a system of marks and means which not only would bring to the attention of the president, once a week, "every single recitation of each student," but which also would inform every parent or guardian, at the end of each session, "of the progress, conduct and punctuality of his son." [16]

High on the list of matters claiming his early attention was that of the condition of the campus. As early as April, 1852, he had reported to the Trustees that he had kept one man constantly employed improving the grounds by removing therefrom some of the trees that "stood so close as to stagnate the air," that obstructed the growth of trees that should remain, and that prevented the growth of grass "without which no Park can be beautiful." If all the woodland owned by the University were properly thinned, he said, a considerable revenue might be obtained by pasturing it. On his request that a landscape gardener be employed to prepare a plan for the improvement of the grounds, the Board deferred action.[17] A year later he returned to this subject, saying that the campus was still an object to which he was devoting much attention, that on it much labor had been expended, a part of which had been done voluntarily by the students and the rest paid for by the sale of wood. "Much remains to be done," he continued, "ere it will be converted from a forest to a park." He renewed his request for a gardener to prepare a plan so that all subsequent work on the grounds would tend to "a harmonious and elegant result." But the Board, still hard pressed to meet its urgent expenses, again deferred action on his recommendation.[18] Malcom now apparently surrendered to the demands of institutional poverty, for in August, 1854, he enumerated among the misfortunes which the University suffered because of its lack of money that of grounds "receptible of the most charming embellishment, [but] lying a mere wood." [19]

In his quest of things that were "practical" rather than esthetic, Malcom was, however, achieving considerable success. One of the most urgent of the instructional needs of the University, as he pointed out to the Trustees in August, 1852, was a collection of specimens in geology and mineralogy which he was then working to acquire. The significance of such a collection, he maintained, could not be overstated, for without the aid of it the teaching of some of the branches of study recently introduced would be as difficult as would be the teaching of natural philosophy without adequate apparatus.[20] In subsequent reports he told of many letters that he and Professor George W. Anderson had written about this matter, and in April, 1853, he announced that instruction in the University would be much improved by the arrival from Paris of a "cabinet of Natural History, Mineralogy and Geology, an extensive herbarium and [a] manakin [*sic*]." [21] These materials had been bought in Paris by Professor George W. Anderson with money privately contributed for the purpose.[22] No small part of the sum thus expended came from the pocket of President Malcom, who, a few months later, was writing exuberantly about the cabinet, saying that, during about a year and without any expense to the University, he had expended some $2,000 in acquiring collections that now placed the University "in front of nearly all Colleges of the U.S. in this particular." It was a note of triumph that he sounded when, in justification of his boast, he remarked that every "topic in the text books on Mineralogy, Geology, Zoology, Botany & Physiology can now be illustrated with actual specimens, scientifically arranged & ticketed." [23]

Meanwhile, and also without cost to the University, President Malcom had been working diligently to acquire a library for the University. We have already seen that, when he arrived on the campus, this library had been no more than started. Thanks to his perception of its need, this library achieved, between 1851 and 1854, a remarkable growth, although in those years the University bought no books. Here was a task to which Malcom brought both enthusiasm and recently acquired experience. During his presidency of the Georgetown College, he had set himself the task, as early as 1841, of transforming a "tolerable" collegiate library into a good collegiate library. Money being unavailable, he resorted to begging for books. He was a persuasive beggar; even his relatives would acknowledge this fact. His method of proceeding is well illustrated by a letter that he wrote on March 12, 1842, to his much loved aunt in Philadelphia, Miss Hannah Poole. To her he said:

> I am to have a box of books & tracts packed at the Tract Depository 21 South 4th St. & if you or Mr. Wheeler have any old volumes to spare, it would be charity to give them to our College Library. It is very small & *any sort of books* will at [least] help fill up the shelves.[24]

By such means he succeeded in collecting a library which, by the standards of that time, was considered superior. Nor did it take him long to accomplish his object. Whereas as late as February, 1844, this library contained only 2,000 volumes, in June, 1848, President Malcom could proudly say to his trustees that the library of Georgetown College, besides having a printed catalogue of more than 5,000 volumes, had become "a Library which would do honor to any College," and which, with his own 1,700 volumes and 500 volumes belonging to the student societies, would give a student in Georgetown College access to more than 7,000 volumes.[25]

What he had done for the library of Georgetown College, President Malcom was determined to do also for the collegiate library of the University at Lewisburg. What he did within a few years for this library compares favorably with what President Thomas Clap did for the library of Yale College during the middle years of the eighteenth century and with what President James Manning did for the library of the College of Rhode Island (now Brown University) during the later years of that century. Once again he resorted to the writing of letters. Before he left Philadelphia for Lewisburg, he prepared, in August, 1851, a form letter reading as follows:

> It is of great consequence that our University at Lewisburg should possess a noble library. It would powerfully tend to draw students, and not only be an incalculable benefit to them while there, but to the Faculty also; enabling them to accomplish researches, otherwise impossible in a secluded location. Indeed, without a respectable library, there can be no respectable College.
>
> Can you spare some of your collection toward this object? You need not be restrained from giving any book by a fear that it may not be worth giving. Any work, above a Spelling book, or a Pamphlet will be welcome, and will be in some way useful. I earnestly beg you to give the University every book you have which is of little or no use to yourself and family.
>
> Please send them to the Publication Society's House, No. 118 Arch Street, with a list of the works, and your name.[25a]

As late as December, 1854, Malcom was still using this form letter, a copy of it in his Scrap Book showing the printed date line "Philad. August 1851" crossed out and the written line "Lewisburg Dec. 1854" substituted for it.[26] Nor did he restrict his begging to the sending of a form letter; once again, on October 23, 1854, he appealed to his "dear and only aunt," saying:

> I believe the Epis. Church has a society for printing & distributing the common prayer & other standard vols of practical piety. Would it not

make a donation of one of each of its publications for our Library where they would be permanently useful to many . . . ?[27]

By persistent begging President Malcom brought quick and abundant returns. In his first annual report, submitted in August, 1852, he could say:

> The steady increase of the Library is an object of constant solicitude, and I have obtained during the year 827 volumes, which nearly double our number of books, many of them . . . the most important we could have, and all will be constantly useful.[28]

By the end of the academic year 1853–54, President Malcom's efforts to build up a library with nothing had so exasperated him that, in his annual report to the Trustees for that year, he spoke sharply:

> Our library [he wrote] is of the utmost consequence to the Institution and though I have more than doubled it both in number of volumes and value, it is yet wholly unworthy of use—Not a book has been purchased since my connection with the Institution, while nearly $400 has been received for it from the assessment on students for its use— I presume it is your intention to appropriate these fees to the support of the Library. . . . I respectfully suggest that $150 be appropriated to binding pamphlets, repairing books, and the subscription for one or two of the most important periodicals.[29]

The Trustees, taking to heart the rebuke administered to them, appropriated $150 for the purpose that Malcom suggested, but they did not establish a fund for the purchase of books for the library. By this time the number of volumes in the collegiate library was 2,560, and one of them, a gift from Dr. C. Seiler, was "an old folio Martyrology of the Baptists" that had come from the press in Ephrata, Pennsylvania, more than a hundred years before.[30]

For three years President Malcom had worked zealously to improve the library, but by the early part of the year 1855 it appeared that his spirited effort for it was beginning to wane. He may have become somewhat disillusioned about it, or he may have decided to give more of his attention to other matters. However that may be, the academic year 1854–55 saw not only the beginning of a slackening of the growth of the library, but also the adoption of a new sort of appeal for books. Heretofore the Catalogue of the University had said little about the library. For the year 1851–52 it had mentioned a library fee of $2 per annum, and for the next year it had affirmed that the University had "a

Library Room," which, as we learn from the Catalogue for 1853–54, was forty feet square. But for 1854–55 the Catalogue not only called attention to the recent growth of the library, but also intimated what the sequel would clearly show—namely, that thenceforth the appeal for gifts of books to the library would be made in the Catalogue of the University rather than in letters bearing the signature of the president of the University. Whatever the reason for such change may have been, President Malcom permitted the insertion in the Catalogue for 1854–55 of a statement reading as follows:

> This branch of the means of instruction afforded by the University [*i.e.*, the collegiate library] has been enlarged during the past three years, by the addition of above 2,000 volumes, and is continually increasing. This increase has been made by the donations of books from a few individuals, the Institution having, as yet, no fund provided for this purpose. The donation of books is earnestly solicited. They may be forwarded either to the President, or to Rev. B. R. Loxly, 118 Arch Street, Philadelphia.[31]

During the next three years the library was neglected, and as late as July 25, 1859, after it had been removed to new quarters on the second floor of the central part of the new University Building (Old Main), it contained only 3,147 volumes.[32] This was the foundation of the collegiate library of the University at Lewisburg.

President Malcom's enthusiasm for an educational institution adequately equipped for effective instruction—great as we have seen that enthusiasm to have been—was no greater than his enthusiasm for promoting the great object of the founders of the University at Lewisburg. That object was to unite the Baptists of Pennsylvania (and presently also the Baptists of New Jersey) in promoting more effectively the cause of widespread evangelization under Baptist auspices. The University would be an important means to that end. Accordingly, he reported joyfully to the Trustees in April, 1853, a general religious awakening in the University during the preceding February that resulted in more than sixty persons' professing "a change of heart." Nor was that all. The University was performing a large amount of home-missionary work by maintaining stations for preaching and by conducting Sunday Schools in nearby towns. "Many of the students," he said, "are engaged either in preaching or Sunday Schools every Sunday, whom I furnish with tracts for distribution"; and about thirty of them, he said, would be employed by various benevolent societies during the spring vacation.[33]

By August, 1854, Malcom was even more enthusiastic about the extent of the Christian influence of the University "both on the contiguous population and on the more distant parts of the State." Besides supplying regularly with preaching four meeting houses and several schoolhouses, students of the University had held several protracted meetings and had conducted Sunday Schools and singing schools in various places. Moreover, the instructors were doing considerable preaching in the community, two of them preaching regularly every Sunday.[34] So extensive did work of this sort become that, after his report of March 25, 1856, in which he explained his desire to build up feeble churches as well as to give proper training to prospective young ministers, the Trustees resolved that, however worthy such work by students might be, they "would by no means encourage their efforts at the expense of absence from any regular duties of the University."[35] Presumably the Trustees believed that Malcom's zeal as a minister of the gospel was affecting adversely his judgment as the administrator of a university.

President Malcom was now in a quandary, and no doubt he felt somewhat hurt by a rebuke that he had not anticipated and that he thought he did not deserve. In his report to the Trustees in July, 1856, a few months after the cautionary utterance of the Trustees, he confessed that, on the advice of the faculty and of others, he had not strictly enforced the rule about the young preachers, although he would have done so had he not believed that the language of the resolution adopted by the Board said more than the Board had intended to say; for, as he observed, strict adherence to the rule would prevent any student from preaching on Sunday unless he could be back in the University in time for prayers on Monday morning. But he promised that thereafter, unless he should be otherwise instructed, he would require "rigid conformity to the rule."[36] He had both the mind and the heart of a good soldier.

Malcom was not "otherwise instructed," but he was given what the Board no doubt considered a clarification of its original resolution on the subject of preaching by students. On two separate days the Trustees reconsidered this matter, and eventually they agreed on a statement affirming "that the resolution in relation to preaching by students adopted at the last meeting of the Board . . . [was and continues to be their] . . . judgment in the premises, and as such, is intended to be administered by the Faculty with neither more nor less of rigidity than may justly be expected in the case of other regulations."[37] With this precious ambiguity the case was closed. What Malcom thought of this "clarification" we have no means of finding out, but we do know that in his subsequent reports to the Trustees we can find no mention of preaching by students.

If Malcom and his Trustees could not always see eye to eye in the matter of preaching by students, they were unanimous in their agreement respecting the basic principle upon which rested the governance of the University. Here, as in similar institutions of that time, the form of government was paternal; in relation to their students the president and the faculty of a college, wherever that college may have been situated, stood *in loco parentis*. There were, of course, differences in the spirit in which collegiate parental rule was enforced. President Malcom informed his Trustees, in August, 1854, that, as a result of ten years of experience in another educational institution, he was satisfied to depend upon the honor and the morality of the students rather than upon a "humiliating system of espionage & mistrust." "I watch very closely," he said, "the first symptoms of idleness or vice, and deal plainly though privately with the individual. Every student knows how he ought to conduct himself, and is not surprized to find himself questioned when he knows he has erred. Generally the result of private admonition is entirely satisfactory, and when it fails the student is removed without public censure." [38] Malcom's reports show that, now and again, he dropped a student for idleness or other misconduct, and also that occasionally he advised parents either to withdraw their sons from the University or not to let them return at the beginning of the next term.

But parental government in colleges comprehended more than the enacting of rules of behavior and of prescribing punishment for infractions thereof. Broadly speaking, it meant a fatherly supervision of the whole life of the student from his admission into college to his graduation therefrom. Such form of government acquires added significance to us when we recall the fact that, as late as the middle of the nineteenth century, students were commonly admitted to the freshman year of college at the age of fifteen, and to the preparatory department of a college at a still earlier age. In President Malcom's time a young man of fifteen years of age, or older, who wished to enter the University at Lewisburg would present his credentials of moral character to the President, who, if he were satisfied with such credentials, would send the candidate to an examiner. After passing his examination, and settling his accounts with the treasurer, he would return to the president, who would then admit him to the University after he had signed an affirmation pledging himself to "observe all the laws of the University at Lewisburg so long as . . . [he remained] a member of the same."

The laws that the newly admitted student had pledged himself to observe touched numerous matters, including emphatically his program of instruction, whether such program led to the degree of Bachelor of Arts or to the degree of Bachelor of Philosophy. In either case the work was prescribed. His hours of study and of recitation were determined by the faculty, subject to the approval of the Board of Trustees. In the early 1850's, these hours were as follows: "From the beginning of the first session to the first of April, . . . from 9 to 12 in the forenoon, from 2 to 5 in the afternoon, and from 6 to 9 in the evening. During the remainder of the year, from 8 to 11 in the forenoon, from 2 to 5 in the afternoon, and from 7 to 9 in the evening." During these hours, except when he was at recitations, the student was required to stay in his room and "apply himself with diligence to his prescribed studies and pursuits." At the end of each session he was publicly examined, and, if he did not "sustain himself," he would be either "conditioned" or required to repeat the work in which he had failed. His instruction was given by text books supplemented by lectures, and both the quality of his recitations and the character of his deportment were reported weekly. These reports were duly entered in a "doomsday book" kept by the president. The average that he received from reports thus recorded determined what, if any, honors a student should receive at the time of his graduation. His commencement oration he must submit to the president at least three weeks in advance of the day of its delivery. If the president should so direct, he must delete from his oration any "objectionable passage"; and any such forbidden passage he must not publicly utter, either absent-mindedly or maliciously, on his day of graduation, the penalty for so doing being forfeiture of his degree. If he received the degree of Bachelor of Arts, he would be entitled three years later (good conduct in the meantime being presumed) to apply for, and on the payment of the required fee to receive, the degree of Master of Arts *in course*—the italicized phrase being a euphemistic rendering of a longer but unexpressed phrase: "in the course of three years." However ridiculous it may seem to us, this practice had become well established in American colleges at that time; in this, as in most other matters, the University at Lewisburg did not wander from traditional paths. No such good fortune, however, was in store for the student who was graduated with the degree of Bachelor of Philosophy. For him there was nothing to look forward to "in the course of three years." He would not be eligible for the degree of Master of Arts—the only master's degree then offered—for he had completed only three years of college work and had never "sustained examinations" in either Latin or Greek.

Equally thorough was the supervision of the spiritual life and the personal conduct of the student. He was required to be present daily at chapel exercises, as well as to "remember the Sabbath day, to keep it holy." On Lord's day mornings he was required to attend public worship, and to provide such evidence of punctual attendance upon such worship as would satisfy the faculty. But attendance at church on Sunday need not mean attendance at Baptist services; he could choose, or his parents could choose for him, which of the evangelical churches in Lewisburg he would attend. But attendance at one such church was obligatory. Even when he was not attending religious services, or not observing study hours, he was not free to indulge himself in riotous living. If he were a law-abiding person, he could not be out of his room after ten o'clock at night; he could not smoke in certain places; and he could not keep intoxicating liquor in his possession unless it had been prescribed by a physician as medicine. He could not attend "forbidden" entertainments in Lewisburg; he could not associate with "vicious company"; he could not gamble, swear, or tell lies; and he must promptly go to his room when he was ordered by a member of the faculty to do so. His room could be entered by a member of the faculty at any time. His freedom to associate with other students in groups was restricted by the rule that voluntary student societies could not be formed and class meetings could not be held without permission from the faculty or from the president. For violating laws of the University he would be punished according to the gravity of his offense. He might be put on probation, or he might, if his offense warranted severe punishment, be expelled by consent of three-fourths of the faculty, the president approving.[39]

Such freedom as the student legally enjoyed—and that freedom would not have been confounded with license—was largely the consequence of the pecuniary stringency of the University. Within certain limits, he could choose his room and decide where and how he would get his meals. Before 1850 all the boarding students—women as well as men—had to occupy rooms and to take their meals in the village; and to get such services they could choose among the places that the faculty approved. By the opening of the year 1850–51, rooms were available to men in the West Wing of the University Building; but the University had no commons, the lack of which it justified by affirming that great advantages were obtained "by not bringing all the students together to board in common." Such advantages, we are told, were easy to recognize. Students thus separated were "less tempted to disorderly combinations, less exposed to the influence of evil example, . . . more likely in a well regulated family, to retain purity and propriety of manners, and in case of sickness receive more suitable attention." The price of board varied from $1.25 to $2.50 a week, although some students, by forming boarding clubs, obtained their food at somewhat lower prices.[40] The principal freedom of a student, however, consisted in his taking chances of not being caught when, because of boredom or an excess of youthful exuberance, he sought excitement by neglecting study hours or by engaging in pranks damaging to the property of the University or unbecoming to what then was conceived to be proper conduct for a young gentleman. Such freedom students everywhere and in all times have greatly appreciated. On the whole, if official reports are to be trusted, the students in the University at Lewisburg were not abnormal in their behavior.

As to the fixed expenses of collegiate life, every student had only the choice of paying them, unless he was the beneficiary of some society, such as the Pennsylvania Baptist Education Society, or unless, under peculiar circumstances, the Trustees saw fit to remit his tuition.[41] The expense of attending the University varied little from year to year through Malcom's administration. For the year 1854–55, the fixed costs in the College were as follows: annual tuition, $30; rent of an unfurnished room in the West Wing, $7.50; library fee, $2; care and cleaning of public rooms, $1; and fuel for public and private rooms, $4. In the Academy the price of tuition was $20, but in the Female Institute, which then was in operation, it was $30.[42]

The Academy, of course, was well established by the early 1850's, but during Malcom's administration its scope was somewhat broadened. Its main function continued to be that of preparing boys either for the Classical or for the Scientific Program in the College; but by the year 1855–56 it was offering, besides the Preparatory Course, a Normal Course that was designed "to prepare young men for teachers in public or select schools." Also, it admitted students who wished to pursue only "miscellaneous studies." By this time, if not before, students in the Academy had the privilege of rooming in the University Building.[43]

President Malcom's main concern in respect to the Academy was its lack of provision for supervising the conduct of young boys who came to it from distant places. To remedy this situation, he recommended, in April, 1853, that the principal of the Academy take charge of the Boarding House and receive into his family all young students "from a distance," and thus manage the Academy as the Female Institute was managed. Although he repeated his request for a reform in the administration of the Academy, the arrangement that he desired was not adopted until after the University Building was completed.[44]

We turn now to another aspect of our subject, an aspect of direct and vital concern to the Board of Trustees. While President Malcom was being much occupied with the internal affairs of the University, the Trustees had been intent, on the one hand, on instituting economies in the operation of the University, and, on the other hand, in prosecuting measures to hasten the completion of the foundation of such an institution as the founders of the University had envisioned. There was urgent need for them to do both these things, but the way to their accomplishment was hard. They needed money, and money was difficult to come by. Subscriptions must be solicited, but, once obtained, they were not easily collected. Since ordinarily subscriptions were obtained on condition that they could be paid in installments, some of them were paid only in part, and some of them were never paid. Consequently, it was hazardous for the Trustees to incur obligations in the expectation that, at a given time, enough money would be available to enable them to meet such obligations. Accordingly, they soon learned to proceed cautiously and to keep agents continually at work seeking new subscriptions and endeavoring to collect money already pledged. Although the agents of the University during those years were assisted by resolutions passed from year to year by the Pennsylvania Baptist Convention and by the Pennsylvania Baptist Education Society and published in their respective minutes,[45] the task of collecting subscriptions and money for the University was not an easy one. Perhaps it was intimate knowledge of such conditions that prompted President Justin R. Loomis to say, in 1865, that the "history of American colleges has been a history of financial embarrassment." [46]

Even greater than the need of economical administration was the need to establish, with the least practicable delay, all the departments of instruction specified in the Resolution of 1845 and to provide buildings that would house adequately all the branches of the University. A university that was ill-housed, ill-staffed, and ill-equipped would not inspire confidence in the Baptists of Pennsylvania, just as a university that operated, as the University at Lewisburg had operated from its beginning, on money advanced by friends could not relieve itself of the burden of uncertainty. Even the patience of so generous a creditor as the chairman of its Board of Trustees, Thomas Wattson, might in time wear thin. Already it appeared obvious that the University was tending to become a community institution.[47] Baptists in Philadelphia, accordingly, might be expected to regret the fact that they had helped to establish a university in a place as small and as inaccessible as Lewisburg then was. It would indeed not be surprising should well-to-do Baptists of the Philadelphia community presently express a willingness to spend a considerable sum of money to get the University removed to a more attractive site than its present one. Agitation for such removal apparently began early in the history of the University, for George Good, a member of the Class of 1852, tells us, as early as December, 1851, that he "heard it intimated that it is beginning to be aggitated [*sic*] whether this institution should be removed to some other location." [48] No doubt this "aggitation" smoldered during subsequent years; by the summer of 1856 the fire was visible for all to see. On July 29 of that year the financial agent and treasurer, Adie K. Bell, submitted to the Trustees as an item of business a proposal, dated April 4, 1856, of one of the Trustees, John P. Crozer, of Chester, Pennsylvania, to give $50,000 for the purpose of "more fully founding and endowing the University," provided that the University be removed to the neighborhood of Chester, in Delaware County. But, in order to receive this gift, the Trustees must not only approve the proposal, but also get before April 1, 1857, the legislation required for removal. In presenting this matter to the Board, Bell remarked that the "offer is noble, liberal, princely, and demands the serious and mature consideration of the board."[49]

Sorely in need of money, the Trustees were now confronted by a grave decision—whether to accept or not to accept the offer, whether to abandon the investment already made in Lewisburg and to begin anew in a community of greater wealth and of larger population. The decision would not be an easy one to make. To the people of Lewisburg, however, this so-called "noble, liberal, princely" offer was anything but that. On the contrary, as expressed in a remonstrance adopted with but one dissenting vote by the Board of Curators on the motion of J. F. Linn of Lewisburg and of David J. Yerkes of Holidaysburg, this offer was as unwise as it was unsettling, as illegal as it would be unfaithful to the people of the Northumberland Baptist Association and elsewhere, people who had made a large investment in an enterprise that they were told was to be situated in Lewisburg.[50] The Trustees, slightly annoyed by the remonstrance of the Curators, debated the offer at length, rejected a motion to postpone action on it, and then, on July 30, 1856, refused the offer by a vote of ten to four. The four who voted for acceptance of the offer were John P. Crozer, William Bucknell, and J. Wheaton Smith, all of Philadelphia, and Adam Johnston of Reading.[51]

The issue of removal not only emphasized the need for the University to set its affairs in order; it also emphasized the need of haste to make the investment in Lewisburg so valuable that no subsequent attempt to remove the University therefrom would be seriously considered. Much had been done since 1851. Economy had been practiced until it hurt, and all the departments envisioned by the Resolution of 1845 had been established; but the University was still poor, and its main building was not completed.

To understand the condition of the University at the time of the removal crisis in 1856, we must return to the year 1851 and follow some of the lines of its development during the next five years. From the beginning of Malcom's administration, the Trustees had sought means to reduce the expenditures of the University. On August 19, 1851, their committee on the report of the treasurer pointed out that the debt of more than $2,000 owed by the School Fund to the $100,000 Fund had increased during the year 1850–51 by $756, and it recommended early action on this matter. The Board, however, postponed such action, but it did abolish the office of superintendent, and it did impose on the president the duties of assistant treasurer as well as those of supervisor of buildings.[52] A year later, however, the Board appointed a special committee and charged it with the duty of reporting forthwith on the expediency of curtailing the expenses of instruction in the University. One day later this committee recommended that, in view of the decreasing income from tuition and of some new commitments that had been made, the two professorships of languages be merged, and that the professorship of belles lettres be dispensed with for the present. Hesitant about taking such drastic action, the Board postponed the recommendation until the meeting in April next, and then again postponed it until the meeting in August of 1853, at which time it voted to postpone the matter indefinitely.[53]

In 1853, however, the Board resorted to several measures to achieve economy. It accepted the resignation of Alfred Taylor, professor of belles lettres, and it left this chair vacant; it turned over to one of its long-time teachers, Norman Ball, to be conducted as a private venture, the Primary Department of the University, and lent him the furniture of the Primary Room; and it combined the duties of the treasurer and those of the financial agent, and persuaded Adie K. Bell to accept this enlarged office.[54] Then, in August, 1854, after Bell had reported that it "appeared" that, since the opening of the enterprise, the School Fund had absorbed more than $9,000 from the $100,000 Fund, and that the Trustees should decide how this money should be refunded, the Board accepted the resignation that George W. Anderson, professor of the Latin language and literature, had submitted on March 31, 1854. It then consolidated the two professorships of languages and elected George R. Bliss to the professorship of the Greek and Latin languages and literature.[55] Whether pressure was put upon Anderson to resign his office, or in the preceding year upon Alfred Taylor to resign his office, we do not know. It is interesting to observe, however, that the recommendation on this subject which the Board declined to accept in 1852 and 1853 had now, by indirect means, been given effect. President Malcom expressed to the Trustees his great regret at Anderson's resignation, but, loyal servant that he was, he bowed before the inevitable and consoled himself with the knowledge that his favorite professor was leaving "without discord." [56]

While they were taking rather drastic measures to reduce the operating expenses of the University, the Trustees were putting into effect other measures to enlarge the scope of its instruction. As early as 1852 they had added another branch (or, as then called, department). This was the Female Institute, a branch not named in the charter but specifically mentioned in the Resolution of 1845. From the opening of the school in the basement of the Baptist Church in 1846, girls as well as boys had been taught in the University. Until 1852 there was coeducation in practice, and as late as 1852 the names of the girls were listed in the Catalogue of the University under the title Female Academy.[57] The moving of the girls into a separate building of their own would not only enhance the prestige of the University; it would also fulfill a promise that Stephen W. Taylor had made to the Baptists of Pennsylvania in 1846—namely, that the young men and the young women would not recite together,[58] although that was what they did do in the Academy between 1846 and 1852, with results not altogether displeasing to a man as precise as was Professor George R. Bliss.[59] What was needed to create in fact a branch of the University for women was money to acquire, or to construct, a building for their use; and money, as we should by this time have learned well, was something not easy for the Trustees to come by in the early 1850's.

When the Trustees met in April, 1852, a letter was laid before them by their temporary chairman. This letter, dated April 16, 1852, was from their permanent chairman, Thomas Wattson, who could not be present, but who told his colleagues of his having learned that a large house owned by James K. Casey and situated in Lewisburg at Second and St. Louis Streets could be bought for a Female Boarding School for $4,200. This matter the Board referred to a special committee, of which President Malcom was a member. This committee recommended, and the Board agreed, that this house should be purchased, provided that it could be had at a price not exceeding $3,500.[60] On August 17, 1852, Malcom reported that the Casey House had been bought for $3,500, payment for which was to be made on August 30. The house, however, was in need of some repairs. The Board appointed a committee with "plenary power" to repair the house, to employ competent teachers for what would be called the University Female Institute, and, when looking for teachers, "to try and get a male Teacher to take charge of the Seminary." [61] Perhaps for pecuniary reasons, the committee, however, settled for a woman as principal, Miss Hadassah S. Scribner, of Littleton, New Hampshire. The Institute opened on October 21, 1852, and by April, 1853, it had more than forty pupils and was in a prosperous condition.[62] As early as August, 1854, the treasurer could report with satisfaction that this department of the University was not a losing concern.[63]

Miss Scribner remained as principal of the Female Institute for two years, at the end of which time, being unwilling to take over and operate the school as a personal venture, she resigned the principalship. She was succeeded by Miss Amanda Taylor, of Northampton County, who agreed, at the end of the first session of 1854–55, to take charge of the boarding department jointly with Mrs. D. E. Kean, who was teacher of mathematics in the Institute. During the first year of Miss Taylor's administration, the Institute became well organized and highly prosperous, to the great delight of the treasurer, who affirmed that theretofore it had "been at loose ends, both in its government and in its course." Now everything was different. Miss Taylor had prepared a curriculum for the primary department as well as for the regular course, and a committee of the Trustees, with the approval of the teachers and the president of the University, had prepared a set of rules for the government of the Institute.[64] Moreover, during this year the Institute had acquired a library and a literary society, and had published its first catalogue.[65] All told, the year 1854–55 had been for the University Female Institute, in a sense that was not subtle, *annus mirabilis.* At the end of that year the committee that was in charge of the Institute was almost ecstatic in describing the progress of the Institute, and, in words that must surely have rung pleasantly in the ears of those who were embarrassed by the poverty of the University as a whole, affirmed that the Institute, from a pecuniary standpoint, "has paid, is paying, and will pay better than any other [department] of the school." Nor was this all. "Its influence on the community," the committee continued, "and the interest of the enterprize throughout Pennsylvania and New Jersey we think can scarcely be overrated. Your committee therefore with confidence ask for it the fostering care of the Board, believing the day is not far distant when it shall not only yield a handsome revenue, but do very much towards building up the entire University." [66]

Such prosperity in the Institute inevitably gave rise to the idea of expansion, and in 1855 the Board of Trustees, on the recommendation of its committee on the Institute, authorized the disposal of the building then occupied by the Female Institute for a price not less than $6,000, provided that the right be retained to continue to use this building until such time as another one might be ready for the Institute to occupy.[67] Less than a year later the committee on the Institute reported that "this department of the University" was still prosperous, still profitable, and filled to overflowing.[68] Such affluence in an outpost to a campus on which pennies had to be squeezed, and on which high aspirations had to be restrained, deserved a reward, and presently it would get it in the form of a new building on a new site that would be closer —but not too close—to buildings frequented by young men on College Hill.

The curriculum prepared for the Female Institute by Miss Taylor and approved by the Board of Trustees provided for a preparatory class for one year and for a three-year regular program consisting, for the most part, of subjects which now would be considered appropriate for high-school study. It made provision also for the optional study of Latin and of such ornamental subjects as music and drawing. The regular course, however, led to a diploma, not to a degree, and graduation did not entitle a girl to pursue further studies in the collegiate department of the University.[69]

The Female Institute, a day school as well as a boarding school, affirmed that its first object was to prepare young women for the "cheerful discharge of the duties of life," a collegiate career being obviously not one such duty. To achieve such object it directed its attention not only to the training of the intellectual powers of young women, but also to the education of their physical systems and of their hearts. It aimed at thoroughness of instruction, it required precise grading of recitations and deportment, and it prescribed public examinations at the end of each session; and, moreover, it exercised watchful care over the health and the morals of its pupils. It required them to take daily exercise in the open air, weather permitting, and it provided a gymnasium for them. Also, it made abundant provision for the spiritual life of its pupils, requiring of each of them a recitation in the Bible "as a daily exercise" and attendance at a daily religious service in school, at a weekly prayer meeting, and at a Bible class once and at public worship twice every Sunday. Pupils who came from a distance were required to board in the school. Their freedom of movement was regulated somewhat more rigorously than was that of the boys. A girl living in the Institute could not expect to be out at night after nine o'clock except by special permission, and ordinarily she could receive calls only on Friday evenings. Emphatically she could not accept an invitation to ride or walk with a young gentleman "without permission from the principal obtained before making the engagement."

A boarding student in the Institute during the academic year 1854–55 paid for tuition, if in the preparatory course, $20 dollars; but, if in the regular course, $30. Each one paid for board, room, lighting, and heating $2.25 a week, and for washing one dollar a week; and each one paid additional, and varying, sums for instruction in optional studies, for use of the library, and for "pew rent." Day pupils were charged a dollar a year for fuel.[70]

Thus the Female Institute was in, but not quite of, the University at Lewisburg. But its peculiar situation, being governed as it was by the same Boards and by the same president as were the other branches of the University, was presumed to give advantages to its pupils that were not enjoyed in other such institutions less favorably situated. Pupils in the Institute were permitted to hear occasional lectures given by professors in the University, and they had access, when occasion demanded, to the laboratories and to the library of the College. On the other hand, advantages to the University as a whole were expected to accrue from this arrangement, for the presence of the girls in the nearby Institute would, as some persons hoped, tend to improve the conduct and to elevate the manners of the boys in the Academy and of the young men in the College.[71]

Even before they had removed the Female Academy from the Academic Building and renamed it the University Female Institute, the Trustees were about the business of establishing in the University a department for imparting instruction in theology. Such a department, although specifically mentioned in the Resolution of 1845, had not been specifically prescribed by the charter, perhaps because Stephen W. Taylor thought that its omission therefrom would make easier the acceptance of the charter by the state legislature. However that may have been, theological instruction in the University was generally desired and widely expected. Accordingly, in a meeting of the Trustees in April, 1851, the general financial agent, William Shadrach, moved that a committee be appointed to report forthwith a plan for the establishment of such a department.[72]

Behind this resolution lay interesting events. Shadrach had been testing Baptist opinion while he had been collecting Baptist pledges in both Pennsylvania and New Jersey. He reported to the Board on a short but successful campaign that he had recently undertaken to solicit in New Jersey subscriptions for the University. For that purpose he had entered that state about the first of November, 1850, but had accomplished little there until he proposed, with the approval of two prominent Baptists in New Jersey, to enlist the Baptists of that state in a specific subscription which, if successful, would entitle them to effective representation in the founding and sustaining of the University at Lewisburg. Accordingly, at a gathering of "friends of Education" in Newark on December 13, 1850, resolutions were passed not only approving a union of Baptists of New Jersey and of Pennsylvania in support of collegiate education, but also sanctioning a proposal that the Baptists of New Jersey should raise the sum of $15,000 to endow in the University at Lewisburg either a professorship of mathematics and natural philosophy or a professorship of the Greek language and literature; and the meeting specifically commended Shadrach to "the friendly regards of the Baptists of New Jersey," and solicited in his behalf their "liberal co-operation." For the purpose of this endowment Shadrach collected in New Jersey, between December 13 and December 25, subscriptions amounting to $3,250.[73] This was the beginning of what presently would become the New Jersey Professorship Fund.

On August 18, 1852, Shadrach reported to the Board that the subscription for the New Jersey professorship was nearing completion, and that the Baptist Convention of New Jersey had "referred" to the New Jersey Baptist Education Society the management of this professorship. Thereupon the Trustees, in order to tighten the union of Baptists in New Jersey and in Pennsylvania in support of collegiate education, voted that the "Brethren in New Jersey" should be represented in the governing of the University by two members on the Board of Trustees and by four members on the Board of Curators, and that the nominations of persons for such offices should be made by the New Jersey Baptist Education Society. They also voted that, as soon as the first installment of the fund for this professorship should be invested, the nominees of the New Jersey Baptists should be entitled to election to their respective posts.[74] On November 13, 1852, the New Jersey Baptist Education Society approved these proposals, and on August 16, 1853, Shadrach reported that the subscription to the fund for the New Jersey professorship had been completed.[75] Nevertheless, presumably because of the slowness of collections and of making investments of what was collected, it was not until August, 1855, that the Trustees of the University elected to membership on their Board the first two nominees from New Jersey.[76] The complete subscription for this professorship was never collected. In August, 1858, the general agent and treasurer, Adie K. Bell, reported that he had received in cash from this subscription the sum of $10,849.[77] Nevertheless, the professorship was established, and in the Catalogue of the University for 1858–59 there appeared under the name of George R. Bliss, for the first time, the title of New Jersey Professor of the Greek and Latin Languages and Literature.[78]

It was after relating his experience in New Jersey in November and December of 1850 that Shadrach called attention to an uneasiness in certain quarters that he had noticed during his travels—a troubled concern about the delay in making provision in the University at Lewisburg for giving proper instruction to young men who were looking forward to careers in the ministry. He then announced that he had obtained $2,000 in unconditional pledges and $1,000 in a conditional pledge toward the endowment of a professorship in theology. He expressed the belief that the entire sum needed to complete this endowment could be obtained during the ensuing summer. Consequently, after his report had been accepted, he moved, as heretofore mentioned, that a committee be appointed on the subject of planning for theological instruction in the University. This committee was appointed, and Shadrach, as a member of it, reported for the committee on the next day, recommending that one professor of theology be appointed, that a course of instruction in theology be given for one or two years to meet the wants of both graduates and non-graduates of colleges, that such instruction be given gratuitously, that a subscription to raise $20,000 to endow a professorship in theology be authorized, and, finally, that the Board affirm that it would be under no obligation to establish such a professorship until an endowment for it of $20,000 be raised. The Board approved this report, and, before adjourning, elected to the new professorship in the making Dr. George B. Ide, pastor of the First Baptist Church in Philadelphia.[79]

But there were delays. The task took more time than Shadrach supposed that it would take, and so it was not until April, 1853, that he could report that, as endowment for the presidency and for the professorship of theology, the sum of $49,380 had been pledged. He now resigned his agency, but was persuaded to continue his labors until the subscription for the New Jersey professorship should be completed.[80] Presumably the concern of the Trustees about effecting economies accounts for the further delay in establishing a professorship in theology. Whatever the reason therefor may have been, it was not until August, 1854, that they appointed a committee to inquire whether Dr. Ide would accept the professorship to which he had been elected, and, in case of his refusal of the offer, to nominate another person for this position.[81] In April, 1855, this committee reported that Dr. Ide had declined the appointment offered him, and, accordingly, it recommended for election to this position the Reverend Thomas F. Curtis, a man thirty-nine years old, a graduate of the Bangor Theological Seminary, the author of a treatise on communion, a former pastor of several churches in the South, and a scholar who was well recommended. Accordingly, on April 26, 1855, the Trustees elected him by a unanimous vote at an annual salary of $1,000.[82] In August of that year the Trustees voted that $20,000 of the endowment recently raised should be set aside for the support of the professorship of theology.[83]

Professor Curtis, a man who did not underestimate his importance and who gave his advice freely, sometimes to those who thought that they had no need of it, asked that his salary be at least $1,150 a year; but, when the Board declined to go beyond its first offer, he accepted the salary of $1,000. The Board also, on August 14, 1855, adopted a program of theological study which presumably had been prepared by Curtis.[84] As explained in the Catalogue for 1855–56, this program consisted of two years for graduates, one year for persons of limited time to give to such study, and, perhaps most important of all, a regular course of three years, to which juniors in the college would be admitted and be permitted, for three years, to study both theological and collegiate subjects. At the end of that period, having finished both their collegiate and their theological studies, they would receive the degree of Bachelor of Arts.[85]

Well before the spring of 1856, Professor Curtis had become a thorn in the side of Professor Malcom, who, on March 25 of that year, requested the Board of Trustees to decide an issue which, as he said, had caused the University much embarrassment. Professor Curtis, said Malcom, understood that his department was to be considered, not as a department like that of natural sciences, but as a theological institution having a faculty distinct from that of the College. After due consideration of the matter, the Board decided that the Department of Theology was "under the immediate care of its own Board of Instruction," and that it had no more "separateness" than any other Department of the Institution.[86] Presumably this assertion means what the Catalogue seems to confirm—namely, that the Department of Theology was a Department in the same sense that the College, the Academy, and the Female Institute were three distinct Departments of the University. Accordingly, neither Malcom nor Curtis was entirely "right." Curtis, however, was not given the title of principal, or director, of the Department of Theology. To the end of his career in Lewisburg he had no title other than that of professor of theology.

The year that witnessed his embarrassment about Professor Curtis—1856—was for Malcom a year for counting woes rather than blessings. By this time he was weary of overwork and of suffering frustrations. In a letter on February 29 of that year he imparted to George W. Anderson, a friend and a former colleague, the information that he would not continue to be president of the University much longer. "I have set my heart on resigning all office[s] at 60 which is but 2 or 3 years off," he said. "Bliss would make a first rate Pres. here & I am only keeping out a better man by holding on." [87] Before that year was ended, his woes had piled high. His discontent because the Board had ignored again and again his recommendation that the Academy be so reorganized as to provide better supervision of young boys away from home was now augmented by painful cases of discipline, by what seemed to him like a rebuke for his emphasis on preaching by students, and by accumulated discontents and inconveniences that arose from the persisting poverty of the University. His faculty had been diminished, the enrollment in the University had shrunk,[88] and the general outlook was gloomy. But that he would retire at the end of the next academic year was, perhaps, something that he did not yet know.

For the University, however, the year 1856 was more nearly a year for renewing hopes than for counting woes. The University then emerged safely, at least temporarily, from the danger of removal, and now many of its supporters were determined to safeguard it against a renewal of such danger. In a word, there arose a new determination to accelerate the pace of action to finish the foundation of the University by completing its essential buildings and by enlarging its endowment. When the investment in buildings became large, the danger of its being abandoned would diminish. Consequently, the major concerns of the Trustees during the next two years were the construction of a more adequate building for the Female Institute and the completion of the main University Building.

The Female Institute, still growing and still prosperous, was rapidly becoming the darling of the Trustees. Accordingly, when the committee of the Trustees on this branch of the University reported in July, 1856, that the Female Institute was still prospering, still making a profit, and now becoming full to overflowing, the Board promptly agreed with the committee's recommendation that it was "absolutely necessary" for the Institute to have a larger and better building on the grounds that had been set aside for such purpose. It accordingly resolved that the building presently occupied by the Institute should be sold for not less than $5,000; that from the proceeds of this sale and of sales of University lots there be appropriated for the erection of the proposed new building a sum not exceeding $15,000; and that, when the sum of $10,000 should be obtained from the sale of "the present property & Lots," a committee should be appointed to plan a building for the Institute and to supervise its construction. Then, ignoring the limitation in the last of these resolutions, it appointed forthwith a committee to give effect to its purpose in this matter.[89]

The work of getting the new building proceeded rapidly. On September 13 the committee sold the building which housed the Female Institute. It then obtained from an architect in Philadelphia the plan of a new building, and on October 24, the day on which it sold for about $5,000 twenty University building lots, it advertised for bids for the construction of the new building, which would be situated in "the Grove, near St. George street." On November 1 the contract for construction was awarded to L. B. Root & Co., of Muncy, for $16,500, the "Messrs. Root making a subscription of $300," and the building was to be ready for occupancy on September 20, 1857. The committee apologized for ordering a building that would cost more than the Board had wished to pay, but it was not reproved for having done so when it explained that it was necessary for it to exceed the limit set by the Board in order to get a building that would be suitable for the Institute. "It will comfortably accommodate some 90 pupils with their teachers," the committee said, and then it called attention to the fact that the kitchen, the dining hall, and the school rooms were sufficiently large to permit an addition to the building of enough sleeping apartments to accommodate as many as 150 boarders.[90] In July, 1857, the committee on this project estimated that the total cost of the new building would be about $17,000, nearly all of which could be paid from the proceeds of the sale of University lots.[91] In July, 1858, the buildings of the Institute were valued at $17,500.[92]

Even before the contract for the construction of the new building for the Female Institute had been let, the building committee of the University had awarded, about the first of October, 1856, a contract to Lewis Palmer, of Lewisburg, for the construction of both the central part and the east wing of the main University Building. The contract price was $34,000.[93] Palmer had achieved some local fame for his work on the new Union County Court House, which is still, after more than a hundred years, an imposing building in Lewisburg.

The effort to complete the University Building had dragged its heels for many years. Because subscriptions were paid very slowly, the building committee did nothing. When the general agent and treasurer reported on August 15, 1854, that he had in the Building Fund more than $7,000 in subscriptions and in the treasury $2,116.03 in cash, the Board appointed a new building committee, with Thomas Hayes serving it as chairman, and instructed this committee to get proposals for the completion of the University Building, but not to enter into a contract for such construction until the sum of $25,000 had been subscribed and as much as $10,000 thereof had been paid into the treasury of the University. Of this subscription the sum of $6,000 must be subscribed in Lewisburg and its neighborhood, a territory "embracing a diameter of ten miles." [94]

Two years later the general agent and treasurer reported that $25,000 in subscriptions had been obtained for the Building Fund, and on the same day, July 29, 1856, the chairman of the committee on this project explained that this sum had been raised "by an extraordinary effort in the Borough of Lewisburg." The sum required to be in the treasury before building operations could begin would, he affirmed, soon be there. The next day, July 30, the Board authorized the building committee to proceed with the work of completing the University Building as soon as the treasurer should certify that he had in hand the sum of $10,000 for such purpose.[95] Before the end of August this committee was advertising that bids for this construction would be received until three o'clock in the afternoon of September 19.[96] Soon after the date for closing bids a contract, as we have already learned, was made with Lewis Palmer. In March, 1857, Adie K. Bell reported that he had on hand to pay for this project $26,442 in subscriptions, but that, to compensate for losses of subscription and to pay for "agency," about $9,000 more would be needed to pay for the completion of the University Building.[97] A few months later he announced that the deficit, including the cost of heaters for the building, would be $10,200.[98]

By the end of July, 1858, the University Building was virtually completed, but the University then lacked more than $8,000 of having enough money to pay what it owed the builder. Moreover, in order to pay for stoves to heat this building, the University would need at least $1,500 more. This deficit, the general agent and treasurer was certain, was the fault of no person connected with the University. The reasons of such deficit, on the contrary, lay in the "revulsions" of business which, in recent months, had stopped in its course the "whole machinery of trade." "Wealth," he continued, "made to itself wings and flew away—all classes of society and every department of business have been made to feel the pressure." In such circumstances to collect money already pledged was difficult; to get new subscriptions was impossible. Accordingly, the Board appointed a committee to report on the subject of the debt owed for the completion of the University Building.[99] A year later, after reporting that the contract for the erection of this building was "nearly completed," the treasurer moved, and his motion carried, that the committee on this building be discharged.[100] The reason therefor, presumably, may be found in a story, published in Lewisburg on March 25, 1859, affirming that President Justin R. Loomis had succeeded in raising by subscriptions the money required [the headline says $10,000] to finish paying for "the last buildings of the University at Lewisburg." [101]

Before this building was completed, even before the new building for the Female Institute was ready for occupancy, Howard Malcom had ceased to be president of the University at Lewisburg. Weariness and ill health no doubt hastened his retirement. As early as January, 1857, he was complaining of excessive work and poor health. "Once," he wrote, "hard work was a pleasure—now it begins to be wearisome—though I can do as much, in a given time, & do it as well, as I ever could—" Moreover, he continued, "My right arm has been almost useless for several months, with rheumatism, & was till lately very painful." [102] Later in the year he suffered a recurrence of the throat trouble that earlier had "silenced" him for years,[103] and this malady seemed to get worse rather than better. Accordingly, as he told his Trustees on July 28, 1857, he resigned an office which they had bestowed upon him by unanimous vote, and in which he had spent "six of the pleasantest years" of his life. The Trustees were not to be outdone by such urbanity. In accepting his resignation they not only expressed sympathy because of his affliction, but also assured him that the University would cherish "with warmest gratitude, the memory of its first President, and [would] fondly hope that his example of gentlemanly urbanity and self-sacrificing toil . . . [would] not be lost upon its future history." [104] The amenities did not stop here. As a parting present the University conferred upon Howard Malcom the honorary degree of Doctor of Laws.[105]

Because of his seniority, Professor Bliss was now made acting president of the University, and in this office he served through the academic year 1857–58. Malcom's successor, Professor Justin R. Loomis, although elected on December 29, 1857, did not assume the duties of his new office until the fall of 1858.[106]

As its second presidency was about to begin, the University seemed to be pervaded by a new spirit, a sense of fulfillment. We perceive this spirit at the end of the academic year 1857–58 in the concluding remarks of the report of Professor Bliss as acting president, in the holding of the commencement exercises in the new University Building, in the introduction of the new president during commencement exercises, and, emphatically, in the summary view of the financial history of the University that was prepared by the general agent for the Trustees and that was by them ordered, on July 27, 1858, to be published.[107] Pervasive was the perception that the University had come to the end of an era; that it had passed safely through a troubled infancy; that the way seemed now to be opening to a desirable future for it. Thus far its accomplishments had not been negligible. It had acquired, or was at the point of getting, its necessary buildings; it now had in operation every branch of instruction prescribed in the resolution adopted by the Northumberland Baptist Association on August 14, 1845; it had sought, and by this time it had achieved, the co-operation of Baptists in New Jersey in the establishment of a New Jersey professorship in the University; it had, thanks to railroad connections, largely overcome the handicap of isolation; it had been steadily encouraged and consistently commended through the years by the Pennsylvania Baptist Convention; and, besides approval, it had received from the Pennsylvania Baptist Education Society pecuniary aid for receiving as students the beneficiaries

An Act
To establish the University at Lewisburg..

Whereas, The Baptists of Pennsylvania as a denomination are not now engaged in the maintenance of any particular College or University in this State; And Whereas, The Chartering of a University to be placed under their patronage, [illegible] and direction, would be a measure well adapted to call forth from all parts of the Commonwealth, [illegible] means and [illegible] efforts in the establishment of sound learning, the efforts of said denomination and thereby promote the general interests of science, literature and good morals; Therefore,

Section 1. Be it enacted by the Senate and House of Representatives of the Commonwealth of Pennsylvania in General Assembly met, and it is hereby enacted by the authority of the same, That there be and hereby is erected and established at or near the borough of Lewisburg, in the County of Union, in this Commonwealth a University, to consist of a primary school and Academy, a College, and such other departments appropriate to a University as the friends and [illegible] of said institution shall from time to time be able to maintain, and that the name and Constitution of the said University shall be and they are as follows —

Article 1. Section 1. The said institution shall be forever called and known by the name of "The University at Lewisburg".

Article 2. Section 1. The said University shall be under the management, direction, government and supervision of a number of Trustees, [illegible] and a number of Curators, not exceeding forty, a quorum of each as hereinafter [illegible].

[illegible]

On February 5, 1846, Governor Francis R. Shunk approved the charter of the University at Lewisburg

The First Baptist Meeting House in Lewisburg, in the basement of which the University at Lewisburg had its beginning

Stephen W. Taylor, the author of the charter of the University

James Moore, Jr., one of the principal founders of Bucknell University

William Bucknell, the man for whom the University was named in 1886

The Academy Building, now called Taylor Hall, was the first building of the University at Lewisburg

Old Main, when completed in the late 1850's, was one of the largest collegiate buildings in the United States

The Building of the Female Institute, now called Larison Hall

The faculty in 1874
Seated—(l. to r.) Professor George R. Bliss, President Justin R. Loomis
Standing—(l. to r.) Professors Francis W. Tustin, Robert Lowry,
and Charles S. James

Baseball team of 1899, with Christy Mathewson second from the right, rear row

Women's basketball team of 1896, with Dr. Mary Moore Wolfe third from the right

The Bucknell Band in the early 1900's

Loomis Field was the scene of many exciting football games, but most of the spectators had to stand

of that society. Now, it seemed, it needed only better support in dollars and in students from Baptists throughout Pennsylvania and New Jersey to silence the accusation of its serving local interests rather than the denominational interests of the Baptists throughout these states. Now, being prepared to give superior service, it could look forward patiently and hopefully to the reaping of an abundant harvest, and, while so doing, console itself with the thought that the "work of founding a University was not the work of a day."[108] It now had both a solid foundation and a goodly heritage.

Part Two

The Challenge of a New America

4

The Troubled Years of War

The history of American Colleges has been a history of financial embarrassment.—*Justin R. Loomis, An Address in 1865.*

President Justin R. Loomis brought to his new office no thought of drastic reform. As the sequel will show, he was a conservative. Although a graduate of Brown University, he emphatically did not endorse President Francis Wayland's "progressive" views on collegiate education. The editor of the *Lewisburg Chronicle* was no doubt correct in his judgment that the choice of Loomis for president of the University at Lewisburg was "eminently safe and judicious." [1] For this office he received a unanimous vote of the Trustees, but not until fourteen ballots had been taken. On October 28, 1857, Thomas Wattson, acting for the committee appointed to nominate a successor to President Howard Malcom, presented the name of the Reverend Samuel B. Swaim, of West Cambridge, Massachusetts; and James Moore, Jr., also a member of this committee, presented the name of Professor Justin R. Loomis. Two ballots were taken, and on each of them Loomis received a majority, but not a large enough majority to be elected. At the next meeting of the Trustees, which was held in Philadelphia on December 29, 1857, a third name, that of the Reverend Arthur S. Train, of Harvard, Massachusetts, was presented. Through the first ten ballots at this meeting, the vote for Loomis varied from four to seven. After the tenth ballot, Swaim's name was dropped; on the eleventh ballot Train received five votes and Loomis received eight; and on the twelfth ballot Loomis received a unanimous vote. He assumed the presidency of the University in the autumn of 1858, and, at the same time, the professorship of metaphysics and moral philosophy.[2]

Loomis was born in Bennington, New York, in 1810. He entered the Hamilton Literary and Theological Institution in April, 1828, withdrew therefrom in 1831, entered Brown University, and was graduated by this institution in 1835. After teaching for a year in Pawtuxet,

Rhode Island, he became a tutor in Waterville College (now Colby) in 1836. Two years later he was promoted to the rank of professor of chemistry and natural history, a position which he held for fourteen years. He was ordained a Baptist minister in 1845. On August 17, 1853, he was elected professor of the natural sciences in the University at Lewisburg, but he did not assume the duties of this office until January, 1854. He held this position until he was elected president of the University. Before coming to Lewisburg, he had traveled in South America, and he had published two textbooks: *Elements of Geology* in 1852 and *Elements of Anatomy and Physiology* in 1853. Both these books passed through more than one edition.[3]

Loomis was neither a gifted speaker nor a graceful writer, but he was recognized as a "thorough educator." [4] He was a vigorous, courageous man of exemplary piety; he was dedicated to the work of his calling; and he gave generously of both his time and his money to works of Christian benevolence. He was much respected, and even admired by some persons; but he never became an object of general affection. Unhappily, he lacked a sense of humor. It would have been impossible for him to poke fun at himself. During his presidency of twenty-one years, the University passed through more than one period of troubles, and, at the time of his retirement, it was deep in a dangerous crisis. A man endowed with a saving sense of humor and with a mind more flexible than his would doubtless have survived these troubles better than he.

In the beginning his requests for changes in the University were not numerous. Pursuant to those which he made in his reports in March and July, 1859, the Trustees promoted Francis W. Tustin from the rank of tutor to that of adjunct professor of languages, authorized a Christmas vacation of ten days, approved the alteration of the Academic Building so as to fit it as a residence for the principal of the Academy and for the boarding of students, appointed, pursuant to a recommendation of the president of Dickinson College, President Loomis as a delegate to represent the University in a united appeal of the colleges of Pennsylvania for legislative aid, and also appointed a committee to consult with a commitee of the Pennsylvania Law School Association on a proposal to establish, in connection with the University, a school of law in Lewisburg. The University, however, never received legislative aid, and it never established a working relationship with a school of law. The intention had been that the proposed school of law in Lewisburg should be self-supporting, but that it should use certain facilities of the University and that upon the graduates of this school the University should confer degrees. For some reason, not now known, this project did not materialize, although Loomis was in favor of it. Also, at their session in July, 1859, the Trustees authorized Professor Bliss to teach courses in the Department of Theology and Professor Curtis to teach courses in the College.[5]

At the meeting of the Board of Trustees in July, 1860, President Loomis reported that the Academic Building had been remodeled, at a cost of about $2,500, so as to provide, "besides the rooms required for School & recitation purposes, sixteen dormitories, a Dining Hall and [a] suitable apartment for a family." Also, he requested, and the Board approved, the appointment of Francis W. Tustin as professor of the natural sciences so as to give the "list of Instructors the appearance of greater fulness and more correctly answer to the facts of the case." Another event of that year, and one that was highly significant for the future, was the delivery by members of the faculty of lectures to the students "on subjects nearly relative to their course of study, though not included in it"; and President Loomis said that it was the "purpose of the faculty to make these lectures more frequent & reduce them to a system as rapidly as possible."

By this time it was plain to those who were permitted to examine its records that the University was getting into pecuniary difficulties of an embarrassing character, for on July 25, 1860, the committee of the Trustees on the state of accounts reported a deficit of $7,062.51. Since there was trouble about getting agents to solicit subscriptions and to collect pledges, an effort was made to persuade Adie K. Bell to add to his duties as treasurer the duties both of general agent and of principal of the Female Institute.[6] This unattractive offer Mr. Bell refused to accept, and with the passing months the pecuniary situation of the University did not improve. In March, 1861, President Loomis reported that "the notes issued to liquidate the final indebtedness of the Building Fund amounting to some $2,300 interest included" were due; that "the salaries for the past term . . . [were] for the most part unpaid, and further that the income for the coming summer . . . [would] probably not meet the expenses." But the Trustees, not knowing what to do, postponed the matter of their indebtedness until their meeting in July, 1861.[7] Before that meeting was held, the country was involved in war.

From its beginning to its end, the Civil War had a somewhat disturbing but, except for a few weeks in 1863, not a disruptive effect upon the University. The coming of this war should not have been a shock either to the faculty or to the students, for the University, chartered in February, 1846, had had its beginning and had reached its early maturity in a period of sectional cold war, during which successive crises were loosening the bonds of American nationality. Consequently, both the faculty and the students had had, so to speak, a time of preparation of hearts and minds for this war; they had passed through disturbing crises, they had discussed the issues which produced these crises, and, whether for this reason, or perhaps for the reason that there were no Southerners in the University, they had become of one mind before the challenge of disunion confronted them. Accordingly, when the war came, there was no "secession" from the University of either students or members of the faculty because of conflicting ideologies. So also of the members of the Board of Trustees, with one exception. The Reverend William T. Brantly, who had become pastor of the Tabernacle Baptist Church in Philadelphia in 1856 and a trustee of the University at Lewisburg in 1860, was, on July 29, 1862, dismissed from the Board of Trustees because, as the official record shows, he had "removed his residence from Pennsylvania to the Rebellious part of the Union." [8] To be specific, Dr. Brantly, a Southerner who had spent his boyhood in Philadelphia and who had been educated in Brown University, had accepted a call to become pastor of the Second Baptist Church in Atlanta, Georgia.[9]

Owing to scanty records, we cannot trace in full the efforts of members of the faculty, whether on rostra or in pulpits, to guide, during the troubled years of the 1850's, the public thought about disturbing contemporaneous issues; but we can discover where their sympathies lay. We know that President Howard Malcom and Professors George R. Bliss and George W. Anderson participated in a public meeting held in Lewisburg on February 21, 1854, to express opposition to the repeal of the Missouri Compromise, and that they also participated in another public meeting, held in the chapel of the University on July 4, 1854, to denounce the enactment of the Kansas-Nebraska Bill.[10] We also know that in 1856 Professor Bliss, in two published letters, not only supported John Charles Frémont, Republican nominee for the presidency, but also committed himself fully to support the Republican principle that there should be no further extension of slavery into American territories.[11] Also, we have other evidence, less trustworthy but easy to accept, that Professor Bliss, a few years later, did some campaigning for Abraham Lincoln.[12]

Naturally the students in the University at Lewisburg could take little part in shaping public opinion; but in their literary societies, in the Academy as well as in the College, they could, and they did, discuss all issues, intramural and extramural, that seemed important to them. Like students before their time and after their time, they were receptive rather than original; and for this reason the records of their doings, being mostly reflections of what was happening about them, are highly important sources of our cultural history. Fortunately, we have in the

Archives of our University the complete minutes of the two collegiate literary societies—Euepia and Theta Alpha—from their formation in 1850 to a time well beyond the period of the Civil War; but, unfortunately, we have the minutes of only one society in the Academy, and these minutes extend only from 1850 to 1854. Nevertheless, from these surviving records we can trace, to some extent, the impact upon the students not only of the disruptive happenings of the 1850's, but also of the war that began in 1861.

Let us begin with the Academic society called Phirhoan, a society which, in the early 1850's, not only debated questions, but also decided each of its debates and recorded all such decisions. On March 1, 1851, it decided that slavery should be abolished in the United States. On March 26, 1852, it decided that, by extending its territory, the United States would strengthen the Union; and on December 3 of that year it decided that the Fugitive Slave Law of 1850 should be repealed. Thereafter, until early in 1854, it turned its attention principally to domestic social questions and to certain aspects of our foreign policy. It decided, *inter alia,* that young men in college should not habitually associate with ladies, that the Maine liquor law should be sanctioned by the people of the United States, that women should not have equal rights with men, and, after two discussions, that "Spirit-Rappings" were "a humbug." As to foreign affairs, it decided that the United States should aid another nation striving for freedom when asked by that nation to do so, but it also decided that it would not be proper for the United States to assist Turkey in the Crimean War. Finally, on March 2, 1854, while the Kansas-Nebraska Bill was under discussion, it decided that our form of government was in danger of being overthrown.[13]

By contrast, the two collegiate societies, although not indifferent to the important problems of women and liquor, were deeply concerned, during the 1850's, with the issues raised by the sectional controversy of that decade. Unfortunately for us, they refrained from recording either their approval or their disapproval of orations delivered before the society, and they passed no judgment as to the outcome of any debate within their respective halls.

For some reason that is not clear, the Euepians were more interested in debating questions of national political concern than were the men of Theta Alpha. During the year 1851, Euepians discussed both the "rightness" of slavery and the desirability of repealing the Fugitive Slave Law of 1850. In 1853 and 1854, when the question of organizing the territories of Kansas and Nebraska was before the country, the Euepians discussed the right of a state to secede from the Union, the constitutionality of a Federal law to prohibit the introduction of slavery into "newly acquired territory," the advisability of enacting the Kansas-Nebraska Bill, and, significantly, the consideration of whether it was "the imperative duty of every American citizen to yield implicit obedience to and as far as it is in his power carry out every law of this Republic." Also, in 1854, the men of Theta Alpha considered whether the signs of the times pointed to a dissolution of the Union, a subject to which they returned in 1858 and again in 1860. In 1854, moreover, they listened to an essay entitled "Our Country's Future."

During 1856, when "Bleeding Kansas" and a Presidential campaign were matters of great interest, the Euepians were debating whether Representative Preston S. Brooks should be expelled from the House of Representatives for his assault upon Senator Charles Sumner, whether the Union should be dissolved, and whether Buchanan would be a better President than Frémont. In the same year the men of Theta Alpha discussed, *inter alia,* the power of Congress to exclude slavery from the territories, and, at one meeting, listened to an oration entitled "Our National Existence in Danger."

Curiously, neither of these societies came to grips in 1857 with the consequences of the Dred Scott decision. In that year and in 1858 they were concerned about the proposed admission of Kansas under the Lecompton Constitution and about the territorial expansion of the United States. In those years both societies discussed the desirability of annexing Cuba to the United States and of making Mexico a protectorate of the United States. In 1859 the two societies discussed, among other things, John Brown's raid on Harpers Ferry, the Euepians asking whether this "outrage" was a natural consequence of slavery, and the men of Theta Alpha asking whether John Brown should be executed for his offense.[14]

The increasing tension produced by the Presidential campaign of 1860, by the election of Lincoln, and, presently, by the secession of several of the Southern states was as emotionally disturbing to the University as it was to the community of Lewisburg; and uncertainty and concern about the course that the Buchanan administration would pursue between the election and the inauguration of Lincoln are reflected as clearly in the activities of the collegiate literary societies as they are in the columns of the newspapers of Lewisburg. Eventually the attack upon Fort Sumter released pent emotions. "The news of Fort Sumter surrendered has thrown us all out of sorts," wrote Elisha Shorkley, a businessman of Lewisburg, in his diary for April 17. "Today a roll appears & names are being rapidly added. Our Flag has been insulted. A requisition from the Present. for *75000 men. War—How full of dread.* Our town [is] in banners & the roll of the drum is stirring to battle."

The next day his entry was as follows: "War and the necessary arrangements seems [*sic*] the idea of all hands. Drums & Banners tell of patriotism. Cold cloudy day. Eighty-four leaving for Harrisburg. . . . Retired at 10 all excitement. I pray there may be no battle." [15]

By April 19 the *Union County Star and Lewisburg Chronicle* was telling even more about the excitement, the banners, and the preparations for war being made in Lewisburg. "American national flags, &c.," it said, "are displayed in Lewisburg, and the feeling appears to be almost unanimous, here, to stand by the Government in its present struggle with a despotism as treacherous as it is cruel." In this issue we find the text of President Lincoln's proclamation of April 15, calling for 75,000 militiamen to put down "combinations" obstructing the operation of Federal laws, and here we learn that of these troops Pennsylvania would be expected to provide sixteen regiments. Here also we learn that a military company, with members from Mifflinburg, Winfield, and other places, had been formed in Lewisburg under the name of the Lewisburg Infantry; [16] that this company's offer of service had been accepted; and that Friday (April 19) had been appointed as the time for its starting to Harrisburg. Finally, we learn that the editors of this newspaper had stopped their press on this day so that they could give "some account" of the departure of eighty or ninety men from Lewisburg "to defend their country's honor and the rights of humanity." These persons, we learn, "rendezvoused at their temporary Armory in Chamberlin's Block, at an early hour, and—preceded by the Republican and the Democratic flags of the last campaign side by side—proceeded about 8½ A.M. to the Railway Depot on foot." There they found assembled about 1,500 men, women, and children, and there the Reverend Thomas M. Reese, of the Methodist Church, addressed the departing soldiers and those who had come to see them off "in most eloquent, manly and patriotic terms."

One week later the *Star and Chronicle* [17] told its readers that not only had Lewisburg provided the first company from the West Branch, but also that a second Lewisburg company (with twenty-five outside members, some from Mifflinburg and some from Hartleton) had been formed under the proposed name of Slifer Rifles; [18] that some Lewisburgers, some former students, and some graduates of the University were enlisting elsewhere; that the ladies of Lewisburg and its vicinity had been invited to meet in the Baptist Church in the afternoon of April 26 "to take means to prepare Surgeon's bandages"; and that the Lewisburg Bridge Company had generously provided free use of its bridge to persons "going to and from the Railway with military companies."

Lewisburg was now in the war, and the University was showing its approval of what the town was doing to forward preparations for fighting. By May 17 the patriotic activities of the University had attracted the attention of the editors of the *Star and Chronicle,* for in their issue of that date they "noticed" not only that "the Female Seminary and University Buildings in Lewisburg have the American Flag displayed," but also that the "College boys are drilled, military fashion, by Capt. J. B. Hutton, formerly a Lieutenant in the Centre County Infantry." [19] An even greater display of patriotism by the University was made nearly three weeks later when, on June 5, the Slifer Guards, "over fifty in number, left Lewisburg for Harrisburg." These men "were escorted by Capt. James Hayes and his troop of forty or fifty on horseback—about an equal number of Home Grays, under Capt. [Jacob] Neyhart—and a portion of the University Company, commanded by Capt. Hutton, whose imitation guns and soldier-like movements commanded special applause. A very large throng assembled at the Depot, when Prof. [George R.] Bliss made some timely remarks to the Volunteers and their friends, and Eld. Rodenbaugh commended them in prayer to the blessing of Almighty God." [20] That night one of these volunteers, writing to the *Star and Chronicle* from Camp Curtin, near Harrisburg, tendered for himself and his associates "hearty thanks to Prof. Bliss for his inspiring words of cheer, to Capt. Hutton for his efficient services, the University Guards, Home Guards, the Troop, and your citizens generally, who kindly escorted us to the Depot to see us off 'rejoicing on our way.' " [21]

This was not the last appearance of the University Guards with their imitation guns, nor was it the last time that members of the faculty of the University would participate in patriotic demonstrations or in other affairs related to the prosecution of the war. Both the faculty and the students took prominent parts in celebrating the Fourth of July in Lewisburg in 1861. President Justin R. Loomis and Professor George R. Bliss served on a committee to procure speakers, and Professor T. F. Curtis served as chaplain for the occasion.[22] The role of the University Guards in this observance was somewhat spectacular. The evening before, they had marched to a hill (presumably present-day College Park) that was then owned by Major John Gundy. Here they pitched their tents, raised the American flag, ate their evening meal, paraded, entertained visitors, and then held a religious service led by their own chaplain. Before retiring for the night, they posted a guard, seven in number, and provided that every hour this guard should be changed, so that each member of the company might perform this kind of duty. Called from their slumber by reveille at four o'clock the next morning, they immediately fell in, marched in parade, and fired a salute of thirty-four guns. Then they were called to morning service, at which they "were favored with the attendance of a detachment from the Female

Institute." Whether the girls remained for breakfast the record does not reveal. However that may have been, after breakfast the University Guards struck their tents, and at about six-thirty o'clock began a return march to College Hill, where they presently arrived "without any casualty, with ranks unbroken, and much pleased with . . . [their] brief campaign." They were now prepared to march, and did march, through the streets of Lewisburg in a long parade, and afterward they received, at the residence of Joseph Meixell, "an elegant Flag." On this occasion both President Loomis and Professor Bliss made appropriate addresses.[23]

Thus far the work of the University had not been much disturbed, and for months thereafter it would be hindered little, because of the war. As late as Commencement Week, July 28 to August 1, 1861, the editors of the *Star and Chronicle* could say that the University had "suffered as little as any other from the times." If it had been situated in one of the states of New England, the University might have pursued throughout the war a course no more disturbing to its work, and no more hazardous, than the one that it had pursued during the spring and summer of 1861. Despite some embarrassment from a temporary dwindling of its enrollment, and considerable discomfort from rising prices, it might well have continued to carry on its work much as it had before the war began. Its professors might have restricted to religious, patriotic, and humanitarian activities their efforts to further the cause of the North, and its students might have confined their efforts to drilling with imitation guns and to debating questions (as they did) touching the rightness of war, the wisdom of important decisions made by President Lincoln, the qualifications of Northern military commanders, the advisability of enlarging our navy, the possibility of British intervention in the war, the wisdom of encouraging mixed schools, the effect of the Emancipation Proclamation, and the wisdom, or lack of wisdom, in presuming that "the production & free use of wine in the United States would not diminish the amount of drunkenness."[24] But such tranquillity for the University at Lewisburg was not to be; for Pennsylvania, with its southern border inadequately defended, was vulnerable to enemy raiding parties, and even to invasion if the Army of Northern Virginia, advancing northward from the Shenandoah Valley, could bypass, out-maneuver, or defeat the Army of the Potomac. Once the enemy had entered Franklin County in force, the way lay open to it through the Cumberland Valley to Harrisburg and the whole Valley of the Susquehanna. Because of a threat of invasion in 1862, because of an actual invasion in 1863, and because of a damaging raid in 1864, the University at Lewisburg, within each of those years, became, willy-nilly, to some extent, a participant in the Civil War.

The first armed participation of the University, made in 1862, was more spectacular than important, for the threat to Pennsylvania in that year arose when the University was not in session, and the threat was of short duration. Between September 3 and September 10, the danger from the northward advance of the Army of Virginia increased so greatly that, on the last-named date, Governor Andrew Curtin called upon all the able-bodied men of Pennsylvania "to organize immediately for the defense of the state." The next day, by order of the President, he called out fifty thousand of the "freemen of Pennsylvania" for immediate service "to repel the now imminent danger of invasion." [25]

Meanwhile, in Lewisburg, Captain George W. Forrest in the North Ward and Captain Charles C. Shorkley in the South Ward had been drilling companies, which, by September 9, were awaiting orders to go to Harrisburg.[26] They did not wait long. In the morning of September 13, Captain Shorkley, with some seventy men from the South Ward, set out for Harrisburg, and in the evening of the same day Captain Forrest, with about forty men from the North Ward, also left for Harrisburg. On Monday morning these groups were followed by other recruits from Lewisburg, some from the South Ward and others from the North Ward. In Harrisburg, in the afternoon of September 14, the Third Regiment of Pennsylvania Militia was formed. It consisted of ten companies. Company A came from Milton. Company B, commanded by Captain Shorkley, was the South Ward Company of Lewisburg, and Company C, commanded by Captain Forrest, was the North Ward Company of Lewisburg.[27]

Except for one person, the University was represented only in Company B. Because the students were then on vacation, this representation was not large; but it was of such character that it attracted considerable notice. It included four students whose academic status, according to the Catalogue of the University for 1861–62, was as follows: one was a freshman, one was a sophomore, one was a senior in the Academy, and one was a member of the Theological Department. Also in this company were two recent graduates of the University. These six persons were residents of Lewisburg.[28] The startling fact about this company, however, is that the president of the University, Dr. Justin R. Loomis, and one of the professors, Charles S. James, were members of it. Although, according to a contemporaneous report, they had both been offered commissions, they declined to serve as officers because of their lack of military experience.[29] They enlisted as privates. President Loomis, however, was made regimental chaplain, and Professor James was chosen to be one of the sergeants of Company B. Corporal Edwin C. Wolfe, of Company C, had been a member of the University in the Class of 1857, but had not finished his course. All told, the University was represented by nine persons in Company B and Company C.[30]

The service of these men proved to be neither long nor hazardous.[31] They were mustered in only for the duration of the emergency, which was virtually ended by the battle of Antietam. On September 24, after twelve days in the army, they were again home in Lewisburg, looking "bronzed and thin . . . [but] in good spirits." [32] They had advanced beyond Hagerstown, and more than once they had stood in battle formation; but they were never under fire. Nevertheless, as the enthusiastic editors of the *Star and Chronicle* remarked in welcoming them home, they "left when real danger threatened—did their duty, patriotically—were successful in their object—had 'a good time' in all respects—and in general will only have to regret that the 'campaign' was so short." [33] The editors of this newspaper might also have said that, for the University, what really mattered was that both President Loomis and Professor James had returned a day before the opening of the fall term.[34]

Nine months passed by before Pennsylvania was again threatened with an invasion. This time there was an invasion, one of the consequences of which was the suspension for six weeks of the work of the collegiate and the theological branches of the University at Lewisburg. This invasion, set on foot soon after the Confederate victory at Chancellorsville, was not unexpected by the North. A great victory for the Confederates in Pennsylvania might well decide the outcome of the war. A victory of such consequence seemed imperatively necessary to the Confederates, for, as General Robert E. Lee remarked to President Jefferson Davis, in a letter dated June 10, 1863, "We should not . . . conceal from ourselves that our resources in men are constantly diminishing, and the disproportion in this respect between us and our enemies, if they continue united in their efforts to subjugate us, is steadily augmenting." [35] Moreover, a successful invasion of Pennsylvania, a land of plenty, would have a wholesome effect upon Confederate soldiers, who often were ill-fed, scantily clad, and, in numerous instances, compelled to march without shoes.[36] Furthermore, the pleasure that such soldiers would experience in teaching the Yankees how discomforting an invasion can be to people whose country is invaded was an added reason for a large-scale Confederate advance into Pennsylvania. We may be certain, I think, that a young Confederate surgeon, Dr. Spencer Glasgow Welch, was voicing a view widely held in the Army of Northern Virginia when, on June 21, 1863, as his northward-moving corps was nearing Winchester, Virginia, he wrote to his wife, saying that he would endure almost anything to have the pleasure of "getting into Pennsylvania and letting the Yankees feel what it is to be invaded." [37]

Naturally, preparations to repel this expected invasion were being made in both Washington and Harrisburg. One action looking to this end was the division of Pennsylvania into two military departments—

the Department of the Monongahela and the Department of the Susquehanna.[38] Scarcely had this action been taken when, on June 15, President Lincoln called into Federal service one hundred thousand of the militia of Maryland, Pennsylvania, West Virginia, and Ohio "to serve for the period of six months from the date of such muster into said service, unless sooner discharged." Of these troops, Pennsylvania's quota would be fifty thousand.[39]

By this time Lewisburg was once again thoroughly aroused. On June 15 a Lewisburg girl, Sally Meixell, wrote in her diary as follows: "Bad war news. Lee's reble [*sic*] cavalry are making a raid in Penna. The militia are called out." That same day Elisha Shorkley wrote in his diary, saying: "The tocsin of alarm is being rung throughout the land. An invasion is threatened and we are all agog again. Business is on the wane and suffers in interest. War meeting." The next day he wrote that the whole town was "afloat on the waves of excitement." Also on June 16 the people of Lewisburg could read in the *Star and Chronicle* an alarm sounded by Governor Curtin on June 15, as well as an impassioned plea by him to prospective volunteers not to hold back for fear that they might be kept in the service for six months, but, in a time when the capital of their state was threatened, to trust his assurance that they would not be held beyond the end of the emergency. "I will accept men," he promised them, "without reference to the six months."

A response from Lewisburg came quickly. There, on the night of June 16, a meeting was held in front of the Lewisburg Bank to make preparations "to send on men AT ONCE for the defence of Pennsylvania." [40] The next morning "a large crowd gathered on Market Street. Capt. T. R. Jones, late of the North'd Co. of the 131st,[41] started with about 50 students from the University, and was followed before noon by Capts. Shorkley and Forrest, with some of those in service last Sept. Additions to these companies were made Wednesday night and Thursday morning. . . . Our College classes are to a man absent. . . ." [42] Thus we learn that Lewisburg was sending out three companies of emergency troops, notwithstanding the fact that, as soon we shall see, not all the classes of the College were "to a man absent."

The morning of June 17 was a busy time for Sally Meixell, who spent several hours working on and directing the making of three haversacks and parts of three others. Her work, however, was interrupted when John Probasco, one of the student volunteers, brought her his photograph. At eleven o'clock she went down the street with Hannah Bright "to see the Militia comps. off." After bidding many of them goodbye, she allowed one of the departing seniors, William Wolverton, to kiss her cheek. Naturally, this was a time when everyone would be expected to be co-operative as well as self-sacrificing, and Sally averred that she had made this concession "to prevent a fuss." However that may be, she remarked, as a clarifying afterthought, that "two town comps." had left that morning, together with "Capt. Jones' comp. of students." "All the College & Academy students enlisted," she continued, "except some seven, one a 'sick copper head,' the others wounded, too delicate, & too young." [43]

Captain Jones's company, unofficially known as the University Guards, proceeded to Camp Curtin. In the evening of June 22, at dress parade, Captain Jones told his company that it had become Company A of the Twenty-Eighth Regiment of Pennsylvania Volunteers.[44] Of the nine other companies in this regiment, two were from Lewisburg. The South Ward Company, commanded by Captain Charles C. Shorkley, became Company D, and the North Ward Company, commanded by Captain George W. Forrest, became Company F.[45] That night Orlando Wellington Spratt, a member of Company A, wrote from Camp Curtin to the *Star and Chronicle* as follows: "Ours is the *third* regiment organized for this emergency. . . . Gov. Curtin is to be judge when the emergency is over. . . . The boys are enjoying excellent health and spirits, and are prepared to perform whatever duty is required of them." [46]

Company A was for some days separated from its regiment. As late as July 3, it was guarding the railroad bridge at Marysville, north of Harrisburg. Presently, however, it set out to join its regiment, which was then at Carlisle.[47] But it appears that it was quickly assigned to special duty, for on July 10 the *Star and Chronicle* reported that Company A, when "last heard from," was on duty as provost guard at Shippensburg. While it was there, a considerable number of Confederate prisoners were committed to its care, and on July 11 the second lieutenant of this company, Professor Charles S. James, passed through Harrisburg in charge of more than a hundred wounded prisoners who were being sent to a hospital in Philadelphia.[48] On July 14 the *Star and Chronicle* reported that, except for Captain Jones's company, the Twenty-Eighth Regiment of Pennsylvania Volunteers, "when last heard from," was in Waynesburg. Eventually, Company A joined its regiment, perhaps in Hagerstown.[49] Soon thereafter this regiment began moving northward.

On July 21, Captain Shorkley, of Company D, writing from a camp near Greencastle, said that his troops had left Hagerstown that morning, and that on July 22 they expected to march to Chambersburg, from which place, he presumed, they would go by rail to Harrisburg. He supposed that they would be home in about a week.[50] He was approximately right. Between Monday evening and Thursday evening, July

27–30, the three Lewisburg companies reached home. Their health had been so good that only three men had been left behind, two from Jones's company and one from Forrest's. Captain Jones's company had returned in squads, between Monday evening and Wednesday evening. The other two companies arrived at five o'clock in the afternoon of Thursday, and found, "in addition to 'Commencement' and the Circus people, a large crowd to welcome them home." [51]

Meanwhile in Lewisburg, as the last week of July drew nearer, there was considerable speculation about the holding of commencement for the graduates of the College. Commencement exercises were scheduled to begin on Sunday night, July 26, with a sermon before the Society of Inquiry, and to end on Thursday, July 30, with the graduation of the Class of 1863.[52] Sometime between July 16 and July 23, President Loomis wrote to the editor of the Philadelphia *Christian Chronicle* as follows:

> Please make the statement in your next paper [July 23] that a part of the Commencement exercises at Lewisburg, from the 26th to the 30th inst., will necessarily be omitted. The Students are all in the army, and there is no present prospect of an immediate discharge. The degrees will however be conferred upon the graduating class. The exercises of the Female Institute will take place, and such other exercises as are not immediately dependent upon the presence of the college classes.

A story incorporating this undated note was set in type for the issue of July 23, but, just as the paper was going to press, the editor received from Dr. Loomis a telegram saying that the boys "would be allowed to come home," and that commencement would be held as usual. Accordingly, the above-mentioned story, although printed, was countermanded by a paragraph conveying the substance of Loomis's telegram and expressing the hope that "a large and enthusiastic gathering [would] greet the Faculty and Students of our noble University." [53]

How early it was known in Lewisburg that the graduating class would be home for commencement, we cannot tell precisely. In its issue for July 18, the Harrisburg *Telegraph* affirmed that preparations were "being actively made to muster out of the service all the three months' and emergency troops now in the field." This statement was reprinted in the *Star and Chronicle* of July 21, and was accompanied by this editorial remark: "We may then expect the Lewisburg Companies home within a week." A day or two thereafter President Loomis knew that the seniors would be home for graduation, but this news was not quickly disseminated in Lewisburg. In its issue of July 24 the *Star and Chronicle* remarked vaguely that, whereas some college commencements in southern Pennsylvania had been "marred by the late invasions," it was "expected that our College Company" would return soon, and that "respectable classes" would be graduated "next week from the University at Lewisburg." As late as July 25, John B. Linn, a lawyer of Lewisburg, wrote to his brother, Captain J. Merrill Linn, saying: "I don't know exactly what the College will do for a Commencement as the Students company cannot possibly be back." [54] But events were moving faster than he knew, for three days later, in another letter to his brother, he could say: "Those of the graduating class of the College company got home . . . last night [July 27]." But thus far, he remarked, the commencement had been a "fizzle," for "no orators" had shown up.[55]

The members of the graduating class were, as we have seen, the first ones of the University Guards to get home. The other students in this company came home, at different times, in groups, one group arriving during the evening of July 29, while the anniversary of the Literary Societies was being observed. Their arrival was described by an observer in these words:

> During the delivery of the oration, ten or twelve of the students, who had by mistake been left behind at Sunbury, in the afternoon, having footed the intervening distance (nine miles,) entered the Hall with a soldierly tread, and of course the orator was obliged to give way to the applause which greeted their coming.[56]

Apparently pressure of some sort had been exerted, perhaps by Colonel Eli Slifer, a Curator of the University and the Secretary of the Commonwealth, to get the graduating class home in time for commencement. We presume that special consideration had been given to these students, because President Loomis, in his annual report to the Trustees, on July 27, after remarking that all collegiate exercises had been suspended when the students left, affirmed that it was "only by very great efforts that they . . . [were] temporarily brought back to fill their places during this anniversary." He hoped, however, that their services would soon be dispensed with.[57]

Even so, not every member of the Class of 1863 was present to receive a diploma on July 30. George Bowman, who was ill, was left in a hospital in Harrisburg, and another student, Harrison B. Garner, a sophomore, remained with him.[58] More intriguing, if less important, is the fact that, for this class, patriotism had paid a big dividend. Not only was the entire class excused from the customary senior examination, but one of them, Harry Flavel Grier, was, for some unspecified reason, excused from giving his commencement oration. As to the others, a sympathetic reporter wrote that, because of "the lateness of the arrival of the class from the army, some had not their orations perfect, but such were excused by every hearer."[59] Somewhat startling, however, is the fact that one of the persons graduated in the Class of 1863, Joseph Phillips Tustin, had not been in the army, and, according to the Catalogue of the University for 1862–63, was not enrolled in the University. Consequently, his appearance at commencement to receive his diploma is to us a minor mystery, but this mystery need not now detain us.[60]

Those who attended this commencement were less numerous "than usual," but, in the opinion of more than one interested observer, there was ample compensation for a relatively small attendance. As one of them wrote: "If the attendance this year has been comparatively small, and the students have been broken from their accustomed amount of preparation, yet this Commencement will ever be regarded as one of the very noblest in the history of the Institution on account of the cause of these things." [61]

Because of numerous questionable statements that have been made about the so-called "Students' Company" of 1863, as well as about the effects upon the University of the wartime crisis of that year, it seems appropriate for us not only to inquire into the composition of this company, but also to ascertain what effect its organization had upon the University. At its full strength, according to a muster roll belonging to Captain Thomas R. Jones, this company consisted of seventy-seven men—three commissioned officers, thirteen non-commissioned officers, two musicians, and fifty-nine privates.[62] Of these, thirty-six (according to the Catalogue of the University for 1862–63) were then students in the University, and twelve others either had been, or presently would become, students therein. Consequently, the term "Students' Company," when used to designate this company, is misleading, for fewer than half of its members were then in the University, and twenty-seven of its members had never been, and would never become, students in the University. There was, however, some justification for calling it the University Guards, a name applied, as we have seen, to a student organization as early as May, 1861. From the standpoint of leadership, no less than from the standpoint of numbers, it was predominantly of the University. Its captain, Thomas Rockafellow Jones, and its first lieutenant, David Montgomery Nesbit, were of the Class of 1862. Its second lieutenant, a veteran of the twelve-day campaign of 1862, was Professor Charles S. James. Four of its five sergeants, five of its eight corporals, and both of its musicians were then students in the University. Finally, twenty-five of its privates were then students in the

University, and twelve others (one of whom was principal of the Academy) either had been, or soon would be, students therein. Thus we perceive that nearly two-thirds of this company were either of the University or in the way of becoming so.

We are now brought to this crucial question: in how many of its branches was the work of the University disrupted, or abandoned, because of the enrollment of its students as emergency troops in 1863? Nearly all the answers that have been given to this question—answers generally given without fear, without imagination, and without much investigation—are disturbingly erroneous. Let us look at the record. According to the Catalogue of the University for 1862–63, there were, during that academic Year, forty-three enrolled in both the College and the Theological Department and forty in the Academy. Of the first-named group, thirty-three enlisted (thirty-two in Company A and one in Company D). Of the forty in the Academy, only four enlisted (two of them as musicians). By classes the enlistment was as follows: in the Theological Department, all four in the second year and two of the four in the first year; in the College, all ten seniors, six of the nine juniors, three of the five sophomores, and eight of the eleven freshmen. Thus in the Theological Department and in the College there were ten who did not enlist. One of these, a junior in the College, was a Burmese student named Shaw Loo. In the Academy, only one in the senior class and three in the junior class enlisted.

From the foregoing figures the situation seems so clear that one might wonder that anyone could misinterpret it. Yet, to give but one of many erroneous or misleading statements about this matter, we read in a contemporaneous document—the Report of the Publication Committee of the Board of Curators for the year ending August 1, 1863—an assertion implying that, since (as the Report says) a "large portion of the students in the Collegiate, Theological, and Academic departments . . . had enlisted in the military service of the United States during the recent invasion of Pennsylvania," [63] these three branches of the University had been closed. But the work of the Academy could not conceivably have been broken up by the enlistment of its principal and four of its forty students. The assistant principal, who did not enlist, and the thirty-six students who stayed behind could have carried on; and there is no reason to think that the work of the Academy was not carried on. We may presume that President Loomis explained this matter fully and accurately when, in his report to the Trustees on July 27, 1863, he said that from the time of the enlistment of the students "all college exercises" had been suspended.[64] Because he said nothing about the suspension of work in the Academy, we may presume that there was no suspension of such work. He no doubt had in mind both the Theological Department and the College when he said "all college exercises," for both the faculties and the programs of these two branches of the University overlapped. Accordingly, we conclude that the Theological Department and the College were temporarily closed because of Lee's invasion of Pennsylvania in 1863, but that neither the Academy nor the Female Institute was then closed, although the work of both may have been adversely affected because some of the girls in the Institute, and perhaps some of the boys in the Academy, sought safety in their homes.[65]

Precisely one year after the exciting commencement of 1863, a Confederate force commanded by General Jubal A. Early pushed into Pennsylvania, burned the town of Chambersburg, and thus once again spread alarm through the Susquehanna Valley. The efforts that were then made to protect Pennsylvania against "other Chambersburgs" were only slightly disturbing to the University. Because it was not then in session, and perhaps also because the threat was soon dispelled, no effort was made, as in 1863, to enlist as a group the students in the University. Nevertheless, on the muster roll of an independent company called into being by this emergency—Captain Bruce Lambert's Cavalry Company—we find the names of five veterans of the University Guards of 1863, as well as the names of four other young men whose names also appear in one or more issues of the Catalogue of the University between 1864 and 1868.[66] Also, we find that a former student of the University, a member of the Class of 1857, enlisted in Lambert's company.[67] The enlistment of these men, however, did not disrupt the work of the University, although among the students who did enlist were four of the eight members of the senior class. Of the other five, one was a junior, one was a sophomore, two were freshmen, and one was a senior in the Academy. After the mustering out of this company on November 25, 1864, most of these "men of the University" returned to their studies. Four of them were graduated in 1865, one was graduated in 1866, and two were graduated in 1868.[68] The other two did not complete their courses in the University.

Having learned what the University did for the military effort of the North during the Civil War, we shall now try to find out what that war did to the University between 1861 and 1865. Some of its effects upon the University were, as we shall see, highly significant.

Perhaps the most obvious consequence of student participation in the war was the bringing to our campus of the Kappa Chapter of the Sigma Chi fraternity, the second such organization to arise in the University. Sigma Chi had been preceded on the campus by Phi Kappa Psi, the Pennsylvania Gamma Chapter of which had been established here in 1855. This chapter, because it tried to monopolize offices and honors, produced so much resentment that, in 1861, seven students, one of whom was Theodore A. K. Gessler, formed a secret society, called Iota, to oppose it. While the University Guards were in camp near Harrisburg, Gessler met Niles Shearer, a member of the Omicron Chapter of Sigma Chi in Dickinson College, and was deeply impressed by the badge that Shearer was wearing and, no doubt, by what Shearer told him about Sigma Chi. This chance contact led to significant action. At a meeting in camp of members of the Omicron Chapter and members of the Iota Society, it was decided that sixteen members of Iota should petition for a chapter of Sigma Chi. They did so, a charter was granted to them on March 1, 1864, and several days later the new chapter was installed in Lewisburg.[69]

This new acquisition was not a gift of pure gold to the University, for now opposition to Phi Kappa Psi had become rivalry with Phi Kappa Psi. So disturbing was this rivalry that President Loomis, on April 10, 1866, sought the advice of the Trustees as to the proper way to deal with it. The Trustees did not sidestep the issue. They forthwith empowered the faculty to exact of each applicant for admission to the University a twofold pledge: first, to renounce any connection that he might have with any secret society associated with the University, and, secondly, to promise not to hold membership in any such society "during his academic life."[70] The enactment, and attempted enforcement, of rules pursuant to this grant of authority would make plenty of trouble for President Loomis in subsequent years.

The aggravation of its problem of fraternities was, however, one of the lesser evils that the Civil War brought to the University. During those years the Trustees were bedeviled by problems that were as serious as they were provoking. Some of them, no doubt, sprang from emotional disturbances; others were the consequence of an adverse pecuniary situation. Some of these problems can be recognized more easily than they can be explained. It is not easy, for instance, to determine how much "the excitement of the times" (to use a favored but silly euphemism of those years) contributed to the discontent manifested by students in the Academy, to the neglect of duty by the principal of the Academy, to the desire of some of the collegiate students in 1862 to transfer to other institutions, or to the resignation of William Bucknell from the Board of Trustees in March, 1863. All this discontent might have arisen if there had been no war. We do not know precisely what caused it. Accordingly, we turn to problems of another sort—problems rooted in a pecuniary situation that had become troublesome before the outbreak of the war and that was aggravated by the war. As far back as August, 1860, the most optimistic statement that could be made about the pecuniary condition of the University was that "the income of the current year . . . [had] about met expenses."[71] The situation was not improving and for several years it would not improve. The University not only was plagued by a debt acquired before the war, but was embarrassed, year after year, by an operating loss. By July, 1862, the debt stood at $16,377.60, all of which was bearing interest. Of this debt the sum of $6,240.43 was owed to the teachers of the University.[72] The enrollment had fallen from a total of 211 in 1860–61 to a total of 185 in 1861–62; and the end was not yet. There had been a loss of students in each branch of the University.[73] To meet some of its most pressing problems, the Trustees had appropriated money from the Endowment Fund.[74]

At a special meeting of the Trustees, on May 5, 1863, the general agent reported for a committee that had been appointed in March of that year to devise a plan for procuring funds for the endowment of the University. The plan that the committee now offered, perhaps with some misgivings, was that of selling enough scholarships to increase the endowment from $58,000 to $100,000. The Trustees, not yet fully persuaded to adopt this plan, deferred action thereon until their next meeting, which would be held in July, 1863.[75]

The University was now well along in the time of its troubles; within a year it would be deep in the harsh winter of its wartime discontents. Wartime inflation was doing its work well. Prices had risen, but for most of those who served the University salaries and wages had not risen. Something had to be done—and done quickly. Accordingly, at the stated meeting in July, 1863, the Trustees accepted the plan proposed by the above-mentioned committee, with this limitation: the sum to be raised by the sale of scholarships would be $45,000. The number of temporary scholarships would be limited to one hundred for those running for eight years, and to fifty for those running for twenty-four years. The perpetual scholarships would not be limited in number. According to this plan, a guarantee of free tuition for one person for eight years would cost $100; a guarantee of free tuition for one person for twenty-four years would cost $250; and a guarantee of free tuition for one person in perpetuity would cost $500. As subsequently explained to the public by a committee of the Board of Curators, these scholarships would be available in any department of the University, and they would be transferable. A perpetual scholarship would be available when the sum of $500 was paid, but no temporary scholarship would be available until the whole sum of $45,000 had been collected.[76]

By the time of the meeting of the Trustees on April 5, 1864, scholarships amounting to $17,000 had been sold, and when it again met on July 26 of that year scholarships to the amount of $21,900 had been disposed of. But the pecuniary condition of the University had not improved, in part, because most of the sales of scholarships represented, as yet, subscriptions rather than cash, and, secondly, for other reasons as obvious as they were real. The enrollment for 1863–64 had risen to 240, an increase of 98 since the preceding year, and this increase had required the employment of additional teachers in the Female Institute. Moreover, indispensable repairs of buildings had taken money that was much needed for other things. Some of the members of the faculty were now petitioning the Trustees for increases in their salaries, and, to add to the embarrassment of the Trustees, the Presbyterian and the Methodist ministers of Lewisburg appeared before them and presented "an appeal from the pastors and churches of Lewisburg to raise the salaries of the Professors." Thus pressed, the Trustees made a few increases in the lower salaries, and they raised the pay of each janitor $2.50 a month. More significantly, six of the Trustees advanced a loan of $5,000 "to pay the pressing needs of the Faculty and teachers." Furthermore, "in view of the greatly increased expenses of living," the Trustees voted that a donation of $100 to each member of the Faculty and to the general agent should be provided by them from their private means. These measures, of course, were palliatives. As a remedy for the existing distress, the Trustees were still committing themselves firmly to the plan of selling scholarships. Accordingly, they not only provided for an additional agent to solicit money, but also invited the President and the professors "to engage in scholarship agency during vacation, the Board paying the necessary travelling expenses."

Such being the case, we are taken aback to learn that, when the Trustees held their next session, on April 4, 1865, President Loomis reported that he had obtained $79,050 on the $100,000 fund. Since he said nothing about scholarships, we are aware that something had happened that was well known to the Trustees but had not been entered in their official record. What had happened? The answer to this question we find in an address that President Loomis made to the students of the University at a meeting held on June 9, 1865, to celebrate the completion of the Endowment Fund. Briefly, what he told them was that, because the "better class of business men" had seriously doubted the expediency of the plan to sell scholarships, this plan, during the preceding autumn, had been abandoned, "or at least put in abeyance till a further endowment could be obtained." Instead of selling scholarships to obtain $45,000, it was now decided to enter upon a campaign to increase, by solicitation for money, the endowment of the University by $100,000.[77]

Since January 1, 1865, President Loomis had given most of his time to soliciting money for the new Endowment Fund, and his report of his success, made on April 4, impressed the Trustees so favorably that they not only empowered him to continue, but also released him from the duties of the presidency during the next term and instructed him, after the needed $20,000 had been subscribed, to "proceed with the collection of the $100,000." [78]

The remaining part of the campaign was speedily and successfully concluded, thanks in part to generous contributions from the people of Lewisburg and to equally generous subscriptions made by students in the University. On July 25, 1865, President Loomis could report to the Trustees that, since their meeting in April, "when there was great doubt whether the endowment could be raised, the requisite sum . . . [had] been subscribed." Moreover, he continued, "a large proportion of the subscription has been either paid in money or has been put into the form of interest-bearing obligations." [79]

This was a time of triumph for President Loomis. The Civil War was now ended, and the University was about to rid itself of the trials and tribulations that that war had imposed upon it. Both the nation and the University, President Loomis could now believe, would have "a new birth of freedom." His conception of the new era was that of a time of affluence such as the University had never before known. Now the old debts could be paid, and henceforth no new debts need be incurred. Now the salaries of those who had served the University well could be increased. Now the chair of belles lettres could be adequately filled, a new professorship of modern languages could be established, and the Department of Theology could be fully manned. All these things he recommended to the Trustees. Moreover, in this new era that was dawning, the University, he believed, could expect, "in a larger sense than heretofore," to become the central point of Baptist denominational interest in Pennsylvania. It should not only provide the Baptist churches of Pennsylvania with educated ministers, teachers, and writers, but it should also do its part to provide professional leadership for the state and to help elevate the public mind thereof pursuant to the views of those of the Baptist persuasion. "If," he admonished the Trustees, "you have men here who can do this work, it is well. If you have not, then there should be no hesitation in removing them and filling their places with men who can. The best talent should be found and should be used *here*." [80] What may have been his purpose in thus challenging the Trustees, we do not know. Perhaps he was only asking for a vote of confidence. Except perhaps by implication, he did not receive it. The Trustees showed no disposition to remove any of the professors or to disregard any of President Loomis's recommendations, but they gave the administration no formal vote of confidence. They did, however, proffer "their heartfelt thanks to the President of the University for his self-sacrificing and persevering labor" in making successful the latest effort to endow the University.[81] Perhaps they thought that that was enough to start the University into a new era equipped, as President Loomis had somewhat naïvely told the students on June 9, 1865, with an endowment that would, if properly administered, preclude the fear of pecuniary embarrassment for the University in the years that lay ahead.[82]

5

Conservatism, Depression, and Crisis

There may be improvement, but that which has stood the test of time is sure to be good if not the best. You will be safe in following it. If you propose improvements bring them forward only after mature deliberation.—*Justin R. Loomis, Baccalaureate Address, 1876.*

By getting for it during 1864–65 subscriptions amounting to $100,133.34, Justin R. Loomis had performed for his University a service that its Trustees would not soon forget. Although from these subscriptions there was a loss of somewhat more than $14,000, the Board not only could pay from the sum yielded by this effort debts amounting to $26,543.20; it also could add to the Endowment Fund of the University the sum of $59,259.22.[1] This was an accomplishment of no slight importance, and for the time being the Trustees could rest from their worries and congratulate themselves on their having chosen for president of their University a man who could get things done. As we already have learned, they thanked him profusely in 1865; but their supreme compliment to him they deferred for two years, and then gave it to him spontaneously. The time was the annual meeting of the Board in 1867, and the occasion was the election of a successor to Joseph Meixell, a long-time, but recently deceased, member of the Board of Trustees. When, on July 24 of that year, the Trustees decided to fill the vacancy on their Board, they gave to Loomis, without his being nominated, six votes on their first ballot. Immediately thereafter they adopted this resolution: "Whereas Dr. J. R. Loomis has been for years the President of the University & by his ability and faithfulness won our confidence & esteem, therefore, Resolved that we make his election unanimous, said election not to be used as a precedent for the election of any employee in the future."[2] The Trustees, as they well knew, had by this action taken a momentous step, for now Dr. Loomis, their principal employee, had become a member of both the governing boards of the University. This was the third honor that the University at Lewisburg had conferred upon him since his election to its faculty. In 1854 the faculty and the Board of Curators had bestowed upon him the honorary degree of Doctor of Philosophy; in 1857 the Trustees, by electing him president of the University, had made him *ex officio* a member of the Board of Curators; and now, in 1867, the Trustees, by electing him to membership on their Board, had made him a voting member of the Corporation. These were honors that most men would covet, but it is doubtful whether Loomis as a member of the Board of Trustees found his way as president of the University as smooth as it otherwise might have been. Now he could be disliked on two accounts: for what he did as president and for what he did as a trustee.

However that may be, the program of expansion and betterment that Loomis had suggested to the Board in 1865 moved slowly towards accomplishment, not because it displeased the Board, but because, between 1865 and 1868, the Trustees were getting rid of debts and adopting measures which, as they hoped, would make it unnecessary for them to incur new debts. The Department of Theology, however, was quickly expanded. When Professor Thomas F. Curtis resigned his professorship in this department in 1865, he recommended the appointment of two or more professors of theology. Others, among them the members of the Board of Curators, were of like mind. Accordingly, in July, 1865, the Trustees elected three new professors, of whom two—Lemuel Moss and Lucius E. Smith—accepted.[3] Since there was not enough work to keep both of them busy in the Department of Theology, each of them taught part time in the College. In July, 1866, it was announced officially that Professor Smith, with the newly established title of Crozer Professor of Rhetoric, was, in addition to his work in theology, filling the long-neglected chair of belles lettres.[4] This arrangement, however, was of short duration, for at the end of the academic year 1867–68 the University discontinued its Department of Theology.

The teaching of theology at the University at Lewisburg had been given up by amicable agreement between the Trustees of this institution and the Trustees of a newly chartered institution in Delaware County, Pennsylvania, that had been named the Crozer Theological Seminary in honor of the late John Price Crozer, a long-time member of the Board of Trustees of the University at Lewisburg and a generous benefactor who recently had endowed in this institution a professorship of rhetoric.[5] Mr. Crozer died in March, 1866, and soon thereafter the members of his family began considering the advisability of endowing in Upland, Pennsylvania, a theological seminary in his honor and of transferring thereto the Department of Theology in the University at Lewisburg. Their inquiry continued, with the knowledge of President Loomis, and in September, 1866, their proposal was approved by the Philadelphia Conference of Baptist Ministers. A few days later President Loomis and Professor Bliss attended in Philadelphia a meeting at which the matter was fully discussed and approved, and at which arrangements were made to confer on this subject with the Trustees of the University at Lewisburg. On November 2 the Crozer family agreed to contribute $275,000 to the establishment and the endowment of the proposed seminary, and on April 4, 1867, they obtained from the state legislature a charter for the Crozer Theological Seminary, which was to be established in Upland, Pennsylvania.[6] On June 12, 1867, the Trustees of this institution met and organized, and on June 21 they established four departments of instruction and decided that the Seminary should open its doors in September, 1868.[7]

Meanwhile an amicable agreement had been reached between the Trustees of the University at Lewisburg and the Trustees of the Crozer Theological Seminary. At a meeting in Philadelphia on December 11, 1867, committees representing the Boards of these two institutions agreed that the University would "make over" to Crozer the work of theological instruction in time for the opening of this institution in September, 1868; that the University would retain all its property and funds for continuing its work other than theological; and that the Seminary would pledge itself not to offer work either of academic or of collegiate character.[8] The two boards approved this agreement—the Board of Crozer on December 24, 1867, and the Board of the University on April 21, 1868. On July 29, 1868, the Trustees of the University voted that the money which heretofore had been devoted to the Department of Theology in this institution would henceforth be devoted to the Collegiate Department, but affirmed that, in the event that the Department of Theology should ever be re-established in the University, the $40,000 of endowment which formerly had been appropriated for its use would be again set aside for its support.[9] The Crozer Theological Seminary began its work on October 2, 1868, when thirteen young men were examined and then admitted to instruction.[10] The Great Enterprise of the Baptists in Pennsylvania was now divided between Lewisburg and Upland.

The discontinuance of the Department of Theology not only resulted in the reduction of the number of professors in the University from six to five; it also affected the thinking of both the Trustees and the president in respect to the future course of the University. As early as July 29, 1868, the Trustees approved a report in which their committee on the reorganization of the work of the faculty had recommended "that the Faculty be at liberty to institute parallel & optional studies in so far as the present teaching force will enable them to do so & as in their judgment it may be desirable, it being understood that there be no reduction in the extent of the course required for graduation." [11] Here is a somewhat ambiguous concession to the new "progressivism" in collegiate education; but, since one of the committee that recommended it was President Loomis, we may rightly presume, I think, that it was intended to open the way to changes of emphasis and of details rather than to changes providing for drastic revision of the Classical Program. Before the founding of the Crozer Theological Seminary, President Loomis would have welcomed a School of Law as an adjunct to the University, and theretofore he had eagerly desired an adequately staffed Department of Theology as an essential part of the University. After 1868, however, he concentrated his attention upon the Collegiate Department, emphasizing its function as that of providing a solid liberal education as a preparation for professional study. Also, he was concerned about the Academy as a feeder of the College, and in 1869, on his recommendation, the Trustees approved the separation of the classical and the English divisions of the Academy. They created a Preparatory Department in which would be offered, under the supervision of the faculty of the College, two years of work as preparation for admission to the Classical Program of the College, and an English Academy which would concern itself, *inter alia,* with preparing students either for admission to the Scientific Program of the College or for teaching in the public schools. Pursuant to this arrangement, the Preparatory Department had its own principal, Professor Freeman Loomis, and formed its own literary society, which was called Euodia.[12] The members of this Department were housed in the University Building. The English Academy also had its own principal, its own literary society, and its own society room and library. Its literary society, called Hermenia, was probably the old Phirhoan Society revived under a new name. Its principal, from 1870 to 1873, was Jonathan Jones, and thereafter William E. Martin, who remained in this office until, in 1894, he was made a professor in the College and librarian for the collegiate branch of the University.[13]

Although for different reasons, President Loomis was perhaps as much interested in the Female Institute as in the Academy. But, despite his approval of the request of the principal of the Institute that the regular three-year course in this institution be made a four-year course, and also despite the fact that the Board of Curators gave enthusiastic support to this request, the Board of Trustees withheld its assent thereto for many years. Not until the year 1878–79 did four-year programs appear in the catalogue of the Institute.[14] The reason for such postponement is not far to seek. Because the Institute was prospering under its existing program, the Trustees presumably were unwilling to experiment with an expanded program which would increase the expenditures of the University. In the matter of housing for the Institute, the view of the Board, however, was forward-looking. When the general agent, in April, 1868, recommended an addition to the Institute Building, to cost not more than $6,000 and to be paid for from the earnings of the Institute, the Board approved the recommendation without question. The contract for constructing what was called the South Wing of the Institute Building was let in 1868, and the building was completed in 1869 at a total cost of $7,874.45. On July 27, 1869, the general agent, in his report to the Trustees on this project, announced that the total cost of the building had been paid, and that a small surplus remained "in favor of the Seminary." [15] Henceforth the Institute could accommodate more students.

As to the College and its programs in the years after 1868, President Loomis, as late as 1876, could say somewhat proudly, perhaps even defiantly, that "the University . . . [had] resisted the temptation to organize professional schools, which . . . [might] be entered with very little preparatory study." It aimed, he continued, to do well "only College work," and the word *College* he was using "in the sense in which the word . . . [had] till recently been understood in this country." He insisted, again as late as 1876, that he was not opposed to change. Noting that collegiate education in the United States had "made great advancement in the last few years," he affirmed that the University had "aimed to keep pace with the times." It had, he maintained, raised the requirements for admission, improved instruction, and expanded its program of studies.[16] Here he was speaking truly, but very generally; and, in order to determine what "progress" the University had achieved during the preceding ten years, we must examine in detail the important changes that it had undergone, especially after the discontinuance of the Department of Theology.

Both Professor Smith and Professor Moss, who had been brought to the University primarily for the purpose of expanding the work of the Department of Theology, withdrew from the faculty after that department was abandoned, and in April, 1869, Robert Lowry, of the Class of 1854, was elected to succeed Professor Smith as Crozer Professor of Rhetoric. This position he held for six years, and, at the same time, he served the Baptist Church in Lewisburg as its pastor.[17] Some two years later, in June, 1871, President Loomis proposed to the Trustees several important changes for improving the work of the University. First of all, he pointed out the need for a gymnasium. This was by no means a novel idea, even in the University over which he presided, and, whether by prior agreement or by coincidence, the President and the Alumni Association, acting separately, presented this proposition to the Board on the same day, June 26, 1871. In the morning of that day, the Alumni Association, desirous of commemorating properly the twenty-fifth anniversary of the University "by something tangible and that will supply a long felt and absolute want," voted to raise enough money to establish a gymnasium "in connection with the University." They also voted to ask the Board's approval of this action. The Board gave its approval by appointing a committee of five and empowering it to act in any way "not involving expense to the Board" and by instructing it to obtain professional advice before deciding upon both the site and the character of the building it proposed to erect.[18] Thanks to this optimistic beginning, the University got a gymnasium—in 1890.

As his second proposal for improving the work of the University, President Loomis suggested that the teaching force be increased by the employment of a professor of Latin and a professor of modern languages. The professor of Latin, George W. Anderson, it will be recalled, had resigned his position in 1854, and in that year Professor George R. Bliss had been appointed professor of both Latin and Greek, a position which he would hold until he withdrew from the University in 1874, when he was succeeded by Professor Francis W. Tustin. It was not until 1875 that the Board re-established the chair of Latin, to which it appointed William T. Grier. In that year Tustin became professor of the Greek language and literature. On the suggestion that a professor of modern languages be appointed, however, the Board acted quickly, appointing to this position on June 27, 1871, the son of President Loomis, Freeman Loomis, and extended for another year his leave of absence to study in Germany.[19]

As his third and fourth proposals for improving the University, President Loomis recommended without comment that there be an increase of salaries for those who served the University and, consequently, a "necessary increase of Funds." If his proposal for enlarging the faculty were realized, he continued, "it would then be possible to have the recitations of the several classes at the same hours, each officer having three recitations daily, saving thus much confusion and disorder." Apparently Loomis was hopeful that his program would soon be put into effect, for, after saying that he would take advantage of the permission given him to be on leave of absence during the ensuing year, he remarked that he hoped to see on his return at least the substance of his recommendations in operation.[20]

During the next five years, the academic offerings of the College were enlarged and improved by the establishment of a Latin Scientific Program and by the introduction of organized lecture courses; and the University as a place for learning and for applying knowledge was made better for persons of studious habits and of literary proclivities by some enlargement of the library and by the founding of a monthly journal conducted by the students. It also was made more tolerable for members of the faculty by modest increases of their compensation. But, as the years passed, the way of improvement became increasingly difficult, owing, in large part, to the depression which began in 1873. A pertinent illustration of this fact is the record of salaries paid to members of the faculty. By the year 1873–74, the salary of the president had risen only to $2,000, and the salaries of the professors ranged from $1,200 to $1,800. Two years later the president's salary was $2,300, and the salaries of the professors, the oldest one of them having resigned in 1874, varied from $1,000 to $1,700. For several years thereafter there was no increase. As late as June, 1880, the salary of the newly appointed president was only $2,000, and that of the senior professor was still $1,700. The other professors, all relatively new, received salaries ranging from $1,000 to $1,200 each.[21] Without money to pay respectable living wages to its faculty, the University could hardly hope to make itself into a superior institution.

Nevertheless, the academic offerings of the University had been somewhat enlarged and their quality had been considerably improved by the establishment of a four-year program in lieu of the old three-year program which had led to the degree, first, of Bachelor of Philosophy, and, later, of Bachelor of Science. The Catalogue of the University for 1874–75 had announced that a new Latin Scientific Program was in the making, and in June, 1875, the Trustees had agreed that such a program should be established, the details of which they referred to President Loomis. Pursuant to this grant of authority, the Catalogue for 1875–76 described fully the new four-year program which thereafter would be pursued by aspirants for the degree of Bachelor of Science. This degree now began to take on the odor of respectability, because henceforth it would be awarded to students who had completed four years of work, and who also, during those four years, had completed all the work in Latin required for the degree of Bachelor of Arts.[22]

The degree of Bachelor of Science had had a peculiar history in the University at Lewisburg. There the three-year program, when it was established in 1851, led to the degree of Bachelor of Philosophy. Through the year 1864–65, the graduates of this program continued to receive this degree, but the Catalogue for 1865–66 tells us that the graduates of this program were entitled to the degree of Bachelor of Science. I have found no authorization for such change, although at some time the consent of the Trustees to so important a change must have been given.

The mystery becomes even deeper when we discover that the Latin Catalogue of the University for 1865 (*Catalogus Senatus Academici*) lists as Bachelors of Science (*Scientiae Baccalaureos*) all the alumni who had not been graduated Bachelors of Arts, and that the similar catalogue for 1872 does likewise for all those through the preceding years not graduated Bachelors of Arts.

However the practice of recording in later years as degrees in science the degrees earned in earlier years as degrees in philosophy may have become established, neither the academic programs of the University at Lewisburg in 1875–76, nor the degrees to which these programs led, could rightly have been called either superficial or reactionary. Many of the distinguished scholars in the best-known colleges of America of that era would have commended these degrees and these programs. To such persons it would have appeared, as it appeared to President Loomis, that the University at Lewisburg had been keeping pace with the times. The contrast between its offerings in 1862 and its offerings in 1875, as President Loomis pointed out, is as interesting as it is informing. Whereas in 1862 the Classical Program contained no courses in modern languages and was embellished by no established lectures, by 1876 it had been enlarged by new courses and enriched principally by required lectures on a variety of subjects. Yet its essential foundation had not been disturbed. This program consisted in 1876 of thirty-six studies extending through four years of three terms each, and the distribution of these studies among subjects or fields was as follows: twelve to Latin and Greek, four and a half to pure mathematics, four to applied mathematics and physics, two and a half to logic and rhetoric, five to natural science, four to modern languages, and four to metaphysics and moral philosophy. Parallel to this program was the Latin Scientific Program of four years, from which, however, the study of Greek was omitted. These were the programs that were taught principally by textbooks, the studies in which the students "recited" to their professors. These "solid" courses, however, were supplemented by continuing instruction in composition and rhetoricals, by required lectures in what President Loomis called a "full course of instruction" in history, and by some instruction, perhaps superficial, in aesthetics and art, the history of philosophy, the history of the English language, natural theology and evidences of Christianity, physical geography, and zoölogical classification.[23]

Lectures by members of the faculty of the University, even apart from such as they may have delivered incidentally in their classrooms, were being given as early as the 1850's. But it was not until after the Civil War that lectures as a means of formal instruction in the University became organized and systematic. As to the beginning of such courses of lectures, our information is fragmentary and imprecise, for the minutes of the meetings of the faculty, the meetings in which such matters were agreed upon and recorded, are not available for the years before 1874–75. From the first published periodical of the collegiate students, however, we learn that during the years 1869–70 and 1870–71 lectures were given by members of the faculty in a University Literary Course.[24] From the Catalogue of the University for 1872–73—but not from any earlier issue—we learn that at least two courses of lectures were prescribed for each collegiate class, and from another source we learn that, in October, 1873, lectures were being given on Thursday mornings. Here was probably the beginning of the long-continued "established" lectures, first described and listed by titles and by lecturers in the Catalogue for 1875–76, that were scheduled to be "given on Thursday mornings at 7½ o'clock," that lasted for one hour each, and that continued through the year. To the seniors in 1875–76, President Loomis lectured on the history of philosophy and on evidences of Christianity and natural theology; to the juniors Professor Charles S. James lectured on English history, and Mr. David Jayne Hill on English literature and criticism; to the sophomores Professor William T. Grier lectured on Roman history and literature, and Professor Freeman Loomis on medieval history; and to the freshmen Professor Francis W. Tustin lectured on Greek history and literature, and Professor Loomis on medieval history. During two of the three preceding years, 1872–73 and 1873–74, "orientation" lectures were given, probably by Professor George R. Bliss, to freshmen on the nature and the aims of the college course, and in these years lectures were given on American history, probably in both years by Professor Tustin. We know that Professor Tustin gave lectures on American history in 1873–74, but at the beginning of the next year, having succeeded Professor Bliss as professor of Latin and Greek, he began to give lectures on Greek history. Accordingly, American history, as a subject for established lectures, was dropped from the schedule. In the year 1881–82, however, the course was re-established, and from that time forward through the year 1884–85 lectures on American history were given by Professor William C. Bartol.[25]

To any charge that the program just described lacked "depth," except possibly in Latin and Greek, President Loomis no doubt would have replied that the purpose of the collegiate Classical Program was to discipline minds and to lay "broad and deep foundations for the superstructure of professional knowledge." It was, he made clear, in the "superstructure" of professional knowledge that "depth" of understanding should be sought, for it was in one's profession that one should strive to attain such specialized knowledge as would be required for achieving eminence. To those who could not, or would not, study Greek, the Scientific Program was available. It was intended to be what in present-day educational parlance would be called a "terminal" program, the reward thereof being the degree of Bachelor of Science. Beyond this reward there was nothing to expect, for upon holders of this degree the University at Lewisburg did not then confer a master's degree. Here, then, were the programs which, in the opinion of President Loomis, were admirably suited to an American college that aspired to "keep pace with the times."

In respect to matters other than its programs of instruction, the University, despite its poverty, had not been standing still. The collegiate library, thanks in part to small annual appropriations for its support, as well as to some gifts, was considerably larger in 1876 than it had been in 1865; but, unhappily, its growth had not kept pace with that of the libraries of other comparable institutions in Pennsylvania. The library of Lafayette College, for example, had by that year increased to 16,000 volumes, that of Dickinson College to 7,765, and that of Gettysburg College to 7,200. Elsewhere in the nation the situation was not different. In New England the libraries of Williams, Amherst, Bowdoin, and Wesleyan had grown considerably; in New York those of Madison, Hamilton, and Union had done well; and in the West those of Marietta, Denison, Illinois, and Shurtleff had made considerable progress. Whatever it may otherwise have accomplished, the University at Lewisburg had not kept pace with the above-mentioned institutions in the matter of increasing the holdings of its library.[26]

In respect, however, to another matter—one of considerable consequence—the University had done very well. By the late spring of 1870 the first number of its first students' periodical publication—the *College Herald*—came from the press. This monthly journal, which was edited and published jointly by the two collegiate literary societies, was the consequence of a third effort to get a students' publication started in the University. Early in 1860 President Loomis had brought to the attention of both Euepia and Theta Alpha a proposal that the students of various colleges unite to publish an undergraduate journal under the name of *Undergraduate*. After considering this matter for a few weeks, both these societies rejected the proposal.[27] Three years later, however, Euepia and Theta Alpha considered, between the end of January and the early part of May, 1863, the matter of their uniting to publish a journal under the name of the *College Monthly*. They agreed that the proposed journal should be edited and managed by joint committees of the two societies, that the subscription price should be fifty cents a year, and that publication should be commenced. But, because the societies fell out about the matter of a publisher, the project was dropped as impracticable.[28] In May, 1870, however, the first number of the first volume of the *College Herald* appeared under a arrangement almost identical with that agreed upon for the proposed *College Monthly* seven years earlier. The editors of the *Herald* announced that this journal would be "the organ of the whole University," and they invited the students of all departments of the University to "join hands around this common interest, and pledge their mutual support." This publishing enterprise was successful; the *College Herald* lasted for more than a decade. Its beginning was propitious, for its first number contained, besides a compendious history of the University by Professor Bliss, news about the Crozer Theological Seminary, news about other colleges and universities, a short story about the University Olympian Base Ball Club "sustained by the students for the purpose of physical exercise," and an announcement that a "College Boat-Club" was in the making. Presently the *Herald* would be discussing, in addition to athletics and other matters of peculiar concern to students, subjects of national concern, such as the coeducation of the sexes, the role of Greek in liberal education, and the significance of the elective system at Harvard.

Nevertheless, regardless of what had been done to improve both life and study on its campus, the University at Lewisburg in the middle of the 1870's was entering a time of hardships and discontents which, within a very few years, would take it into the first really threatening crisis of its existence. Discontents had accumulated through the years, especially since the end of the Civil War; but the new hardships were merely the old hardships in a later time—they sprang from the persisting poverty of the University. The fund raised by President Loomis in 1864–65 had not, as he had hoped it would, brought either affluence to the University or contentment to those who served it. Expressions of dissatisfaction and of unrest were coming from students, from the Alumni, from the Board of Curators, and perhaps also from Baptists generally throughout Pennsylvania; and members of the faculty could hardly have been contented with heavy schedules for which they were not adequately compensated.

Underneath the various disagreements and frustrations, however, lay a disquieting malaise, a growing and a gnawing apprehension that the University was not, despite the assertions of President Loomis to the contrary, keeping pace with the times. The "times" were as interesting as they were upsetting. By the middle 1870's the United States was well advanced in the Great Transformation which, before the end of the century, would make it a country not only highly industrialized and considerably urbanized, but also a country so powerful that presently it would be recognized for what it undoubtedly had become—one of the great powers of the world. The expanding American industries, the rising American cities, the increasing American population, and the impact upon America of new ideas flowing in from Europe—these forces broke the cake of American custom, and from the whirls and swirls of such disturbing forces there was coming into being a new American society in which appeared needs and inclinations for the satisfaction of which the conventional American collegiate education seemed ill-adapted. Voices calling for changes in American collegiate education were becoming strident, and their demands were getting more and more support. Most of the changes being asked for were not novel; the New Education had been, as we have seen, proclaimed by reformers before the Civil War. But these early reformers, for the time being, accomplished little. By the decade of the 1870's, however, the pressures for educational reform in the United States were being strengthened by the forces which, rapidly since the Civil War, were transforming the America that had been preponderantly agricultural in its economy and largely rural in its outlook into an America whose economy was becoming preponderantly industrialized and whose way of living and of thinking was becoming increasingly urbanized.

To solve all the problems created by the Great Transformation—problems that were economic, problems that were social, problems that were intellectual and spiritual—something more, many thoughtful Americans were coming more and more to believe, would be needed than the traditional collegiate education with its heavy emphasis upon Latin, Greek, and mathematics. A society as dynamic as the American society was becoming, an economy enlarging as the American economy was enlarging, could hardly be satisfied with a required collegiate education revolving about such genteel things as Bullion's *Greek Grammar, Tacitus on Germany, Demosthenes on the Crown,* Wayland's *Moral Philosophy,* and Butler's *Analogy*. However well the studies prescribed for the degree of Bachelor of Arts might serve those who were seeking careers in the traditional professions of medicine, law, and theology, they seemed to many Americans anachronistic—almost laughable—in an age in which increasingly young men were seeking careers in industry, transportation, and trade. For them knowledge of science and of its applications seemed more relevant to the needs of their time than knowledge of Plato, Aristotle, Horace, and Cicero. Indeed, the battle for the New Education in post-Civil War America was, broadly speaking, on the one hand, a battle for education emphasizing science rather than the classics, and, on the other hand, a battle for recognition of equality not only between the two programs, but also among all the subjects offered in either of them. The principal means by which the reformers hoped to topple Latin and Greek from their positions of preëminence was, first of all, that of winning for the students freedom to elect studies, and, secondly, that of gaining acceptance of the new dogma that all the studies offered in collegiate programs, or at least many of them, should be considered equal in respect to their value for disciplining the mind and for storing it with useful knowledge. It was not enough that, even before the Civil War, some of the colleges had met some of the demands of the reformers by crowding new studies into the Classical Program, by establishing a scientific school outside the college—Harvard, Yale, and Dartmouth are examples—or by establishing a parallel Scientific Program within the college. These, to the genteel, were inferior programs that led to substandard degrees, and thus deprived the recipients thereof of a truly liberal education, an education which, to those dedicated to the traditional collegiate way, or to those who had a vested interest in the classics, could be obtained only by a program which, *inter alia,* required a heavy concentration in Latin and Greek, the subjects which, so their argument ran, were preëminently important in imparting both the discipline and the knowledge that set apart those who were liberally educated.[29] Consequently, the way to achieve the freedom in American collegiate education that the reformers sought was to break the classical monopoly by compelling Latin and Greek to compete with other subjects for acceptance in an open educational market; and the way to establish such free and democratic competition was to win general acceptance of the principle of elective studies.[30]

This principle was not new in 1865—far from that—but before the Civil War it had made little headway in American collegiate circles. Before the end of the 1860's, however, two things of transcendent importance for American collegiate education had happened, one in the state of New York and one in the state of Massachusetts. In 1868 Cornell University, an institution founded in part on a land grant provided by the Federal Government pursuant to the Morrill Act of 1862, had opened its doors, with Andrew D. White as its president, in Ithaca, New York; and a year later Charles W. Eliot, a young man whose training had been in science, was inaugurated president of Harvard University in Cambridge, Massachusetts. For many years thereafter many Americans who were interested in education looked, some with grave apprehensions and others with high expectations, at the course of events in Ithaca and in Cambridge.[31] In the experiments going on in both these places the University at Lewisburg was deeply interested, and no doubt perceptive friends and admirers of this institution saw in Cornell a remarkable fulfillment of an earlier prediction of their own President Malcom, and in the Harvard of Charles W. Eliot the way to the fulfillment of the gospel of democratic educational reform according to Francis Wayland.

Here we need not anticipate the course of the great debate about American higher education during the 1880's and the 1890's, and here we need not anticipate the time, then not far distant, when in many American colleges and universities students after four years of study of subjects other than the classics would receive a baccalaureate degree with untroubled conscience—free from the fear of ever waking from restless slumber to weep over the remorseful thought that they could not read Greek. The victory of the reformers would be almost a total victory.

Nor need we at this point concern ourselves with two other important questions which were beginning to confront American colleges—the question whether colleges should be transformed into universities and the question whether women should be admitted to the privileges of collegiate education on a footing of equality with men. Or, to put this latter question as Stephen W. Taylor would have put it: whether young ladies and young gentlemen should pursue the same course of studies, recite together in classes, and, at the end of four years, receive the same degree. It was this question, as we shall see, that had more practical importance for the University at Lewisburg than had the question whether this institution should remain a university in name only or become a university in fact as well as in name.

To those who were interested in collegiate reform no other person in American educational circles during the last three decades of the nineteenth century was so much in the public eye, or so successful in getting his ideas adopted, as was Charles W. Eliot, who, notwithstanding considerable opposition, had become the president of Harvard at the age of thirty-five. His liberal views on education were well known to informed persons—hence the opposition to his election—but his persistence, his courage, and his administrative ability were yet to be learned. In his inaugural address, delivered on April 19, 1869, he left no doubt as to his main purpose.

> This University [he affirmed] recognizes no real antagonism between literature and science, and consents to no such narrow alternatives as mathematics and classics, science or metaphysics. We would have them all and at their best. . . .
>
> The elective system fosters scholarship, because it gives free play to natural preferences and inborn aptitudes, makes possible enthusiasm for a chosen work, relieves the professor and the ardent disciple of the presence of a body of students, who are compelled to an unwelcome task, and enlarges instruction by substituting many and various lessons given to small, lively classes, for a few lessons many times repeated to different sections of a numerous class. The College therefore proposes to persevere in its efforts to establish, improve, and extend the elective system.[32]

This determination, persisted in for a generation or more, not only in time gave Harvard a system of instruction that Eliot desired, but also through many years made Eliot and Harvard objects of national attention, and thus invited, on the one hand, condemnation, and, on the other hand, the highest form of praise—namely, imitation. Harvard could not be, and was not, ignored.

Because lack of space forbids it, the fascinating national controversy about elective studies during the last quarter of the nineteenth century can not here be told even in effective outline. It remains only to say that, as early as 1871, students in the University at Lewisburg were discussing the purpose of collegiate education; that in April, 1872, an article entitled "The Elective System of Harvard College" appeared in the *College Herald;*[33] that in three issues of the *Herald* for that year—those of June, July, and October—a full-page advertisement of Harvard's educational offerings appeared; and that in subsequent issues of the *Herald* during the 1870's the subject of collegiate education was not neglected. In 1875 David Jayne Hill, valedictorian of the Class of 1874 and now a tutor in the College, published in the *Herald* an article entitled "The Elective System," in which he called attention to two classes of educators who were then, as he said, striving for ascendancy. One class spoke for the disciplinarians; the other, for the utilitarians, who favored the elective system. Of this system, if it permitted students freely to choose their own subjects, Hill had a low opinion; and, although he argued that every college should offer such a variety of courses as would satisfy the "needs of all classes of persons," he maintained that the "selection, order, and arrangement of studies" should be left to those who "hold in view the respective claims and due proportion of discipline and information." [34] Perhaps this statement expressed accurately the view of those in the University who favored moderate reform. Throughout much of the decade of the 1870's it appears that, if the *College Herald* reflected accurately the views of the students, there was on the campus no general discontent among the students with the course that the University was then pursuing. The discontent arose first among the alumni and in the Board of Curators, a body in which, by this time, the alumni were strongly represented.

This discontent no doubt sprang in part from the pecuniary situation that kept the Board of Trustees closely confined to the way of cautious conservatism. From its beginning the University had had pecuniary difficulties, and its pecuniary situation during the Civil War, as we have seen, had become acute. The subscription raised at that time by President Loomis did not yield enough to safeguard the University against future pecuniary difficulties, particularly those that arose during the depression that began in 1873. As early as January of that year, President Loomis had suggested to the Trustees the desirability of their making an effort to increase the endowment of the University, for the members of the faculty were then finding it impossible to meet their current expenses without performing "outside labor." In June, 1873, he reported that there had been no increase in the endowment during 1872–73, and he suggested that "during the incoming school year or by its close the proper period will arise for presenting the University's claims to the Baptists of the State." [35] It was during Commencement Week in 1874 that an enthusiastic meeting of Trustees, Curators, and alumni was held in the College Chapel for the purpose of setting on foot "a grand forward movement" to obtain a sum of money that would adequately endow the University and the Baptist schools of Pennsylvania. Enthusiasm ran high, and it was proposed to raise the sum of $500,000.[36] As subsequently explained by the Committee on Publication of the Board of Curators, it was proposed that of the money to be thus raised "three hundred thousand [should be] for the University at Lewisburg, and two hundred thousand [should be] for the Academies originated by the denomination. The advanced standard and enlarged scope of College studies [it affirmed] now requires additional teachers and various other aids. The salaries of teachers need to be increased, to meet the demands of the times. . . . The proposed endowment, within two years, with present means and facilities, can be easier raised than was the first endowment of the central institution at Lewisburg." [37]

Never did a prophecy fall flatter than this one fell. Despite elaborate organization, including a well-paid secretary, and despite extensive and appealing advertising, the campaign, at the end of two years, was a complete failure. Midway in the campaign the Board of Curators, reporting to the public through its Committee on Publication in July, 1875, set forth clearly the progressive, forward-looking program that the proposed new endowment was expected to sustain.

> The demand for immediate advancement [this committee declared] is imperative, in founding new professorships, in furnishing an adequate remuneration to professors and teachers now in the service, in the enlargement of the library, and the increase of facilities in the scientific department. Such enlargement becomes necessary, from the advanced requirements of the age, and also by the actual and contemplated advance of other institutions occupying in part the same field. We must advance or lose our relative standing as an educational institution. This would be disastrous and fatal. But the outlook is hopeful. It has been decided that the least we can worthily attempt for Lewisburg, as our Centennial offering, is to add *three hundred thousand* dollars to its endowment.[38]

One year later a report on the proceedings of commencement in 1876 announced the complete failure of the campaign in the following magnificent understatement:

> The Endowment Fund has not grown so rapidly as the friends of the institution had hoped. Owing to the financial embarrassment of the times, and the extreme difficulty of raising funds for even so worthy an object, the Rev. E. W. Bliss, the Centennial Secretary, tendered his resignation to the Board of Trustees.

The total amount raised during this campaign was less than $10,000.[39]

The failure of the Centennial campaign marked a turning point in the efforts to bring the University "up to date." A sense of frustration now seemed to lay hold of the friends of the University, and, seeking a reason for such an untoward course of affairs, many of these friends concluded that something must be wrong with the administration of the University, an administration that was out of step with progress, an administration that looked backward rather than forward. Such views, no doubt, were strengthened as everybody, during the next three years, saw the University slipping rapidly into a dangerous crisis. Between 1875–76 and 1878–79, the enrollment declined steadily in all branches of the University—in the College from 74 to 44, in the Preparatory Department and in the Academy from 64 to 26, and in the Female Institute from 98 to 65.[40] The pecuniary situation of the University grew steadily worse. In January, 1877, because of a "deficiency in the payment of endowment interest," the general agent was authorized to borrow, if necessary, $2,000 to pay salaries. In June of that year the general agent reported that the finances of the University had been "more difficult to manage than during any previous year." In the matter of collecting subscriptions already made, he accomplished little because of the "closeness of money," but the acknowledgment by subscribers of their willingness to pay was encouraging to him. He asked of the Board authority to borrow "about $2,000" in order to pay salaries.[41]

During the next two years the financial situation of the University did not improve. The death of the general agent, J. A. Kelly, in December, 1877, caused considerable embarrassment, but Adie K. Bell again took charge of the financial affairs of the University and reported thereon to the Board in June, 1878. The outlook was not bright. An investment in the form of a loan on real estate in Chicago had gone wrong, and the loss to the University was known to be considerable. Eventually, it amounted to more than $20,000. The needs of the University had become urgent, and the means to fulfill these needs were wanting.

Improvements by grading the campus during the preceding year had cost about $4,000, but President Loomis had paid for most of this work from his own meager resources. The Female Institute needed refurbishing, and elsewhere there was need of repairs; and for operations during the coming year it appeared that, "over and above" the expected receipts, there would be need for as much as $4,000. "It would be folly amounting to crime," the general agent told the Trustees, "to enter upon another year without fully counting the cost." [42] But the University did continue its work, and a year later the treasurer reported that the debt unprovided for amounted to $3,016.83. One measure of economy adopted during this year was the reunion of the Preparatory Department and the English Academy to form, once again, the University Academy.[43] But this action had contributed little to the relief of the pecuniary stringency. Presumably the University had been scraping along by borrowing from its Endowment Fund to pay current expenses. By December, 1879, the situation did appear to be really serious, for the Board then voted that because of the loss of money in the Chicago investment, the School Fund should be allowed to borrow, with interest at six per cent on the loan, $6,000 from the Endowment Fund; and the Board took note of the fact that a large amount of interest was owed to the Endowment Fund.[44] To some persons it may have appeared that the University was rapidly skidding into bankruptcy.

Meantime, discontent with the programs of the University and with their operation had mounted. It was becoming clear, without as well as within the University, that sentiment was growing in favor of some of the dogmas of the New Education. The editor of the *National Baptist,* after the commencement of 1878, dwelt at length on this subject. To the general question raised by the alumni at that time as to how the University could acquire a larger place in the sympathies of the state and of the Baptist denomination therein, his answer was that it should take a forward view. He would have its work so enlarged as "to meet the wants, not alone of the learned professions, and especially of the ministry, but of the industrial classes" as well. He would have it extend its privileges to both sexes alike. "We can conceive of no harm or even risk," he said, "but rather of great good and decided economy, in uniting in one class all who are pursuing the same study." He believed that the "governing body" [*i.e.,* the Board of Trustees] should more adequately represent the state and the denomination, that the membership of both governing boards should be frequently renewed, and that the "governing powers" should show more faith in the public by publishing the annual reports of both the president and the treasurer. Finally, in a summary that amounted to a peroration, he affirmed his belief that

> the University should be in the fullest sense abreast of the age, should be instinct with the genius of the Nineteenth Century, ready to avail itself of whatever has been approved by experiments elsewhere, ready also to lead the way in paths not yet trodden. . . . We would have . . . [it] adopt the guidance of large general principles; we would have it believe in the future as well as in the past, and believe that the future is vastly grander than the past; we would have it believe less in the anchor, and more in the compass and the heavenly bodies. . . .[45]

A few weeks later the Committee on Publication of the Board of Curators, after reciting facts, good and bad, about the University during the preceding year, concluded its report in these words:

> The general outlook of the University . . . is not as encouraging as could be wished. The number of students is small. Dissatisfaction with the administration of affairs has alienated many of the Alumni. . . . We cannot but regard the present as a very critical period in the history of the University—a time which calls for the greatest wisdom and devotion of the friends of higher education within the limits of Pennsylvania and New Jersey. We beg all, whatever their differences of opinion, to rally to the support of the University and to labor earnestly to bring in the day of larger and better things.[46]

No doubt it was in the hope of bringing in "the day of larger and better things" that the Reverend Augustus H. Lung, a member of the Class of 1853 as well as a member of the Board of Trustees, proposed on June 24, 1879, for adoption by the Board, a resolution affirming that

> Whereas, more advanced studies in the Natural Sciences are desirable in our collegiate course, therefore, Resolved that we recommend to the Faculty to so change the curriculum as to allow students, who have passed the Sophomore year, to pursue elective studies in the Natural Sciences as equivalents to studies in the languages, as far as the teaching force will allow.

This resolution the Board laid on the table "for the present." [47]

There were other things that nourished discontent among the alumni. Much of their discontent between 1876 and 1879 revolved about two things—the failure of their efforts to get a relaxation of the rule in respect to fraternities and the failure of their efforts to get more effective representation of the alumni on the Board of Trustees.

The question of fraternities, as we have seen, had become acute by the end of the Civil War, and the answer to this question that was then given was to starve the fraternities by requiring, as a condition of admission to the University, an affirmation of prospective students that they would not join such societies. The fraternities, however, instead of folding up, went underground; and those who joined fraternities were confronted by the question of whether they had been morally dishonest. Once in 1872, and again in 1873, the Board had been petitioned to rescind this pledge, but had declined to do so. In June, 1872, after receiving a petition signed by a large number of alumni asking that the pledge be done away with, the Board sought the advice of the faculty on this subject. Professors Bliss, James, Tustin, and Lowry being "all strongly condemnatory of secret societies in College," the Board, after prolonged discussion of the matter, voted to maintain the existing pledge. A year later, in response to a similar petition from the Alumni Club of Philadelphia, it reaffirmed its decision of 1872.[48] Subsequently, in respect to this subject, there arose a *cause célèbre*—namely, the refusal of the faculty to recommend for graduation Jonathan Follmer Strieby, of the Class of 1875, because of his violation of his pledge not to join a fraternity. Three years later the Class of 1875 memorialized the Board of Trustees on this subject, requesting that the degree of Bachelor of Arts be conferred upon Strieby. This request the Board referred to the faculty, and in September, 1878, the faculty voted not to change the decision on this matter that it had made in 1875. Presumably because of persistent pressure, the Board of Trustees, on June 24, 1879, although still believing that secret societies were injurious to undergraduates, decided that it would be expedient for it to commit the "enforcement of the whole matter to the wisdom and discretion of the President and College Faculty." Being at last persuaded, however reluctantly, that collegiate fraternities were riding the wave of the future, the Trustees, it appears, decided to "save face" by passing the buck to the faculty. Pursuant to this grant of authority, the faculty, deciding also to roll with the wave of the future, unanimously recommended Strieby for graduation.[49] Here conversion was as complete at it had been sudden.

Less easy of solution, because on this subject there could be no passing of the buck, was the problem of giving the alumni more influence in the Board of Trustees. By June, 1875, in response to a request from the alumni that the Board fill every vacancy in its membership with "a candidate nominated by the alumni" until such time as at least one-third of the members thereof should be alumni, the Board, although rejecting the "method" proposed, accepted as its policy "the plan of filling every third vacancy in its numbers by electing one from the ranks of the Alumni, until the proposed one-third representation shall be had." It reserved, however, the right to deviate from this procedure if "peculiar and important emergencies" should arise.[50] The Board had granted the request for alumni representation, but it had reserved the right to determine who the alumni representatives should be.

But the alumni were not through. Presently they turned to the Board of Curators, a body which, by the middle 1870's, they virtually controlled. The Curators were not happy about their role in the governance of the University. Theirs was a position of honor, not a position of authority. As early as 1869 they had exhibited restlessness about their lack of power, and had proposed that committees of the two governing bodies discuss the advisability of having one board to manage the University.[51] Nothing came of this proposal, but in 1870 the Curators proposed to the Trustees that the charter of the University be so amended as to vest in the Curators the power to employ and dismiss teachers, to supervise the government of the University and the instruction therein, and to direct the general affairs of the University; but the power to fix and pay salaries should remain vested in the Board of Trustees. The Trustees refused to concur in "a change so radical," and expressed their doubt as to whether "experience proves that it is often wise to separate the fixing and paying [of] salaries from the appointing and governing powers." [52] Here the matter was dropped for the time being. But the disturbing events of the three years immediately following 1875 led the Curators to bring up once more the question of "modernizing" the charter of the University. In June, 1878, they proposed that the two governing boards unite in getting amendments to the charter that would make possible "closer and more necessary" co-operation of the two boards, especially in the making of decisions affecting the election and dismissal of teachers, the enforcement of discipline, the making of changes in the general curriculum, and the methods of instruction in the University. This proposal the Trustees referred to a committee that was instructed to study it and to report its conclusions a year later.[53]

The reference in the foregoing proposal to the election and the dismissal of teachers called sharply to mind a decision of the preceding year that did much to polarize the discontent with the existing regime and to hasten the collapse of Loomis's administration. On June 26, 1877, President Loomis committed the greatest blunder of his career when, in a special communication to his fellow Trustees, he preferred against Professor Charles S. James charges alleging that James had probably never done full justice to his department, that in giving attention to a private business and in neglecting to stay during study hours in his room in the College he had contributed to a demoralizing situation, and, finally, that his attitude to Loomis had made the personal relations of the professor and the president highly unpleasant. In respect to the last-named matter, Loomis affirmed that James would do anything to thwart the efforts of Loomis, "provided he could do it under the protection of concealment." For two years, he said, he had refrained from bringing before the faculty any subject which "seemed capable of being used by him to damage the government" of the University. Since such a situation could not continue without damage to the University, and since there seemed no possibility that the faculty as then constituted would be harmonious, he referred the matter to the Board for its decision, saying that he did not wish his "position, interests or feelings [to] stand in the way of settling the question on its merits." [54] Loomis had written with a pen that he had dipped in gall, and the nature of his charges were such, as he well knew, that the Board would be compelled to choose between him and James. The University was not large enough for both. Would the Board slant its decision in favor of one of its members, a person who had deserved well of their consideration?

Since it could not ignore charges as serious as those laid before it, the Board appointed a committee to confer with Professor James on this subject. At a special meeting of the Board on July 24, this committee reported that it had attempted, in conference with Loomis and James, to effect a reconciliation between them. To the suggestion of the committee that they endeavor to work together during the coming academic year, President Loomis had replied that no such arrangement would be practicable, and Professor James had denied the charges made against him, and proposed to read to the Board his reply to these charges. This reply, undated, dealt with the charges at considerable length, and, notwithstanding his belief that he had vindicated himself, he concluded his remarks by saying that he would resign if it were made "plain" to him that his "presence in the Faculty works against the best interest of the College"; but, he frankly told the Board, he was unwilling to leave the College "under the shadow of charges unproven, unfounded and unjust." After considering his defense, the Board resolved that the retirement of James from the faculty would be "desirable for the best interests of all concerned," and requested his resignation. The Board was divided on the issue; of the twelve Trustees present, nine voted for the resolution and three against it. The committee appointed to inform James of this action had been instructed to tell him that, if he would consent to resign, the part of the resolution requesting his resignation would be expunged from the minutes of the Board.[55] At another special meeting of the Board, held September 3, 1877, the Trustees were informed that James had refused to resign, that he had submitted a letter affirming his belief that his resignation would be injurious to the College, and that the Board could not legally remove him "except for sufficient cause, established after a fair trial, with specific charges proved by competent testimony in . . . [his] presence." In proof of his affirmations, he submitted extracts from two court decisions bearing on his cause, together with a testimonial signed by more than a hundred persons consisting of members of the Board of Curators, members of the Alumni Association, and friends of the University. After considering at length the evidence before them, the Trustees decided (eight for, two against, one not voting) that the connection of Professor James with the University should be "determined for the causes set forth by the President of the University in his special report to the Board" in June, 1877; and it appointed a committee of three members of the Board to inform Professor James that the Board "no longer desire[d] his services." Before adjourning, the Board requested the present faculty to "carry on the work of instruction in the University until the Professorship of Mathematics be filled." [56] So far as the Board was concerned, the James affair was now closed; but for months to come there would linger in the minds of many persons who knew of this affair the belief that Professor James, whatever his faults may have been, had been dismissed from his position without due process of law.

Professor James did not give up the fight. At a special meeting of the faculty on September 5, 1877, President Loomis presented a communication in which a committee of the Trustees told of the action taken by the Board in respect to Professor James, and he also conveyed to the members of the faculty the regret of the Board that, for the time being, additional duties would be imposed upon them by virtue of the dismissal of Professor James from his post. At this same meeting Professor Francis W. Tustin, secretary of the faculty, read a letter in which Professor James said that he did not admit the legality of the action taken by the Trustees in dismissing him, and that he held himself ready "to do duty by the assignment of the Faculty, as heretofore." To this request the faculty replied that, because of the action that the Board had taken in respect to him, it did "not feel at liberty" to assign any work to him.[57] Thereafter Professor James pleaded his cause with the family of the University at large,[58] and eventually took it to the courts of Pennsylvania.

By the time of commencement in June, 1878, *l'affaire James* had caused widespread commotion and had aroused untold resentment against the Loomis administration. Recognizing this state of affairs, President Loomis, on June 25, 1878, submitted his resignation as president of the University with the stipulation that it take effect at the end of the academic year 1878–79.[59] Meanwhile, the Reverend A. Judson Rowland had presented to the Board of Curators resolutions disapproving the action of the Board of Trustees in dismissing Professor James, and expressing the belief that James should be given an opportunity to meet his accusers face to face in a trial properly conducted. In the course of the discussion of these matters, a letter to the Curators from the secretary of the Philadelphia Club of Lewisburg Alumni was read. It informed the Curators that this club, on June 17, 1878, had resolved that, since there existed "on all sides a profound dissatisfaction with the state of things in our Alma Mater," and since "this dissatisfaction appears to be justly chargeable to the line of policy and general conduct of the University pursued by the President," it was persuaded that the time for a change had come, and, accordingly, it requested that, at the earliest practicable date, action be taken to insure the retirement of Loomis from the office of president of the University. Presently, when information was received that Loomis had submitted his resignation, the Board of Curators, after permitting the withdrawal of the papers under consideration, passed resolutions urging the Trustees to make this resignation effective at once and to reopen the case of Professor James.[60]

In the afternoon of the same day, June 25, the Alumni Association passed resolutions informing the Trustees that it was "the sentiment of the Alumni" that the resignation of Loomis should be so accepted as to take effect at once, and the Association recommended also that the Board reconsider its action in dismissing Professor James from the faculty of the University.[61]

The Trustees, however, refused to be intimidated. To both the Board of Curators and the Alumni Association they replied, in respect to one resolution, that they had accepted the resignation of the president to take effect at commencement, 1879, before the request to do otherwise "was before . . . [the Board] for action," and, in respect to the other resolution, that they considered it "unwise and without hope of good results" to reopen the case of Professor James.[62]

A few weeks later the Committee on Publication of the Board of Curators gave wide publicity to its belief that the James case should be reopened, to the fact that both the Board of Curators and the Alumni Association had urged the Trustees to make the resignation of President Loomis effective at once, and to the committee's assertion that the "summary dismissal" of Professor James had increased disaffection within the family of the University.[63]

As a matter of law, the James affair was finally terminated in the courts of Pennsylvania. After the Trustees, in June, 1878, had elected George Morris Philips to the professorship from which James had been dismissed,[64] the way was open to Professor James to petition the Court of Common Pleas of Union County for a writ of *quo warranto* against Philips for the purpose of ascertaining whether James had been legally removed from his chair and Philips was legally entitled to occupy it. James won his case in the Union County Court,[65] but on appeal the Supreme Court of Pennsylvania reversed the judgment of the lower court on the ground that, pursuant to a law of Pennsylvania of June 14, 1836—the law on which James was relying—a writ of *quo warranto* could not be issued against a mere "servant, employee or agent of the corporation," but only against officers of the corporation. Since the court held that a professorship is not a corporate office, James had no standing in court under the law upon which he had relied. He was, in effect, just an employee of a Pennsylvania corporation known as the University at Lewisburg.[66]

The reaction to the Board's removal of Professor James on the strength of the charges that President Loomis had preferred against him was as incomprehensible to the Board as it no doubt was disturbing to Loomis. The committee of the Board that recommended the acceptance of the resignation of President Loomis remarked that, in so doing, it had yielded to what appeared "to be the leadings of divine Providence, conscious that the services of President Loomis may never be estimated, or properly requited by the friends of our University." [67] What impressed the members of this committee was the knowledge they possessed that Loomis had done much for the University; and their view of the matter is understandable. Loomis had served the University faithfully through difficult times of war and depression; he had given to it generously of his time and his money; and he also had served faithfully the Baptist denomination in Pennsylvania, of which the University was an important agency.[68] Yet, under his direction, the University had not grown, and the Baptists of Pennsylvania—not to mention those of New Jersey—were not firmly united in their support of it. At the solicitation of Baptists in southwestern Pennsylvania, the legislature, on March 14, 1871, had chartered a college to be established at or near Jefferson in Greene County, and to be known as Monongahela College. The charter of this institution was much like that of the University at Lewisburg; among other things, it provided for the government of the college by a Board of Curators as well as by a Board of Trustees. Also, it was empowered to establish a female seminary, "and such other departments appropriate for primary study and theological learning, as the patrons and managers of said college shall find themselves able to maintain." [69] Although this college expected to draw support from West Virginia and from eastern Ohio, as well as from western Pennsylvania, it never prospered, and during its relatively short life it was not a serious competitor of the University at Lewisburg. But its very existence was proof of the fact that not all Baptists in Pennsylvania were wholeheartedly devoted to their institution in Lewisburg. Accordingly, since the University appeared to be dragging its heels, to be serving local rather than state interests, and even to be unsympathetic to the new needs of a new era, it seemed to many persons not unreasonable to fix responsibility for this untoward situation upon the man who was guiding the operations of this institution. It was easy to think, as it was easy to say, that, given the changing times in America, Loomis was not young enough, not enlightened enough, not flexible enough, not imaginative enough, and not lovable enough to direct the University in a time which offered rare opportunities to it to move rapidly toward the realization of the high goals to which it aspired. It was easy for those who disliked him to say that Loomis had no doubt outlived his usefulness as president of the University before he made the supreme blunder of preferring charges against Professor James. Nor did the fact that in the James affair he was a Trustee appealing to fellow Trustees to choose between him and James help his position within the family of the University; for in this family the notion was coming to be held that the Board of Trustees, like Loomis, was to some extent guilty of looking backward rather than forward, and that the Board's support of Loomis in this affair was based upon sympathy for a like-minded fellow trustee rather than upon a rational desire to see to it that one who had been accused of wrongdoing was not deprived of his position without due process of law. It is difficult, however, to determine how much of the support that James received was based upon the desire to keep James in the faculty of the University and how much of it was based upon the desire to support James as a means of getting rid of Loomis.

Whatever may be the truth about the James affair, it is beyond question, I think, that the belief had become widespread that the University had fallen into the grip of persons who were unsympathetic to progress. Such belief, indeed, had infected the students, and was no doubt faithfully expressed in an editorial that appeared in the students' magazine at the beginning of the year 1880. Here we read that

> The University at Lewisburg has emerged from the gloom of fogyism and the shadow of precedent, and although weak from a long existence under these evils, nevertheless under the guidance of President Hill it is making rapid progress in those directions which are characteristic of the live Colleges of the present day.[70]

Only technically did President Loomis's administration extend to commencement in 1879. No doubt dispirited by the obvious and widespread evidence of his repudiation, he arranged to hear during the first term all the recitations for which he was responsible during the academic year 1878–79, and at the meeting of the Board of Trustees in December, 1878, he requested and received leave of absence without pay until the end of the academic year. Professor Francis W. Tustin, being the senior professor, served as acting president for the rest of Loomis's term.[71] Before the end of that academic year, however, the University had acquired a new president, and his duty it would be to lift the University, if that could be done, from the pecuniary, intellectual, and spiritual depths to which it had fallen and to help it acquire at least some of the characteristics that students were then coming to accept as the hallmark of a "live" educational institution.

6

Reorganization and Revival

An institution of learning must adapt itself to the public by which it is surrounded, and to which it looks for support. . . . We need not, with our present equipments rightly utilized, turn any young man or woman away from the doors of this University. We have here facilities for furnishing instruction in any non-professional study. I would make no distinction of sex, as regards a choice of study. I would not require of every student that he should pursue a certain curriculum, though I would strongly advise it, and would not grant a degree without it.—*David Jayne Hill, Inaugural Address, June 25, 1879.*

David Jayne Hill was elected president of the University at Lewisburg on March 11, 1879, at a second special meeting of the Trustees held for the purpose of choosing a successor to President Loomis. At the first of these meetings, on December 27, 1878, the Reverend P. S. Henson, pastor of the Memorial Baptist Church in Philadelphia, was elected and was voted an annual salary of $3,300. But his election had not been by unanimous vote; one person had voted for Professor David Jayne Hill, and three had cast blank ballots. Because Henson declined the office tendered him, the Trustees were obliged to hold a second meeting to choose a president. At this meeting two nominations were made: Professor N. L. Andrews, of Madison University, and Professor David Jayne Hill, of the University at Lewisburg. On the first ballot Hill received twelve of the fifteen votes cast, and on the second ballot he received all the votes. He was offered an annual salary of $2,000, and he would be required, if he accepted the office, to occupy, at an annual rental of $320, the house which the Trustees recently had bought from President Loomis. By virtue of his new position, he also would become professor of metaphysics and moral philosophy. In the autumn of 1879 he was ordained a Baptist minister.[1]

Professor Hill was not yet thirty years old. He was born in Plainfield, New Jersey, on June 10, 1850, the son of the Reverend and Mrs. Daniel T. Hill. He entered the University at Lewisburg in 1870, and four years later he was graduated with the highest honors of his class. In 1874 he became a tutor in his alma mater, a year later he became an instructor, and in 1877 he was elected Crozer Professor of Rhetoric, a position which he still held in 1879. He had risen rapidly in the faculty of the University, and already he was becoming widely known as an educator and as a man of letters. He had published two textbooks: *The Science of Rhetoric* (1877) and *The Elements of Rhetoric and Composition* (1878), both of which continued to be used well into the twentieth century. Also, in the year of his election to the presidency, he had brought out in the series called *American Authors* two volumes, one on Washington Irving and the other on William Cullen Bryant.[2]

The election of Professor Hill marked the beginning of a new era in the history of the University, which now, deep in a disturbing crisis, was passing the baton from an old man to a young man; and the young man, the first alumnus to be so honored, did not shrink from the difficult task that he was being asked to perform. To a group of citizens of Lewisburg who came to his home on the night of March 17 to congratulate him on his election, Professor Hill, who not yet had accepted the offer, spoke not only as a man aware of the great responsibility being thrust upon him, but also as one hopeful, even confident, of the progress of the University in the era that lay ahead.

> A new chapter of its history [he affirmed] is about to be written. You are properly solicitous about this important matter. . . . I believe that with the revival of business now approaching we may indulge great hopes of increased prosperity. Our institution must reach out its arms for the young men and women of this State, and its resources must be augmented to meet the demands of the present age. Let us have your confidence, your encouragement, your good words, and your hearty co-operation, and we shall achieve such success that you will look with pride upon the University at Lewisburg.[3]

Three days later David Jayne Hill wrote his acceptance of the presidency of his alma mater.[4]

Besides the exuberance and the abundant energy of youth, Hill brought to the performance of his new duties many and varied talents. His ability was as great as his *savoir-faire* was abundant; his understanding as deep as his mind was flexible; his articulateness as precise as his literacy was broad; his gift of speaking well as great as his gift of writing gracefully. Moreover, his quiet humor tempered his seriousness of purpose, and his affability enhanced his personal charm. Inclined by temperament and by training to moderation, he had become wise beyond his years. Consequently, his view of collegiate education, though forward-looking, was not radical. He would not willingly preside over a revolutionary change in the curricula of the University, but rather over moderate changes therein that, in his opinion, would put the University in step with the progress of the era. He, of course, could not then know that, within two years, he would play a leading part in bringing about a revolution in management that would open the way to a rapid change of Old Lewisburg to New Lewisburg. But he did know that much was expected of him, and he could not help knowing that nothing short of complete success would satisfy his ambition.

Within the family of the University the young president-elect was accepted sincerely and wholeheartedly. From both students and alumni his reception was as enthusiastic as it was flattering. One of the editors of the *College Herald,* looking forward a few days to Hill's inauguration, remarked that he need not speak of the qualifications of the president-elect for so important a trust as the one that he was about to receive, for he needed no eulogy. "All feel [he wrote] that a great and noble spirit is about to take the helm and guide our beloved University safely through the surges and breakers of all opposition. . . . High hopes are also entertained of the future prosperity of the University. Already [he continued] some who were somewhat indifferent to the welfare of the Institution are quickened into new activity, and are pledging their hearty co-operation to the interest of the University." [5] With equal enthusiasm the officers of the Alumni Association accepted the new president of the University. In their notice to members of the Association of the forthcoming inauguration of Hill at the commencement in 1879, they urged that all former students attend in a body to present "their foremost brother" to the University as the gift of the alumni. Moreover, the alumni were told in this notice that upon them there now rested "a large responsibility" for the future of the University, and their presence at the inauguration, they were assured, would show that, by being faithful to their alma mater, they were being loyal to her new president.[6]

Outside the University, in the press and elsewhere, the president-elect was enthusiastically acclaimed, both within and without the Baptist denomination. The nature of his welcome, since few illustrations thereof can here be given, can perhaps best be shown by an occasion when persons without the family of the University united with persons within that family to give him a rousing reception on May 20, 1879, a few weeks before his inauguration, at a meeting of the Social Union in Philadelphia. Here, speaking to a group which included members of the Alumni Association, members of the faculty of the University, and others prominent in the Baptist denomination, he gave a sketchy preview of some things about the University that he subsequently elucidated more fully in his inaugural address. To achieve its maximum of effectiveness, he said, the University should cultivate better relations with the public, increase its facilities for instruction, and, emphatically, enlarge its endowment. An increase of its endowment by a quarter of a million would, he felt certain, double the effectiveness of the University.[7]

On June 25, 1879, the day of his induction into office, he gave in a formal address a rounded expression of his educational philosophy and a full statement of what earlier he had merely sketched in outline concerning his conception of the needs of the University that must be met to permit this institution to achieve the goals that had been set for it. Accepting as soundly liberal the view expressed in John Milton's *Tract on Education,* he affirmed that modern life demands men—men of knowledge, men of power, men abreast of their age, and, "above all else," men of high character: "men who can be trusted with the management of great interests." To prepare men of that sort for their tasks in life, the University had been founded, and in its efforts to accomplish its purposes it had pursued such a curriculum as might yet be found in "the best American colleges." For its operations the University at Lewisburg, he said, had a large field—Pennsylvania, New Jersey, Delaware, and Maryland—and also a commendable history and resources that were "by no means contemptible." But, he continued, it had great and urgent needs, for it "must keep pace with the advances of the age." Of the urgent needs of the University, the first, in his opinion, was

> the united effort of all its friends to increase its efficiency and the number of its students. . . . If [he continued] one half the energy that has been expended in fault-finding and complaint had been put forth in promoting the interests of this institution, there would be more prosperity and fewer regrets. . . .

Another urgent need of the University was, he thought, really a cluster of needs which he assembled under the heading of more adequate facilities for instruction. "In the higher branches of knowledge," he said,

> much subdivision is necessary, in order to insure thoroughness. The University should have a chair of history, political economy, and constitutional law. The department of natural sciences requires two professors, one of physics and one of natural history. A larger place should be made for English philology and literature. Separate laboratories for students in the experimental sciences should be constructed and equipped. The library

> should be liberally endowed, in order to provide for its continuous growth. An astronomical observatory should be erected. The Academy should be placed on the same basis as Colgate Academy at Hamilton, with a full and special corps of instructors. The young ladies of the Institute should enjoy the same advantages as the young men of the College, both as to the extent and thoroughness of their course of study.

Such, then, was the program which President Hill had formulated to put the University at Lewisburg in the way of making its proper contribution to the fulfilling of the needs of modern life. To carry out this program, as he carefully pointed out, a "liberal endowment" would be needed; and he looked forward hopefully to the day when a generous friend would double the usefulness of the University, and thus help to provide for the people of Pennsylvania "a free Christian education." [8]

As to policy, he was equally explicit. The University, he said, would pursue a policy that would be both "broad and progressive." It would be "generous and confiding" to its friends in Lewisburg.[9] It would welcome in its aims and actions the increasing influence of the alumni. It would adapt itself to the public to which it looked for support, providing "efficient instruction in any non-professional study," and, in respect to choice of studies, it would make no distinction on account of sex. Moreover, it would grant a degree only to those who had completed a prescribed curriculum, not "for various studies at the option of the learner." To the idea of complete freedom for students to choose the subjects for disciplining and furnishing their minds he was firmly opposed, for, with President Martin B. Anderson, of the University of Rochester, he agreed that young collegians were not qualified to choose "the course of study which is best for a liberal education." Accordingly, during his administration complete freedom in electing studies would not be allowed students who sought a degree from the University at Lewisburg. In respect to this matter, President Hill was more in accord with the current practice at Yale or at Princeton than with the currently evolving practice at Harvard.[10]

Neither the acclaim that he had received as its new president, nor the indisputable evidence that the alumni had acquired new faith in and new hope for their alma mater, had alleviated the pecuniary crisis into which the University was sinking. In fact, during the next two years, this crisis would become so bad that the very continuance of the University would be called in question. In June, 1879, the treasurer had reported a deficit of $3,016.83 for which no provision had been made, and a year later the Trustees authorized a loan of $4,000 from the Endowment Fund to the School Fund. Moreover, in December, 1880, another loan from the Endowment Fund was authorized to "meet current expenses." Also, the Trustees, now apparently much disturbed by the deteriorating pecuniary condition of the University, appointed a committee for the purpose, *inter alia,* of considering "the present condition of the University, and [of] suggest[ing] to the next annual meeting some definite measures necessary to be pursued in the future." Nothing was, or perhaps could be, done, for as late as October, 1881, the treasurer, after reporting a lack of money in the School Fund, was authorized by the harassed Trustees "to pay the Professors out of any money in his hands." [11]

Meanwhile, agitation for changes in the charter had continued. Responding to the challenge made when, in June, 1879, the Reverend A. Judson Rowland, in behalf of a committee appointed by a meeting in Philadelphia of friends of the University, presented to them two drafts of a revised charter, the Trustees appointed a committee of seven to confer with a like committee of the Curators on the subject of "changes in the charter." [12] A year later these two committees, having met twice and reached an agreement, reported unanimously in favor of so amending the charter as, *inter alia,* to abolish the Board of Curators; to vest the full power of governing the University in a board of trustees consisting of not more than thirty-five members, of whom four-fifths should be Baptists in good standing; and to restrict the term of a trustee to five years. Furthermore, the committees recommended that the Trustees appoint a committee to work with a committee of the Curators to get the required legal sanction for such proposed amendment of the charter. The Trustees, however, contented themselves with recommending that, at the time of their next semi-annual meeting, the Trustees and the Curators hold a joint meeting for the purpose of considering proposed changes in the charter. On December 29, 1880, the day set for the joint meeting, the Trustees agreed that they would consult the Curators "in a meeting of conference, and not for the purpose of being bound by any action of said joint meeting." [13]

No record of the above-mentioned joint meeting can be found in the Minutes of the Trustees, but in the Minutes of the Curators, under date of June 28, 1881, there is recorded, presumably as an *aide-memoire,* a resolution adopted by the joint meeting in Philadelphia on December 29, 1880. This resolution provided for the appointment of a committee, consisting of three Trustees, three Curators, and President Hill, "to mature such a plan of reorganization" as would, in the opinion of the committee, "secure the largest measure of cooperation and prosperity"; and this committee was instructed to provide, at the earliest practicable moment, a printed copy of their plan for each of the respective members of the two governing boards of the University.[14] Whether this committee did or did not mature such a plan, we do not know; but we do know that, even weeks before the time that their report would be due, the matter which they had under consideration had ceased to be important, as a resolution adopted by the Curators on June 28, 1881, readily discloses to anyone informed about the affairs of the University at Lewisburg at that time. This resolution—the last one adopted by the Curators—reads as follows:

> That we hereby express our sympathy with the movement now being made to secure an addition of $100,000 dollars [*sic*] to the Endowment Fund, and that we pledge our hearty cooperation with the appointed agent, Dr. G. M. Spratt, in his efforts to raise this amount.[15]

If the movement thus endorsed proved to be successful, action would be taken to abolish the Board of Curators; and, as the sequel will show, it was successful.

Behind this resolution lay more than a story of pecuniary distress and of sheer accident. The story, in part, is one of reconciliation and of fulfillment; the reconciler was the young president of the University, the reconciled was a former trustee of the University, and the fulfillment was the rise of two related families to prominence in the history of Baptist education in Pennsylvania. In this affair the new president of the University became deeply involved.

During the first two years after his inauguration, President Hill found himself, willy-nilly, increasingly concerned with the mounting crisis in the pecuniary affairs of the University. Regardless of what might be happening in the sphere of business generally, prosperity, as we have seen, did not come to the University. In his efforts to remedy this situation, President Hill presently thought of an earlier friend of the University, William Bucknell, a Philadelphia man of means, who, nearly twenty years before, had turned his back upon the University by withdrawing from its principal governing board. Upon this man President Hill brought to bear so successfully all his personal charm and all his persuasive power that Mr. Bucknell was induced, once again, to take a hand in the affairs of an institution that he earlier had abandoned. Perhaps his decision to do so was made easier for him by the fact that, in 1868, thanks to the wealth and the generosity of the Crozer family, an important part of the Great Enterprise had been removed from Lewisburg to Upland, Pennsylvania, there to be re-established and enlarged as the Crozer Theological Seminary in tribute to John Price Crozer, the father of Mr. Bucknell's second wife. In 1856 both Mr.

Crozer and Mr. Bucknell, as Trustees, had voted to remove the entire University to a site in Delaware County. Thus, perhaps, the frustration of an aspiration of earlier years now had been effaced, and the way had become smoothed to a renewal of Mr. Bucknell's support of that part of the Great Enterprise which had remained in Lewisburg. By this time, moreover, thanks to the coming of transportation by rail, Lewisburg was much less isolated than it had been in the 1850's. However that may be, on April 2, 1881, Mr. Bucknell signed a paper that President Hill had drafted for him, and, by so doing, pledged himself to give to *a* Board of Trustees of the University at Lewisburg, "hereafter to be agreed upon," the sum of $50,000, provided (1) that $100,000 be derived from the present endowment of the University by liquidating all its assets except its buildings and its real estate in the campus in Lewisburg; (2) that an additional $50,000 be raised; (3) that all the property of the University be placed in the hands of one governing board to be "chosen by the new subscribers"; (4) that all the claims against the University be met without "impairing the funds above named"; (5) that Mr. Bucknell's subscription should fall due and be paid in cash only when the other prescribed funds should be raised; (6) that the present Board of Trustees accept this offer within three weeks from April 2, 1881; and (7) that the whole project be completed before November 1, 1881.[16]

The Trustees, meeting in a special session on April 21, 1881, "gratefully" accepted this offer, and promised to do their best to fulfill all the conditions laid down by Mr. Bucknell. They designated President Hill as their special agent in this matter and appointed a committee to assist him. Subsequently this committee employed the Reverend George M. Spratt to solicit $50,000 in subscriptions.[17] This was the price that they were willing to pay to rescue the University from impending insolvency.

Once again Baptists in Pennsylvania were being put to a test comparable to that in 1846 of raising $100,000 in order to give effect to the charter of their proposed University, or to that in 1864–65 of removing serious subsequent distresses of the University by raising another $100,000. That the crisis confronting the University in 1881 was acute, no informed Baptist in Pennsylvania would have denied. A time of vital decision had come. Calling the offer of Mr. Bucknell as wise as it was generous, the editor of the *National Baptist* affirmed that now was the time to find out whether Baptists in Pennsylvania actually wanted a University—the time when they must decide whether to raise the sum of $50,000 within the specified time, or to compel the University to close its doors. "That this is really the alternative," he said, "we are informed by the best authority. The income from present funds does not meet expenses, and the charter prohibits any appropriation of endowment funds for current outlay." [18] By June, 1881, when he learned that Mr. Bucknell would be liberal in interpreting his conditions and that Dr. Spratt, "the invaluable Secretary of the Education Society," would be in charge of the campaign to raise the required sum, the editor of this magazine wrote optimistically about the project, saying, however, that "the two points on which the success of the movement" would largely turn were Philadelphia and Lewisburg. He "believed" that Philadelphia would do its part, and he "trusted" that Lewisburg and Union County would "not be behind." [19]

That the foregoing statements about the approaching insolvency of the University were responsible utterances we are compelled to believe. On this point, for example, President Hill was as explicit as he was persistent. Speaking before a meeting of the Pennsylvania Baptist Education Society in Reading, Pennsylvania, in October, 1881, he remarked:

> More than a year ago the Treasurer said to me that unless we could raise $50,000 additional, the doors must be closed. I was nonplussed. The Faculty met again and again for prayer. We felt that we were a lighthouse whose oil was exhausted.[20]

More than eight years later, soon after the death of Mr. Bucknell, Dr. Hill, who was then president of the University of Rochester, reaffirmed his earlier view of the intensity of the crisis at Lewisburg at the beginning of the 1880's.

> No one so well as myself [he wrote] can now realize the condition of affairs at Lewisburg in 1880. This is not the place to picture that situation; but we cannot rightly appreciate one of the many benevolent actions of Mr. Bucknell without knowing that the situation was very desperate. He saved the institution from closing its doors.[21]

Because of good planning, good publicity, and no doubt favorable responses to such calls for unity as were made at the meeting of the Alumni Association in June, 1881, the campaign was successful. At that meeting of the Association the Reverend A. Judson Rowland, who theretofore had been adversely critical of Loomis's administration, pleaded for co-operation and for a "burial of all past differences" as to location, policy, and other matters.[22] Nor was he alone in making such pleas. The progress of the campaign showed that many Baptists of Pennsylvania wanted to preserve their University and that they wanted it to be adequately supported. At a special meeting of the Trustees on October 12, 1881, Dr. Spratt reported that more than $30,000 in subscriptions for new endowment had been raised, and three months later, when he could report that the full sum had been raised, he was cordially thanked for his efforts. Consequently, at a special meeting on February 14, 1882, the Trustees adopted the measures needed to complete the arrangements for complying with the conditions of Mr. Bucknell's "endowment offer." [23]

It remained to choose a new Board of Trustees and to make new bylaws pursuant to the charter which was now in process of being amended. Such actions were taken at special meetings in March and April, 1882. At the March meeting President Hill, speaking for the committee that had been designated by the "new owners" to make nominations for a new board, presented the names of twenty persons who had been approved that day. Thereupon, one by one, the old Trustees resigned and were replaced by persons on the list of nominees. Eight of the old Trustees, however, were retained as members of the new Board. Among those not retained were Adie K. Bell, Justin R. Loomis, and James Moore, Jr., all of whom had given many years of service to the University. At the meeting in April Adie K. Bell resigned the office of treasurer and was replaced by David P. Leas. Also, a committee on the revision of the bylaws was appointed and instructed to have its report ready, if possible, by the meeting in June.[24] At that time, the charter having been legally amended and other arrangements having been completed, the reorganization of the University was completed by the election of officers of the new Board. William Bucknell became chairman, A. Judson Rowland became secretary, and David P. Leas became treasurer.[25] Also, as a part of the reorganization, the Board established four standing committees: Instruction and Discipline, Buildings and Grounds, Finance, and Publication.

In Baptist circles in Pennsylvania, while the reorganization of the University was in progress in 1882, there was considerable interested, and some interesting, comment on the situation. Then it was that the expressions *Old Lewisburg* and *New Lewisburg* came into use. One commentator remarked that, pursuant to an agreement between Mr. Bucknell and the Old Trustees, January 1, 1882, would mark the end of the Old Lewisburg; and he "respectfully" suggested that the new Trustees, after the requisite changes in the charter had been completed, enter to take charge of "The Bucknell University." Here, I think, was the first public suggestion that the name of the University be changed. However that may be, the aforesaid commentator was certain that the future of the University would be in the care of "business men of large means and enlarged views," men who would conduct all its affairs "on strictly business principles."[26] Less tactful and more resentful of past happenings was a commentator who characterized the outgoing managers of the University not as men whose means were large and whose views were enlarged, but as men who emphatically stood in need of "more means, and especially more 'brains' "—men who had lost the confidence of "our men of means and brains."[27]

Such utterances, of course, did not pass unanswered. Adie K. Bell, as spokesman for those of the old regime who had "resigned out," acknowledged that the "Lewisburg of the future" would be a New Lewisburg —new in its charter and in its management, and new in its "ownership." "The old Board of Control," he said, "were required to abdicate, and those naming the new Board of Trustees are those who gave the last $100,000; hence the new owners." But the new Board, he frankly admitted, was both wise and strong. Nevertheless, he insisted, with perhaps a trace of bitterness, that the Lewisburg of years gone by had done "a good work." "Its management," he confessed, "may have lacked brains and business capacity, but they lacked means in a much larger degree." Nor could he resist the temptation to say that, of those "resigned out," the University never had had a truer friend than James Moore, Jr., nor a more "unselfish, wholehearted" servant than Justin R. Loomis.[28] Bell's statement was as factually accurate as his expression of it was emotionally restrained. The management that was leaving had been a victim of adverse circumstances more than it had been an exhibit of incompetent action. Nor would those who had been crowded out to make room for others who had "means and brains" henceforth be disloyal to the University. On the contrary, from the "back seats" they would occupy they would rejoice in the prosperity of the New Lewisburg, even though their wounds of pride might never be bound up.[29]

The reorganization gave to the University the generous benefactor of whom David Jayne Hill had dreamed. Much of the money for reviving the University and for improving its facilities between 1882 and 1890 came from William Bucknell, the principal "owner" of the New Lewisburg. He was now *paterfamilias*. During his chairmanship of the Board of Trustees, no campaign was made to raise money for the University, apart from the desultory efforts of the Alumni Association to collect money to pay for a gymnasium. Mr. Bucknell made gifts to the collegiate library and to the library of the Institute; he endowed prizes for women in the Institute, and he established twenty scholarships for men in the College; he made gifts to the Endowment Fund; he gave an organ for use in the chapel; and he made gifts for the improvement of existing buildings and for the erection of new buildings. All told, as we learn from the Catalogue of the University for 1889–90, he had contributed to the general fund since 1881 "one hundred and fifteen thousand dollars, and for scholarships and prizes about twenty-five thousand dollars." Thanks in large part to these gifts, President Hill was able to provide much of what he had thought that the University needed as early as 1879.[30]

In making gifts for the purchase of books and for the endowment of scholarships, Mr. Bucknell never lost sight of certain of his fixed convictions. On a personal bookplate which today may be seen in any one of numerous books in the library of the University, he affirms that

> In this presentation he gives his testimony that works of fiction are not the kind of reading most profitable for young persons who are preparing for the earnest work of life.[31]

So, too, of the scholarships which he made available to "worthy young men" in the College of the University. The recipient of each of these scholarships, besides demonstrating ability, must be a member in good standing of a Christian church, must "conform to high standards of morals and courteous deportment in all respects," and must not be addicted to the "use of spirituous liquors or tobacco in any form." [32]

Not uncharacteristically, Mr. Bucknell provided that the first building which he would give to the University should be a chapel. The gift for this building—at first called Reunion Hall but presently dedicated as Bucknell Hall—the Trustees accepted in June, 1885, with "gratitude and affection"; and in proof thereof they prescribed that, upon the completion of this building, "all the Students of the University and all the Instructors in the University be required to attend morning chapel in the new hall." [33] But their supreme expression of gratitude and respect they reserved for another time. At their annual meeting in June, 1886, the Trustees, after interrupting their proceedings to attend "the opening of Bucknell Hall," subsequently reassembled, and (their chairman being absent) resolved unanimously that "the name of this Institution be changed from the University at Lewisburg to Bucknell University." [34] Mr. Bucknell accepted this honor.

During the next four years, Mr. Bucknell's gifts to the University came abundantly and often. First of all was a gift of $10,000 for an astronomical observatory on which, as the *University Mirror* announced as early as October, 1886, the work of construction was ready to begin.[35] In May, 1887, the *Mirror* published an article in which Professor William C. Bartol not only affirmed that the gift for the observatory would be adequate for its purpose, but also gave a somewhat detailed description of the contents of the new building.[36] The Observatory Building was dedicated at a meeting held in Bucknell Hall on June 28, 1887, at which time an address was delivered by Professor Leonard Waldo, of Yale University.[37] In the afternoon of that day the Trustees voted that astronomy should be a required study in the College.[38]

Still other gifts followed. At the meeting in June, 1887, the Trustees announced that Mr. Bucknell had given $50,000 to the Endowment Fund since the preceding meeting of the Board. Before another academic year had passed, Mr. Bucknell had made an additional gift of $25,000 in observance of his seventy-seventh birthday.[39] This money was used to pay for the erection of East Hall, contiguous to the Academy Building, and for another building (presently called the Bucknell Cottage) that would serve as an annex to the Institute Building. East Hall, which was principally a residence for men, contained also a recitation room and apartments for a teacher. Both these buildings were constructed during the year 1888–89, and both were accepted by the Trustees at their meeting in June, 1889.[40]

Before his death on March 5, 1890, Mr. Bucknell had made provision, or at least had intended to make provision, for the renovation and enlargement of the President's House and for the erection of a Chemical and Physical Laboratory. The work on the President's House was completed before commencement in 1890, but the Laboratory Building, constructed during the academic year 1890–91, was not reported to be completed until June, 1891. On June 23 of that year it was presented to the University by members of Mr. Bucknell's family, who were thanked by the Trustees for having carried out Mr. Bucknell's wish in respect to this matter, although "not under the least legal obligation to do so." [41]

Meanwhile, other and important changes—particularly changes affecting the curricular offerings of the University—had been under way. These changes illustrate, as perhaps no other changes could, the moderation of Hill's administration, for they were kept within the bounds of an unchanging general purpose—namely, that of imparting sound instruction in all non-professional studies. By the year 1887–88, students outside the Classical Program could choose between a Latin Scientific and a Greek Scientific Program, and those in the Classical Program in that year could choose from more than twice as many elective studies as had been available to them eight years earlier.[42] Yet the University continued to offer *pro merito* only the degrees of Bachelor of Arts and Bachelor of Science, and the purposes of the two programs remained unchanged. The Classical Program, which, as the Catalogue for 1879–80 tells us, aimed to provide "a liberal education in the classics, the sciences, the arts and literature," embraced, "substantially, the studies of the established college curriculum, with the addition of such branches as modern life seems to demand." To meet the demand of modern life, there had been added recently modern languages, English literature, and constitutional law as *required studies,* and Anglo-Saxon, comparative zoology, and analytical chemistry as *electives.* The Scientific Program, which required ten terms of Latin and "all the other studies of the Classical Course, except Greek," was intended to provide a "thorough training" in the work offered. A so-called eclectic program, which led to no degree, was available to students who wished, and who were prepared, to pursue selected studies.[43]

Such, then, were the offerings during the first year of Hill's presidency. Nine years later, as we learn from the Catalogue for 1887–88, the Classical Program had added as additional required studies medieval and modern history of Europe, comparative zoology, and anthropology, and as elective studies practical astronomy, microscopic botany, American literature, Italian, Spanish, analytical chemistry, calculus, biology, civics, and New Testament Greek; and now in the Scientific Program students could choose, for the first time, between eight terms of Latin and eight terms of Greek. Interestingly enough, in the selection of optional studies in either the Classical or the Scientific Program, the choices could be made only "with the approbation of the Faculty."[44]

An innovation of more than passing interest, that of naming and numbering departments of instruction, appeared for the first time in the Catalogue for 1879–80, the first "large" Catalogue of the University.[45] Herein are listed these departments: English Language and Literature, Latin Language and Literature, Greek Language and Literature, Modern Languages, Pure and Applied Mathematics, Physical Sciences, Political Economy and Constitutional Law, and Mental and Moral Philosophy. Eight years later there were ten such departments, the first four (the language departments) being unchanged, and the remaining six consisting of Medieval and Modern History, Physics and Chemistry, Mathematics and Astronomy, Organic Science, Mental and Moral Sciences, and Economics and Politics.[46] From a faculty of six professors, including the president, in 1879–80, there had been expansion to a faculty of seven professors, including the president, and one instructor in 1887–88. The work for the faculty to do had been expanded more than the number of the faculty had been increased. Professor Freeman Loomis, for example, was now professor of modern languages and history, and librarian. Moreover, the department of Economics and Politics had no professor, and in 1887–88 Enoch Perrine, Crozer Professor of Rhetoric, taught, in addition to rhetoric and literature, both economics and American civics.[47] The day of "excessive specialization" had not yet dawned on the recently christened Bucknell University.

Accompanying the "textbook" studies were courses of scheduled lectures in which all the members of the faculty, including the president, participated. These Thursday morning lectures, beginning immediately after chapel exercises, were well established by 1879, and they were continued through Hill's administration, and beyond. Also, beginning in 1881, Monday morning lectures were scheduled. Broadly speaking, all these lectures dealt with subjects which students did not specifically study in textbooks for the immediate purpose of "reciting" to their professors. Naturally, the subjects of these lectures varied as the "textbook" studies varied or increased in number, and as interest in scientific subjects mounted with the passing years.[48]

One new scheme for promoting learning was introduced by vote of the faculty during the first year of Hill's administration. It was called "honor examinations," and in practice it was substantially what today would be called "individual reading" or, perhaps, "honor courses." It provided that any student having an aggregate average of nine (*i.e.,* 90 per cent) in all his studies of the preceding term could take special work prescribed by the professor in any department of the College. If, during the term of such special study, he achieved an average of nine in all his studies, and passed "before a committee appointed by the Faculty" a satisfactory examination in his voluntary study, his work in the voluntary study not only would be credited to him in the Catalogue of the University, but also, after the year 1879–80, would be considered in the awarding of honors at the time of his graduation.[49] This program was in operation as late as the year 1915–16, but it was then called "Extra Studies." [50]

Curricular changes, however, did not stop here. During the 1880's, when the urge to "university" pretensions among American colleges was strong because their faculties, their alumni, and their friends not only were agog about educational news that then was coming out of Germany, but also about the rise of the first American universities which they had been watching more or less uneasily,[51] the members of the Alumni Association of the University at Lewisburg came up in June, 1886, with a suggestion which, if it had been given effect, would have made the Catalogue of their alma mater read as if it had come from an institution that was something more than a university in name only. Briefly, the Association gave expression, not altogether coherently, to its "sense of approval as to the conferring of degrees of M.A. & Ph.D., that they be granted upon examination, and that courses be established under direction of the Faculty and be published in the Catalogue." [52]

This suggestion the faculty received and discussed in all seriousness, and in October, 1886, voted to insert in the forthcoming Catalogue a statement affirming that the faculty had the proposal under "favorable consideration." [53] Having designated on November 13, 1886, Professors Francis W. Tustin, George G. Groff, and Enoch Perrine as a committee on this matter, the faculty, on December 18, 1886, listened to, discussed, adopted, and referred to the Committee of the Trustees on Instruction and Discipline a report from the aforesaid committee recommending the discontinuance of the degree of Master of Arts *in course,* and the establishment of programs leading to the degrees of Master of Arts and Doctor of Philosophy, either of which would be conferred upon a candidate after he had fulfilled the prescribed residential requirements, had presented an acceptable thesis, and had passed a satisfactory examination. Accompanying these recommendations of the committee was a suggestion from the committee, which the faculty approved, that "various appliances" for pursuing post-graduate study would be needed to attract students to any post-graduate program that the University might adopt.

As a means of helping the Trustees to a proper decision about this matter, the faculty requested its secretary to send them, in addition to the foregoing recommendations, the catalogues of Vanderbilt University, Syracuse University, and Illinois Wesleyan University, so that they might get "an idea of what the Faculty have in mind in the contemplated Post-Graduate Study and Degrees." [54] Upon receiving this material, the Trustees, presumably neither thrilled nor amused, voted, in January, 1887, to refer the communication back to the members of the faculty for further study; and then, by way of imparting to them a lesson in protocol, assured them that, if they so desired, they might "renew their proposition through the President of the University at the next meeting of the Board." [55] There is no evidence that the faculty gave further consideration to this matter.

From this diverting digression we return to the subject of undergraduate instruction, which was then, and would continue to be, the essential work of the University. Such being the case, the College of the University not only was much concerned about the academic program of the Academy, its principal "feeder," but, by the middle 1880's, was also concerned about the instructional program of the Female Institute, which now was becoming another feeder of the College. The work of the Academy, which had been restored to its original condition by a merger of the Preparatory Department of the College and the English Academy in 1878, remained nearly constant during the ensuing decade. Its function was to prepare prospective collegiate students for admission into the freshman class of the College and to prepare other students either for business or for teaching.[56] The work of the Female Institute, however, was more complex, and to this subject we now turn.

For the year 1879–80 the Female Institute, besides its traditional programs, was offering three four-year programs—*viz.,* Latin Scientific, Scientific Art, and Classical, the last-named being equivalent to the program "pursued in the best of American colleges." [57] Three years later this rather elaborate set of offerings had been shaken down to three programs: one preparatory, one "regular," and one collegiate. A full collegiate program, either classical or scientific, was available under the supervision of the professors of the College; but each of these courses, notwithstanding, led only to a "suitable diploma," not to a collegiate degree.[58] By 1884–85, however, both these courses led to a regular collegiate degree. The Female Institute was now becoming, in part, a college for women, for here the women pursuing collegiate studies leading to a degree lived with other women not pursuing such programs, and all residents of the Institute were subject to the laws thereof.[59] The Institute also was becoming, in part, a feeder of the Academy, for the Catalogue of the University for 1887–88 affirms that graduates of the preparatory program in the Institute could pursue in the Academy such additional work as they would need to qualify them for admission to the freshman class of the College.[60]

This growing complexity and intermingling of instructional programs within the University was, to no slight extent, the consequence of the acceptance by the University of both the principle and the practice of coeducation, a principle which, incidentally, was not a novel one in Lewisburg in the early 1880's. As early as 1871, a writer had argued in the *College Herald* that women were as much entitled to education as were men, but that it would be better for them to be educated in colleges for women.[61] The next year two events touching this subject made considerable noise on the campus. One was the news that Cornell had admitted women with the same rights and privileges that men received; the other consisted of remarks made by Professor George R. Bliss before the National Baptist Educational Convention. Here Professor Bliss, recalling his experiences of coeducation in the earliest days of the University at Lewisburg, testified that, through the sophomore and junior years, young ladies could participate "in the studies of young men in college . . . on about equal terms." [62] The interest in this subject continued through later years, and the *College Herald,* from time to time, revealed what other colleges and universities were doing about this matter. Late in 1877 it noted that the University of Pennsylvania had opened its doors to women; that New York University would soon open its doors to women, not on equal terms, but on condition, first, that the young women recite after the young men had finished their work for the day, and, secondly, that, unlike the men, they "pay a tuition fee"; and, finally, without an expression of approval or of disapproval, that at Cornell President Andrew D. White had reported that "the ladies stand ten per cent higher than the gentlemen." [63]

In the course of the discussion of the subject of coeducation, one writer, as early as the beginning of 1874, came up with "one thing certain" about this subject—something that, with the passing of years, probably converted more hard-boiled businessmen and hard-pressed administrators to the cause of coeducation than any argument about equal abilities and equal rights. This "thing certain" was that the instruction of men and women together in the same studies would be more economical than the instruction of them apart in the same studies. "It would," he said, "require but one set of teachers, one library, [a] single collection of natural history, and but one set of chemical, astronomical, and philosophical apparatus." [64] But there were other arguments. Somewhat more than three years later the Board of Curators accepted from one of its committees a report affirming, *inter alia,* that it was "so palpably self-evident that the young ladies committed to our care should have the opportunity of a more extended training, either in the College or in a course substantially equivalent to it, that we hardly think it open to debate." [65] This argument for "either-or" was made at a time of growing financial crisis for the University, when any expansion of the program of the University would have seemed highly imprudent. Perhaps for that reason Professor George G. Groff, in December, 1879, when the University was deep in its most disturbing crisis, presented in a meeting of the faculty of the College the application of Lydia F. Groff for admission, on examination, to sophomore standing in the College. On a motion to recommend to the Trustees that the College be opened to women prepared for its regular work, the faculty divided: two for the motion and three against, the president not voting but being opposed to the adoption of the motion. One of the reasons for the opposition was the belief that the existing circumstances of the College did not warrant a public discussion of this matter. Professor Groff thereupon withdrew the application.[66]

While the University was being reorganized during the next three years, discussion of the subject of coeducation continued, and numerous decisions thereon were made, throughout the nation; and on the campus in Lewisburg echoes thereof were heard.[67] In 1881 Professor Groff and Jonathan Jones, principal of the Female Institute, debated this question with considerable acerbity in a national magazine of the Baptist denomination.[68] A turning point in the controversy as it affected the University at Lewisburg came in June, 1882, when the Board of Trustees instructed its Committee on Instruction and Discipline to consult the faculty and report in the ensuing January on the changes that would be required to permit the students of the Institute and those of the Academy "to recite together." [69] There is no record showing that anything came of this instruction; but a year later, when the Board instructed the president "to take steps to secure the joint instruction and recitation of the students of the three schools so far as this may be made practicable and advantageous," action was taken.[70] President Hill presented this matter to the faculty on September 5, 1883, and the faculty voted to admit to the freshman class, for the purpose of pursuing studies in the Classical Program, two young women who were graduates of the Peddie Institute, Hightstown, New Jersey. The president then announced that "the Senior Class in Psychology in the Institute would recite with the Senior Class in College; and the Chemistry class in the Institute would recite (both these classes of young ladies reciting daily) with the Sophomores in College—the classes in the Institute are to attend at the 'Hill.' " [71]

This was prelude to more important action. In June, 1884, the Trustees voted that students in the Institute should, so far as practicable, recite with the classes of the College, and, with their blessing, referred to the faculty the matter of arranging a supplementary program of study that would permit graduates of the Institute to obtain the degree of Bachelor of Science.[72] To this request the faculty responded graciously. On September 27, 1884, it discussed a recommendation, presented by Professors George G. Groff and Albert E. Waffle, that "the young ladies attending College be admitted to College standing in full in connection with the classes to which they would properly belong, and that they be allowed all the class privileges of College students." It was understood, of course, that young ladies entering the College, unless they lived with relatives in Lewisburg, would board and room in the Institute and be governed by the laws thereof, and that they would not be permitted to join the collegiate literary societies. Final action in this matter was postponed because of the absence of President Hill, and, after his return, was deferred for various reasons until, on January 17, 1885, it was unanimously adopted.[73] On June 23, 1885, the Trustees authorized President Hill to make such a combination of classes as would, in his judgment, achieve "economy in the Teaching force." [74] On the next day the University for the first time graduated a woman, Miss Chella Scott, who received with honors the degree of Bachelor of Science, and who was permitted at commencement to deliver an Oration of the First Class.[75]

Legally, the University now had coeducation, but many years would pass before the process of integration would be completed. Time would be required to dissipate deeply rooted prejudices against the free mingling of the sexes; time would be required also to remove widespread prejudices against the admission of women to unrestricted use of the library and to their being accepted to membership in various and sundry organizations on a footing of equality with men; and, emphatically, time would be required to reconcile men to the fact that frequently the intellectual attainments of women were superior to their own. In 1895 the *Bucknell Mirror* was arguing for a separate reading room for women,[76] and as late as 1902 the author of an editorial in the collegiate newspaper was complaining that the men of the College were getting a "bad break." Women were receiving better marks than men, he affirmed, because men who took "tough" subjects and who participated in all functions pertaining to the College were at a disadvantage in competing with women who specialized in subjects that were easy for them, and who never questioned the minor omniscience of their teachers.[77]

In this period of reorganization and of revival, nothing perhaps better illustrates the emerging New Lewisburg than an upsurge of interest in the library that was comparable to that which President Malcom had aroused in the early 1850's. Such revival of interest was no doubt greatly pleasing to President Hill, who, in addition to his other duties, had served the University as librarian from 1874 to 1879. However that may be, it is more to the point to observe that, during Hill's administration, the library, as perhaps never before, had become a subject of discussion both by members of the faculty and by students. There was discussion about the size and the adequacy of its holdings, discussion about the need of greater accessibility to its collections, discussion about keeping the library open more hours in the day, discussion about the need of an endowment for the library, and, emphatically, discussion about the need for adequate administration of the library. As never had been the case before, both students and members of the faculty began talking about the proper role of the library in a collegiate institution that was aspiring to meet the "demand of modern life."

The revival of this interest in the library coincided with the beginning of Hill's presidency, and the academic year 1879–80 became, in a meaningful sense, *annus mirabilis* for the collegiate library of the University. The reason therefor was not merely the election of Hill to the presidency of the University, for behind this event, during the early and the middle 1870's, influences had been at work, on the campus in Lewisburg and elsewhere in the nation, to stir up interest in libraries. One of these influences was widespreading collegiate journalism. In Lewisburg the *College Herald,* dating, as we have learned, from 1870, had by writings of its own staff and by news of happenings on other campuses that it derived from its exchanges, promoted interest not only in the collegiate library of the University at Lewisburg, but also in collegiate libraries generally; and the publication in 1876, under the sponsorship of the United States Bureau of Education, of a work entitled *Public Libraries in the United States of America: Their History, Condition, and Management* brought to people everywhere in the United States a wealth of material about libraries of all sorts in their country, and, more importantly, facilities for making comparisons of the respective holdings of libraries in any given category. Thus this work tended, to some extent, to make libraries a newsworthy subject.

Three events in 1879 helped to advertise, and to some extent to relieve, the needs of the collegiate library of the University at Lewisburg. One of these was the raising by friends of a sum of money sufficiently large to permit the University to buy from its retiring president, Justin R. Loomis, his library of valuable works.[78] This was a courtesy which, some twenty years earlier, it had not been able to extend to its first president when he retired. The second event was the gift to the University during Commencement Week of a library of 1,700 volumes that had belonged to the late Reverend S. J. Creswell, a trustee of the University from 1856 to 1864. This gift from Mr. Creswell's children the Trustees accepted with profound gratitude, and ordered that it "be kept in a section of the Library by itself." [79] The third event, and in respect to the future of the library perhaps the most important one of that year, was the adoption by the Alumni Association, during Commencement Week, of a resolution requesting each alumnus and each friend of the University to contribute during the current year one book or more to the collegiate library. To give effect to this resolution the Association appointed, under the chairmanship of the Reverend W. H. Conard, Class of 1862, a committee to co-operate with President Hill in a campaign to get books for the library.[80] The so-called "Conard Plan" was well advertised, and it no doubt was largely responsible for the unusual growth of the library during the next two years. One of the largest contributors in these years was William Bucknell, of Philadelphia, who gave, partly in books and partly in cash for the purchase of books, the sum of $700; and thus there came into being a "Bucknell Alcove" in the library. From 1881 onward to the end of Hill's administration, the library grew slowly, partly by gifts and partly by small annual appropriations for the purchase of books, until by the year 1887–88 it contained "about nine thousand bound volumes, besides several thousand unbound pamphlets." [81]

Meantime there had been discussion about the need for a fund to purchase books, a fund which Professor George G. Groff, a consistent friend of the library, insisted should not be less than $25,000.[82] Eventually, before the end of Hill's administration, such a fund did come in the form of a bequest from an alumnus of the University. At their meeting in January, 1887, the Trustees announced that a considerable bequest to the library was coming from the estate of the late Dr. William H. Backus, Class of 1853. This bequest, the income of which was to be used for the purchase of books, came gradually through many years. As of June 30, 1961, it amounted to $42,291.88.[83]

We return to the year 1879, and we do so for the purpose of recording the fact that, in September of that year, at the very beginning of Hill's administration, the professors and the students, after more than six years of agitation by the *College Herald,* formed an association for establishing and maintaining a reading room in the College. For five years this room was supported by subscriptions, but from the beginning of the year 1884–85 it was maintained by the University, and, for that reason, could thenceforth be used by the students without the payment of a fee. The possession of a reading room, moreover, suggested the desirability of keeping the library open daily, and even for several hours each day. From 1886–87 forward the library was kept open daily, but, at least until the middle 1890's, we do not know, except for a few months in 1887, for how many hours each day.[84]

By the middle of the academic year 1886–87, at least a year and a half before the end of Hill's administration, it had become evident, if we judge by writings that had appeared, and still were appearing, in the *University Mirror,* that both the faculty and the students of the University had come to regard the library as a workshop that should be open for many hours each day, that its holdings should be adequate and completely catalogued, and that its collections should be in charge of a competent librarian who would see to it that the materials in his custody would be, to those who needed them, accessible by day and by night. To obtain such a library, three things would be needed—namely, a substantial endowment, a usable catalogue, and a full-time librarian; and of these three the students, beyond doubt, desired most of all a full-time librarian.[85] By this time an endowment for the purchase of books was in prospect, a catalogue of the holdings of the library was about to be started, and, if the *University Mirror* had not been incorrectly informed, a full-time librarian was about to assume his duties. This person, a brother of President Hill, was Isaac N. Hill, who, on June 23, 1885,[86] had been named assistant principal of the Academy, a position which, according to the Catalogue of the University, he continued to hold until the end of the academic year 1886–87. There is no official record of his being appointed librarian for the College.

Officially, Professor Enoch Perrine was librarian for the College from January, 1886, until June, 1887. Since 1879 there had been several librarians. Professor William T. Grier, immediate successor to David Jayne Hill, served from September, 1879, until his death on October 24, 1884, when, it appears, he was succeeded by Professor Albert E. Waffle, who withdrew from the University at the end of the academic year 1884–85. From the opening of the last-named year, Professor Frank E. Rockwood served as librarian until the coming, in January, 1886, of Professor Perrine, who, so the official record tells us, continued to fill that position until June, 1887, when, by vote of the Trustees, "the Library was added to the work of Professor Freeman Loomis." [87]

Nevertheless, despite the clarity of the official record in respect to the succession of librarians, the *University Mirror* announced, in January, 1887, that Isaac N. Hill had "been appointed to the position of College Librarian," and in April, 1887, it was loud in its praise of Hill's accomplishments as librarian, affirming that he "is now busily engaged in making a very complete catalogue of the books," and that he had been keeping the library "open during the entire day for reading, consultation, and drawing of books." By June some at least of the students, believing that the Trustees could "do no better thing than to make the office of librarian permanent," petitioned them to retain Mr. Hill as librarian. But the Trustees were not persuaded to do so, and, as we have seen, returned to the older practice of making the office of the librarian a part-time job for one of the professors.[88] However the fact of Isaac N. Hill's being in charge of the library from January to June, 1887, may be accounted for, there can be no denial either of his being at least *de facto* librarian during those months, or of his having served the students of the College so well that never again would they be fully satisfied with a librarian who gave only a small part of his time to the work appropriately belonging to a librarian.

Significant as it was, the growing interest in improving the library and in putting its resources to better use was, however, but a prominent aspect of a broader and a deeper interest in the University as a whole. From the middle of the 1880's forward, there was considerable discussion both of the recent accomplishments and of the current needs of the University; and, on the whole, the tone of such discussions was optimistic. Naturally, those who viewed the matter realistically perceived that Bucknell University, with its many lacks despite its recent considerable progress, had not yet become a first-rate institution; but it was not difficult for them to believe, especially if they called Bucknell their alma mater, that this institution was in the way of becoming first-rate. Widespread, indeed, was the feeling that Hill's administration, in bringing into being a New Lewisburg, had advanced this institution far beyond the ideals and the accomplishments of the Old Lewisburg. Such, indeed, is the impression emphatically given, among other writings, by the leading editorial, entitled "The Growth of Our University," that appeared in the *University Mirror* for June, 1888. Here the writer contrasted the enrollment in all branches of the University at the beginning of Hill's administration with the enrollment in all branches therein in 1887–88, and he observed considerable growth; here he enumerated important new subjects that had been incorporated into the programs of instruction, and here he affirmed that, although greater scope had been given to elective studies, the required curricula had not been debased; and here also he called attention to an enlarged faculty, better methods of instruction, more laboratory practice, a better and more serviceable library, twenty free scholarships in the College, more collegiate prizes to encourage efforts, new buildings and an improved campus, and, not least, an enlarged endowment. All this had been accomplished during the nine years of Hill's presidency, and it seemed wonderful to behold.

Broadly speaking, all the foregoing assertions are true, but they do not warrant the inference either that Bucknell University had been caught in the whirlwind of the New Education, or that, in consequence of such changes, it now was knocking on the door of academic excellence. Neither of these assumptions would be true. The administration of Hill, instead of going the way of radicalism, had chosen the way of enlightened conservatism. It had gone modern, but neither in a riotous way nor in a pejorative sense. It still held fast what it believed experience to have proved good. It had not abolished the study of Greek, and it had not done away with daily compulsory chapel. It had not downgraded the classics in order to upgrade the sciences. Here, as late as 1888, no one could earn a degree without passing courses in either Latin or Greek. Here there had been no drift toward uncontrolled electives, as at Harvard; here there had been a drift toward controlled electives, but not toward more and varied parallel programs, as at Cornell. Here the system of paternal government had persisted, although, as administered in Hill's administration, it had been "mild but efficient." [89] Here the one big innovation—the only substantial break with the past—had been the adoption, under gentle pressure from the Trustees, of both the principle and the practice of coeducation.

In still other ways the University at the end of Hill's administration seemed much like what it had been at the beginning of that administration. Here, of course, we are not concerned with the fact that the power to govern the University, divided between two boards in 1879, had become concentrated in one board by 1882. Here we are concerned only with matters that would impress students or casual observers. Consequently, we observe that here, as late as 1888, attendance at church on Sundays was still required of all students, and here the annual day of prayer for colleges continued to be observed. We observe also that here the traditional system of marks and of awarding honors at graduation had not been changed, and that, *mutatis mutandis,* commencement in 1888 was a repetition of commencement in 1880. Here also we observe that the cost of attending college had not changed much. Whereas here in 1879–80 tuition, room-rent, fuel, and the like cost $65 per annum, in 1887–88 the cost of such things was $80, principally because the cost of tuition had been advanced from $36 in the former year to $50 in the latter year. Moreover, whereas here in 1879–80 boarding in clubs cost from $1.25 to $1.75 a week, and in private families $2.50 a week, in 1887–88 boarding in clubs cost students from $1.50 to $2.25 a week, and in private families $3.00 a week.[90] Finally, as to enrollment, whether in the College, the Academy, or the Female Institute, the figures show that, between 1879 and 1888, there had been revival rather than large growth. It is true that, whereas the total enrollment in the University in 1879–80 was 171, of whom 51 were in the College, the total enrollment in the University in 1887–88 was 228, of whom 74 were in the College.[91] But it also is true that here in 1871–72 the total enrollment in the University was 266, of whom 79 were in the College, and that here in 1872–73 the total enrollment in the University was 267, of whom 71 were in the College.[92] Thus it can clearly be seen that, at no time during Hill's administration, was the enrollment in the University as large as it had been in the years immediately preceding the depression of 1873. Accordingly, we must conclude that Hill's administration was for the University a time of revival rather than a time of remarkable progress either in accepting the New Education or in increasing its enrollment. The conservatism of David Jayne Hill in his later years developed logically from the conservatism of David Jayne Hill in his earlier years.

What, then, had produced the pronounced optimism as to the future of the University and the widely held belief that Hill, who already apparently had accomplished so much, had made himself all but indispensable to the continued well-being of the University? The reasons therefor are no doubt both numerous and varied, but foremost among them, I think, was the perception that a young man, as dynamic as he was personable, had reversed a tendency which was, in the opinion of persons well informed, pushing the University into insolvency. Moreover, working with a generous patron whom he had found, he had repaired and strengthened the fiscal foundation of the University and had unified and simplified its government. Furthermore, he had shown no antipathy to change, although he had insisted on controlled change. Finally, as teacher, scholar, author, alumnus, and president of the University, he had raised enormously the prestige of his alma mater both at home and throughout the nation. By winning national recognition for himself, he had conferred honor upon the institution that had graduated him with high honors, that had elected him to its staff of teachers, and that, finally, in a time of peril, had called him to become its chief administrative officer. The principal service of Hill's administration, it seems, had been that of stirring up in the hearts and minds of the students, the alumni, and other friends of the University the feeling that their institution was destined neither to backwardness nor to inferiority, but that, if it were adequately staffed, properly housed, adequately endowed, and ably administered, it would, in the years that lay ahead, become a newer Lewisburg worthy of high distinction and capable of great accomplishment. To persons holding such views, Hill had become a symbol of competence and of progress—a leader who had been tried and found not wanting.

Accordingly, since the Lewisburg of the future had been set in motion by a man whose most fruitful years were presumably yet to come, there should be no cause for surprise that, when rumors got afloat near the end of the academic year 1887–88 that Hill was being sought as successor to Dr. Martin B. Anderson, the distinguished but now aged president of the University of Rochester, those who were most concerned about the well-being of the University at Lewisburg should feel both sorrow and apprehension at the prospect of his leaving the presidency of this institution. There can be little doubt, I think, that the *University Mirror* was voicing views widely held when, in complimenting "Rochester friends" for their good judgment in wanting Hill, it also remarked that it could not "but owe them a grudge for any attempt to entice Dr. Hill from his post of duty" in Lewisburg.[93] Nevertheless, on the recommendation of President Anderson, David Jayne Hill was unanimously elected, on June 18, 1888, to be the next president of the University of Rochester.[94] A day later President Hill informed William Bucknell of what had happened, and on June 20, in replying to Hill, Mr. Bucknell expressed his great regret at hearing such news, assured Hill that the Trustees were unanimous in their eagerness to have him remain in his present position, and expressed the hope that Hill, before accepting the offer from Rochester, would discuss the matter fully with all the members of the Board of Trustees.[95]

To the Trustees of Bucknell University, at their annual meeting on June 26, 1888, Hill announced his election to the presidency of the University of Rochester; and to this announcement they replied that, because they would consider his departure the greatest loss that the University could suffer, they would pledge themselves to do everything in their power to "increase the strength and efficiency of the University," that they would give him a leave of absence with pay for a year, and that they would see to it that their Committee on Finance took "measures for building a President's House." [96] Hill was duly impressed by this show of confidence in him, but, being ambitious to go on to larger tasks, he decided on July 8, 1888, after he had talked with President Anderson, that he would accept the offer from Rochester.[97] Like Bucknell, Rochester had offered him a year's leave of absence so that he could study in Germany. On July 9, 1888, he wrote a letter of resignation to the Trustees of Bucknell University, requesting that his resignation take effect on September 1 of that year. At a special meeting on July 18, 1888, the Trustees reluctantly accepted the resignation and designated as acting president of the University Professor George G. Groff, who served in this office during the academic year 1888–89.[98]

7

On the Hill and in the Grove

[Voted] That a social gathering, inexpensively conducted under the general management of the President & General Agent take place at the Female Institute not oftener than once a term.—*Minutes of the Trustees, July 29, 1868.*

The *Herald* is as large as any publication in the United States, edited and published by the enterprise of undergraduates alone. . . . Subscriptions will be received at any time.—*College Herald, November, 1872.*

Some of the young ladies now spend their leisure hours in manipulating the racket and tossing the ball.—*University Mirror, June, 1887.*

Nov. 2nd, 1888. No society owing to big blazing bonfire and lively time on the campus in honor of the great foot ball victory over Dickinson College. Score Bucknell 18. Dickinson 8.—*Minutes of the Theta Alpha Society, November 2, 1888.*

Thus far we have been concerned principally with the history of Bucknell from the standpoint of those who founded it and of those who administered it. With their problems and their accomplishments we have become somewhat familiar. There is, however, another, and a very important, aspect of the history of this institution—the story of its day-to-day operations and of the behavior of both its teachers and its students, at work and at play, whether on the Hill, where stood the buildings of the College and the Academy, or below the Hill in the Grove which sheltered the building into which the Female Academy had moved in 1857. To this subject we now turn.

Our task will not be easy, and what we may accomplish with much effort will leave something to be desired. The chief reason therefor is that, at every turn, we are embarrassed by the lack of suitable materials for writing such a story—the lack of personal diaries and letters, of periodical publications for the earliest years, of complete records of organized activities of the students, of complete records of the Baptist Church in Lewisburg, and, finally, of the minutes of the faculty before September, 1874. But from the limited materials available we shall endeavor to sketch in outline for the decades of the 1870's and 1880's a story that could not be written by consulting the minutes of the Trustees and the Catalogues of the University.

Let us begin with the faculty of the College, a small group of men upon whom, together with the president who also was a professor, rested the burden of administering the regulations of the College, of organizing and imparting the collegiate instruction, and of supervising the activities, curricular and extracurricular, of the collegiate students. Because it was small, the faculty operated without standing committees; it met frequently, not only for the purpose of recording the "averages" of the students, but also for the purpose of performing other tasks. In its meetings it gave, from time to time, special examinations to students; planned contests for prizes and designated the winners thereof; dealt with various and sundry matters of discipline; scheduled, at appropriate times, "recitations," lectures, and term examinations; and, once a year, made arrangements for the activities of Commencement Week, which, by 1870, came in the last week of June. In brief, the collegiate faculty in those years dealt with much business which now would be transacted by standing committees, by deans, and by the president.

We have no record of meetings of the faculty before September 7, 1874. But at the meeting on that day, which began at seven o'clock in the evening, the faculty probably did substantially what it had done at its first meeting in each of the preceding years, with the difference that, at this meeting, it was required to choose a new secretary. Professor Charles S. James resigned, and Professor Francis W. Tustin was chosen to succeed him. James was the third secretary to the faculty. He had been preceded by Professor George W. Anderson, the first secretary, and by Professor Justin R. Loomis, the second secretary, who succeeded Anderson in 1854 and retained the secretaryship until he was elected president of the University. At the above-mentioned meeting the faculty was largely concerned with matters pertaining to the opening of the autumn session of the University.[1]

The new secretary, who was professor of the Greek language and literature, served the faculty well in his newly acquired office until his death on April 14, 1887. Not only was he alert and meticulous; he also was, *mirabile dictu,* an excellent penman. Moreover, informed as he was by a sense of historical values, he had a broad and liberal conception of what would be useful in a book of minutes of the faculty; consequently, he recorded, besides actions taken by the faculty, numerous facts and happenings that are important in the history of the University. Thanks to such perception, we here may learn, *inter alia,* of the deaths of persons within the family of the University; of happenings in the community of interest to the University; of the goings and the comings of the president; and of such administrative matters as, for example, the distribution of students between the two collegiate literary societies, Euepia and Theta Alpha. Accordingly, the record that Professor Tustin kept as secretary to the faculty is one of the valuable sources of the history of the University.

But, details apart, the most interesting entries in this record for students of our time are those pertaining to the schedules of recitations and of lectures. Here we learn that, for the year 1874–75, every working day in the University began with chapel exercises at 7:15 in the morning; that classes for recitation were held at 7:30, at 11:00, and at 4:00; and that each recitation lasted for an hour. Eight years later, however, the working day began with the chapel exercises at 8:15, and classes for recitation were scheduled at 8:30, 11:15, and 4:00.[2] In subsequent years, as the offerings of the College were increased by the introduction of elective studies, the schedule became longer. As shown in the Catalogue for 1887–88, classes for recitation were scheduled at 8:30, 9:30, 10:00, 11:15, 3:00, and 4:00.[3] Naturally, the larger number of periods for recitation disrupted the old program of required study hours during the day. So much, then, for the scheduling of classes. The matter of scheduling lectures, which has been dealt with elsewhere, need not detain us.

Next to the recitations and the lectures, the most important academic affair on the Hill was no doubt the annual Commencement Week. Although the time for it since 1851 had been shifted from August to July and then to June, the spirit which informed it and the program which justified it changed but little through the years. During this week there were examinations preparatory to the promotion of classes and to the admission of students into the College; there was the annual meeting of the Board of Trustees and, before 1882, the annual meeting of the Board of Curators; there were the anniversaries of the Alumni Association and the Alumnae Association; and, before the end of the 1880's, there was, to a greater or less extent, participation in the affairs of this week by every branch of the University, by the collegiate literary societies, by the Society for Moral and Religious Inquiry (before 1882), by the Senior Class, and by the Pennsylvania Baptist Education Society. Two important exercises of the week, however, remained in respect to both time and nature constant, or nearly so—that is, the baccalaureate address delivered by the president on the Sunday morning preceding commencement, and the commencement exercises on Wednesday morning, followed by the Corporation dinner in mid-day and by the president's reception in the evening. Another event of the week that was equally constant was the procession to the commencement exercises. Before 1886, the Boards, the faculty, the alumni, the students, and faithful friends of the University assembled on the morning of commencement day at nine o'clock in the Baptist Church, listened to official announcements, and then marched in procession to the place on College Hill (which from 1858 was Commencement Hall on the third floor of Old Main) where the exercises would be held. Beginning with 1886, the processions started from Bucknell Hall.[4]

In the years which presently concern us, no Commencement Week since 1879 was so important as was that of 1889. This week was noteworthy not only because it, like that of 1879, was the time of the inauguration of a new president, but also because the commencement of 1889 was the last one that William Bucknell attended. Of the procession at that commencement, a reporter has left us an account as follows:

> At 9 A.M. the students assembled in Bucknell Hall, where the names of those promoted and those upon whom degrees have been conferred were read. A procession of the classes as they now stand was then formed. The undergraduates marched to the foot of the steps on the brow of the hill and then halted and faced while the graduates and alumni passed through with bared heads up to Commencement Hall, and took their seats upon the platform. The Honored Mr. Bucknell was again loudly applauded as he was led to a seat by the acting president.[5]

The commencement exercises in 1889, were, *mutatis mutandis,* what commencement exercises had been in preceding years. Those who were graduated with honors delivered orations of either the first class or of the second class, the difference being, substantially, that between *magna cum laude* and *cum laude*. How early the practice of thus classifying the orations began, we do not know. The first mention of it in the Catalogue appears in the issue for 1875–76, but that was not the year of its beginning. In a detailed report of the commencement of 1874, we read that five of the eight graduates of that year "were assigned first class orations, a larger proportion than any previous class has received." [6] As of the present time, this is the extent of our information on this subject. We do know, however, that from the beginning the one who stood highest in the graduating class delivered the valedictory, and that the one who stood next to him delivered the Latin salutatory. Ordinarily at commencement a few degrees of Master of Arts *in course* would be granted, and, more often than not, a few honorary degrees would be conferred. Also, as a part of the exercises of commencement, prizes that students had won during the year were awarded.

Incomplete though it is, our information relating to the activities of the faculty of the College is much fuller than such information as we have about the doings of the teachers in the Academy. Unhappily, no records, if any were made, have been preserved of the meetings of the teachers in this branch of the University. Perhaps no formal meetings of these teachers were held, for the staff of the Academy, apart from the professors who did some teaching therein, was very small. Moreover, since few of the annual reports of the principal of the Academy have been preserved, we have little or no material from which to describe the activities therein as fully as we can describe the activities within the College. It is otherwise, however, in respect to the Female Institute, for this branch of the University had a sizeable staff of its own that held meetings regularly and preserved a record thereof. To this record we now turn.[7]

At least through many years the teachers of the Institute ordinarily met once a week to record grades, to discuss, if need be, the intellectual shortcomings of students, and to report such misdemeanors as had come to their attention. Generally speaking, the reported offenses or improprieties of some of the girls, although they were infractions of the rules, do not seem particularly abominable to our generation.[8] One of the more frequent offenses was that of "clandestine communication with students of the College," and for such offenses girls, now and again, were sent home. But apparently no serious punishment was inflicted upon either of two girls who, on March 4, 1878, were reported guilty of infractions of rules—one for "walking with one of the College students from lecture Thursday morning," and the other for "disturbing the peace of the Baptist Church and Congregation by eye-communication" with a young man. But, by and large through the years, the young ladies in the Institute were so obedient to the rules thereof that they evoked from their teachers words of commendation more often than words of disapproval.

By the academic year 1886–87, however, when the practice of holding chapel exercises in common for all the students in the University was begun, and when the practice of integrating classes was well under way, new problems of discipline were posed for the principal of the Institute. In that year Miss Mary Brown was teaching in both the Institute and the Academy, and certain classes of the Institute were reciting either in the Academy or in the College.[9] Such arrangements raised doubts and apprehensions in the minds of women who had been brought up in the belief that, for purposes of education, young men and young women should be kept apart. On the existing situation Mrs. Katherine B. Larison, the principal of the Institute, in a summary statement that was inserted in the book of minutes of the teachers of the Institute, wrote on December 23, 1886, that, although the experiment of combining classes had not been "entirely successful," it would continue through the year.[10] Whether or not Mrs. Larison liked it, the practice would continue year after year, although in 1888, and again in 1889, she and her associates in the Institute tried to keep as many recitations as possible in the Institute.[11] But nearly everybody, sooner or later, becomes reconciled to changes, and Mrs. Larison was pleased to note that five "collegiate students" had entered the Institute in September, 1888;[12] and an entry in the minutes of the teachers of the Institute for December 18, 1889, affirms that the result of combining the "Rhetorical exercises" of the Institute with those of the Academy was so satisfactory as to warrant the continuance of the practice. Such consolidation was a necessary consequence of—indeed a primary reason for—the acceptance of the principle of coeducation; and presently most persons would learn to like it, as presently also those who were incorrigibly "other directed" would be silenced by death.

Other affairs touching the education of students for which the professors and the other teachers in the several branches of the University were responsible were the scheduled public exercises, frequently called "exhibitions," that were more or less regularly required of certain classes. The holding of such exercises was a logical consequence of the continuing emphasis that the University placed upon declamation and composition, or, in the parlance of the era, rhetoricals. Such public appearances were the equivalent of examinations in writing and expression, and they could be regarded by the students either as a reward for work well done or as a punishment for work not well done. In any event, they were curricular, not extracurricular, performances; and upon them the University set great store.

Annual exhibitions by the junior class date from at least 1855—probably from an earlier date; and by 1857 public exercises were being held by the senior class of the Academy, by the junior class of the College, and by the students of the Female Institute. Through the years thereafter the program changed only in detail, its general purpose being to give representation in such performances to all three branches of the University; but always in the College the exhibition was given by the same class. During the later years of the 1880's, such exercises were given by the "middle class" of the Academy, by the "middle-year class" of the Institute, and, persistently, by the junior class of the College.[13]

From our brief consideration of the role of professors and teachers in the routine operations of the University, we now turn to the subject of extracurricular activities of the students. With the passing of the years, such activities assumed increasing importance; they confirmed the students in loyalty to their alma mater, and presently they gave them the feeling that they belonged to an institution that was moving in the main stream of modern educational developments.

As late as the 1870's, the literary societies in the College, in the Academy, and in the Female Institute were the principal organizations of the students. There were, as we have learned, two such societies in the College, and, during a part of the period that we are now considering, two in the Female Institute. During the 1870's, there was one in the Preparatory Department of the College and one in the English Academy; and, after the union of these two preparatory branches in 1878, there was one in the Academy until 1888, when a second one was formed.[14] Of all these, however, the most important were the collegiate societies, which maintained a spirited rivalry. Their subjects of debate during the 1870's and the 1880's touched upon virtually all the controversial issues of American higher education of that era, and, at the same time, upon many of the pressing social and political problems and upon some of the disturbing religious issues that confronted the emerging New America. Before the end of the 1880's, however, it was becoming obvious that these societies were entering a period of decline. By this time the students in the College were acquiring other and varied interests, and in competition with these interests the literary societies were playing a losing game.[15]

Despite their rivalry, however, the collegiate literary societies did, on occasion, co-operate in giving public programs; but joint debates between teams representing these societies, although some were held,[16] never aroused the interest nor acquired the significance that debates of such character acquired between teams representing, for example, the literary societies in the University of Wisconsin.[17] But from the beginning Euepia and Theta Alpha did co-operate, more or less successfully, in choosing an orator to represent them in one of the most important exercises of Commencement Week. In those years the annual oration before the literary societies, an oration not infrequently delivered by a person of considerable eminence, was as important as was later the address delivered before the graduating class on commencement day. But the most significant example of the co-operation of the literary societies, as has been mentioned heretofore, was that of establishing in

1870 a monthly publication. In consequence of an agreement reached on March 5, 1870, that the proposed paper be edited by a joint committee of two from each society, and be managed by a joint committee of one from each society, the *College Herald* appeared in May, 1870, as "the organ of the whole University." Its editors appealed for support both to the students and to the alumni.

The advantages to the students and to the University of having a periodical publication were many. In the first place, such a publication tended to bring closer together the students in all the branches of the University: to make them aware that here was something which they all had in common. Emphatically did this become so when, in April, 1874, there appeared for the first time in the *Herald* a column of "Seminary Items" contributed by a member of the senior class of the Female Institute. As the editors then remarked, "The ladies now speak for themselves through their chosen correspondent." Nor was this all. There was a continuing appeal in this periodical to the alumni in general for support of the *Herald,* and the provision therein from the beginning for a column of "Crozer Items" bore witness to the fact that not a few graduates of the University were going to Crozer Theological Seminary to prepare themselves for the gospel ministry. The bond between Crozer and the institution from which it had emerged became very close when, in 1870, Crozer invited the graduates of the former Department of Theology in the University at Lewisburg to accept "all the privileges of the graduates" of Crozer.[17a]

There were other advantages to the students and to the University from having a monthly periodical. The *College Herald* gave to some students opportunities to write or to edit, and to others the opportunity to manage a business enterprise; it gave to the editors the privilege of approving or of condemning the conduct of students, as well as the opportunity to trade both compliments and disparaging observations with the editors of similar publications in other institutions; and it provided for both students and members of the faculty a forum for the expression of views on issues of importance, whether local or national, and for pointing out both the needs and the accomplishments of the University. In brief, it helped to develop a community opinion about various and sundry matters of current significance. Even more important, perhaps, was the fact that a monthly periodical put the students of the University in relatively close touch with happenings on collegiate campuses throughout the United States. Soon the *Herald's* list of exchanges became large, and from the numerous periodicals that came to his desk the exchange editor culled for the readers of the *Herald* educational news of great interest to students of that time. Accordingly, by reading their own periodical the students in the University at Lewisburg learned of what was exciting, inspiring, or depressing on both Eastern and Western campuses.

But there came a time when co-operation between Euepia and Theta Alpha broke down, and for this reason the *College Herald* ceased publication with its issue for December, 1880. For thirteen months thereafter the students of the University were without a publication. After it became clear that the literary societies could not be so reconciled as to resume publication of the *Herald,* a committee of the students asked the faculty, in December, 1881, to approve a constitution and bylaws that some of the students had drawn up for the government of an association of students "to provide for the publication of a College paper." The faculty approved the project on condition that the publication be brought out monthly and that it not be discontinued without the consent of the faculty.[18] Pursuant to this arrangement, there was formed "an association of all the collegiate students, who have sufficient interest in the matter to join the association and subscribe for the paper"; and, under the sponsorship of this association, a board of six editors and a business manager brought out in February, 1882, the first number of the *University Mirror,* a monthly journal which proved to be an acceptable and an enduring successor to the *College Herald.* The *Mirror* aspired "to reflect, as perfectly as may be, the doings and facts of interest concerning the College and '*her boys,*' both those who still linger in her halls and those who have gone forth to contend in the battle of life." [19] But the *Mirror* did more than that; it reflected, to some extent, the "doings and facts of interest" of all branches of the University.

The *Mirror* during the 1880's, perhaps even more than the *College Herald* during the 1870's, promoted ideas and undertakings at the same time that it was reflecting activities and aspirations. In general outlook, however, the policies of the two periodicals were almost identical, as the nature and the variety of what they reflected were very similar. Perhaps the most significant things that they promoted were physical training and athletic sports.

Apart from our knowledge that the girls in the Institute, almost from the beginning, were instructed in gymnastic exercises in a gymnasium of their own, and that in the new South Wing of their building, completed in 1869, they were instructed in such exercises in a larger and better gymnasium,[20] we have little information about physical training or physical exercise in the University before 1870. We do know, however, that during the 1850's, before the completion of Old Main, students in the College sometimes "cut study hours" to play what Professor George R. Bliss called "barn ball" against the east end of the West Wing of the unfinished building.[21] We also know that, as early as 1866, students in the College erected in the rear of Old Main, "about where the sun dial now stands," a crude outdoor gymnasium consisting of a cross bar resting on the tops of two sawed-off trees. From this bar were suspended rings and a trapeze. After a few years this "gymnasium" collapsed.[22]

Meanwhile, baseball had appeared on the campus, and by May, 1870, the Olympian Baseball Club, as we have seen, was flourishing.[23] During that year and the next, baseball saw its first "palmy days" at the University. Between May 9 and October 7, 1870, the University team played and won six games with outside teams. During the next two years, enthusiasm for this game remained high, and the record made by the University team appears to have been creditable. On October 3, 1872, the sophomores held a big celebration in honor of the First Nine.[24] By this time, however, baseball as a major sport was getting a rival. In December of that year football, which had not been introduced as late as December, 1871, was said to be a chief sport.[25] These two, baseball and football, thus early became and remained during the 1870's and the 1880's the leading athletic sports. Only one other sport, boating, aspired to equality with them. In the spring of 1873, amidst great excitement, this sport made its first bid for prominence in the University,[26] but interest in it soon declined.

During the middle years of the 1870's, interest in baseball declined, perhaps because in 1874 baseball with "outside" teams was forbidden; but in October, 1877, the *Herald* was predicting the emergence of a baseball club that would rival the old Olympian Club in its best days. Moreover, the women were now becoming interested in this sport. At a game played on September 22, 1877, between a team of juniors and freshmen and a team of seniors and sophomores, the "ladies from the Seminary, and a number from town, added *eclat* to the occasion by their presence." [27]

A step forward in athletics was taken when, either late in 1881 or early in 1882, an Athletic Association was formed, an association comparable to the one formed at about the same time to publish the *University Mirror*.[28] This Athletic Association was expected not only to raise money to support athletic sports, but also to arrange contests and see to it that suitable teams were chosen. Presently, however, interest in athletic sports declined, and the Athletic Association became inactive. But in 1886, after accepting an invitation to join the Intercollegiate League of Eastern Pennsylvania, this association reorganized and recruited a new membership. Although the above-mentioned league died aborning because Franklin and Marshall soon withdrew from it, some baseball games were played in 1886 by particular arrangements of teams that had proposed to join this league. In that year the University played games with the Pennsylvania State College and Dickinson, but, in general, its performance was not impressive, despite its having acquired new brown-and-white uniforms.[29]

The next year, 1887, baseball stock was "very low" in Lewisburg,[30] but in 1888 the University team, reclad in uniforms consisting each of an orange and blue cap, grey pants and shirt, blue stockings, and an orange belt—a combination highly pleasing to the editors of the *University Mirror* [31]—had some success, the "crowning event" of the season being the defeat of the State College team on its own grounds by a score of 9 to 6.[32] The next year the baseball team expanded its schedule as much as it raised its aspirations. In 1889, under a student manager appointed by the Athletic Association, it played a full schedule of games, including a series that required it to be away from home for several days. It left Lewisburg on May 4, and before it returned it had lost a game each to the University of Pennsylvania and to Media Academy, and had won a game each from Swarthmore, Gettysburg, and Dickinson. During the entire season the team won ten of the fifteen games that it played.[33]

By this time, moreover, football was emerging as a more glamorous game than baseball. For a few years, beginning late in 1872, football had been received with considerable enthusiasm by the collegiate students, and through several years of the 1870's Euepia and Theta Alpha had played match games rather regularly. But football, like baseball, suffered a decline before the end of that decade, and a new interest in the game apparently was not aroused until, soon after the formation of the Athletic Association, the football team acquired "new, strong, and beautiful uniforms." [34] By this time, moreover, football had become an intercollegiate sport on the campus in Lewisburg. In 1882 the University lost a game to the State College,[35] and in 1883, despite an afternoon given by the faculty to the students to put the field in better condition, the University lost a game on Thanksgiving to Lafayette by a score of 59 to 0.[36] Then came another lapse of interest in football which, with a corresponding lapse of interest in baseball, led one of the editors of the *Mirror* in June, 1886, to explode in words as follows:

> It reflects very much to the discredit of our University [he wrote] that seldom in its history has it had a first-class Athletic Association. Many of them have been instituted, but few of them have received the attention which would place them on an equal footing with those in the higher colleges. Our base ball teams are never able to cope with those from institutions even of less repute than ours. Our foot ball teams, which, how-

ever, are a thing of the past, always suffered defeat. In none of our athletic sports are we gloriously proficient. This is a burning shame. But where lies the difficulty? The Faculty do all in their power to lend spirit and vim to our enterprises. They take a deep interest in them all. This spring they have contributed munificently to aid us in a financial way. Some have joined the boys' association. They grant us innumerable privileges in the way of 'hours off' to practice and play, and even encourage us with their presence at the games. The fault lies in us. We do not practice.[37]

Whether because of this tongue-lashing, or for other reasons, the athletic situation in the University began to improve in 1887, and in the autumn of 1888 football at Bucknell was beginning to come into its own.[38] The faculty continued to show its interest in this game, for in October of that year it permitted the football team to be absent from Tuesday to Friday of one week, and in November it permitted it to be absent on a Friday and a Saturday to play at Cornell University.[39] The year 1888 turned out to be a good one for athletic sports at Bucknell, for in the spring its baseball team won six of the nine games that it played, and in the autumn, after losing to Lafayette and Lehigh, its football team "practically sunk State College" and won triumphantly from Dickinson by a score of 18 to 8. This last-named victory not only broke up a meeting of Theta Alpha, but also no doubt inspired Edwin Faulkner to write exultantly that Bucknell no longer was "without creditable representation in the college athletic world." This was indeed so great a victory that students celebrated it with "a jolly big bonfire on the victorious arena." [40] Major athletic sports had now come of age at Bucknell, even though a gymnasium was still an aspiration, and even though, as the *Mirror* complained, the attitude of the students at Bucknell to athletics was distinctly inferior to that of the students at Lafayette, Lehigh, Princeton, and Yale.[41]

Boating as a sport had not in the meantime achieved major importance. Although it was under discussion as early as 1870, boating did not get a start until the organization on April 5, 1873, of the Undine Boat Club, a name which, however, was soon changed to Lewisburg University Boat Club.[42] The excitement attending the arrival on May 9 of a boat for this club was likened by one writer to the "approach of an elephant into a country village." Everybody came out to see the boat, and many students then showed an eagerness to take part in the sport of boating.[43] A year later the boating club had forty-seven active members and owned two craft, "a six-oared boat, and a double scull." [44] But interest in boating soon dwindled, as interest in other sports then declined, although the *College Herald* believed that in the autumn of

1876 there was somewhat of a resurgence of interest in athletics in the University.[45] But the resurgence, such as it might have been, did not revive boating as a sport. By the spring of 1882, the "boat" was in need of repairs, and a year later the *Mirror,* nonplussed because of the neglect of the opportunities offered for boating in Lewisburg, confessed that this activity, as a "healthful exercise," was almost unknown to the students of the University.[46] In April, 1884, there was talk of "organizing a boat crew," and as late as April, 1889, the *Mirror,* observing that the ladies of the Harvard Annex (the forerunner of Radcliffe) proposed to put a four-oared crew on the Charles River, declared that these ladies had more pluck than the men of Bucknell University. It seemed odd to the exchange editor of the *Mirror* that Bucknell could not have at least "one four-oared shell." [47] But, although Bucknell seemed destined not to have a crew, boating for exercise or for pleasure did become popular with some of its students in the early summer of 1889. The editor of "Locals," writing in the *Mirror* for June of that year, affirmed that

> Boating is at present one of the most popular sports, not only among a large number of College students, but also among the members of the Institute. The students of Bucknell [he reaffirmed] do not appreciate good rowing advantages. Clubs should be organized.[48]

Of the lesser sports in the University, some no doubt were adopted during the 1870's and the 1880's because gymnastic exercises were not available. Croquet, which was said to be, before 1871, "the prevailing form of dissipation" on the campus, was presumed to be dying out during the summer and the autumn of 1871.[49] Somewhat patronizingly, the *College Herald* had called it "a game better suited to ladies, small boys, and invalid clergymen than to healthy young men," who needed something more strenuous than what, in western parlance, would be called a "squaw game." [50] Interestingly enough, after 1871 we hear no more of croquet as a game for the boys, but as late as May, 1873, it was still a popular game at the Female Institute.[51]

Winter sports, such as coasting and skating, were also appreciated by the students, although the opportunities to practice them varied with the severity of the winters. Skating was one of the chief sports in December, 1872, as it also was a favorite activity of both boys and girls in February, 1889. In winters that admitted of them, as in 1884 and 1889, sleighing parties were held, either by classes or by other groups. A favorite destination of such parties in 1884 was the Great Western Hotel in Vicksburg.[52]

Of the lesser recreational sports that were suited to both young men and young women, tennis had become the most popular by the middle of the 1880's. "Lawn tennis," the *University Mirror* affirmed in May, 1885, "has come to be a very popular game at the University. Two new courts have been made on that part of the campus which was recently filled. They answer their purpose much better than the old courts, and their surroundings are far more agreeable." [53] Although acknowledging in the autumn of 1886 that the collegiate tennis players were "very expert," the *Mirror* advised these players not to be in a hurry to engage in "match games," lest they experience the "sad fate" of the baseball club. The enthusiasm for this game was now laying hold of the girls, and in the summer of 1887 they were expressing their thanks for two handsome "lawn tennis equipments" on the grounds of the Institute; and in May, 1888, their thanks for fine tennis courts were even more profuse. At the same time, on the back campus on top of the Hill, a tennis court was being prepared for the boys of the Academy. Finally, in November, 1889, the *Mirror* could report that in the College interest in tennis was growing, that the number of tennis players had increased threefold during the three preceding years, and that, for "a small institution" like Bucknell, tennis was "the 'dandy' game." A few months earlier the first edition of the collegiate yearbook, *L'Agenda,* had listed four tennis clubs and, incidentally, a Bucknell Bicycle Club.[54]

Journalism and athletic sports were not the only spheres of interest in which the students of the University made use of their organizing talents. Before the end of the 1880's, their extracurricular activities had been extended to music and to new aspects of religious activity; and a new policy in respect to social fraternities had permitted the older fraternities to come above ground and a new one to be formed.

Music had been from the beginning a special concern of the Female Institute, but instruction in music in the College and the Academy, when given, had been incidental, if not accidental. But as early as 1870 the *College Herald* was "pleased to hear of the establishment of the College Glee Club," an organization which, as it affirmed, had been a long-felt want on the campus.[55] Apparently this club did not flourish, for more than four years later the *Herald* was saying that such an organization was being contemplated. Thereafter it seems that the glee club was from year to year a hit and miss affair, being sometimes organized and sometimes not. By the middle eighties, however, it was attracting considerable attention. Late in 1885 it was "warned" by the girls of the Institute to beware of a rival club in the Institute. But the glee club in the Institute, if one then actually came into being, was even more shadowy than the one in the College had been. But from 1885 on, the College each year had a glee club in action, one which gave a concert in the

Watsontown Baptist Church in June, 1886, and one which, in 1888, gave a concert for the benefit of the Tustin Gymnasium Fund, and other concerts for the benefit of Baptist churches in Watsontown, Montgomery, and Winfield. Yet in the spring of 1889 the exchange editor of the *Mirror* was lamenting the fact that, whereas the freshmen of Yale had a glee club of twenty-six voices, the students of Bucknell University had one of only four voices; and he yearned for the good old days of preceding years when the University could "boast of an organization worthy of the name of a glee club." In the autumn of that year the *Mirror,* although still lamenting the fact that Bucknell was not on a par with other colleges in respect to its glee club, was glad to announce that such a club had been organized again.[56]

But the tide was about to turn. In 1887 Elysee Aviragnet was employed as professor of music and as teacher of romance languages in the Institute, and in 1890 he became director of the newly created Institute of Music.[57] The increasing emphasis upon the study of music in the University, together with the competence and the popularity of Professor Aviragnet, led, during the 1890's, to the rise of numerous musical organizations, some for women in the Institute, some for men in the College and the Academy, and at least one, the University Orchestra, led by Professor Aviragnet, for both men and women.

While many of the students of the University were much occupied with the above-mentioned organizations, some of the students continued to be concerned with organizations formed for religious purposes. Bucknell was still a denominational institution, still dedicated to the service of the Baptist denomination—one proof of which was an affirmation by President Hill, in the spring of 1886, that religion "should have a place in all education, because there is no true education without it." [58] Consequently, the traditional emphasis on daily chapel exercises, on church attendance on Sundays, on frequent prayer meetings, on promoting revivals, and on the meticulous observance of the annual day of prayer for colleges was not lessened.[59] By 1882, however, the old Society of Inquiry, as we have seen, had been replaced by a branch of the Y.M.C.A. in the College, and seven years later a branch was organized in the Academy. Meanwhile, in 1885, a branch of the Y.W.C.A. was formed in the Institute, and by 1887 it was directing in the Institute all devotional meetings, all Bible classes, and all missionary and other benevolent work. As early as 1886, the Institute had a "mission band" which, in April of that year, gave an entertainment to raise money to help educate a Burmese girl whom this band had "taken under its special care." [60]

Also in 1886, under the inspiration of a conference of students directed by Dwight L. Moody at Mount Hermon, Massachusetts, in July, 1886, and continued in subsequent years at Northfield, there began the organization at Bucknell of what came to be called the Volunteer Band for Foreign Missions. This organization, in aim a successor to the old Society for Inquiry, attracted both men and women, and it was flourishing by the early 1890's.[61]

If we now look at the social life of the students, we shall find that no small part of it centered in entertainment provided by the Female Institute and in affairs promoted by the literary societies and the classes of the College and of the Academy. It was at affairs provided by these organizations that, under proper chaperonage, the young men of the University met their "class sisters," and the young women in the Institute met their "class brothers." Such social entertainment had begun long before 1870, and within a few years of its founding the hospitality of the Female Institute had become somewhat disturbing to those who were required to pinch the pennies of the University. Accordingly, on July 29, 1868, the Trustees voted that a social gathering, "inexpensively conducted under the general management of the President & General Agent, take place at the Female Institute not oftener than once a term."[62] Presumably this was the official authorization for what became the celebrated soirees of the Institute, events to which many came to look forward with considerable eagerness. One such entertainment, held in December, 1878, was described by one of the male students in these words:

> The hearts of the College and Academy boys were made glad last week, by receiving an invitation to attend the semi-annual Soiree at the Seminary, on Saturday evening, December 13. . . . The programme consisted of fine essays, written and delivered by members of the Middle Year class, interspersed with instrumental and vocal music. . . . Next came the sociable, the greatest treat of all, when the students who enjoy so little the society of the fair sex, were permitted to bask, for a short season, in the sunlight of their presence, an opportunity which we embraced with alacrity. . . .[63]

No other social affairs on the campus were reported so consistently, or praised so highly through the years, as the soirees of the Female Institute.

If the hearts of many of the boys were made glad by attendance at the soirees, the hearts of not a few of them were made sad when the seniors of the Institute entertained, as frequently they did, their "brothers" of the senior class of the College. One of the editors of the *College Herald,* speaking in the autumn of 1873 for those who had not been invited, wondered why he and the other boys of the "lower classes" were denied the "refining pleasure of association" with their "class sisters." Freely acknowledging that he was no "strenuous advocate" either of coeducation or of the "cell and cloister method" of education, he expressed the hope that an Aristotelian "golden mean" might be found that "would destroy the barbarous roughness of colleges, and the insipid nothingness of female seminaries." [64] After him came other editors who held similar views, and one of them, writing in January, 1880, expressed his contempt for an arrangement which permitted the girls of the Institute who lived in the town to associate with the boys of the College, but denied such privilege to the girls who were so unfortunate as to be living in the Institute.[65] Problems like these would in time, if not solved, shrink in importance because of the wholehearted acceptance of the practice of coeducation.

But entertainment by the "Sems," as the women of the Institute were familiarly called, was not a one-way affair. The boys also entertained the girls. The literary societies, in the College as well as in the Academy, invited them occasionally both to their meetings and to the public programs which they presented. And the girls naturally would be invited to public debates between teams representing Euepia and Theta Alpha. Also classes in the College, and probably also classes in the Academy, entertained, from time to time, their class sisters at dinner. One delightful illustration of this practice is that of the junior class, which, in the winter of 1882–83, "previous to the soiree, . . . in connection with the work of decoration, gave their class sisters a supper. Everything," so we are told, "was gotten up in first class style. The greatest variety was procured that the best caterer in town could furnish." [66] Some five years later, in January, 1888, other young ladies of the Institute expressed their gratitude to the young gentlemen "who gave them the double pleasure of a sleigh ride and an oyster supper on Saturday, January 14th. It proved [to be] the social event of the season." [67] Further illustrations of such affairs would unduly clutter our story without adding to our understanding of an intriguing practice.

Another organization that was used by some men of the College to provide entertainment as well as to elevate themselves to positions of social and political leadership on the campus was the social fraternity, which enjoyed its first years of freedom during the 1880's. The ban on fraternities, it will be recalled, had been lifted in 1879. Then it was that the two fraternities then on the campus, Phi Kappa Psi and Sigma Chi, came out of the caverns of their captivity; and three years later they were joined by another fraternity, Phi Gamma Delta. That they made their power felt in campus affairs there can be no denying, for in June, 1882, prompted by what he had read in an exchange periodical, the exchange editor of the *Mirror* frankly acknowledged that only two of the six editors of this periodical were "non-frats": and four months later the exchange editor of the *Mirror* wrote that the three fraternities were competing with one another for leadership. In the spring of 1883 a correspondent on the campus wrote to a newspaper in Williamsport, saying that the three fraternities were not only prosperous, but also were "exceedingly jealous of any others being started." [68]

Regardless of their rivalries and of their striving for power, the fraternities on the campus of the University at Lewisburg, at least by 1883, were helping to provide entertainment for some of the students. Our record of their social doings is fragmentary, but the nature of their social activities is at least suggested by a story, published in February, 1883, saying that Phi Kappa Psi had given a sleighing party; by another story, published in October, 1885, saying that this fraternity had given its "fall reception to the young ladies of the town"; and by still another story, published in March, 1886, saying that Sigma Chi recently had given a reception "to its lady friends," for which occasion the Sunbury orchestra had provided the music. By this time social fraternities were securely established on the campus, but they had not been fully welcomed by all the students of the University.[69]

Social entertainment within doors was supplemented by recreational frolicking outdoors. Throughout the 1870's and the 1880's, outings by students of the University were popular. Generally, but not always, the trips were taken by classes, and also generally, but not always, the place visited was either Montour Ridge or Blue Hill. The latter was perhaps the more popular place. Late in the spring of 1870 the sophomores spent a Saturday on Montour Ridge, ate a huge meal, and then erected "upon the apex" of the hill a memorial mound.[70] The next year, on April 15, while the freshmen were at the foot of Montour Ridge, the sophomores were enjoying themselves at Blue Hill. In May, 1872, the freshmen, most of them wearing high hats and some of them carrying canes, celebrated at Blue Hill.[71] And so, with variations, there were many outings through the years. In May, 1874, the girls of the Institute passed a day at Blue Hill, and the collegiate freshman class went by train to Laurelton and there passed a day by fishing, shooting, ball-playing, and the consuming of "two square meals." On June 1, 1877, the girls of the Institute left Lewisburg in wagons, at seven-thirty in the morning, for a day's outing at Montour Ridge.[72]

The practice of taking such outings continued during the 1880's, but with one difference. As early as June 14, 1882, the collegiate seniors were picnicking with their class sisters at Blue Hill, and we are told that not only did they make "the romantic hill resound with mirth and laughter," but that also the bands of every town serenaded them as they "passed on their pleasure-boat." At the same time, on a "distant hill," the juniors were picnicking with their class sisters. Six years later the pattern had not changed, for on Decoration Day in 1888 young women of the Institute and young men of the College were picnicking at Blue Hill.[73]

Also in the 1880's outings for some students became trips for learning as well as for pleasure when Professor George G. Groff took them on field trips. Professor Groff had served the University during 1876–77 as an instructor in chemistry, and then, after an absence of two years, had returned to accept the position of professor of natural sciences, a position which, under a slightly changed title, he retained until his death on February 18, 1910. Professor Groff was a doctor of medicine, but he preferred to teach rather than to practice his profession. He was a man of many and varied interests, restless, able, and dedicated to the task of diffusing widely scientific knowledge. He preferred the New Education to the Old Education, and he declared bluntly that more attention should be given to science and less attention to the classical languages. Almost compulsively he lectured on or wrote about many things; and soon he was in demand as a speaker, not only in Pennsylvania, but in distant places—in the South and in the Pacific Northwest. Emphatically was he committed to the idea of new methods of teaching, and so he pleaded for adequate laboratories, for an adequate museum, and for an adequate library.[74] One of the devices of teaching on which he set great store was the trip for observation, and the variety of his purposes in making such trips may be illustrated by a few that he conducted in the middle 1880's. In the autumn of 1885, a group of twenty-three students accompanied him on a visit to a cave in Centre County, a visit which the senior class of the Institute called a "delightful affair"; and a few days later he took the Class of 1886 on a tour of instruction and pleasure to the coal mines of Mount Carmel. The next autumn, as we are told by the *University Mirror,* the senior class accompanied him down the river "and noticed many interesting facts concerning the earth's crust." [75]

The faculty as a whole, now and again, contributed to the joy of the students at being released from routine duties. The faculty was not averse to giving the students some time off for worthy causes, or even for exciting events, such as putting the athletic field in suitable condition for a forthcoming game, or attending the annual fair of the Union County Agricultural Society. Nor was it opposed to giving them, on a highly important occasion, a whole day off, as it did on May 15, 1873, so that they could attend a Sunday School convention then being held in the Lewisburg Baptist Church. Such concessions were, of course, dispensations of grace, not recognition of vested rights, and they showed clearly that those who manipulated the paternal system by which the University then was governed were not devoid either of a feeling of sympathy for youthful desires or of a sense of humor when confronted by things as they were.[76]

In their quest of recreation or of excitement, students on the Hill raised problems that were never raised by students in the Grove, for on the Hill there were young men of whom at least some were more or less intent on maintaining a tradition of rowdyism which they conceived essential to the collegiate way of life. In the summer of 1871 the *College Herald,* looking back upon the "tricks" of students in earlier years, when property of the College was defaced and when rooms of the students were "torn out," could rejoice that better times had come.[77] Yet it did not believe that the day of rowdyism was entirely past, and the years lying ahead would show that in this belief it was right. The University would continue to be embarrassed by the tooting of tin horns, even at women, by hazing in one form or another, and by other barbarous practices. But by the end of the year 1871–72 the *Herald* believed that such things as "hazing, wrangling, rushing, and the like" were becoming outmoded in Lewisburg; and six years later one of the editors of the *Herald* was rejoicing because the Class of 1878 had abandoned the indignity of hazing. The effect seemed to be almost too good to be true, yet he regretted the lessening of the deference "formerly accorded by under-class men to their superiors in class rank." Civility, he had learned, had its price.[78]

Such rejoicing was premature, for in June, 1879, the Board of Curators recommended that the Trustees and the faculty "take all needful steps to prevent the barbarity known as 'hazing.' " This recommendation the Trustees endorsed and passed on to the president and the faculty. This action was taken at the beginning of the administration of President Hill, who, by combining firmness with kindness and understanding of adolescent psychology, accomplished much in the way of eliminating barbaric conduct from the Hill. As a token of their respect for him, the senior class, on December 22, 1879, presented to him a gold-headed cane. In accepting this gift President Hill thanked the donors for their confidence and allegiance, and for the absence of "customary college barbarities" during recent months. By the end of the year 1881–82, much seemed to have been accomplished. Hazing had been discontinued the year before, and more recently, at the request of the president, the boys had given up the "horn-tooting business." Such accomplishments, wrought more by a "law of love than by cast-iron restraints," so astounded one of the editors of the *University Mirror* that he announced the restoration of his faith in students, saying, "College boys want to be treated like men with hearts and intellects, and when so treated are always ready to grant a reasonable request from their instructors." [79]

Again such optimism proved to be somewhat premature. Even so popular a man as President Hill could not eradicate, once for all, practices that were widespread and deeply rooted. Students in Lewisburg did not wish to be different; they had been behaving like students elsewhere. In the issue of the *University Mirror* for March, 1882, one can read that the students at the University of Cincinnati had asked their president to resign; that fourteen sophomores, convicted of hazing, had been suspended by the University of California; that twenty-three students at Princeton had been indicted for rowdyism and for defacing property; and, lastly, that a suit for $10,000 had been brought against each of eight students at Bowdoin for hazing a fellow student. Nor was this all. We are told on credible authority that, during the 1880's, both hazing and horn-tooting were not uncommon practices in colleges in New England.[80]

The year 1882–83 witnessed in Lewisburg a recurrence of hazing and of rowdyism in general, principally, it seems, through the activity of a "gang" called "Texas Rangers"—an organization, as described by the *University Mirror,* of "the boys who are possessed of a superabundance of animal spirits." This gang of "nocturnal raiders" not only so aroused one student in the West Wing that he came out one night "armed with an axe and clad in his toga," threatening to "clean out the crowd," but it also collided with the administration, and one of its members was required to withdraw from the University. Nor was the end yet. In 1885 the "Rangers" reorganized, but, as the *Mirror* learned, during the evening of the reorganization nothing was damaged except "the plug hat of the Principal of the Academy and the coat of a victim, seized by the above named dignitary." By 1886 the "diabolical meanness" of hazing had been greatly lessened, and by 1889 the *Mirror,* observing an unusually good feeling between the freshmen and the sophomores, predicted once again that hazing in Lewisburg was "a thing of the past." [81] He should have said that the situation was improved; the problem of hazing had not yet been solved.

Not all the odd behavior of the students, however, was either harmful or barbaric. The oddities of dress that students sometimes affected were as harmless as they were amusing. In June, 1871, the seniors "came out" with silver-headed ebony canes bearing appropriate inscriptions, and a year later they were wearing "plugs" and "swallow-tails," and were carrying canes. In the spring of 1879 the sophomores were wearing large sombreros, and in April, 1884, the juniors were wearing "white plugs."

In January, 1886, the seniors appeared in silk hats, but were discomfited when they saw a few freshmen wearing the same sort of apparel. In that year the juniors "sported" snakewood canes having silver handles.[82]

Another matter relating to dress was more serious. Even as late as the 1880's, the practice of wearing the traditional academic costume by the graduating class at commencement had not hardened into an established custom on the campus in Lewisburg. Apparently, in the beginning, caps and gowns had been worn, for in August, 1854, the Trustees, after voting unanimously that it would be inexpedient for the graduating class to wear gowns at commencement, reconsidered their vote and then tabled the resolution. But in 1871 a reporter, writing of the commencement of that year, remarked that the speakers on the stage looked "neat and attractive. 'Swallow tail coats,'" he continued, "had supplanted the black and silk gowns, so prominent upon former occasions. A few of these by-gone days, however, were still visible, doubtless retained to add impressiveness to the scene." Also in 1872, as the *College Herald* tells us, the seniors "turned their backs scornfully upon everything that looks like a gown," and one of the editors of the *Herald* hoped that "the popish garment" had gone "'where the woodbine twineth.'"[83] Nevertheless, the question of gowns at commencement was up again in 1879, and the Trustees referred the matter to the discretion of the faculty. But the faculty, in respect to this matter, did no more than vote against the wearing of gowns by members of the faculty on such occasions. If the practice of wearing gowns had not been resumed in the later 1870's, we cannot help being puzzled by an editorial in the *College Herald* of February, 1880, in which the writer, counting the blessings that had come to the University under the new administration of President Hill, affirms that one of these blessings was the abandonment of "the useless and absurd habit of wearing a gown or swallow tail, at Commencement." Accordingly, we conclude, tentatively, that this matter, as late as the 1880's, was in a state of unstable equilibrium. But, as the years went by, "exchange news" in successive issues of the *University Mirror* revealed the fact that other colleges and universities were adopting the "academic cap and gown"; and presently Bucknell, in this as in other matters, would follow suit. The change, which came near the end of the school year 1890–91, was perhaps hastened by the appearance in the *University Mirror* for May of that year of the statement that "Caps and gowns are in great demand by our best colleges and universities for Commencement." Be that as it may, we read in the June issue of the *Mirror* for that year that the "Seniors were measured for caps and gowns last week," and that "Strawbridge & Clothier, of Philadelphia, will furnish the same." Then, as if to clinch the matter, the *Mirror,* in its issue for July, 1891, affirmed that the Class of 1891 had "introduced the caps and gowns as the apparel for graduation and all presented a very pleasant aspect." But the faculty apparently was not yet ready to follow suit, for as late as June, 1899, the Trustees, on motion, requested the faculty "to wear cap & gown during commencement exercises." On November 13, 1899, the faculty voted to comply with this request.[84]

As harmless also as any practice of oddness in dressing was the practice of burning textbooks after certain studies had been completed. Here was a practice that long had prevailed at the University of Michigan and that was a "picturesque ceremony" at some of the colleges of New England, and perhaps elsewhere, during the 1880's.[85] In 1882, and again in 1884, the "victim" of the students in the University at Lewisburg was analytical geometry, whose ashes after each cremation were buried in the Grove of the Institute. The ceremony of cremation in the evening of April 4, 1884, under the auspices of the Class of 1886, was especially elaborate. At eight-thirty a procession headed by a marshal on horseback, accompanied by fifty students, began a march through the streets of Lewisburg. Also in the procession was the Lewisburg Band, which was followed by the catafalque drawn by four horses, guarded by the "Texas Rangers," and followed by six pall bearers. Then, in turn, came the Class of 1886, the Class of 1887, and the students of the Academy. At Third and Market the procession halted, and here the corpse of the tyrant Anna was cremated. After the ashes had been put into an urn, the procession reformed and proceeded to the "Seminary Grove," where the "earthly remains of the departed Anna Lytical were interred with solemn ceremonies." The affair was, as the *Mirror* proudly affirmed, an exhibition of "commendable class spirit," and one of the best performances ever given by the College. Less impressive were similar exercises held in the spring of 1886, when, to the strains of music that were "purely classic," books of geometry, novels, and rhetoric were burned.[86] Thereafter we read no more of exercises held for the cremation of books.

There were two other practices of students in the period with which we are now dealing that deserve to be mentioned—one a persistent practice of questionable merit, the other a short-lived practice of much utility. The first of these was the continuing publication of burlesques of public performances. Such things could be, and apparently frequently were, both insulting and degrading. What the *University Mirror* said about the burlesques in the spring of 1886 will make clear this point. The one that appeared on the night of the junior exhibition, the *Mirror* affirmed, was a " 'dirty sheet,' as usual," and a month later it said that the burlesques of the spring term of that year had "created quite a sensation." [87] The other practice—that of each graduating class to plant a tree on the campus—was started before 1870, was discontinued in 1871, and was revived in 1878.[88] After the last-named year, however, we hear no more of this practice.

During the later years of the 1880's, as the students of the University became increasingly conscious of the fact that their institution was moving into the main stream of collegiate life in the United States, it was all but inevitable that soon there would appear both college yells and college colors on the campus in Lewisburg. As early as December, 1885, the girls of the Institute had published a yell—"We excel! we excel! Jolly girls—Sem. at L." [89] We hear no more of this yell, perhaps for the reason that it soon was made useless by the change of the name of the University. So also of a class yell proposed and published in January, 1886—"We yell! We yell! U. at L. U. at L. Eighty-nine! Every time!" [90] A college yell—"Rah! Rah! Rah! U. at L.!"—was published in July, 1886.[91] Then in November, 1887, there appeared, seemingly without earlier notice, this "college cry" on one of the advertising pages of the *University Mirror*—"Yah! Yah! Yoo!!! Bucknell! B.U.!! Wah—hoo! Hoo—wah! Bang!!!" However it may have originated, it quickly caught on. It was repeated in October, 1888, in a story describing a football victory for Bucknell, and in April, 1889, the exchange editor of the *Mirror* offered a year's subscription to the *Mirror* to any student in the Department of Music in the Institute who would set to music this "celebrated 'war-whoop' " of the University. On October 22, 1909, the faculty approved this yell as an appropriate one for the University, and it appeared in the Catalogue of the University for the year 1909–10.[92]

More precise is our knowledge of the origin of the colors of the University. On October 1, 1887, students of Bucknell, having become increasingly aware of the fact that other colleges and universities were becoming known by their colors, voted that orange and blue should be the colors of their University. On October 17 the faculty approved this choice, and on January 12, 1888, the Trustees gave their approval. Here was an added stimulus to institutional pride. "In the adoption of a combination of colors peculiarly her own," the *University Mirror* remarked, "Bucknell has added another of the bonds which help make the University family one in spirit as in name. We have many reasons," it continued, "to be proud of our institution. We need not be ashamed to flaunt her 'orange and blue' in the face of any one." [93]

Here was the note upon which the decade of the 1880's was ending for Bucknellians. Much had been accomplished since the summer of 1879. Students, in particular, had expanded their activities, had compared themselves with students elsewhere, had criticized their own buildings and programs, and had persuaded themselves that the way to better things lay open to them and their University. Before the end of the year 1887, even the fence which had through long years enclosed the "sacred precincts" of the Institute had been removed.[94] Time, they believed, surely was on the side of Bucknell, and more and better things than had thus far been acquired were yet to come. Among the better things which the students had been acquiring were improved conditions of living. During the year 1869–70, the Institute Building had been heated by hot air and lighted by gas, and by 1883 the introduction of water into this building had, in the opinion of the teachers, "added much to the comfort of the inmates." Three years later, when the introduction of steam heat made for the first time "the Institute comfortably warm," the principal of the Institute vouched for the rejoicing of all persons in that branch of the University.[95] Meanwhile, comparable improvements had been made in the residential halls for men, and the spirit of thankfulness for such improvements found expression in November, 1886, in a statement in the *Mirror,* saying that, since water pipes were being laid from the town to the College, the men of the Hill soon would have "all the conveniences in this line which are enjoyed at any other first-class institution." [96] Accordingly, even though the progress of the 1880's had not brought a gymnasium to the campus, the students, the alumni, the faculty, and the friends of Bucknell, although recognizing fully the fact that their institution could not in a few years become a Harvard, a Yale, or a Princeton, were, nevertheless, eager to believe that there was "dawning for the University a more glorious era of prosperity" than this institution had ever known before.[97]

Part Three

An Era of Transition

8

Thirty Years of Promotion

The new regime is quite evident in chapel to those who were accustomed to the old order of things.—*University Mirror, IX (October, 1889).*

I was convinced that by enlarging the scope of the school we could bring in a large body of students intending to follow other callings than the ministry, and thus build up a strong body of lay alumni, some of whom would inherit or achieve wealth and could furnish in the next generation a solid financial basis.—*John Howard Harris, Thirty Years as President of Bucknell.*

If a college has a Board which either will not or cannot furnish a large proportion of the funds needful for growth, its development will be arrested.—*John Howard Harris, Thirty Years as President of Bucknell.*

John Howard Harris, of the Class of 1869, was elected president of Bucknell University by a unanimous vote of the Trustees. He was not their first choice. In October, 1888, they had elected Dr. George M. Philips, a former professor in the University, who declined the offer; and in March, 1889, they had elected the Reverend John Humpstone, of the Class of 1871, who also declined the offer. Accordingly, on May 22, 1889, when they met again in special session, they accepted, on the recommendation of William Bucknell, a relatively young man who, more than two years before, had been elected a trustee of the University, an office which he would continue to hold through his presidency of the University, and beyond.[1]

To his new task Dr. Harris brought twenty years of educational experience, a fondness for hard work, considerable ability, and more than ordinary energy; and he also brought administrative talent and maturity of judgment. He was born in Indiana County, Pennsylvania, on May 21, 1847; he had served as sergeant in the Union Army during the later months of the Civil War; and he had entered the University at Lewisburg in 1865. Upon his graduation therefrom in 1869 with the degree of Bachelor of Arts, he became the founder and the principal of the Keystone Academy in Factoryville, Pennsylvania. Under his guidance this institution, which was opened in the autumn of 1869 in the lecture room of the Baptist Church in Factoryville, became a preparatory school of considerable size and of no slight influence. It was in promoting and administering this institution that Harris acquired the experience that stood him in good stead when he became president of Bucknell University. Moreover, he had been ordained a Baptist minister in 1872, and, in addition to his duties as principal of the academy, he had served the Baptist Church in Factoryville as its pastor from 1880 to 1889. In 1883 Lafayette College had conferred upon him the honorary degree of Doctor of Philosophy.[2]

On June 25, 1889, during Commencement Week, Dr. Harris was inaugurated. In his address [3] on that occasion he made reasonably clear his views on collegiate education. He had been brought up in the classical tradition, but twenty years of experience in administering an academy had brought him to virtual acceptance of the New Education. He was favorably disposed to what was happening in Harvard, and he dreamed of doing in Lewisburg, Pennsylvania, something comparable to what Andrew D. White had done in Ithaca, New York.[4] Although still believing the "primary object" of education to be the acquisition of "power" through discipline, he was not committed to the studies traditionally used to achieve that object. On the contrary, he would select from branches "equally valuable for discipline" those which would keep the student in touch with his own times and with his own country: the constitution of the United States, for example, rather than the constitution of Athens; modern languages, especially English, rather than Latin and Greek, although the classical languages he would not discard. Because he perceived that the present is rooted in the past, he would not break with the past; and he would be very unwilling for any student to leave the University without having required a knowledge of the historical development of each branch of learning that he had studied. Yet reverence for the past, he believed, should not blind one to the accomplishments of the present or to the demands of the future. To meet the needs of the present and the future, he would pay particular attention to the natural sciences, and he would accept without question the practice of coeducation. Indeed, the nature and the scope of the program of the University would be determined by the value of subjects for discipline and knowledge, by the needs of the constituency of the University, and by the ability of the University to do the work well. Finally, a "sound physical basis" for the development of men he did not question, and he expected to see available in Lewisburg in the near future a gymnasium "in charge of a competent director."

As to policy, the new president was no less clear. The education offered by Bucknell would be Christian education. "The influence of the Christian life," he said, "should pervade all instruction and every admonition." Accordingly, the University should have teachers who were both proficient and Christian, and he proposed, by the aid of fellowships, to prepare promising graduates of the University for service as teachers therein. "Other things being equal," he affirmed, ". . . the best men for us are our own men, and with the founding of these fellowships, other things will usually be equal." Moreover, the services of the University, in his opinion, should be more widely extended. To that end he would maintain cordial relations with the affiliated academies, and with them he would endeavor to stir up an educational revival in Pennsylvania; and, as a means of furthering that purpose, he would continue to rejoice because no test of party, creed, nationality, race, or sex need be passed for entrance into the University; and he would not lose hope that soon the day would come when, because of established scholarships, no young man or young woman would be kept away from the University because of the lack of means to remain therein. Finally, he would have the University, by stimulating among the people a greater desire for education, create a larger demand for what the University could supply. "We will," he averred, as if formulating a slogan to guide his future action, "press upon the people's attention the value of the work done here." This affirmation turned out to be one of the guiding principles of a long administration that was much concerned with the task of promotion, and, as a consequence of such promotion, the University would be changed both in its organization and in its programs of instruction.

Having been inducted into office, President Harris took charge of the University, and soon no one doubted that there was a new president on the campus. He was Bucknell's last president of the old school—pastor, teacher, administrator, and counselor acting in *loco parentis;* but he was old-schoolish in an unorthodox way. He was not contented with things as they had been, or were. He was not averse to making changes, and, when he thought that changes were needed, he made changes, frequently without bothering other persons about the matter. The spirit of the new regime was quickly perceived and, at least openly, applauded. As one student remarked at the beginning of the autumn term in 1889, the changes that had been made for conducting chapel were as "evident" as they were "truly refreshing." Singing now came first, he said, with the choir facing the audience, and at the dismissal of chapel "the ladies rise first, the collegiates next, and the academics last." [5] The discipline that Harris had received in military service he had not forgotten; he had become used to giving orders and to seeing to it that these orders were obeyed. Presently, as every one in due time would find out, Harris would set in order other and larger things; for he had conceived for the University an institutional development which would make his role as president thereof resemble more that of a man directing a burgeoning business enterprise of his era than that of an old-time college president presiding over a small college in an era of small things, when a professor of Greek was as much exalted as, in a later era, a successful coach of football would be wildly acclaimed.

The dominating personality of President Harris affected not only the students and the members of the faculty, of which he was one; it affected also the members of the Board of Trustees, of which he also was one. As a member of the Board, he was, in 1889, assigned to its Committee on Buildings and Grounds; by 1894 he had been made *ex officio* a member of each of the four standing committees of the Board.[6] Legally an employee of the Corporation of which he was a voting member, he was in practice a trusted associate of his fellow trustees, and by them was authorized to see to it that the University was administered and promoted pursuant to their wishes, frequently expressed in general terms. After the death of William Bucknell, early in 1890, the influence of Harris in the Board increased; and for thirty years he retained the confidence of his fellow trustees, in part, because they approved of what he wanted to do for and with the University and also, in part, because they admired him for getting done what practicably could be done. What, in broad outline, happened to the University during those thirty years, we shall now endeavor to ascertain.

Throughout his administration the major object of President Harris was to increase the number of students in the University. This object, he believed, he should seek first of all, and then other things would be added unto the University. Consequently, it became necessary not only for the University to offer something that would attract students to its campus, but also for its administration to advertise, widely and persistently, what the University had to offer. Too long the University had suffered because it had not been well known. Accordingly, during the first year of the administration of President Harris, a long-promised gymnasium for men was constructed and dedicated, and a significant change in the programs of study was made, first, by providing that the established Scientific Program, in its Latin as in its Greek division, should no longer lead to the degree of Bachelor of Science, but that thenceforth, reconstructed as a Philosophical Program, it should lead in both its divisions to the degree of Bachelor of Philosophy; and, secondly, by creating a new four-year Scientific Program which, "uncontaminated" by any requirement in the classical languages, should lead to the degree of Bachelor of Science.[7] Here, then, for the first time in its history, Bucknell University was offering a more or less respectable program that would carry students to a more or less respectable degree by a more or less respectable route that bypassed both Latin and Greek. Now a bell was ringing for the New Education at Bucknell, and thenceforth, with the passing of the years, its peals would become louder. But, except for an increase in the number of elective studies offered, the program just described was continued unchanged until after the opening of the twentieth century.

Meanwhile, President Harris had undertaken with enthusiasm the work of pressing "upon the people's attention" the kind of education that Bucknell could provide. His program for advertising the University was varied, imaginative, and persistent. He himself was an effective advertiser, spending many years in preaching, Sunday after Sunday, to Baptist congregations throughout the state and elsewhere. His program of advertising, moreover, comprehended close relations of the University with the alumni, and between January, 1891, and January, 1892, an agreement was reached between the Trustees and the alumni whereby the Alumni Association was empowered to nominate one of its number to fill any vacancy in the representation of the alumni on the Board. Such nominee, however, must be elected by the Trustees pursuant to their bylaws.[8] Nor was this the full extent of the advertising program. His program comprehended also close—even intimate—relations of the University with Baptist academies in Pennsylvania and in New Jersey which were expected to continue to serve as "feeders" of the College in the University. This, of course, was not a novel idea, but not before the administration of Harris had the Trustees of the University taken official action intended to establish a close bond of interest among these institutions. In January, 1891, the Trustees approved the recommendation of President Harris that there be "a closer relation of the College" not only with the Western Pennsylvania Classical and Scientific Institute, the Keystone Academy, and the Hall Institute, situated, respectively, in Mount Pleasant, Factoryville, and Sharon, Pennsylvania, but also with the South Jersey Institute and the Peddie Institute, situated, respectively, in Bridgeton and Hightstown, New Jersey. The Trustees also instructed Harris to put this decision into effect.[9] He did so by inserting in the

Catalogue of the University for 1890–91 a statement affirming that the above-named Pennsylvania academies were affiliated with the University, and that the president of the University was a lecturer on ethics in all these schools.[10] Nor was this the full extent of co-operation, for in the catalogue of the Keystone Academy for 1890–91 Professors George G. Groff and Enoch Perrine are listed with President Harris as lecturers in this institution.[11]

The most widely used form of advertising employed by the University, however, and no doubt in the long run the most effective, was that of the printed word. This form of advertising had been started during the time of Stephen W. Taylor, when "circulars" and other notices about the University had been printed in newspapers, when leaflets describing the University had been circulated with the minutes of Baptist associations in Pennsylvania and in New Jersey, and when advertisements had been carried in both religious and secular periodical publications. Such advertising was continued through the years. Furthermore, until the reorganization of the University in 1882, the Board of Curators through its Committee on Publication had published in select newspapers of the state annual reports on the work and on the prospects of the University. From 1882 on, the responsibility for informing the public by an annual report was vested in the Trustees,[12] who, presumably, delegated this task to the Board's Committee on Publications with the understanding, no doubt, that the work would be done largely by the administration of the University.

In 1889, before Harris had been selected president of the University, the advertising of the University was accelerated when William C. Gretzinger, of the Class of 1889, became business manager of the University. Within a year, or less, he was being called registrar, the first person to bear that title; but the Trustees did not officially sanction the use of this title until January, 1892.[13] But, title or no title, Gretzinger, from 1889 until his death in 1909, was the right-hand man of President Harris, and during those years one of his principal duties was that of directing, in all its aspects, the publicity of the University. As early as 1892 it was reported that the larger number of students then in Bucknell was owing to the personal efforts of Harris and Gretzinger.[14] What those efforts in the way of distributing printed materials had become ten years later we may perceive in a report that Gretzinger sent to President Harris on May 16, 1902 (the basis of the report made in that year to the Board of Trustees by its Committee on Publications).[15] Whichever of these reports we study, we learn that the University was then issuing catalogues and pamphlets, that it was inserting paid advertising in daily and in weekly newspapers, in religious periodical publications, and in the publications of preparatory and normal schools, that it maintained a news service, and that it profited by the circulation of the several publications of the students. A year later we are specifically told that the University was issuing a quarterly bulletin, of which the annual Catalogue was one issue, and that it was sending out thousands of mimeographed letters. During the preceding year it had spent the sum of $1,638.89 for printing and advertising. Presumably the Trustees believed that this money had been well spent, for they "heartily approved" the report in which their committee affirmed that the "efforts of the President and Registrar in keeping the interests of the University before the people are worthy of all praise." [16]

Such approval meant of course that the advertising of the University was producing desirable results, and the most important result that it had sought was an increase in the enrollment of the University. So great was the increase within a few years that nobody would have dared question the methods of the administration. It was in the College especially that the growth had taken place, and the growth had been steadily upward: from 71 in 1889–90 to 103 in 1890–91, to 171 in 1894–95, to 315 in 1899–1900; in those same years the total enrollment of the University advanced from 285 in 1889–90 to 384 in 1890–91, to 431 in 1894–95, to 487 in 1899–1900. Three years later, in 1902–03, the increase was even more remarkable: 408 in the College and 577 in the University.[17] And so it continued through subsequent years, the trend being always upward. In no year was there a loss in the University as a whole. At the end of twenty years of effort, President Harris, in a special report to the Board of Trustees on June 22, 1909, could say:

> It may not be out of place to mention that through the successful efforts of our many friends, the attendance [in the College] has been increased from 71 to 547; the faculty from 8 to 25; the number of courses given from 54 to 263; and the sum of $420,000.00 has been collected, including the present effort.[18]

Six years later he could say that the entering class numbered 246, "by much the largest class" of freshmen that the University thus far had received, and that some of the classes were overcrowded, a fact which revealed the need for more teachers.[19] For 1916–17, the year after the Academy, and two years after the Female Institute, had ceased to exist, the total enrollment in the College was 715. The Catalogue for 1917–18 traced the growth of the College by periods as follows: in 1890—71; in 1895—171; in 1900—315; in 1905—475; in 1910—527; and in 1917—715.[20] Here was a record in which, justifiably, President Harris could take considerable pride.

The continuous and rapid growth of the University created a need for more money to pay for new buildings, to provide more equipment, and to pay the salaries of additional teachers. Accordingly, at a meeting on January 8, 1891, the Trustees not only empowered its Committee on Buildings and Grounds to collect money for the construction of new buildings, but also authorized President Harris to inquire about getting assistance from the National Education Society (no doubt meaning the American Baptist Education Society) in case an effort should be made to increase the endowment of the University.[21] Nothing came immediately of the first of these authorizations, but something soon came of the second one. Because the American Baptist Education Society showed a willingness to contribute $10,000 on condition that an additional sum of $90,000, "clear of all expense," be raised by friends of the University, a campaign to enlarge the endowment of the University seemed practicable.[22] By Commencement Week, 1891, rumors were afloat to the effect that the University had started, or soon would start, a movement to raise $100,000 for its endowment fund.[23] Actually, at their meeting in June, 1891, the Trustees referred the matter of raising more endowment to their Committee on Finance "for immediate consideration," and then, on the recommendation of this committee, authorized the officers of the Board to sign an application to the American Baptist Education Society for a subscription of $20,000 on condition that the University raise an additional $80,000.[24]

At a special meeting held on July 20, 1891, the Trustees, on the recommendation of President Harris that the need for so doing was great, and that the prospect of success was encouraging, authorized a campaign to raise $100,000 and appointed a committee of three of their members to get subscriptions to this fund.[25] The American Baptist Education Society promised to contribute to this campaign $10,000.[26] The labor of raising the required sum proved to be difficult, and almost a year elapsed before the campaign was completed. To obtain the required sum, hard work was done in Lewisburg, in the University, in Philadelphia, and elsewhere. All told, the sum of about $6,000 was raised in the University, part of it being subscribed by classes in the College, part of it by students in the Academy, and $25 of it by the Phi Kappa Psi fraternity.[27] By June, 1892, the sum of about $72,000 being in sight, most of the Trustees doubled the amounts that they had pledged. Then the campaign moved quickly to its end; early in July the chairman publicly announced that the full subscription had been completed; and the Philadelphia *National Baptist,* which published this announcement, remarked that now Bucknell would be able "to enter upon an era of renewed prosperity and to enlarge its teaching force, now sorely overtaxed." [28]

Apart from a lesser campaign to obtain $40,000 to endow a chair of instruction in the English Bible—a campaign proposed by President Harris and approved by the Trustees on July 30, 1892 [29] —the attention of those concerned with the management of Bucknell now turned to the subject of buildings. By the summer of 1896 the Trustees had approved for construction as soon as practicable buildings that had been recommended as follows: a dormitory to accommodate 100 men in the College, a dormitory to accommodate 50 women in the College, a dormitory to accommodate 50 boys in the Academy, and an extension of Bucknell Hall, the chapel of the University; and in order to expedite this work the Trustees instructed their Committee on Buildings and Grounds to submit at the next meeting of the Board plans for the construction of these buildings and estimates of the cost thereof.[30]

During the next year, a priority for the construction of buildings became established. In June, 1897, the Committee on Buildings and Grounds recommended, first, the construction of a heating plant, and after it, in order, the erection of a dormitory for men of the College, a dormitory on the Institute grounds for women of the College, and an additional building for the boys of the Academy; and the committee submitted preliminary plans for the proposed men's dormitory and for the proposed women's dormitory.[31] There were exasperating delays, but by the summer of 1898 the plan for a new dormitory for collegiate men was approved. The plan for the women's dormitory was referred back for some changes.[32] On January 12, 1899, the Trustees authorized their Committee on Finance to arrange for the construction of the men's building with the least practicable delay, and the contract therefor was soon let. On April 3, 1899, ground was broken for this building, which for nearly sixty years would be called West College.[33] After being completely renovated and refurbished, it was renamed Rush H. Kress Hall in 1960.

While the construction of this building was under way, the work of raising money to pay for it was proceeding. The cornerstone was laid on June 20, 1899, and the building, which was dedicated during Commencement Week in June, 1900, was opened to students at the beginning of the autumn term in that year. It was built of brick, and was four stories in height, one hundred and forty feet long, and forty-two feet wide. In the south end of the first floor a room, thirty by forty feet, was set aside for the use of the collegiate Y.M.C.A.[34] At the time of its dedication not all the money needed to pay for this building had been raised. On June 20, 1899, President Harris had reported that John D. Rockefeller, through the American Baptist Education Society, had pledged $15,000 to this enterprise on condition that the University raise an additional $60,000. The Trustees gratefully accepted Mr. Rockefeller's offer, and pledged themselves to comply with the conditions that he had laid down. By June, 1900, more than $45,000 of the required money had been subscribed, and eleven days later, as President Harris reported to the Board on January 10, 1901, the full sum had been "secured in good & valid subscriptions." [35]

This matter was scarcely out of the way, however, before President Harris, on June 18, 1901, began reminding the Trustees of the "pressing need of an additional endowment of $100,000." Being now perhaps hardened to such things, the Trustees were not taken aback by this announcement; on the contrary, they authorized Dr. Harris to take the preliminary steps required for raising this sum of money.[36] He lost no time in doing so, and on January 9, 1902, the Committee on Finance could report the promise of a subscription of $25,000 from the American Baptist Education Society on condition that the University raise an additional sum of $75,000. In June, 1902, the financial agent of the University, the Reverend Calvin A. Hare, reported subscriptions to this effort amounting to $67,264.50, and reminded his employers that the campaign must be closed by the end of the year. It was completed in time to get the grant from the Baptist Education Society. On January 8, 1903, President Harris, in a printed statement, announced that the work had been completed on December 31, 1902.[37] Presumably the money for the subscription of $25,000 by the American Baptist Education Society came as a gift from Mr. Rockefeller, for in July, 1902, William C. Gretzinger, acknowledging the receipt of $50 contributed toward the endowment fund of $100,000, remarked in English having a "Pennsylvania Dutch" flavor: "You well understand Mr. Rockefeller pays in his money pro rata, that is, for every dollar subscribed and paid, he remits to us his share, after making a statement, so any amount we are short, we do not receive a proportional amount from him." [38] President Harris was much pleased at the outcome, not only because some of the subscriptions were relatively large, but also because more than half of the sum that the University was required to raise had been contributed by members of the Board of Trustees. There was, he reported, one subscription "for $25,000, one for $10,000, four for $5,000 each, two of $2,500 each, one of $2,000, eight of $1,000 each and a large number of subscriptions of smaller amounts. Eight members of the Board had contributed $40,000." [39]

By this time, according to the calculation of President Harris, Bucknell University had become a million-dollar concern.[40] For that reason, and also no doubt for the further reason that the successful outcome of his effective promotion and efficient administration had bolstered his self-confidence, he believed that the time had come to make "large plans" for the University. Accordingly, on January 8, 1903, in the report in which, as we have seen, he announced the successful completion of the campaign to raise an additional $100,000 for the endowment of the University, he set forth in comprehensive outline his program for the future development of Bucknell. Unhappily, a copy of this report has not been preserved, but from a variety of sources we are able to derive information that permits us to understand the substance of it.

As summarized in the Minutes of the Trustees for January 8, 1903, it proposed the enlargement of the campus, more buildings for the University, a further increase of endowment, the establishment of fellowships and scholarships, and the creation of a loan fund. Also, it embodied suggestions "with reference to the securing of money for these objects." The Trustees were not put out of countenance by what some persons would have called this gross impertinence; on the contrary, they approved the proposals and authorized President Harris to carry them toward fulfillment as rapidly "as possible." [41] Presumably they had by this time acquired as much confidence in Dr. Harris's Aladdin's lamp as had an editorial writer for the weekly collegiate newspaper, the *Orange and Blue,* who, affirming that Dr. Harris had asked for a million and a quarter dollars to meet needs of the "immediate future," took pride not only in the thought that the University had become so useful as to need so much money, but also in the thought that a task so difficult as this one should be proposed for the University. His own belief, however, was that "the successful conclusion to which Dr. Harris and his associates have brought similar efforts augurs well for the success of this one also." [42]

From his quotations from, and his comments on, his Report of 1903 that appear in his *Thirty Years as President of Bucknell,* we learn more specifically what Dr. Harris had in mind in asking for a larger campus, more buildings, and more endowment for the University. As to the first of these, he was persuaded that a campus of "thirty acres" was much too small for the Bucknell that he envisioned; in fact, he thought that an enlargement of two hundred acres would not be unreasonable. Part of this increase of land he wished to use as a campus for the Women's College, which, he believed, could not properly develop unless it had its own "campus of a hundred acres, buildings costing $500,000, and a million dollars [of] endowment." Of the additional buildings that the University needed, he proposed, first of all, one for the library, and he believed that one costing $100,000 would not be too large. But, since the cost of maintaining so large a building would be out of proportion to the cost of maintaining the total plant of the University, he was willing to settle for a building for the library costing $50,000, but one so planned that its capacity could be doubled when there should be need for its expansion. The other buildings that he asked for were residential halls, one for men and one for women, each one to cost about $50,000. To the endowment of the University, he believed that at least a million dollars should be added so that the University could pay salaries that would permit it to keep its able professors and to make needed grants to worthy students of limited means.[43]

In this report Dr. Harris pointed out the desirability of getting specific endowments, each of which "would bear and perpetuate the name of the donor, or of some person designated by him." Specifically, he suggested that a department could be endowed for $100,000 "and upward," that a professorship could be endowed for $50,000, that a fellowship could be endowed for $10,000, that a scholarship could be endowed by a gift of $1,000 to $5,000, that a loan fund should be established for the benefit of students, and that a fund for the retirement of superannuated professors would be highly desirable.

Finally, in order to raise the money needed to construct the buildings that he had proposed, to purchase the land that was desired, and to enlarge the general endowment by at least a million dollars, Dr. Harris proposed that, from time to time, efforts be made to raise money by general subscription, by large gifts from wealthy persons, and by legacies.[44]

Of the buildings recommended in this report, the first two to be obtained were a building for the library and a residential hall for women. Agitation for a separate building for the collegiate library had continued through long years, but the matter never got beyond suggestions until, on June 23, 1903, the Trustees approved and sent to Andrew Carnegie a communication about "a library building" that Dr. Harris had laid before them.[45] What reply, if any, was received to this communication, we do not know. But we do know that on January 14, 1904, pursuant to the suggestion of Dr. Harris that "the request to Mr. Carnegie for $50,000 for [a] library building be renewed," the Trustees not only gave their approval to this suggestion, but also authorized the taking of "such measures as might be deemed wise . . . to secure Mr. Carnegie's interest in the University." Also at that meeting the Trustees took preliminary measures toward getting a "new building for [the] girls," but this subject we shall deal with in a subsequent paragraph.[46]

The second appeal to Mr. Carnegie was at least moderately successful, for on March 11, 1904, Dr. Harris received from Mr. Carnegie's private secretary a letter saying that Mr. Carnegie would gladly contribute

$30,000 for the construction of a library building for Bucknell, provided that the University would adequately support the library that it would house. Plans for such a building were quickly obtained from a firm of architects in New York and on May 17 were submitted to Mr. Carnegie. On June 3, 1904, Mr. Carnegie sent word from Skibo Castle, in Scotland, that, provided that the cost of the building "shown in the plans" be kept within the amount that he had promised, the plans were approved, and that his cashier in Hoboken, New Jersey, would honor requests for money to pay for the building. On June 21, 1904, the Trustees instructed Dr. Harris to tell Mr. Carnegie that his offer "was gratefully accepted." [47]

The task of getting this building constructed was assigned to Frank E. Burpee, who was then instructor of Greek in the Academy. Ground was broken for it on June 21, 1904, the cornerstone was laid on October 20 of that year, and the building was dedicated on June 20, 1905, during Commencement Week.[48] The description of it which appears in the Catalogue for 1906–07 reads as follows:

> The building is sixty-four feet by ninety, built of pressed brick, and trimmed with brownstone. The center, thirty feet by ninety, is used as a reading room. At the height of sixteen feet there is a gallery extending around the room. The sides, each fifteen feet by ninety, are divided on the first floor into rooms of special collections and for offices. The second and third floors will be used for stack rooms. The building will accommodate about 150,000 [100,000] volumes.[49]

With the erection of the new building for the library there proceeded almost *pari passu* the construction of a new residential hall for women. In January, 1904, President Harris, reporting that at the beginning of the year some forty students had been denied admission because of lack of accommodations for them, affirmed that the "most imperative need" of the University was a building for women; and he suggested that a building on the plan of West College could be put up for them at a cost of $50,000. Since such a building would be financially productive, he recommended that plans for its construction be prepared without delay, and that consideration be given to the matter of paying for it with conditional gifts on which interest would be paid to the donors as long as they lived. The Board, approving this suggestion, instructed its Committee on Finance to submit plans for such a building at the next meeting of the Board. But the plans were not ready at the time of that meeting, and it was not until January 12, 1905, when President Harris pointed out the "very great need of an additional building for the Institute" and outlined plans for financing its construction, that the

Trustees authorized the Committee on Buildings and Grounds to erect the building at a cost "in the neighborhood of $20,000." But, as had been the case with buildings built theretofore, that "neighborhood" expanded as the construction of the building proceeded. In June, 1905, when the building was nearing completion, President Harris said that it would permit the University to accept some sixty more students, but that its cost, including all the fixtures and the furnishing, would be about $30,000. The reason for the increase was that the basement had been finished into four recitation rooms and eleven music rooms, "and the attic into a gymnasium 36 x 128 feet." [50]

The new residence for women was completed at about the same time that the Carnegie Building was ready for occupancy. Both these buildings had been constructed under the supervision of Mr. Burpee. Because the plan for financing the dormitory for women by conditional gifts did not materialize, this new building did not receive the name of a donor.[51] Through long years it was called the New Cottage, but after the death of Dr. Harris in 1925 it was named Harris Hall.

In the same report in which he spoke of the approaching completion of the new hall for women, President Harris mentioned not only the urgent need for constructing for men a new dormitory similar to West College, but also the equally urgent need for increasing the productive funds of the University. Accordingly, he suggested that a preliminary inquiry be made to determine whether it would be advisable to attempt to raise $100,000; and, if such sum could be raised, he recommended that $30,000 of it be used for the construction of a new dormitory, the foundation of which might be built in the autumn of 1905 and the entire building be completed and ready for occupancy in the autumn of 1906.[52] But action in this matter was less rapid than Dr. Harris desired. In January, 1906, however, he was authorized to begin a canvass to raise $50,000 for the construction of a new dormitory for men that would be called East College, the pledges for which would become binding when one-half of the total subscription had been made. The construction of the building was to begin when authorized by the Committee on Finance. On June 19, 1906, Dr. Harris reported that more than $23,000 had been obtained in subscriptions for East College, and, under authority then given him, the ground on which the building would be erected was broken that afternoon. The plans for East College were drawn by Professors Charles A. Lindemann and Frank E. Burpee, and Mr. Burpee was appointed supervisor of its construction.[53]

The construction of the building, however, proceeded gradually during a period of at least three years. On January 10, 1908, the Committee on Buildings and Grounds reported to the Trustees that work on East

College had been "discontinued with the finishing of one story for the use of students and of the Electrical Laboratory and four other rooms in the first story," and President Harris reported at the same time that the indebtedness on this building, which amounted to about $19,000, was offset by pledges of about the same amount. But work was resumed on East College during 1908, and in the autumn of that year the *Orange and Blue* could report that twenty-eight "new rooms were opened this fall in East College, so that there is an increase in the number of men enrolled"; and this statement was confirmed on January 14, 1909, when the Committee on Buildings and Grounds reported that the "second story of East College with twenty-eight rooms has been furnished and all the rooms are occupied." Thus far, this committee continued, the cost of the building had been $46,571.45, and the amount paid in only $31,257.45; and it estimated that at least $30,000, "in addition to some $6,000.00 [of] old subscriptions regarded as good," would be needed to complete the building. By the payment of $5,000 Samuel A. Crozer had made possible the resumption of work on the building; and, encouragingly, President Harris reported at this meeting that he had obtained $16,000 in subscriptions towards the $30,000 needed to complete the building.[54]

Thereafter the work on the building proceeded rapidly, and by Commencement Week, 1909, East College, now capped by the observation tower given by the Class of 1909, appeared to be a completed building; and this appearance presumably had become reality when, in September, 1909, the collegiate newspaper announced that East College had been finished, "with four floors now available for students' rooms and the top floor utilized as a draughting room." Somewhat puzzling, however, is the report of the Committee on Buildings, made on January 12, 1911, which reads as follows: "The East College Building has been completed and occupied, the total cost having been $62,088.78, of which $3,288.52 is unpaid, but provided for." [55]

As early as June, 1909, when the success of East College had been assured, President Harris reminded the Trustees that, since six major efforts had been made during the preceding ten years to raise money for the University, it would be necessary to wait "for some time" before making another large-scale effort. "I suggest," he said,

> that the next effort be for increasing the endowment. We have now reached a point where we can stop increasing in the way of buildings, except that an enlargement of the chapel is greatly needed. The present chapel furnishes seats for only one-half of the College students and so requirements of attendance cannot be enforced. I submit herewith a plan

> for such enlargement. It is thought that this enlargement, which will cost about $20,000[,] may be obtained from one or at any rate, a few persons, without a general canvas[s].

This report the Trustees received and placed on file.[56]

The "some time" suggested by President Harris turned out to be about eighteen months, for on January 12, 1911, having reported to the Trustees that he "was engaged in a movement" to increase the endowment of the University pursuant to authority previously given him by the Board, he was instructed to proceed in this work under the direction of the Committee on Finance. A year later the University was again deep in a major effort to raise money, principally for the purpose of increasing its endowment, but partly for the purpose of liquidating an indebtedness amounting to more than $48,000. More than half of this indebtedness consisted of sums yet unpaid on the newly constructed dormitories: $3,000 on the East College for men and more than $22,000 on the New Cottage for women. The plan for financing the New Cottage had not turned out as President Harris had anticipated that it would. As the treasurer reported to the Trustees on January 11, 1912,

> It was expected when the Women's College [*i.e.,* the New Cottage] was erected that a certain party would pay the whole cost as a Memorial, but failure to sell a property delays the payment. The amount, however, is secured by will, but it is judged best, however, to pay off liabilities and this amount when it comes in can be added to endowment.

Meanwhile, the treasurer was authorized to borrow, from time to time, such sums as might be needed to carry current indebtedness while the movement then under way to raise additional money for the University was being carried to completion. As summarized by the Committee on Finance, it was proposed by this movement to raise money, first, "to pay off all liabilities, and second, to increase the endowment by the addition of not less than $112,000. This [the Committee continued] will make the endowment total $507,750, and the productive investment $850,-750." [57]

The foregoing statement reveals the fact that the University had decided to endeavor to raise more than the $100,000 which had been contemplated for its Fund of 1911. The reason for so doing was the promise of help from the General Education Board, an organization which John D. Rockefeller had founded in 1902 as an agency for dispensing his gifts for the promotion of education in the United States.[58] Theretofore Mr. Rockefeller had restricted his gifts for education to

Baptist institutions and had used as his agency for making such gifts the American Baptist Education Society. In an offer dated October 27, 1911, the General Board had proposed to contribute to the funds of the University $35,000 provided that the University would raise, not later than July 1, 1913, the sum of $25,000 in addition to the $100,000 that it earlier had contemplated raising. This offer from the General Board was accepted by the Trustees of the University, who, on January 11, 1912, specifically promised that $40,000 of the $160,000 to be raised would be used to complete payments on buildings already constructed, that $8,000 of it would be used to discharge other indebtedness of the University, and that $112,000 of it would be added to the endowment.[59] The additional $60,000 came to be known as the Endowment Fund of 1913.[60]

In January, 1913, President Harris reported to the Trustees that the Fund of 1911, amounting to $100,633, had been completed on December 18, 1912, and that of the amount thus far raised in the total effort the sum of $68,525 had been contributed by members of the Board of Trustees. By Commencement Week, in June, 1913, there still remained somewhat less than $5,000 to be raised; but at the meeting of the Board on January 8, 1914, President Harris reported that the full sum had been subscribed within the time limit and that the result had been accepted by the General Board. "The sum of $1622.00 needed to make up the amount required at the close," he said, "was pledged by Mr. Leas, in addition to the $15,000 previously pledged by him." [61] The man whose generosity Dr. Harris had thus acknowledged, David Porter Leas, was a member of the Class of 1863, and he had served the University as treasurer since its reorganization in 1882. For his generosity he was given a vote of appreciation by his fellow members of the Board of Trustees.[62]

Their greatest plaudits, however, the Trustees reserved for another "fellow member," John Howard Harris, who was then in the twenty-fifth year of his service as president of Bucknell. No doubt touched by this thought, and presuming that this latest effort would be the culmination of President Harris's strenuous promotional labors for the University, the Trustees expressed to him "their great appreciation" for "his splendid work, untiring zeal, and unremitting energy" in bringing to a successful conclusion "this most disagreeable, exciting and laborious canvass." Nor was this all. Before adjourning, they appointed a committee of five of their members to provide, in June, 1914, a suitable memorial of "the twenty-fifth anniversary of Dr. Harris as President of the University." [63]

The celebration took place in Commencement Hall on the morning of June 16, the day before commencement. There were four principal speakers: Professor Enoch Perrine for the faculty, David Porter Leas for the Trustees, the Reverend Theodore A. K. Gessler for the alumni, and Dr. Martin G. Brumbaugh, of Philadelphia, for the state as a whole. Through their praise of various and sundry things that Dr. Harris had done for the University, there ran a common theme that was heavily emphasized—namely, the great material advance of Bucknell: an advance in the number of its students, in the number of its buildings, in the increase of its curricular offerings, in the growth of its library, and in the enlargement of its endowment. To those who were listening it must have appeared that these speakers were documenting a remark in an editorial that appeared that morning in *Commencement News*—namely, "Dr. Harris has, through his perseverance and conscientious work, raised the rank of Bucknell to one of the best institutions of learning in our country." The ceremony concluded with the presentation by the Class of 1914 of a portrait of Dr. Harris that had been done by William H. Leavitt.[64]

The speakers at the commemoration did not dwell upon everything that Dr. Harris had accomplished during the preceding twenty-five years, and of course they could make no precise prediction of what he would do thereafter. His career at Bucknell was not yet ended. For those who preferred seeing to hearing, the current published guide to "Points of Interest About the University," especially if such persons were aware of its implications, brought them face to face with the most significant consequences of the promotional work of Dr. Harris. In this guide attention was called, *inter alia,* to the art gallery in the Cottage of the Women's College, to the biological museum on the second floor of the Carnegie Building, to the observation tower on East College, to the drawing rooms on the top floor of East College and on the first floor of the East Wing of the Main Hall, to the physical and electrical laboratories in the basement of East College, and to the mechanical and engineering shops and engine rooms in the "building in the rear of the Gymnasium."[65] This last-named building has not yet been dealt with in this chapter. It was begun in the autumn of 1900 and was completed during the academic year 1901–02. It was called the Heating and Lighting Plant until the year 1903–04, when its name was changed to Physical Laboratory. From the beginning its main story had accommodated the Department of Physics, the heating and lighting plant being placed in the basement. So firmly did the name Physical Laboratory attach itself to this building that it continued to be used after the physical laboratory had been assigned to share with the electrical laboratory the basement of East College in 1909 and the floor which this department formerly had occupied was being used for "shop work." [66]

Another building for which Harris was in part responsible, and which heretofore has been only mentioned, is the Tustin Gymnasium that had long been in contemplation for men. The dedication of this building, one year after Dr. Harris had assumed the presidency of Bucknell, marked the end of at least twenty years of agitation for a men's gymnasium. The subject of a collegiate gymnasium appeared in the first issue of the *College Herald,* in May, 1870, and agitation therefor continued during subsequent years. Before long the construction of such a building became an object of alumni concern, but not much was accomplished toward the realization of such an undertaking until 1886 when, stimulated and perhaps somewhat embarrassed by William Bucknell's gift to the University of both a Chapel and an Observatory, the Alumni Association set to work earnestly to raise money to pay for the erection of a gymnasium. It formed a building committee that was headed by Professor Francis W. Tustin, and after Tustin's untimely death in the spring of 1887 it decided to name the proposed building in honor of Professor Tustin. As his successor in this effort, it named William E. Martin, Principal of the Academy. The work of collecting money proceeded slowly, but, on the rather urgent recommendation of President Harris, the Committee of the Trustees on Finance in July, 1889, authorized the beginning of the construction of what would be the Tustin Gymnasium. In the autumn of 1889 ground was broken for this building. During the next few months the *University Mirror* followed eagerly the course of construction, and the *Commencement News* of June 25, 1890, announced that, on the preceding day, the Tustin Gymnasium was dedicated, although the building was not fully completed and was not entirely paid for.[67]

After 1914, still other buildings were acquired by the University. A foundry, requested by Professor Frank E. Burpee, was authorized in June, 1912, and completed by January, 1915.[68] Also in this period the University began the practice of acquiring near the campus additional houses as residences for women. In January, 1916, the Trustees were informed that nineteen collegiate women and two teachers were occupying "the house" on Fifth Street that recently had been fitted up as a residence for women of the College. Presumably this was the building listed in the Catalogue for several years as the Annex.[69] But there was one building, or rather addition to a building, that Dr. Harris persistently sought but did not obtain. That was an addition to Bucknell Hall which would make this building adequate as a common chapel for all the students in an institution that had outgrown the calculation of accommodations that had seemed reasonable in William Bucknell's time. As late as February 7, 1919, however, the Trustees voted that "the Chapel be enlarged as soon as practicable for the purpose of providing a meeting place where the students may assemble for such purposes as may be desirable." [70]

Besides the acquisition of new buildings and of additional endowment, President Harris had been moderately successful in getting fellowships and scholarships for the University. Perhaps the most significant of these was the fellowship that Charles Miller, of Franklin, Pennsylvania, established in 1893 to permit a graduate of Bucknell University to pursue post-graduate studies in the University of Chicago.[71] This fellowship was continued for ten years. The first recipient of it, Ephraim M. Heim, a man who subsequently had a long career as professor in the University, was chosen for this honor by the faculty on March 20, 1894; and his fellowship was renewed through the year 1896–97. Among other recipients of this fellowship were Mary Belle Harris, who acquired the degree of Doctor of Philosophy, and Llewellyn Phillips, a man who subsequently had a long career in the University, first as professor and then as dean of the College.[72]

In 1902, shortly before the above-mentioned fellowship was discontinued, Mr. Miller established four scholarships for students in Bucknell, and soon thereafter, in the year that the graduate fellowship was discontinued, he increased the number of the scholarships to ten. These scholarships he maintained through the year 1918–19.[73] Still other scholarships, some of them endowed, were established during the Harris regime, the most important of them being the Livingston Scholarships which were created in 1893 when the Pennsylvania Baptist Education Society transferred to the University its Livingston Fund in exchange for twenty-two scholarships, each with an endowment of $500. These scholarships were for ministerial students.[74] Other enduring scholarships were the Philadelphia Alumnae Scholarship, founded in 1903 by a gift of $1,000 from the Philadelphia Alumnae Club for the benefit of worthy young women of Philadelphia,[75] and the Weaver Scholarships, endowed with $10,000 during the year 1917–18 by Dr. Joseph K. Weaver, of the Class of 1861, for the benefit of worthy students.[76]

In respect to one matter, however, that he had proposed in his Report of 1903, President Harris had been conspicuously unsuccessful. He had not acquired any endowed professorships. About 1912 he had appealed, without result, to Mrs. Russell Sage for $50,000 to endow a professorship, just as, in 1907, he had applied to her, also without result, not only for $50,000 for the construction "of a Y.M.C.A. building suitable for Chapel purposes," but also for $50,000 for the endowment of such a building.[77] Equally unsuccessful was his appeal in 1912 to Andrew

Carnegie for $50,000 to establish a Carnegie Professorship of Electro-Technics, on condition that the University raise an additional $150,000. To this request Mr. Carnegie replied that he had given a library building to the University.[78]

Not only had Dr. Harris been interested in getting a building for the library of the University; he had been interested also in promoting the growth and the effective use of the library. Apart from the grant for the construction of the library building, his greatest service to the library was perhaps performed in 1894, when he obtained the transfer of William E. Martin from the principalship of the Academy to a professorship in the College. Professor Martin was assigned a part-time teaching schedule in the College, and he was expected to give the greater part of his time to the library. This appointment was a happy one. Although without professional training for the task, Professor Martin brought to his labor as librarian so much enthusiasm, imagination, and energy that he quickly won and long retained both the support of the students and the admiration of his colleagues. From 1894 until his death in 1922, he worked in season and out of season to enlarge the collections of the library and to make these collections more serviceable. He was as enthusiastic a beggar for the library as President Malcom had been long years before, and consequently, despite its inadequate appropriations, the library during his administration grew in size, improved in quality, and acquired a workable card catalogue. By the year 1905–06, when it moved into the new Carnegie Building, it contained, besides many pamphlets, about 26,000 volumes. During the next decade, however, its rate of growth was relatively slow. By the time of our entrance into the First World War in 1917, it contained, besides "many thousand pamphlets," somewhat more than 30,000 volumes. It had not kept pace with the growth of the institution of which it was a part; it had not kept pace with the growth of the libraries of the better collegiate institutions in the Northeast; and, emphatically, it had not kept pace with the growth of the libraries of some of the Pennsylvania institutions with which Bucknell was competing for students.[79]

The twenty-fifth year of Dr. Harris's presidency marked the end of the large promotional efforts in which he had been involved. No extensive program to raise money was undertaken between the end of the effort for the Fund of 1913 and our entrance into the First World War.[80] In June, 1916, the Trustees authorized Dr. Harris to get an additional endowment of $25,000 to support "religious work connected with the University," [81] and in March, 1917, the Alumni Association, in imitation of the Brown University Loyalty Fund, was considering the establishment at Bucknell of an Alumni Fund to be used for increasing the salaries of the members of the faculty. The Association had become painfully aware of the fact that, at Bucknell, salaries were "amazingly small." But by October, 1917, this matter was deferred because of the demands of the war in which the country was then engaged.[82]

The entrance of the United States into the First World War brought to Bucknell, as to other American colleges and universities, problems of the gravest character. In June, 1917, the Committee of the Trustees on Finance, anticipating both a loss of students at Bucknell and an increase in the cost of supplies, strongly recommended a reduction of expenditures, "but not below what is necessary for the efficiency of the College work." [83] In January, 1918, President Harris reported that a falling off in attendance of 230 had caused a serious loss of revenue and, consequently, a reduction in the number of teachers, the postponement of increases in the salaries of members of the faculty, and the deferment of some improvements. In June of that year the Trustees granted leaves of absence to several members of the faculty, two of whom, Professor Norman H. Stewart and Professor Benjamin W. Griffith, were to serve with the Y.M.C.A. in France. Also Dr. Harris presented a plan, which the Trustees approved, that led to the establishment, later in that year, of a Student Army Training Corps on the campus; and on January 9, 1919, the Trustees approved an action that Dr. Harris had taken for the establishment at Bucknell of a Reserve Officers' Training Corps.[84]

The fighting was now ended, and Bucknell was facing not only postwar problems, but also the coming of a new era. In the solution of the problems consequent on the changes wrought by the war, however, Dr. Harris would have nothing to do; several months earlier he had served notice that he would give up the presidency of Bucknell at the end of the academic year 1918–19, although he expected to remain, and was permitted to remain, as a member of the faculty.[85]

Thus was ending a thirty-year administration which, in this chapter, I have dealt with as a large-scale promotional enterprise. It was also a demonstration of how one man, in the spirit and in the manner of an old-time college president, administered for thirty years an institution which, thanks to intelligent and persistent promotional efforts, was transcending in size and in activities the typical American college of earlier years.

In his administration of Bucknell, Dr. Harris had had few helpers. From the beginning, as we have seen, he had an efficient business manager, who soon came to be called a registrar. Upon him President Harris leaned heavily. From January, 1898, he had had a dean of the College, but the duties of this office had been nominal rather than burdensome. The title was established because the illness and absence of Freeman Loomis, the senior professor, made it seem necessary for some person to be designated to "act as presiding officer in the absence of the President." Accordingly, Professor Frank E. Rockwood was appointed dean of the College, a position which he held until his retirement in 1917. In June, 1918, Professor Llewellyn Phillips was named as his successor.[86]

It may well be that considerable responsibility rested upon another dean who also served as the principal of the Female Institute. When Mrs. Katherine B. Larison resigned the principalship of the Institute in June, 1897, the Trustees voted that her successor should be dean of the College of Women. Accordingly, this position was first held by Miss Eveline Judith Stanton, whose title, however, appeared in the Catalogue as dean of the College Women. When Miss Stanton resigned this office in June, 1904, Thomas A. Edwards, principal of the Academy, was appointed as her successor with the title of dean of the Women's Department and professor of pedagogy. This title he bore until his death in December, 1914, although the Trustees, on June 20, 1905, had renamed the Department of Women the College of Women. On June 15, 1915, Miss Anna R. Carey was appointed dean of the Women's College, although, oddly enough, her title appeared in the Catalogue as dean of the Department of Women.[87]

No doubt the disruptions produced by the war then in progress, as well as his own awareness that he was getting old, persuaded Dr. Harris of the desirability of his retiring as the end of the era which he represented drew nigh. He knew very well that the old-time college president, like the kind of college that the old-time college president had administered, belonged to the past. Bucknell had ceased to be a small college. Accordingly, in a printed report embodying his resignation of the presidency of Bucknell, Dr. Harris reviewed some aspects of his administration and offered some suggestions for the guidance of those who would continue his labors.

While Bucknell had been growing in numbers year by year during the last three decades, President Harris observed, the duties of the president of Bucknell had not been lessening. Whereas in standard colleges, as he pointed out, the president did no teaching, the practice had been otherwise with him at Bucknell. He had taught six days in the week, and sometimes seven. Also, he continued, whereas in a standard college the dean is charged with most of the details of administration, he, "following the plan of a small college," had himself attended to such work through the years as the College was growing from an enrollment of 71 to an enrollment of 715. He advised that the successor to Dean Rockwood be required to perform the work usually done by a dean in a standard college, and that after his own retirement the work of his successor be made to "conform" to that of a president of a standard college. No other sensible person, he seemed to be implying, would do all the things that President Harris had done.

Finally, after reminding the Trustees that through many years he had taken the full responsibility for the current finances of the University, as well as for the subscriptions for new buildings and for new endowments, he turned to the subject of the Board of Trustees, a subject of recurring interest to him during his presidency. This body, he thought, should be self-renewing as well as self-perpetuating, "one fifth going out each year." As to the sort of men who should serve on the Board, he had a firm conviction which he had cherished through the years. That conviction he now passed on to his associates on the Board of Trustees in these words: "It is of the utmost importance that we get as many men of means and liberality on the Board as possible. In raising the million dollars additional endowment which is imperative if the College is to maintain its rank and one fourth as much in building and equipment, the trustees should be able and willing to furnish one half." [88]

Dr. Harris had not delivered a farewell address: the time for his so doing had not yet come. But to his associates on the Board of Trustees he had delivered in broad outline some account of his stewardship, and his principal advice disclosed to them the fact that, as he had begun his service to the University with the determination to promote, *inter alia*, its material growth, so he was now, twenty-nine years later, approaching the end of this service much concerned about the promotional labors that would need to be done after his time. For another year he would perform administrative duties at Bucknell, but his work of "building up" his alma mater he was now waiting to pass on to other hands.

9

From Old Ways to New Ways

To avoid femininizing the whole Institution, almost sure to happen in a college of liberal arts which admits women, I introduced Jurisprudence, Biology and the four engineering courses, Chemical, Civil, Electrical and Mechanical. Into the Women's College I introduced Household Economics.—*John Howard Harris, Thirty Years as President of Bucknell.*

Bucknell is proud of her elective system.—*Commencement News, June 21, 1905.*

At this season of the year when the alumni gather and plan for the future of their Alma Mater something should be done to secure for this institution a chapter of Phi Beta Kappa.—*Commencement News, June 20, 1911.*

Owing to changed conditions, it was voted to sanction the beginning of the study of Greek in the College classes—allowing the candidate full credit.—*Minutes of the Faculty, January 8, 1918.*

To attract students to Bucknell, President Harris, during the first twelve years of his administration, relied upon an academic program which, superficially, disclosed no abrupt break with the past. Between 1889 and 1901 the program operated pursuant to the general aims proclaimed for the University during most of President Hill's administration—namely, "to impart sound instruction in all non-professional studies" and to impart such instruction through "the studies of the established college curriculum, with the addition of such branches as modern life seems to demand." [1] These aims, however, meant one thing to Hill and another thing to Harris. What divided these men in respect to educational practice was a difference in their understanding of what modern life demanded of collegiate education. To meet this demand, they both used the two favored devices of educational reformers of that era, elective studies and parallel programs; but they used these devices in different ways. Hill used the elective principle sparingly; Harris used it somewhat lavishly. Hill began and ended with two programs leading to undergraduate degrees, one of them requiring the study of both Latin and Greek, and the other requiring the study of either Latin or Greek; Harris, on the other hand, began with three programs leading to undergraduate degrees, one of which required no study of either Latin or Greek, and he ended with ten such programs, most of which required no study of Latin or Greek. After 1901 Harris opened wide the doors of the University to both professional and technological studies, and by 1919, the year of his retirement, his curricular changes had so undermined the traditional conception of what should be required for the degree of Bachelor of Arts that thenceforth students in Bucknell University could win that coveted degree without bothering themselves about either Latin or Greek. By this time, at Bucknell as at many other American collegiate institutions, the New Education had achieved a complete victory.

During the 1890's, as the number of elective studies increased from year to year, and as these studies more and more encroached upon the older required subjects, President Harris was loudly applauded in the publications conducted by the students of the University. "The curriculum of studies is constantly being revised to meet the demands of the times," the editor of the *University Mirror* proclaimed in 1891, and such changes, he maintained, had "raised Bucknell to the standing of a first-class University"; [2] and a few months later a contributor to the *Commencement News* affirmed that there was no longer any need to argue whether a classical program of study was either superior or inferior to a scientific program. "Those who affect contempt for classical learning," he said, "can leave it for the more practical pursuits of science." [3] By the end of the year 1893–94, forecasts of later emphasis upon professionalism were evident in the boasts of the editor of the *Commencement News* that, during the year just ended, a chair in Hebrew (a professional concession to pre-ministerial students) had been established, a course in civil engineering, with special attention to "city surveying," had been introduced, and a program preparatory to medical studies had been set on foot.[4] During the year 1894–95, as the editor of the *Mirror* affirmed, "forty-four required courses have been given, thirty-seven elective courses, nineteen honor courses, and twelve lecture courses of one hour a week. The system [he continued] has greatly increased the interest of the students in their work, and has nearly doubled the amount of work done." [5] Now we understand how it was possible to expand so extensively the curricular offerings of the University without greatly increasing the number of instructors. Both the lecture courses and the honor courses were so conducted that they required no meetings for recitations. At a banquet of the Philadelphia Bucknell Alumni Club on December 5, 1898, President Harris called "especial attention" to the fact that one hundred students were then "taking honor work." [6] The general effect of all such curricular changes the editor of the *Commencement News* summed up at the turn of the century in these words: "Old courses have been enlarged and broadened and one new chair has been established. Young instructors, full of energy and new ideas, have been added to the faculty. Old classical moorings have been left and now the institution is pervaded by the new scientific spirit." [7]

The drifting away from the old moorings during the 1890's can be easily traced in the issues of the Catalogue of the University for that decade. In 1889–90, all the studies of the first two years of the Classical Program were required, as were two of the three studies of all three terms of both the junior and the senior years. For each of the three terms of the two last-named years, one study could be chosen, with the approval of the faculty, from three electives. Also in that year, in the other two programs leading to degrees, the Philosophical and the Scientific, the same plan was followed in respect to electives.[8] By the year 1893–94, most of the studies in the junior and senior years of the Classical Program had become elective, and in the Philosophical Program, the one leading to the degree of Bachelor of Philosophy, the number of terms required in either Latin or Greek had been reduced from five to four. Two years later studies in the Classical Program were required only in the freshman year and in two terms of the sophomore year, and by 1899–1900 only the studies of the freshman year and of one term of the sophomore year were required; and in this program neither Latin nor Greek was required beyond the second term of the sophomore year. In that year four terms of either Latin or Greek were still required in the Philosophical Program. As to elective studies, choices in any one of the three programs leading to degrees could be made only with the "approbation of the Faculty." [9] The Bucknell system of elective studies never became a system of completely free elective studies.

With the opening of the new century a "big shift" in both thought and practice was under way at Bucknell. The Catalogue for 1900–01 was the last one to contain the statement that the University aimed to "impart sound instruction in all non-professional studies," and it was the first one in many years to omit from the descriptions of its programs leading to degrees a general statement about elective studies. It also was the first one to affirm not only that candidates for the degree of Bachelor of Arts "must present at least three courses in German and French," but also that candidates for the degree of Bachelor of Philosophy and of Bachelor of Science must present at least "four courses of German and French." In each of the three programs leading to undergraduate degrees, "thirty-six courses, each of one term five hours a week[,] must be presented, as well as the prescribed work in oral and written Expression, the former of which extends through two years of the course and the latter through four years." [10]

During these years, the Academy, now operating under the "form" system which President Harris had introduced, continued to be concerned with preparing its pupils for college, for teaching, or for business; and to do so it offered through the year 1899–1900 two four-year programs; Classical Preparatory and Scientific Preparatory. The next year it began to offer three programs—namely, Classical, Latin Scientific, and Scientific; and it continued to offer these programs as long as the Academy existed. In the Academy a student could, at any time, be prepared for any program that the University was offering.[11]

The Female Institute, besides its work in music and art, began with the year 1891–92 to offer three five-year programs: Literary, Classical, and Latin Scientific. Those who completed the Classical Program could be admitted to the sophomore class of the College as candidates for the degree of Bachelor of Arts, and those who completed the Latin Scientific Program could be admitted to the sophomore class of the College as candidates for the degree of Bachelor of Philosophy. Whether students who completed the Literary Program could be admitted to the College, we are not told. In any event, the Institute, at the opening of the new century, had become, and for a decade and a half would continue to be, a finishing school for women, a school to prepare women for college, and, to some extent, a junior college for women.[12] We shall return to this subject before the end of this chapter.

Officially, the "big shift," which had been incubating for several years, got under way in June, 1901, when the Trustees felt free, now that the statement about "non-professional subjects" had been removed from the Catalogue, to refer to President Harris the matter of affiliating the University "with Medical Colleges, Law Schools & Seminaries." [13] Accordingly, the faculty began the academic year 1901–02 by putting into the class schedule two courses in law, one a two-hour course in criminal law, to be taught by Frederick E. Bower, an attorney of Lewisburg, and the other a three-hour course in real property, to be taught by Albert W. Johnson, who also was an attorney of Lewisburg; [14] and in the Catalogue for 1901–02 there was described for the first time the Department of Law, staffed by three lecturers, Judge Harold M. McClure, Mr. Bower, and Mr. Johnson. In this description we read that the subjects offered were "those usually given in the first year of the best law schools," that a certificate would be given for work of very high quality that was done in this department, and that credit for work done in courses in law, to the amount of one year's work, would be counted toward the degree of Bachelor of Arts.[15] This department had come to stay. It retained its place in all the issues of the Catalogue through the year 1918–19, and classes for lecturers on law were being scheduled by the faculty as late as the year 1917–18.[16]

Also in the Catalogue for 1901–02 there is described for the first time a Department of Medicine, staffed by two professors and an assistant professor in the University and by three lecturers who were practicing physicians, and offering "the Preparatory studies and most of the non-clinical studies of the first two years of the courses required in the Medical Colleges." Enrollment in such studies was restricted to students in liberal arts, who were given assurance that each of them would have at his disposal an adequate laboratory in which he would have the opportunity to "dissect the whole human body." [17] But the Department of Medicine at Bucknell, unlike the Department of Law, did not prosper, although the registrar was saying, in September, 1903, that a student taking the medical preparatory work at Bucknell could "cut off one year in the best Medical Schools of the country." [18] Some two years later, however, he was saying that Bucknell was offering only a preparatory course in medicine, and that students no longer were admitted to advanced standing "in the best medical schools" except from other "recognized medical schools"; and he expressed very strongly the opinion that students should receive a "general College and Biological training" before entering a college of medicine.[19] Meanwhile, in the Catalogue for 1903–04, the former Department of Medicine was described as the Medical Preparatory Department. Four years later no courses were listed for this department, and in the Catalogue for 1908–09 neither courses nor instructors were listed for this department.[20] By this time the Medical Preparatory Department had been absorbed by the Department of Organic Science (succeeded in 1910–11 by the Department of Biology), and all the work preparatory to medicine that was available to students in Bucknell University was being given by the staff of this department.

A new emphasis upon another aspect of professionalism—that of education, or training for teaching—appeared in the Catalogue for 1902–03. Here, too, was something which had been in the making for more than a few years. For long years before the time of President Harris, the preparation of students for teaching had been one of the concerns of the Academy; and in the spring of 1889 Professor George G. Groff, then acting president of the University, made provision in the Academy for a course in the theory and practice of teaching that was taught by a visiting instructor.[21] Such work was not neglected by President Harris, who was as eager to find professional or vocational occupations for graduates of Bucknell as he was to persuade students to enter Bucknell for collegiate training. As early as the autumn of 1893, he was giving to juniors a one-hour lecture course on the history of education, and a year later he was offering also an honor course in the philosophy of education. During the year 1897–98, he was offering for the first time a regular course in psychology.[22] These three courses he continued to offer for the next four years. In the Catalogue for 1900–01, the president's department, theretofore known as the Department of Mental and Moral Philosophy, was called for the first time the Department of Philosophy; and it embraced the subjects of psychology, philosophy, ethics, theism, and education.[23] Two years later the program in education, now a division in the Department of Philosophy, had been expanded to nine courses, consisting of the history of education, the psychology of education, the philosophy of education, comparative and child psychology, school administration, and courses of methods in American history, Greek, Latin, and mathematics. Accompanying the descriptions of these courses were statements affirming that graduates of Bucknell University, after three years of experience in teaching, could receive state teachers' certificates in Pennsylvania; that students who took at least eight courses in education would be entitled to receive a certificate showing that such work had been done; that there would be no additional charge for the courses in education; and, finally, that a registry of graduates of Bucknell who wished to teach was being kept as a means of aiding "Boards of Control" in finding prepared teachers. For the benefit of such graduates, friends of the University were requested to notify the president of the University of teaching positions that were waiting to be filled.[24] Here we see the beginning of a teacher-placement office at Bucknell, and, as was the case with many other things in the time of Dr. Harris, the beginning was in the office of the president of the University.

The program of education, as described above, was continued with little change for fourteen years. In 1904 Thomas A. Edwards, who had been principal and teacher of Latin and Greek in the Academy for ten years, was made professor of pedagogy and dean of the Department of Women. He held this position until his death in December, 1914.[25] Not long after Llewellyn Phillips had been appointed as his successor, there appeared in the Catalogue for 1916–17 the first description of an independent Department of Education, which was offering a program of twelve courses, three of which were courses in methods. Accompanying the descriptions of these courses were statements affirming, *inter alia,* not only that graduates of Bucknell could get from the state of Pennsylvania teachers' provisional certificates, good for three years, but also that, after three years of successful teaching in Pennsylvania, they could get permanent state certificates. Certification to teach could also be obtained by graduates of Bucknell in New York, New Jersey, "and all other states which issue certificates to the graduates of any college." [26]

Of all the curricular changes made during the administration of President Harris for the purpose of encouraging or of promoting professional study, none was perhaps more significant than the introduction into the College of programs of instruction in engineering. Civil engineering led the way, and it had had its beginning as early as 1894 in a course in surveying taught by Albert B. Stewart.[27] This course was a part of a modest program which the Department of Mathematics had introduced in "surveying, city surveying, and civil engineering." [28] By 1902 this small program had been expanded into a four-year program leading to the degree of Bachelor of Science in Civil Engineering—the first "differentiation" that Bucknell made in the degree of Bachelor of Science.[29] As early as March 20 of that year, the registrar wrote that arrangements had been made to introduce such a program in September, 1902, and in June, 1902, the Trustees gave their approval to this program, a program which they believed to be "equivalent to the corresponding course in the University of Pennsylvania and other institutions of like grade"; and they decreed that the studies for the freshmen and the sophomores in this program should begin in 1902–03, and that the rest of the program should begin in 1903–04.[30] The full four-year program was printed in the *Orange and Blue* on November 17, 1902, was mentioned in the collegiate magazine in January, 1903, and was approved by the faculty on September 12, 1903. The first degrees of Bachelor of Science in Civil Engineering were awarded in June, 1907.[31]

The success of the work in civil engineering opened the way to other programs in engineering. A four-year program in electrical engineering was started in September, 1905, and the degree of Bachelor of Science in Electrical Engineering was first awarded in June, 1908.[32] On October 22, 1909, the faculty discussed and approved two more engineering programs, one of them leading to the degree of Bachelor of Science in Chemical Engineering and the other to the degree of Bachelor of Science in Mechanical Engineering. Both these programs were published in an issue of the *University Bulletin* early in November, 1909, and were immediately explained and approved in the collegiate newspaper. The new program in chemical engineering provided for fewer elective studies than had the old program in chemistry which it replaced, and it also required two years of physics instead of one. The program of mechanical engineering, on the other hand, was much like that of electrical engineering for the first three years, but some changes were made in the senior year. Perhaps its most distinctive feature was its requirement of four years of "shopwork." [33] Bucknell now had the equivalent of a School of Engineering, although no such name was officially given to it. Nevertheless, the *Orange and Blue* affirmed, as early as 1909, that "the introduction of the new courses" of that year put "the School of Engineering at Bucknell . . . on a par with the best." [34] However that may be, the degree of Bachelor of Science in Chemical Engineering was first awarded in June, 1913, and the degree of Bachelor of Science in Mechanical Engineering was first awarded in June, 1914.[35]

By this time a new quasi-professional program, one that would have a special appeal to many women, was getting under way in the University. During the year 1912–13, lectures and demonstrations were offered in "general cookery," and this modest offering proved to be the beginning of a program of home economics. These lectures were given during the winter term by Mrs. Anna B. Scott, the "expert in Domestic Art of the [Philadelphia] North American." [36] Some months elapsed, however, before a consistent program of home economics was adopted. The required approval for such a program was obtained from the Trustees on January 8, 1914, when President Harris reported that both interest and attendance in the Institute could be increased "by adding courses in cooking sufficient to enable our graduates to fill positions in that line in the public schools," and when the Committee of the Trustees on Instruction, endorsing the proposal of President Harris, recommended that a new teacher in cooking be employed because, as it affirmed, "occasional lectures" in this subject would not meet the demand.[37] Accordingly, there appeared in the Catalogue of the University for 1913–14 a new two-year program in domestic science, a program which began in the autumn of 1914 and continued through the year 1916–17. Students who enrolled in this program were recognized as students in the College.[38] In January, 1917, the Trustees approved a four-year program in household economics leading to the degree of Bachelor of Science, and they gave this program dignity by establishing it as a division in the program of General Science. Degrees earned in this new division were awarded for the first time in June, 1919.[39]

While new programs of study were being introduced, and new subjects were being admitted into older programs, the departments of instruction were being affected in various ways. Some new departments arose, and the older departments, to a greater or less extent, changed in content; and some of them took on new names. The changes in four of the departments we have already examined; it remains to see what happened to the others. During the thirty years of Harris's administration, the four departments of languages—Latin, Greek, English, and modern—experienced changes in content but retained their original names. Other departments acquired either modified or wholly different names. The Department of Medieval and Modern History of 1889–90, for example, became the Department of History in 1900–01, the Department of Elocution and Oratory of 1889–90 became the Department of Rhetoric and Oratory in 1902–03, and the Department of Organic Science of 1889–90 became, after the death of Professor George G. Groff, the Department of Biology in 1910–11. The subjects of chemistry and physics, which were united in one department in 1889–90, were separated in 1902–03, when chemistry became independent and physics became lost. A year later, however, physics turned up in the Department of Mathematics, where it still had its resting place as late as 1918–19. By this time the largest department in the University was the Department of Mathematics, which had been the Department of Mathematics and Astronomy before 1895–96. In 1918–19 it contained sixty courses and had a large teaching staff. It had become large not only because it contained the courses in physics, but also because it contained most of the courses offered in three of the programs in engineering. No departments of engineering were established before the retirement of President Harris. The Departments of Chemistry and of Biology also became large, the former in part because it contained most of the courses offered in chemical engineering, and the latter in part because of the premedical program of the University.

A few other departments of instruction remain to be examined. Some of these were short-lived. The Department of Hebrew, for example, arose in 1892–93 and made its last appearance in 1897–98, and the Department of Biblical Literature arose in 1893–94 and disappeared after the year 1899–1900. Two other departments, both of which had arisen before 1900, deserve some notice. They were long associated with the names of Professors Ephraim M. Heim and William E. Martin, both of whom lived beyond the end of Harris's administration.

The Department of Economics and Politics (later the Department of Economic and Political Science) was, as we have learned, established before 1889–90, but as late as that year it was still without a professor. In 1890–91 it became one of the "charges" of Dr. Enoch Perrine, professor of English, who kept it through 1891–92, and thereafter continued to teach a course in economics through the year 1897–98. Two years later, Ephraim M. Heim,[40] a graduate of Bucknell who had done advanced work in the University of Chicago, was listed as the professor in this department, and this position he held until his death in 1930.

The department which had been created for Professor William E. Martin in 1894 was first named the Department of Logic and Anthropology. Its name was changed several times. By 1901–02 it had become the Department of Logic and Sociology, by 1904–05 the Department of Sociology, and by 1913–14 the Department of Sociology and Logic, the name which it retained beyond the close of Harris's administration. The relation of sociology to this department is as interesting as it is complex, for this subject was taught in the University before it became a part of any department therein. From the year 1894–95 through the year 1897–98, Dr. Heman Lincoln Wayland, editor of the *Examiner,* delivered at Bucknell a course of lectures on sociology, and this course was continued through 1903–04 by Dr. Lemuel Moss,[41] who earlier had been a member of the faculty of the University. For two years after it was established, the Department of Logic and Anthropology offered no course in sociology. But in 1896–97 it began to offer such a course as an elective for juniors and seniors, and by 1900–01 it was offering three courses in sociology, one of which was the course of lectures by Dr. Moss. By the year 1901–02, a year that marked the beginning of significant curricular changes in the University, the word *sociology* had replaced the word *anthropology* in the title of Professor Martin's department. Equally interesting is the fact that, in the year 1898–99, Professor Martin began to offer a course in the history of art, and thus laid the foundation for the Department of Art of later years.[42]

Expansion of curricular offerings was accompanied by the addition of new programs of study leading to degrees. These programs no doubt were intended in part to control the choice of electives by students, but in part they were intended, as President Harris later confessed, to keep the University somewhat "masculine." In his reminiscences he affirms that, in order to "avoid feminizing the whole Institution," he introduced programs in jurisprudence, biology, and four branches of engineering.[43] Three of these—Jurisprudence, Biology, and Chemistry—were described for the first time in the Catalogue for 1903–04. They were all essentially "masculine" programs. The one in jurisprudence, which contained a slight requirement in Latin and Greek and led to the degree of Bachelor of Arts, was intended to compete with the Classical Program. It emphasized law, political science, economics, philosophy, history, literature, and mathematics, and was particularly planned to attract young men who were interested in law, business, or public affairs. The programs in biology and in chemistry, on the other hand, led to a bachelor's degree in science. Neither of them contained a requirement in either Latin or Greek.[44]

Accordingly, by 1903–04 students in Bucknell could choose any one of seven undergraduate programs, two of which led to the degree of Bachelor of Arts, one to the degree of Bachelor of Philosophy, and four to a bachelor's degree in science. With the addition of two more programs in engineering in subsequent years, and the creation of a four-year division of domestic science in the program of General Science, students at Bucknell could, by the year 1916–17, choose from ten undergraduate programs, seven of which led to a bachelor's degree in science.[45]

During these years of change, a problem in respect to degrees arose in the Female Institute because that institution was becoming various things to various women. Not all the work that it was offering had a clear relation to the work of the College. For the women who completed in the Institute either the Classical or the Scientific Program the door to the sophomore class in the College was open. But the situation was otherwise for women who completed the Literary Program of the Institute and then decided to pursue a collegiate career. Their problem was solved when the Trustees, on January 12, 1905, voted that graduates of this program could, by completing eighteen courses of study in the College, receive the degree of Bachelor of Letters; [46] and the Catalogue for 1904–05 specified that this additional work should be done in the "College of Liberal Arts." [47] At the commencement in June, 1905, two persons were awarded the degree of Bachelor of Letters. Not many acquired this degree. It was awarded for the last time in June, 1912, although then, oddly enough, it was called Bachelor of Literature.[48] By that year the Institute was approaching the end of its career.

Because of the curricular changes heretofore described, the way to the degree of Bachelor of Arts became increasingly easy to those who could not, or would not, stomach much Latin and Greek. Until the year 1902–03, only those who pursued the Classical Program could receive this degree. In November, 1902, however, the faculty voted that a candidate for the degree of Bachelor of Philosophy could, by offering "eight courses [later increased to nine] in either of the ancient classical languages," receive the degree of Bachelor of Arts.[49] The program in Jurisprudence, introduced the next year, also led to the degree of Bachelor of Arts, despite the fact that it had no requirement in Greek. Moreover, by 1908–09 candidates for the degree of Bachelor of Philosophy could get the degree of Bachelor of Arts by offering either nine courses in Latin or Greek, or, "in addition to the required work in Latin or Greek," nine courses in a modern language; and by 1915–16 the Catalogue made perfectly clear the fact that one of these modern languages could be English.[50] Furthermore, by this time the requirement of Greek in the Classical Program did not extend beyond the second term of the sophomore year, nor the requirement in Latin beyond the first term of that year.

The condition of the Department of Greek worsened with the passing years so much that the faculty, on January 8, 1918, sanctioned, because of "changed conditions," a beginning course in the study of Greek—"allowing the candidate full credit" therefor; [51] and the Catalogue for 1917–18 tells us, for the first time in the history of the University, that students could begin the study of Greek in the College.[52] Between 1914–15 and 1917–18, the enrollment in classes in Greek had become pitifully small, and most of the students that the professor of Greek, Thomas F. Hamblin, was then teaching were enrolled either in Greek history or in Greek Masterpieces, courses which required no knowledge of the Greek language.[53] The Department of Latin had suffered less, for in the issue of the Catalogue for 1917–18 we learn that there still were "four terms of required work in Latin and eleven of elective" in the Classical and Philosophical Programs.[54]

Not only were the requirements for the bachelor's degree affected by curricular changes made during Harris's administration; the requirements for the master's degree underwent what might well be called revolutionary changes, one of which was the adoption of a program leading to the master's degree *pro merito* and the other the discontinuance of the practice of awarding a master's degree "in course." The introduction of post-graduate work leading to an earned master's degree presumably had its beginning in June, 1891, when the faculty requested, and the Trustees approved, a plan by which graduates of Bucknell might pursue advanced courses leading to the degrees of Master of Arts, Master of Philosophy, and Master of Science.[55] Before this time the degree of Master of Arts had been granted either "in course" after three years or had been awarded *honoris causa,* and for some time thereafter it would continue to be so offered. By the year 1902–03 this degree was no longer being given "in course," but as late as June, 1917, a degree of Master of Arts was conferred *honoris causa.*[56]

Statements made in the minutes of the faculty, in issues of the Catalogue beginning with that of 1891–92, and elsewhere make reasonably clear the changing requirements for the earned master's degree. We are told that in 1894 the program leading to this degree consisted of nine courses, three of which must be taken in one department, that the work could be pursued in residence or out of residence, and that the program was restricted to graduates of Bucknell only because of the large number of undergraduates in the University. By vote of the faculty in October, 1900, the program was opened to graduates of other colleges. In November, 1902, the faculty approved the granting of both a bachelor's and a master's degree at the end of four years of study, provided that the candidate therefor had completely forty-five full courses, had achieved the standing of *summa cum laude,* and had received no grade below 90 in any of his courses.[57] Earlier in that year the faculty had voted that the degree of Master of Arts would be conferred upon those entering after June, 1902, only "on examination in studies recommended by the Faculty." [58] A year later the faculty decided that the residential requirement for the master's degree could be satisfied either by one year of non-professional work in any university "of standing" or by two years of work in any professional school "of standing." [59] By the year 1909–10 it was requiring that two-thirds of the work for a master's degree be done in one department, and this requirement was in force as late as the year 1918–19.[60]

In the year 1902–03 the University ceased to offer the degree of Master of Philosophy, but by the year 1906–07 it was offering, besides the degrees of Master of Arts and Master of Science, the professional degrees of Civil Engineer and Electrical Engineer.[61] The practice of awarding an earned advanced degree after a year of post-graduate study was now well established in Bucknell University, but as yet no department of advanced studies had been organized, and as late as 1918–19 no visible administration of such a program existed outside the office of the president, the person to whom inquirers about advanced degrees were requested to turn for "particulars." [62]

By such institutional expansion and curricular growth as we have examined, the faculty naturally had been considerably influenced. It had increased greatly in size. Whereas in 1889–90 there were eight professors (including the president) and one instructor, in 1917–18, the first year of our participation in the First World War, there were twenty professors, seven instructors, and four lecturers. In that year no member of the faculty held the rank of assistant professor, but that title was in use. It had been conferred upon Nelson F. Davis in 1899 and had been borne also by some other men who subsequently became full professors. The rank of associate professor was not used in the University during the administration of President Harris. Alongside the faculty, but not altogether distinct from it, the "administration" had grown, but not excessively. The administrative work that was being done in 1889 by a professor-president, a full-time business manager (soon to be called registrar), and a part-time librarian was being done in 1918 by the same professor-president, the dean of the College, the dean of the Department of Women, the dean of the Summer School, a registrar, a superintendent of buildings and grounds, and a part-time librarian. The registrar excepted, all these persons were giving a part of their time to teaching.

Some change also had taken place in the professional preparation of the faculty. In 1889 all the professors held the degree of Master of Arts, presumably granted "in course," and three of them also held honorary degrees of Doctor of Philosophy, one of which had been awarded by Bucknell to Freeman Loomis, who had passed two years in advanced study in Germany.[63] Professor George G. Groff, who was an honorary Doctor of Laws, also held, as we already have learned, the earned degree of Doctor of Medicine. The one instructor in that year, Miss Ada Carlton Groom, held only the degree of Bachelor of Arts. By 1918 all except eight of the professors held either professional or doctoral degrees. Of the doctoral degrees so held all but five were honorary and of the five that were not honorary three had been awarded *pro merito* pursuant to a peculiar idea that soon was abandoned. In 1901 Ephraim M. Heim and in 1902 Henry T. Colestock each received from Bucknell the degree of Doctor of Philosophy for work done in the University of Chicago; and in 1903, without specifying the reason therefor, the faculty voted to confer upon Nelson F. Davis the degree of Doctor of Science *pro merito*.[64] Accordingly, these three degrees do not appear in the records of the University as honorary degrees. The two members of the faculty who then held the earned degree of Doctor of Philosophy from other institutions were Lincoln Hulley (Chicago, 1895) and Floyd G. Ballentine (Harvard, 1903). President Harris encouraged the members of his faculty, particularly the younger ones, to continue their graduate studies, and after the close of his administration two of the younger professors and several of the instructors of the year 1917–18 acquired the earned degree of Doctor of Philosophy. Eventually one of them, Benjamin W. Griffith, received a doctor's degree from the University of Paris.

Before the First World War, American universities had not completely supplanted European universities, especially those of Germany, as places of advanced study for Americans. Consequently, some members of the faculty of Bucknell after 1900, like some members of this faculty in earlier years, went to Germany to study, although no one of them acquired a degree from a German University. Of those who went abroad to study, the pioneer was Freeman Loomis, who was in Germany between 1870 and 1872.[65] Subsequently, George G. Groff was there in 1886, Frank E. Rockwood in 1888, and William G. Owens in 1889.[66] After 1900, G. L. C. Reimer, Paul G. Stolz, and Leo L. Rockwell studied in Germany.[67] As noted above, Professor Griffith studied in France.

By the end of the nineteenth century, if not earlier, the lavish distribution of honorary degrees by American colleges and universities was being sharply called in question in this country. Emphatically was this true in respect to the degree of Doctor of Philosophy. Increasingly professors and other teachers who had earned this degree in reputable institutions were being annoyed by the knowledge that, for no reason that was obvious, some of their colleagues were being decorated with the degree of Doctor of Philosophy, either by the institutions which employed them or by other institutions operating under a gentlemen's understanding that such courtesies ought to be exchanged. Before long the practice of not granting honorary degrees of Doctor of Philosophy would become one of the criteria for determining the academic respectability of an American college or university.

Like other such institutions, Bucknell from its beginning had not been averse to the granting of honorary degrees. By the end of the nineteenth century, it had acquired a long list of honorary alumni, most of them Doctors of Divinity, Doctors of Law, or Masters of Arts; but it had still other kinds of honorary doctors on its list: one of civil law, one of music, four of science, and seventeen of philosophy.[68] To three members of its faculty it had awarded *honoris causa* the degree of Doctor of Philosophy: to Justin R. Loomis in 1854, to Francis W. Tustin in 1879, and to Freeman Loomis in 1889. But after 1893 it never again awarded this degree *honoris causa,* and in 1899 the faculty pledged itself not "to grant an honorary degree of Doctor of Philosophy or any Bachelor's degree except upon work done." [69] Thirteen years later, in order "to comply with the regulations of the Education Department of the State of New York for registration as a recognized institution," the faculty in a recommendation which the Trustees approved on June 18, 1912, reaffirmed this pledge, saying, "The bachelor's degree in arts, science, philosophy or literature and the doctor's degree in philosophy will not be conferred *honoris causa.*" [70] But the giving and the receiving of other honorary degrees continued. During the 1920's, several older members of the faculty of Bucknell received honorary degrees from another institution, and in 1924 Bucknell conferred upon one of its recently appointed professors the honorary degree of Doctor of Literature.[71]

Meetings of the faculty during the administration of President Harris were less frequent than such meetings had been in earlier years. Because of the greater number of students, weekly meetings of the faculty for the purpose of recording grades became, as President Harris said, impracticable, and so regular meetings of the faculty were held at the beginning and at the end of each term, and special meetings were called when necessary. "The meetings," President Harris wrote without either irony or humor, "were strictly for business, whereby much time was saved and harmony promoted." [72] During his administration, the book of minutes of the faculty bulged not only with schedules of lectures, of recitations, of examinations, and of commencement exercises, but also with lists of students admitted and with lists of students graduated. Accordingly, it has great statistical value, but the minutes of the faculty of this era do not sparkle as do the minutes of an earlier era when Francis W. Tustin was secretary.

As in earlier eras, so also in that of John Howard Harris, schedules of recitations and of lectures made by the faculty are of great interest to us, for they tell us when classes were held and lectures delivered, what each instructor was teaching and how heavy or how light was his teaching schedule. Ordinarily a teaching schedule consisted of fifteen hours. Three times a year such schedules were made, for the University then operated, as it had from the beginning, pursuant to a three-term system. As the years went by, the schedules of classes became longer, and by the spring term of 1917 the hours for holding classes were as follows: 8:15, 9:15, 10:15, 11:15, 1:15, 2:15, 3:15, and a night class for students studying "Bills & Notes." [73] Courses of lectures for the four classes, each such course to be given by a member of the faculty, were scheduled for 8:15 on Mondays. Through long years, as we recall, such lectures had been given on Thursday mornings, immediately after chapel. In the course of time lectures were scheduled for both Mondays and Thursdays, but from 1895 on such lectures were given on Monday mornings only.[74]

We turn now to the subject of students and their concerns during President Harris's administration. Students in those years could hardly help being interested observers, as most of them no doubt could hardly help being eager supporters, of the institutional change and curricular growth that appeared to be opening to them new avenues to varied and richer lives. For them everything was changing; even the procedure for admission was modified as the years went by. Whereas in earlier years the problem had been that of making examinations for admission convenient for those who wished to take them, the problem in later years became that of finding ways to admit students without their taking such examinations. Throughout Harris's administration the old practice of holding an examination on Monday of Commencement Week for admission to the College was continued, and from 1890 on another such examination was held before the opening of the autumn term in September.[75] But the practice, begun at the suggestion of the Alumni Association in June, 1881, of also holding in Philadelphia, Pittsburgh, Harrisburg, and Scranton "local" examinations for the admission of students was discontinued after 1900.

Already, however, the procedure for admission was undergoing a change. Even before the time of Harris a few students had been admitted to the College on the "certificates" of the principals of respected academies, but not until the academic year 1896–97 was a statement about this matter printed in the Catalogue. In that Catalogue we are told that the University would admit without examination, besides the graduates of its own preparatory schools, the graduates of Pennsylvania

State Normal Schools and the graduates of preparatory schools of high grade; and by the year 1901–02 the graduates of approved high schools were also being admitted without examination.[76] Most significant, however, of all the changes in respect to admission was the one announced in the Catalogue for 1902–03. Here we are told that the University would accept certificates of the College Entrance Examination Board for the Middle States and Maryland.[77] This Board had been organized late in 1899, largely through the efforts of Charles W. Eliot and Nicholas Murray Butler,[78] and not later than the beginning of 1902 Bucknell had become a member of it, for on February 4 of that year the faculty elected Professor Frank E. Rockwood to represent the University on this Board.[79] Subsequently, in 1906–07, the University announced that, in addition to the foregoing certificates, the University would accept both the certificates of the State Board for Examining Candidates for Registration as Students of Law and the Regents' certificates of the State of New York.[80] Accordingly, we may safely presume that, well before the end of President Harris's administration, a great many students were being admitted to the College each year without formal examination.

The cost of attending the University increased somewhat with the passing years. Oddly, from our standpoint, the cost of tuition in 1918–19 was only $50 a year, which was what it had been in 1889–90.[81] Living costs, however, had advanced, and well before 1918 students were required to pay various and sundry fees, the number and the amount thereof depending upon their respective programs of study. During the year 1899–1900, men who lived in the College Building were charged (tuition included) $90 a year, and men who roomed in the town were charged $75. These charges did not include board, for, outside the Academy, the University did not operate a dining room for men. In this same year boarding students in the Academy, if they lived in the Main Hall, were charged (tuition included) $185 a year, and, if they lived in East Hall, $230; and also in the same year students who were boarders in the Female Institute were charged (tuition included) $230 a year.[82] In 1918–19 men who roomed in College buildings were charged (without board) $160 a year, and regular boarding students in the Women's College were charged $375 a year.[83] Before this time both the Academy and the Institute had ceased to exist.

Changing conditions in this era affected profoundly the interests of students that found expression in organized activities. Some of their older organizations continued to function, but numerous new ones, as soon we shall see, arose as reflections of the increasing diversity of the interests of the students. Moreover, in this period as never before, the spirit of promotion informed the thinking of the students, who boasted in their publications of the progress toward excellence that their institution was making, but who also, at the same time, revealed their awareness of its lack of some things without which no college could be first-rate. For them, in this period, a principal reason for striving was not to keep up with the Joneses, but to catch up with them. To be both frank and blunt, students of Bucknell in this period were to some extent afflicted with an inferiority complex.

Among the older organizations, the four classes continued to function with considerable vigor, notwithstanding the increasing number of students and the growing diversity of instructional offerings. The class organizations were fostered by the administration, and as late as 1919 a date for the election of class officers was still being published in the calendar of the University.[84] Numerous ceremonies associated with one or another of the classes arose from time to time, but few of them hardened into enduring traditions. Early in the twentieth century the annual freshman-sophomore "rush" was attracting considerable attention. Of this affair in 1906 the collegiate newspaper affirmed that it "not only engages the attention of the student body, but attracts numbers of the citizens of the town to the Hill on the day of the occurrence. From year to year its recurrence is looked forward to and it has assumed a place in the student's calendar almost equal in interest to Commencement."[85] However that may have been, this affair, if it long persisted, soon lost its value as news. So also of the "annual moving up pee-rade" of the freshman class, a noisy procession of freshmen in pajamas, of which we catch a fleeting glimpse in 1913, although we are told that this procession by that time had been an annual occurrence for several years.[86]

More interesting and more significant were two exercises of the senior class. One of these, called the mantle ceremony, was begun by the Class of 1899, and it persisted at least through the year 1909.[87] It was a dignified ceremony held during Commencement Week as a symbolic turning over of "power" by the graduating class to a representative of the class immediately below it. "The most beautiful and most pleasing of Bucknell's traditional exercises is the mantle ceremony," we are told in the morning edition of the *Commencement News* for June 21, 1905. "A member of the Senior class bestows a Mantle upon a representative Junior. This Mantle is symbolic of the power, dignity, and importance of the Seniors which from this time for one year become attributes of the succeeding class." Yet this ceremony, if it were continued more than a few years, also lost its value as news.

More enduring, it appears, than any other practice by a class (that of the publication of *L'Agenda* by the junior class being no exception) has been the practice of the senior class to leave a parting gift to the University. The history of this practice is far from clear. It is known that the Class of 1865 gave a tree, and that its example was followed by several subsequent classes. The Class of 1875 inserted as its memorial an inscribed block of granite in the wall to the left of the principal entrance to Old Main, the Class of 1880 decorated Commencement Hall, and thereafter for several years the giving of books to the library became a common practice of graduating classes. The Class of 1901 planted a maple tree near the entrance to the campus from University Avenue, and by this time the practice of giving a class memorial was firmly established. The Class of 1902 gave "the marble posts at the chapel entrance to the grounds," and through subsequent years classes made gifts of physical objects that varied both in character and in size. The clock on the top of what then was West College (now Kress Hall) was, for example, the gift of the Class of 1907.[88] Somewhat unusual was the gift which the Class of 1956 made to endow a lectureship to be awarded annually to a member of the faculty of Bucknell in recognition of inspirational teaching.[89]

The older collegiate literary societies, Euepia and Theta Alpha, like similar societies in the Academy and in the Female Institute, had lost much of their early influence before the beginning of Harris's administration. Although they persisted into the twentieth century, their existence was precarious, despite the numerous efforts that were made to point out the advantages of such societies.[90] In 1895 the collegiate women organized such a society of their own, the Zeta Society, and in June, 1897, the faculty granted this society representation equal to that of Euepia and Theta Alpha on the platform when the annual lecture was delivered before the literary societies during Commencement Week.[91] But, despite all the "promotional" labors to keep them alive, and despite joint meetings of the societies of the Academy and the Institute, the literary societies in all the branches of the University gradually faded out. As early as December, 1895, the editor of the *Bucknell Mirror* put his finger upon the real cause of their decline when he wrote that half of the meetings of the "University Literary Societies were broken up this term by entertainments and socials connected with the school."[92] By this time students had acquired numerous interests, and many of their new interests seemed to them more important than the older literary interests. *L'Agenda* of 1906 carried a memorial notice of the Zeta Society.[93] Euepia and Theta Alpha lingered on for a few years, but the last lecture before these societies during a Commencement Week was delivered in 1908.[94] In 1912 both of these societies were revived and reorganized, and apparently about this time the Zeta Society also was revived, but they did not regain their former vitality. Their names appeared in the Catalogue for 1916–17, but in no subsequent issue thereof.[95]

Another student organization that flourished during the administration of President Harris was the social fraternity, and in that era fraternities enriched the social life of the campus, improved the living conditions of many students, and to some extent set one group of students against another. Like the elective system of studies, Bucknell accepted fraternities and sororities, but both the elective system and the system of fraternities and sororities were regulated by the faculty. On March 11, 1898, the faculty approved "An Act for the Regulation and Improvement of College Fraternities" which affirmed that, after April 1 of that year, no student in the College could join a fraternity during his first year, nor until he had completed the work of the freshman year; and, moreover, it also affirmed that he could be received into a fraternity only on a certificate from the president of the University showing that he was eligible to membership therein. It provided also that no student should be pledged to a fraternity except pursuant to the foregoing specifications, that no person should be admitted into the College as a freshman or as a special student who, after the posting of this act, should have become a member of any fraternity, and, finally, that no secret fraternities formed by classes would be permitted in the College. This act applied to both sororities and fraternities, and, with some minor additions and modifications, remained the law governing fraternities and sororities at Bucknell during the administration of President Harris.[96] Essential facts about the emergence and the continuance of fraternities and sororities at Bucknell have been preserved in successive issues of *L'Agenda.*

The organization that tended more than any other in this era to strengthen the bonds which were uniting the students was the one which, beginning on March 10, 1897, published the *Orange and Blue,* a weekly collegiate newspaper which became the *Bucknellian* on November 8, 1915, and which is still being published under that name.[97] Its appearance made necessary a change of policy for the *Bucknell Mirror,* which had begun publication as a monthly under the name of *University Mirror* in 1882 and had continued, soon after its name was changed in 1893, as a semi-monthly. The *Mirror* became, more or less, a literary magazine and continued to appear through May, 1906. It was revived in October, 1921, but lasted only through the issue of June, 1923.

The students of this period had other publications, two of which were annuals: the yearbook, *L'Agenda,* and the *Students' Hand Book,* a guide to the University which the collegiate Y.M.C.A. had been publishing since 1893. Still another publication of that era, one which made clear the fact that the students in the College were not yet completely "integrated," appeared for the first time in December, 1915, under the title of *Bucknell Women's Journal.* It was a quarterly magazine edited and published by the women of the College. It was discontinued after the issue of June, 1918.

To complete the list of publications by students in the University during that era, attention must be called, first of all, to a monthly paper called *Der Zeit-Geist,* published by students of the Academy between 1910 and 1914, and, secondly, to an irregular, mysterious, gadflyish pamphlet which appeared from time to time, between 1907 and 1918, under the name of the *Woodpecker*. In spirit, but not in format, the *Woodpecker* was a legitimate offspring of the "burlesques" of earlier years.

The activity which was best advertised by publications conducted by students, which perhaps concerned more students than any other activity, and which produced more headaches for both the faculty and the Board of Trustees than even the fraternities produced, was the activity of athletic sports. Some years before Harris became President of Bucknell, such sports had entered this institution to stay. Accordingly, the problem of athletic sports had become one not to do away with, but one to live with. It was, moreover, a problem that broadened and became more troublesome with the passing years, thanks in large part to the "prestige" that a college then was presumed to acquire by having winning teams. Since Bucknell had large aspirations to become recognized as first-rate, it would have its share of troubles arising from the participation of its teams in intercollegiate athletic sports. In general, the "big problems" that it faced are easy to define. From the standpoint of the faculty and the administration there was the problem of so controlling such matters as to maintain high academic standards, to prevent students from "over-participating" in athletic events, and to keep the Athletic Association from becoming insolvent; from the standpoint of the students there was the problem of getting enough money to improve the athletic grounds (now called Loomis Field), to pay for adequate coaching, and to defray various and sundry expenses; and from the standpoint of the Trustees there was the problem of "legislating" in such ways as to preserve the standing and well-being of the University and to prevent students from being "taxed" against their will to help support something which they either disliked or thought that they could not afford to support.

Adequate regulation of athletic sports was a problem that was not peculiar to Bucknell; it had become a national problem. By the early 1890's the nation was becoming appalled at the number of persons who were maimed or killed in football games. In January, 1894, Professor George G. Groff, a member of the faculty of Bucknell and a physician, called the game "barbarous and rough," and the "travesty of athleticism." [98] About a year later President Charles W. Eliot of Harvard affirmed that this game, "as now played," was "unfit for college use." [99] Yet six years later he thought that the situation was greatly improved, and that Harvard had discovered a plan to regulate sports that other institutions would accept.[100] But time would show that Eliot had found no certain cure for all the evils of intercollegiate athletics; and it was in a time when abuses in intercollegiate athletic sports were many that such sports came of age in Bucknell University.

At Bucknell, between 1889 and 1919, football, baseball, basketball, track, and tennis became intercollegiate sports in which students might earn the letter "B"; and the most glamorous of these was football.[101] Here there is no space, as here there is no need, to trace through this period the history of each of these sports at Bucknell. From 1897 on they were promoted by the collegiate newspaper, and their accomplishments and their failures were published therein; and a summary of each year's athletic history was recorded in *L'Agenda* and, more fully, in the *Commencement News.* Accordingly, since such information is thus obtainable, it remains only to show how the problems of athletics at Bucknell were dealt with during the administration of President Harris.

The Tustin Gymnasium, available in 1890, made possible the linking of physical education with athletic sports. Here athletes could keep themselves in training during the months of winter, and here also gymnastic exercises could be taken by other students, or could be forced upon them. A director of the gymnasium was employed for the year 1890–91, and from that year forward exercise in the gymnasium was required of all students, the men taking theirs in the Tustin Gymnasium and the women taking theirs in their own "Calistheneum," which was the top floor of the building now called Harris Hall.[102]

Beginning with the year 1892–93 and continuing through the year 1898–99, at least two instructors, or directors, were employed for the gymnasium, one of whom, Harvey F. Smith, served for two years before entering upon training that prepared him to become a distinguished surgeon; and these men served also as coaches of athletic sports. During the year 1899–1900, George W. Hoskins began at Bucknell a career as physical director that lasted through the year 1910–11.[103] He coached several sports, one of which was football. Whether he was coach of football during all those years, we cannot be certain; but as late as 1906 it was still the practice at Bucknell for the physical director to coach the football team, although he might be assisted in this work by any alumnus whom the Athletic Association saw fit to select.[104]

One of the interesting consequences of using the gymnasium for the training of athletes in winter was the rise at Bucknell, in 1895, of the game of basketball. This game was introduced by William C. Gretzinger and Charles Firth as a winter sport "primarily as an aid to football" by "keeping men in good trim during the winter"; but, as one writer tells us, the "need of a winter sport assured it a permanent place on our athletic calendar." [105] It quickly became a major athletic sport for men.[106] Nor was this all. Soon basketball was "taking the Bucknell girls by storm," and in January, 1896, a writer for the *Bucknell Mirror* suggested that the girls' team be allowed to use the Tustin Gymnasium because the girls' gymnasium was "too small for practice." [107]

By the beginning of the year 1898, the faculty had made at least two enduring regulations in respect to participation by students in athletic contests. One of these, which appeared in the Catalogue for 1890–91, provided that the Athletic Association could not arrange any "match games" without the consent of the faculty.[108] The other, approved on January 6, 1898, was much broader in scope. It barred from participation in any extracurricular activity, including that of being a member "of any contesting athletic team," every student who was not free of all academic deficiencies.[109] Ten years later, in another regulation applicable only to athletic affairs, it forbade not only participation in athletic contests as a member of a University team, but also membership in the Athletic Association, to any person not "regularly registered" in the College and carrying at least seventeen hours of work a week.[110] In other words, athletic floaters or adventurers were not wanted at Bucknell.

In still other ways the faculty acted to control athletic sports. It determined the number of games that could be played on any trip, and it also determined the number that could be played in any season.[111] In the course of time it acquired an important voice in the affairs of the Athletic Association. Pursuant to the constitution of this Association that was adopted in December, 1906, it was entitled to two memberships on the executive board of the Association, but was not empowered to elect these members.[112] This arrangement left something to be desired, for the Athletic Association obviously needed strict supervision in respect to its fiscal affairs. The faculty did not obtain effective participation in the affairs of the Athletic Association until June 20, 1911, when the Trustees approved a plan adopted earlier by the faculty that vested, subject to the control of the faculty, the management of athletics at Bucknell in an executive committee elected annually and consisting of three members of the faculty chosen by the faculty, two members of the Alumni Association chosen by that association, and two undergraduate students elected by the Athletic Association. Also, the plan empowered the faculty to appoint one of its members on the executive committee to serve as comptroller to supervise the finances of the Association. The secretary of the executive committee was empowered to supervise all the correspondence of the Association.[113] The faculty elected Professors Ephraim M. Heim, Thomas F. Hamblin, and Benjamin W. Griffith its representatives on the "Athletic Board" and appointed Professor Griffith the "financial comptroller" of the Athletic Association.[114] A year later President Harris reported to the Trustees that the new arrangements were working well.[115] They were still in operation at the end of his administration.

To finance their athletic operations the students had struggled through many years to find adequate means. Their Athletic Association, a voluntary body whose membership was open to any student on the payment of one dollar annually, was not uniformly well supported. Occasionally it did well; frequently it was embarrassed by debt.[116] In 1898 some of the students sought relief by asking the Trustees to add to the tuition bill of each student the sum of $5 for the benefit of the Athletic Association. The Trustees refused such aid, as they did again two years later.[117] In 1905 the Association tried, with some success, the plan of selling season tickets for $5 each.[118] Eventually, the Association aroused the sympathy of one group of the alumni. In 1911 the Bucknell Club of Pittsburgh requested that such a fee be charged, but the Trustees, after months of consideration, voted in January, 1912, that the cost of "competing teams" should be defrayed by money obtained from the voluntary purchase of tickets.[119]

In the summer of 1913 the idea of maintaining all the major activities of students by a budget supported by a compulsory annual fee of $10 was under discussion at Bucknell, and by the beginning of 1915–16 such a budget, resting on voluntary contributions, was in operation.[120] It was not entirely successful, but nothing better was worked out before June, 1918, when the Trustees voted that intercollegiate athletics be dispensed with for the duration of the war.[121] But the subject of a compulsory budget was up again in 1919, and on June 23 of that year the Trustees referred the matter to their Committee on Finance.[122] In October, 1919, the *Bucknell Alumni Monthly* announced that the compulsory fee had been authorized, and that henceforth all students at Bucknell would be "taxed $10.00 for the support of the most prominent student activities." [123]

Because of the broadening of interests in an era characterized by change, life on the campus of Bucknell by 1919 had become more varied, more interesting, and more urbane. Psychologically and emotionally, despite an increasing diversity of activities, the "Hill" and the "Grove" in that year were more nearly one than they had been in 1889. Now all the students had become collegiate students, for both the Academy and the Institute had ceased to exist, and the Women's College, unlike the Institute, designated only a place of residence for collegiate women, not a particular branch of the University. Now, except for a few activities, the men and the women of Bucknell were pursuing their extracurricular activities in common. The "Bucknell spirit," moreover, had given them more yells and more songs. The list of yells in the *Students' Hand Book* for 1915–16, although still headed by the old "Yah! Yah! Yoo!," included, *inter alia,* "Ray! the Team!" and "Give-er-ell! Bucknell!" Furthermore, the songs of Bucknell, including "Dear Bucknell," that had been published in 1897 by the class of that year had been superseded in 1913 by a more comprehensive collection, edited by Professors William C. Bartol and Paul G. Stolz and published through the generosity of David Porter Leas, the treasurer of the University, under the name of *Bucknell Song Book.*[124] It was from this book that the Glee Club in 1915 published a pamphlet of songs called *Selections.*

Nevertheless, despite enormous change, there were still some things in the routine of life on the campus in 1919 that were reminiscent of earlier years. Attendance at chapel at the beginning of each working day was still required of all students, as was also attendance at religious services every Sunday. One thing of earlier days, however, had been missing for several years before 1919—the Day of Prayer for Colleges. In his reminiscences President Harris says that, when the Y.M.C.A. "adopted a Sunday service with the same purpose as the Day of Prayer," he decided, in 1897, to make a change from a one-day observance to a "week of religious inspiration and instruction." [125] But as to the date of this change his memory failed him, for the annual sermon before the Y.M.C.A. was being preached earlier than the beginning of his administration, and the Day of Prayer for Colleges retained its place in the calendar of the University as late as 1908–09.[126] Be that as it may, the work of the Christian Associations continued through these years and perhaps, socially as well as spiritually, gained in significance. Beginning with the year 1912–13, the Y.M.C.A. had a full-time secretary.[127] But it never acquired a building of its own.

The conduct of the students also showed improvement. Rowdyism on the Hill had been greatly reduced before 1919. No longer, for example, was there "horn-tooting" at visitors on the campus. "Thanks to some refining influence at work among our students," the *Bucknell Mirror* affirmed in October, 1893, "the 'Texas Rangers,' the 'Night Hawks' and all such barbarous organizations belong to the past." [128] With the passing years even the troublesome practice of hazing was brought under control, and by 1914 the sophomores were denied the right to haze the freshmen. This "duty" was taken over by the upperclassmen, and was used by them to discipline freshmen who had "done something contrary to the laws and customs of the college," and who would not "listen to proper reasoning." [129] By this time, indeed, important steps toward self-government had been taken. The Women's Student Government Association, which became effective on March 31, 1913, established on November 5 of that year an "honor system" which not only bound each girl in the Association neither to give nor to receive "illegitimate aid" in an examination, but also obligated the Association to enforce the rules of that system.[130] Meanwhile on the Hill the Senior Council, a small group of seniors appointed by the president of the senior class, had come into being during 1913–14. It consisted of a representative from each of the fraternities and of two representatives from the non-fraternity group. It met once a week for the purpose of discussing and settling "matters pertaining to the student life 'on the Hill,' which do not come directly under faculty supervision." It appears that it did its work well, and within a short time it was said to be "recognized as the student governing body at Bucknell." [131]

Beginning early in the 1890's, new interests, some of them ephemeral, found expression in newer kinds of clubs or societies on the campus of Bucknell. These organizations ranged from a Chess Club in 1893, a Pedestrian Club in 1896, and a variety of contemporaneous musical clubs to various and sundry clubs or societies which foreshadowed some of the departmental "honor societies" of a later era. A Chemical and Physical Society was formed in 1891, a Natural History Society in 1894, and a French Club in 1894.[132] After the opening of the new century, the forming of new organizations by students continued, the new clubs and societies ranging in kind from the T Square Club in 1901 to *Der Deutsche Verein* in 1906, to the Rifle Club in 1915, and to the Campfire Girls in 1917.[133] Significant expressions of a growing professional outlook, moreover, were shown in the rise of the Medical Society in 1908, the Law Club in 1909, the societies of the four engineering groups formed at different times, and the Intercollegiate Debating League formed during the year 1911–12.[134] Of the organizations of earlier years, the ones that seemed to be most stable after 1900 were, besides the dramatic clubs, Frill and Frown and Cap and Dagger, the Band, the Bucknell Orchestra, and the Men's Glee Club.[135] The one organization toward which the faculty, alumni, and students continued to look longingly was the Phi Beta Kappa Society. As early as 1902, the Alumni Association appointed a committee to see about getting a chapter of this society for Bucknell. In June, 1903, the faculty approved not only a petition for such a chapter, but also a "scholarship society" for students of Bucknell. This society, it was hoped, would obtain "recognition as a chapter of Phi Beta Kappa." [136] But all efforts to obtain for Bucknell a chapter of Phi Beta Kappa were unsuccessful until nearly forty years later, when Bucknell had come somewhat closer to being the "Greater Bucknell" dreamed of in the era of John Howard Harris.

Part Four

New Orientations

President Howard Malcom
1851–1857

President Justin R. Loomis
1857–1879

President David Jayne Hill
1879–1888

President John Howard Harris
1889–1919

President Emory W. Hunt
1919–1931

President Homer P. Rainey
1931–1935

President Arnaud C. Marts
Acting 1935–1938
President 1938–1945

President Herbert L. Spencer
1945–1949

President Horace A. Hildreth
1949–1953

President Merle M. Odgers
1954–1964

In 1932 an early morning fire destroyed the central part of Old Main and gutted the wings

Old Main was restored in 1937, and its central part was named Daniel C. Roberts Hall

Looking backward and forward

During the Centennial observance, Bucknell coeds reënacted the bicycle race of by-gone days

Notables at the Centennial Commencement, shown with Herbert L. Spencer (left), president of the University, included (l. to r.) George W. Maxey, a justice of the Supreme Court of Pennsylvania, Edward Martin, governor of Pennsylvania, and Martin Clement, president of the Pennsylvania Railroad Company

The Vaughan Literature Building

The Davis Gymnasium and the Freas-Rooke Swimming Pool

The Charles A. Dana Engineering Building

The F. W. Olin Science Building

The Ellen Clarke Bertrand Library

The James S. Swartz Hall, one of the residences for men

The William H. Coleman Hall, Bucknell's largest classroom building

10

Reorganization and Modernization

Bucknell should keep to the guiding purpose expressed by Arnold of Rugby: first, religious and moral principle; secondly, gentlemanly conduct; thirdly, intellectual ability.—*Emory W. Hunt, Report to the Trustees, 1919–1929.*

During the administration of President Hunt, great freedom has been given to the faculty to conduct and develop the University along democratic lines.—*Memorials of Bucknell University, 1919–1931.*

The most striking change in educational thought, during these twelve years, appears in the fact that the dominant trio in 1919, Greek, Latin, and mathematics, is wholly eliminated from the list of subjects prescribed in 1931.—*Memorials of Bucknell University, 1919–1931.*

As President Harris had foreseen, his successor would be the chief administrator of a changing Bucknell University. Whether he wished to be so or not, the new president, like Harris before him, would of necessity be a promoter; for a growing university would need more money to provide more buildings, more teachers, and better accommodations for a larger and a more demanding body of students. The post-war changes at Bucknell began quickly and continued throughout the decade of the 1920's. By 1930 Bucknell had become larger, more prosperous, more modern, and more widely recognized than ever before. Its campus had been much enlarged (as President Harris had hoped that it would be), its physical plant had been expanded and improved, its library had grown and had become more serviceable, its teaching staff had been enlarged and had become more competent, its programs of instruction had been adjusted to meet important demands of a new era, and its faculty as never before was participating in the internal administration of the University.

The man who presided over these changes was Dr. Emory William Hunt, a minister and an educator, whose preceding career had been strikingly similar to that of Dr. Howard Malcom, the first president of Bucknell. Dr. Hunt was born in East Clarence, New York, on February 2, 1862. He was graduated by the University of Rochester in 1884 and by the Crozer Theological Seminary three years later. From 1887, the year of his ordination, until 1902, he held pastorates in Toledo and in Boston. In January, 1902, he became president of Denison University, a position which he left in June, 1913, to become general secretary of the American Baptist Foreign Missionary Society. From 1915 until 1919, he was pastor of the First Baptist Church in Newton Center, Massachusetts. In the meantime, he had received two honorary degrees: that of Doctor of Divinity from Denison in 1901 and that of Doctor of Laws from the University of Rochester in 1902. On February 2, 1919, he was elected, and on June 4 of that year inaugurated, president of Bucknell University.[1]

To this task Dr. Hunt brought in a difficult time not only experience and maturity of judgment, but also, like Howard Malcom before him, urbanity, *savoir-faire,* and a goodly store of both wit and humor. He would have need of these qualities, for from the beginning he was confronted with a task of reorganization and expansion in a time when endowment at Bucknell was meager and when neither tuition nor salaries had been adjusted to inflated prices. In 1919 Bucknell was in urgent need of more money to meet the demands of the post-war years. The problem of finance, however, was one whose solution the Trustees should take the lead in seeking. Consequently, during the first few months of the academic year 1919–20, the faculty, with the approval and co-operation of President Hunt, turned its attention to the matter of internal reorganization, something which, as not a few persons thought, was long overdue.

Numerous changes that reflected a new spirit of administration came rapidly during 1919–20. They began on June 4, 1919, when the Trustees approved a statement of principles and plans which Dean Llewellyn Phillips had submitted to their Committee on Instruction at a meeting on April 24, 1919, which Dr. Hunt had attended. This statement, approved by this committee and referred to the Trustees, affirmed, *inter alia,* that

> The administration of the University shall be conducted by Committees of the Board and Faculty. The President of the University shall be ex

officio a member of every Committee of the Board and Faculty; the Dean a member of the Faculty Committees only.

Although this statement designated ten committees of the faculty that should be appointed, it specified that these principles and plans should "be put in operation by the Faculty at their first meeting in the autumn of 1919 with such modifications as . . . [might] be deemed desirable." [2]

The faculty lost no time in exercising its newly acquired authority. At its first meeting of the year 1919–20, besides voting that it would meet regularly on the first Wednesday of each month, it appointed four committees, and in subsequent meetings it increased this number to eight.[3] Largely because of the assiduous work of these committees, the faculty had so altered the internal administration of the University before the end of February, 1920, that the Catalogue of the University for 1919–20 presents a strange contrast to the Catalogue for 1918–19. From the Catalogue carrying such changes we learn that thenceforth the exercises of chapel would not open each working day at eight o'clock, but would be held from 10:05 to 10:25 A.M., each student being required to attend them only twice a week; that a new system of grading by letters would replace the old system of grading by numbers; that the two-semester system would replace the three-term system; that the requirements for admission to college would be altered; that the program in General Science would be abandoned; that the degree of Bachelor of Philosophy would no longer be granted; and that "the particulars" about advanced courses would be transferred from the office of the president of the University to the Catalogue of the University. Nor did the changes end here. We observe that the "General College Orders" of Harris's time had now become "General Regulations," and that under this rubric there was no requirement, as formerly there had been, of attendance "upon public worship in some church in town on Sunday." [4] We also observe significant changes in the organization of departments of instruction and in the program of courses leading to the degree of Bachelor of Arts; but these matters we shall deal with at some length hereafter.

Here, then, was a sweeping reorganization—a plunge into the surging waters of modernization which were expected by many to carry Bucknell rapidly to the goal of greatness that it coveted. But, before we examine more fully the matter of curricular modernization, we must ascertain what was being done to solve the urgent problems which confronted the management of Bucknell in the early 1920's, problems which had to be solved if Bucknell were to continue its advance toward the day when, in the words of President Hunt, Bucknell University would "be out-ranked by not a single similar institution in America." [5]

Ironically, especially from the standpoint of Dr. Harris, who now was a member of the teaching corps, as well as a member of the Board of Trustees, the cause of the most urgent problems confronting the administration of the University was the large number of students. No longer did Bucknell have to work hard to get students for its College. Thanks to the rising prosperity in the country, the number of collegiate students rose year by year—from 765 in 1919–20 to 904 in 1922–23, and then, for the first time, to more than 1,000 in 1924–25.[6] More students required more teachers, and together more students and more teachers created a housing problem which was greatly troubling President Hunt during the academic year 1922–23. At the end of that year, in his annual report to the Trustees, he confessed that the enrollment of the students was so large that it "had become a source of embarrassment."

> In spite of real efforts to scrutinize and curtail our list [he said], the enrollment this year exceeds nine hundred college students. . . . We are not only making no effort to increase this number but are making a careful inquiry into the quality of our new students. . . . Our problem is most acute with reference to the young women. . . . This year we have had to decline applications from enough qualified young women to fill another large dormitory.[7]

The problem of housing, however, was not merely one of providing adequate living quarters for young men and young women; it comprehended also the provision of adequate buildings to care for all the things and all the activities resulting from the presence of these young men and young women as well as for the increasing numbers of those who were to teach these students.

Next to the problem of housing, the "most vital" problem then confronting Bucknell, in the opinion of President Hunt, was "to retain and make adequate provision" for teachers of "established power and faithful service." In order to get suitable replacements for those who left, or to get teachers for new positions being created, it was necessary, he said, to pay higher salaries than formerly had been paid; and consequently, for the time being, an injustice was being done to those older in service whose salaries would not be proportionately increased. He pleaded that this injustice be removed as quickly as possible. As a means of solving this problem, he recommended that the campaign then under way to double the endowment of the University be completed at the earliest practicable moment. Without more money to pay higher salaries, Bucknell would not be able, he was certain, to compete on equal terms with colleges having smaller enrollments and larger endowments.[8]

As we have already learned, Bucknell in 1922–23 was engaged in a campaign to raise money. This campaign had been under way for some time. At their meeting in January, 1920, the Trustees had appointed a committee to organize a campaign to raise money for Bucknell and to co-operate with the Board of Promotion of the Northern Baptist Convention.[9] Consequently, the campaign for Bucknell in 1920 became merged with the New World Movement of the Northern Baptist Convention, which planned to raise the sum of $100,000,000. Of this sum, $28,000,000 would be set aside for educational purposes, and Bucknell's share of this sum, if the campaign should be completely successful, would be $1,500,000. It became, however, the "duty and responsibility of Bucknell to raise, by a separate campaign, as large a percentage of the $1,-500,000 as is possible."[10] The program progressed well for a time, and in June, 1920, the Trustees were so optimistic about getting all this money that, in their eagerness to solve the housing problem of the University, they showed a willingness to borrow money not only for the purpose of making extensive improvements of the existing physical plant of the University, but also for the purpose of enlarging this plant; and President Hunt was hopeful that, within four years, this campaign would result in a large increase in the endowment of Bucknell by raising the $450,000 that Bucknell needed for matching a conditional gift of $200,000 promised by the General Education Board for the enlargement of Bucknell's endowment.[11] But the New World Movement of the Northern Baptist Convention, after five years of effort, did not achieve the goal that it had set for itself. Consequently, Bucknell received from this campaign only $259,745.68 from the Northern Baptist Convention and $77,096.53 from contributions of alumni and of friends of the University. From this total yield of $336,842.21, the sum of $58,600 was allotted to the endowment fund of the University, and most of the rest, as we shall see, was used to pay for land and buildings.[12]

Meanwhile, the Trustees, although they had not forgotten the need to double the endowment, could not ignore the increasing pressure exerted upon them by some of the alumni to provide better athletic facilities for the University. Consequently, at their meeting on December 23, 1922, they combined the two objects of endowment and athletic facilities by authorizing the beginning, early in January, 1923, of a campaign to raise $1,000,000 for endowment and $500,000 for a stadium, with the proviso that, until April 1, 1924, the campaign for the stadium should have right of way. In the meantime, Dr. Joseph R. Wood, who had been employed as assistant to the president of the University, would proceed quietly to prepare the way for the campaign for the endowment after the money needed for a stadium had been subscribed.[13]

John T. Shirley, a matriculate of the Class of 1909, was put in charge of the campaign to raise money for the stadium, and, as stadium commissioner, was requested to rely for advice upon a committee of seven persons, four of whom would be Trustees of the University.[14] Under Mr. Shirley's direction, the campaign was prosecuted with vigor. "The services of the Ward, Wells, Dreshmann, and Gates Co., with Mr. A. C. Marts as active agent, were secured. Mr. Marts, in conjunction with Commissioner Shirley, and backed by the hearty support of the Trustees of the University, President Hunt, and prominent alumni, laid plans for and executed an active campaign with headquarters in all the principal cities where there were alumni bodies."[15] In his report for 1922–23, President Hunt commended the attitude of the alumni in respect to this matter, saying that the alumni had "proposed to construct a gymnasium and stadium together with a practice field which . . . [would] provide for general participation in athletics by the student body, the whole construction to cost five hundred thousand dollars"; and he was pleased to note that "the citizens and alumni of Lewisburg and Milton [had] pledged fifty thousand dollars and the undergraduate students more than fifty thousand dollars to this total."[16] By March, 1924, the sum of $430,087 had been subscribed for this object, and the contract had been let for the construction of what soon would become the Memorial Stadium of Bucknell University.[17]

By this time the campaign for additional endowment had been well started. As early as October, 1923, Dr. Wood was reported to be making progress in this undertaking, one of the major objects of which was to raise, by December 31, 1925, the sum of $450,000 in order to get the promised grant of $200,000 from the General Education Board.[18] This campaign was organized and directed by Arnaud C. Marts, who, as we have seen, had assisted in raising money for the stadium; and, thanks to the grant by the General Education Board of a year's extension of time, the campaign was successful, and Bucknell received the full grant from the General Education Board.[19] Largely as a result of this campaign, and of the contribution of $58,600 from the campaign begun in 1920, the endowment of Bucknell, according to the treasurer of this institution, was increased from $568,625.50 on June 3, 1920, to $1,299,-930.87 on June 1, 1929.[20]

While the campaigns to raise money had been in progress, and afterward, the landed possessions and other physical property of the University had been greatly increased, partly by purchases and partly by gifts; and on, or near, the campus old buildings had been improved and new buildings had been erected. Accordingly, we now turn to the subject of the acquisitions of land and of buildings by the University during the presidency of Dr. Hunt.

The Trustees began to acquire properties during the summer of 1919, and at their meeting on January 23, 1920, the treasurer reported the purchase of the residence on St. George Street of the late Charles J. Wolfe and of the property formerly owned by the late Dr. George G. Groff. The Wolfe house, which cost $9,000, had been furnished, and was accommodating about twenty young women. "The need of this building," the treasurer affirmed, "is seen in the fact that the University . . . [was] paying rent for rooms in private houses to take care of the overflow of students." For the Groff property, "comprising a brick dwelling, four acres of ground, and a small barn," the sum of $8,000 was paid. The Groff house, since it was occupied by the Forum Fraternity, which wished to obtain from the University a three-year lease of it at a rental of $320 a year, was helping to solve, and would continue to help solve, the problem of housing students; [21] but the enduring value of this acquisition lay in the fact that the University had obtained control, on the eastern slope of the "Hill," of a valuable property not only contiguous to its original holdings, but also possessing a substantial building which later would serve as an infirmary for men.

But by all odds the most valuable landed property adjoining the campus that the University acquired in this period was the Miller farm, bought in 1920 for the sum of $55,000. This large tract, consisting of 170 acres, adjoined the campus on the south and the west, and its acquisition thus opened the way to the University to expand beyond the cramped quarters in which through many years it had been confined. The agreement to purchase this farm, made by the Committee on Finance before May 10, 1920, was approved by the Trustees at a special meeting on that date.[22] Its acquisition fulfilled the hope for an adequate campus that Dr. Harris had in mind when, in 1903, he made his notable report to the Trustees on the needs of the University.

Nine years later another farm, consisting of ninety acres adjacent to the Miller farm on the west, was acquired, largely through the efforts of Judge Albert W. Johnson, a member of the Board of Trustees. This land was to be paid for by private subscriptions, and it was to be used for a golf course—something which the Trustees had had in contemplation since at least 1920. In December, 1929, after some pledges had been made toward paying for this property, William H. Thompson, a member of the Board of Trustees, offered to complete the payments on it, provided that the pledges amounting to $3,800 that Judge Johnson had obtained be paid, that the golf course be constructed and operated under a committee chosen by the Trustees of the University, that this course "be distinctly a part of the athletic equipment of the University," and that membership in the organization which would operate this course be open to the students, the faculty, the alumni, and the interested residents of Lewisburg and its vicinity. This offer the Trustees accepted by a unanimous vote, and the property thus acquired was entered on the books of the University as of July 1, 1932, at a valuation of $9,500, with an appended note saying that "it was purchased with a gift of $6,000 from William H. Thompson, of Hightstown, New Jersey, a member of the Board, and [with] collections by the trustee golf committee of which Judge Albert W. Johnson was chairman to the amount of $3,756." The work on this course was in progress by the spring of 1930, and on October 31 of that year the Bucknell Golf Course was dedicated. It was then, and it has remained, a private course in the sense that membership in the club which operates it must be limited, but the club has always endeavored to serve, as far as possible, all the golfers of the community of Lewisburg.[23]

The largest acquisition of land by the University during the 1920's was not, however, an extension of the campus of the University. It consisted of two contiguous tracts of undeveloped land lying along the Potomac River, between Alexandria and Mount Vernon, in Fairfax County, Virginia. It came to the University in 1923 as two gifts, one of about 594 acres from James S. Swartz, chairman of the Board of Trustees, and the other of about 250 acres from his friend, Henry J. Loftus, who wished his gift to be a memorial to his deceased wife, Sara Josephine Loftus. This land the University held as a speculation through many years. As late as the summer of 1930, nearly a year after the Great Depression had started, it refused an offer of $750,000 for this property, no doubt for the reason, as President Hunt wrote in 1929, that some of the Trustees who had been "studying the disposition of it . . . [said] that there . . . [was] a possibility that it [might] bring to Bucknell a million and a half of dollars." [24] The story of the disposal of this land will appear in a later chapter of this book.

We now return to the building problem of Bucknell during the 1920's. The expectation of soon acquiring money from the campaign that the Northern Baptist Convention had under way in 1920, together with the opportunity given by the purchase of the Miller farm to erect buildings on more desirable sites than the University theretofore had possessed, persuaded the Trustees, as we have seen, to borrow money, as early as the summer of 1920, for the purpose of starting a building program for the University. Accordingly, on June 15 of that year, they not only made relatively large appropriations to continue the work of modernizing old buildings that they had started in January of that year, but also authorized the borrowing of $100,000 to pay for a part of a proposed Engineering Building. The first wing of this building, intended primarily for the use of the Department of Mechanical Engineering, was the first building to be erected on the former Miller farm. Under the supervision of Professor Frank E. Burpee, its construction was begun in May, 1921, and by March, 1922, it was so far advanced that classes were meeting in it. It was fully equipped during the summer of 1922. Its cost, including equipment, was $106,157, nearly all of which sum was paid with money obtained by the campaign of 1920 for endowment and equipment.[25]

This wing of the new Engineering Building was the first contribution by new construction to the solution of the housing problem of the University. The second contribution, an enlargement of the Chemical Building, was the consequence of an authorization, given by the Trustees in December, 1920, to borrow $30,000 for this purpose. This enlargement, which added forty-five feet to the length of the Chemical Building, was ready for occupancy in the autumn of 1921. To pay most of the cost of this improvement, the sum of $30,600 was taken from the receipts of the campaign of 1920 for endowment and equipment.[26]

Of all the building projects carried out by the University during the 1920's, the most expensive by far was that of the stadium. We have already learned how subscriptions were obtained for what was intended to be a combination of gymnasium, stadium, and playing field. For this project considerable work of grading and filling was done on a site that came to be known as the North Field, adjacent to the cemetery of Lewisburg. Subsequently, when the desirability of having two athletic fields became apparent, a new site for the stadium, approved by the Trustees on June 8, 1923, was selected south of what is now Moore Avenue. Here preparations were made to construct a stadium apart from a gymnasium which eventually would be built on the North Field; and here, between March and October, 1924, the stadium was erected. It was completed in advance of October 18, Homecoming Day, and, just before the starting of the football game for that occasion, Charles P. Vaughan, chairman of the Bucknell Stadium Commission, presented the deed of the stadium to J. Warren Davis, vice-chairman of the Board of Trustees.[27] As to the outcome of the game which followed this ceremony, we find in the diary of E. B. Riehl, a citizen of Lewisburg, this terse report: ". . . attended the first game of football in the new stadium this afternoon played between Bucknell and Lafayette. A great many people there. . . . Score: Bucknell 3, Lafayette 21." [28]

The completion of what may be called the project of the stadium, if we overlook the fact that eventually the University had to pay about one-fourth of the cost of this proposed gift of the alumni to their alma mater, was made during the year 1927–28, when the grounds of the stadium were enclosed by a fence costing $8,923.46; when in the autumn of 1927, two bronze tablets bearing the names of 601 Bucknellians who had served in the late World War—some of them in the Ambulance Units S. S. U. 524 and S. S. U. 525—were fastened to the stadium, which now became Bucknell's Memorial Stadium; and, lastly, when on June 5, 1928, the Christy Mathewson Memorial Gateway to the grounds of the stadium was dedicated. On this occasion the principal address was delivered by Judge Kenesaw Mountain Landis, the so-called "czar" of baseball. This memorial to the late Christy Mathewson, a famous pitcher for the New York Giants and a matriculate of Bucknell's Class of 1902, had been made possible by the contribution of $22,064.95 by the two major baseball leagues. The contribution of the University to this project was relatively small.[29]

The projects to complete the undertaking of the Memorial Stadium were, from the standpoint of a bookkeeper or of a banker, small parts of the large building program undertaken by the University between 1927 and 1929, a program which, for the most part, was carried out with borrowed money. In respect to monetary outlay, two other projects of this program were minor; but in the plan were projects for two large buildings, long needed to provide adequate rooming and boarding facilities for the Women's College, which became possible only because the Trustees were willing to incur a large indebtedness.

Of these four projects, the first to be completed was an infirmary for men. On June 8, 1926, the Trustees authorized the remodeling of the former Groff house for this purpose. Nearly a year later, at a meeting of some of the Trustees in Philadelphia on April 29, 1927, the widow of the late Dr. Samuel Lewis Ziegler offered to purchase this building, equip it as an infirmary, and then give it to the University as a memorial to her late husband, a Bucknellian of the Class of 1880, a member of the Board of Trustees of his alma mater, and a highly distinguished ophthalmological surgeon. Her only restriction on the gift was that no part of the infirmary should be used for living quarters by a resident physician. The Trustees gratefully accepted this offer, and, while Mrs. Ziegler was having the building for the infirmary enlarged and equipped, they were having erected alongside it a bungalow as a residence for the physician of the University. On June 5, 1928, the Ziegler Memorial Infirmary was dedicated, the address being delivered by J. Warren Davis, a member of the Board of Trustees and a long-time friend of Dr. Ziegler.[30]

The second of the lesser housing projects during 1927–28 was a botanical building with an attached greenhouse. For this project the Trustees, on December 17, 1927, had appropriated a sum not to exceed $15,000. Under the direction of Professor Burpee, this building was constructed and made ready for occupancy in the autumn of 1928. According to the records of the treasurer of the University, its total cost, including the greenhouse and all the furnishings, was $35,804.93.[31] As described at the time of its occupancy, this building was one of two stories, constructed of "red brick with stone foundation, steel skeleton, sound-proof floors and walls, and slate roof," the basement of which contained a recitation room, a storeroom, a photographic dark room, and three laboratories. The main floor contained a lecture room, a library, a general botanical laboratory, a storage laboratory, and an office. The greenhouse was divided into three sections, one for instructional work and the others for purposes of research.[32]

The major building erected during 1927 and 1928 was a new dormitory for women. It had long been needed, and a building for this purpose had been under careful consideration for at least a year before the Trustees, in December, 1926, appointed a committee with power, *inter alia,* to procure the erection of a women's dormitory.[33] Under the direction of Professor Burpee, work on this building was started in January, 1927, and in June of that year the Trustees authorized the borrowing of $300,000 for its completion, with the expectation that, by thus providing housing for about 150 women, they would make practicable the gathering "upon the campus [of] all women students who . . . [were then] rooming in apartment houses and in private dwellings." Although not then entirely completed, this building was occupied in February, 1928, by about 140 women. Its total cost, including furnishings, was $276,-870.24.[34] It was the largest and the most desirable of the buildings then available as residences for women of the University. In the beginning, it was called "The New Dormitory," but about a year and a half after the retirement of President Hunt, it was renamed, as the Catalogue of the University for 1932–33 tells us, Hunt Hall, "in honor of Emory William Hunt, D.D., LL.D., D.C.L., president of the University from 1919 to 1931."[35]

Since the Trustees were determined to accommodate all the women of the University with adequate dining facilities as well as with adequate housing, they authorized, in June, 1927, further investigation of the "matter of an addition to the Women's dining hall and kitchen or the building of a dining hall" at a cost of $75,000 to $100,000. On December 17, 1927, they approved the erection of a "women's dining-room not to exceed a cost of $60,000."[36] The need for such a building was urgent, for, as the *Alumni Monthly* tells us, in February, 1928, the "semites"[37] were then "dining in several 'shifts' in the old building dining room."[38] The new dining hall, like the new dormitory and the botanical building, was erected under the supervision of Professor Burpee. It was completed during the Christmas holidays, 1928–29, and was ready for use when the women returned from their mid-winter vacation in that year. It was joined to Larison Hall by a corridor. Its cost, like the cost of most of the other buildings erected for the University, was greater than had been anticipated. According to the treasurer of the University, the total cost of this building, including its furnishings, was $69,983.54; and to this sum should perhaps be added the expenditure of $11,644.19 made for improvements of the kitchen during 1928–29.[39]

The University was now at the end of an expensive building program which, except for Mrs. Ziegler's contribution to the Memorial Infirmary and the contribution of the baseball leagues to the Memorial Gateway, had been completed without the benefit of special gifts. The expenditures during the early years of the 1920's for what the treasurer called "Equipment Items" had been met, as we have seen, largely from receipts of the campaign that Bucknell had conducted in co-operation with the Northern Baptist Convention. Of the money received from this campaign the sum of $171,903.83 had been applied partly on the purchase of the Wolfe house, the Groff property, and the Miller farm, and partly on the cost of enlarging the Chemical Building and of constructing the first wing of the Engineering Building.[40] But the obligations incurred for building operations between January 20, 1927, and December 2, 1929, could not be met in a similar way. These later obligations, together with the obligations amounting to $125,000 that the University had taken over from the Stadium Commission, totaled $592,795.42, a sum which the treasurer had reduced by May 31, 1930, to $470,679.79.[41]

By the summer of 1929 those who were managing the affairs of the University were fully persuaded that the large debt incurred on account of recent building operations in behalf of the University must be paid off as quickly as possible. Accordingly, no objection was made when, in June of that year, the treasurer of the University recommended that ten per cent of the gross income of the University "be henceforth set aside each year to reduce loans now existing and to take care of the interest charges on the same." This proposal, as the secretary recorded in the minutes of the Trustees, was "duly carried." [42] At the same meeting President Hunt, in a ten-year report to the Trustees, expressed his belief that the University "should not incur any further indebtedness on account of construction." This recommendation he made despite his knowledge of certain needs of the University that were "acutely felt"—the need for a new gymnasium for men so that the Tustin Gymnasium might become available for use by the women, the need for an assembly hall large enough to seat all the students of the University, and the need for a recitation hall that would solve the pressing problem of scheduling classes. "We are grateful for what has been done," President Hunt concluded, "and we look forward with hope to the future." [43]

The changes, heretofore described, that were enlarging and modernizing the physical plant of the University were accompanied by other changes that affected in significant ways the Board of Trustees, the administration and the faculty, the curricular offerings, and the students of this institution. It would not be wide of the mark to say that, between 1919 and 1931, the Board of Trustees became somewhat streamlined, that the administration accepted new responsibilities, that the faculty acquired a new sense of its importance, that the programs of instruction were revolutionized, and that the students acquired a broader freedom not only in respect to their personal behavior, but also in respect to their extracurricular activities and to their courses of study leading either to the cultural degree of Bachelor of Arts or to the more or less technical degree of Bachelor of Science in one or another of its seven differentiations in the curricular system of Bucknell University. To these matters we now turn.

A spirit of reform and an impatience for change were abundantly evident at Bucknell in 1919, when this institution was moving rapidly into the post-war era. This spirit affected the Trustees as its affected others, and in part no doubt it helps to explain the fact that, on June 23, 1919, the Trustees appointed a committee to recommend not only changes that ought to be made in the charter, but also changes that might be needed in their own bylaws.[44] They moved deliberately in this matter, however, but by August 16, 1926, the charter had been liberalized by the adoption of an amendment providing that the number of trustees might be increased to twenty-five, that a quorum should consist of seven, and that, instead of four-fifths, not more than three-fifths of the trustees need be members of regular Baptist churches. Even more liberal was the amendment of December 16, 1929, which provided that the number of trustees could be increased to forty, that a quorum should consist of fifteen, and that only a majority of the Trustees need be members of regular Baptist churches.[45] These amendments eased the way to the getting, as President Harris had recommended in his report of June 3, 1918, of "as many men of means and liberality on the Board as possible." [46] Whether or not Dr. Harris's recommendation had implied a reduction of Baptist membership on the Board in order to tap more wealth for the University beyond the bounds of the Baptist denomination, we need not pause to inquire. There can be no doubt, however, of the effect of another suggestion that he had made in the above-mentioned report in respect to the composition of the Board—namely, that one fifth of the Trustees should go out of office each year. On December 19, 1925, the Trustees decreed that the members of their Board should be divided into five groups, and that, beginning in June, 1927, one group should be elected each year for a term of five years.[47] Such, then, were the contributions that the Trustees made during the 1920's to the modernization of their Board. Dr. Harris, however, did not witness any of these changes, for he had died in Scranton on April 4, 1925.[48]

Equally modern were the changes in the administration of the University during the presidency of Dr. Hunt. The University itself had been transformed a few years before 1919, having lost two of its branches, the Academy and the Female Institute. When Dr. Hunt became president, it consisted only of the College and the School of Music, a professional school which offered diplomas but not degrees; and a significant step toward the absorption of the School of Music into the College began on September 21, 1921, when the faculty of the College voted to establish in the College a Department of Music that would be permitted to offer three courses for which collegiate credit would be given.[49] In effect, as President Hunt intimated in January, 1922, Bucknell University was a college burdened with the name of university, and he was certain that, "at least for the present, . . . [it could] do its best work by being a first-class college." [50]

To administer this institution, President Hunt had in the beginning added a recorder to his staff, and, as the enrollment increased, as the faculty became larger, and as the management became more complex, he added other administrative officers; and with the passing years the list of administrative assistants became longer and longer. By 1930, the new officers on the administrative list were, in addition to the recorder, a comptroller, a college physician, and a dean of freshmen. The office of comptroller had been established by the Trustees on July 10, 1924, in part for the purpose of providing better means to collect the pledges made in behalf of the Stadium Fund.[51] But the comptroller had other fiscal duties to perform, and with the passing years his office increased in importance. The first comptroller was Dayton L. Ranck, of the Class of 1916, who became treasurer of the University after the death of Dr. John T. Judd in November, 1931. The college physician was added to the staff during the year 1926–27, and the dean of freshmen was added thereto during the year 1930–31.

Among the new assistants in administration was the alumni secretary, whose name and title appeared for the first time on the administrative list in the year 1924–25. His office had evolved from the office of publicity director which the Trustees had established in 1919. The first publicity agent, Albert O. Vorse, was appointed by the Committee on Finance on July 9, 1919, with the understanding that his duties would be defined by the president of the University. The duties assigned him were, principally, to serve as secretary of the Alumni Association and to edit the

Alumni Monthly. After a few months, Vorse was succeeded by Leo L. Rockwell, who performed for a few years the duties of this office in addition to his teaching duties. In 1924 Alfred G. Stoughton was named the first full-time secretary of the Alumni Association.[52] The relations of this association with the University during the 1920's became closer than they had been before, in part because the alumni secretary was on the campus, and in part because, beginning with 1921, there had been an annual Homecoming Day.[53] One of the significant consequences of this closer relationship was the establishment, during the year 1930–31, of an Alumni Fund, the first report of which, on June 9, 1931, showed that gifts from 721 of the alumni to their alma mater amounted to $5,232.11.[54]

Naturally the expansion of the faculty during the 1920's was greater than that of the administration, and President Hunt, in his decennial report, remarked with some satisfaction that the development of the physical plant of the University had been paralleled by "internal changes . . . even more important for the real purposes of the college." Among these changes he pointed to the expansion between 1919 and 1929 of the teaching force—from twenty-six to thirty-six professors, from none to two associate professors, from four to fifteen assistant professors, and from seven to nineteen instructors. This increase had been made necessary not only because of the coming of more students than ever before, but also because of the introduction of new courses "to keep pace with the discoveries of science and to meet the changing emphasis in knowledge and thought." Also important, as President Hunt remarked, had been the advance within seven years of the salary of a professor from $2,000 to $3,500, and he expressed the hope that soon it would be possible for "teachers of worth to receive more than this."[55] Still another benefit, although President Hunt in his report did not mention it, was the provision that the Trustees made in 1927 for group insurance for the faculty.[56]

A considerable improvement in the qualifications of the faculty between 1919 and 1929 had been achieved, owing, as President Hunt pointed out, to the liberal policy of assisting younger members of the staff to complete their work for the degree of Doctor of Philosophy. Because of this policy, twenty members of the faculty took leaves of absence, between 1919 and 1931, to pursue advanced studies, and ten of them acquired the degree of Doctor of Philosophy.[57] Whereas the number on the faculty in 1919–20 who had earned this degree was very small, the number on the faculty in 1930–31 who possessed it was nineteen; and also on the faculty in the last-named year were five assistant professors and one instructor who subsequently earned this degree.

A much better trained faculty than that of 1919, President Hunt soon discovered, was necessary if Bucknell was to gain the national recognition that it coveted. In his correspondence with officers of the Association of American Colleges and of the American Association of University Women, he learned that an inadequately trained faculty and too much "inbreeding" in the faculty were considered undesirable by national accrediting agencies. Thus it appeared that one of President Harris's favored policies—that of recruiting members of the faculty from the graduates of Bucknell—was proving to be damaging to the best interests of the University. Furthermore, President Hunt learned that the principal objection made by the officers of the American Association of University Women to the recognition of Bucknell, besides that of "a large amount of inbreeding," was the lack of scholarly preparation of women on the faculty. But considerable improvement, combined with persuasive evidence that the University would continue to move "in the right direction," led to the accreditation of Bucknell by the Association of American Colleges on November 12, 1927, and by the American Association of University Women in the spring of 1931.[58] In his comment on the last-named accreditation, the editor of the *Bucknell Alumni Monthly,* in April, 1931, remarked: "All Bucknell women graduates are now eligible to full membership in this noteworthy organization through its many local branches in the various cities of the country." [59]

Meanwhile, significant things had been happening to the University in its sphere of academic affairs. The big changes in the organization of its curricular offerings, as we noted earlier in this chapter, took place during the year 1919–20; thereafter the programs of instruction were refined and enlarged to meet certain urgent demands of a dynamic era. These programs were adapted in 1919–20 to the two-semester system, which went into operation in the autumn of 1920, and they were based upon the requirement of fifteen units of secondary work for admission to college. For undergraduate students, the programs of instruction led, on the one hand, to the degree of Bachelor of Arts, and, on the other hand, to the degree of Bachelor of Science in biology, in four branches of engineering, and in home economics. Each of the programs leading to the degree of Bachelor of Science contained more required courses than the program leading to the degree of Bachelor of Arts required. Among the requirements in the scientific programs were courses in physical education, English composition, and a modern foreign language.[60] The drastic change (or reform, as many would have said) took place in the program leading to the degree of Bachelor of Arts, and to this subject we must given particular attention.

After 1919–20, to be graduated Bachelor of Arts by Bucknell a student would be required to complete 128 credit hours in addition to a requirement in physical education. Of these hours, fifty-eight were required, and, except for three courses in philosophy, were to be pursued during the freshman and sophomore years. The requirement of fifty-eight hours, however, was a minimal requirement. Some students were obliged to take more than the minimal requirement of six hours in foreign languages in order to fulfill the general requirement for graduation of four years' work (including preparatory work) in foreign language; and students who did not elect an ancient language were required to study Ancient Civilization. Moreover, a student who began a foreign language in college was required to pursue this language for at least two years. But, in general, the prescribed work was intended for the freshman and sophomore years, and during the junior and senior years the student was expected to devote his time principally to a major and two minors, the choice of which he was obliged to make, subject to the approval of the dean and of the professors concerned, not later than the second semester of his sophomore year. Under the new dispensation, a major consisted of eighteen hours in one division (or subject) in one of the three groups embracing the curricular offerings available to the candidates for the degree of Bachelor of Arts. Roughly speaking, these groups comprised, respectively, languages, religion and the social disciplines, and mathematics and the sciences. A minor consisted of nine semester hours in one division (or subject), and both minors must be chosen outside the group which contained the major; and neither a prescribed course nor any course of the freshman or the sophomore year could be counted toward either a major or a minor.[61] The main purpose of this program, it would seem, was to accomplish the objects sought by Harvard in its program during President A. Lawrence Lowell's administration—namely, those of concentration and distribution, objects which, it was hoped, would eliminate the evils which had arisen in respect to the choice of subjects under President Eliot's system of free electives.

But those who reorganized the program leading to the degree of Bachelor of Arts at Bucknell had also in mind another object, which was that of destroying, root and branch, the old requirement of some knowledge of classical languages for this degree. The way to the accomplishment of this object was opened when the faculty, by two separate votes, one on December 2, 1919, and the other on January 16, 1920, decreed that in Bucknell University, Latin would no longer be required for either the degree of Bachelor of Science or the degree of Bachelor of Arts, or for entrance into programs of courses leading to either of these degrees.[62] As a requirement for the degree of Bachelor of Arts, knowledge of Greek, except in the Classical Program, had been abandoned, as we have seen, during the administration of President Harris. Presumably the passing years brought, at least to most of the members of the faculty, no feeling of remorse for having put Latin on skids, for in 1931 the committee of the faculty appointed to prepare the *Memorials of Bucknell University, 1919–1931,* took pride in, and apparently was not rebuked for, pointing out twice in this publication that, among the "important subjects" required for the degree of Bachelor of Arts, the "dominant trio of 1919, Latin, Greek, and Mathematics," had been wholly eliminated; and it considered this fact the "most striking change in educational thought" at Bucknell during the preceding twelve years.[63]

By 1931 the program adopted in 1919 for the degree of Bachelor of Arts had been modified, but not fundamentally changed. Now the requirement for graduation had become the completion of 124 semester hours, "including four hours in physical education," and these hours must be accompanied by at least 124 quality credits, to be earned by getting three such credits for each semester hour graded A, two such credits for each semester hour graded B, and one such credit for each semester hour graded C.[64] The requirement of quality credits appeared for the first time in the Catalogue for 1925–26.[65] By 1931, moreover, the major consisted of twenty-four semester hours in one division of a group, and each of the two minors consisted of twelve hours, one of which could be taken in the same group as the major. By that year also the three groups of subjects in 1919 had expanded into five groups, mathematics having become one group, and history, economics, sociology, and political science having become another. Also there had been some changes in the extent of the requirement in certain subjects. The requirement in English had been raised from six to twelve hours, the requirement in foreign language had been raised from six to nine hours, and the requirement of six hours in history had been changed to fifteen hours in history, economics, sociology, religion, and political science. The requirement in mathematics had been reduced from eight to three hours, the requirement in science had been reduced from ten to six hours, and the requirement of nine hours in philosophy had been changed to six hours in philosophy and psychology. The six hours in science, however, must be taken "in the same science and in courses which include[d] laboratory work." Finally, provision had been made by 1930–31 for a major in social science, consisting of twelve hours in history and of six hours each in economics, sociology, and political science.[66]

In the programs leading to the degree of Bachelor of Science, some significant changes were made between 1919 and 1931. The program in home economics was discontinued, and two new programs—that of education and that of commerce and finance—were adopted. By 1931, the number of semester hours required for this degree varied from program to program, that in biology being 140, that in engineering being 146, and that in education and in commerce and finance being each 124. In all these programs the number of hours above given included the requirement in physical education.[67]

Requirements for the master's degree and for the professional degrees offered in engineering were first set forth systematically in the Catalogue for 1920–21. Here we are told that one year of work in residence was required for the master's degree, but that graduates of Bucknell might do this work *in absentia,* although they would not be awarded a master's degree until they had been graduated for at least three years. To attain this degree a candidate was required to complete, with a grade not lower than B, thirty semester hours of an advanced character, of which a major of eighteen hours must be in one department. All the courses pursued for this degree would require the approval of the head of the department in which the major was chosen, and of the committee on advanced degrees. To receive one of the professional degrees, the candidate must be a graduate of Bucknell of five years' standing, must have practiced his profession for five years, and must have submitted a satisfactory thesis; but membership of "an approved grade" in one of the principal engineering or technical societies might be offered as sufficient evidence of the fitness of a candidate to receive such a degree. These requirements were still in force in 1931.[68]

Requirements for the master's degree, however, underwent significant modifications during the 1920's. Beginning with the Catalogue for 1924–25, all the courses offered by the University were so numbered that those suitable for advanced study could be easily ascertained. All the elementary courses were numbered below 200, all the intermediate courses were numbered between 200 and 299, and all the advanced courses were numbered 300 or above. Moreover, regulations which became effective on September 1, 1927, prescribed that, although credits toward a master's degree should be earned in the most advanced courses, at least twelve such hours might be earned in the less advanced courses numbered between 200 and 299; that the graduate major must be in a department in which the candidate had completed twelve hours before beginning his graduate work; that the twelve hours required in addition to the major should be in the same department as the major, or in a department "in which the work . . . [could] be related" to that of the major; that the head of the department in which the major fell might substitute the writing of a thesis for three hours of required work; and, finally, that an examination, which might be oral, would be given to "test the candidate's general knowledge of the major subject." In general, a year in residence was required for the master's degree, but residence for one semester and one summer session or for three summer sessions would be accepted as a fulfillment of this requirement. A maximum of six semester hours earned in any approved college or university could be counted toward this degree.[69] These requirements were changed but slightly during the next four years. By 1931, however, the candidate for a master's degree could earn eighteen hours in courses numbered between 200 and 299, but he was required to pass an examination which might be both written and oral, and he was obliged to fulfill a residential requirement of one semester and two summer sessions, or of four summer sessions in which he had earned twenty-four credits of graduate character.[70]

The process of adjusting the academic programs of the University to the changing demands of a new era naturally affected the departments of instruction. Here, however, we have space to describe only the most important departmental changes during the period with which we are now dealing.

Both the Department of Law and the Department of Home Economics were discontinued during the first half of the 1920's. The Department of Law was listed for the last time in the Catalogue for 1920–21, and three years later the Department of Home Economics offered for the last time a program leading to a degree; but thereafter, through the year 1928–29, there was a limited offering in home economics. The last degrees in this program were conferred in June, 1926.[71] In one way or another, however, new departments appeared. By 1925 the Department of Economics and Political Science had been separated into two departments, and by 1928–29 the newly established Department of Economics had been so much expanded that, in that year, it was offering a program leading to the degree of Bachelor of Science in Commerce and Finance. This degree was conferred for the first time in June, 1932.[72] In 1927 the subjects of philosophy and psychology were separated, and an independent Department of Psychology emerged. By 1931 it was offering seven courses. The Department of Music, which, as we have seen, had been restricted to three courses in 1921–22, was offering by 1931 twenty-four semester hours; but not more than eighteen hours of music could then be counted toward the degree of Bachelor of Arts.

At least four departments grew up during the 1920's. One of these, the Department of Physical Education, acquired added significance in 1926 when John D. Plant became director of physical education. The Department of Sociology and Logic, which as late as 1922–23 was listing only five courses, became the Department of Sociology in 1924, and by 1931 it was offering eleven courses. Equally significant had been the growth of the Department of Religion. In the Catalogue for 1919–20, there were listed four courses in the Bible, one of them being Professor Hamblin's course in New Testament Greek. Four years later this program was expanded and designated the Department of Religious Education, a title which persisted until, in the Catalogue for 1930–31, it gave way to that of Department of Religion. By the year 1925–26, this department was offering courses in four groups—namely, Biblical literature, religious history and thought, Christian social ethics, and religious education techniques; and in 1931 this program had not been changed in any significant way. Majors in this department were required to take courses in all four of its groups. But the greatest departmental growth of all in this period, perhaps, took place in the Department of Education, which as late as 1922–23 was offering only six courses. The next year, however, it was offering a full program, and, beginning with the year 1924–25, students in the University might pursue a program of study leading to the degree of Bachelor of Science in Education. This degree was conferred for the first time in June, 1925.[73] The rapid and extraordinary expansion of this department revealed the fact that Bucknell had become deeply engaged in the work of preparing teachers for service in the public schools.[74]

An analysis of the changing content of the work offered by the various departments of the University is beyond the scope of this chapter. It should be said, however, that the Department of Art in the College had expanded from an offering of one course in 1919–20 to an offering of three courses in 1930–31, and that a division of journalism in the Department of English appeared for the first time in 1924–25. By 1931 this division was offering seven courses, and students were then permitted to count six hours in journalism toward a major in English and three hours in journalism toward a minor in this subject. The Department of Military Science and Tactics soon went with a new wind of sentiment.[75] It had emerged in 1919 as an expression of the war-time patriotism, but it lasted for only a few months. It is not mentioned in the Catalogue for 1920–21. Finally, it might be well to recall the fact that the subject of physics and each of the branches of engineering had appeared, respectively, as independent departments in the year 1919–20.

Some of the benefits of instruction offered by the University were extended during the 1920's to persons who could not become full-time students on the campus. They were so extended by the establishment of both a Summer School and an Extension Division. A summer session had been started in 1915, with Dr. Nelson F. Davis serving as its dean, and it had been continued each summer through 1918, and possibily also through 1919.[76] After being discontinued for four years, it was revived in 1923, and thereafter such a session was held continuously.[77] The Extension Division also was established in 1923. The instruction in this division was at first given either by regular members of the faculty or by "non-resident members of the Extension Faculty"; but, beginning with the autumn of 1927, such instruction was given only by full-time members of the faculty on the campus. In 1928 John H. Eisenhauer, of the Class of 1905, joined the faculty as associate professor of education and was made director of both the Summer School and the Extension Division.[78]

All the programs of instruction, whether they were offered on the campus or off the campus, depended for their effective operation upon an adequate library. Happily, the administration of President Hunt was a time when the library was growing and becoming modernized. Professor William E. Martin, who had been librarian since 1894, died on May 22, 1922, and his daughter, Miss Eliza Martin, succeeded him without any teaching obligation. Except for Isaac N. Hill, who had served as librarian *de facto* for a few months in 1887, she was the first full-time librarian of the University. Although she had been an assistant to her father in 1921–22, she was not fully trained as a librarian. Yet she entered upon her work with so much enthusiasm and with so much understanding that, before the end of a decade, the library of Bucknell had become larger, more serviceable, and essentially modern in its procedures.

To make the library more nearly adequate to the increasing demands of a growing institution, Miss Martin sought, and in 1923 obtained, an annual budget; and by 1931 the holdings of the library had increased by purchases and gifts, some of which were large, to considerably more than 50,000 titles, besides the uncatalogued material, some of which, although not in demand for current instruction, was more valuable than Miss Martin had thought. Moreover, in order to make these collections more usable, she gradually recatalogued the library according to the classification of the Library of Congress. On June 1, 1931, she reported that the recataloguing of current and new material was virtually completed. "The uncatalogued section," she said, "consists chiefly of older, less called for matter," and, as if to emphasize the magnitude of the task that had been completed during 1930–31, she remarked that "9000 cards have been added to the catalog, an increase of 3063 over the number added last year." She also catalogued, sooner or later, all the departmental collections of books, one of which, the Enoch Perrine Memorial Collection in the Department of English, had accumulated by 1931 more than a thousand volumes. Finally, by the end of the 1920's she had acquired a staff of trained assistants to serve the needs of those who used the central library.

To complete the task of modernization to which she had directed her efforts, it remained for her to make the collections of the library more accessible to the students, to the members of the faculty, and to others who chose to use them. Accordingly, she established in 1923 a branch library in the Women's College for the benefit of the women who were then denied the use of the central library at night; she encouraged and extended the practice of reserving books for the use of students in various courses; and, emphatically, she co-operated with those who wished the library to be open every day of the week.

From 1922 to 1930, the library was open daily (Monday through Friday) to all students from 8:00 A.M. to 5:30 P.M., but to men only from 7:00 P.M. to 10:00 P.M. It was closed from Saturday noon until Monday morning. On March 5, 1930, the faculty voted that the library should be open on Saturday afternoons and requested that it be open on Sunday afternoons as soon as arrangements therefor could be made. Such arrangements were soon made, for a year later Miss Martin reported that the library had been opened for two hours on Sunday afternoon "with gratifying results." By September, 1933, the women had been given access to the central library during all the hours, day and night, that it remained open.

By the end of President Hunt's administration, the Carnegie Building was ceasing to be adequate to the needs of the University. No one perceived this fact more clearly than Miss Martin, who, in her report for 1930–31, called attention to the need of a new building for the library "more accessibly located." This was not just a routine remark. A year later, in her first report to President Hunt's successor, she returned to this subject, saying: "The securing of a new building within the next few years is one of the imperative needs of the college. With this in mind your librarian has planned vacations to include the visiting of new college and university library buildings. Fifteen of these have been carefully inspected during the year." But, as she then well knew, her hope for a new building must be deferred until the lifting of the Great Depression which was then embarrassing the University in all its operations.[79]

It remains to glance at those for whose benefit the University exists—the students. For them no less than for the faculty, life at Bucknell during the 1920's became more expensive, and no doubt more comfortable and pleasant, than it had been through the years before the late World War. Fraternities and sororities flourished as never before; between 1919 and 1931, the faculty approved the establishment of nine fraternities and of five sororities. All told, by 1931 Bucknell had twenty-four fraternities and sororities, and in that year it was presumed that seventy-five per cent of the students at Bucknell were members of fraternal or of sororal societies.[80]

The cost of attending college increased considerably during the administration of President Hunt. For men the minimal charge in 1920–21 for tuition, student budget, and furnished room (but not board) was $126 a semester; and for women who received similar accommodations and board the cost was $226 a semester, with an added cost of $7.50 to each one who had a room either in Bucknell Cottage or in the New Residence Hall (later Harris Hall).[81] Five years later the minimal charge for men for such accommodations was $165 a semester, and for women with board the minimal charge was $300.[82] By 1930–31, such charges had advanced to $190 a semester for men and to $350 a semester for women. The price of tuition had then become $150 a semester.[83] Meanwhile, the fee for the student budget, which had been $16 a year in 1921–22, with $10 allotted to athletic sports, had become $25 a year in 1930–31, with $12 allotted to athletic sports.[84] Beginning in 1926–27, an infirmary fee of $6 a semester was also required.[85]

As the allocation of the income from the fees paid by students reveals, athletic sports were the most expensive activities in which the students were engaged during the 1920's; in those years the emphasis upon football was heavy, and some direct aid to athletes was given by the Trustees.[86] Subject to the regulations of the faculty, the control of athletic sports was in the hands of the Athletic Association, with the general direction thereof vested in a committee consisting of the president of the Athletic Association, the president of the University, two members of the faculty "chosen by the faculty or appointed by the President of the University," and twelve alumni appointed by the Trustees. The business management of the association was entrusted to a graduate manager.[87] By 1929–30, the term *Athletic Council of the College* had replaced in official publications of the University the term *Athletic Association.* This council consisted of fifteen members—namely, the president of the University, three members of the faculty appointed by the president of the University, the football captain and another undergraduate student selected by the Senior Council, and nine other persons not officially connected with the University, of whom six were required to be alumni. These nine members were nominated by the Council and elected by the Board of Trustees. The business management of the Athletic Council was in the hands of a graduate manager, who, from 1925 forward, was Professor Benjamin W. Griffith.[88] Keeping the Athletic Council out of debt was one of the annoying problems connected with the athletic operations of the University during the 1920's.

Student government at Bucknell in the 1920's, if it differed from such government there during the preceding decade, differed in spirit rather than in form. Presumably, more attention was paid to the opinion of the students in President Hunt's administration than had been paid to it in

President Harris's time. At the end of the 1920's, the Student Council (apparently an alternative name for Senior Council) consisted of the presidents of sixteen fraternities and a representative of the unorganized students. It was recognized as the "highest authority in student activities and government," being subject only to the president of the University. A related body, the Senior Tribunal, consisted of representatives of the fraternities and of the unorganized students, with the vice president of the senior class serving as its president. Its duty was to police the men's campus. The Women's Student Government Association continued to operate during this period. All these organizations were expected to cooperate with the faculty in maintaining order and in preserving the traditions of the University "both on and off the campus." [89]

Publications which the students supported during the 1920's differed somewhat from those which the students had supported in the years immediately preceding the late World War. Of the earlier publications, the *Bucknellian* and the *Commencement News* continued their operations through the 1920's, as did also the *Handbook* published by the Y.M.C.A., and the yearbook, *L'Agenda,* published by the junior class. New publications of that decade were the *Belle Hop,* a humorous magazine, which appeared for the first time in December, 1923, as the replacement of the old *Bucknell Mirror,* and the *Bucknell Journal of Education,* which first appeared in January, 1927, as the official journal of the Bucknell Education Club. Also new was *Bucknell Verse,* an annual volume containing poems written by students. The first volume of this work was published in 1926.

The other organized activities in which students of the University participated between 1919 and 1931 differed little in their general character from those in which students of the preceding decade had participated. At the beginning of the 1930's, there were debating teams for both men and women, and there also were separate dramatic clubs until, on April 15, 1931, Frill and Frown, the women's club, merged with Cap and Dagger, the men's club, under the name of Cap and Dagger.[90] In the sphere of music, the organizations comprehended separate glee clubs for men and women, a college band, and a college orchestra. The Y.M.C.A. and the Y.W.C.A. also were flourishing, and the Y.M.C.A. acquired for the first time a professionally trained, full-time secretary, when Forrest D. Brown came to the campus in April, 1930.[91] At one time or another during the 1920's, numerous clubs reflecting diverse academic interests of students were in operation. Some of these had survived from earlier years, but not a few of them were newly formed. Among the new ones were the Kent Pre-Legal Club and the Spanish Club, both established in 1923; the Sociological Society and the Educational Society, both formed in 1925; and the Commerce and Finance Club, organized in 1928. The societies of the engineering students, dating from earlier years, continued to flourish, or at least to survive. Especially noticeable at the beginning of the 1930's was the number of specialized honorary societies, eight of which were listed in the *Blue Book* for 1930–31, the former *Students' Handbook* which, in 1931–32, was named the *Freshman Handbook*. One thing, however, noticeably was lacking. In a list of varied organizations, which at Bucknell by 1931 had become rather long, one organization that had been eagerly sought for many years was not to be found. Despite earnest efforts that it put forth during the 1920's, efforts in which President Hunt eagerly participated, Bucknell University did not then succeed in getting a chapter of the Phi Beta Kappa Society.[92] Its petition for such a chapter received much support in that decade, but not enough to win for it, at that time, this coveted prize.

11

Depression and Recovery

The citizen of the new age just ahead of us must have a broad social point of view, and above everything else he must have a strong sense of duty and of social and moral obligation.—*Homer P. Rainey, Baccalaureate Address, 1932.*

The educated men and women acquire inner resources which give them poise and calmness in prosperity, courage and vision in adversity. The world about you may turn to ashes in your very grasp, but these treasures within you are now yours forevermore. —*Arnaud C. Marts, Baccalaureate Address, 1938.*

For two years after expressing his wish to retire from the presidency of Bucknell, Dr. Emory W. Hunt remained at his post. The committee appointed to look for a new president took plenty of time to perform its task, and the Trustees, at a meeting on December 21, 1929, approved this committee's recommendation that Dr. Hunt's resignation should not be accepted until his successor had been chosen and installed.[1] A year later, however, with no successor to him yet in sight, the Trustees promised to release him in June, 1931, permitting him, in the meantime, "to take whatever vacation he might desire." In order that the University might at all times have a directing head, they designated one of their number, Charles P. Vaughan, to serve as acting president during any absence of Dr. Hunt, and, after his retirement, until his successor had been inducted into office.[2] Mr. Vaughan's time of service, however, was short, for a new president was elected on June 8, 1931, was on hand before the opening of the academic year in September, and was inaugurated on November 13, 1931.[3]

The newly chosen president, Homer Price Rainey, was a young man of wide and varied experience. He was born in Clarksville, Texas, on January 19, 1896, and, after being graduated Bachelor of Arts by Austin

College in 1919, served as an instructor in that institution for three years before entering the University of Chicago to specialize in school administration. It was in this university, as he remarked in 1931, that he "laid the background in theory" for his educational ideas.[4] In August, 1924, he received from the University of Chicago the degree of Doctor of Philosophy, and thereafter, for three years, he was a professor of school administration in the University of Oregon. In 1927 he became president of Franklin College, in Indiana, a position which he was still holding when he was elected president of Bucknell University.[5]

Besides abundant energy, much enthusiasm, and lofty principles, Dr. Rainey brought to Bucknell a developed philosophy of education and a clear conception of the role which he thought that a college of liberal education should play in the American educational system. He emphatically did not agree with those who were saying that the college of liberal arts was doomed, for, in his opinion, "the values of a genuine liberal culture" were more needed in the 1930's than at any other time in our national history.[6] But there was, he acknowledged, serious need to redefine the function of a liberal college and to revamp its program so as to enable it to meet the demands of the time. The "function of a liberal education in our democratic society," he affirmed, "is to educate men to direct our society toward worthy human, social, moral, and spiritual ideals." To so educate them, liberal education, he believed, must make them not only intelligent about every aspect of contemporary life, but also about their environment "to the degree that they can control and direct it toward chosen goals." [7]

To achieve results as far-reaching as these, the liberal college, he pointed out, must concern itself with all the arts—must, indeed, begin with landscaping and architecture, for, to him, it seemed axiomatic that a beautiful campus is needed to set "the tone for everything else." Within the curriculum, moreover, the same encouragement should be given to "the expressive and creative functions" of all the arts as is commonly given to all the sciences. There should be on the faculty of a liberal college creative artists as well as researchers in science—teachers of literature, for example, who create literature, teachers of history who write history, and so on through all the arts: from music to the social sciences, and from health, recreation, and physical education to ethics, morality, and religion. "A college," he concluded, "will really function when it reaches the level of creative productivity in all fields." [8]

Naturally, as he made perfectly clear, such a goal could be achieved only by reducing the heavy teaching schedules commonly imposed upon members of a collegiate faculty. Such a reduction, he believed, could be achieved if colleges were to put less emphasis upon teaching and more emphasis upon learning. "College teaching," he insisted, "could be reduced 50 per cent with fine results, if students were made to assume that much additional responsibility for their education," and the result would be not only the substitution of a better educational philosophy for a worse one, but also the release for creative effort of "much of faculty energy, now used for drudgery." [9]

President Rainey lost little time in setting in motion a program of reform at Bucknell. On November 9, 1931, the faculty endorsed "the proposal of President Rainey to the Board of Trustees that a survey of the institution be made," and the minutes of the meeting of the Trustees on December 19, 1931, tell us that "President Rainey . . . made a very instructive report to the Board of the present condition of the University and his recommendations for its future." [10] Elsewhere we read that, with the approval of the Board of Trustees, President Rainey began, in January, 1932, "a comprehensive plan for a sweeping survey of Bucknell," a survey intended to gather information to be submitted to an "investigating committee" which later on would be invited to the campus. Such was the news sent out to the alumni in February, 1932.[11]

Two months later the leading editorial in the *Bucknell Alumni Monthly* was entitled "The Present Survey," an editorial in which the author affirmed that everywhere alumni and friends of the institution were inquiring about the Bucknell survey; and he answered them by saying that Bucknell

> is examining herself, her inmost workings, her financial structure, academic programs, courses, teaching methods, grading, examinations, buildings, and complete organization. The giant task is being directed by President Rainey as he seeks facts and figures upon which to base a future policy for the entire University.[12]

Moreover, the editor submitted to the readers of the *Alumni Monthly* some questions touching major policy which President Rainey had raised, and on which he solicited "advice and opinion." In the same issue of the *Alumni Monthly*, President Rainey, in a letter to the alumni, affirmed that, in the chaotic period in which Americans were living, Bucknell, like other American colleges, must transform itself in order to "keep pace with changing social demands." The survey then in progress, he continued, was being conducted by ten committees of the faculty, each committee dealing with a specific problem; and the desired information thus being gathered would, in due time, be submitted "for study, evaluation, and recommendation" to two of the ablest men in American education: Dr. Charles H. Judd, dean of the School of Education in the University of Chicago, and Dr. M. E. Haggerty, dean of the

School of Education in the University of Minnesota. He promised to keep the alumni informed about the progress of the survey.[13]

By the middle of July, 1932, the survey had been completed, the experts had completed a three-day visit to Bucknell for conferences, had studied nine reports prepared by committees of the faculty, had gone home carrying with them fourteen questions concerning the University, and, in a report to Dr. Rainey, dated July 14, 1932, had submitted their answers to these questions in the form of recommendations.[14] These recommendations, presented to the faculty on September 10, 1932, were, at the suggestion of President Rainey, referred by the faculty to the president and the chairmen of the survey committees for further study.[15] There was need for these recommendations to be carefully considered, for some of them, if adopted, would upset long-established, and therefore much cherished, routines of behavior. But they were not all of this character; some of them were above the plane of controversy, and to these we shall first give attention.

Pleased with the results accomplished in the recent survey, Deans Judd and Haggerty recommended in their report, first of all, that the University maintain a committee for a continuing study of institutional improvement. Then, in respect to administration in general, they strongly recommended for Bucknell a "single collegiate organization directly under the administration of the president," rather than separate collegiate divisions within the institution; but they did recommend the creation of an administrative division concerned with all matters relating to the students apart from instruction and curricula. "Such a division," they said, "would assume most of the obligations now devolving upon the offices of the Dean of Freshmen, the Registrar, the Dean of the College, the Dean of Women, the Director of the Health Service, the Director of Religious Work and certain faculty committees concerned with student problems." As to further institutional needs, they recommended that the University adopt the accounting system devised by the president and the comptroller, and that it also develop a comprehensive building program suited to the purposes that it was endeavoring to achieve, remembering in so doing to give first consideration to a new and better located building for the library and not forgetting that a new gymnasium "would be in the interests of the entire student body."

Most important of all the recommendations that Dean Judd and Dean Haggerty made were those pertaining to the curricula of the University. On this subject they advised the creation of a Lower Division, consisting of the work of the first two collegiate years, in which emphasis would be placed on general education, and of an Upper Division, consisting of the work of two years and of three years, leading, respectively, to a bachelor's and a master's degree, with specialization in the field of major interest. Also, they advised that the twenty-seven existing departments of instruction be replaced by four divisions—namely, biological sciences, physical sciences (including engineering), social sciences (including psychology and education), and the humanities (including music and other fine arts). They recommended, furthermore, an expansion of the current curricular offerings in music and "in the plastic, graphic, and related fine arts." Finally, they proposed that the summer school be continued, that the work of extension be not expanded, and that the two-semester system be not replaced by the four-quarter system.

More numerous, and equally pertinent, were their recommendations touching the faculty. On this subject we learn that salaries of the faculty should be "substantially" increased, but not made equal for all of the same rank, since in the giving of increases the "really competent men" should be recognized. We learn also that great care should be taken in recruiting new members of the faculty, particular attention being given to enlarging the number of those who received their training "in institutions other than Bucknell University," for, in the opinion of both Dean Judd and Dean Haggerty, there was "an undesirable percentage of men whose major or only training" had been obtained at Bucknell University. Moreover, we are told that there should be a reduction of hours in teaching schedules, the median not to exceed twelve, although ten hours would be "a more desirable standard." Also, scholarship in the faculty should be encouraged, for such scholarship would be a first step in encouraging scholarship among the students, although the scholarship of the students might also be encouraged by "supplementary techniques," such as "generous public recognition by the faculty and students of high scholarship among students," the improvement of examinations, and the offering of "honors courses" or of courses in independent study for students of superior ability. Finally, we learn that a satisfactory system of retirement should be provided for members of the faculty.

Lastly, on one of the most sensitive subjects touching collegiate institutions, that of policy in respect to intercollegiate athletic sports, we find that the recommendation of Dean Judd and Dean Haggerty was as emphatic as it was precise—namely,

> that Bucknell University [should] accept and adhere strictly to the recently adopted requirements of the Association of the Middle States and Maryland in reference to intercollegiate athletics. This would mean the abolition of athletic scholarships and [of] the subsidizing and recruiting of athletes. Such action would be in line with current trends throughout the country and in the interests of the whole body of students.

Such, then, was the report referred for study by vote of the faculty to President Rainey and a special committee appointed for this purpose. On November 1, 1932, the report of President Rainey and of this committee was read to the faculty, and eight days later, at a special meeting, the faculty voted to accept in principle the reorganization of the college, with the exception of the departments of engineering, into a Lower Division and an Upper Division, with the requirement of passing a comprehensive examination on work done in the Lower Division for admission to the Upper Division. On November 16 the faculty approved the curriculum for the first two years, which, for the most part, consisted of prescribed work, including several survey courses and a requirement of a reading knowledge of a foreign language. Also at this meeting, the faculty approved the reorganization of the curricular offerings into five groups, the first consisting of English and the foreign languages; the second, of history and the social sciences; the third, of the physical and biological sciences, together with astronomy, mathematics, and physical education; the fourth, of philosophy, psychology, religion, art, and music; and the fifth, of the programs in engineering.[16] In the Catalogue of the University for 1932–1933, these groups would be called, respectively, the Language Group, the Social Science Group, the Natural Science Group, the Philosophy and the Arts Group, and the Engineering Group.[17] On November 30 President Rainey was authorized by the faculty to appoint not only the administrative chairman of each of the foregoing groups, but also to appoint a director of each of the general survey courses, all such appointments to take effect immediately "so far as the plan of reorganization is concerned." Before the close of this meeting, President Rainey announced the appointment of Professor Harry W. Robbins as chairman of the Language Group, of Professor Robert L. Sutherland as chairman of the Social Science Group, of Professor Frank M. Simpson as chairman of the Natural Science Group, of Professor George B. Lawson as chairman of the Philosophy and the Arts Group, and of Professor Sihon C. Ogburn as chairman of the Engineering Group.[18]

Two other important actions were taken by the faculty on November 30. One of these was its decision that all applicants for admission to the University should be graduates of secondary schools, that they should be admitted on the basis of their qualifications to do collegiate work as determined by generally accepted criteria, and that the administrative work of admitting them should be handled by the registrar. Also, the faculty voted at this meeting that the standing committees on admission, attendance and standing, curriculum and courses, registration, rules and regulations, and summer session and extension work be abolished, and that henceforth their functions be vested in a University Council, consisting of the president of the University, the dean of the College, the dean of freshmen, the director of the summer session and of extension work, the registrar, the chairman of the committee on advanced degrees, and the chairmen of the five faculty groups, "all ex officio." [19]

The new program had now been accepted in principle; it would be fully described in the forthcoming Catalogue of the University, and it would apply to the class that would be admitted in September, 1933. The change was momentous, and it had come quickly. Even President Rainey was mildly astonished. On February 9, 1933, he wrote to the president of Knox College, saying, "The fact is that we have abolished about everything we had and have almost started *de novo*. The process has been real breath-taking for some of the more conservative members of the organization, but I think we have made some rather unusual progress and I am enthusiastic about our program for the future." [20]

For the information of the alumni, and of others, President Rainey used a full page of the *Alumni Monthly* for December, 1932, to explain the new program for Bucknell. Its essential purpose, he said, was to clarify the "present confusion of programs which is caused by attempting a multiplicity of functions," and to concentrate the resources of Bucknell upon its "primary function." "The attempt has been made," he continued, "to free the first two years, in so far as possible, of pre-professional and professional work, and thus offer our students the opportunities of a broad general education in the lower division; and, in turn, the last two years are freed entirely for concentration, pre-professional, and professional specialization. . . . The program for the first two years is built around the idea of orientation and is made possible by the use of general or survey courses. . . . It should be noted in this program [he continued] that sufficient time has been left in both years for students to begin the prerequisite and pre-professional courses. The new program will not in any way hamper or delay a student in beginning his pre-professional training in any field." He also called attention to the new requirements for admission to the University, to the reorganization of the twenty-seven departments into five divisions, and to the newly created University Council, which, he said, would "coordinate the entire plan and work of the University." Then, in a peroration intended to appeal to the pride of Bucknellians, he concluded his remarks in these words:

> Bucknell is pioneering in educational developments. The changes effected by the foregoing steps are among the most comprehensive since the founding of the University. The educational world will watch with keen interest the unfolding of the future work of students at Bucknell.[21]

Not all the "breath-taking" changes at Bucknell during the year 1932, however, were comprised in the academic program described above, for on April 6 of that year the faculty, on the recommendation of Dean Rivenburg, voted to abolish the four-year program of the School of Music leading to a diploma in music, and, in lieu thereof, to establish in the College a major and a minor in music to be counted toward either the degree of Bachelor of Arts or that of Bachelor of Science, the major to consist of twenty-four hours, of which twelve hours should be acquired in theoretical music, and the minor to consist of fifteen hours, of which nine hours should be theoretical work. It was further provided that the registrar should conduct the correspondence with the prospective students in music, that the committee on registration should register such students as it registered students in other subjects, and that the records of all students in music should be kept in the office of the recorder.[22] These changes were to become effective in September, 1932. Apropos of this matter, President Rainey remarked that "Colleges of Liberal Arts are coming to realize that they do not deserve the name unless they incorporate the Arts as a fundamental part of their program." [23] By thus transforming the School of Music into a department in the College, the faculty removed the last trace of the "old" University; now the College and the University had become one and the same, although, for some time to come, the expressions *School of Music* and *Dean of the College* would, understandably but anachronistically, continue to be used.

Still another change, begun in 1932 and completed in 1933, became a vital aspect of the "revolutionary" reorganization of Bucknell. This change, as President Rainey explained it to the alumni, was intended to make the campus "as architecturally beautiful as possible" and to give the new educational program of the University "its fullest and richest expression." [24] To plan this change, the services of an architect would be required, and on October 21, 1932, the Trustees, by unanimous vote, chose as the architect of the University Jens Fredrick Larson, a man recommended to them by President Rainey as one who, for thirteen years, had been "the architect for Dartmouth College, and also the architect who laid out a complete plan for Colby College." [25] Mr. Larson was expected to devote a full year of his time to the development of a general plan for Bucknell, and then he would make a "miniature model of the future campus" of Bucknell, a model which would be displayed in a conspicuous place on the campus. Also, during this first year of planning, as President Rainey pointed out, there would be constructed "a utility classroom and office building to meet the . . . [existing] emergency for classroom space and offices for the faculty," and he expressed the hope that this building would be completed by September, 1933.[26]

President Rainey's mention of an existing emergency called sharply to mind the fact that the Bucknell Plan was being started under unfortunate conditions in a time of deepening depression. On August 27, 1932, a fire had destroyed the central section of the University Building (Old Main) and had seriously damaged both its West Wing and its East Wing.[27] In this fire, as President Rainey reminded his faculty on September 15, 1932, the University had lost "twelve of . . . [its] twenty-seven classrooms, practically all of . . . [its] administrative offices with the exception of those of the Comptroller, dormitory rooms for approximately one hundred boys, and the only assembly hall on the campus." To compensate for these losses, he continued, the following arrangements had been made:

> Additional classrooms have been provided in the Engineering Building, the Biology Building, the Botany Building, in the basement and library of Hunt Hall, and in the basement of Harris Hall. Every effort will be made to make these temporary quarters as serviceable as possible. The administrative offices have all been set up on the first floor of West College. . . . The boys who had engaged rooms in Old Main have been provided for in East and West Colleges. The schedule of classes has been changed in the following manner: There will be four class periods in the morning beginning 'on the hour' at 8 o'clock and closing five minutes before the hour until 11:55 A.M. The Assembly periods will be on Tuesdays and Thursdays at 12:05 P.M. in the Baptist Church. Lunch at 12:45. Afternoon classes will begin at 1:30 and continue until 4:30, thus providing an additional class period in the afternoon schedule.[28]

Even greater embarrassment was threatening, for, as President Rainey also told his faculty on September 15, a decreasing enrollment had "caused a serious budgetary problem," which would require rigorous economy, and which might, he hinted, necessitate a reduction of salaries.[29] By this time the decline in the enrollment had become disquieting—from a total in 1930–31 of 1,185, with a freshman class numbering 387, to a total in 1932–33 of 1,069, with a freshman class numbering 307.[30] In the income from tuition, room, and board in this short period there had been a decrease from $521,952 to $462,458, an alarming loss in view of the fact that from this source the University was then getting about ninety percent of its income.[31] Disturbed by this decline, the Trustees, in June, 1932, had authorized the employment of three persons to solicit students, a practice which had not been necessary since the time of President John Howard Harris.[32] The result of such solicitation, however, had been disappointing. Nevertheless, President Rainey gave the faculty what comfort he could by expressing "the sincere hope" that the budget for the coming year could be balanced by economies that would not include a reduction of salaries.[33]

But a reduction of salaries was not far off. On November 18, 1932, Earl A. Morton, a member of the Committee of the Trustees on Finance, warned President Rainey that a reduction of salaries was impending. "I regret," he wrote, "the necessity of making such a suggestion as I well know our better teachers and professors are underpaid. The budget, however, must be balanced if you are to continue to have banking accommodations." [34] The other Trustees were of like mind, and on December 17, 1932, voted a reduction of ten per cent in salaries, wages, and pensions, effective as of December 1 of that year.[35] This was an unwelcome Christmas gift to those who were serving the University, and, unfortunately for the new academic program, some of those who were affected by the reduction associated their pecuniary misfortune with certain features of the new program to produce a state of mind far from favorable to what, a few months later, would be called Bucknell's "New Deal."

Such, then, was the unhappy situation as the new program for the University was coming into being. Yet the program moved forward. On February 8, 1933, Mr. Larson explained to the faculty his plans for the architectural development of the University,[36] and on July 19, 1933, ground was broken for the new Literature Building, which would be paid for with money obtained from the company that had insured Old Main. This building, only three-fifths of which would now be constructed, would be the first one in the proposed new quadrangle of the University,[37] and, in the course of a few years, it would be called the Vaughan Literature Building.[38] It was ready for occupancy by classes early in March, 1934, and its auditorium, as the editor of the *Alumni Monthly* informed his readers, "received its first assemblage on St. Patrick's Day, March 17, when more than four hundred bankers of District Four of the Pennsylvania State Bankers Association were the guests of the University." [39]

Meanwhile, action had been taken to extend the academic part of the new program of Bucknell into the Wyoming Valley, where, on September 14, 1933, the Bucknell University Junior College was opened in rented quarters on Northampton Street, in Wilkes-Barre, Pennsylvania.[40] This project had had its beginning in the spring of 1933, when, after a visit to schools in the Wyoming Valley, Dr. Frank G. Davis, professor of education in Bucknell University, had suggested to President Rainey the idea of establishing a junior college in that part of Pennsylvania.

Somewhat later he renewed this suggestion, and took three superintendents of schools from that valley to Lewisburg to help persuade President Rainey that a junior college would be useful to the people of the Wyoming Valley.[41] President Rainey then asked Professor Davis to make a careful investigation of the feasibility of such a project, and, after receiving from him a favorable report[42] on May 22, 1933, presented on that day to the Trustees of the University a plan for the establishment of a junior college in Wilkes-Barre. This project the Trustees approved "upon the condition that the initial enrollment reach approximately seventy-five students." [43] The plan, accordingly, was put into effect with a group of teachers chosen principally from the faculty in Lewisburg.

The Junior College was established as an integral part of Bucknell University; its students were students of Bucknell University, and its faculty was a part of the faculty of Bucknell University. On the appointed day, it opened auspiciously, with an enrollment considerably larger than had been expected. "Students there," President Rainey told the faculty in Lewisburg on September 16, 1933, "are receiving the same program as students on our own campus, and every effort is being made to see that the quality of work done there is in every way equal to that upon our campus here." [44] But the Junior College, which had been expected not only to pay its own way but also to serve as a "feeder" to the upper classes in Lewisburg, became, after the first year, a financial "headache" to the University; and it so remained until the year 1937–38, when its financial condition became sufficiently good for Dean Romeyn H. Rivenburg to remark that it was at last "on an even keel." [45]

As the new instructional program was going into effect, in Lewisburg and in Wilkes-Barre, President Rainey, in a communication to the faculty on September 16, 1933, pleaded for the co-operation needed to make it successful, saying, *inter alia,*

> This is the beginning of . . . our third year together. . . . The two years that have passed have been years of transition. They have been years of study and reorientation. They have also been years . . . of enforced retrenchment. In them much has happened. We have survived a thoroughgoing self-survey. We have suffered the loss of our most cherished building. We have thoroughly reorganized the administration, curricula, and student life of the institution. We are beginning our work this year with an entirely new program. . . . We have the first building in that program under construction. We have launched a junior college in Wilkes-Barre that opened for the first class this week with one hundred fifty full-time students. . . . I am well pleased with the curricula that we have established. I am delighted with the splendid survey courses which our various committees have evolved. . . . The success of this work is now dependent

upon our ability to make them function creatively in the education of our students. This is a tremendously difficult, but yet, a significant task. It is admittedly an experiment and a new venture for Bucknell. It is only a beginning. Mistakes and defects will begin to appear immediately upon our trial of it. . . . I beg of you to make every effort to make it successful, and I assure you that we shall not hesitate to make whatever readjustments that may seem to be desirable when the need for them arises. The new program will not work automatically. Its success depends upon our sympathetic cooperation and efforts.[46]

Readjustments were not long in coming. Discontent with the new program rose as the depression deepened, the enrollment declined, and money became scarcer. Accordingly, during the year 1934–35, some changes in the new academic program were made with the approval of President Rainey. Among other changes, the word *survey* was dropped from the names of the general introductory courses, and "the methods of conducting one-man courses" was left to "the discretion of the instructors concerned." [47] Moreover, as Dean Romeyn H. Rivenburg tactfully explained to the alumni in January, 1936, the heavy concentration of required work in the Lower Division had made the new curricula "inelastic, inflexible and unsatisfactory to students and professors, because they did not provide sufficient opportunity for students to begin in the Lower Division work in which they expected to major in the Upper Division, or to begin pre-professional work in which many students were supremely interested." Accordingly, changes were made which permitted some required work to be taken either in the Upper or the Lower Division; and, as a further attraction to students, two new four-year programs were added, each one of them leading to the degree of Bachelor of Science in Commerce and Finance—one a secretarial program and the other a program in commercial education for those intending to teach commercial subjects. Such changes, Dean Rivenburg believed, had accomplished their purpose: they had eliminated the "rigidity" of the first curricula adopted, and, at the same time, had conserved "to the highest possible degree" the liberal values of the new program.[48]

But the end was not yet. The Great Depression was still pressing heavily upon the University in 1934–35—the most difficult year of all for Bucknell—and there were grave personal apprehensions and gnawing grievances in the faculty which the record of enrollment and of institutional income did nothing to remove. From a total enrollment in 1933–34 of 992, with a freshman class numbering 253, there was a decline to a total enrollment in 1934–35 of 891, with a freshman class of 253;

and for these years the decline in income from tuition, room, and board was from $359,312 in 1933–34 to $340,028 in 1934–35.[49] Morale fell lower as money became scarcer. Accordingly, on October 5, 1934, the faculty, by a secret vote, selected a Committee of Five "to work with the administration and the Finance Committee of the Trustees on the financial problem."[50] On December 12, 1934, this committee made a preliminary report, which was laid upon the table "for further consideration and study," and the committee was continued.[51] This report contained recommendations for the "improvement of student and faculty morale" and proposals for effecting economies without dismissing members of the faculty and for increasing the enrollment. The committee rightly saw that, if the problem of a declining enrollment could be solved, the financial troubles of the University would "largely disappear."[52]

Thanks to an extraordinary campaign to get more students, the University, in September, 1935, enrolled the largest freshman class in its history.[53] Once again the outlook was encouraging. Accordingly, the Committee of Five, in the report which it laid before the faculty on November 6 of that year,[54] confined its recommendations to matters concerning the faculty and "its internal organization," believing that its suggestions thereon, if adopted, would "go a long way toward creating a better morale and a smoother, happier working arrangement." Its recommendations were ostensibly aimed at the "undemocratic" character of the University Council and the Five Groups, but the implication is strong that at least some of these recommendations were "running interference" for the wounded pride of persons who had been deprived of departmental chairmanships under the old dispensation and denied larger chairmanships under the new dispensation. However that may be, the committee recommended that the University Council of ten persons be replaced by an Administrative Council, consisting (1) of the president of the University, the dean, the treasurer, and the registrar, and, for certain purposes, the librarian, the dean of women, the director of the Junior College, and the director of the Summer Session, and (2), when concerned, members of departments and groups. It also recommended that the Five Groups be replaced by Twelve Interest Groups, within which departmental heads should be recognized, and, beginning a year later, except in departments having fewer than three members, be elected for a two-year term. Finally, it was recommended that a Faculty Advisory Committee, without administrative duties, be formed by the election of one member from each of the Twelve Interest Groups for a term of two years. These were the major recommendations. As minor recommendations, the committee proposed that a committee on public relations be established, that the committees on advanced standing, catalogue, schedule, and scholarships be recognized as administrative committees, and that the membership of the standing committees of the faculty on advanced degrees, chapel, freshman week, honorary degrees, and library be changed gradually, "but in such a way as not to destroy the effectiveness of the work."

This program for restoring morale the faculty, on November 20, 1935, adopted without change.[55] Thus we see that the academic program of the New Plan, with the adjustments heretofore mentioned, had been retained, but that the agencies originally established for administering this program had been replaced by other agencies which, as perhaps most members of the faculty would have said, were more democratic and more nearly representative of the varied opinions within the faculty.[56]

By this time Dr. Rainey had ceased to be president of the University. His resignation came unexpectedly, at the beginning of the year 1935–36. He resigned because he had been invited to become director of the newly created American Youth Commission, an agency financed by the General Education Board and operated under the sponsorship of the American Council on Education.[57] Reluctantly, he submitted his resignation of the presidency of Bucknell at a special meeting of the Trustees on October 5, 1935, and with equal reluctance the Trustees accepted his resignation, to become effective on October 15 of that year, ordered that his remarks explaining the reasons for his resignation be spread upon their minutes, and forthwith elected him to membership on their Board. In his remarks relating to his resignation, Dr. Rainey reminded the Trustees that, as president of Bucknell, he had endeavored to achieve two major objects—first, "to build for the University an educational program that was adequate to meet the demands of contemporary life, and one which . . . [would be] in harmony with the traditions and ideals of Bucknell," and, secondly, "to lay the foundations for an adequate financial support for the future needs of the University in terms of a well-trained and efficient personnel, and adequate material facilities." He expressed his faith in the "fundamental soundness" of Bucknell, one proof of which was that, in the autumn of 1935, the institution was in better financial condition than at the beginning of his administration, an improvement which had been achieved during difficult years of depression without any reduction of the teaching staff of the University. As parting advice to them, he urged the Trustees to complete the restoration of Old Main at the earliest practicable date and also, during the "years leading up to the one-hundredth anniversary," to concentrate their efforts "upon the improvement of the financial support of the University." [58]

Before adjourning this special meeting, the Trustees voted unanimously that a member of their Board, Arnaud C. Marts, a businessman of New York City, should be Dr. Rainey's successor.[59] Although Mr. Marts at once declined this offer, the pressure upon him to accept became so heavy that he sought escape from his difficulty by consenting to serve for a few months as a part-time acting president of Bucknell. Accordingly, at another special meeting, held on October 25, the Trustees, again by a unanimous vote, made him "Acting President of Bucknell University for the school year ending June 30, 1936." [60] Thus, as he told the alumni of Bucknell in November, 1935, a "quick turn of unexpected events catapulted" him into a position that would require him to commute between New York and Lewisburg—"with side trips to . . . [the] Junior College at Wilkes-Barre." In order that his new responsibility might not become unbearably heavy for him, he had insisted that not only should he be allowed to give only half of his time to the presidency of Bucknell, but also that the academic duties of this office should be assumed by the dean of the University, Dr. Romeyn H. Rivenburg, who would thus become, as Mr. Marts said, the "real leader of the students and faculty." [61]

There now began at Bucknell a partnership of two men of high ideals but of different temperaments, a partnership that was destined to last through nearly ten years. In age, the dean and the new president were separated by fourteen years. Whereas the dean in 1935 was past sixty and somewhat hampered in his physical movements, the president was still on the sunny side of fifty, energetic, resourceful, and capable of bouncing many balls simultaneously. While he was playing the role of promoter *par excellence,* the dean was concerned with the administration of the academic program and with internal discipline. Moreover, because he shared to some extent the duties of the presidency, Dean Rivenburg made both annual and semi-annual reports to the Trustees, and his very comprehensive, very meticulous, very proper, and very sober reporting during President Marts's administration is replete, *inter alia,* not only with valuable information about such things as increasing enrollments, efforts to elevate the standard of scholarship, and progress of the University in general, but also with generous praise of what President Marts was doing for the University. Only once in these reports did he surrender to what he would have called "the spirit of levity." In his semi-annual report in December, 1940, in an effort to illustrate the relatively onerous demands that the University was then exacting of its students, he quoted, though disapproving the language, a remark made to his secretary by a "harassed Senior," who said: "You have to work like hell for three years to stay in, then work like hell the fourth year to get out. Don't tell the Dean I said so." [62] Sooner or later, however, every such relationship must end; and, as this one was drawing to its close, President Marts expressed not only his heartfelt thanks to Dean Rivenburg for his "noble and splendid service," but also his hope that, in years to come, historians of Bucknell would say that "between the two" of them, they "were a good college president." [63] They both retired in June, 1945, the dean because of age, and the president because he wished to give his full time to his business in New York City.[64]

To his new task as college president Mr. Marts brought admirable qualities—high intelligence, comparative youth, eagerness to work, and a flexible mind. Nor was this all. He possessed extraordinary tact in dealing both with persons and with groups; he was skillful in effecting organization; he had acquired both ease and style in the sphere of public relations; and he was gifted with a persuasive manner that enabled him to lift people above themselves and to set them working in behalf of the higher things of life. His example of industriousness was so infectious that, as soon we shall see, he had persons of all sorts and of all ages working together for Bucknell. Moreover, his dedication to high ideals and to Christian philanthropy was so obviously sincere that there could be no questioning his integrity. When he said that, despite the demands of his own business, he had accepted the presidency of Bucknell because he was attracted to "the youth of America, the promise of a better world," no one doubted him; and, at about the same time, when he urged the alumni of Bucknell to "keep true to the ideals and aims and dreams" of their student days, admonishing them that true happiness could be found "only on the upper highways of life, on the intellectual, cultural and spiritual highways to which Bucknell, with constancy of purpose, points her sons and daughters," he won their applause and enlisted their support.[65] So also with the faculty and the students. His acceptance in his newly acquired dominium was as complete as it was speedy.

President Marts clearly perceived the problem which would confront him during what he supposed would be his eight months at Bucknell University. Deep discouragement had settled upon the campus of the University, discouragement resulting from four years of declining income, from a reduction of salaries and wages, and from the burden of a heavy debt inherited from the expansive years of the late 1920's. This situation he faced cheerfully and courageously, in part no doubt because he perceived in the large entering class in September, 1935, at least a temporary reversal of the downward tendency. However that may be, he set for himself the task of restoring the confidence of the faculty, the students, the alumni, and the friends of Bucknell in their institution, first, by getting the University "moving" again, and, secondly, by helping to find "the right man" for its permanent president. The pressure of immediate problems, however, kept him working harder at the first than at the second of these objects. As a contribution toward the restoration of confidence during his short tenure, he decided to do his utmost to rebuild Old Main; to endeavor to find new friends for Bucknell and to keep alive old friendships; to help get another record-breaking class for September, 1936; to help start a "constant flow" of bequests and gifts, both for endowment and for the construction of new buildings that were much needed; and, lastly, to work to help the Junior College "establish itself on sound organizational foundations." [66] In his efforts to accomplish these objects, he gave generously of his time and of his talents, and, as his tenure of office lengthened, he also gave more and more of his means. Naturally, he did not say publicly that he would seek for Bucknell relief, and ultimately a considerable measure of security, by getting for it a Board of Trustees consisting, for the most part, of liberally disposed men of large worldly means. But, like President Harris before him, he firmly believed that the members of a Board of Trustees should contribute generously, even lavishly, to the support of a philanthropic institution which had been entrusted to their management.[67] Within a very few years, he had on his Board of Trustees more than a few men of great means and of a benevolent spirit that would have overwhelmed Dr. Harris, had he lived to see what these men were doing for Bucknell.

When the Trustees met in December, 1935, they quickly learned that their acting president had not been inactive. In a "very interesting report on the situation relative to Old Main," he announced, *inter alia,* that, for the reconstruction of this building, the sum of $101,500 had been subscribed, most of it by members of the Board of Trustees; that the approximate cost of completing this work would be about $375,000; and that this sum should be fully subscribed before the work of reconstructing the building was started. Also, upon his recommendation, the title of Dean Rivenburg was changed from dean to vice president and dean, the bylaws of the Board of Trustees were so amended that an Executive Committee thereof might exercise the full power of the Board when the Trustees were not in session, and, finally, approval was given by the Trustees to his appointment of thirteen special committees of their Board, each of which would be concerned with a problem of particular concern to Bucknell University.[68]

President Marts was now giving increasingly of his time to the work of raising money for the reconstruction of Old Main. In January, 1936, he announced a gift for this purpose of $10,000 from Daniel C. Roberts, of Wilkes-Barre, a retired businessman and recently found friend of

Bucknell who had been elected a member of its Board of Trustees in June, 1935. He also announced at this time that it would cost $160,000 to reconstruct the central section of this building, and $105,000 to rebuild and equip each one of its two wings. "Somehow," he said, "the way must be found this Spring and Summer to put this fine old building, rich in tradition, back into its vital service of youth." [69] But money for so large an enterprise was not then easy to come by. In the issue of the *Alumni Monthly* for February–March he was obliged to announce that the sum subscribed for this purpose had risen to only $114,000, but in the next issue of this periodical, that for April–May, he could say, happily, that the sum had been increased to $130,000, which was more than enough to rebuild one part of Old Main. Also, he made known at this time that a general appeal was being made to the alumni for contributions to help bring Old Main back into the service of their alma mater, and he permitted others to announce the fact that, since this work had proceeded less rapidly than he had hoped, he had consented to extend the term of his service to Bucknell for an additional six months.[70] He had now crossed the Rubicon; henceforth, as he became more deeply involved in projects to promote the recovery of the University, he would find it increasingly difficult to give up a job whose end could be approached but never fully reached.

Work on Old Main was soon proceeding rapidly. By July, 1936, its West Wing was "being rapidly rebuilt," subscriptions from the alumni to the Old Main Fund were coming in, and it seemed likely that work on the East Wing of this building could be started as soon as work on the West Wing was completed.[71] In October of that year President Marts told the alumni that the finishing touches were being put on the West Wing, and that additional gifts from a few of the Trustees, amounting to $80,000, had made it feasible to let the contract for the restoration of the East Wing without delay. One-half of this sum had been donated by Daniel C. Roberts.[72] In the November issue of the *Alumni Monthly,* President Marts conveyed this good news to Bucknellians everywhere:

> The restoration of the West Wing of Old Main is now complete. The first floor is being used for the University's administrative offices and the second, third and fourth floors are men's dormitories. It is a lovely building. The outer walls remain as they were for nearly ninety years, while the interior is new and fire-proof and modern. The contract has been let for the similar restoration of the East Wing. The latter work will be completed about April, 1937. Meanwhile, the Old Main Campaign continues, in the hope that enough more funds can be collected soon to let the contract for the Central Section. About $75,000 more than the amount already subscribed will be required.[73]

By February the work on Old Main was progressing well, although the construction was not quite keeping pace with President Marts's expectations.[74] There was then still lacking about $58,000 of the sum needed for the completion of the Central Section of Old Main, but in April, 1937, this lack was removed by a gift of $57,500 from a "modest friend of Bucknell," who eventually was identified as Daniel C. Roberts. With the fund for the restoration of Old Main now complete, President Marts could write exuberantly: "The West Wing is already in use; the East Wing will be completed by June first, and the walls of the Central Section are now being built." [75] By July, the East Wing was completed, and the walls of the Central Section were "up to the third story." [76] On Homecoming Day, November 13, 1937, the Central Section of Old Main, now fully restored, was dedicated as the Daniel C. Roberts Hall, in honor of the man to whom, as President Marts remarked, Bucknell owed "this beautiful and lovely building." Mr. Roberts was present at the ceremony of unveiling in the lobby of this building a bronze plaque proclaiming him "a friend of ambitious youth and a generous benefactor of humanity." [77]

This was a beginning; already something else was under way. Some seven months earlier, at a special meeting of the Board of Trustees on April 3, 1937, President Marts, after authorization had been given for the construction of the Central Section of Old Main, had announced that "the next effort . . . would be to raise about $400,000 to build a new gymnasium," and also that, "in the near future," the Engineering Building, which had been started in 1922, should be completed "at a cost of about $150,000." Accordingly, the Trustees authorized their president and the chairman of their Board, Judge J. Warren Davis, to "open the books" of the University for gifts to both of these projects.[78]

The first gift toward the building of a gymnasium was highly encouraging. In June, 1937, President Marts announced to the Trustees that one of their number, Daniel C. Roberts, had given, in addition to the $97,500 that he had contributed to the reconstruction of Old Main, one thousand shares of the stock of the Woolworth Company, worth $53,000, to the fund for the gymnasium.[79] "This gift," President Marts told the alumni in July, 1937,

> has given us courage and stimulus in our efforts for a new gymnasium. When the fund grows sufficiently to make the new gymnasium possible, it will be erected on the North Playing Field, with its back to the Cemetery, facing toward "the Hill." Tustin Gymnasium, which has served the men of Bucknell so faithfully and well for nearly fifty years, will then be re-fitted for another half century's service as a Women's Gymnasium.[80]

Gifts for this building came rapidly from nine other Trustees, and on July 31, 1937, the Executive Committee of the Board "empowered and directed" the proper officers of the University to execute a contract for the construction of the proposed gymnasium.[81] Accordingly, as early as September, 1937, the laying of the cornerstone of this building was celebrated in ceremonies featuring a radio address by Judge Kenesaw Mountain Landis, who spoke from the studios of the National Broadcasting Company in Chicago.[82] The work on what was intended to be the first section of the gymnasium proceeded rapidly, and in March, 1938, President Marts announced that the commencement exercises in June of that year would be held in the newly completed gymnasium, at which time the building would be named and dedicated. "A few weeks ago," he continued, "when we came to a crucial decision as to certain very vital questions of design, equipment, and finish, the largest contributor to the building fund sent us word that each of the questions should be decided in favor of the *best* way to build a gymnasium regardless of cost. With his message he sent enough additional funds to pay the increased costs which follow such decisions. 'I want the Bucknell Gymnasium to be the best anywhere,' he said, and that is what it is to be." [83] The "largest contributor" was Daniel C. Roberts. By previous agreement between President Marts and Mr. Roberts, who refused to have the building named for himself on the ground that one building named Roberts was enough for Bucknell, the gymnasium was dedicated on June 13, 1938, as the Davis Gymnasium, an honor unexpected by the chairman of the Board, Judge J. Warren Davis, whose labors in behalf of this building had been noteworthy. Also, at this commencement, the honorary degree of Doctor of Laws was conferred upon Mr. Roberts, who, two days before, had been elected honorary chairman of the Board.[84]

Before this time, work had been started on the modernizing of the Tustin Gymnasium, and in July, 1938, President Marts was pleased to remark that this building was being renovated and remodeled, and that Loomis Field was being redesigned to provide two hockey fields and four tennis courts for the use of the women.[85] On October 6 of that year, both the Tustin Gymnasium and Loomis Field were turned over, with appropriate ceremonies, to the women of Bucknell.[86] A month later, in commenting on the completion of the Davis Gymnasium and on the remodeling of the Tustin Gymnasium, President Marts remarked that these modern facilities of physical education at Bucknell had been made possible by the generosity of "a score of Trustees who gave well over $200,000 for the two buildings." [87]

By this time Mr. Marts had been president of Bucknell University, in the full sense of that title, for about nine months. His decision to drop the word *acting* from his title came in the train of his growing fondness for the work that he was doing for Bucknell and, perhaps more particularly, because of an almost overwhelming display of affection for him. During the exercises at chapel, on the morning of December 16, 1937, Ambrose Saricks, a graduate student from Wilkes-Barre, presented to Mr. Marts a petition, signed by virtually all the students of the University, requesting their acting president to accept the title of president, and pledging to him their "loyal support in years to come." [88] A similar sentiment prevailed among the members of the faculty, and among others who knew of his work at Bucknell, including the members of the Board of Trustees. At a meeting of the Board, two days after the petition of the students was presented, the chairman of the Board read this petition to his colleagues, and "all the members of the Board joined in making the same request." [89] Mr. Marts was deeply touched by these expressions of loyalty and of affection, and more especially by a letter, dated January 25, 1938, in which Judge Davis, expressing what he said was the unanimous desire of the Trustees, urged him to drop the word *acting* from his title and to decide for himself how much or how little of his time he would give to Bucknell. "We would rather have you," Judge Davis said, "as our leader at Bucknell only one day a week than anyone else we know for seven days a week," whether as president or as acting president; but, he added persuasively, "It would make us all feel happier to drop the word 'acting.'" Under such pressure, Mr. Marts finally surrendered, promising in a letter to Judge Davis on March 22, 1938, to do his "small part at this crucial time when the world forces of liberty and brotherhood and righteousness need the redoubled devotion of us all." But he begged that no inaugural be held for him; and there was none.[90]

Mr. Marts's decision to become president of Bucknell was announced by Judge Davis during the exercises at chapel on April 7, 1938, and this announcement not only evoked tremendous applause from those who heard it, but also brought forth, in the "final edition" of the *Bucknellian* of that day, a front-page streamer, reading, MARTS BECOMES NEW PRESIDENT.[91] It also brought forth, at a meeting of the faculty in the afternoon of that day, a renewed pledge to him of the "unreserved allegiance" of the members of the faculty in a resolution, saying,

> we will do all that lies within our power to maintain the highest standards of teaching efficiency and scholarly achievement; . . . we will ever place the larger interests of the University above personal considerations; and . . . we will do our utmost to bring the University above personal

considerations; and . . . we will do our utmost to bring the University to the favorable attention of the state in which it is located and of the nation which it serves, thereby making it possible for President Marts to carry forward the constructive program he has initiated in the full confidence that he has the complete cooperation of his teaching staff.[92]

The change of title affected others more than it affected Mr. Marts. His work proceeded as usual. Before November 13, 1937, he had received from Mr. Roberts a gift of $50,000 toward the completion of the Engineering Building, the cost of which he now estimated at $200,000.[93] In June, 1938, the Board authorized the finishing of this building as soon as enough money therefor should become available; in July the architect was busy with plans for this building; and on September 29, 1938, at exercises featuring a radio address by Dr. Albert Edward Wiggam, ground was broken "for two new wings to be added to the Engineering Building" at a cost of $275,000, the raising of which sum had been recently completed by an additional gift of $100,000 by Mr. Roberts, who, together with one other member of the Board, had assumed the total cost of making this improvement. "These additions," President Marts said, "will enable us to bring all four Engineering Departments under one roof and to give each Department increased space and much additional instructional and laboratory equipment." [94] The enlarged Engineering Building was dedicated during commencement exercises in June, 1940.[95]

For the time being, the big building program on the campus in Lewisburg was now completed, although a new building for the library was in contemplation when the time for resuming construction should become propitious. But the big buildings constructed since 1935 were not the only contributions that had been made to the more adequate housing of the University. The construction of a small service building and the acquisition of various houses adjacent to the campus had proceeded *pari passu* with the construction of large buildings. The service building, intended to give the Department of Buildings and Grounds a centralized headquarters and to provide space for workshops being maintained in the basement of Harris Hall and in the basement of West College, was authorized in April, 1937, and was constructed near the Tustin Gymnasium during the summer of 1938.[96] Other buildings were required for other purposes. To provide dining facilities for boys whose parents wished their sons to dine under the supervision of the University, the Judd house on South Sixth Street was acquired, and an addition to it during the summer of 1939 provided a dining-room that would seat eighty-eight men.[97] This was but one of several houses that the University acquired during the 1930's and early 1940's, either on St. George Street or on, or near, South Sixth Street, most of which buildings it remodeled for use as residences for women. One of these buildings became a house for women of the faculty, and another, a former residence of Professor William G. Owens, became an honor house occupied by fourteen women of the senior class. Still others—the Gundy House, the Martin House, and the Co-operative House—also became residences for women, and in the summer of 1941, in expectation of losing male students because of the draft instituted in that year, the University remodeled three other houses for the use of additional women who had been admitted as freshmen of the Class of 1945.[98]

The major building program on the campus in Lewisburg had been paralleled by a program to get adequate housing for the Junior College in Wilkes-Barre. This new institution, which had been occupying rented quarters since 1933, and which had been burdening the University with annual deficits since 1934, President Marts from the beginning made one of his principal concerns. He had never favored the establishment of the Junior College, first, because he thought that it was too far away from the main campus, and, secondly, because he thought that it was too great a financial risk for the University to assume. Accordingly, when he became acting president of a Junior College that was a *fait accompli,* he planned to build it up, to arouse local pride in it, and, eventually, to transfer the control of it to the people of the Wyoming Valley.[99] The Junior College had been of some service to the University in Lewisburg. In a time of crisis, it had provided employment for some members of the faculty whose retention otherwise might have become impracticable, and, for at least a year or two, it contributed a considerable number of students to the upper classes in the University. But, by and large, it was not greatly loved by the faculty in Lewisburg, not only because it soon began to lose money, but also because it appeared to some members of the faculty to be a potential Siberia. Consequently, had they known President Marts's attitude to the Junior College, they would have loved him even more than they did.

Early in 1937 the Junior College received as gifts its first two buildings, and in the autumn of that year it moved from its rented quarters on Northampton Street to Conyngham Hall and Chase Hall, former palatial residences on South River Street—the former presented by Mr. and Mrs. John M. Conyngham and the latter by Admiral and Mrs. Harold R. Stark.[100] Presently, the Junior College received other buildings—a residence for its director, presented by Mr. and Mrs. Fred J. Weckesser in 1938, and, in 1941, the magnificent Kirby residence, presented by Allan P. Kirby as a memorial to his father and mother.[101]

Meanwhile, the Junior College had been accredited by the Pennsylvania State Council on Education and had become a member of the Association of Junior Colleges, and in December, 1937, the Trustees of Bucknell University had approved the appointment for it of a Board of Trustees, consisting of fifteen members. In June, 1938, President Marts told the Trustees that he had announced in Wilkes-Barre "that the Junior College would be built up as a home college, with local control, and as soon as a responsible local Board of Trustees felt themselves able to take over the operation of the Junior College, Bucknell would permit them to do so." [102] By this time the Junior College was not only moving into the sphere of prosperity, but also was well started on the way leading to its independence. It did not, however, receive a charter of its own until after the war, which, as early as 1938, was looming on the horizon.

The getting of more and better buildings—an accomplishment which Dean Rivenburg, as early as December, 1938, called a "modern miracle of our day"—was only a part of President Marts's program for Bucknell.[103] He was deeply interested in making financial provision for the future of the University, and he was much disquieted because its old indebtedness and the recurring annual deficits of the Athletic Council were consuming each year in payments of interest thousands of dollars which, in his opinion, should be used for the "enrichment" of teaching. Accordingly, in December, 1937, he proposed that the Trustees adopt a four-year program, pledging itself (1) to complete the building program then in progress, (2) to pay the debt of the University and "plow back" into the enrichment of its work the money then being paid out as interest, and (3) "to set an ever normal enrollment figure of 1200 students" and maintain this number. This last point concerned him greatly, for he was persuaded that, thanks to the declining birth-rate and a decreased immigration, collegiate enrollments might begin to fall off about 1941.[104] To maintain such "ever normal enrollment," he appealed to the alumni for assistance in getting each year a class of four hundred "quality" freshmen, who, "in accordance with the traditional ratio between the sexes at Bucknell of two men students to one woman student," would comprise about 267 men and 133 women. To facilitate this work, the registrar, he said, had appointed as director of admissions a young alumnus, Lee Francis Lybarger, Jr., of the Class of 1928, to co-operate with the committees of alumni on the admission of freshmen that were being organized in Pennsylvania and in adjoining states.[105]

The capital debt of the University, which in December, 1938, amounted to $358,000, had been causing President Marts no end of worry. The burden of servicing this debt—$25,000 to $30,000 a year—he called unbearable, but he was pleased to report that a committee working to raise money to liquidate this debt had acquired subscriptions amounting to $178,000. He persuaded the Trustees not to undertake the construction of any more buildings until the indebtedness was wiped out, and also, characteristically, he prevailed upon them to affirm that, when building operations should be resumed, "a new Library Building should be next in order." [106] But the complete removal of the debt and the erection of a new building for the library were farther away than President Marts then suspected.

In his planning for the future security of Bucknell, President Marts, by 1940, was looking forward to a larger endowment for it than it then had. In a memorandum that he prepared in October of that year, he said that the University should endeavor to get, besides "a new library, a new science building, a new auditorium, a new chapel, the completion of the Davis Gym, [and] a new power plant," an increase in its endowment from about $1,500,000, which it then had, to $5,000,000; and all these things it should get, if possible, before its one-hundredth anniversary in 1946, the date beyond which he was not then planning.[107] But, thanks to circumstances beyond his control, none of these things was to be acquired by 1946. The largest accession to the endowment during his administration came from the completion in 1937 of a merger, which had been under way for several years before he became president of Bucknell, of Bucknell University with the Western Pennsylvania Classical and Scientific Institute, at Mount Pleasant. By this merger, Bucknell received not only the property of the institute, but also an endowment fund of $85,586.22, which would be known as the LeRoy Stephens–Mount Pleasant Endowment and Scholarship Fund.[108] Considerable sentiment clustered about this merger, for the so-called Mount Pleasant Institute through long years had been an important "feeder" of students to the University, and its president, also through long years, had been LeRoy Stephens, of the Class of 1868, who for many years had served as a member of the Board of Trustees of the University.[109]

But all these things—buildings, the liquidation of indebtedness, financial solvency, and the enlargement of endowment—President Marts regarded merely as means to ends: the gaining of greater recognition for Bucknell in educational circles, the encouragement of the faculty to maximal performance in teaching and in scholarship, and the upholding, as he said again and again, of "an ideal toward which all students and faculty might devote their enthusiasm and energy to a noble purpose for life together on our 'Three Hundred Acres Set Apart.' " [110] Bucknell, he averred, needed "continued growth in high idealism. We have [he affirmed] made splendid progress in that direction—students, faculty, alumni—but I long for continued progress in order that we may feel that our students are learning ways of decency and honor, and not simply learning to be smarter." [111] In this statement of purposes, President Marts was, in effect, saying that he was in cordial agreement with the aspirations of his immediate predecessor, Dr. Homer P. Rainey. In respect to such matters, what one began and the other carried on we can here describe only in sketchy outline.

In his efforts to enhance the prestige of the University, President Marts gave much thought and no little effort to raising the quality of its engineering education. Adequate housing for the four branches of engineering that Bucknell was offering would, he perceived, only partly accomplish this object. To win adequate accreditation for Bucknell's engineering education, it would be necessary to strengthen the engineering faculty, to improve the administration of the four branches of engineering, and to revise the curricular offerings in engineering. These things he quickly accomplished, and the goal which he sought in curricular revision rested upon his belief, as he said very clearly in the introduction to a Bucknell bulletin on engineering in 1940, that the "function of the college is to train the mind and the personality, rather than the hand. The manual skills [he affirmed] can be quickly acquired by those who have become masters of the basic precepts—and of themselves." [112]

In December, 1939, Dean Rivenburg reported to the Trustees that, on October 20 of that year, the Engineers' Council for Professional Development had accredited at Bucknell civil, electrical, and mechanical engineering. "This was a happy ending of a long trail," he said. "For the last three years [he continued] President Marts has planned and executed in masterly fashion, including the revision of all the Engineering curricula, and the building of the Engineering Building, to bring about the complete accreditment of the Bucknell Engineering Department[s]." The American Institute of Chemical Engineers, which inspected and accredited chemical engineering, had deferred its examination, Dean Rivenburg continued, until the Department of Chemical Engineering should be installed in the new Engineering Building.[113] On October 18, 1942, this department also was fully accredited.[114]

Another yearned-for recognition—one which Bucknell had endeavored, unsuccessfully, for more than thirty years to get—President Marts sought and obtained within five years. This was a chapter in the Phi Beta Kappa Society. Here the story of this accomplishment must be told in a few words. On December 14, 1939, at the annual dinner party given to the faculty and the administration by the Women's Student Government Association, President Marts announced that Bucknell had been nominated for a chapter of Phi Beta Kappa.[115] This announcement Dean

Rivenburg passed on to the Trustees in his report of June 8, 1940, saying, *inter alia,* that this accomplishment had been largely the consequence of President Marts's "unremitting efforts for a number of years."[116] The nomination was approved at the Triennial Meeting of the United Chapters on August 30, 1940, and on November 7 of that year the Mu Chapter of Pennsylvania, Phi Beta Kappa, was established on the campus of Bucknell University with elaborate ceremonies featured by two principal addresses, one by Miss Marjorie Nicholson, president of the United Chapters of Phi Beta Kappa, and the other by Dr. Frank P. Graves, a former president of the University of the State of New York. On this occasion, keys were awarded to seventeen charter members of the Mu Chapter.[117]

Still another coveted organization was established on the Bucknell campus during the academic year 1940–41. On February 16, 1941, about three months after the ceremonies at the installation of the chapter of Phi Beta Kappa, all the members of the C.E.A., a local honorary society for women, were initiated into the new Bucknell chapter of Mortar Board, a national honorary society for women.[118]

The desire for prestige, as well as for the improvement of teaching and scholarship, underlay President Marts's concern about the library of Bucknell. In the years immediately preceding his coming to the campus, the library, despite the depression, had been growing, partly by purchases and partly by gifts; but its need for more books and more periodicals was still as great as its need for more adequate quarters. To the solution of this problem President Marts brought his usual enthusiasm and his extraordinary skill in organization. One of his first services to the library was to help organize a group of friends to promote the interests of the library. As early as the autumn of 1933, the editor of the *Bucknell Alumni Monthly* had written that an effort was under way at Bucknell to "form a 'Friends of the Library Association' patterned after similar organizations at other colleges."[119] But no progress was made toward forming such an organization until President Marts, with the hearty support of the librarian, Miss Eliza J. Martin, took the matter in hand. By September, 1936, he was making preparations for a meeting to be held in Lewisburg on October 10 of that year for the purpose of forming a group to be known as "The Friends of the Library" of Bucknell. The meeting was held as scheduled, and the society was formed. This organization, under the presidency of Norman E. Henry, of Pittsburgh, made large and significant contributions to the library during the next five years; and in November, 1936, it brought out the first issue of its bulletin, *Bibliotheca Bucnellensis.*[120]

In the remarkable growth of the library that was then getting under way, Miss Martin participated for only a short time. She died in July, 1938, and was succeeded by Harold W. Hayden, Bucknell's first fully trained librarian. Under his administration, thanks in large part to returning prosperity, the collections of the library increased fairly rapidly—from a total of 68,772 catalogued volumes in the year 1938–39 to a total of 94,826 catalogued volumes in the year 1943–44. Such growth, of course, increased the congestion in the Carnegie Building, and by 1939 the librarian was reporting that, with a "normal growth of between five and seven thousand volumes each year, we can not hope to handle them many more years in the present building as there is no other stack space available." [121] Nevertheless, the library remained "in the present building" until 1951, and it continued to grow.

Meanwhile, President Marts had taken two additional steps toward encouraging the systematic development of the library. During the year 1938–39, the library was a subject of discussion in several meetings of the faculty, and in the autumn of 1939, the Faculty Advisory Committee, pursuant to a suggestion made by President Marts, took under its consideration the matter of formulating a policy for the library. Before the end of October in that year, a member of this committee had drafted in outline "Proposals for a Policy for the Library of Bucknell University," which were approved enthusiastically by President Marts, adopted by the Faculty Advisory Committee, and, after discussion, were approved by the faculty on January 11, 1940.[122]

These proposals rested upon a few basic assumptions—namely, that Bucknell would remain small (about 1,300 students); that it would continue to be coeducational; that its library should reflect interest in its own history as a church-related institution; and, finally, that "a good college, no matter how small it may be, needs a large library." Pursuant to the foregoing considerations, it was proposed that purchases of books and of other materials should be made in part from the standpoint of the needs of the students and in part from the standpoint of the needs of the faculty. The details of these proposals can not here be presented, but it may be said that, except as they have been adapted to two new changes in outlook—that is, an increase in the number of students to 2,400 or more and the widening of the scope of institutional interest to include offerings in Eastern Civilization—these proposals still serve as guiding principles in respect to the growth of the library.[123]

President Marts's second step toward encouraging the growth of the library, which perhaps in the long run was his greatest contribution to it, was his opening the way to the acquisition of a new building for the library. His own observations, the annual reports of the librarian, and adverse criticisms of the crowded quarters of the library from those who inspected Bucknell with a view to recommending it for a chapter of Phi Beta Kappa easily persuaded him that this was a matter which should not be further postponed. Accordingly, after getting the approval of the Trustees, in December, 1938, of his suggestion that the "next building" should be one for the library, he started a campaign to raise money for that object.[124] He appealed, on the one hand, to the alumni of the University, and, on the other hand, to the Friends of the Library. In a letter to the alumni, in January, 1939, after describing the congestion in the Carnegie Building, in which the space for shelves could not be enlarged, he affirmed that the library must have "a new and enlarged building" in order to enable it to "keep pace" with the demands made upon it. "A fine library," he wisely remarked, "is the heart of a modern college." [125] To the Friends of the Library he made a similar appeal in October of that year, promising them that, as soon as practicable, a new building for the library would be erected and, by way of encouragement, informing them that a generous friend had already contributed $50,000 to a fund for such a building. "The New Library Building," he continued,

> will be the central point of the Bucknell Campus of the future. It will be on the high plateau between the Engineering Building and the Memorial Stadium, facing north. All the important buildings to be erected on the Bucknell Campus for the next hundred years are planned on an axis or cross-axis in relation to the new Library. The Library will be the heart and center of Bucknell for generations to come.[126]

Having thus sought to arouse the interest of both the alumni and the Friends of the Library in the campaign that he was starting, President Marts prepared, apparently late in the autumn of 1939, a more detailed and a more intimate appeal in the form of a "confidential statement" to be presented to the Trustees and to a few other friends of the University —that is, an appeal to men and women of both means and influence from whom he might expect substantial contributions to a worthy cause. Informed by what the librarian told him would be required to make the library adequate to the needs of 1,300 students, he wrote as follows:

> It is generally agreed in educational circles that a college of our size and quality should have from 100,000 to 150,000 books in its library. . . . We have 69,842 books catalogued and on the shelves. In addition, we have 27,000 books which we are obliged to keep boxed up because we have no shelves for them. . . . A good College Library should provide enough seats so that 25%–40% of its students could be seated at any one time. This means [that] we should have from 315 to 520 seats in our library, but we

> now have only 170 seats, and it is impossible to provide more in our present library building. A college of our size should subscribe to 650 periodicals each year. Bucknell subscribes to 411 periodicals, and the Periodical Room in our present Carnegie Library will not admit of expansion. A college should spend at least $25 per student per year on its library—for new books, for binding and rebinding, for staff salaries, and for general operations, exclusive of light, heat, and janitor service. By this standard, Bucknell should spend at least $32,000 per year on our library. Our present library budget is $21,180.01.

Moreover, he pointed out that, in comparison with the libraries of colleges in general, and more particularly in comparison with the libraries of nine other colleges generally regarded as competitors of Bucknell, the library of Bucknell left much to be desired. Accordingly, he concluded that the library of Bucknell needed a new building which, with adequate furnishings and equipment, would cost about $350,000; and that, furthermore, the library of Bucknell needed an additional endowment of $250,000. For the construction of a new building, he remarked in conclusion, he had already received from three "generous friends" gifts amounting to $150,000.[127]

This campaign, however, soon came to a halt. Although President Marts could report to the alumni in May, 1940, that one of the Trustees had recently made a gift of $80,000 to the Library Building Fund,[128] the deteriorating international situation required, a few months later, that the "books be closed" to contributions to this fund. Not until December, 1945, were these books again opened; [129] and before that time Mr. Marts had ceased to be president of Bucknell University.

Even greater than President Marts's desire to improve the condition of the library was his persistent eagerness to encourage the members of his faculty to strive for excellence in both teaching and scholarship. Accordingly, he saw to it that, in September, 1936, one-half of the "cut" that had been made in faculty salaries in 1932 was restored, and that, in March, 1937, the other half was restored.[130] Furthermore, he favored the enlargement of the teaching staff as much as was practicable; he approved the granting of leaves of absence for advanced study or for research; and he worked hard to raise money that could be used for increasing the salaries of members of the faculty. But during his presidency, and beyond, the salaries of members of the faculty at Bucknell, through no fault of his, remained relatively low. One of the much desired things, however, that was accomplished in the interest of the faculty and of the staff of the library during his administration was the adoption of a retirement plan. The plan that was put into effect was approved by the Trustees in December, 1938, and became effective on April 1, 1939.[131] For members of the faculty on that date, participation in the plan was optional; for those who joined the faculty thereafter, participation would be compulsory. Pursuant to a request of the faculty, expressed in a resolution adopted on May 6, 1937, the plan provided that each member of the faculty participating in the plan should contribute to the retirement fund five per cent of his salary, and that the University should contribute a like sum. The plan was to be operated through the Teachers Insurance and Annuity Association of America.[132]

To a plan promoted by two members of the faculty in 1937 for the purpose of encouraging productive scholarship at Bucknell, President Marts gave his enthusiastic support, and, when such an organization was effected in 1938, an organization soon to be called the Bucknell Scholars' Club, he attended its monthly meetings, and, as honorary president, presided over its sessions. Foremost among the objects of this organization were, first, the bringing together of interested members of the faculty for a monthly dinner, which would be followed by the reading of at least one scholarly paper by a member of the group, and, secondly, the beginning, as soon as practicable, of the publication of a series of studies by members of the faculty under the general title of *Bucknell University Studies*. At the first meeting of this group, held in the Hotel Lewisburger on March 10, 1938, two papers were read: one by Professor Philip L. Harriman, entitled "The Dream of Falling," and the other by Professor C. Willard Smith, entitled "Imagery in Robert Browning's Poetry." The price of the dinner that evening was seventy-five cents.[133] Thereafter this club met regularly, and Dean Rivenburg reported to the Trustees on June 10, 1939, that this group, which met on the first Thursday evening of each month, had held "ten meetings in a little over a year, at which nineteen papers based on research" had been read.[134]

Despite the looseness of its organization, the Bucknell Scholars' Club proved to be both effective and enduring. Its membership has always consisted of such members of the faculty as are present at a given meeting of the club. It has adopted no written constitution, and it has kept no minutes of its meetings; and, *mirabile dictu,* its members have paid no dues. From this group there presently emerged a periodical publication, the *Bucknell University Studies,* which published only papers prepared by members of the faculty of Bucknell. The first issue of the *Studies* was brought out in 1941. Further publication was suspended because of the Second World War, but the periodical was revived in 1949 and continued until 1954, when, after a reorganization, it emerged in 1955 as the *Bucknell Review.*

It remains to say a few words about the students at Bucknell during the second half of the decade of the 1930's. From 1935 to the coming of the war in 1941, the "problem" of students was not, as it had been from 1930 to 1935, one of getting adequate enrollments; on the contrary, it was, in the opinion of President Marts, a problem of getting able students who did not need a great deal of "aid" in the form of scholarships or work, of assuring such students adequate facilities for study and instruction, of providing for them adequate opportunities for recreation and wholesome social activities, and of upholding before them the ideal of "a noble purpose for life." [135] In an effort to solve this problem, President Marts gave much of his time, much of his energy, and no slight amount of his personal means.

To keep the enrollment at 1,200 students in residence proved to be impracticable. Despite the raising of standards for admission and the dropping of a considerable number of students for poor scholarship, the enrollment rose from 1,322 in 1937–38 to 1,426 in 1938–39, but dropped to 1,423 in 1940–41.[136] During those years, the cost of attending Bucknell remained virtually unchanged. The cost of tuition continued to be $10 a semester hour through the year 1940–41, and the cost of a furnished room in either West College or East College remained at $120 a year as late as 1941–42; but a furnished room in the reconstructed Old Main in the last-named year cost $170.[137] The student budget fee of $25 a year remained unchanged during those years, as did also the infirmary fee of $14 a year. In 1940–41, board in the men's dining hall, which was not available in 1935–36, cost $230 a year.[138] For women, board and furnished room had increased in most of their houses from $400 to $500 a year in 1935–36 to $450 to $500 a year in 1940–41.[139] By 1942–43, however, the cost of tuition for "the normal degree requirement" had risen to $400 a year.[140]

The general pattern of organized activities of the students had become well established before the opening of the decade of the 1930's, and President Marts was not concerned about changing this pattern. What he particularly sought was a greater emphasis on "wholesome social facilities" for the students and the giving of a "moral and religious direction" to their lives. "What is the use," he asked in 1938, "of educating a generation of 'smart' men and women" and of discovering that "their smartness is being used to develop their lives along immoral and selfish lines? I put more of myself and my thought and energy and personality into endeavors along these lines [he continued] than into all of the rest of my endeavors at Bucknell." [141] From the beginning of his presidency, he had presided regularly at the weekly exercises at chapel, had delivered the baccalaureate address for each graduating class, and had encouraged the students to assume responsibility for their own government through the Student-Faculty Congress, a body consisting of eighteen students and twelve members of the faculty that had been formed in 1933 to supervise the activities of the students.[142] Moreover, in order to improve the work of counseling students and to relieve Dean Rivenburg of the additional duties that had been imposed upon him when, for reasons of economy, the office of dean of students had not been filled after Dr. J. Hillis Miller had resigned from that office in 1935, he approved the appointment, in June, 1937, of Dr. Robert L. Sutherland, chairman of the Department of Sociology, as a part-time dean of men.[143] Nor did his concern about the well-being of the students end here. As a means of helping seniors and graduates to find employment, he established, in the spring of 1937, a general placement bureau, and appointed an alumni advisory committee to assist it.[144] This bureau, it appears, was markedly successful, for in June, 1940, Dean Rivenburg reported that, under the direction of Paul Hightower, secretary to the president, it had placed more than ninety per cent of the graduates of the preceding year who had applied to it for help.[145]

As a further means of developing the spiritual life of the students and of enlarging their opportunities for social activities, President Marts "put up the money" in 1937 to purchase a tract of about twenty-eight acres near the village of Cowan, about seven miles west of Lewisburg, to be used as the site for a lodge which he hoped could soon be erected by the Christian Association; [146] and also, in 1940, he instituted the practice of holding annually on the campus a Religion-in-Life Week. In announcing the first of these affairs, to be held on February 18–22, 1940, he said, "The war in Europe has brought to college students a haunting uncertainty, a deep desire to take hold of some fixed and eternal value in life to which they can cling in a world of hate and disorder. I hope that our 'Religion in Life' program will help many of our young men and women to find deep and abiding foundations on which they can build lives of strength and beauty." [147] Moreover, as a contribution to the entertainment of the students, he had provided money in 1938 for the purchase of a "motion picture apparatus" in order that they might have weekly shows of their own "on the Hill." [148]

His concern extended also to the athletic contests of the students. Because of the interest which they had for most of the students, athletic sports during the 1930's, as earlier, were too important to be disregarded by the president of Bucknell. The situation in respect to such matters had been troublesome during President Rainey's administration, when Bucknell was making an effort, conformably to the rules of eligibility adopted by the Association of Colleges and Secondary Schools of the

Middle States and Maryland,[149] to get rid of certain practices which had given Bucknell the reputation of being an advocate of, as well as a participant in, "big-time" football. President Marts was heartily in sympathy with the idea of "de-emphasizing" intercollegiate football at Bucknell by arranging the schedules of the University so that it would play games only with institutions of its own size and class. By so doing, he hoped not only to get rid of the annoying annual deficits of the Athletic Council, but also to remove an obstacle which, he had been told, had stood in the way of Bucknell's getting a chapter of Phi Beta Kappa. Moreover, he looked forward to a time when athletic sports at Bucknell could be integrated with physical education, and when all the students of this institution, women as well as men, would be participating in programs of intramural sports. He did not object to intercollegiate games, and he did not object to giving scholarships to promising boys who wished to play football, but he did oppose the practice of recruiting athletes for the purpose of creating teams to play "big-time" games.[150] Accordingly, in 1937, when Albert E. Humphreys was employed to coach football, he was also made an instructor in physical education; and he taught classes in that department during the second semester of each year. As the editor of the *Alumni Monthly* truly remarked, the election of Humphreys to "two posts" was "an innovation in the athletic program at Bucknell." [151] Still another new development, if not exactly an innovation, was made when President Marts, casting about for some means of solving the problem of athletic debts, brought about the formation, on June 8, 1940, of the Bison Club. The "first and immediate undertaking" of this club was to find means of paying off "a long standing debt." [152] Moreover, the Trustees, interestingly enough, voted unanimously on the day of the formation of the Bison Club to authorize the treasurer of the University to incorporate "into the University's business operations the transactions of the Athletic Council, and, in effect, . . . [make] this work a department of the University's activities." [153]

By this time the shadow of the war that had begun in Europe was lengthening and darkening. Since September, 1939, President Marts had been telling the students at Bucknell that "the leadership for that better world of civilized living" was probably shifting permanently from Europe to the Western Hemisphere, and he urged them, in this time of "crisis and challenge," to work with a deeper consecration for the building of a "world of intelligence, of moral integrity, of Christian brotherhood." [154] After the passage of the American selective service act, he advised them not to enlist in the armed services, but to continue their education and to wait for the draft. In April, 1941, he himself was "drafted" by Governor Arthur H. James to become executive director of the Defense Council of Pennsylvania; but, despite this new call to duty, he continued to give a part of his time to his business firm of Marts & Lundy and another part to Bucknell.[155] Through the months that followed, even after the formal entrance of the United States into war, he continued to urge the students at Bucknell to keep at their work until they were called to the service of their country. But the coming of war, late in 1941, brought to an end a remarkable decade in the history of Bucknell, a decade in which this institution, under the leadership of President Rainey, had adopted and put into operation a new academic program, and then, under the leadership of President Marts, had emerged from the years of depression with confidence restored, with facilities greatly improved, with an enhanced prestige, and with renewed faith that it was advancing on the highway leading to the goal of high accomplishment.

Part Five

The Challenge of a Changing World

12

Through War and Its Aftermath

The ultimate goal of college education is not merely vocational —it is cultural. It should be the creation in each of its students of those attitudes and abilities which make for the fullest appreciation of life, and for the greatest service to that world in which the student finds himself.—*Herbert L. Spencer, Inaugural Address, June 23, 1945.*

Our independent colleges are probably the greatest assurance we have against the complete control of all education by government. But let no one delude himself that the preservation of first-class independent colleges is going to be an easy task.—*Horace A. Hildreth, Inaugural Address, April 29, 1950.*

After the entrance of the United States into the war, in December, 1941, Bucknell moved rapidly from a state of preliminary preparation to a state of complete preparation to meet the problems of war. One aspect of the transition is shown by the fact that, whereas in October, 1940, a course in the training of civil pilots was being offered as an extracurricular subject by Professor Warren D. Garman, of the Department of Mechanical Engineering, after the outbreak of war this course was expanded into a program called Civil Aeronautics Administration War Training Service, and was continued until the summer of 1943.[1] In general, the University was now confronted by a two-fold task: that of giving its utmost service to the Federal Government and, at the same time, of maintaining an enrollment that would permit it to operate without dismissing members of its faculty and without incurring a deficit. The first important step toward accomplishing this task was taken when the faculty, on January 14, 1942, voted to adopt accelerated programs requiring the division of the academic year into three terms, beginning, respectively, in June, September, and February. The consequence of this action was to provide, first, an accelerated program permitting students in liberal arts, biology, physics, education, and commerce and finance to complete their college work in three years, and, secondly, a program that would permit students in engineering and in chemistry to complete their college work in less than three years. The accelerated programs, which began in June, 1942, were required of students in engineering, but were optional for other students.[2] Also, on March 5, 1942, the faculty approved a two-year aeronautics program, and also voted that, for the duration of the war, physical education should be required for both juniors and seniors.[3] A special announcement of the accelerated programs was printed in the Catalogue of the University for 1941–42, and by May, 1942, a new bulletin describing the wartime measures at Bucknell had appeared under the title of *Meeting the War Emergency at Bucknell*.[4]

Although there was "a great fluctuation" in its enrollment during 1942–43, the University incurred no deficit in that year. "We started in October with 1317 students," Dean Rivenburg reported in May, 1943, "graduated 104 seniors on January 30, enrolled 1291 students the first week in February, including 49 freshmen, and had nearly 225 men called by the Army Air Corps and the Army Enlisted Reserve during the second semester, leaving a total of 972 students at present." [5] Despite the recent losses, the prospect looked favorable for the ensuing year, for Bucknell had been selected to receive six hundred trainees who were in the Naval V-12 Program. These students were housed in the men's dormitories, and, in order to provide dining facilities for them, the University acquired and fitted up as a mess hall the house on University Avenue which formerly had been occupied by the Sigma Phi Epsilon fraternity.[6] This accession of trainees, together with an increased number of women, permitted the University to operate fairly satisfactorily throughout the war.

Because the trainees in the V-12 Program occupied the men's dormitories, the University rented four fraternity houses for men who were civilians; but, beginning with the November term, 1943, two of these houses were being used as residences for women. One year later, three fraternity houses—those of Phi Gamma Delta, Kappa Sigma, and Sigma Alpha Epsilon—were accommodating eighty-six women. "The experiment of putting women in the men's fraternity houses with large dormitories and double-decker beds, although questioned at first, has proved a decided success," Dean Rivenburg reported in June, 1944. "The freshman girls have been charmed with the houses and hate to give them up for the Women's College dormitories next year." [7]

In the meantime, the war was having a pronounced effect upon the faculty. During the year 1942–43, the change was striking, for, as Dean Rivenburg reported, the Catalogue for that year did not list the names of twenty-five members of the faculty whose names had appeared in the Catalogue for 1941–42.[8] Moreover, because of the V-12 Program and of the increase in enrollments in engineering, mathematics, and physics, several members of the faculty in liberal arts were being shifted, during the year 1943–44, to teaching positions in departments other than their own; and some emergency appointments had to be made to meet the demands in physics and in engineering. But, on the whole, as Dean Rivenburg reported, the year 1943–44 for Bucknell was as successful as it was extraordinary. "In spite of unusually difficult conditions," he told the Trustees, "Bucknell has gone through the year with the largest enrollment in her history, with the largest income in her history, and with the most unusual group of new students—Navy, Marines, and civilians—in her history." The large enrollment, moreover, had not, as he affirmed, led to any sacrifice of academic standards. At the end of the July term, sixty-four naval trainees had been dismissed because of their poor scholarship, and, at the end of the November term, forty-five more had been dismissed for the same reason. But the accomplishments of that year, Dean Rivenburg frankly confessed, had been bought at a heavy price.

> The accelerated continuous program at Bucknell, 48 weeks of college a year [he said], is taking its toll from our professors, a heavy toll from the older men and some of the younger ones. At present, seven of the Bucknell professors, five of them heads of departments, are not in good health. As soon as the Navy College Training Program is discontinued, the 16-week summer session should be dropped for the sake of both professors and students.
>
> In my judgment [he continued] as soon as possible after the war, the University should plan to increase the salaries of the faculty. In comparison with really high grade colleges and universities, the Bucknell salaries are low. . . . Not only should the salaries of the faculty be increased after the war, but in my judgment there is pressing need for a larger faculty. . . . Our professors have done wonders with heavy loads, but it is important that the University be strengthened after the war by providing a larger faculty for its student body. This, as I see it, is one of the outstanding needs of the University.[9]

The matter of increasing the salaries of the members of the faculty and of the members of the staff of the library President Marts brought to the attention of the Trustees in December, 1944, and from them received approval of the following resolution:

> That when Bucknell shall resume the two semester college year, and as soon thereafter as the enrolment of civilian students reaches again the "ever-normal level" of 1200, it is the policy and intent of the Board that the salaries of all teaching members of the faculty, and the library staff, shall be increased ten per cent.[10]

In the meantime, President Marts had been giving attention to other matters of concern to the University. In February, 1943, he accepted a commission as captain in the United States Coast Guard and transferred his headquarters from Harrisburg to Washington, D.C.; but he continued to keep his finger on the pulse of the University. One of his major concerns was to continue the preparations, begun in 1936, for observing in 1946 the One Hundredth Birthday of Bucknell. In preparation for that event, one of the most important things to do, he believed, was to pay off the "old capital debt," which now amounted to approximately $285,000. In May, 1942, the Trustees had appointed a committee to direct a "special effort" to pay off this debt before the centennial celebration in 1946; and, in 1943, a general campaign was announced that would have for its object the raising enough money to pay this debt. To this campaign, which was expected to be completed by July, 1943, contributors were asked to make their pledges on a twenty-five-month basis, so that all the money would be paid before February 5, 1946. Each contributor was asked to buy one or more shares of a birthday gift to Bucknell, each such share to cost $100 and to be paid for at the rate of four dollars a month.[11]

To the promotion of this campaign, President Marts contributed to the *Alumni Monthly* a two-page message in which he said, *inter alia,* that, in planning for the future, the most important thing to do was to remove the debt which had burdened the University for nearly twenty years. "We have paid out in interest alone during the last fifteen years," he said, "approximately $249,000, almost as much as the total present indebtedness. The annual interest is even yet approximately $15,000." The removal of this debt at a time when further building for the University was impracticable he considered nothing more than "good sound business policy." And he pointed out that, with this debt removed, the University hoped soon to resume the building program that had been interrupted by the war. "The buildings we hope to erect after present conditions have changed [he said] will be a new library, an auditorium, a science building, an enlarged music building, an addition to the Vaughan Literature Building, the renovation of Bucknell Hall for a little chapel and student church, a social science building, the completion of the Davis Gymnasium, and the renovation of the Carnegie Library for use as a student activities building." [12]

The campaign to raise the "birthday gift" was not completed as soon as its promoters had hoped that it would be. In June, 1943, President Marts announced that two-thirds of the required amount had been pledged, and he urged that efforts be made to remove the debt entirely "while the National income is up at present levels." [13] In June, 1944, the chairman of the Board of Trustees announced that subscriptions amounting to $274,295.75 had been obtained, and that of this sum payments amounting to $164,220.25 had been made; and in December, 1945, he could report not only that the indebtedness of the University had been reduced to $9,000, but also that funds now in hand were more than adequate to pay this sum.[14] In other words, the One Hundredth Birthday Gift to Bucknell University had been oversubscribed.

Other matters pertaining to the centennial celebration of the University had also received the attention of President Marts, one of them being the writing of a history of the institution. As early as December, 1941, the Trustees had authorized him to appoint a person to write such a history,[15] and a year later they were told that Dr. Lewis E. Theiss, professor of journalism in Bucknell University, would devote the next four years to this task.[16] Also, in December, 1944, the Trustees authorized their chairman to appoint a general committee to plan an appropriate centennial celebration, and President Marts was made chairman of this committee.[17]

Not the least of the concerns of President Marts during the four years of war was the carrying forward of his plans to make the Junior College in Wilkes-Barre an independent institution. In December, 1943, he explained to the Trustees the policy that he had thus far pursued in respect to this matter, saying that, when he discovered in 1935 that the University had incurred a debt of $30,000 on account of the Junior College, which for three successive years had operated at an annual loss of $10,000, he decided not to take either of the two easy courses—that is, closing it or continuing it as a "missionary" enterprise of Bucknell, but to take the course of building it up with a view to its becoming an autonomous institution. What had been thus far done for the Junior College, he said, had been done with this object in view. Accordingly, he asked the Board's opinion about the advisability of encouraging the Board of Trustees that had been appointed for the Junior College to apply, at the appropriate time, for a charter that would permit this institution to carry on apart from Bucknell. The Trustees approved this policy "and ordered that the minutes of the Board should record such approval." [18] On June 26, 1947, this institution, which then was offering four years of collegiate work, was chartered as Wilkes College.[19]

By the spring of 1944, President Marts was also turning his attention to the matter of planning for the post-war years at Bucknell. In March of that year he appointed three committees of the faculty and the administration to make recommendations on this subject. In making the post-war plans, he said, "we are thinking in the first instance of hundreds of Bucknellians now in war service who will, we hope and believe, return to their Alma Mater to complete their college educations after victory has been won. We are anxious that they shall return to a Bucknell Campus which is alive to their educational needs, and prepared to help them resume their training without loss of time or motion." [20] Interestingly enough, President Marts at this time was still clinging to the notion that Bucknell would continue to remain about as large as it had been before the war, and that its major post-war task would be "to give the finest education possible to the 1,300 young men and women who are selected and qualified to take advantage of the offerings available at Bucknell. Bucknell [he continued] will make such adjustments in curriculum and program as prove necessary to remain abreast of changing conditions." [21]

At this time, President Marts was undoubtedly much concerned about opening the way for his successor to take over the direction of the post-war policy of Bucknell, for at the next meeting of the Trustees, in June, 1944, he submitted his resignation as president of Bucknell University, with the earnest request that he be released from the duties of the presidency as soon as his successor could be installed.[22] With great disappointment the Trustees received this announcement, and they temporarily placed the resignation on the table to await the report of a "special committee" to be appointed by their chairman. President Marts was made chairman of this committee.[23]

Events moved rapidly toward the end of the existing administration. At the close of a meeting of the faculty on November 15, 1944, Dean Rivenburg, after reading a long report on the academic status of the University, announced his retirement at the end of the current academic year; and he repeated this announcement at a meeting of the Board of Trustees on December 16 of that year.[24] Also at the last-named meeting, President Marts, as chairman of the "special committee," recommended that Dr. Herbert L. Spencer, president of the Pennsylvania College for Women, be elected president of Bucknell University. With "deep sorrow and regret," the trustees now accepted the resignation of President Marts and elected Dr. Spencer as his successor.[25] Three days later, at the annual dinner given by the Women's Student Government Association of Bucknell, President Marts presented Dr. and Mrs. Spencer to the students and the faculty of the University; and, in introducing Dr. Spencer, he said that, in June, 1945, he would hand over to President Spencer the seal of the University "with great assurance for Bucknell's future." [26]

Dr. Spencer was installed as the eighth president of Bucknell on June

23, 1945. For this ceremony, he was presented to the chairman of the Board of Trustees by the retiring president, Dr. Arnaud C. Marts, as "Bucknell's new leader, a gentleman fully worthy by his own nature and character, by his training and experience and intellect, to lead Bucknell in its one-hundred-year-old mission of inspiring and teaching and guiding youths in the pathway of growth and fulfillment and of service to God and to human brotherhood." [27] This introduction was no overstatement, for Dr. Spencer was a man of long, varied, and successful experience as an educator. He had been graduated Bachelor of Science in Engineering by the Carnegie Institute of Technology in 1921, but not long thereafter he entered upon a career in education. He received the degree of Doctor of Philosophy from the University of Pittsburgh in 1934, and during the academic year thereafter he served as dean of the College of Arts and Sciences in that institution. In 1935, he was chosen president of the Pennsylvania College for Women, the position which he was still holding when he was elected president of Bucknell University.[28]

Dr. Spencer brought to Bucknell no desire to revolutionize either the administration or the programs of study of this institution. Fundamentally, he came not to change, but to fulfill. In general, he approved and admired the work of his immediate predecessors, and he was eager to carry on and develop what they had begun. As he remarked in his first letter to Bucknellians, it was his desire to carry out, in the years to come, "all the plans and ideals" that President Marts and all Bucknellians wanted for Bucknell. "I assure you," he said, "that I am most anxious to make Bucknell one of the finest colleges in America." [29] In his inaugural address, he expressed his belief that the academic programs of Bucknell would not, as a consequence of the war, be "revamped materially." He expressed emphatically his belief in "the smaller institutions" and in the "need for a division of emphasis" between the two lower and the two upper years of college, affirming that the program of the first two years should be devoted to a "broad cultural program in the humanities, arts, and sciences," and that such specialized training as the student required should be reserved for the last two years. Moreover, he insisted that Bucknell should strive for excellence in its undergraduate teaching. He was keenly aware of the problem of "the returning veteran," but, contrary to some evidence on this subject that had been gathered, he thought that the returning soldiers would not be "content with the pure vocational outlook." On the contrary, he believed that, in addition to the skills which they would need to earn a living, they also would want "the solace which the humanities offer." Accordingly, the greatest problem confronting Bucknell would be, in his opinion, not only to find room for "the large number of young men and young women" who wished to pursue collegiate studies, "but also to provide the kind of curricula . . . to give them a proper balance of professional and liberal arts training." [30]

President Spencer was right in his forecast. The big problem of his administration was the problem of the G.I.'s. It was, moreover, a problem of many facets. Adequate housing must be provided for a great many students, some of whom were married; and competent instruction and satisfactory classroom facilities were urgently needed. A large body of students required a large faculty, and all the persons in the service of an enlarging Bucknell University would need higher salaries than ever before, because of the mounting post-war inflation. Accordingly, on a much larger scale, the big problem that confronted President Spencer was like the big problem that had confronted President Hunt during the early years of the 1920's.

The general apprehension that the enrollment of men during the academic year 1945–46 would be small was quickly dispelled. In December, 1945, President Spencer reported to the Trustees that 1,439 students were enrolled, of whom 353 were naval trainees. There were 636 women in residence and seventy-five commuting, and there were 202 male civilian students in residence and 173 living off the campus. There were approximately 200 returned veterans, and of these about forty were married. President Spencer told the Trustees that, if the naval training program were continued, it would be impossible for the University to enroll as many returning soldiers as it had planned to accommodate. Accordingly, the Trustees voted that the naval training program should be terminated on February 28, 1946, and that the Navy should be given an adequate expression of Bucknell's gratitude for having been permitted to participate in the Navy's general training program during the late war.[31]

By March, 1946, the G.I. rush to Bucknell was well under way. The enrollment then was somewhat more than 1,600, and for September an enrollment of 2,000 was expected. Consequently, as President Spencer pointed out in June, 1946, there was an urgent need for additional housing and classroom facilities and for more instructors and larger salaries to pay them. In order to help prepare the University to meet this state of affairs, the Trustees authorized Dr. Spencer to negotiate with the Federal Government for the procurement of housing facilities for members of the faculty who would be added to the teaching staff of the University because of the influx of returning veterans.[32] At about the same time, the new president was telling the alumni of Bucknell that, of the 785 veterans then on the campus, more than half were former students of Bucknell. To accommodate so many students, he said, the facilities of the University were being extended "to the utmost."

> We have [he continued] reconverted the Navy mess hall into a men's dining hall in which 425 students now take their meals. We hope also to alleviate the housing shortage which has been especially acute in the case of married couples. Work has already begun on the construction of fifty emergency housing units allocated to Bucknell by the Federal Public Housing Authority. These units, consisting of reconverted Army barracks, will be placed on college property directly across from the Davis Gymnasium, along the state [Federal] highway.[33]

While these preparations were being made to overcome the housing crisis, other preparations were under way for the ceremonies that would constitute the climax of the centennial observance of the University at commencement time in June of 1946. The preparations for this observance, as we have learned, had begun in 1936, when Bucknellians celebrated the ninetieth anniversary of their alma mater with a nationwide radio broadcast. "At that time," as President Marts wrote in January, 1943, "a few of us made a quiet covenant with ourselves that we would do everything in our power to enable Bucknell to celebrate its 100th Anniversary in 1946, as one of America's greatest small colleges." [34] The centennial observance was formally begun with charter-day exercises on February 5, 1946, during which, in Lewisburg, the payment of the debts of the University was celebrated by the burning of the last of Bucknell's notes;[35] it reached its climax "with formal academic exercises" at the ninety-sixth annual commencement of the University on June 29 of that year; [36] and it closed with the Homecoming celebration on October 26, 1946, when, appropriately, the football team of Bucknell defeated the football team of Lafayette by a score of 29 to 0.[37] At the commencement in June, the major address had been given by a distinguished journalist and biographer, Douglas Southall Freeman, who was awarded the honorary degree of Doctor of Letters. Numerous other honorary degrees were awarded on that occasion, one of them to Dr. Arnaud Cartwright Marts, who was honored as the man who "found Bucknell a struggling institution" and who "left it free from debt and nation-wide in prestige." [38] Before the end of the year 1946, *The Centennial History of Bucknell,* written by Dr. Lewis E. Theiss, Class of 1902, was published. It received its first notice in the *Bucknell Alumnus* for September, 1946, and was advertised in the issue of this magazine for December of that year as "now available" at $3.50 a copy.[39]

By this time Bucknell was beginning the first academic year of its second century with the record-breaking enrollment that had been predicted for it.[40] In December, 1946, President Spencer told both the Trustees and the alumni that 2,043 students were enrolled, of whom more than 1,200 were veterans. Despite this influx, Bucknell was endeavoring to maintain high academic standards and to adjust its curriculum so as to enable the University to meet the post-war demands upon it. Before this time, moreover, the "emergency housing unit" for the families of fifty married veterans had been completed, and another project which would provide homes for the families of sixteen members of the faculty was nearing completion.[41] The first of these projects was named Bucknell Village, and near it there was constructed, in 1947, a temporary dormitory to house forty-eight men. The second of these projects, called the Faculty Court, consisted of four permanent apartment buildings which had been acquired from the Federal Government. They had been built near Port Henry, in the state of New York, but had not been occupied because of "the abrupt ending of the war." They were dismantled, removed to Lewisburg, and were there rebuilt and fully occupied in the early days of January, 1947.[42]

Nor were these projects the only instances of emergency building on the campus of Bucknell. During the calendar year 1947, Bucknell obtained four temporary buildings by the allocation of surplus buildings by the Public Works Administration. For the acquisition of such buildings without cost to the University, "except for service connections and other site expenses," the Trustees had given their consent on December 7, 1946. "When erected, these temporary buildings," President Spencer wrote in March, 1947, "will give us additional space for classes in physics, biology, commerce and finance, and music. Work has already begun on the construction of an annex to the men's infirmary under this program." The temporary buildings erected at that time to provide more classrooms were called the Social Science Building, the Physics Laboratory, and the Temporary Music Building.[43] They were all used well beyond the era of the G.I.'s.

By October, 1947, a program looking toward the enlargement of both the endowment and the physical plant of the University was under way. It was called the Second Century Development Program, and it set as goals for the University to achieve by 1960 an increase of the endowment of Bucknell to $10,000,000 and the enlargement of the physical plant of the University by the addition thereto of nine permanent buildings, which, besides a new heating plant, were listed as follows: a building for the library, the completion of the Davis Gymnasium and the addition thereto of a swimming pool, a science building for chemistry and physics, a chapel-auditorium, the completion of the Literature Building so as to house the fine arts, a social science building, an alumni inn, and a students' community center. In announcing this program, President Spencer affirmed that Bucknell intended to remain a college of liberal arts and sciences, with an enrollment of 1,500 men and women. "When the G.I. emergency ends," he said, "we hope to reduce our enrollment to this figure. Bucknell does not desire to grow larger, but it does desire to grow better. Through this long-range program, we hope to make it as fine a liberal arts college as any institution of its size in America." [44]

The impetus toward a drive for additional endowment had already been provided by "one alumnus," who offered to give to the endowment of Bucknell $1,000,000, which he would pay in installments of $25,000 for each $100,000 contributed by others.[45] The "one alumnus," who then wished to remain anonymous, was Rush H. Kress, Class of 1900, who made this offer at a meeting of the Board of Trustees on December 7, 1946.[46] Hereafter, we shall read more of Mr. Kress's generosity to his alma mater.

An "immediate crisis created by the need for a new heating plant" obliged the committee on the Second Century Development Program to begin its work by starting a drive to raise $400,000 for the construction of a new plant.[47] The problem of a heating plant was one of long standing. As early as June, 1941, the Trustees had appointed a committee to inquire about this matter, and it reported in December of that year that a new power plant would cost about $300,000, an expenditure which the University at that time was unable to undertake.[48] In June, 1944, however, President Marts told the Trustees that the time had come when definite action about the heating plant must be taken, and in December of that year the chairman of a special committee on this subject reported that "the experimental boiler had been removed from the engineering building to replace the two obsolete boilers" in the heating plant, and that, at least for the time being, the "power and steam situation" had been cared for.[49] In June, 1946, the Trustees voted that $60,000 a year be spent for five years to improve the heating plant, but during the next year the situation became so critical that, in June, 1947, the Trustees appointed a committee to consider the matter of obtaining a new power plant; [50] but, while efforts to raise money for this project were being made, the University, as a precautionary measure, had acquired a "scrap locomotive" from the Central Railroad of New Jersey to provide steam "in the event of a breakdown of the University's boilers." A photograph that appeared in the issue of *The Second Century* for February, 1948, showed workman erecting steam and water lines to connect this locomotive with the heating plant.[51] But by June, 1948, the campaign to raise money for the construction of a new heating plant had produced

$334,184, ground for the proposed building had been broken, and the new plant was completed and put in operation in February, 1949, although it was not then wholly paid for.[52]

In the meantime, other significant changes had taken place. The enrollment had continued to increase. From a total of 2,045 in the first semester of 1947–48, it rose to a total of 2,305 in the first semester of 1948–49, and, a year later, to a total of 2,412.[53] During this period, moreover, the faculty had been considerably enlarged. Between July, 1945, and December, 1946, it increased in size from 94 to 131; but, as Dean William H. Coleman, successor to Dean Rivenburg, pointed out, the increase had been so small that, on the "basis of our present enrollment of 2043," there had been established a "student-faculty ratio of 15.93, which was much above the desirable norm of from 10 to 12." [54] There were further additions to the faculty as the months went by, but, despite the concern of the Trustees about this matter, the increase in the salaries of the members of the faculty had been relatively slight, principally for the reason that, as yet, the University had neither increased its endowment substantially nor advanced very much its charge for tuition. Whereas for the year 1946–47 the cost of tuition "for the normal degree requirement" was still $400 per annum, for the year 1950–51 the cost of tuition therefor had risen only to $500 per annum. The Trustees, however, did take one action looking toward the raising of the morale of the faculty. When President Spencer, in December, 1948, requested that they stimulate the scholarly productions of members of the faculty by making an appropriation looking toward the establishment of a University Press, the Trustees responded by appropriating the sum of $600 to permit the revival of the *Bucknell University Studies*,[55] a publication which, as we have learned, had been suspended on the outbreak of the Second World War.

Paralleling the efforts to make adequate provision for the housing and the instruction of a greatly increased body of students were efforts by which, during the last half of the 1940's, the University formulated its educational objectives, revised some of its instructional techniques, enlarged its curricular offerings, and, perhaps, increased somewhat its prestige as an educational institution. In September, 1946, Dean Coleman announced that, since December, 1945, committees had been at work appraising the educational objectives of the University and, in the light of such objectives, were planning curricular changes which, he anticipated, would go into effect in the autumn of 1947. Whatever such changes might turn out to be, the curriculum of the University, he was certain, would "be conservative in content, modern in method and in keeping with the ideals that motivated the founders of the University at Lewisburg." [56]

On May 19, 1947, the faculty adopted resolutions to put into effect a revised program of liberal arts applicable to all candidates for the degree of Bachelor of Arts who entered the University after June 1, 1947; to establish a permanent committee on academic standards; to permit the development by a special committee of an interdepartmental integrating course to be introduced in February, 1948; and, finally, to authorize the administration of the curriculum pursuant to a policy affirming that, "as a progressive Christian institution," Bucknell University should provide for its students a program which would encourage

1. the fullest possible development of the qualities and abilities essential to an effective career as a member of a democratic society;
2. the acquisition of knowledge and skill necessary for professional and personal success; [and a]
3. development into a well-rounded member of society, with social seriousness, spiritual interests, and active participation in affairs of the community, the nation and the world.[57]

The changes made in the program leading to the degree of Bachelor of Arts were changes of detail. The four fields of concentration were retained, but some changes were made in the required work, the "approximate average requirement" henceforth to be ten hours in English, ten hours in a foreign language, ten and a half hours in art, music, philosophy, psychology, and religion (with work to be done in four departments), ten hours in natural science, and twelve hours in social science.[58] The introductory course in each of the modern foreign languages was elevated from a course of three hours to a course of five hours; and, in order to give women an opportunity to increase their proficiency in French, German, or Spanish, a French House, a German House, and a Spanish House were established during 1946 and 1947. Each of these houses, which accommodated from eight to fourteen women, had for its hostess a French, a German, or a Spanish woman.[59]

The most significant change in the academic program at this time, however, was the introduction of an advanced integrative course—called the University Course—the purpose of which was to "endeavor to clarify the basic interrelations of areas and aspects of study or culture." Of this innovation President Spencer remarked that "Here at Bucknell in the University Course we propose to bring the scientists, the artists, and the philosophers together to show students how the various points of view are related." [60] This course, of which Dr. W. Preston Warren, professor of philosophy, was co-ordinator, was listed as "350" in the offerings of the Department of Philosophy. It was described as an interdepartmental course, "with several members and visiting lecturers participating," and directed specifically to this question: "How can we use the record of man, achievements of science, and our own intellects to act with effectiveness for the good of man and society?" [61]

The curricular offerings of the University were extended by the adoption, in May, 1948, of two four-year programs in music, one of them leading to the degree of Bachelor of Music and the other to the degree of Bachelor of Science in Music Education.[62] One year later the offerings were further enlarged by the adoption of a four-year program leading to the degree of Bachelor of Science in Elementary Education.[63]

While the University was acquiring a new heating plant and was revising its curricular offerings, some of its trustees were engaged in negotiations which ultimately led to the increase of the endowment of the University by more than a million dollars. These negotiations were conducted with a view to the disposal of the property of the University in Fairfax County, Virginia, that it had acquired, as we have learned, by two gifts in 1923. In May, 1934, the University had sold for $100,000 that part of this property, consisting of 260.41 acres, which lay between the Mount Vernon Memorial Highway and the Potomac River. This money, coming as it did at a time when the University was deep in the Great Depression, was like a gift from heaven. It was used in part to help defray the cost of the new Literature Building, "in part to retire notes that had fallen due, in part to pay for a needed enlargement of the campus, and in part to pay certain current expenses." Because of this addition to its income, the University postponed an anticipated cut in salaries and wages.[64]

Not until the opening of the 1940's were negotiations begun for the sale of what remained of this property, and in May, 1949, after prolonged and difficult efforts, the University made a contract for the gradual disposal of this land for purposes of development. During the next six years, this contract, under the supervision of O. V. W. Hawkins, a member of the Board of Trustees, was fulfilled. In June, 1955, Mr. Hawkins told the Trustees that all their Virginia property had been disposed of, and that "the proceeds of this sale amounted to $1,080,-390.30." [65] At this meeting the Trustees voted that a new dormitory for men, which was then nearing completion, should be named the James S. Swartz Hall in honor of the principal donor of the Virginia lands, from the sale of which the University had greatly profited.[66] Incidentally, the memory of Bucknell's ownership of these lands has been perpetuated by the naming of one of the developments thereon Bucknell Manor and also by the naming of a school which serves the people living within this development the Bucknell Elementary School.[67]

A few months before it completed the contract for the disposal of its property in Virginia, the University was brought face to face with the report of a thoroughgoing survey of the University that was intended to provide a basis for the re-evaluation of the objectives of this institution and to point the way to the improvement of its organization and its administration. This survey, the report of which was dated December 3, 1948, had been made at the request of Rush H. Kress by Booz, Allen & Hamilton, management counsel with offices in New York, Chicago, and Los Angeles, and the report thereof was laid before the Trustees at their meeting on December 4, 1948. It was accepted and referred for study to a special committee of the Trustees that was instructed to report thereon at a subsequent meeting of the Board. Mr. Kress was thanked profusely for having provided the money to defray the cost of this survey.[68]

The report of the survey now before the Trustees was as "hard-boiled" as it was thorough. Although it pointed out numerous "favorable aspects" of the subject under review, it nevertheless showed that Bucknell needed to put its administrative house in order, that it needed to improve its planning "at all levels," and, finally, that it needed to "embark on a long-range financing project" if it were "to continue its second century of development." Specifically, it affirmed, *inter alia,* that the plan for the development of the University was "not based on factual planning," that an unfavorable faculty-student ratio existed, that a "major function of the university," "intercollegiate athletics," was "administered by a semi-independent council," that the faculty was not productive in scholarly research, that the physical facilities were inadequate, and that the endowment was much less than it should be.

In general, the surveyors were persuaded that at Bucknell funds had been inadequate for maintaining an educational program of superior quality, that the "basic source" of current income—tuition and fees—was insufficient, and that plans of procedure had not been based on "a predetermined educational program." Consequently, they pointed out that the physical plant of the University was in need of repairs and of reconditioning that would cost $700,000, and that the salaries that Bucknell was paying would "require an estimated 10% blanket increase to bring them in line with those of other universities." Moreover, they advised that a needed reduction of the present student-faculty ratio of eighteen to one to a proposed ratio of twelve to one would require an increase of fifty per cent "in the instructional salary expense of the university."

As to the desire of the University to reduce its enrollment to 1,500, the surveyors were of the opinion that such action would be impracticable. They pointed out that, as matters then stood at Bucknell, the "break-even point" was 1,900 to 2,000 students, and they implied that an enrollment somewhat larger than that should be maintained. They pointed out, for example, that, whereas education of high quality could be provided at Bucknell for 2,400 students with an additional endowment of $7,925,000, such education for 1,500 students could not be provided unless there could be an additional endowment of $7,650,000.

In respect to administrative reorganization, the recommendations of the surveyors were forward-looking. They advised that the University be divided into three schools—namely, arts and sciences, engineering, and business administration, each one to have its own dean. They further recommended the appointment of a vice president for education, a vice president for business, a director of student affairs, and a director of athletics and of physical education, the one last-named to be responsible to the vice president for education. Emphatically, they recommended that the Athletic Council should neither administer athletic events nor select either the director of athletics or the coaches. "Such personnel," they maintained, "should be selected in the same manner as other faculty members of the university." [69]

The committee of the Trustees that was appointed to study the report of the Bucknell Survey and to make recommendations for action thereon decided that most of the recommendations of the surveyors could not be adopted until the income of the University had been substantially increased. For the most part, the members of this committee approved the recommendations in the report, although they pointed out the fact that a few of them were not relevant to the objectives of Bucknell, and they suggested that the report be accepted as "a challenge to all connected with the University to secure the additional endowment necessary to afford to future students of Bucknell a program meeting the objectives of the University." Presumably, they were thus recommending this report as a handbook for those who were promoting the program of second-century development for Bucknell.[70]

When the Trustees met on March 5, 1949, to receive the report of their special committee on the Bucknell Survey, they were confronted by another matter of extraordinary importance, for their chairman read to them a letter, dated February 28, 1949, in which Dr. Spencer submitted his resignation of the presidency of Bucknell in order to accept the position of executive director of the Samuel H. Kress Foundation in New York City. Although Rush H. Kress, an honorary member of the Board of Trustees and a generous benefactor of the University, assured the Trustees that, in consequence of Dr. Spencer's acceptance of this new position, the University would be "greatly benefited," the Trustees generally accepted the resignation reluctantly and authorized their chairman to appoint a committee to seek a successor to Dr. Spencer.[71] At their meeting in June, 1949, they elected Dr. Spencer a member of their Board.[72]

The report of the special committee on the Bucknell Survey was unanimously adopted, and the chairman of the Board was authorized to appoint the committees that might be needed to put into effect such sections of the report as the special committee of the Trustees had recommended as practical. Also, the chairman reminded all the members of the Board of their responsibility to see to it that the Bucknell Survey became "a practical matter to the college." [73]

By June, 1949, the committee that had been chosen to find a successor to Dr. Spencer had reached no decision in this matter. Accordingly, the Trustees appointed their chairman, Joseph W. Henderson, to serve as acting president of the University.[74] But his term of service was short, for the Trustees, at a special meeting in Philadelphia on August 11, 1949, elected by unanimous vote Horace A. Hildreth, a former governor of Maine, as president of Bucknell University.[75] Dr. Hildreth was in Lewisburg in time for the opening of the academic year 1949–50.

Although Dr. Hildreth, like President Marts, had not been trained as an educator, he brought to his new position, as President Marts had also brought before him, relative youth, unusual alertness, and a broad experience in public affairs. But, whereas President Marts's experience had been largely in philanthropy, Dr. Hildreth's had been principally in politics. To his new task, moreover, Dr. Hildreth brought keen eagerness for work, deep earnestness of purpose, forthrightness in thought that led to frankness in expression, and a disciplined mind that demanded precise definitions of the proper functions in the University of the Trustees, the faculty, and the administration. He had been graduated Bachelor of Arts by Bowdoin College in 1925 and Bachelor of Law by the Harvard Law School in 1928. He had practiced law, had served in the legislature of Maine, and, between 1945 and 1949, had completed two terms as governor of Maine.[76] Accordingly, in September, 1949, the chairman of the Board of Trustees introduced him to the alumni of Bucknell as "a distinguished citizen, a successful businessman, an outstanding public servant, and a far-seeing executive, who we are confident will provide intelligent and devoted leadership to Bucknell in these crucial early years of her second century." He urged the alumni to show Dr. Hildreth that "the problem of placing Bucknell at the top among co-educational liberal arts colleges" was one that concerned them as well as him.[77]

At his first meeting with the faculty, on October 5, 1949, Dr. Hildreth related the circumstances of his appointment as president of Bucknell and said that he had accepted the position because of the challenge that it presented to him. He also said that he had come without fixed opinions, that he would take time to absorb as much information about his job as possible, and announced that his conception of this job could be summed up in three words: organize, deputize, and supervise. On the subject of instruction he expressed the opinion that good teaching should be supplemented by research and scholarly publications. The financial problem was, he thought, the most serious one that was then facing collegiate institutions, an assertion which he subsequently discovered to be emphatically true of Bucknell, for he told the Trustees, at their meeting in December of that year, that this was the "primary problem" of the institution whose management had been entrusted to their care.[78]

As one means of improving the financial condition of Bucknell, President Hildreth soon turned his attention to the task of persuading the alumni of this institution to increase their annual giving to their alma mater.[79] Accordingly, by the autumn of 1950, a full-time secretary of the Alumni Association, John H. Shott, had been employed, and one of the tasks with which he was particularly charged was that of increasing the Alumni Fund. "I have no hesitancy," President Hildreth said in December, 1950, "in setting as a goal for our Alumni Secretary the building up of our Alumni Fund to the point where 50% or more of our Alumni contribute each year to the Alumni Fund, which should bring to the college an annual income of $50,000 a year. At present about 15% of our Alumni give about $15,000 a year." [80]

Also, as a means of increasing the financial resources of the University, President Hildreth obtained, during his second year as president of Bucknell, the appointment of Alfred H. Fenton, a journalist of much experience, as director of development for Bucknell. The establishment of such an office, it will be recalled, had been strongly urged by those who had conducted the recent Bucknell Survey, and the appointment of a person to fill such a position had been urged upon the Trustees at their meeting in March, 1949, by Rush H. Kress, who said that "if such an individual were engaged, he would pay the necessary salary for a period of five or ten years." [81] Mr. Fenton was employed for a term of five years, and his salary was paid by Mr. Kress. On May 7, 1952, President Hildreth announced to the faculty that the title of Mr. Fenton had been changed from director of development to assistant to the president, but that no change had been made in either the nature or the extent of his duties. It was expected, Dr. Hildreth said, that the new title would facilitate Mr. Fenton's getting "admittance to friendly audiences to whom the former title was somewhat anathema." [82]

The increase of the annual income of the University was, of course, intended to be a means to various ends, and one of the ends that called for speedy attainment, as President Hildreth clearly perceived, was that of raising the salaries of the instructional staff of the University. In order to make an increase feasible, the Board of Trustees, on the recommendation of President Hildreth, approved on December 9, 1950, the raising of the annual tuition at Bucknell from $500 to $600, the new rate to become effective in September, 1951.[83] In a letter of explanation to the parents of students, President Hildreth, on January 9, 1951, said that, despite "careful planning and thrifty housekeeping," the advancing costs of operating the University had at last forced the making of a decision either to raise the rates or to curtail the service to the students. Accordingly, he said, "we have reluctantly determined to adjust our charges so that they will cover at least a portion of our increased operating expenses." [84] Two increases in the salaries of members of the faculty came rather rapidly in the train of the foregoing decision. Because, in the light of developments during the subsequent decade, the salaries then paid seem pitifully small, they are, as a matter of curiosity to present-day members of the faculty of Bucknell, herewith presented to show not only the amount that was then being paid to persons in the different ranks of the instructional staff of the University, but also the scale of salaries in each rank.[85]

	Spring of 1949	Spring of 1953
Professors	$4,300 to $4,700	$4,500 to $5,500
Associate Professors	3,799 to 4,200	3,900 to 5,000
Assistant Professors	3,200 to 3,600	3,300 to 4,300
Instructors	2,400 to 3,100	3,000 to 3,700

Meanwhile, as he reported to the Trustees on December 8, 1951, President Hildreth had been giving considerable attention to the problem of determining the interrelationship of the faculty, the administration, and the trustees.[86] Such definition he achieved after more than two years of discussion and controversy, some of which was as acrid as it was animated. The upshot, however, was the appearance, late in 1952, of a printed *Handbook for Faculty and Administrative Officers,* a booklet which incorporated not only the traditional "Faculty Memoranda," but also a statement, written by a special committee of the Trustees, which formulated and defined the "Traditions, Principles, and Policies of Bucknell University." [87] Herein are set forth the position of the University in respect to religion, academic freedom, and educational objectives, and the respective powers and duties of the faculty and the Trustees pursuant to the charter, together with the commitments of the

University in respect to such important matters as tenure, leaves of absence, and retirement.

Bucknell University, the Trustees herein affirm, "has a religious heritage" to which it adheres. "It is," they continue, "very definitely a progressive, church-related, but not church-controlled, institution," but, from its beginning, it has been a "liberal college," for no religious sentiments have ever stood in the way either of the employment of a person to serve as a member of the faculty or of the admission of a person to the rights and benefits of instruction in the University. Furthermore, they say, the University has been equally liberal in the matter of according academic freedom. "The faculty," the Trustees affirm, "will have the utmost freedom in its teachings to present fully and fairly all phases of any subject under discussion, subject always to the interests of the nation, universally accepted social practices, truth, decency, integrity, loyalties and good taste." Moreover, the members of the faculty "will have the privilege of engaging in research and publishing their findings as long as such activity does not interfere with teaching duties and responsibilities to the students." Finally, the Trustees say, the proof of the commitment of Bucknell to the principles of freedom and of research may readily be found in the history of the institution.

The educational objectives of the University, formulated a few years earlier, the Trustees here reaffirm as follows: First, to maintain an educational program that will provide "the fullest possible development of the qualities and abilities essential to an effective career as a member of a democratic society," and, secondly, to make possible the "acquisition of knowledge and skill necessary for professional and personal success."

As to the vital question touching the relation of the faculty to "the power to govern" the University, the Trustees make abundantly clear the fact that, as the charter prescribes, the "ultimate power and responsibility" for the operation of the University is vested in the Board of Trustees. Moreover, as they point out, such powers and responsibilities the Trustees can not lawfully surrender, but they can—and they do—delegate "the administration of their responsibilities" to the president, the faculty, and the administrative officers of the University; and, in order that those whose power it is to govern may be properly informed, the advice of the faculty is eagerly sought in respect to matters pertaining to the operation of the University, in proof whereof they reaffirm a statement, made in January, 1952, wherein President Hildreth gave his approval of the representation of the faculty on every committee at Bucknell. Nevertheless, lest there be some misunderstanding, the Trustees firmly assert that "there is no important field in which the faculty is the exclusive policy-making body of the University," and, unless the Trustees disapprove, the final decision respecting action to be taken on the campus rests with the president of the University, the chief executive officer of the Trustees of this institution.

Furthermore, in the statement under consideration, the Trustees set forth the general qualifications required of persons for election to membership in the faculty of the University and for the promotion of a member of the faculty to a rank higher than the one he holds; and in it they affirm, moreover, that "Tenure may be assumed after four years [of] service at Bucknell as associate professor or professor or twelve years as assistant professor." Also, they prescribe the conditions under which leaves of absence may be granted, and they affirm, furthermore, in respect to retirement, that the optional age, both for a member of the faculty and for the college, is sixty-eight, and that the compulsory age is seventy.

One of the consequences of the emotional and intellectual turmoil that attended the preparation of the *Handbook for Faculty and Administrative Officers,* a consequence as significant as it is interesting, was the adoption by the Trustees on December 6, 1952, of a resolution, recommended by President Hildreth and a member of the Board of Trustees, inviting the faculty "to choose annually a full professor who had served at Bucknell not less than four years to sit at regularly stated meetings of the Board of Trustees as the guest of the Trustees, with full power to speak and report to the Faculty." [88] Professor C. Willard Smith, secretary to the faculty, was the first representative of the faculty to attend meetings of the Trustees pursuant to this resolution.[89]

No less troublesome than the problem of defining the interrelationships of the faculty, the administration, and the Board of Trustees was the long-continued problem of the administration of athletic affairs at Bucknell. For those who were charged with the duty of balancing the annual budgets of the University, the central fact about which the conduct of athletic affairs at Bucknell revolved was the inability of the athletic program to pay its way. Year after year the Athletic Council, a semi-autonomous body, had incurred a large deficit, and, in consequence thereof, year after year the administration had run a high temperature. There were, of course, other aspects of this problem, one of the most important of which was the matter of giving "aid" to students who showed promise of becoming good athletes. This problem, however, after prolonged discussion in the early part of President Hildreth's administration, was put in the way of what promised to be solution when the Board of Trustees, on December 8, 1951, adopted a resolution affirming that "the program of athletics at Bucknell University shall be administered in the same manner as other departments of the University, including the selection of personnel and the fixing of compensation therefor." Moreover, the president of the University was charged with the duty of creating an Athletic Advisory Committee, consisting of one student, one member of the faculty, one member of the administration, and four alumni, of whom three would be appointed by the Bison Club. The old Athletic Council was abolished, but all its members were made honorary members of the new Advisory Committee.[90] This arrangement, it will be recalled, conformed to a recommendation in the report on the survey that was made in 1948 by Booz, Allen & Hamilton.

Last in this presentation, but not least in importance, was the problem of enrollment that confronted President Hildreth early in his administration. By 1950, after the outbreak of war in Korea, this problem became, essentially, one of getting from the body of young men subject to the military draft enough students to support adequately the program of the University. This matter President Hildreth had discussed with the Executive Committee of the Board of Trustees on November 3, 1950, and this committee had authorized the "application to the proper military officers for the location of an R.O.T.C. or other armed service training unit at Bucknell," with the proviso that all freshmen entering the University be required to enroll for such training.[91] This recommendation the Trustees approved at their meeting on December 9, 1950, and, at the same time, voted to accept a recommendation of the president to "increase the enrollment of women students as facilities may permit." [92] Accordingly, pursuant to this grant of authority, a Department of Military Science and Tactics was established in the University, and, beginning with September, 1951, its program of military instruction was required of entering freshmen. The basic course consisted of two years of work, upon the completion of which a student, if he should be recommended for further training, would be permitted to elect the advanced course of two years.[93]

At the same time that negotiations were in progress to bring to Bucknell a program of military training, the construction of the second building in the program of development for the second century of Bucknell was moving toward completion. The erection of this building, which would house the growing library of the University, was the most important event of President Hildreth's administration. This project, which, as we have seen, had been set on foot by President Marts, was well under way before the entrance of the United States into the Second World War; and, when it was resumed in 1945, the need for such a building had become distressingly great. The way to the final gifts which would make possible the erection of this building President Marts had opened on the eve of the war, and after the war, while he was serving the University as a member of the Board of Trustees, he widened and improved this way. What he had done to promote the fulfillment of this project he explained to Roy G. Bostwick on February 1, 1946, in a letter which reads, in part, as follows:

> Back in 1940, Joe Dent, of the class of '20, who has a responsible position in the Guaranty Trust Company, told me about one of the wealthy men of this city, named Herbert Bertrand, and through Joe's acquaintance with Mr. Bertrand we discussed with him the suggestion that he come on the Bucknell Board of Trustees. He took the matter under favorable consideration; but before our arrangements were completed, Mr. Bertrand was taken ill and died suddenly about the year 1942. He left a very substantial estate to his widow.[94]

Mrs. Bertrand never forgot the offer that had been made to her husband, and eventually she expressed an interest in a suggestion made to her by Mr. Dent that she contribute a sum of money that would permit the construction of a new building for the library of Bucknell as a memorial to her late husband. Accordingly, early in February, 1946, Dr. Marts and Mr. Dent prepared the draft of a letter requesting such a gift and sent this draft to President Spencer for his information. This letter President Spencer approved without change, and on February 12 he signed a copy of it and sent it to Mrs. Bertrand. On February 26 of that year, in an answer to this letter, Mrs. Bertrand announced her intention to give $200,000 toward the construction of a new building for the library of Bucknell. She requested that this building be named The Ellen Clarke Bertrand Library and that its main reading room be called the Herbert Bertrand Room.[95]

This was Mrs. Bertrand's first gift to Bucknell. Other gifts which were needed to offset the rising cost of construction were, however, delayed because of the effort that was then under way to raise money for the construction of the new heating plant. On April 21, 1949, President Spencer wrote to Mrs. Bertrand, saying that the heating plant had recently been completed, that the library building fund amounted to $557,869.88, and that he hoped that the construction of the proposed building for the library would soon be started.[96] A few weeks later Dr. Horace A. Hildreth succeeded Dr. Spencer as President of Bucknell and took up the work of increasing the fund for the construction of the library to $700,000, the sum now estimated to be necessary for this purpose. From the summer of 1949 onward for several months, the architect of the University was engaged in perfecting plans for the new building, and in April, 1950, President Hildreth told the Executive Committee of the Trustees that these plans should be completed by May of that year. At this meeting, the Executive Committee formally approved the name of Ellen Clarke Bertrand for the new building and called attention to the fact that its main reading room should be made a memorial to the late Herbert Bertrand.[97] On June 10, 1950, President Hildreth reported to the Trustees that a recent gift of $100,000 from Mrs. Bertrand completed the sum needed for the construction of this building. Accordingly, the Board authorized the making of the necessary contracts with the Sordoni Construction Company for the erection of the building at an estimated cost of $700,000.[98]

This accomplishment President Hildreth made the highlight of his letter to the alumni in September, 1950, saying,

> I know that you will share my pleasure in the knowledge that Bucknell's new library will soon become a reality. An additional gift of $100,000, received on the eve of the University's 100th Commencement in June, made possible the letting of the contract and ground for the structure was broken June 16. Construction is moving ahead on schedule and, barring unforeseen delays, the library will be completed and ready for occupancy next spring. As announced earlier, the building will be called the Ellen Clarke Bertrand Library, in honor of Mrs. Herbert Bertrand of New York City. The main reading room will be designated as a memorial to Mrs. Bertrand's late husband, who died in 1942. . . .[99]

The cornerstone of the new building for the library was put in its place at a ceremony held on February 24, 1951, and the building was dedicated on June 9, 1951, the guest of honor being Mrs. Bertrand, who had been elected a member of the Board of Trustees in the preceding December. The moving of books from the Carnegie Building to the new building had begun on May 21, 1951, but the formal opening of the library in its new quarters was delayed until the beginning of the new academic year, when a five-day library weekend was held between September 26 and September 30. It was featured by an address delivered on September 26 by Dr. Louis Booker Wright, director of the Folger Shakespeare Library in Washington, D.C., who spoke on the subject "Book Collectors—American Style." At the convocation in the morning of that day, Dr. Wright was awarded by Bucknell the honorary degree of Doctor of Humane Letters.[100]

Meanwhile, in the spring of 1951, the Bucknell Development Council, an outgrowth of the Second Century Development Program, had been organized by the recently appointed director of development, Alfred H. Fenton, "to serve as an advisory council as well as a corps of salesmen." The plan of operation for development, as the editor of the *Bucknell Alumnus* told his readers in March of that year, calls for an equal division of effort between those activities designed to bring immediate results and those designed to bring future funds. Already [he said] Mr. Fenton is preparing presentations to certain foundations and industry and at the same time is assisting Dr. Joseph W. Henderson in the reactivation of Bucknell's Bequest Committee.[101]

The program of development in respect to new buildings, although in substance it had been generally well known for a long time, the Trustees, at their meeting on June 7 and 8, 1952, approved in its latest listing of projects by their Committee on Buildings and Grounds. However, their approval did not commit them irrevocably to the order in which the projects were listed, which was as follows:

A chapel building, a science building, the front of the Davis Gymnasium, a swimming pool, a dormitory for men, a dormitory for women, a food-service building (providing facilities for processing and for storage), the remaining wing of the Vaughan Literature Building, a social science building, a student union, and a music school.[102]

Of the two objects toward which the Development Council principally directed its efforts during 1952 and 1953, the first was the remodeling of Taylor Hall, in which, after the death on February 1, 1952, of a highly esteemed alumnus, Dr. S. Dale Spotts, it was proposed that there be established a Spotts Memorial Auditorium. The second object for which it worked was the raising of money for the erection of a new dormitory for men.[103] But, before either of these projects reached fruition, Dr. Hildreth had ceased to be president of Bucknell. On May 1, 1953, he submitted his resignation to the Board of Trustees on the assumption that the Senate of the United States would confirm his nomination as ambassador from the United States to Pakistan. This letter was presented to the Board at its meeting on May 9, 1953, but the Trustees deferred action thereon until their meeting in June, when, the nomination of Dr. Hildreth having been confirmed, they "regretfully accepted" the resignation.[104] Their chairman then announced that, at the luncheon of the alumni on the preceding day, June 6, Dr. Hildreth had said that he intended to return to the University every cent of compensation that had been paid to him for his service as president of Bucknell University. He gave as his reason for so doing the fact that he and Mrs. Hildreth were "so devoted to Bucknell, and so proud of it, that . . . [they wanted] to be in the position of having given . . . [their] services to Bucknell without any compensation therefor." [105] In its comments on what Dr. Hildreth had done during his short administration to improve the financial condition of the University, the Bucknell Development Council pointed to this act of generosity "as an example of what Bucknell can come to mean to one man and his family."[106] On November 14, 1953, Dr. Hildreth was elected to membership on the Board of Trustees.[107]

To serve as acting president until such time as a successor to Dr. Hildreth could be found, the Trustees once again chose their chairman, Joseph W. Henderson, and to represent him on the campus they appointed Dean William H. Coleman to serve as vice president in charge of academic affairs and the treasurer of the University, Dayton L. Ranck, to serve as vice president in charge of administration. All these appointments became effective on July 1, 1953.[108]

13

Rebuilding the University

In the improvement of an American University there is no beginning and no end. It must go on, and in going on, it must move forward. It cannot move forward in part, but must move forward on all fronts.—*Merle M. Odgers, in "About Bucknell," 1958.*

While the committee appointed to find a successor to Dr. Hildreth was still engaged in its task, the efforts to renovate existing buildings and to get money for the construction of a new dormitory for men continued. At the meeting of the Trustees in November, 1953, the Committee of the Trustees on Buildings and Grounds reported, *inter alia,* that, since the meeting in the preceding June, the Senior Honor House had been completely remodeled, additional rooms had been completed in Bucknell Cottage, and thirty rooms had been remodeled in Larison Hall. Nor was this all. The chairman of the Board instructed a special committee to "make all necessary arrangements and plans for the program which would include the New Dormitory and Taylor Hall projects," both of which were of the utmost importance.[1] A renovated Taylor Hall was much needed by the Department of Biology, and a new dormitory was especially needed for the housing of freshman men. The essence of the problem of housing men President Hildreth had explained, nine months earlier, in a letter to one of the Trustees in these words: "We now house 600 men in dormitory space originally designed to house 300 men." The University, he said, had not, despite its growth, built a men's dormitory since 1908; but, he added hopefully, "Mr. [Rush H.] Kress has offered us $100,000 whenever we have obtained gifts of $400,000 from any sources whatsoever for a new men's dormitory." [2]

Although it contributed nothing directly to the solution either of the problem of renovating Taylor Hall or of erecting a new dormitory for men, an announcement made on January 15, 1954, at a special convocation in the Davis Gymnasium, gave a decided impetus to the program of Second Century Development. At this convocation, as one writer affirmed, "the University and community were thrilled with the electrifying news that a gift from the Olin Foundation of $900,000 . . . [would] permit the early construction of a new science building to house the departments of chemistry, physics, and mathematics."[3] Never before had Bucknell received so much money in a single gift. Despite its being a surprise to most persons, this gift was the result of negotiations which had been under way for about a year and a half. In making the presentation to Joseph W. Henderson, chairman of the Board of Trustees, Dr. Charles L. Horn, president of the Olin Foundation, remarked that the Olin Foundation had first become interested in Bucknell through one of its graduates, Rowland Henry Coleman, son of Dean William H. Coleman. On June 3, 1952, in a letter to Dr. Horn, Dean Coleman explained the need of Bucknell for a science building; and, months later, after much correspondence, several conferences, and an inspection of the campus of Bucknell, the Olin Foundation made the gift of a building which, besides an auditorium seating more than two hundred persons, would have classrooms, laboratories, and offices.[4] For his success in getting this building for the University, Dean Coleman was thanked profusely both by the faculty and the Trustees.[5]

Work on the new building proceeded according to schedule. Ground for its construction was broken on June 12, 1954,[6] the ceremony of laying the cornerstone was conducted on June 11, 1955,[7] and the completed building was dedicated with elaborate ceremonies on Convocation Day, September 28, 1955, at which time two principal addresses were given and six honorary degrees were awarded. The morning address, on the subject of "Science, Scientist, and Civilization," was delivered by Dr. John C. Warner, president of the Carnegie Institute of Technology, and the evening address, on the subject of "Benjamin Franklin and his Scientific Friends," was delivered by Dr. Leonard W. Labaree, Farnham Professor of History in Yale University.[8] A subsequent grant from the Olin Foundation of $109,518 in 1959 made possible an addition to this building that consisted of "four classrooms, a seminar room, and six offices." This addition was formally opened in December, 1959.[9]

The ceremony of dedicating the new Olin Science Building was presided over by a new president of Bucknell University, Dr. Merle Middleton Odgers, who was elected to this position at a special meeting of the Trustees on June 24, 1954.[10] Dr. Odgers, however, did not come to the campus until December 1, 1954, at which time he was warmly welcomed at a special convocation in the Davis Gymnasium.[11] He went eagerly to work. He was never formally inaugurated, for he considered such a ceremony expensive, time-consuming, and unnecessary. To his new duties he brought maturity, a thorough discipline in classical scholarship, and many years of experience in teaching and in administration. He had received from the University of Pennsylvania the degree of Bachelor of Arts in 1922 and the degree of Doctor of Philosophy in 1928. After teaching Latin in his alma mater for several years, he served that institution as dean of the College of Liberal Arts for Women from 1933 until 1936, when he was elected president of Girard College, a position which he still held when he was chosen president of Bucknell. He had traveled extensively, had participated in public affairs, and had published books. Accordingly, he came to Bucknell as a man both of letters and of affairs.[12]

Perhaps because he did not deliver an inaugural address, President Odgers began his work at Bucknell without making a general pronouncement concerning either his educational philosophy or the policies which he expected to pursue; but he did circulate among friends, as early as January 3, 1955, a confidential memorandum which he thought might, with some modifications, become "a sort of sailing chart" for a few years. In this memorandum he urged strongly the need to increase the salaries of members of the faculty, and he also urged the need of measures to promote economy, to encourage efficiency, to avoid undue expansion of the faculty, to maintain adequate communications, and to increase the endowment of the University.[13] Five months later, in a report to the Board of Trustees, he recommended a policy for guidance as follows:

> College and university enrollments will show striking increases in the next ten or fifteen years. During that time,
>
> Bucknell University will attempt to adhere to a policy of controlled expansion.
>
> It will consolidate its numerous gains of the recent past.
>
> It will further strengthen the Faculty and its facilities.
>
> It will raise its academic standards and increase its attention to student welfare.
>
> It will strive to provide some of the leadership needed in higher education in America.
>
> It will undergo a planned development and not a mushroom growth.[14]

The philosophy underlying his policies was gradually made clear as his program of action gradually unfolded. Bucknell he conceived to be, fundamentally, a "teaching institution," which should not become a center of sponsored research; but "individual investigation and scholarly writing" would not only be welcomed but also, whenever possible, would be encouraged. "We know that this kind of effort," he said, "enriches teaching and we welcome it." [15] By November, 1958, his program for the Bucknell of Tomorrow—a program which he summarized and reaffirmed in 1961—was finally completed. It

> proposed a controlled growth for Bucknell only as funds and facilities permit with an ultimate enrollment of approximately 2500 undergraduate students. It proposed that our job is the laying of good foundations, that as an undergraduate institution focusing on basic liberal education we add no new special vocational programs and no graduate study to the level of the Ph.D., and that we encourage research but clearly recognize that teaching is our main task. It also proposed to strengthen what we are now doing in the liberal arts, the professional curricula, and the programs leading to the master's degree. It proposed that as a strong educational institution determined to attain its fullest strength Bucknell establish its Tomorrow upon (1) a superior teaching faculty, adequately compensated for superior work, (2) a student body carefully selected on the basis of talent and capacity to benefit from our academic life, (3) an entirely adequate physical plant, and (4) adequate funds. This has been and is our sailing chart.[16]

Thus guided and thus equipped, Bucknell, he believed, should move forward to better things. This view he advanced forcefully in an address at the dedication of Coleman Hall on January 17, 1959, saying,

> Our chief avenue for development in strength at Bucknell is qualitative: whatever is sub-standard, we must raise to standard; whatever is standard, we must make superior; whatever is superior, we must carry to excellence. This is not a matter of party or creed; this is the good American doctrine of constant progress toward the fuller life.[17]

By this time, the Program for Second Century Development had made, under his leadership, extraordinary progress in achieving the foregoing aim. For several years before 1959, the University had been in the process of rebuilding its physical plant, of scrutinizing both its aims and its curricular offerings, and of striving to achieve the prestige which comes from excellence in performance. It had made substantial progress in renovating existing buildings and in making provision for new buildings. At the meeting of the Trustees on May 8, 1954, the special committee on the projects for the new dormitory and the renovation of Taylor Hall reported that the work on Taylor Hall was scheduled to be done during the summer of 1954, and that the new dormitory for men should be completed by September, 1955. "The site of the new dormitory," the committee reported,

> has been satisfactorily decided, and the financing is to be handled as follows: $400,000 to be raised by the Board, including $75,000 now in hand and a gift from Mr. Kress of $100,000 contingent upon receipt from other sources of the remainder; and borrowing of the remaining necessary funds from receipts from the Virginia land transaction, amortization to be made

through dormitory rentals. This means that $225,000 must be raised by fall, when it is hoped that construction may be begun.[18]

By the middle of September, the construction of the new dormitory was begun, and at the meeting of the Trustees on November 13, 1954, progress on its construction was reported. This building, called the James S. Swartz Hall, was dedicated on October 15, 1955.[19] Also, it was reported to the Trustees on November 13, 1954, that the Olin Foundation had made an additional grant of $19,000 to complete the equipment of the Olin Science building, which then was in course of construction.[20] Moreover, at that meeting the Trustees approved recommendations of their Executive Committee that a food-service building be erected, that plans be made for the improvement of both West College and East College, and that a committee be appointed to study the potential uses to which the Chemistry Building and the Physics Annex might be put. They referred to their Executive Committee the decision about constructing a Field House, the name then given to a proposed addition to the Davis Gymnasium; [21] and on April 23, 1955, this committee authorized not only the building of this addition, which was to be used for "chapel programs," but also the making of alterations in the Chemistry Building and the remodeling of the Music Building and the Music Annex for use in the autumn of 1955 as dormitories for women.[22]

Because of the foregoing authorizations, President Odgers, in his *Report for the Academic Year 1954–55,* could say:

> The summer of 1955 was a busy one because of remodeling, renovation, and construction. The Olin Science Building, the James S. Swartz Hall, and the rear addition of the Davis Gymnasium were being finished. The old Chemistry Building became a Music and Art Building. The old Music Building and its annex were completely modernized and a new section connecting them was erected, so that Carey House, as it is now renamed, is a dormitory for 36 freshmen women. The Physics area of East College has been made over into office space and the Physics annex serves the Psychology Department for laboratory space. The Food Storage Building, which now provides a modern pasteurization plant for our Dairy in addition to three refrigerated storage rooms, was completed in the summer of 1955.[23]

Meanwhile, President Odgers had concerned himself with the matter of raising the salaries of members of the faculty and with the creation of the kind of administration "needed for the successful operation of the many and complicated business affairs" of an institution which was no longer small. From the Executive Committee he had received on January 12, 1955, authorization to advance salaries as follows: $500 for professors, $400 for associate professors, and $300 for assistant professors. These increases became effective on March 1 of that year.[24] Moreover, the Executive Committee accepted the recommendation of President Odgers that, as circumstances permitted, the maximum salary for professors should be advanced to $7,000 a year, the sum which he thought would be about equal to $3,500 in 1939, and that the maximum salary in each of the other instructional ranks should be advanced comparably.[25]

In the matter of reorganizing the administration, President Odgers was authorized to appoint a director of engineering, whose major duty would be that of raising money for engineering education, and also to appoint, effective on July 1, 1955, "an officer to head the business functions of the University, probably with the title 'Assistant to the President.'" Moreover, since the vice-president and treasurer, Dayton L. Ranck, would retire from the treasurership at the end of the academic year to become vice-president and director of development, the president was authorized to appoint in his place Donald B. Young as treasurer and comptroller of the University. Incidentally, since the officer in charge of the business functions of the University would no doubt be called assistant to the president, the title of Alfred H. Fenton, who had been assistant to the president in the preceding administration, was changed to assistant to the vice-president and director of development.[26] At the next meeting of the Executive Committee, held on April 23, 1955, President Odgers announced that John Frederick Zeller, III, had accepted the position of assistant to the president, and that Dr. Mark C. Ebersole, assistant professor of religion, had been appointed chaplain to the University. He was authorized at this meeting to engage Rear Admiral Ernest McNeill Eller (Ret.) as director of engineering and to negotiate with John C. Hayward with a view to engaging him as dean of student affairs.[27] Mr. Hayward accepted the offer of this position. On September 1, 1955, the organizational chart of the University showed that the president of the University expected to keep in touch with all aspects of the functioning of the University through the assistant to the president, the chaplain, the dean of student affairs, the vice-president and dean, and the vice-president and director of development. A year later this chart showed only two changes: the vice-president and dean had become vice-president and secretary of the Bucknell Study, and had been superseded in his former office by a new dean of the University.

Reorganization of the administration and expansion of the physical plant had proceeded *pari passu*. During the year 1955–56, the buildings being remodeled or newly constructed that President Odgers had mentioned in his report for 1954–55 were brought into use—the Olin Science Building, Swartz Hall, the addition to the rear of the gymnasium, and the food-service building being new buildings, and the Music House and its annex and the old Chemistry Building being remodeled for use, respectively, as a dormitory for women and as a new home for the Departments of Music and Art. Moreover, before the end of the first semester of the academic year 1956–57, three other projects under construction were completed—the Freas-Rooke Swimming Pool, a new wing of the Davis Gymnasium; the Cowan Center, a development promoted by the Christian Association; and the front section of the Davis Gymnasium, the construction of which was authorized on April 28, 1956.

The Freas-Rooke Swimming Pool was the gift of two of the Trustees, A. Guy Freas and Robert L. Rooke. Ground was broken for its construction on November 5, 1955, and the building was dedicated on the night of October 19, 1956, "with a program that included 'an aquatic exhibition.' " [28] This pool, available for the use of both men and women, made possible at Bucknell a new major sport, in which some students of Bucknell have won national distinction for themselves and for their alma mater.

Cowan Lodge (or, as it came to be called, Cowan Center) was the fulfillment of a dream of twenty years. As has been noted in a preceding chapter, President Marts, soon after he came to Bucknell, acquired a tract near the village of Cowan for the use of the Christian Association. Here, he hoped, an adequate lodge would soon be constructed, but through many years the Christian Association was compelled to get along with the old buildings on its Cowan property. It was not until November, 1954, that the Trustees of the University authorized the Christian Association to conduct a campaign to raise $50,000 for the building of a lodge at Cowan, and it was not until May, 1956, that work on a lodge thereat was begun. The new building was officially opened on September 13, 1956, but was not formally dedicated until October 28 of that year.[29] As the editor of the *Bucknell Alumnus* wrote, the new lodge

> contains a large lounge and meeting room, 25 × 48 feet. On one end is a dormitory for men. On the other is the modern kitchen, two rooms for chaperones, and a dormitory for 28 women. Designed by Jens Larson, and constructed by the Sordoni Construction Company (both of whom donated their services), the building is in keeping with [the] college architecture.

Many persons had made contributions toward the construction of this building, the largest of them being a gift of $5,000 by the Bucknell Mothers' Association.[30]

The front section of the Davis Gymnasium, like the wing thereof called the Freas-Rooke Swimming Pool, was a gift of several of the Trustees, Robert L. Rooke, A. Guy Freas, and Senator Andrew J. Sordoni. It provided "an entrance lobby with ticket booths, a lounge, eight offices, a classroom, team locker and shower rooms, and a women's rest room." It was completed in the autumn of 1956.[31]

The year 1956—*annus mirabilis* for the improvement of the physical plant of Bucknell—was the tenth year of Bucknell's second century, and the University, so to speak, paused for a moment to review its accomplishments of the preceding ten years and to get its bearings for a further advance into that century. In June, 1956, it brought out an illustrated brochure entitled *Two Decades of Decision: Review, 1946–1956* [and] *Preview, 1956–1966,* in which is shown expenditures, between 1946 and 1956, amounting to $4,749,00 for new buildings, remodeled buildings, and other improvements at Bucknell; and in which also is shown in a preview for the next ten years the need for four new buildings to be constructed at a cost of $4,800,000 and the further need for new endowment amounting to $5,000,000—in other words, roughly, "a ten-million dollar plan." [32]

During the preceding ten years, as this brochure reminds us, the assets of the University had more than doubled—from slightly less than six million dollars in July, 1946, to "well over twelve million dollars" in June, 1956, a considerable part of which, as we have seen, was "represented by five large buildings, a number of smaller buildings, and extensive improvements in the physical plant." Endowment, too, during the same period had more than doubled—from $1,595,035 on July 1, 1946, to $3,309,259 in June, 1956. This large gain in assets had come in gifts from the alumni, from the Trustees, from foundations, from a widened "circle of friends," and from the sale in Virginia of lands that had been given to the University in 1923.

Encouraged by such evidences of progress, and having a "deep faith in Bucknell's future," a committee of the Trustees, after studying the needs of the University for the next ten years, resolved, as this brochure reveals, to "set up five major objectives" for the next decade—namely, a chapel-auditorium, endowment for the salaries of members of the faculty, a social science building, the completion of the final wing of the Vaughan Literature Building, and a new dormitory for women. Because the need for all the building projects herein specified was urgent, no "order of desirability" was established.

The first one of the "major objectives" for the next decade to be achieved was a large building for classrooms, offices, and a Little Theater, which came as the second gift of the Olin Foundation to the University. This gift, announced by Dr. Charles L. Horn at the alumni luncheon during the weekend of commencement in June, 1957, amounted to $1,475,000; and Dr. Horn said that the new building which this money would be used to construct would be called Coleman Hall, in honor of Dr. William H. Coleman, formerly vice-president and dean of the University, who now had become vice-president of the University and secretary of the Bucknell Study. The proposed Coleman Hall, intended to house eight departments of the University, would face the Vaughan Literature Building, and thus would occupy a prominent place in the new academic quadrangle of the University.[33]

Predicting that this grant would set off "a chain reaction," President Odgers said that it had made "self-evident" the need to complete the Vaughan Literature Building and thus "round out this westward movement of the academic and administrative affairs of the University." But the effect, he continued, would not stop with the improvement of facilities for instruction and with the enhancement of the architectural beauty of the campus; it also would open to Bucknell the way to have, for the first time in its history, a men's residential quadrangle; for the construction of Coleman Hall, as he pointed out, would permit the removal of the Department of Economics from the first floor of West College, and the completion of the Vaughan Literature Building would make possible the removal thereto of the administrative offices from Old Main and from the ground floor of East College. Accordingly, he concluded, the latest Olin grant would "provide both a challenge and an inspiration to all of us to achieve the things that this gift puts within our grasp." [34]

More than a year's time was required for the building of Coleman Hall. On October 12, 1957, ground for its construction was broken; on June 7, 1958, the ceremony of laying its cornerstone was held; and on January 17, 1959, the building was officially dedicated, at which time President Odgers remarked that the gifts of the Olin Foundation to Bucknell had "strengthened in unprecedented magnitude the University's facilities in the physical and social sciences, the humanities, and the theatre arts." He also said that Dr. William H. Coleman "richly" deserved the honor of having his name bestowed upon a building which would mean "so much to the University that for so many years has meant so much to him." As a part of the ceremony of dedication, there was placed in the main lobby of Coleman Hall a bronze plaque bearing an inscription which affirms that this building was constructed by the Olin Foundation, Inc., in honor of William H. Coleman, "teacher, scholar, and gentleman, who has served Bucknell since 1924 as professor of English, dean of the college, and vice president." [35]

For Bucknellians who could not witness the ceremonies of dedicating the new building and of walking through its rooms and corridors, the *Bucknell Alumnus* published this description of the new Coleman Hall:

Coleman Hall houses the Departments of Economics, History, Political Science, Sociology, Education, Psychology, Philosophy, and Religion. The building, the second largest building on the Bucknell campus (Davis Gymnasium is larger in cubic feet) is 365 feet long, covering 77,000 square feet of space.

It is completely air-conditioned and contains 33 classroom units including: two amphitheatre-type lecture halls; a television studio for classroom use of closed-circuit television; a room specially equipped for instruction of elementary teachers; two accounting laboratories; a psychology laboratory; typing and business machines rooms; eight seminar rooms; a small animal room, separately heated, ventilated and air-conditioned for psychology research; a darkroom; three departmental storerooms; and forty-nine faculty and departmental offices, including a suite for use by Dr. Coleman.

The University Theatre, which is the central unit of Coleman Hall, seats 514 persons. The central stage house rises approximately 45 feet above the stage floor to accommodate the flying of scenery, a fixed movie screen, and a double asbestos fire curtain. On either side of the main stage are wagon stages to permit easy scenery changes. A part of the large forestage is removable. The removable section provides a cover for the orchestra pit, which will be uncovered only for musical productions.[36]

By the time of the laying of the cornerstone of Coleman Hall, the "chain reaction" predicted by President Odgers was taking place, for on June 7, 1958, the Trustees accepted the proposal of the John Price Jones Company, Inc., of New York City, to study Bucknell's "obligations and opportunities in the world today, and its potential for meeting these obligations and opportunities in the near future." In September, 1958, this company recommended that Bucknell "launch an intensive campaign covering all segments of its constituency" for the purpose of raising $1,850,000, of which sum $750,000 would be added to the endowment of the University, $850,000 would be expended for the completion of the Vaughan Literature Building and for the remodeling of other buildings "to provide more dormitory accommodations for men," and $250,000 would be used for operating expenses and for the maintenance of the annual Alumni Fund during the three-year period when the pledges made during the campaign were being paid. The company recommended that the campaign begin on October 13, 1958, and end on December 2, 1959, with activity suspended during the months of July and August, 1959.[37]

The recommendations of the John Price Jones Company were, in general, accepted, and on October 23, 1958, President Odgers, in a written statement, gave the faculty of the University advance notice of the approaching campaign, saying:

> You will be interested in the fact that on Saturday, October 25, guests at the Alumni luncheon will hear the first public announcement that Bucknell University is launching a $1,850,000 capital-funds campaign as the next major step in our ten-year ten-million-dollar development plan, announced in 1956 and already well begun. . . . This announcement will be made by authority of the Board of Trustees and after careful study by professional counselors. . . .
>
> From now until February, we shall make preparations and solicit initial gifts. From February until June, we shall be soliciting corporations and foundations, and seeking special gifts. From early next September until the end of 1959, the intensive general solicitation will be carried out on the campus, in the community, and among the general alumni.[38]

By early November, 1958, the campaign for the Dual Development Fund, the second step in Bucknell's ten-year (1956–1966) development plan, was well started by the release of a brochure, called *The Bucknell of Tomorrow,* which President Odgers had prepared. Herein he restated and reaffirmed the goals of Bucknell in a changing world. The Bucknell of Tomorrow, he said, will "be the same, but better." It will, he continued, seek its ends not "by academic fads," but by continuing to be "mainly an undergraduate teaching university of the liberal arts and sciences," concentrating its efforts on "the basic education which is the source of satisfying domestic, professional, and community life, and the foundation for specialized training." The job of Bucknell, he insisted, "is the laying of good foundations," not that of becoming a "major center of research." Bucknell, he affirmed, is not interested either in special vocational programs or in the expansion of its current program of work leading to the degree of Master of Arts, and, emphatically, it is not interested in "indiscriminate size." But controlled growth, he said, "is another matter," and he made clear the fact that he was not out of sympathy with the current planning which envisaged for Bucknell a body of about 2,500 undergraduate students, or, in other words, an expansion of its present enrollment by about twenty per cent.

To achieve the goals which it sought, Bucknell, as President Odgers in this brochure made abundantly clear, needed to acquire certain "foundations," the most important of which he called "a superior teaching faculty, adequately compensated for superior work, just as the 'key' people in general industry are rewarded." Three other foundations which appeared to be necessary he enumerated as, first, a body of students "selected" because of their ability to benefit from what Bucknell has to offer them; secondly, a physical plant adequate to the needs of the University; and, lastly, enough money to guarantee it the enjoyment of "freedom from want." [39]

The campaign for the Dual Development Fund was so planned as neither to burden the alumni nor to interfere with the Alumni Fund, which had, in the recent past, become an important source of income for the University. Accordingly, pursuant to an agreement with the Alumni Board, the managers of this campaign determined "to ask each alumnus for a single substantial pledge in the fall of 1959, payable over a three-year period." Each alumnus making such a pledge would be listed for three years as a contributor to the Alumni Fund. To compensate for the losses that would be incurred by the temporary cessation of annual giving, as well as to provide for the cost of the campaign, the sum of $250,000 had been included in the total goal of the Dual Development Fund, and from this sum the University would draw for three years to cover amounts normally coming in from the Alumni Fund and from other annual giving programs affected by the campaign for the Dual Development Fund.[40]

After the arrangements to preserve the Alumni Fund had been made, the Trustees appealed to the alumni and friends of Bucknell to give generously for the purpose of meeting the challenges posed by three generous gifts to Bucknell, one of which was the offer of the S. H. Kress Foundation to contribute to the endowment of Bucknell $1,000,000 to be paid in installments of $100,000 for every $400,000 obtained for this purpose from other sources. Here, then, was a bonus of twenty-five per cent on every $400,000 raised for the endowment of Bucknell. The second challenge came from the grant made by the Olin Foundation for the construction of Coleman Hall. "When we accepted the gift of Coleman Hall," wrote two of the Trustees in 1959, "we committed ourselves to the completion of Vaughan Literature Building so that it will equal Coleman Hall in dimensions and match it in design. Only by this completion can the necessary architectural symmetry [of the new quadrangle] be achieved." Lastly, there came a third challenge when "The Lindback Foundation, bearing the name of a former Honorary Chairman of the Board of Trustees, . . . offered a gift of $125,000, contingent upon raising an equal sum," the understanding being that the sum of $250,000 thus obtained would be used to endow a professorship in business administration.[41]

The campaign proceeded without untoward incidents. By June, 1959, the Trustees were told that the sum of $552,133 had been received toward the goal of $1,850,000,[42] and a year later this goal had been fully reached. At the annual Alumni luncheon on June 4, 1960, President Odgers announced, somewhat enigmatically, "We are over the goal, but there is still no touchdown." He then explained this puzzling utterance by saying that, whereas receipts and pledges had exceeded what had been sought for endowment, the amount needed to finance the building half of the dual objective of the campaign "was $350,000 short." Accordingly, he continued, "We must raise this additional $350,000 because some of our largest gifts were made on the condition that we complete projected buildings. We cannot meet the challenges and conditions of our building objective by taking money from the endowment side on which we are over to balance the side on which we are under, since it is not possible to convert monies designated for endowment by their donors, nor can we afford to forfeit endowment matching units provided by the Kress Foundation." [43] In the meantime, the goal of the campaign had been raised to $2,200,000 to take care of this problem, and the campaign to raise this additional sum was proceeding.

At the meeting of the Trustees on December 3, 1960, it was reported that $2,159,197.46 had been raised, and the reporter was hopeful "that the revised goal of $2,200,000 would be reached soon." [44] It was soon reached, for on February 8, 1961, the chairman of the Financial Committee of the Trustees, Harry G. Schad, wrote as follows: "Our campaign has gone 'over the top' and we owe and shall express grateful appreciation to those who answered our appeal toward the achievement of, first, our goal of $1,850,000 and next, the new goal of $2,200,000." [45] The report on the campaign shows that the effort had achieved, in cash and pledges, $1,106,217.88 for endowment, $954,238.81 for building, and $250,000 for maintaining the continuity of annual funds. The campaign had exceeded the "final goal" by $110,456.69.[46]

One of the gifts contingent upon the raising of the additional $350,000 for building purposes was a grant of $400,000 from the Charles A. Dana Foundation, of New York City, half of which was for endowment and half for buildings.[47] Still another gift that came during the campaign, although it was not a contribution to the Dual Development Fund, was a bequest from Mrs. Ellen Clarke Bertrand, who died on July 12, 1960. During the later years of her life, Mrs. Bertrand, now a faithful member of the Board of Trustees of Bucknell University, had made generous contributions to the support of Bucknell; but her bequest was so magnificent that it made her the greatest contributor to Bucknell in all its history. Her total contributions to Bucknell, as reported finally to the Trustees in June, 1963, amounted to $6,876,907.91, of which more than $6,000,000 had been credited as endowment for the Ellen Clarke Bertrand Library. Thanks to her large bequest, "which came as a benediction at the end of the capital gifts effort," the University had acquired considerably more than the $5,000,000 additional endowment that had been projected by the Trustees in 1956.[48]

The benefits to be derived from the Dual Development Fund were not deferred until the campaign was completed. At their meeting during the weekend of commencement in June, 1960, the Trustees decided to proceed with the construction of the new wing of the Vaughan Literature Building. Accordingly, by July of that year the contract for the new Administration Center had been let, and on October 22, as "one of the highlights of the Homecoming" celebration in 1960, the ceremony of laying the cornerstone was held.[49] In May, 1961, most of the administrative offices were moved into this new wing of what had now become a part of the Vaughan Literature and Administration Building.

During this year, other acquisitions of the University were of considerable value. One of these was the College Inn, which through many years had been operated by Mr. and Mrs. Guy Payne. Pursuant to an agreement made with the Paynes in 1959, the University took over the College Inn on January 1, 1961, and gave Mr. and Mrs. Payne an annuity and the right to occupy an apartment in this building as long as they desired to do so.[50] The University now was operating two "recreational centers," for in 1948 it had opened the Bison,[51] at the foot of the hill, for such purpose.

From the academic standpoint, however, one of the most important acquisitions of the University during the calendar year 1961 was a computing center, which was installed in the Dana Engineering Building and was open for inspection on Homecoming Day on October 14 of that year. In part a gift from the National Science Foundation, but in much greater part a gift from two of the Trustees, A. Guy Freas and Robert L. Rooke, the new computing center was called the Freas-Rooke Computing Center.[52] By January, 1962, thanks to a grant of $11,000 from the Atomic Energy Commission, the "capabilities" of the new center had been augmented by the purchase of an analogue computer, which was "available for use by all the instructional departments within the University." [53]

Still another acquisition that was housed in the Dana Engineering Building, as President Odgers pointed out in his *Report for the Academic Year 1960–61,* was a bituminous laboratory in the Department of Civil Engineering. This laboratory was acquired through "the generosity of the Bituminous Concrete Association of Pennsylvania." [54]

Meanwhile, the work of remodeling older buildings had been in progress. Since the first floor of West College had been given up by the Department of Economics when Coleman Hall was opened, and since administrative and business offices in Old Main and on the second floor of the Carnegie Building would be moved to the new Administration Center, much remodeling was as unavoidable as it was urgent to prepare this relinquished space for new uses. Accordingly, the Trustees, at their meeting in June, 1959, approved "the renovation of West College . . . [that] summer by the Sordoni Construction Company," the financing to be done by borrowing from the endowment funds at the rate of five per cent.[55] By the end of that summer, this building, completely refurbished, was ready for occupancy, and a year later it was renamed the Rush H. Kress Hall, in honor of one of the most generous benefactors of his alma mater.[56] A few months earlier, in April, 1960, the Executive Committee of the Trustees had voted to finance the remodeling of East College by borrowing $300,000 on short-term notes, and by "taking $100,000 from Dual Development cash, and the remaining $130,000 from anticipated operating surplus." This building was remodeled and refurbished during the summer of 1960, and in December, 1961, it was renamed the Harland A. Trax Hall, in honor of a generous alumnus and a faithful member of the Board of Trustees.[57] Meanwhile, during 1959–60, the Carnegie Building had been remodeled so as to provide temporary offices on the second floor for the alumni secretary and the director of development; and, after the removal of these offices to the new Administration Center, in May, 1961, this floor was reconditioned for the use of the Department of Geology and Geography.[58] On the first floor of this building more space was provided for the University Bookstore [59] and for offices for the Placement Bureau.[60] The ground floor of the Botany Building, heretofore occupied by the Department of Geology and Geography, now became the new quarters of the Christian Association.[61] Also in the summer of 1960, the top floor of Harris Hall, once used as a gymnasium for women, was remodeled for use as a dormitory,[62] and during the autumn of that year a new wing was added to the Tustin Gymnasium, which, as we have learned, had become a gymnasium for women in 1938.[63]

No new buildings were erected during the summer of 1961, but two important jobs—one of renovation and the other of reconstruction—were completed. The work of renovating Taylor Hall was finally completed,[64] as was also the restoration of the roof and tower of the Ellen Clarke Bertrand Library. The last-named job was one of considerable magnitude. It consisted of replacing the roof and of restoring the tower that had been destroyed by a fire on December 24, 1960. Advantage was taken of this need for restoration to make minor changes in the building, the most important of these being the construction of nine more studies for members of the faculty and the air-conditioning of the entire building. The cost of restoration was approximately $330,000, of which the sum of $180,000 was derived from the proceeds of fire insurance, and the remaining sum of $150,000 from the income of the Bertrand Fund. During the summer of 1961, the work was completed, and in September of that year, when the students returned to the campus, they "were greeted once again by the lighted tower of the Ellen Clarke Bertrand Library." [65]

The year 1962 saw additional changes in both the physical plant and the grounds of the University. The Ziegler Infirmary, after the Trustees of the University had authorized a contract with the Evangelical Community Hospital in Lewisburg to provide a suite of rooms for Bucknell's use as an infirmary, became the Ziegler Memorial Dispensary. Here the director of the Medical Service of the University maintains an office, and here registered nurses are on duty "on a 24-hour basis . . . throughout the academic year." [66] Also, in May of that year the Executive Committee of the Trustees approved the allocation of land from the farm of the University to permit the enlargement of the University golf course from nine to eighteen holes. Work on this addition began in the summer of 1962, and, somewhat more than a year later, it was presumed that the enlarged course might be ready for use by June, 1964.[67] Still another improvement planned for the summer of 1962, and no doubt the most important one to be undertaken at that time, was the renovation and enlargement of the Bucknell Observatory. The outcome of this undertaking was unexpected, for, while repairs to the building were under way, the collapse of one of the walls made it advisable to raze the entire building and to begin preparations for the construction of a new building on a different site. In December, 1962, the Trustees authorized the construction of a new building for an observatory, provided that grants be obtained to pay at least half the cost of its erection. After receiving a grant of $50,000 from the National Science Foundation for this purpose, ground for a new building was broken on April 2, 1963, and by the autumn of that year a new observatory, situated "on high ground near the Stadium" and costing approximately $200,000, was in use.[68]

For the University the year 1962 was noteworthy also for the promulgation of a new projection of immediate needs of Bucknell—a "blueprint," so to speak, for the years 1962 to 1972. Behind this promulgation lay an interesting development. As early as June, 1961, the Trustees had approved a program for raising $12,700,000 to meet the increasing needs of the University.[69] As one means of promoting this program, a large Development Council, consisting of about one hundred alumni and other friends of the University, was formed, and it held its first meeting on November 17 and 18, 1961, to discuss not only the needs of the University, but also ways and means of meeting these needs. Early in June, 1962, the Trustees modified their earlier program by providing, within their estimate of $12,700,000 for the needs of Bucknell, a "readjustment" that allocated a larger sum than was originally intended for the building of a student center and that reduced the sum originally estimated for a chapel, which was "now planned for use as a worship center only rather than as a chapel auditorium." [70] This revision was incorporated in an illustrated brochure which appeared later that month, and which provided a subject for discussion at the next meeting of the Development Council in the autumn of 1962.[71]

As set forth in this brochure, the new capital needs of the University between 1962 and 1972 would consist, first, of $7,000,000 for endowment, of which $2,000,000 would be designated for scholarships; secondly, of three major buildings—namely, a chapel with a seating capacity of about seven hundred, a dormitory for women, and a campus center; and, thirdly, of three lesser projects—namely, the completion of the remodeling of Harris Hall, one of the older residences for women, the construction of a Science Research Center as an annex to the Charles A. Dana Engineering Building, and the erection of a one-story building, containing five classrooms and the offices needed by the director of admissions, which would connect Coleman Hall and the newly constructed Administration Center. The procedure for raising $5,700,000 for erecting new buildings required, presumably, no discussion; but the procedure for raising a much larger sum for endowment—$5,000,000 to support superior instruction, a euphemism for higher salaries for members of the faculty, and $2,000,000 for the endowment of scholarships—was a different matter, for, to the public in general, a name on a building on the campus of Bucknell would seem more inviting than a handsome receipt for a contribution to a fund mentioned in the annual reports of the treasurer of the University. Accordingly, it was suggested in the brochure above mentioned that the need for promoting "superior teaching" at Bucknell could be met by the endowment of twenty professorships at $250,000 each, and that the need for scholarships could be met by the endowment of one hundred scholarships, each producing $1,000 a year, that would permit the University "to maintain equality of opportunity for qualified, but needy, students." Endowed scholarships for students and endowed chairs for professors could, like buildings, be named for the persons who endowed them.[72]

The first step toward realizing the objectives of the projection of 1962 was taken when, at the fiftieth reunion of his class on May 31, 1963, the chairman of the Executive Committee of the Board of Trustees, Robert L. Rooke, announced his intention to provide money to build for the University a chapel which, in honor of his parents, would be named the Charles M. and Olive S. Rooke Chapel. At the same time, his class, as a memorial gift, contributed $10,000 to be used toward the construction of a portico of this building. Work on the new chapel began early in October, 1963, the ceremony of laying the cornerstone for it was held on November 16 of that year, and the date for dedicating this building has been set for October 25, 1964. The new chapel, which will seat somewhat more than seven hundred persons, will be equipped with an expensive organ, and the building, in addition to the main chapel, will have on its south side a small one-story wing, which will contain offices for the chaplain, a reception room, and a meditation room equipped with an altar, a lectern, and an electric organ.[73]

Ironically, as some persons would think, Bucknell, after waiting long years for such a gift, finally received an adequate chapel four years after chapel exercises had ceased to be compulsory for its students. Beginning with the year 1960–61, when such services ceased to be required, a weekly devotional service was conducted each Sunday morning, at eleven o'clock, in the University Theater in Coleman Hall with the expectation that it would "deepen the religious life of the students of the University." [74]

During the summer of 1963, the University acquired other properties and continued its work of remodeling older properties. The Judd house on University Avenue, recently purchased, was remodeled to provide additional apartments for members of the faculty, and, among other improvements, the dining-room of the Women's College was converted to cafeteria service.[75] Moreover, in April, 1963, the University accepted as a gift from the S. H. Kress Foundation an interest in a tract of six hundred acres at Huckleberry Hill, near Newfoundland, Pennsylvania, in the Pocono Mountains. This property the University expects to sell for the benefit of its endowment.[76]

Although the enlargement and the improvement of its physical plant during the 1950's had absorbed much of its attention, the University during that decade had been equally interested in increasing its endowment, for income from endowment was becoming increasingly a need for the support of instruction. Accordingly, the endowment of the University, during this decade, increased slowly but encouragingly, advancing from a book value of $4,613,987.84 at the end of the fiscal year 1957 to a book value of $5,792,043.64 at the end of the fiscal year 1960.[77] This fund had been substantially aided not only by the liberal offer of Rush H. Kress to give to the endowment fund one dollar for every four dollars contributed by others,[78] but also by a grant, announced in December, 1955, of $538,100 from the Ford Foundation. Since this grant had been made for the purpose of increasing the salaries of members of the faculty, President Odgers said that it would inspire the University to continue its efforts "to achieve a satisfactory salary scale for the dedicated men and women whose teaching is, after all, the very heart of an educational institution." [79] The contribution of the Dual Development Campaign to the endowment of the University we have already mentioned.

Between the end of the fiscal year 1960 and the end of the fiscal year

1961, the endowment of Bucknell nearly doubled, thanks, in large part, to the munificent bequest of Mrs. Ellen Clarke Bertrand, whose gifts to the University have already been noted. Nor was this the end. From a book value of $11,279,847.40 at the end of the fiscal year 1961, the endowment increased until, on June 1, 1963, its book value "stood at $13,049,-021.20, and its market value at $16,883,256.74." [80] In December, 1963, the treasurer of the University reported to the Trustees that the book value of the endowment had become $13,316,583.03, and that, as of November 20 of that year, the market value thereof was $17,282,316.66.[81]

An enlarging endowment would justify increases in salaries and wages, and the raising of the salaries of the members of the faculty had at the beginning of his administration been, and throughout his administration it continued to be, one of the major concerns of President Odgers. This concern of his informed much of his correspondence with members of the Board of Trustees, and it recurred again and again in his public pronouncements and in his annual reports. His reason for this concern was not far to seek: adequate salaries were needed to get and retain superior teachers, and superior teachers were needed to put Bucknell in the way of achieving excellence in its academic programs. "I felt in December 1954," he wrote in his *Report* for 1962–63, "that first attention and continuing attention must be given to faculty salaries," which he had found to be very low.[82] In his second *Report,* which was for the year 1955–56, he observed that, even after substantial increases had been made, salaries for members of the faculty had been, and continued to be, low.[83] Three years later, despite the fact that rather large increases had been made, he affirmed in his *Report* for 1958–59 that the salaries of members of the faculty were "still in need of substantial improvement." [84] In his *Report* two years later, however, he expressed pleasure at the progress which Bucknell had made in increasing the compensation of the members of its teaching staff, saying that a study of the salaries of academic persons in Pennsylvania during the preceding year had shown "that among the ten institutions with enrollments in the 1500–3000 range Bucknell stands in third place for its full professors in relation to maximum salaries, average salaries, and fringe benefits, second place for its associate professors, and first place for both its assistant professors and its instructors." [85]

The constant urging of President Odgers that the salaries of members of the faculty be raised was not without its effect upon the Trustees. On February 25, 1958, the chairman of the Committee of the Trustees on Finance, after studying a "survey" which President Odgers had sent him, commented as follows:

> My review of the salary survey which you sent to me was far from comforting. First, our own salaries are substantially below the average for all sixty-two institutions. . . . In our own group of twelve institutions we are below the average for each rank by 9.3%, 7.8%, 4.7%, and 2.4%. The changes you plan to make in September will reverse this position so that we would be above the averages by 4.3%, 7.3%, 9.4%, and 9.6%. However, the other institutions undoubtedly will raise their salaries at the same time, with the result that our relative standing probably will not be greatly improved in next year's survey.[86]

Nevertheless, about two years later, President Odgers could say to the author of the foregoing quotation that Bucknell's "average for instructors exceeds the general average by $500, for assistant professors by $500, and for associate profesors by $100, but [that] it is under the average for full professors by $100. Salaries [he continued] still need improvement but we are in a relatively better position than we used to be."[87]

The foregoing increases in salaries had, in fact, justified optimism for the future. By November, 1957, the new ranges, minimum to maximum, had been established by ranks as follows: instructor, $3,700 to $4,600; assistant professor, $4,100 to $5,550; associate professor, $4,600 to $6,300; and professor, $5,350 to $7,500. By 1961–62, the ranges were as follows: Instructor, $4,800 to $6,800; assistant professor, $5,800 to $8,500; associate professor, $6,200 to $9,200; and professor, $6,500 to $11,500.[88] At the beginning of the year 1963–64, President Odgers could write on this subject as follows: "Our maximum and median salaries this fall for full professors are $13,000 and $10,000, as compared with $5,500 and $5,200, respectively, in 1954–55; similarly, our maximum and median for instructors are $7,000 and $6,000 as compared with $4,000 and $3,500, respectively. Our budgeted faculty salary roll for 1963–64 totals $1,642,700, whereas the corresponding figure for a somewhat smaller faculty ten years ago was $574,000."[89] Interestingly enough, a study of the operational expenses of the University between the year 1954–55 and the year 1959–60 shows that, whereas in those years the part of the total budget allotted to instruction and research increased from 33 per cent to 36 per cent, the part of the total budget allotted to administrative and related expense decreased from 23 per cent to 20 per cent.[90]

In still other ways the condition of the faculty improved during the administration of President Odgers. Opportunities for research were increased by enlarging the sum of money available for summer-school grants to members of the faculty,[91] and, with the passing of the years, individual grants from the National Science Foundation and other foundations made possible the carrying on of projects of research in biology, chemistry, education, and psychology.[92] Such research the administration encouraged, despite the fact that Bucknell conceived its function to be superior teaching rather than the promotion of research. But, as the administration recognized, the two are inseparable; and perhaps the best expression of the recognition of this fact appeared in the president's *Report for the Academic Year 1958–1959* in these words:

> Because Bucknell is primarily an undergraduate institution, we are much concerned about getting faculty members who are superior teachers. Accordingly, we put teaching ability ahead of promise of research scholarship. Naturally, we do our best to get teachers who excel as teachers and who also are highly competent as research scholars. We believe that no person, no matter how gifted he may be as a teacher, can long continue to be an inspiring teacher unless, in addition to his teaching, he is constantly engaged in scholarly reading and in research. We think that every teacher ought to publish, as often as he can, either scholarly monographs or scholarly articles and reviews in order that he may profit by the comments thereon of other scholars in his own field.[93]

Four years later, in his *Report for 1962–1963,* President Odgers observed that a greater emphasis was "being placed on research and scholarly work"; and, after noting that members of the faculty of Bucknell had published about fifty articles and books during the year, that forty of them had been invited to read papers before meetings of professional societies, and that the University during the year had "received from foundations and other agencies funds for research and development projects to the amount of $457,762," he concluded that "Bucknell must continue to take cognizance of the increased emphasis on scholarly and research work within higher education generally." [94] But, still believing that special recognition should be given for excellence in teaching, he rejoiced when two endowments were established at Bucknell to support such recognition: one an annual lectureship established by the Class of 1956 as an award to be given each year to a member of the faculty of Bucknell for inspirational teaching, and the other an establishment by the Christian R. and Mary F. Lindback Foundation of annual awards, first made in 1961, to three members of the faculty for distinguished teaching. The first holder of the Class of 1956 Lectureship was Professor Manning Smith, of the Department of Chemistry, and the first three recipients of the Lindback awards were Professor Harold W. Miller, of the Department of Classics; Professor James A. Gathings, of the Department of Political Science; and Professor J. Orin Oliphant, of the Department of History.[95]

The condition of the faculty was improved in other ways during the administration of President Odgers. The granting of leaves of absence was liberalized, the matter of tenure was sharply defined and, for assistant professors, the time required to get tenure was lowered from twelve to nine years; and retirement and "fringe benefits" were increased. All these, and other matters of concern to members of the faculty, were carefully set forth in a meticulous revision of the *Handbook for Faculty and Administrative Officers* that had been brought out in 1952. The revision of this pamphlet appeared in 1963 under the title of *Academic Organization of Bucknell University, 1963*.

Two other matters touching the members of the faculty that were of continuing concern to President Odgers were, first, the so-called "student ratio" and, secondly, the professional preparation of each member of the faculty. On the first of these matters, he wrote in his last *Report* as follows:

> Each institution seems to have its own method of arriving at the faculty-student ratio. For better or worse, our method excludes members of the faculty on leave and part-time members from the number of the faculty, and it includes only full-time undergraduates in the number of students. Ten years ago, in 1953–54, our ratio was 12.8 (1812 students and 142 teachers). In 1962–63 the ratio was 13.1 (2333 students and 178 teachers). With a low of 12.6 in 1954–55 and a high of 14.4 in 1958–59, our average for the ten years is 12.8 (2084 students and 163 teachers).

As to the other, he remarked in the same *Report* that, "in spite of an increase in the number of the members of the faculty from 142 to 178, the percentage of the members holding the Ph.D. degree has risen from 43.0% in 1953 to 52.8% in 1962." [96]

To the increases in the salaries of members of the faculty, the contribution of the students in tuition and fees became larger with the passing of the years. Whereas from the autumn of 1955 through the academic year 1956–57 the annual comprehensive charge for all women and for freshman men in residence was $1,500, of which $700 was charged for tuition, from 1957–58 forward this charge increased from year to year. From $1,750 for 1957–58, the comprehensive charge for women and for freshman men in residence advanced to $2,000 for 1960–61, and to $2,150 for 1963–64; and the Catalogue for the last-named year announced that the comprehensive charge would be $2,250 for 1964–65 and $2,400 for 1965–66. The cost of tuition, which was a considerable part of the comprehensive charge, rose from $700 for 1956–57 to $900 for 1957–58, to $1,150 for 1960–61, and to $1,250 for 1963–64. It will be $1,500 for 1965–66.[97]

As it became increasingly expensive for students to remain in Bucknell, so it also became increasingly difficult for students to gain admission to Bucknell. At the end of the year 1956–57, the registrar was relieved of the duty of admitting students, and an Admissions Office was established, of which Fitz Walling became director, and Robert A. Newcombe became assistant director.[98] By this time, moreover, it was "the testimony of students and faculty alike" that the University was expecting more than ever of its students "in the way of intellectual interest and achievement." [99] Yet the competition to gain admission to Bucknell remained keen, and, although the greater part of those admitted came from Pennsylvania, New York, and New Jersey, there was a sizable representation from New England and a good sprinkling from many other states of the Union and from not a few foreign countries.[100] Of the freshman class admitted in 1959, there were 443 men and 240 women; of the freshman class admitted in 1960, there were 489 men and 274 women; and of the freshman class admitted in 1963, there were 452 men and 277 women. With the passing years, as the cost to students kept mounting, the University increased its aid to freshmen: from $25,000 in 1960, to $30,000 in 1961, to $43,600 in 1962, and to $56,000 in 1963; and in each of these years these direct grants by the University were supplemented by awards that came from other sources.[101]

The development of a plan of organization for students' affairs during President Odgers's administration followed rather closely recommendations made in the report of Booz, Allen & Hamilton. A newly appointed dean of student affairs was given supervision of the counseling service, the health and medical services, the Christian Association, and the offices of the dean of men and the dean of women. As "the supreme executive and legislative instrument" for directing the life of the students at Bucknell, the Student–Faculty Congress, an organization dating from the early 1930's, was retained, as was also the Women's Student Government Association with its three branches, a senate, a house of representatives, and a judicial board. As a parallel organization to the Women's Association, there was formed in 1954 a Men's Student Government with three branches, consisting of a house of representatives, a house executive board, and a judicial council.[102] Because of disturbing events, early in 1962, about an invitation from a group of students to a "controversial speaker" to appear upon the campus, a University Committee on Student Affairs, approved by the Trustees on June 1, 1962, was established to formulate policies pertaining to the establishment and activities of student organizations. This committee consists of three members of the faculty elected by the faculty of the University, three members of the administration appointed by the president of the University, five students elected by the Student–Faculty Congress, and the dean of student affairs, who serves as chairman of the committee. "No student organization may use the name or facilities of Bucknell unless it holds formal recognition from this committee." [103]

By this time, moreover, President Odgers was working toward the completion of the administrative reorganization that he had started in 1954–55. In June, 1961, in keeping with a recommendation strongly urged in the report of Booz, Allen & Hamilton, President Odgers announced the establishment within the University of three colleges: the College of Arts and Sciences, the College of Engineering, and the College of Business Administration. This reorganization, he said, "implies no change in the character, objective, and basic structure of the University as we know it." On the contrary, he continued, its purpose was to increase the effectiveness of administration, to provide greater benefits for students, and to "strengthen the possibilities of financial support for each of the colleges." This change, moreover, he emphatically affirmed, was not an invitation to rapid expansion of the University. On the contrary, the program for Bucknell that was set forth in *The Bucknell of Tomorrow,* in November, 1958, continued to be the "sailing chart" for the University. Therein, as he again pointed out, was proposed a "controlled growth for Bucknell only as funds and facilities permit[ted] with an ultimate enrollment of approximately 2500 undergraduate students."

> We believe [President Odgers concluded] that a strong college of arts and sciences is essential to the welfare of this or any American University. We believe that the students of professional schools within a University profit by a connection with an institution which is centered in the liberal arts. In establishing three schools it is felt that the College of Arts and Sciences will benefit because of its larger opportunity to develop its program homogenously without close identification with professional curricula.
>
> Prestige [he continued] will be added to engineering and business education by establishing their curricula in individual schools; . . . [and] . . . at the same time none of the colleges will lose the advantages such semi-autonomous divisions have when they are integrated parts of a University.

Professor Mark C. Ebersole, assistant dean of the University, became dean of the College of Arts and Sciences; Professor Russell A. Headley, chairman of the Department of Economics and Business Administration, became dean of the College of Business Administration; and Professor Herbert F. Eckberg, director of engineering, became dean of the College of Engineering. Dr. Karl D. Hartzell remained dean of the University and "chief adviser to the President on educational matters." [104]

The administrative reorganization of the University, however, was not yet completed, although it came closer to completion a year later, when President Odgers, again following a recommendation in the report of Booz, Allen & Hamilton, as well as a more recent recommendation of an evaluating committee of the Middle States Association of Colleges and Secondary Schools, announced in June, 1962, with the approval of the Board of Trustees, the establishment of the office of vice-president for academic affairs, the occupant of which would be in direct charge of the academic programs in all the colleges of the University. The office of dean of the University was discontinued. Dean Ebersole was appointed to the newly created office of vice-president for academic affairs, and Dr. Leon Pacala, associate professor of religion, became dean of the College of Arts and Sciences. Also, at this time, the director of development was given the title of vice-president for development.[105]

One further step remained to complete the administrative reorganization, and this was taken in the autumn of 1962, when a University Council and an Administrative Council, both of which had been approved by the Executive Committee of the Board of Trustees, were established in the University with the expectation, as President Odgers said, of improving "both vertical and horizontal communication and . . . [of helping] in the continuing study" of the University, "its progress, and its stability in a rapidly changing national environment." The establishment of such councils had been recently recommended by the evaluation committee of the Middle States Association of Colleges and Secondary Schools, although, as President Odgers reminded the faculty, these councils were bodies toward the acceptance of which the evolution of Bucknell had been trending "even without the happy confirmation of a group of visitors." [106] In any event, the action taken was an important one, for, as we read in the *Academic Organization of Bucknell University, 1963,*

> The University Council is the senior academic body of the University. It is responsible for studying and developing, for recommendation to the President or to the Board of Trustees, matters relating to the academic affairs of the University. It reviews proposals and recommendations initiated by other academic bodies and committees of the University. It is composed of the chairmen of all departments of instruction, the deans of the three colleges, the Dean of Student Affairs, the Director of Admissions, the Librarian, the Registrar, the Vice President for Business and Finance, the Vice President for Development, and the President and the Vice President for Academic Affairs, who serve as chairman and vice chairman respectively.

Equally important, perhaps, as an agency for promoting the interests of the University is the Administrative Council, a body

> responsible for studying and developing, for recommendation to the President or to the Board of Trustees, operational programs, policies and procedures that can most effectively and economically serve and advance the objectives and goals of the University. It is composed of those members of the administrative staff appointed by the President, the Secretary of the University Faculty, three professors on tenure elected by the University Faculty, and the President and Vice President for Business and Finance who serve as chairman and vice chairman respectively.[107]

Before these administrative agencies had come into existence, two advisory bodies, apart from the large Development Council, had been established as "adjunct organizations" to help promote the growth of "a consensus of support and of a unity of thought and action" in matters pertaining to the progress of the University. The Engineering Advisory Committee had met annually since 1956, and the Advisory Committee for Economics and Business Administration had met annually since its formation in 1959. These committees, in the opinion of President Odgers, were of considerable value because they gave to the administration of the University "a desirable interchange between the campus and the world of business, the professions, and the government."[108]

The year 1962–63, the one in which President Odgers virtually completed his program of administrative reorganization, was the year in which he made his last annual report to the Trustees. In October, 1963, at the first meeting of the faculty of the University for the year 1963–64, he announced his intention to retire from the presidency of Bucknell in the summer of 1964. Accordingly, in his last annual report, he glanced backward over recent years—backward to remarkable changes that had taken place in the University since the autumn of 1954: the growth of the physical plant, the increase of the endowment, the improvement of the collections of the library, a broadening of the outlook of the University and a better understanding of its aims, an increase in the assets of the University amounting to nearly $20,000,000, an operating budget that had increased "2.46 times" and an appropriation for the salaries of members of the faculty that had increased "2.55 times"—and then he expressed his gratitude "to have had a part in the great development," which, as he generously remarked, "your Board has sparked."

> I have [he concluded] genuinely enjoyed participating with many of our Trustees in many tasks. Bucknell has strong foundations. I knew it first many years ago as an institution with a reputation for good teaching. We

> still enjoy the reputation for handling well what is our main task, teaching. We think that we carry on that main task even better than formerly. But we did need advances on a number of fronts, physical and fiscal as well as educational. It was this conviction that drew me to Bucknell. Bucknell presented, and still presents, a strong challenge. There is much still to be done. My successor, whoever he may be, should feel, and no doubt will feel, that challenge.[109]

Dr. Odgers served as adviser and secretary to a special committee appointed by the chairman of the Board of Trustees to recommend a new president for the University. After several months of effort, this committee presented as its nominee Dr. Charles Henry Watts, II, who was elected by unanimous vote of the Trustees in February, 1964, to be president of Bucknell University from August 1, 1964. Dr. Watts, who was then thirty-seven years old, had been graduated Bachelor of Arts and Doctor of Philosophy by Brown University, had served his alma mater as professor of English and as dean, and, since 1962, had been executive associate and director of the Commission on Administrative Affairs of the American Council on Education. At the time of his election, Dr. Watts remarked, *inter alia,* that "President Odgers has during his tenure achieved significant increases in the University's capacity to fulfill its ambitions. He will be a hard man to follow and his influence will continue in the foundations for future growth which he has established. Bucknell's future should be an exciting one, with a strong tradition of fine teaching in the liberal studies and with an equally strong tradition of public service. Its contributions in the fields of education, engineering, and the sciences are well recognized. It is of a size and structure which should enable it to meet successfully the challenges of the years ahead." [110]

Of the "foundations" which President Odgers helped to lay for the future growth of Bucknell, it remains to examine those which are neither physical nor fiscal, and to this subject we turn in the closing chapter of this book.

14

Looking Inward and Outward

The Bucknell Study was a University-wide project which was undertaken in the spring of 1955 and which was brought to an end by the reorganization of the University Administration in 1961. This University-wide project was undertaken at the suggestion of President Merle M. Odgers as a means of laying a firm foundation for the administration which he was inaugurating. It has involved virtually the entire faculty, numerous administrators, and, in earlier stages, a number of selected students.—*Karl D. Hartzell, in a Statement dated December 6, 1961.*

In the summer of 1963, Bucknell increased its contribution to international education. In addition to the Summer Institute for Foreign Students, a contract was signed with the Agency for International Development of the State Department. Under the terms of this contract, our College of Engineering is assisting the Catholic University of Córdoba, Argentina, to improve its undergraduate engineering education.—*Merle M. Odgers, Report for the Academic Year 1962–1963.*

To Bucknell University, as to all other American colleges and universities, the years that followed the cessation of the fighting which was supposed to end the Second World War brought uncertainty and uneasiness. There was not, and there could not be, a return to "normalcy." The world, on the threshold of an era of nuclear power, was in turmoil. The old order was dissolving; new nations were arising; the balance of power was broken, in the East as in the West. The world had become divided ideologically, and the Soviet Union and the United States of America, the two great powers in the emerging new order, were waging a "cold war" to determine which of them would win the allegiance of the uncommitted peoples of the world. Nor was the situation stable in America. Here the dislocations caused by the war, the rising post-war inflation, and the struggle for effective social and economic democracy had raised grave domestic issues. Accordingly, it was all but inevitable that, in such a time, thoughtful Americans should be looking both inward and outward—all but inevitable that Bucknell University should re-examine its heritage, try to define its aims and purposes, and seek to determine what it should offer to America and to the world in a time of neither peace nor war. The consequences of its looking inward and outward in these years we shall now endeavor to ascertain.

From 1945 forward, a continuing investigation of Bucknell was carried on, and sooner or later all aspects of the University—from the composition and functioning of the Board of Trustees to the composition and functioning of the faculty and the administration—were sharply scrutinized. A survey of the University by experts in 1948 brought forth, among other things which heretofore we have noted, a recommendation that the charter of the University be so amended as to eliminate therefrom a provision requiring that a majority of the Trustees be "members of regular Baptist Churches." Members of the Board of Trustees, according to this recommendation, should be selected, not because of religious affiliation, but because of their ability "to make a valuable contribution to the conduct of the university." [1] To most members of the Board of Trustees, however, this recommendation appeared to be too much of a break with the past. Accordingly, at a special meeting on March 5, 1949, the Board accepted from the special committee that it had earlier appointed to study the report of the survey the recommendation that no change in the charter be made "at the present time," but that "a serious effort" be made, "as new members are elected to the Board," to obtain "members of the Baptist Church who will make a contribution to the University's Board." [2]

But a few years later the Trustees, accepting the established fact that Bucknell long since had ceased to be primarily of the Baptists and for the Baptists, voted unanimously at their meeting in June, 1953, that the charter of the University be so changed that the provision therein requiring that a majority of the Trustees be Baptists be replaced by a provision requiring only that "at least" one-fifth of the Trustees be "members of Baptist Churches." [3] Thus for Bucknell the way was widened to sources of wealth beyond the bounds of the Baptist denomination. But, on the same day that they approved this change in the charter, the Trustees adopted a resolution affirming

> That Bucknell University, recognizing the change in the denominational complexion of its Board of Trustees, records its continuing purpose to remain always a Christian educational institution. Due to its historical background and relationship, Bucknell University appreciates the importance of maintaining a close connection with the American Baptist Convention and the Pennsylvania State Baptist Convention and desires to continue to serve these Conventions and their objectives.[4]

Since 1953, President Odgers has at least twice publicly reaffirmed this position of the University. In April, 1958, in calling attention to the fact that Bucknell was not participating in a campaign of the American Baptist Convention to raise money for the "support of higher education," he stressed the fact that Bucknell for a long time had been "a nonsectarian or interdenominational" college. "The majority of our Board of Trustees and of our faculty and administrative staff [he said] are non-Baptists and fewer than ten per cent of our students are Baptists." But he insisted that Bucknell "has been and is a Christian college," and that the "liberal Baptist tradition has been Bucknell's Christian tradition." This tradition, he maintained, had "pointed the way to the interdenominational cooperation that has prevailed for many years on the Bucknell campus and to the potentialities of Christian unity, of emphasis on what unites rather than what divides our neighbors." [5] Again, in 1960, when the University made its chapel service voluntary and decided to hold it each Sunday morning at eleven o'clock, President Odgers explained this action as a recognition of changed conditions, and as a decision that was made in the belief "that through the Sunday University Chapel services the corporate worship of the campus will be enriched and that the religious tradition of the University will be reinforced." [6]

Of perhaps even greater concern to most friends of the University during the post-war years were the continuing adaptations of Bucknell's curricular offerings to changing demands of a new and fast-moving era. In this sphere of its activities, the changes during the 1940's, including the introduction of a course in integrative education, did not stop questioning about the educational program of the University. Whither was Bucknell trending? What should be its major objective? What should Bucknell offer to a continually increasing number of students? Were the students of Bucknell becoming broadly educated? What contributions to research should the faculty of Bucknell be expected to make? These were some of the questions which were uppermost in the minds of persons concerned about the well-being of Bucknell during the academic year 1953–54, when Dean William H. Coleman was preparing the way to a comprehensive survey, by members of the faculty, of the educational program of the University. "It is," Dean Coleman then remarked, in justification of the proposed survey, "essential, periodically, that an institution of higher learning take stock of its academic resources—not simply for the sake of change—but to insure that it is functioning at maximum efficiency." [7]

The discussions held pursuant to the plans for the foregoing investigation provided the foundation of a general survey of the University that President Odgers proposed. This survey, which came to be called the Bucknell Study, was intended, as President Odgers remarked in his *Report for the Academic Year 1954–55,* to be "a self-study of the aims, the curriculum, and the educational policies of the University." Such a study, he believed, would lead not only to an "improved offering," but also to economies in the operation of the University.[8] It got under way gradually. On February 28, 1955, President Odgers told the faculty that he had in mind such a study, to be made either by a small group of the faculty financed by a grant which he was seeking, or "by a much larger group that, working over an extensive period of time, would attempt to assess the situation and to suggest means for improving existing conditions." [9] Some two months later, Dean Coleman announced to the faculty plans for "the continuation of the study of curricular and other academic problems of the University and the establishment of a special program of general self-study to be undertaken in the near future." [10] The Bucknell Study got officially under way on October 5, 1955, when President Odgers announced to the faculty the names of the members of the Core Committee that he had appointed "as a result of an official request for nominations from the Faculty" to work with him and Dean Coleman in planning the study; and he made perfectly clear the fact that the study would be pursued whether or not financial aid for its prosecution was received from the Carnegie Foundation.[11] No grant was made to the University to support this study.

The first work of the Core Committee was the drafting of a statement of the objectives of the University. This statement President Odgers, as chairman of the Core Committee, presented to the faculty on May 2, 1956, and two weeks later the faculty, after considerable discussion, approved these objectives,[12] which, as they have since appeared in successive issues of the Catalogue of the University, read as follows:

> Bucknell is committed in the Christian tradition to provide the means and opportunity for the intellectual development of students of qualified preparation and character to the end that they may become mature and responsible members of society.

> Bucknell endeavors to impart to the student the principles of inherited knowledge and culture and to bring the student to an awareness of his own talent. As a center of independent thought Bucknell is dedicated to the cause of free and responsible inquiry and to seeking the truth wherever it may be found.[13]

As early as December, 1955, President Odgers had reported to the Executive Committee of the Board of Trustees that the Bucknell Study was undertaking a survey of the "University's academic program," and he recommended that Dr. Coleman, who would retire in June, 1956, from the deanship of the University, be retained as vice-president and secretary of the Bucknell Study. The Trustees approved this recommendation,[14] and, with Dr. Coleman giving his full time to this project, the year 1956–57 proved to be the first one during which the Bucknell Study made considerable progress.[15] In an article published in January, 1957, for the purpose of informing the alumni about the nature, the scope, and the progress of this study, Dr. Coleman said that President Odgers had appointed two central committees for the Study: a General Advisory Committee, consisting of twenty-three members chosen from the faculty, the Board of Trustees, the administrative staff, and the alumni, with President Odgers serving as its chairman, and an Executive Committee composed of selected members of the General Advisory Committee and headed by Dr. Karl D. Hartzell, successor to Dr. Coleman as dean of the University. The General Advisory Committee was expected to "advise the President initially with regard to the proper areas of study, and subsequently with respect to the conduct of the study and the implementing of its recommendations," and the Executive Committee was expected to "co-ordinate the processes of the study and screen all major recommendations to be submitted through the President to the appropriate bodies (faculty, trustees, and administrative officers)." The General Advisory Committee, as a result of its deliberations in two meetings, recommended that the Bucknell Study "be organized around three principal committees"—namely, one on the students, one on the curriculum, and one on the faculty. As explained by Dr. Coleman,

> The function of the Committee on the Student Body will be to determine from data in the college offices, questionnaires, and other means the major characteristics, organization and activities of the Bucknell student body to determine what changes, if any, are desirable in the present situation, and to determine the quality of the finished product (our graduates), and how it may be improved.
>
> The function of the Committee on the Curriculum will be to examine what is being taught, how it is being taught, and the relevance of the

> material presented in the classroom to the needs of individual students, and the requirements of our modern culture. It is hoped that the goals of the University will be reflected in the knowledge, judgments, and developed abilities of its graduates.
>
> The function of the Committee on the Faculty will be to appraise our faculty in terms of its quality, recruitment, functions, and conditions of work. From this examination, we hope, will come greater insight into just what it is that makes a great faculty, and a deeper appreciation of the contributions of the faculty to the educational stature of the University.[16]

Despite Dr. Coleman's illness, which began in November, 1957, and presently forced his retirement from the University, the work of the Study continued under the direction of Dean Hartzell, and by the autumn of 1958 President Odgers could report that it was "far past its midpoint," and that considerable progress had been made "in the areas of the faculty and the curriculum." Thus far, he said, the Study had more than justified itself. Its role, he continued,

> is only to recommend, though many ideas developed and conclusions reached during the Survey have already been made effective. Even if the recommendations of a specific nature be few, the Study has enabled the University to know itself better and, to use the phrase of a professor, it has "jarred us out of our smugness." Actually our campus has less smugness than many, but it is good to know that the Study has jarred what we have.
>
> None of us can fail to be impressed by the willingness of committees and individuals to spend hours and hours on the many aspects of the Study. Personally, I am not merely gratified, I am hopeful about the possibilities. The hard work of Dean Hartzell and of others connected with the Bucknell Study will surely bear some fruit. The investigations have been many-sided and the results should benefit Bucknell in no small way.[17]

The extent of the involvement of the faculty in the Study is explained in a statement prepared by Dean Hartzell on December 6, 1961, a copy of which is filed with the reports of the Study that are preserved in the Archives of the University. "A major aim," he said, "was to involve as many members of the faculty as were interested and able to make a contribution." Accordingly, the Committee on the Student Body had sub-committees dealing, respectively, with admissions, academic counseling, student attitudes, student government and fraternities, non-academic counseling, and extracurricular activities; the Committee on the Curriculum had sub-committees studying, respectively, core courses, programs for graduate and undergraduate degrees, the function of the major, exceptional students, testing devices, curricular balance and relevance, and intellectual achievement and student values; and the Committee on the Faculty had sub-committees which concerned themselves with the composition of the faculty, teaching efficiency and effectiveness, the contribution of the teacher to the total program of the University, and the working conditions of teachers. From the activities of all these committees there emerged, eventually, not a few reports which made a substantial contribution to the betterment of the University. All told, the Bucknell Study, Dean Hartzell concluded, had provided the faculty "with a challenge to have a fresh look at fundamentals," to reconsider established practices, and to be "imaginative and original in proposing courses of action" that would improve the educational program at Bucknell.

> Getting a faculty to reach a consensus on anything except the need for higher salaries and lighter teaching loads [he acknowledged] poses a major challenge to anyone or any group. Faculties do not arrive easily at collective decisions, partly because people who think otherwise are not fundamentally happy when they are caught agreeing with their colleagues, since agreement appears to be the negation of originality for all but one person in a group, and for academicians, originality and individuality are cherished possessions.[18]

From time to time, President Odgers publicly acknowledged the accomplishments of the Bucknell Study. In his report for the year 1959–60, he noted the operation for the second year of its recommendation that the seniors be given the Graduate Record Examination Area Tests; he called attention also to the establishment of the "first units of the Honors Program," and the appointment of an "Ad Hoc Curriculum Committee," which, he said, had functioned "steadily and well"; and, finally, he remarked that so many improvements emerging from the Study had been so quietly adopted by departments, the faculty, and the administration that it was difficult to "assemble a final report" on the Study, because, fortunately, as he believed, suggested improvements had not waited for the completion of the Study.[19]

On the subject of the faculty, one of the three principal topics of the Bucknell Study, a result of more than temporary significance was achieved. The report of the Study on the organization of the faculty, a report embodying a complete revision of the *Handbook* of 1952, was, with amendments, approved by the Trustees in respect to matters touching their authority on June 2, 1962, and subsequently it was printed under the title of *Academic Organization of Bucknell University, 1963.*

This subject, however, has been touched upon in the chapter immediately preceding this one.

In respect to the curriculum, the Bucknell Study produced reports on three subjects which may have lasting effects on the curricular programs of the University. One of these reports, which recommended the establishment of a permanent committee on the curriculum, the faculty approved in April, 1959, as it also approved at that time a recommendation that the president of the University appoint an *ad hoc* committee on this subject preparatory to the establishment of the permanent committee on the curriculum. With the organization of three colleges in the University in 1961, each of which would have a committee on its curriculum, there was established, as Dean Hartzell pointed out, "the principle that the mechanics of curricular change should be regularized and lodged with members of the faculty appointed by the Deans of the respective Colleges and working closely with them." [20]

On the second of these curricular subjects, that of an Honors Program, there were two reports, one recommending in principle the establishment of an Honors Council and an Honors Program, which the faculty approved in April, 1959, and the other proposing a permanent Honors Program, prepared by the Honors Council, which the faculty approved in January, 1961.[21] The approval of the first of these reports, as President Odgers noted, had "led to the development of colloquia for freshmen and sophomores" in the autumn of 1959 and also to the offering of "special sections in a number of lower-division courses." Of the outcome of this venture, he was optimistic, for, as he said, the experience of other institutions had been that successful Honors Programs not only affected the "attitudes of students," but also stimulated the faculty to better teaching.[22]

During the first year of the Honors Program, two colloquia—that is, "seminars in which selected books are discussed and individual papers are presented"—were offered, one for a group of fifteen selected freshmen and the other for a like number of selected sophomores. The first of these colloquia, extending through two semesters, dealt with the mind of man and its development, and the second one, also extending through two semesters, dealt with the nature of man. The program as a whole was "intended to provide for able students the deeper and more significant educational experiences commensurate with their intelligence and desire for knowledge." Students who pursued such work successfully would have the opportunity to be examined in the senior year for graduation with general honors. The program, moreover, extended beyond the colloquia which opened the way to graduation with general honors; it comprehended also "honors sections" which were being arranged in certain freshman or sophomore courses, together with programs then under preparation in certain departments that would lead successful participants in such programs to graduation with departmental honors.[23]

The Honors Program was expanded in 1961, and for the academic year 1961–62 three colloquia were offered for the purpose of exploring "problems and subjects of general interest" which, ordinarily, would not be dealt with in the offerings of the departments of the University. One of these, dealing with American thought and expression, was offered to fifteen selected freshmen; the other two, one dealing with society, culture, and politics in Renaissance England, and the other dealing with late classicism and early Christianity, were offered to two groups, each one consisting of fifteen selected upperclassmen.[24] In his report on this academic year—1961–62—President Odgers noted that fifty-nine students had been enrolled in the "honors colloquia," and that five were candidates for general honors and five for departmental honors in 1963. "To date," he said, "only three have been graduated with departmental honors and none as yet have been graduated with general honors." He observed, however, that "362 students participated in special honors sections of regular departmental courses during the same period even though they were not formally enrolled in the General Honors Program." [25]

For the academic year 1962–63, the Honors Program was further expanded, a general-honors thesis being added to the three colloquia offered. Of the Honors Program for this year, President Odgers reported as follows:

> The Honors Program in the College of Arts and Sciences has been expanded. Supported by nine departments, a total of 461 students were enrolled in Honors offerings in special Honors sections. In June 1963, for the first time, the University awarded general honors to students receiving degrees. Departmental honors were also awarded as in the past.[26]

One year later the Honors Program had been so expanded that it consisted of four colloquia in addition to the general-honors thesis. One of these colloquia, dealing with the subject of American thought and expression, was conducted for fifteen selected freshmen; the other three, dealing, respectively, with modern views of man, political and legal obligation, and variational principles of physics, were each conducted for fifteen selected upperclassmen.[27]

Probably the most significant of all the results of the Bucknell Study was the revision of the curriculum leading to the degree of Bachelor of Arts. This revision, approved by the faculty in May, 1961, became effective in September, 1962.[28] In justification of this new program, which emphasizes both humanistic and scientific points of view, there was inserted in the Catalogue of the University a statement reading as follows:

> The end and aim of all liberal studies is the orientation and development of an intelligent and responsible individual. These studies are the starting point and the constant preoccupation of men and women who are committed to a belief—the belief that knowledge for its own sake is important, and that the study of perfection is worth all the trouble it takes. A student who elects liberal studies as his major interest in college has set his foot upon the path of highest personal achievement. In the world beyond college walls he discovers his great practical advantage, for he has laid the foundations of an understanding of his cultural heritage, of the contemporary world, of the hierarchy of values, and of himself. . . .
>
> For the student who has professional ambitions, and who therefore faces the prospect of three to six years of specialized graduate study, the curriculum of liberal studies is invaluable. Increasingly the leading graduate schools of the United States, as well as the officers in charge of special training programs in industry, are demanding a liberal education as a qualification for admission.
>
> Liberal education is not incompatible with specialization. It is liberal education that gives specialization broader usefulness. . . . It enhances balance of judgment and depth of understanding, and tends to generate in the specialist the indispensable qualities of resourcefulness, creative imagination, and leadership.[29]

The subjects which fall within the category of prescribed work for candidates for the degree of Bachelor of Arts are classed in three divisions—humanities, social sciences, and natural sciences and mathematics—and the emphasis upon the humanities is heavy. These requirements, prescribed for the first two years, consist of 34 to 43 hours in the humanities, with particular emphasis upon English, foreign language, and history; twelve hours in the social sciences (economics, education, political science, psychology, and sociology), with a year's work in one and a semester's work in each of two others: and 12 to 16 hours in the natural sciences and mathematics, one-half of which must be taken in a laboratory science. The junior and senior years of the program are devoted to the major and to electives.[30]

During the years of the Bucknell Study, the University Course continued to operate as a program of integrative education. With the aid of a grant from the Carnegie Foundation for the Advancement of Teaching in July, 1953,[31] the original course was expanded into a program of four courses,[32] but soon thereafter it became for juniors and seniors a sequence of three interdepartmental courses dealing, respectively, with the sciences, the humanities, and the major philosophical systems. In this sequence, as the program is officially explained,

> the student examines the major fields of human knowledge in regard to their basic differences and interrelationships. The sciences—physical, biological, and social—are investigated in terms of their problems and provinces, their common and special methods, and some of their central principles. A few major philosophical systems are examined for their adequacy in relating the sciences and the humanities, and in providing an intellectually mature basis for individual and social action.[33]

The inward looking at Bucknell during the later years of the 1950's was not restricted to the offerings in the liberal arts; it comprehended also the program in economics and business administration. Thanks to a grant of $25,000 from the Ford Foundation, this department, before the end of the academic year 1959–60, was well advanced in the task of improving and enlarging its offerings.[34] By this time a student in this department could choose a major in economics leading to the degree of Bachelor of Arts, or a major either in accounting or business administration that would lead to the degree of Bachelor of Science in Business Administration. If he majored in economics, and worked for the degree of Bachelor of Arts, he took thirty hours in economics, with required courses in basic economics, fundamentals of economic measurement, organization of the industrial economy, historical analysis, governmental policies affecting the economy, and international economic policies; if he majored in accounting, he took twenty-four hours in accounting and eight hours in business law, and he could take all the hours needed in economics and business administration to qualify him for the C.P.A. examination in his state; and, finally, if he majored in business administration, he took at least forty-eight hours in economics and business administration, and he was expected to become "adept at using the devices provided by economic analysis." [35]

During these years of intellectual fermentation at Bucknell, some changes also were made in engineering education. These changes, however, tended not toward modification of objectives, which had been established as early as the academic year 1951–52, but toward liberalization of curricular offerings. The objectives of 1951–52, still firmly held in 1963–64, are as follows:

> (1) to develop a broad understanding of engineering fundamentals and to provide the best possible technical education in the profession of chemical, civil, electrical, and mechanical engineering; (2) to give the student in engineering an adequate conception of his place in society; (3) to make available to qualified students an introduction to the principles involved in basic engineering research; and (4) to present an adequate program for students desiring to work for the Master's Degree.[36]

Also, in the year 1951–52, the four branches of engineering, with the approval of the faculty given on March 5, 1952,[37] took a long step toward integrating their programs with the program of liberal arts by establishing a five-year program in both engineering and liberal arts. This program, intended to help meet a growing demand for engineers "who have a broad cultural background," provided for the granting of a degree of Bachelor of Arts at the end of four years, and of a degree in engineering at the end of five years. In this program, the courses for students in chemical, civil, electrical, and mechanical engineering were the same for the first two years, and before the end of this period the student selected his "field of specialization." [38] Twelve years later this program is still intact, although the Catalogue of the University for 1963–64 provides the notation that, ordinarily, "the chemical engineering students will take their Bachelor of Arts major in chemistry, and the other engineering students will take their Bachelor of Arts major in mathematics." [39]

By the late 1950's, indications of changes in the curricular offerings of the departments of engineering began to receive notice in the annual reports of the president of the University, who noted that, during the academic year 1958–59, all engineering students at Bucknell would be required for the first time to take the University Course.[40] Two years later, in the autumn of 1961, he wrote on this subject as follows:

> The Engineering curriculum has been undergoing modification in the past two or three years which has definitely demonstrated the feasibility of core courses in the basic engineering sciences. This past year, a common course was developed in Thermodynamics. Large lectures and small recitation groups were also used for the first time in Statics, thereby making it possible to save faculty time. In place of a single required University Course sequence, two- and three-course sequences in several of the humanities and social sciences have been added as alternative elective patterns, giving both breadth and depth in these areas. The College of Engineering has increased the use of computers to include the freshman, junior and senior years.[41]

One year later President Odgers quoted from remarks of the dean of the College of Engineering, Captain Herbert F. Eckberg, on a growing tendency in engineering education. Said Dean Eckberg:

> The five-year, double degree program is considered the best program for engineering students. This program combines the broad education available in the College of Arts and Sciences with the professional program given in the College of Engineering. It may well be the foundation of engineering education of the future. The program is difficult, and only the best students should attempt it.[42]

For the year 1962–63, the president reported, with obvious satisfaction, not only that the double-degree in engineering was still being offered, but also that Dean Eckberg had affirmed that progress had been made "in opening fields other than Mathematics and Chemistry to students in the double degree program." For the degree of Bachelor of Arts, he said, "students in this program may now major in Economics, Physics and other subjects." [43] In the autumn of that year, moreover, Dean Eckberg, in a review for the Bucknell Engineering Alumni Association of the progress in the program of engineering education at Bucknell since 1957, said that

> The curriculum had been under constant review with emphasis increasing in the area of the engineering sciences. To make room for study in depth of thermodynamics, mechanics, heat transfer, electricity, etc., descriptive courses have been largely eliminated. Courses in thermodynamics common for all departments have been introduced as well as changes in the methods of teaching some of the courses.[44]

Nor was this all. By this time "Social-Humanistic Electives" were available to both juniors and seniors in the four normal four-year programs in engineering.[45]

Such evidences of liberalization in engineering education were no doubt heartening to President Odgers, although the changes thus far made fell short of what he had proposed in October, 1957, as "A Design for Excellence" at Bucknell. This design would comprehend the whole program of undergraduate education at Bucknell—liberal education as well as professional education—a program "planned to produce broadly educated men and women" regardless of their special interests. To accomplish this object, he would integrate with education in the liberal arts the training of those seeking careers in engineering, teaching, medicine, or business; and he would work "steadily and without compromise" toward an undergraduate education leading to a single degree, that of Bachelor of Arts. Specialization, he said,

> would develop out of such undergraduate education but would not monopolize it. We would maintain rapport with specialized work but would not permit it to reduce the humanities, the social studies, or the basic sciences to a fringe. So substantial would be the amount of an undergraduate's work in these fields, whatever his objective might be, that with educational integrity we would have no hesitation in conferring upon him the arts degree.[46]

Such being the goal toward which he was looking, it is understandable that, despite the "advances on a number of fronts, physical and fiscal as well as educational," he would remark, in the autumn of 1963, that, at Bucknell, there was "much still to be done." [47]

The inquiring spirit fostered by the Bucknell Study brought forth, from time to time, investigations and reports on matters related to education at Bucknell but not considered as essential parts of the Bucknell Study. One such report, dealing with the program of graduate study in the University, was drafted for a special committee on this subject by Dr. Philip L. Harriman, professor of psychology. It was immediately given effect by the administration, and it was subsequently used as part of a larger report of the University to the Middle States Association of Colleges and Secondary Schools. This report, which affirms that "A graduate program in those departments having an adequate staff, with access to good research facilities, is decidedly a worthwhile part of the total program at this university," points out, nevertheless, that the "major responsibility of faculty members and administrators" at Bucknell "is the continued improvement of the undergraduate programs." [48]

But, since limited graduate study is to remain an integral part of the academic program at Bucknell, the report recommends, even at the risk of thereby curtailing the offerings to graduate students and of reducing the enrollment of graduate students, that

> (a) standards of admission to candidacy for a Master's degree be immediately raised; (b) the supervision of the curricula be henceforth entrusted to the Dean of the University and the Committee on the Graduate Program; (c) those University officers who maintain full and complete records for undergraduate students and alumni accept responsibility for the keeping of full records for candidates for Master's degrees and those who are graduated with the M.A. or the M.S.; and (d) all other aspects of the graduate programs, including the appointment, supervision, and evaluation of faculty members, be henceforth placed upon a comparable basis

> with that pertaining to the undergraduate curricula. The intent of this broad recommendation is to raise the qualitative standards of our graduate-degree programs.[49]

The accepted recommendations of this report appear in the Catalogue of the University for 1962–63. Since, for various reasons, the report did not recommend the establishment, "at this time," of a Graduate School at Bucknell, graduate work was put under the supervision of the vice-president for academic affairs, who was assisted by a co-ordinator of graduate studies. The vice-president for academic studies also was made chairman of a newly appointed committee on graduate studies. Pursuant to the recommendation of the report, requirements for admission to graduate study were raised so that a candidate for admission to graduate standing must have received from an accredited college or university either a bachelor's degree equivalent to one offered by Bucknell, "or certification of corresponding achievement from an institution abroad." Furthermore, to acquire graduate standing he must have received at least "a general undergraduate grade-point average of 2.500 on a scale of A = 4.000, and a grade-point average of 2.500 (a) in the field of the undergraduate major, *and* (b) in the proposed graduate major." Finally, except for some deviations in business administration, education, and psychology, the candidate must have completed an undergraduate major or minor of at least eighteen hours in the department of his proposed graduate major.

As minimal requirements for graduation with a master's degree, the candidate must present at least thirty semester hours, of which at least eighteen must be in the department of his major; also, he must obtain a cumulative grade-point average of 3.000 (grade of B) for all the work that he attempted; and, if a candidate for the degree of Master of Arts, he must demonstrate a reading knowledge of an approved foreign language. A master's thesis, except by the determination of a department, has not hitherto been required for a master's degree at Bucknell, but it will be required of all students who enroll after September 1, 1964.[50]

In the train of the labors involved in the Bucknell Study came the task of making additional reports to be submitted to a visiting committee appointed by the Middle States Association of Colleges and Secondary Schools to make an "evaluation" of Bucknell University. Bucknell had been accredited by this association as early as 1921, and such accreditation had been reaffirmed as late as 1951. Accordingly, since the accreditation of Bucknell was not in question, the Association decided to follow a new procedure in respect to Bucknell—it purposed now to examine not all the aspects of the operations of Bucknell, but only five "areas" of its program which were of particular concern to Bucknell and which had not received full attention in the recently completed Bucknell Study. The areas agreed upon for evaluation, in the light of the declared objectives of the University, were teaching, extracurricular activities, the library, communications, and graduate study—all of which, except the last-named, were matters involving differences of opinion, and, in some instances, clashing emotional attitudes. Nevertheless, it was agreed that in April, 1962, a committee on evaluation appointed by the Association should visit the campus "to counsel with the faculty and administration of the University," and, "possibly, suggest areas for continued study." [51] In a sense, therefore, the preparation for the visit of this committee was a continuation of the work of the Bucknell Study.

For several months before April, 1962, committees of the faculty and administration were engaged in preparing reports on the five so-called areas to be examined by the visiting committee. The making, revising, and editing of these reports consumed much time, provoked acrimonious discussion, and disclosed within the University misunderstandings as well as divisions of opinion which were not excluded from the reports submitted to the committee on evaluation. Consequently, in its report on its visit to Bucknell, the committee on evaluation took cognizance of such differences and made some recommendations intended to improve "communication," to dispel misunderstandings, and to promote more effective co-operation within the University; and several of its recommendations were quickly given effect. This report, President Odgers remarked, would "be helpful in spite of [our] disagreements with parts of it. We shall [he said] never be deaf to those who lend advice and make an encouragingly constructive study of our advances and our shortcomings, past, present, and future." [52]

In general, the report of the committee on evaluation was commendatory of Bucknell's achievements. "There is," it says,

> little question that Bucknell is achieving in great measure the goals which it has set for itself. Only five areas of the total life of the University were intensively surveyed, but it was not possible to study the reports submitted, to be a guest of the institution for almost three days and to meet and talk at length with students, faculty, and members of the administration without getting the "feel" of the institution and realizing that despite certain drawbacks, and no college or university is without these, it is functioning well within its approved parameters. The undergraduate programs are well taught to good students; the graduate programs offered are clearly not an excessive drain on its resources and [are] fully warranted in terms of the region in which the University is located; the library is adequate for both the undergraduate and graduate programs; the plant is

> an excellent one, albeit the projected campus center is badly needed; and faculties and facilities are of high order.[53]

The continuing inward looking which had led to the significant administrative and curricular changes heretofore described was accompanied by constant outward looking which has led, and still is leading, to important changes in the relations of the University to the nation and to the world. In fact, much of the internal change described above had been the consequence of raising questions about the role of the University in a nation called in the post-war world to assume responsibilities as heavy as they were unwonted. What should Bucknell University contribute toward the solution of the problems, at home and abroad, that had been raised by the emerging new order? This was a leading question at Bucknell, as at other American colleges and universities; and, as thus phrased, this question was merely another way of asking what adjustments should be made in the way of life at Bucknell.

One of the important adjustments that the University made to the new era was the opening of ways to superior students to pursue their collegiate careers, in part, away from the campus of Bucknell without disrupting the programs which they had planned for themselves. The first of these, called the Washington Semester program, became available to students at Bucknell in the autumn of 1952, as a consequence of an arrangement which the American University in Washington, D.C., had made to accept from a considerable number of American colleges of liberal arts students who would live on its campus for a semester and study under its supervision. Pursuant to this arrangement, a few selected upperclass students at Bucknell are permitted each year to spend a full semester in Washington, "taking courses and receiving academic credit as though they were taking the same courses on the Bucknell campus"; and, for their benefit, special projects of study are assigned, seminars are scheduled, and counseling is provided by the American University. The principal advantage of this arrangement is that it gives to students pursuing their collegiate studies away from Washington an opportunity "to utilize source materials and to learn at first hand about governmental institutions" in the nation's capital.[54]

The success of the Washington Semester induced Bucknell, early in the 1960's, to make similar arrangements with two other Universities, one of which is Drew University. To some qualified upperclass students of Bucknell this arrangement "provides an opportunity for the study of international organizations through a direct contact with the United Nations and related agencies in New York City, [and to spend two] days each week of a semester in the immediate vicinity of the United

Nations under the supervision of a member of the Drew University faculty." In addition to the seminars and other projects on international organization, students participating in this program take enough courses at Drew University to make a full semester's work. For a semester's work of this sort, a student will receive fifteen hours of credit at Bucknell. Only juniors and seniors may participate in this program.[55]

The other arrangement, which was made with Howard University, provides for an exchange by means of which a limited number of students in Bucknell University may spend one or both semesters of the junior year at Howard University in Washington, D.C. Students of Bucknell who participate in this program enroll at Howard University and pay tuition and fees to that institution. The credits which they earn there are automatically transferred to Bucknell. This program was arranged for the benefit of students "interested in social and intracultural relations." [56]

Another consequence of its outward looking has been Bucknell's participation in the widespread effort to solve the national problem of improving the qualifications of American secondary-school teachers, particularly teachers of science, of mathematics, and of foreign languages. This participation has consisted, principally, of offering summer institutes supported either by grants from foundations or by subsidies from the Federal Government. Since 1957, when it offered the first of these programs, Bucknell has so increased the number of its summer institutes that, in recent years, it has had, besides courses for teachers of science, of mathematics, and of foreign languages, special offerings for teachers of history, of the social sciences, and of the engineering sciences.

Work of this sort was started at Bucknell with a grant in 1957 from the National Science Foundation of $53,000, a sum which made available at Bucknell fellowships for fifty high-school teachers for instruction in a six-week institute directed by Dr. Lester Kieft, chairman of the Department of Chemistry. Thus it was that Bucknell entered a program which was begun in 1953 by the National Science Foundation "to encourage the high school teachers to improve subject-matter mastery of science and mathematics." [57] Accordingly, Bucknell became one of numerous institutions that participated in this program, its latest grant for such an institute being one for the summer of 1964.[58]

As the years went by, the National Science Foundation broadened its program. In 1959 Bucknell received from this foundation an additional grant for a summer institute in science for high-school boys who had completed their junior year, and two years later it received from the same foundation still another grant, this one for an institute in engineering sciences for teachers in colleges. All these institutes proved to be so successful that, in January, 1964, Bucknell could announce that it had received from the National Science Foundation a grant for the eighth summer institute in science and mathematics, a grant for the sixth summer institute in science for high-school students, and a grant for the fourth summer institute in engineering sciences for college teachers of physics and of pre-engineering courses.[59]

Another grant to Bucknell for an additional institute came for the third time in 1964 from the United States Office of Education. This subsidy, first granted in 1962, amounted to $58,000 for an institute that would enroll forty high-school teachers of Spanish and French.[60]

Two other summer institutes, featuring history and the social sciences, were in progress at Bucknell in the early 1960's. They, too, were supported, at least in part, by grants from foundations. The older of these—the Institute for Asian Studies—was begun in 1958 in co-operation with the Asia Society, the Asia Foundation, and the Japan Society. In a sense, this institute was an extension into the summer session of a program of non-Western studies that was begun at Bucknell during the academic year 1958–59. One of its major purposes was to broaden the understanding of secondary-school teachers in the United States.[61] The other of these institutes—the Institute of American Studies—began in 1960 with a grant of $10,000 from the Coe Foundation, and, with the Coe Foundation still its principal sponsor, it has scheduled its fifth session for the summer of 1964. Accompanying the first grant from the Coe Foundation, made on November 10, 1959, was a statement saying that the money thus given was to be used solely to help establish "summer refresher courses in American Studies for selected teachers and professors." The departments of history, political science, and economics have co-operated in conducting this institute.[62]

Outward looking at Bucknell led not only to the establishment of opportunities for qualified students at Bucknell to do a part of their collegiate studying on other campuses in the United States and to the establishment on the campus of Bucknell of institutes to improve the education of teachers who were preparing pupils for college; it led also to the opening of the door to qualified students at Bucknell to do a part of their collegiate studying abroad. In the year 1953–54, the University adopted the policy of "allowing qualified students to study abroad at any accredited university while receiving credit toward the Bucknell degree." In 1954–55, four Bucknell juniors were abroad pursuant to this program, one of whom was at the University of Edinburgh, and four others were abroad during the next year, one of them at Silliman University, in the Philippine Islands.[63] The idea of passing the junior year abroad laid hold of more and more students with the passing years, and, in October, 1959, it was announced that eleven students from Bucknell had been given permission to pursue such study.[64] By that time the University had found it necessary to define very clearly its policy in respect to the Junior Year Abroad, although, oddly enough, no statement of such policy appeared in the Catalogue of the University before the issue for 1962–63.

The statement of policy in respect to the Junior Year Abroad that was issued by Dean Karl D. Hartzell in October, 1959, provides, *inter alia,* that students must get permission to study abroad if they wish to be considered students of Bucknell while they are away; that their work abroad "should constitute a full year's work at the institution the student attends, and should supplement his major field at Bucknell," and that Bucknell would give credit for such work "only upon certification by the appropriate university officer abroad of the student's performance in the final examination in each course." Moreover, this statement affirms that students "studying at institutions in other countries are representatives of Bucknell University and are expected to exemplify high standards of personal conduct and to possess outstanding academic ability and capacity for application." [65]

As the Catalogue of the University for 1963–64 reveals, the conditions regulating the study abroad of students during their junior year are as follows:

> The College permits qualified students to spend the junior year abroad whenever such an arrangement would be a justifiable part of the student's program. . . . Students who are qualified for this opportunity, having complied with all the regulations governing it, are considered as enrolled in Bucknell, and listed as being on leave for foreign study. Such leaves may be granted by the Dean of the College of Arts and Sciences to students who have achieved an academic average of 3.000, or better, for four semesters in Bucknell.[66]

Still another opportunity for students of Bucknell to study abroad was provided for the first time in the summer of 1962, when Bucknell, in cooperation with the National Student Association, offered two courses of study in Florence under the direction of Dr. F. David Martin, professor of philosophy in Bucknell University. Both courses were in philosophy, one for graduate students and the other for undergraduates. Students who participated in this institute were housed in a building on the campus of the Cavour Institute.[67] Other students of Bucknell have gone elsewhere in Europe to study. Pursuant to agreements between Bucknell on the one hand and the University of Bonn and the University of Caen on the other hand, one student in Bucknell may be exchanged each year with a student in Bonn and a student in Caen; and, by special arrangements of one sort or another, a sprinkling of students from other European countries may be found each year on the campus of Bucknell. Also, pursuant to a program conducted by the Department of State, a few students each year are now coming to Bucknell from countries in Africa.[68]

Some of the professors of Bucknell, like some of the students of this institution, have been abroad in recent years, a few for purposes of research and others as Fulbright lecturers. One professor went twice to countries of southern Asia on Fulbright appointments, and two others spent two years each in Italy on similar appointments. But the greatest contribution of Bucknell to the education of foreigners has been given on the campus in Lewisburg, in part to students from abroad who have been regularly enrolled in the University, and in part to a special summer institute which came into being during the later months of the Second World War.

The Bucknell Institute for Foreign Students was established in 1944 as the Bucknell English Institute, the name by which it was known through the year 1950. In the beginning, it was both of and for students from Latin America, whose initial problem of orientation to life and study in this country was that of acquiring an adequate knowledge of the English language. To give them such knowledge was the essential purpose of the institute, and this continued to be its essential purpose until after 1950, when there came to the institute more and more European students whose grasp of English was better than that of most students from Latin American countries. Accordingly, the institute began to put more emphasis on "introducing the foreign student to the peculiarities of the American system of education and to American customs and manners." Because the institute had changed in composition and, to some extent, in purpose, its name was changed to Bucknell Institute for Foreign Students.[69]

During its second decade, this institute enrolled more and more students, who came from nearly every part of the world. In its twentieth session, during the summer of 1963, it offered two programs—one of eight weeks and one of four weeks—in which were enrolled 135 students who came from thirty-nine countries. The eight-week session emphasized instruction in English; the four-week session concerned itself with instruction in orientation to American culture and academic life. As the present director of the institute has said, the purpose of the institute in recent years has been

> (1) to provide intensive work in English through the media of classroom work, lectures, language laboratory practice, and "conversational hours," so as to prepare the foreign student linguistically for academic study in

this country; (2) to acquaint the foreign student with academic and administrative practices and procedures in American colleges and universities; and (3) to introduce the foreign student to social, cultural, and economic aspects of life in the United States.

In recent years, the University of Arizona and the University of Kansas have organized comparable institutes for foreign students, and in the preparing of the programs of each of these institutes the director of the Bucknell Institute for Foreign Students, Professor Harvey M. Powers, served as consultant.[70]

One of the most interesting ventures that Bucknell has made in the sphere of international affairs is called the annual Burma-Bucknell Weekend, a time when Burmese and American friends of Burma get together. This extraordinary arrangement had its beginning in an international party held on the campus of Bucknell on April 2–3, 1949, reached a climax in 1958, and has been flourishing ever since under the auspices of the Christian Association of Bucknell University. Senator Theodore Francis Green, of Rhode Island, who was an honored guest at the Weekend in 1957, expressed the belief that such an affair was "unique in American education," and that associations such as the Burma-Bucknell Weekend provided "are of a most satisfying and rewarding nature." [71]

Bucknell's interest in Burma dates from the beginning of the University at Lewisburg, for one of the founders of Bucknell, Eugenio Kincaid, was an American missionary to Burma, who was home on leave during the beginning years of this institution. The interest of the University at Lewisburg in Burma was strengthened when a young Burmese student, Maung Shaw Loo, entered the Academy of the University at Lewisburg in 1858, and, six years later, was graduated by the College in its Class of 1864. Subsequently, Shaw Loo took a degree in medicine and then returned to Burma to practice his profession. There, in 1929, he died at the advanced age of ninety-one. Meanwhile, the religious and educational relations of Bucknell with people in Burma had become stronger and more cordial with the passing years.[72]

By 1958, when it celebrated its tenth anniversary, the Burma-Bucknell Weekend had become a matter of considerable interest to the government of the Union of Burma as well as to the government of the United States. On this occasion, Bucknell University was host at extraordinary ceremonies to many distinguished guests and to the Burmese students residing in the eastern part of the United States. During these ceremonies, the University, on the morning of March 1, held a special convocation in recognition of the tenth anniversary of the independence of the Union of Burma, the tenth anniversary of the Burma Bucknell

Weekend, and the one-hundredth anniversary of the admission to the University of Maung Shaw Loo, Bucknell University's first overseas student. At this convocation the address was given by William O. Douglas, an associate justice of the Supreme Court of the United States, and honorary degrees were conferred upon Mr. Justice Douglas and His Excellency U Win, ambassador from the Union of Burma to the United States. At the banquet held that night, addresses were given by the Honorable Horace A. Hildreth, former president of Bucknell and former ambassador from the United States to Pakistan, and by His Excellency U Thant, who then was ambassador from the Union of Burma to the United Nations. At this banquet, also, Ambassador U Win presented to Bucknell University, as a gift from the President of the Union of Burma, a silver bowl bearing this inscription: "The Burma-Bucknell Bowl, March 1, 1958, symbolizing 100 years of friendly relationship between the people of Burma and Bucknell University: awarded annually in recognition of a significant contribution to the ideal of brotherhood and good citizenship." The annual "award" of the bowl is a formal recognition of service performed; the bowl remains as a permanent exhibit in the main foyer of the Ellen Clarke Bertrand Library.

One of the highly honored guests at the Tenth Bucknell-Burma Weekend was the only surviving daughter of Dr. Maung Shaw Loo, Miss Lizabeth Shaw Loo, who flew from Rangoon to Pennsylvania for the occasion. During her sojourn in Lewisburg, she presented to the University an oil portrait of her father, which now hangs in the Bucknell Treasure Room.[73]

The Sixteenth Burma-Bucknell Weekend, held on March 13–15, 1964, brought to the campus of the University the usual number of distinguished visitors, Burmese and American, including the Burmese ambassador to the United States, His Excellency U On Sein, as well as a representative from the Department of State of the United States. This was the sixth Weekend that Ambassador U On Sein had attended.[74]

One of the latest of Bucknell's contributions to education abroad began on August 1, 1963, when the University signed a two-year contract with the Agency for International Development of the Department of State providing that, in consideration of a grant of $300,000, Bucknell University would assist the Catholic University in Córdoba, Argentina, to develop an undergraduate program in engineering and to train an engineering faculty for that institution. Of the above-mentioned grant, $80,000 will be spent to equip electrical and metallurgical laboratories.

Pursuant to the provisions of this contract, Bucknell has sent, for two years of service in Córdoba, a member of its staff in electrical engineering and a professor of metallurgical engineering; and it has accepted for further study in engineering in Bucknell University several qualified students who have studied for four years in the Catholic University of Córdoba. "These participants," Dean Eckberg said, in an address before the American Society for Engineering Education at the University of Maine in June, 1964, "are under contract to return to Catholic University as full time faculty members after receiving their bachelor and master degrees here."

At the end of the first year of the experiment in Córdoba, Dean Eckberg expressed the view that a small engineering college, like that of Bucknell University, could participate successfully in the increasingly important work of assisting "developing nations in the area of technical education. I feel [he continued] that our work is producing good results, not only [in] the development of engineering education in one foreign institution, but also in gaining friends for the United States in an important country to the South of us." [75]

The activities described in preceding paragraphs illustrate rather than enumerate all the varied activities which have been bringing Bucknell in recent years into closer relations with matters of international concern than the University maintained in the years before the late war. The expansion of such activities so impressed President Odgers that, in his report covering the academic year 1959–60, he devoted five pages to a discussion of "Our World Responsibility." He was much impressed not only by the fact that students from countries the world over were enrolling for study in Bucknell University, but also by the fact of the "outward flow of American students"—for study, for work, or for travel. Bucknell, he said, is

> now sending each year ten or twelve young men and women abroad for the junior year. They go in programs sponsored by other American colleges in France, Germany, Spain, Italy, and other lands, or through direct arrangements with universities in England and Scotland. Others enroll for summer courses at universities in Mexico and Europe. During the past two summers many Bucknell students have traveled through Europe with tour groups organized by members of the faculty. Other tours, extended in concept to emphasize specific educational objectives, are in prospect for the future.

Moreover, he said, the world was bearing in upon Bucknell "at a great many points" through its curriculum, "both through courses and programs expressly oriented to international concerns and through ideas and materials that inject themselves" into various subjects taught in the University. Such pressure, he was certain, was being exerted upon all American colleges and universities, and he warned that continuing pressure for "more activity on the international front" should be examined in the light of the "central objectives for which the university exists." A university, he reminded his readers, like an individual, could do so much that it would do nothing well. Nevertheless, he believed with a spokesman of the Department of State that the university must move with the nation, which "has been carried to the four corners of the world." The "extremely worthwhile activities" that have brought students and members of the faculty of Bucknell into contact with international affairs he called commendable, and he believed that they should not be discontinued. "Yet," he continued,

> I think [that] we would have to admit that each of these activities has emerged as a result of some partial view of our world responsibility and opportunity. In a world in which it is increasingly "impossible to distinguish between the national and the international," we need increasingly to view as a whole the curricular and extra-curricular programs of the University as they give expression to our sense of purpose. This is a challenge which comes with increasing force to the front of our minds and to which we shall be giving direct attention.[76]

The pressure for further participation by Bucknell in matters of international concern continued to increase, and, as President Odgers noted in his report on the academic year 1962–63, the vice-president for academic affairs in Bucknell University, Dr. Mark C. Ebersole, was recommending that Bucknell increase its "emphasis on international affairs." To be educated as a citizen of the world, Dr. Ebersole argued, every student should be acquainted not only with the civilization of Europe, but also with the civilization of at least one country of Asia. To that end, he urged that Bucknell consider the matter of expanding its Junior Year Abroad and of instituting "a special program in Asian or, perhaps, more specifically, Japanese studies." [77]

Accordingly, as it advances into the decade of the 1960's, Bucknell University remains troubled in spirit. It is still looking inward and outward—inward to try to determine what provisions it should make to accomplish its declared purposes, and outward to try to determine its responsibilities to the nation and to the world. Again and again through the years it has courageously confronted dangerous crises, and again and again it has responded becomingly to the challenges posed by these crises. The crisis that it confronts today is stupendous: the challenge which this crisis poses is all but appalling. But today, Bucknell, faithful to its tradition, is still inquiring and still aspiring.

Notes

CHAPTER ONE

[1] "To the Patrons and Friends of the University at Lewisburg," *Lewisburg Chronicle,* January 24, 1849.

[2] A representative expression of this idea appeared in 1836 in one of the Baptist Education Societies in words as follows: "God has never designed that his gospel shall be extended over all the earth, except by the agency of the Christian ministry. The word of God and the living teacher take the lead in the system of means employed for the renovation of the world, and the consummation of the kingdom of Christ." Baptist Education Society of the State of New York, *Nineteenth Annual Meeting, 1836* (Utica, 1836), 10. At a meeting of the Society for Moral and Religious Inquiry of the University at Lewisburg on December 7, 1856, H. B. Johnson was scheduled to make a report entitled "Human Agency in the World's Evangelization." *Lewisburg Chronicle,* December 5, 1856.

[3] Speaking in the House of Representatives on March 3, 1852, in favor of a bill to grant homesteads, John L. Dawson said, *inter alia:* "The American Government is the great pioneer in the cause of freedom. By the force of republican principles and of unexampled success, it has advanced in nationality until it is now hailed as a beacon-light for every continent, and a star of hope for every people." Quoted in the *Lewisburg Chronicle,* April 21, 1852. For a fuller expression of these views, with adequate documentation, see the following articles by the author of this book: "George Simpson and Oregon Missions," *Pacific Historical Review,* VI (September, 1937), 216–222; "The American Missionary Spirit, 1828–1835," *Church History,* VII (June, 1938), 125–137; "Eastern Contributions to Baptist Beginnings in the Upper Mississippi Valley," *Bucknell University Studies,* I, No. 3 (1949), 1–21.

[4] B., "Present Encouraging Aspects of the Unevangelized Parts of the World," *Panoplist,* XVI (February, 1820), 55; Antipas, "The Favorableness of the Present Age for the Success of the Christian Enterprise," *Spirit of the Pilgrims,* I (December, 1828), 619–622; anon., "Study of Greek Literature," *American Quarterly Register,* V (February, 1833), 236.

[5] *American Quarterly Register,* VI (August, 1833), 67.

[6] "The East and the West," *New-York Observer,* February 13, 1830. The literature dealing with the subject of the menace of "Popery" in the American West is vast and varied. As examples, see "The Kingdom of the Beast," *New-York Observer,* October 20, 1827; "The Grand Conspiracy," *New York Evangelist,* November 29, 1834; and W. C. Brownlee, *Popery: An Enemy of Civil and Religious Liberty; and Dangerous to Our Republic* (New York, 1836). See also John Todd, *Colleges Essential to the Church of God: Plain Letters Addressed to a Parishioner in Behalf of the Society for the Promotion of Collegiate and Theological Education in the West* (New York, 1847), 11, and Clifford S. Griffin, "Converting the Catholics: American Benevolent Societies and the Ante-Bellum Crusade Against the Church," *Catholic Historical Review,* XLVII (October, 1961), 325–341. On the subject of anti-Catholicism in the United States in general, see Ray A. Billington, *The Protestant Crusade* (New York, 1938).

[7] "Review of the [Fifth] Report of the A. H. M. Society," *Quarterly Christian Spectator,* III (December, 1831), 515; Western Baptist Educational Association, *Second Annual Report of the Executive Committee, 1834* (Boston, 1834), 7. For a view of the

"barbarizing" tendency of the West, see Horace Bushnell, *Barbarism the First Danger: A Discourse for Home Missions* (New York, 1847), 22–23.

8 M. N., "Signs of the Times," *Panoplist,* XIV (April, 1818), 153. See also Charles C. Cole, Jr., *The Social Ideas of the Northern Evangelists, 1826–1860* (New York, 1954), 232–233.

9 Antipas, "The Favorableness of the Present Age for the Success of the Christian Enterprise," *loc. cit.,* 623.

10 *Boston Recorder and Telegraph,* XVI (June 22, 1831), 97; "Review of Sprague's Lectures to Youth," *Quarterly Christian Spectator,* II (December, 1830), 653.

11 *Boston Recorder and Telegraph,* June 16, 1830, quoting from the *Philadelphian.*

11a Donald G. Tewksbury, *The Founding of American Colleges and Universities Before the Civil War, with Particular Reference to the Religious Influences Bearing Upon the College Movement* (New York, 1932), chap. 2.

12 J. Orin Oliphant, ed., *Through the South and the West with Jeremiah Evarts in 1826* (Lewisburg, Pa., 1956), 12.

13 Pennsylvania Baptist Education Society, *Minutes, 1854* (Philadelphia, 1854), 6.

14 J. Orin Oliphant, "The American Missionary Spirit, 1828–1835," *Church History,* VII (June, 1938), 128.

15 Christian Spy [pseud.], "National Societies," *Boston Recorder and Telegraph,* July 28, 1826.

16 Oliphant, ed., *Through the South and the West with Jeremiah Evarts in 1826,* 13.

17 *Ibid.,* 14. On the expansion of Christianity in Europe and the United States during the nineteenth century, see, in general, Kenneth Scott Latourette, *A History of the Expansion of Christianity: The Great Century,* A.D. *1800*—A.D. *1914 . . .* (New York, 1941), IV, *passim.*

18 On the subject of American Baptist colleges and American Baptist benevolent societies as of the year 1836, see I. M. Allen, ed., *The Triennial Baptist Register, No. 2—1836* (Philadelphia, 1836), 25–84.

19 A. D. Gillette, ed., *Minutes of the Philadelphia Baptist Association, from* A.D. *1707 to* A.D. *1807, Being the First One Hundred Years of its Existence* (Philadelphia, 1851), *passim.*

20 Philadelphia Baptist Association, *Minutes, 1832* (Philadelphia, 1832), 5.

21 *Ibid., 1833,* 10–11.

22 *Ibid., 1834,* 10–11; Boston *Christian Watchman,* May 24, 1833.

23 Boston *Christian Watchman,* August 8, 1834.

24 Philadelphia Baptist Association, *Minutes, 1834* (Philadelphia, 1834), 7–8.

25 Central Baptist Convention for Education Purposes, *Minutes, . . . 1834* (Philadelphia, 1834), 5–7.

26 *Ibid.,* 8–10.

27 New Jersey Baptist Association, *Minutes, 1835* (n. p., n. d.), 4.

28 *Triennial Baptist Register, No. 2—1836,* 74.

29 Central Union Association of Independent Baptist Churches, *Minutes, 1834* (Philadelphia, 1834), 10–11.

30 *Ibid., 1835,* 5, 13–15.

31 *Ibid., 1836,* 27.

32 New Jersey Baptist Association, *Minutes, 1835,* 4.

33 New Jersey Baptist State Convention, *Minutes, 1836* (Trenton, 1836), 4.

34 *Ibid., 1837,* 5, 11.

35 *Ibid., 1839,* 5, 28.

36 New Jersey Baptist Association, *Minutes, 1839* (Burlington, 1839), 2.

37 *Triennial Baptist Register, No. 2—1836,* 75.

38 *Laws of the General Assembly of the Commonwealth of Pennsylvania, . . . 1835–36* (Harrisburg, 1836), 293–295.

39 *Triennial Baptist Register, No. 2—1836,* 75.

40 Philadelphia Baptist Association, *Minutes, 1836* (Philadelphia, 1836), 11.

41 *Ibid., 1837,* 17.

[42] *Ibid., 1839,* 20; Philadelphia *National Baptist,* August 5, 1869, 4.

[43] John H. Raymond, "Sketch of the History of the New York State Baptist Education Society," in the Baptist Education Society of the State of New York, *Twenty-Fifth Annual Meeting, 1842* (Hamilton, 1842), 40. As late as 1845 the Pennsylvania Baptist Education Society (*Minutes,* 1845, 4) was aiding thirty students, and of these twenty-eight were at Hamilton.

[44] Howard D. Williams, The History of Colgate University to 1869 (Doctoral Dissertation, Harvard University, 1949). Consulted with the permission of Dr. Williams.

[45] *Ibid.,* 49; Board of Correspondence [later Board of the New York Baptist Theological Seminary] of the Baptist Education Society in Philadelphia for the Middle States, Minutes, March 8, 1813—November 16, 1848 (Archives, Colgate University), 86–87; Baptist Education Society of the State of New York, *Sixth Annual Meeting, June 4, 1823* (Hamilton, 1823), 5–18.

[46] Hamilton Literary and Theological Institution, *Catalogue, 1844–45* (Hamilton, 1844), 22; Tewksbury, *op. cit.,* 44.

[47] Bronson, B. F. *et al.,* eds., *The First Half Century of Madison University, . . .* (New York, 1872), 377–379.

[48] Philadelphia Baptist Association, *Minutes, 1841* (Philadelphia, 1841), 15–16, 18.

[49] *Ibid., 1842,* 20–22.

[50] Northumberland Baptist Association, *Minutes, 1832* (n. p., n. d.), 2.

[51] *Ibid., 1840* (Muncy, Pa., 1840), 5.

[52] *Ibid., 1839,* 2.

[53] *Ibid., 1841,* 7.

[54] *Ibid., 1843,* 12.

[55] *Ibid., 1844,* 6–7.

[56] *Ibid., 1845,* 8.

[57] *Ibid.,* 11.

[58] *Ibid., 1846,* 16.

CHAPTER TWO

[1] Northumberland Baptist Association, *Minutes, 1846* (Lewisburg, 1846), 12.

[2] *Ibid.,* 11–12.

[2a] Eugenio Kincaid returned with his family from Burma in 1843. Philadelphia *Baptist Record,* May 10, 1843.

[3] In a reminiscent paper dated April 10, 1878, James Moore, Jr., told of his role in the founding of the University at Lewisburg. Here he affirmed that he "was the first person who thought of founding a Baptist College at Lewisburg." This paper is published in full in the *Bucknell Mirror,* XVI (December 10, 1896), 49–53.

[4] Stephen W. Taylor, A Brief History of the Origin of the University at Lewisburg (Ms.). This history was prepared at the request of the Board of Trustees (August 25, 1849) and approved by the Board on April 18, 1850. It was copied into the Book of Minutes of the Trustees immediately preceding the charter, and it was also copied into the Book of Minutes of the Curators. The original manuscript is in the office of the treasurer of the University.

[5] See a letter signed D and dated at Hamilton, New York, on August 20, 1845, in the Boston *Christian Reflector,* August 28, 1845; also an anonymous letter dated at Niagara Falls on August 22, 1845, in the *New York Recorder,* August 28, 1845.

[6] Taylor, A Brief History. The pages of this manuscript are not numbered.

[7] Walter N. Wyeth, "Stephen W. Taylor, LL.D.," *Bucknell Mirror,* XVIII (May, 1899), 172–178; *Union County Star and Lewisburg Chronicle,* October 26, 1860; Howard D. Williams, The History of Colgate University to 1869 (Doctoral Dissertation, Harvard University, 1949), 121–122.

[8] An Old Resident [George R. Bliss], "Sketch of the History of Our University," *College Herald,* I (May, 1870), 2.

[9] Taylor, A Brief History.

[10] Philadelphia *Christian Chronicle,* August 5, 1846; letter from George W. Anderson, in the *Christian Chronicle,* October 28, 1846, and reprinted in the Pennsylvania Department of Internal Affairs, *Monthly Bulletin,* XXIII (December, 1954), 20–23; Thomas Wattson's letter (October 3, 1846) describing a visit to Lewisburg, in the *Christian Chronicle,* October 7, 1846. See also Isaac N. Loomis to Mr. and Mrs. H. Harvey, October 19, 1847. Original letter in the Archives of Bucknell University.

[11] J. Orin Oliphant, "How Lewisburg Became a Canal Port," Northumberland County Historical Society, *Proceedings,* XXI (August, 1857), 37–66.

[12] University at Lewisburg, *Catalogue, 1853–54,* 19.

[13] Stephen W. Taylor to Samuel Wolfe, January 24, 1846. Original letter in the Archives of Bucknell University.

[14] *Ibid.*

[15] *Journal of the Senate of the Commonwealth of Pennsylvania, . . . 1846* (Harrisburg, 1846), 70, 89, 117–118, 146, 148.

[16] Taylor, A Brief History.

[17] The charter is printed in full in the *Lewisburg Chronicle,* February 14, 1846.

[18] *Laws of the General Assembly of the Commonwealth of Pennsylvania, . . . 1846* (Harrisburg, 1846), 32–35. The creation of two governing boards, in one of which provision was made for members who were not Baptists, no doubt was advantageous in the beginning. It provided places of prominence for more persons than could have been made available on one board, and it made feasible the giving of recognition to prominent men in Lewisburg who were not of the Baptist persuasion. But such division of powers created problems, and it is significant that, in the reorganization of 1882, all powers to govern were vested in a single board. As early as August 26, 1850, the Trustees discussed, but did not approve, a proposal that the charter be so changed that the power of the Curators in the matter of granting degrees be transferred to the Trustees. Minutes of the Trustees, August 26, 1850.

[19] University at Lewisburg, Minutes of the Trustees, February 14, 1846.

[20] Taylor to Samuel Wolfe, January 24, 1846.

[21] Taylor to Samuel Wolfe, March 9, 1846. Original letter in the Archives of Bucknell University.

[22] Taylor, A Brief History.

[23] *Ibid.*

[24] Philadelphia *Christian Chronicle,* September 23, 1846.

[25] *Ibid.*, October 14, 1846.

[26] *Ibid.*, December 9, 1846.

[27] *Ibid.*

[28] *Ibid.*, November 25, 1846.

[29] "Professor Taylor commenced teaching school today in the baptist church." J. Merrill Linn, Diary, October 5, 1846. Archives of Bucknell University.

[30] Northumberland Baptist Association, *Minutes, 1844* (Muncy, 1844), 15; Philadelphia *Baptist Record,* January 24, 1844.

[31] *Church Manual: Containing an Historical Sketch of the First Baptist Church, in Lewisburg, Pa. . . .* (Lewisburg, 1885), 2; John T. Judd *et al., History of the First Baptist Church in Lewisburg, Pa. . . .* (Lewisburg, 1894), 7–8.

[32] Minutes of the Trustees, December 26, 1846.

[33] Isaac N. Loomis to Mr. and Mrs. H. Harvey, October 19, 1847; J. Merrill Linn, Diary, October 15, 1847. George Good, who had just entered this school, wrote in his Diary, under date of October 17, 1847: ". . . Recited Bullion's Greek grammar to Lumas [Loomis] at 10 min past 11. . . ."

[34] Taylor, A Brief History.

[35] Philadelphia *Christian Chronicle,* October 28, 1846.

[36] J. Merrill Linn, Diary, *passim.* Of the examinations at the end of this term,

Eugenio Kincaid wrote as follows: "The examination of our school closed to-day [August 24]—it continued for three days, and was one of the most thorough examinations I have ever attended. . . . I hope some one who has a little leisure will give the 'Chronicle' a minute account of this examination, so creditable both to instructors and pupils. Another Professor is to be on in October. . . ." Philadelphia *Christian Chronicle,* September 1, 1847.

[37] *Supra,* note 33. George Good, on October 23, 1847, as he tells us in his Diary of that date, "recited to Asst Lumas [Loomis] in vocal music."

[38] J. Merrill Linn, Diary, October 20–21, 1847; Franklin H. Lane, "The Early Days of Euepia," *Bucknell Mirror,* XVIII (March, 1899), 121.

[39] Elsewhere we read: "There is now upwards of one hundred students under the charge of Professor Taylor, and more expected. From all appearance, it is destined to be equal if not superior to any University in the United States." *Lewisburg Chronicle,* October 30, 1847.

[40] J. Merrill Linn, Diary, May 31, 1848, and *passim.*

[41] Minutes of the Trustees, August 23, 1847, and January 1 and February 1–2, 1848.

[42] In the Catalogue of the University for 1855–56, p. 21, we read: "This building is on the University Hill, sixty by eighty feet, three stories high, and basement. . . ."

[43] *Lewisburg Chronicle,* January 24, 1849; Minutes of the Trustees, April 18, 1849. In 1851 the Trustees appropriated the sum of $120 to pay the First Baptist Church of Lewisburg for the use of its basement "by the High-School." Minutes of the Trustees, April 15, 1851.

[44] The report of the Curators for the year 1847–48 shows the institution to be highly prosperous. Ten young men were prepared for the sophomore class in the College and sixteen were prepared for the senior class in the Academy. The report bestowed lavish praise upon Stephen W. Taylor for working well "in inconvenient rooms, without necessary apparatus, and where we considered it noble condescension in him to labor." It announced the fact that Taylor had been elected to the chair of mathematics and natural philosophy, "to rank next to the President in the Faculty, and, until that office is filled, to be the Presiding Officer of the University." *Lewisburg Chronicle,* October 20, 1848.

[45] Minutes of the Trustees, May 2, 1848.

[46] *Ibid.,* January 19, 1849.

[47] Philadelphia *Christian Chronicle,* April 5, 1848.

[48] Minutes of the Trustees, January 19–20, 1849.

[49] An official notice, signed by the secretary of the Board, George F. Miller, said that the meeting would be held on January 18, 1849. "It is hoped," the notice reads, "that the trustees will all be in attendance, as important business will be laid before the Board which will require immediate action." *Lewisburg Chronicle,* January 10, 1849. George R. Bliss, who had come from New Brunswick, New Jersey, to attend this meeting, recalled in an address to the Alumni Club of Philadelphia on January 15, 1874, that twenty-five years ago that night "he started upon his first trip to the wilds of Pennsylvania, there to aid in establishing an institution that has since become the pride of its founders." *College Herald,* IV (February, 1874), 63.

[50] George W. Anderson was elected professor of Latin.

[51] Minutes of the Trustees, January 18, 1849. Bliss accepted his appointment on February 8, 1849, and Anderson accepted his on April 17, 1849. See also *The First Half Century of Madison University (1819–1869), or the Jubilee Volume. . . .* (New York, 1872), 158, 237, 267.

[52] Minutes of the Trustees, January 20, 1849.

[53] By this time the Board had decided to erect a dormitory before it constructed the central part of the University Building. The "wing" referred to here became known as the West Wing of this building.

[54] Minutes of the Trustees, April 19, 1849. Also, see in the *Lewisburg Chronicle,* April 25, 1849, an abstract of the proceedings of this meeting.

[55] See in the *Lewisburg Chronicle,* October 3, 1849, an abstract of the proceedings of the Board during its meeting in August, 1848.

[56] *Lewisburg Chronicle,* September 11, 1850.

[56a] On May 2, 1848, the Trustees appointed a committee "to inquire in relation to a transfer of a sufficient portion of Land from William H. Ludwig and also concerning a transfer of a tract known as the University Land from the owners to this Board." See subsequent actions taken by the Board in respect to this matter. Minutes of the Board, May 2–3, and August 28, 1848, and August 19, 1849.

[57] Minutes of the Trustees, August 26–27, 1850. See also Mary Bartol Theiss, "The Homes of Bucknell's Presidents," *Bucknell Alumni Monthly,* X (October, 1925), 9–11.

[58] *Lewisburg Chronicle,* September 11, 1850.

[59] Taylor, A Brief History.

[60] Minutes of the Trustees, August 25, 1849. "Philosophical apparatus" was equipment used for conducting what today would be called experiments in physics.

[61] *Ibid.,* April 17, 1850.

[62] *Ibid.,* August 26, 1850.

[63] *Ibid.,* August 24, 1850. Mrs. George W. Anderson, writing to her mother-in-law in November, 1850, said that her husband was very busy, "for they have a senior class this year and the work of the President is divided among the three Professors. George has at present Natural Theology in addition to the classes in his own department." Maria F. Anderson to Mrs. R. D. Anderson, November 11, 1850. Original letter in the Archives of Bucknell University.

[64] [George R. Bliss], "Sketch of the History of Our University," *College Herald,* I (May, 1870), 1. J. Merrill Linn, in his Diary under date of May 21, 1850, volunteered this unchivalrous information: "There are lots of young ladies going to the Institution, none that are handsome."

[65] There is a photostatic copy of this Circular in the Archives of Bucknell University. The Circular appeared in the *Lewisburg Chronicle,* September 25, 1850. For an account of the textbooks used in the University during the academic year 1851–52, see *Bibliotheca Bucnellensis,* 1962–63, II, n. s., 24–34.

[66] On the growth of the collegiate library during the Taylor era, see J. Orin Oliphant, *The Library of Bucknell University* (Lewisburg, Pa., 1962), 3–9, and works therein cited.

[67] For a comprehensive study of collegiate literary societies in the United States before 1876, see Thomas S. Harding, College Literary Societies: Their Contribution to Education in the United States, 1815–1876. Doctoral Dissertation, University of Chicago, June, 1957 (available on microfilm). On the role of the literary societies in one of the colleges of Virginia, see George J. Stevenson, *Increase in Excellence: A History of Emory and Henry College* (New York, *c.* 1963), 169–175.

[68] University at Lewisburg, *Catalogue, 1850–51,* 23.

[69] *Laws of the University at Lewisburg, Pennsylvania. Enacted 1851.* [Second edition, revised.] (Printed for the University, 1855), 24.

[69a] In October, 1897, the students of the Academy adopted a constitution for the "new Calliopean" society. This society was named after "Bucknell's first society, Calliopean, established Dec. 4, 1847." *Orange and Blue,* October 12, 1897.

[70] *Lewisburg Chronicle,* June 13, October 10, November 7, 1849.

[71] Oliphant, *The Library of Bucknell University,* 19–21.

[72] Theta Alpha Society, Minutes, December 28, 1850.

[73] Phirhoan Society, Minutes, 1850–54.

[74] Robert Lowry to William T. Biddle, March 4, 1850, in the Letter Book of the Society for Moral and Religious Inquiry. See also Society for Inquiry of the Hamilton Literary & Theological Institution, *Annual Report, March, 1837* (Utica, 1837), *passim.*

[75] Henry K. Rowe, *History of the Andover Theological Seminary* (Newton, Mass., 1933), 114.

[76] On this subject generally, see Oliphant, *The Library of Bucknell University,* 21–25, and the works therein cited.

[77] University at Lewisburg, *Catalogue, 1851–52,* 22.

[78] Minutes of the Trustees, August 24, 1850.

[79] Madison University, Constitution and Minutes of the Board of Trustees, August 22, 1850. Archives of Colgate University.

[80] Jesse Leonard Rosenberger, *Rochester and Colgate: Historical Backgrounds of the Two Universities* (Chicago, *c.* 1925), chap. 3.

[81] Both of these letters are in the Archives of Colgate University.

[82] Taylor to Spear, December 20, 1850; Taylor to Alva Pierce, December 23, 1850. Archives of Colgate University.

[83] Taylor to Thomas Wattson, December 20, 1850. Minutes of the Trustees, April, 16, 1851.

[84] Madison University, Constitution and Minutes of the Board of Trustees, February 5, 1851; Taylor to Spear, February 14, 1851. Archives of Colgate University.

[85] Minutes of the Trustees, April 16, 1851.

[86] Note 83, *supra.*

[87] Taylor to Henry Tower, May 14, 1851; Taylor to Spear, May 14, 1851, with a postscript dated May 31, 1851. Archives of Colgate University.

[88] Minutes of the Trustees, April 16, 1851.

[89] George W. Anderson to Mrs. R. D. Anderson, November 29, 1851. Original letter in the Archives of Bucknell University.

[90] Minutes of the Trustees, August 21, 1851. John Houseknecht, a student in Taylor's High School during its first year, wrote to his parents in Muncy, Pennsylvania, on December 7, 1846, as follows: "Proff. Taylor is the greatest critic that graces the theatre of learning. A student cannot make the slightest mistake without being detected and shown his errors." Original letter in the Archives of Bucknell University. J. Merrill Linn, who was one of Taylor's students for five years, spoke highly of Taylor in 1846, but in May, 1850, he contrasted him unfavorably with Professor Bliss, saying that, whereas Bliss was simple and humble, Taylor was pompous and egotistical. J. Merrill Linn, Diary, October 26, 1846, and May 17, 1850. But in 1876, in an address before the Alumni Association of the University at Lewisburg, he spoke of Taylor in the highest terms, saying, *inter alia,* "His admonition never hurt the most sensitive. His reproof never marred the self-respect. His patience was unwearied." *Lewisburg Chronicle,* August 25, 1876.

[91] Taylor to Spear, May 31, 1851. Archives of Colgate University.

[92] Minutes of the Trustees, August 20, 1851.

[93] George Good, Diary, August 11, 1851.

[94] J. Merrill Linn, Diary, July 22, 1851.

[95] *Ibid.*, August 16, 1851; Lewisburg *Democrat,* July 29, 1851.

[96] "Commencement Exercises of the University at Lewisburg," Lewisburg *Democrat,* August 26, 1851.

[97] University at Lewisburg, Minutes of the Curators, August 19, 1851.

[98] *Lewisburg Chronicle,* August 27, 1851.

[99] Lewisburg *Union County Whig,* August 28, 1851.

[100] J. Merrill Linn, Diary, August 20, 1851.

[101] *Bucknell Alumnus,* XXXV (September, 1950), 21.

CHAPTER THREE

[1] University at Lewisburg, Minutes of the Trustees, July 28, 1857.

[2] *Necrological Report Presented to the Alumni Association of the Princeton Theological Seminary, at its Annual Meeting, April 29, 1879, by a Committee of the Association* (Philadelphia, 1879), 13–14; *Historical Catalogue of Brown University, 1764–1804* (Providence, 1905), 549; Philadelphia *National Baptist,* April 3, 1879, 1.

[3] Cincinnati *Cross and Baptist Journal,* August 7, 1840; Leland W. Meyer, *Georgetown College: Its Background and a Chapter in Its Early History* (The College, 1929), 72.

[4] Philadelphia Fifth Baptist Church, Minutes (1840–1848), No. 3, 231, 236–238, 306–307. American Baptist Historical Society, Rochester, New York.

[5] Cincinnati *Cross and Baptist Journal,* September 18, 1835; *Historical Catalogue of Brown University,* 549.

[6] University at Lewisburg, Minutes of the Trustees, August 15, 1854.

[7] University at Lewisburg, *Catalogue, 1856–57,* 20.

[8] Minutes of the Trustees, July 29, 1856.

[9] *Ibid.,* August 19, 1851. This Scientific Program was very much like one that was offered in Georgetown College. *Catalogue of the Officers and Students of Georgetown College, Kentucky, 1848–49* (Cincinnati, 1849), 11.

[10] *Report of the Corporation of Brown University on Changes in the System of Collegiate Education, Read March 28, 1850* (Providence, 1850), 50, 52, 74. See also Wayland's *The Education Demanded by the People . . .* (Boston, 1855).

[11] Advertisement in the *Lewisburg Chronicle,* September 24, 1852. Some two years later the Board approved Malcom's proposal to change the Classical Program by "omitting some portion of Latin and Greek, and introducing more of the Physical Sciences." Minutes of the Trustees, August 16, 1854.

[12] Minutes of the Trustees, August 17, 1852.

[13] *Ibid.,* August 15, 1854.

[14] Frederick Rudolph, *The American College and University: A History* (New York, 1962), chap. 6; R. Freeman Butts, *The College Charts its Course: Historical Conceptions and Current Proposals* (New York, 1939), chap. 8.

[15] *Reports on the Course of Instruction in Yale College; by a Committee of the Corporation and the Academical Faculty* (New Haven, 1828), 6, 7, 30. See also Rudolph, *op. cit.,* 130–135, and Butts, *op. cit.,* 119–125.

[16] Minutes of the Trustees, August 17, 1852.

[17] *Ibid.,* April 20 and August 17, 1852.

[18] *Ibid.,* April 19, 1853.

[19] *Ibid.,* August 15, 1854.

[20] *Ibid.,* April 20, 1852.

[21] *Ibid.,* April 19, 1853.

[22] On Malcom's gift and on Anderson's trip to Europe, see the documents printed in the *Lewisburg Chronicle,* August 28, November 26, and December 24, 1852. See also Malcom's Scrap Book, American Baptist Historical Society.

[23] Minutes of the Trustees, August 16, 1853.

[24] Malcom's Scrap Book.

[25] Philadelphia *Baptist Record,* February 18, 1844; Louisville *Baptist Banner,* July 12, 1848.

[25a] Malcom's Scrap Book.

[26] *Ibid.*

[27] Howard Malcom to Hannah R. Poole, October 23, 1854. Malcom's Scrap Book.

[28] Minutes of the Trustees, August 17, 1853.

[29] *Ibid.,* August 15, 1854.

[30] *Ibid.*

[31] University at Lewisburg, *Catalogue, 1854–55,* 21.

[32] Minutes of the Trustees, July 27, 1859. On Malcom's contribution to the library of the University at Lewisburg, see J. Orin Oliphant's *The Library of Bucknell University* (Lewisburg, Pa., 1962), 9–15.

[33] Minutes of the Trustees, April 19, 1853.

[34] *Ibid.,* August 15, 1854.

[35] *Ibid.,* March 25, 1856.

[36] *Ibid.,* July 29, 1856.

[37] *Ibid.,* July 30, 1856.

[38] *Ibid.,* August 15, 1854.

[39] *Laws of the University at Lewisburg, Pennsylvania. Enacted 1851* (Lewisburg, Pa., 1851). These laws, slightly revised, were reprinted in 1855.

[40] Circular appended to the *Laws of the University,* cited above.

[41] There was no charge for instruction in the Department of Theology.

[42] University at Lewisburg, *Catalogue, 1854–55,* 23, 32.

[43] *Ibid., 1855–56,* 21–22.

[44] Minutes of the Trustees, April 19, 1853, and March 25, 1856.

[45] See, for example, the Pennsylvania Baptist Convention, *Minutes, 1851–55* (Philadelphia, 1851–56), *passim,* and the Pennsylvania Baptist Education Society, *Minutes, 1853–54* (Philadelphia, 1853–54), *passim.*

[46] Justin R. Loomis, *An Address Delivered June 9, 1865, in Commencement Hall, of the University at Lewisburg, Pa., before the Students of the Several Departments, on the Occasion of their Celebrating the Completion of the Endowment Fund* (Lewisburg, 1865), 13.

[47] Board of Curators, "Annual Report of the Committee of Publication," *Lewisburg Chronicle,* August 8, 1856.

[48] George Good, Diary, December 13, 1851.

[49] Minutes of the Trustees, July 29, 1856.

[50] University at Lewisburg, Minutes of the Curators, July 29, 1856; Board of Curators, "Annual Report of the Committee of Publication," *Lewisburg Chronicle,* August 8, 1856.

[51] Minutes of the Trustees, July 30, 1856.

[52] *Ibid.,* August 19–21, 1852, *passim.*

[53] *Ibid.,* August 18, 1852, and August 16, 1853.

[54] *Ibid.,* August 16–17, 1853.

[55] *Ibid.,* August 15, 1854.

[56] *Ibid.*

[57] University at Lewisburg, *Catalogue, 1851–52,* 16; Harriet E. Spratt, "University Female Institute: Historical Sketch," in O. W. Spratt, ed., *Historical Sketch of the University at Lewisburg . . .* (Philadelphia, 1877), 32.

[58] Philadelphia *Christian Chronicle,* October 14, 1846.

[59] [George R. Bliss], "Sketch of the History of Our University," *College Herald,* I (May, 1870), 1; Franklin H. Lane, "The Early Days of Euepia," *Bucknell Mirror,* XVIII (March, 1899), 122.

[60] Minutes of the Trustees, April 20–21, 1852.

[61] *Ibid.,* August 17–18, 1852; *Lewisburg Chronicle,* May 21, 1852.

[62] Statement by Thomas Wattson, *Lewisburg Chronicle,* October 8, 1852; Howard Malcom, "Semi-Annual Report," Minutes of the Trustees, April 19, 1853.

[63] Minutes of the Trustees, August 15, 1854.

[64] Report of the committee on the Female Institute, Minutes of the Trustees, April 17, 1855; *Lewisburg Chronicle,* October 13, 1854.

[65] On libraries in the Female Institute, see Oliphant, *op. cit.,* 29–33; *Catalogue of the University Female Institute, 1855* (Lewisburg, Pa., 1855).

[66] Minutes of the Trustees, August 14, 1855.

[67] *Ibid.,* August 14, 1855.

[68] *Ibid.,* July 29, 1856.

[69] *Ibid.,* April 17, 1855; *Catalogue of the University Female Institute, 1855,* 13–14.

[70] *Ibid.*

[71] Statement by Thomas Wattson, *Lewisburg Chronicle,* October 8, 1852.

[72] Minutes of the Trustees, April 15, 1851.

[73] *Ibid.*

[74] *Ibid.,* August 18, 1852.

[75] New Jersey Baptist State Convention, *Minutes of the Twenty-Third Anniversary, . . . and of the Fifteenth Annual Meeting of the New Jersey Baptist Education Society, . . . November 13th, 14th, 15th and 16th, 1852* (Burlington, 1853), 27–28; Minutes of the Trustees, August 16, 1853.

[76] Minutes of the Trustees, August 14, 1855.

[77] *Report of the Board of Trustees of the University at Lewisburg to the Patrons and Friends of the University* (Philadelphia, 1858), 7.

[78] University at Lewisburg, *Catalogue, 1858–59,* 5.

[79] Minutes of the Trustees, April 15–16, 1851.

[80] *Ibid.*, April 19, 1853.
[81] *Ibid.*, August 16, 1854.
[82] *Ibid.*, April 17 and April 26, 1855; *Lewisburg Chronicle,* May 11, 1855.
[83] Minutes of the Trustees, August 14, 1855.
[84] *Ibid.*, August 14, 1855, and March 25, 1856.
[85] University at Lewisburg, *Catalogue, 1855–56,* 6–8.
[86] Minutes of the Trustees, March 25, 1856.
[87] Original letter in the Archives of Bucknell University.
[88] The shrinkage was principally in the College, from 80 in 1853–54 to 65 in 1856–57. Without the beneficiaries of the Pennsylvania Baptist Education Society, the enrollment would have been much smaller. During those years the enrollment in the Female Institute increased from 41 to 70.
[89] Minutes of the Trustees, July 29, 1856.
[90] *Ibid.*, March 25, 1857; *Lewisburg Chronicle,* October 24, October 31, and November 14, 1856; *ibid.*, July 24 and August 14, 1857.
[91] Minutes of the Trustees, July 28, 1857.
[92] *Ibid.*, July 27, 1858.
[93] *Lewisburg Chronicle,* October 3, 1856.
[94] Minutes of the Trustees, August 15, 1854.
[95] *Ibid.*, July 29–30, 1856.
[96] *Lewisburg Chronicle,* August 26, 1856.
[97] Minutes of the Trustees, March 24, 1857.
[98] *Ibid.*, July 28, 1857.
[99] *Ibid.*, July 27, 1858.
[100] *Ibid.*, July 26, 1859.
[101] *Lewisburg Chronicle,* March 25, 1859.
[102] Howard Malcom to Hannah R. Poole, January 11, 1857. Malcom's Scrap Book.
[103] Cincinnati *Cross and Baptist Journal,* September 18, 1835.
[104] Minutes of the Trustees, July 28, 1857.
[105] University at Lewisburg, Minutes of the Curators, July 28, 1857.
[106] Minutes of the Trustees, December 29, 1857.
[107] *Ibid.*, July 28, 1858; *Lewisburg Chronicle,* July 10 and July 30, 1858; *Report of the Board of Trustees of the University at Lewisburg to the Patrons and Friends of the University* (Philadelphia, 1858).
[108] *Report of the Board of Trustees* . . . (Philadelphia, 1858), 6.

CHAPTER FOUR

[1] Edit., "President of Lewisburg University," *Lewisburg Chronicle,* January 1, 1858.
[2] University at Lewisburg, Minutes of the Trustees, July 28, October 28, and December 29, 1857; University at Lewisburg, *Catalogue, 1857–58,* 4.
[3] *Historical Catalogue of Brown University, 1764–1904* (Providence, 1905), 168; *First Half Century of Madison University, 1819–1869* (New York, 1872), 212; Minutes of the Trustees, August 17, 1853, and August 15, 1854.
[4] *Lewisburg Chronicle,* January 1, 1858.
[5] Minutes of the Trustees, July 26–27, 1859. The minutes of the meeting of the Board in March, 1859, were presumably lost. They were not entered in the book containing the minutes of the other meetings of the Board. For the report of the Committee of Publication for the Curators on the academic year 1858–59, see the *Lewisburg Chronicle,* August 12, 1859.
[6] Minutes of the Trustees, July 25, 1860.
[7] *Ibid.*, March 26, 1861.
[8] Minutes of the Trustees, July 24, 1860, and July 29, 1862. On July 27, 1859, Dr. Brantly had been elected a member of the Board of Curators, but his seat on this Board was vacated when he became a trustee. University at Lewisburg, Minutes of the

Curators, July 27, 1859, and July 31, 1861. See also the *Union County Star and Lewisburg Chronicle:* July 27, 1860; July 2, 1861; September 9, 1862.

9 William Cathcart, ed., *The Baptist Encyclopaedia* (Philadelphia, 1881), 128.

10 Accounts of these two meetings in Lewisburg in 1854 are embodied in a long story on "Kansas A Free State" that appeared in the *Union County Star and Lewisburg Chronicle,* February 8, 1861.

11 See two "open letters" that Professor George R. Bliss addressed to Senator William Bigler. *Ibid.,* October 24 and 31, 1856.

12 John Humpstone, "In Memoriam: The Reverend Professor George Ripley Bliss, D.D., LL.D.," *Bucknell Mirror,* XII (June, 1893), 116.

13 University at Lewisburg, Phirhoan Society, Minutes, March 1, 1851–March 2, 1854.

14 University at Lewisburg, Euepia Society, Minutes, *passim,* and Theta Alpha Society, Minutes, *passim.*

15 Elisha Shorkley's diary is in the Archives of Bucknell University.

16 The Lewisburg Infantry was mustered into service on April 20, 1861, for three months, as Company G of the Fourth Regiment of Pennsylvania Volunteers. After completing its tour of duty, it arrived in Lewisburg on July 27, 1861. *Union County Star and Lewisburg Chronicle,* July 30, 1861. For the muster roll of this company, see *ibid.,* May 17, 1861, and Samuel P. Bates, *History of the Pennsylvania Volunteers . . .* (Harrisburg, 1869), I, 47. J. Merrill Linn, Class of 1851, University at Lewisburg, served as second lieutenant in this company.

17 Hereafter in this chapter the *Union County Star and Lewisburg Chronicle* will be cited as *Star and Chronicle.*

18 When organized, this company was given the name of Slifer Guards, in honor of Colonel Eli Slifer, a businessman of Lewisburg, who was then serving as Secretary of the Commonwealth of Pennsylvania.

19 John Bowen Hutton, of Milesburg, was a freshman in the University at Lewisburg in 1860–61. In 1863 he served as a sergeant in the University Guards (Company A, Twenty-Eighth Regiment, Pennsylvania Volunteers). *Star and Chronicle,* June 26, 1863.

20 The Slifer Guards, commanded by Captain Thomas Chamberlin, became Company D of the Thirty-Fourth Regiment, Fifth Pennsylvania Reserve. Bates, *op. cit.,* I, 678–680. In November, 1861, Colonel Eli Slifer sent as a present eighty "gummed blankets" for the use of the men in this company who were without such equipment. *Star and Chronicle,* November 22, 1861.

21 This letter was signed "T. G. O." It was written by Thomas G. Orwig, who was subsequently elected second lieutenant in Company B of Campbell's Artillery. *Star and Chronicle,* June 21, 1861.

22 *Ibid.,* June 21 and 28, 1861.

23 *Ibid.,* July 9, 1861.

24 In 1863 Professor T. F. Curtis served as treasurer of the Soldiers' Fund of Lewisburg. This fund was raised and maintained by voluntary subscriptions, and its purpose was to provide assistance to the dependents of enlisted men. Professor Curtis subscribed $100 to this fund in 1863. *Star and Chronicle,* June 19 and 23, 1863. In 1863 both President Loomis and Professor Bliss were commissioned as "delegates" by the United States Christian Commission, and after the battle of Gettysburg they both went to Gettysburg and served as nurses to wounded soldiers. Lemuel Moss, *Annals of the United States Christian Commission* (Philadelphia, 1868), 605, 609; *Star and Chronicle,* July 7 and 17, 1863; Lucy R. Bliss, "The Days of 'Sixty-Three," *Bucknell Alumni Monthly,* VII (December, 1922), 4; John Humpstone, "In Memoriam . . . ," *loc. cit.,* 116; Euepia Society, Minutes, 1861–65, *passim;* Theta Alpha Society, Minutes, 1861–65, *passim.*

25 Harrisburg *Pennsylvania Daily Telegraph,* September 11 and 12, 1862.

26 *Star and Chronicle,* September 12, 1862. Elisha Shorkley, in his diary for September 8, 1862, wrote that military affairs were "all the rush," and that there was drilling "in both wards, & full companies too." Three days later he wrote in his diary as follows: "The excitement is intense. At 9 we haul the fires of the Foundry & quit the routine of

business for that of soldiery." Elisha Shorkley served as a corporal in Company B, Third Regiment, Pennsylvania Volunteers. His brother Charles commanded this company.

27 *Star and Chronicle,* September 19 and 30, 1862; Bates, *op. cit.,* V, 1153–1154.

28 The six persons were as follows: Charles Spyker Wolfe, freshman; Henry F. Grier, sophomore; G. Barron Miller, senior in the Academy; Edwin H. Ranney, Theological Department; William L. Nesbit, '60; and Orlando Wellington Spratt, '61.

29 Philadelphia *Christian Chronicle,* September 18, 1862. President Loomis, it appears, actually performed some service as a soldier. In a letter dated at Camp McClure on September 16, 1862, "R," of Company C, wrote as follows: "One of the most interesting features in camp life to me thus far has been the ease with which men fall into the routine of camp duties. A Rev. editor, formerly a pastor of one of our churches, visited the camp this morning—but imagine his surprise to find himself brought to a 'Halt!' by the venerable President of the University at Lewisburg, out on guard!" Presumably "R" was John Randolph, principal of the Lewisburg Academy. *Star and Chronicle,* September 24, 1862.

30 The muster rolls of Companies B and C are printed in the *Star and Chronicle,* September 30, 1862, and the muster rolls for the entire regiment are printed in Bates, *op. cit.,* V, 1153–1156. In the last-named work it is said (p. 1153) that the Third Regiment was organized on September 11–13, 1862, and was mustered out on September 23–25, 1862. See also William L. Nesbit, "The First Emergency," *Bucknell Alumni Monthly,* VII (May, 1923), 4–5.

31 Two privates in Company C, Samuel L. Beck, Jr., and Walter G. M'Mahon, who were employees of the *Star and Chronicle,* prepared a brief day-by-day account of the activities of Companies B and C (with particular reference to Company C) that was published in the *Star and Chronicle* of September 30, 1862.

32 *Star and Chronicle,* September 24, 1862.

33 *Ibid.* General George B. McClellan, in a message to Governor Curtin, dated September 15, 1862—8 A.M., announced a "complete victory" at South Mountain and congratulated the governor "on the gallant behavior of the Pennsylvania Reserves." *The War of the Rebellion,* Series I, XIX, Pt. 2, 305–306.

34 It was announced, as early as September 19, 1862, that both the University and the Lewisburg Academy would open at the appointed times, notwithstanding the absence of President Loomis and Professor James from the University and of Principal John Randolph from the Lewisburg Academy. *Star and Chronicle,* September 19, 1862. In Philadelphia, on September 25, it was announced that President Loomis and Professor James would be "relieved" in time to return for the opening of the fall term of the University. Editorial, "Lewisburg University," Philadelphia *Christian Chronicle,* September 25, 1862. In a telegram to General H. W. Halleck, dated September 23, 1862, Governor Curtin said that the Pennsylvania militia had been disbanded. *The War of the Rebellion,* Series I, XIX, Pt. 2, 352.

35 *Ibid.,* XXVII, 881.

36 The story of Confederate raiding in Pennsylvania before the battle of Gettysburg is told perceptively by Professor Edwin B. Coddington in "Prelude to Gettysburg: The Confederates Plunder Pennsylvania," *Pennsylvania History,* XXX, (April, 1963), 123–157.

37 Spencer Glasgow Welch, *A Confederate Surgeon's Letters to His Wife* (Marietta, Ga., 1954), 56.

38 *The War of the Rebellion,* Series I, XXVII, Pt. 3, 54–55.

39 *Ibid.,* 136–137.

40 *Star and Chronicle,* June 16, 1863.

41 Captain Thomas Rockafellow Jones, of Company C, 131st Regiment, Pennsylvania Volunteers, was mustered into service on August 14, 1862, and was mustered out with the company on May 23, 1863. Bates, *op. cit.,* IV, 230. This company was organized in Northumberland County under the name of "Northumberland County Tigers." *Star and Chronicle,* June 19, 1862.

42 *Star and Chronicle,* June 19, 1863.

[43] Sally Meixell's comment about the enlistments is not entirely accurate, as the sequel will show. Her diary is in the Archives of Bucknell University.

[44] *Star and Chronicle,* June 26, 1863.

[45] For muster rolls of these companies, see Bates, *op. cit.,* V, 1239–1241, and *Star and Chronicle,* June 26 and August 4, 1863. Under the heading of "Good for Union County," the Harrisburg *Pennsylvania Daily Telegraph* of July 1, 1863, said: "Another large company, numbering 140 or 150, composed principally of the business men of Lewisburg, arrived here last night. Union County at present has three companies in the fortifications opposite the city, commanded by Captains Shorkley, Jones and Forrest. The latter gentleman is the present Postmaster of Lewisburg. Union county has furnished more men than her quota already, and men are still offering their services."

[46] *Star and Chronicle,* June 26, 1863. In this letter Spratt said that the members of this company had taken the following oath: "I do solemnly swear that I will bear true faith and allegiance to the United States of America, and that I will serve them honestly and faithfully during the *existing emergency* for service in this Department, against all their enemies and opposers whomsoever; and that I will observe and obey the orders of the President of the United States, and the orders of the Officers appointed over me, according to the rules and regulations of the government of the Army of the U.S."

[47] *Star and Chronicle,* July 7, 1863.

[48] *Ibid.,* July 14, 1863.

[49] On the movements of Company A, and especially on the exaggerated assertion that this company had "saved Harrisburg," see the article by William L. Nesbit in the *Bucknell Alumni Monthly,* VII (March, 1923), 2. Nesbit's assertion that Harrisburg was saved, not by emergency troops, but by the withdrawal of Confederate troops to join the main Confederate army, is, in general, substantiated by the report of General R. E. Rodes, C.S.A., on the Gettysburg campaign. *The War of the Rebellion,* Series I, XXVII, Pt. 2, 551–552.

[50] Charles C. Shorkley to Elisha Shorkley, June 21, 1863. This letter is owned by Mrs. Ruth Bliss, Carpenteria, Calif.

[51] *Star and Chronicle,* July 28 and August 4, 1863; diary of Elisha Shorkley, July 30, 1863.

[52] *Star and Chronicle,* July 24, 1863.

[53] Philadelphia *Christian Chronicle,* July 23, 1863.

[54] J. Merrill Linn Papers, Archives of Bucknell University.

[55] *Ibid.*

[56] Correspondence, by a "Friend," in the Philadelphia *Christian Chronicle,* August 6, 1863.

[57] Minutes of the Trustees, July 28, 1863.

[58] *Star and Chronicle,* August 4, 1863.

[59] *Ibid.*

[60] See the story on the commencement exercises, *ibid.*

[61] Philadelphia *Christian Chronicle,* August 6, 1863.

[62] The muster roll of Company A is printed in O. W. Spratt, ed., *Historical Sketch of the University at Lewisburg, and Report of the Twenty-Sixth Annual Commencement, Lewisburg, Pa., June 23–28, 1876.* Published by the Society of Alumni (Philadelphia, 1877), 25. Unhappily, the students in this company are not distinguished from the other members. Accordingly, since Company A is here called "The Students' Company," the impression given by this muster roll is that the company was exclusively a company of students. Recently Bucknell University has acquired the certificate of discharge of Charles A. Stone, a junior, who served as a private in Company A. From this certificate we learn that he was twenty-three years old when he enlisted, that he was enrolled on June 16, 1863, "to serve during the emergency," that he was discharged in Harrisburg on July 27, 1863, and that he was "paid in full" by the paymaster of the United States. Mr. Stone was graduated in the Class of 1864.

[63] *Star and Chronicle,* August 28, 1863.

[64] Minutes of the Trustees, July 28, 1863.

[65] We know that the work of the Female Institute was somewhat disrupted, because, by the end of June, 1863, twenty-five of its fifty-nine students had gone home "on account of the war excitement." By July 10 the teachers in the Institute had quit making weekly reports because of "the rapid decrease of the school consequent upon the war excitement and the irregularity of classes." University at Lewisburg, Minutes of the Teachers' Meetings of the Female Institute, June 30 and July 10, 1863. There is no indication, however, that the work of the Institute was discontinued. It is conceivable, also, that some of the students in the Academy went home "on account of the war excitement," although we have no record of their doing so.

[66] The five members of the University Guards of 1863 were Thomas A. Gill, George D. Kincaid, John B. Probasco, Clement B. Low, and Leroy Stephens. The other students were Theophilus E. Clapp, John Sexton James, Hiram M'Gowen, and Charles S. Wolfe.

[67] James H. Eldredge. The muster roll of this company, which was in service from August 12, 1864, to November 25, 1864, is printed in Bates, *op. cit.*, V, 1339.

[68] John Sexton James tells his recollections of service in Lambert's Cavalry in "War Clouds in the Sixties at Lewisburg," *Bucknell Mirror,* XVII (June 10, 1898), 112–116.

[69] Bucknell University, *L'Agenda, Published by the Junior Class . . . for the Year 1888,* 40; Joseph Cookman Nate, *The History of the Sigma Chi Fraternity, 1855–1925* (Published by the Fraternity [1927?]), II, 189–203. Of the sixteen charter members, the following had served in the University Guards in 1863: Thomas F. Curtis, Theodore A. K. Gessler, Harrison B. Garner, John S. Hutson, John B. Hutton, John Ritner, Thomas M. Shanafelt, and Robert A. Townsend.

[70] Minutes of the Trustees, April 10, 1866.

[71] Annual Report of the Committee on Publication of the Board of Curators, *Star and Chronicle,* August 24, 1860.

[72] Minutes of the Trustees, July 29, 1862.

[73] *Memorials of Bucknell University, 1846–1896* (Published by the University, Lewisburg, Pa., 1896), 25.

[74] Minutes of the Trustees, March 31, 1863.

[75] The Trustees had reason to be wary of such a proposal. They knew about an unfortunate experience that Jefferson College had had in selling scholarships, and they may well have been calculating the dangers involved in selling "permanent" scholarships. On the distressing experience of American colleges and universities in respect to the sale of scholarships, see Frederick Rudolph, *The American College and University: A History* (New York, 1962), 190–192. See also G. Wallace Chessman, *Denison: The Story of an Ohio College* (Granville, *c.* 1957), 54–55, 212–213.

[76] Annual Report of the Committee on Publication of the Board of Curators, *Star and Chronicle,* August 28, 1863.

[77] Justin R. Loomis, *An Address Delivered June 9, 1865, in Commencement Hall, of the University at Lewisburg, Pa., Before the Students of the Several Departments, on the Occasion of Their Celebration of the Completion of the Endowment Fund* (Lewisburg, Pa., 1865), 12. The Trustees did not discontinue their efforts to sell certificates of scholarships, for in July, 1865, they "Resolved, That the General Agent in connection with the Committee on Scholarships be instructed to continue the sale of scholarships until the original limits be reached—that all monies arising therefrom be added to the Endowment—and those having paid and hereafter paying being entitled to use their certificates forthwith." Minutes of the Trustees, July 25, 1865. Apparently the University in subsequent years was not so much embarrassed by its scholarships as many other educational institutions were by theirs. It seems that it made no serious effort to collect the subscriptions that had been made for scholarships. In July, 1869, the general agent reported that forty-five scholarships were outstanding, of which thirty were actually in use. Of these only three were perpetual. In 1877 he reported that twenty-eight scholarships were outstanding, of which twenty-four were in use. Of these four were perpetual, eight were for twenty-four years, and sixteen were for eight years. Minutes of the Trustees, II, 249, 373. This was not an excessive burden for the University to carry. As

late as 1906, however, at least one eight-year scholarship was in use at Bucknell. It had been sold on September 11, 1865, for $100, and it guaranteed the purchaser, C. Mozley, "his heirs and assigns free tuition for one pupil in either department of the University at Lewisburg, for eight years." This certificate has recently been acquired by the Archives of Bucknell. The first endorsement on it, made on January 13, 1903, affirms that "Three years of the within scholarship have been used to date." Subsequent endorsements show that this scholarship was in use as late as the autumn of 1906.

78 Minutes of the Trustees, April 4, 1865. In his address before the students on June 9, 1865, President Loomis said, apropos of the decision to raise $100,000 for endowment: "The work was begun in January last, and was prosecuted with more of prayer than faith." Loomis, *op. cit.*, 12. While Loomis was engaged in this work, Professor Bliss, once again, served as acting president of the University.

79 Minutes of the Trustees, July 25, 1865. For a statement by a committee affirming that Loomis had obtained "reliable subscriptions," see the *Lewisburg Chronicle,* June 9, 1865. The Annual Report of the Committee on Publication of the Board of Curators for 1864–65 is printed in the *Lewisburg Chronicle,* August 18, 1865.

80 Minutes of the Trustees, July 25, 1865.

81 *Ibid.*

82 Loomis, *op. cit.*, 13.

CHAPTER FIVE

1 University at Lewisburg, *Abstract of Treasurer's Report, June 1, 1879,* 13.

2 University at Lewisburg, Minutes of the Trustees, II, 215.

3 *Ibid.*, II, 151–155, 169; University at Lewisburg, Minutes of the Curators, July 23, 1865.

4 Minutes of the Trustees, II, 179.

5 *Ibid.*, II, 130–132.

6 Philadelphia *National Baptist,* November 14, 1867, 1; *Laws of the General Assembly of the State of Pennsylvania, . . . Session of 1867. . . .* (Harrisburg, 1867), 766–767.

7 Crozer Theological Seminary, Minutes of the Trustees, I, 21; Philadelphia *National Baptist,* November 14, 1867, 1.

8 Crozer Theological Seminary, Minutes of the Trustees, October 16, 1867, I, 29.

9 University at Lewisburg, Minutes of the Trustees, II, 219–221, 236–237.

10 Crozer Theological Seminary, Minutes of the Trustees, June 8, 1869, I, 43.

11 University at Lewisburg, Minutes of the Trustees, II, 235, 237.

12 *Ibid.*, II, 243, 260; University at Lewisburg, *Catalogue, 1869–70,* 16, 22; Freeman Loomis, "Classical Preparatory Department," in O. W. Spratt, ed., *Historical Sketch of the University at Lewisburg . . .* (Philadelphia, 1877), 27; Philadelphia *National Baptist,* April 22, 1869, 4.

13 William E. Martin, "Historical Sketch of the Academy," in O. W. Spratt, ed., *loc. cit.*, 30–31; Minutes of the Trustees, III, 198.

14 Minutes of the Trustees, II, 241–243, 261; University Female Institute, *Catalogue, 1878–79,* 17.

15 Minutes of the Trustees, II, 204, 218–219, 224, 247–248.

16 O. W. Spratt, ed., *op. cit.*, 9–11.

17 Minutes of the Trustees, II, 243; First Baptist Church of Lewisburg, Record B, April 21 and July 2, 1869.

18 Minutes of the Trustees, II, 282–283, 284, 291.

19 *Ibid.*, II, 284, 294, 347, 352.

20 *Ibid.*, II, 284–285.

21 *Ibid.*, II, 327, 377, 471.

22 University at Lewisburg, *Catalogue, 1874–75,* 12; Minutes of the Trustees, II, 351; University at Lewisburg, *Catalogue, 1875–76,* 13–15.

23 Justin R. Loomis, "Historical Sketch," in O. W. Spratt, ed., *loc. cit.*, 9, 11.

[24] *College Herald,* I (May, 1870), 5; *ibid.,* I (March, 1871), 8.

[25] University at Lewisburg, *Catalogue, 1872–73,* 13–17; *College Herald,* IV (October, 1873), 31; University at Lewisburg, *Catalogue, 1875–76,* 18; *ibid.,* 1881–82, 33; *ibid.,* 1884–85, 25.

[26] J. Orin Oliphant, *The Library of Bucknell University* (Lewisburg, Pa., 1962), 49–55.

[27] Euepia, Minutes, February 25 and March 3, 1860; Theta Alpha, Minutes, February 18, February 25, March 10, 1860.

[28] Euepia, Minutes, January 31, February 28, March 14, May 2, 1863; Theta Alpha, Minutes, February 14, March 16, March 17, 1863.

[29] Frederick Rudolph, *The American College and University: A History* (New York, 1962), chaps. i–xi *passim.* See also an excerpt from President Charles W. Eliot's Report for 1892–93, in *Harvard Graduates' Magazine,* II (March, 1894), 375.

[30] Rudolph, *op. cit.,* chap. xiv.

[31] Morris Bishop, *A History of Cornell* (Ithaca, *c.* 1962), chap. v; Samuel Eliot Morison, *Three Centuries of Harvard* (Cambridge, 1936), chap. xiv; Walter P. Rogers, *Andrew D. White and the Modern University* (Ithaca, 1942), 98–99; 213–214.

[32] *Addresses at the Inauguration of Charles William Eliot as President of Harvard College, Tuesday, October 19, 1869* (Cambridge, 1869), 29, 41–42.

[33] Quivis, "Criticism of the College System," *College Herald,* II (May, 1871), 3–4; C., "The Elective System of Harvard," *ibid.,* II (April, 1872), 5–6.

[34] D. J. H., "The Elective System," *ibid.,* V (February, 1875), 57–58.

[35] Minutes of the Trustees, II, 316, 322.

[36] O. W. Spratt, ed., *The University at Lewisburg: Report of the Twenty-Fourth Annual Commencement, Lewisburg, Pa., June 19–24, 1874* (Philadelphia, 1874), 20–21.

[37] *Ibid.,* 34–35.

[38] Philadelphia *National Baptist,* July 29, 1875, 1; *Lewisburg Chronicle, July* 16, 1875.

[39] O. W. Spratt, ed., *Historical Sketch of the University at Lewisburg . . . ,* 45–46, quoting from the annual report of the Board of Curators of the University at Lewisburg, in the Philadelphia *National Baptist,* September 7, 1876; Minutes of the Trustees, June 27, 1876, II, 367; *Lewisburg Chronicle,* August 25, 1876.

[40] *Memorials of Bucknell University, 1849–1896* (Lewisburg, Pa.), 27–28. After 1869 the enrollment in the Academy had declined, and the principal, William E. Martin, writing in 1876, had ascribed the decrease, in large part, not only to the rise of new academies in Pennsylvania and in New Jersey since 1869, but also to the founding of Monongahela College in "the remote Southwest." The further decline after 1873, however, may be attributed, at least in part, to the conditions which were causing a decline in enrollments in the other branches of the University. William E. Martin, "Historical Sketch of the Academy," in O. W. Spratt, ed., *Historical Sketch of the University at Lewisburg . . . ,* 31.

[41] Minutes of the Trustees, II, 368, 370, 372.

[42] *Ibid.,* II, 413, 424–425; University at Lewisburg, *Abstract of Treasurer's Report, June 1, 1879,* 14.

[43] Minutes of the Trustees, II, 449, 454–455; advertisement, signed by William E. Martin, in the *Lewisburg Chronicle,* December 26, 1878.

[44] Minutes of the Trustees, II, 462.

[45] Edit., "University at Lewisburg," Philadelphia *National Baptist,* July 4, 1878, 4.

[46] *Lewisburg Chronicle,* August 1, 1878.

[47] Minutes of the Trustees, II, 455.

[48] *Ibid.,* II, 303–304, 311, 325–326.

[49] Minutes of the Trustees, II, 430, 450; Minutes of the Faculty, June 25, 1875, II, 23, 107–108, 145–146.

[50] Minutes of the Trustees, II, 347–349.

[51] *Ibid.,* II, 257, 262.

[52] *Ibid.,* II, 274, 277.

[53] *Ibid.,* II, 431–432.

[54] *Ibid.,* II, 377–380.

[55] *Ibid.*, II, 381, 386–402.
[56] *Ibid.*, II, 403–406.
[57] Minutes of the Faculty, II, 72–76.
[58] A copy of a printed pamphlet of twenty-nine pages, in which Professor James presented his case to "The Alumni and Other Friends and Patrons of the University at Lewisburg," is in the Archives of Bucknell University. This pamphlet was dated at Allentown, Pennsylvania, on May 10, 1878.
[59] Minutes of the Trustees, II, 413.
[60] Minutes of the Curators, June 25, 1878.
[61] Minutes of the Trustees, II, 432.
[62] *Ibid.*, II, 436–437.
[63] *Lewisburg Chronicle,* August 1, 1878; Philadelphia *National Baptist,* July 25, 1878, 4.
[64] Minutes of the Trustees, II, 430.
[65] *Lewisburg Chronicle,* May 5, 1881.
[66] Philips v. Commonwealth *ex rel.* James, 90 Pa. St. Rep. at 394 (June 16, 1881). See also Edward Elliott and M. M. Chambers, *The Colleges and the Courts . . .* (New York, 1936), 73, 347.
[67] Minutes of the Trustees, II, 433–434 (June 25, 1878).
[68] President Loomis played a significant part in the construction of the new building for the First Baptist Church of Lewisburg, the cornerstone of which was laid on July 24, 1867. Not only did he serve as architect and superintendent; he also performed considerable manual labor on the building. When workmen refused to slate the roof of the spire of the building, Loomis did the work satisfactorily and expeditiously. Minutes of the Trustees, II, 213; *Lewisburg Chronicle,* June 21, 1867, and April 26, 1872; Philadelphia *National Baptist,* March 3, 1870, 1; and *College Herald,* II (May, 1871), 6. See Professor William E. Martin's tribute to Loomis in the Minutes of the Faculty, June 24, 1898, III, 50–54.
[69] *Laws of the General Assembly of the State of Pennsylvania, Passed at the Session of 1871 . . .* (Harrisburg, 1871), 342–346. See also *College Herald,* I (March, 1871), 10, where it is affirmed that the first session of this college would begin on the 24th of April, 1871. In 1882, Professor Charles S. James was elected president of this college, and served as such for a short time. *University Mirror,* I (May, 1882), 61.
[70] *College Herald,* X (January, 1880), 100.
[71] Minutes of the Trustees, II, 439, 443.

CHAPTER SIX

[1] Minutes of the Trustees, II, 443, 445–446; Philadelphia *National Baptist,* January 23, 1879, 5, and *ibid.,* March 20, 1879, 4; *Lewisburg Chronicle,* March 13, 1879; Autobiography of David Jayne Hill (Confessions of a Grandfather, chap. viii, 154), a typescript in the Archives of Bucknell University.
[2] *Bucknell Alumni Monthly,* XV (April, 1932), 7–8.
[3] *Lewisburg Chronicle,* March 20, 1879. The text of his remarks, as published in the *College Herald,* IX (March, 1879), 54, differs slightly from the text published in the *Lewisburg Chronicle,* the one here used.
[4] Philadelphia *National Baptist,* March 27, 1879, 4.
[5] *College Herald,* IX (June, 1879), 76.
[6] A copy of this notice is in the Papers of David Jayne Hill (Clippings and Memorabilia, 1876–1892) in the Library of the University of Rochester.
[7] An undated clipping from the Philadelphia *National Baptist,* in David Jayne Hill's Scrap Book, Archives of Bucknell University.
[8] The printed text of Hill's inaugural address, clipped from a newspaper, is in his Scrap Book, Archives of Bucknell University.
[9] See D. J. Hill, "A Letter to the People of Lewisburg," in the *Lewisburg Chronicle,* March 4, 1880.

10 *Ibid.* Hill's views on the New Education were not fundamentally unlike those expressed by President James McCosh, of Princeton, in *The New Departure in Education, Being a Reply to President Eliot's Defence of it in New York, Feb. 24, 1885* (New York, 1885), *passim.* On this subject, in respect to Yale, see George Wilson Pierson, *Yale College: An Educational History, 1871–1921* (New Haven, 1952), I, 66–94; and on the same subject, in respect to Harvard, see Samuel Eliot Morison, *Three Centuries of Harvard, 1636–1936* (Cambridge, 1936), 341–343. As a contribution to the "lighter" side of this matter, the *University Mirror* (IV, February 1885, 70) reprinted this story: "Sixty Harvard Freshmen have abandoned their Latin, eighty their Greek, and one hundred their Mathematics. None of them, however, have dropped base ball or boating, and college culture is therefore safe.—Ex."

11 Minutes of the Trustees, II, 449, 474, 477, 478, 493.

12 *Ibid.*, II, 453, 457.

13 *Ibid.*, II, 468–470.

14 Minutes of the Curators, June 28, 1881.

15 *Ibid.*

16 Minutes of the Trustees, II, 478–481; Hill's Autobiography, chap. xxiv, 494–495.

17 Minutes of the Trustees, II, 481, 484; *Lewisburg Chronicle,* June 30, 1881.

18 Edit., "The Crisis for Lewisburg," Philadelphia *National Baptist,* April 28, 1881, 264.

19 Edit., "The Present Duty," Philadelphia *National Baptist,* June 16, 1881, 376; *ibid.*, July 14, 1881, 441.

20 *Ibid.*, October 27, 1881, 680.

21 David Jayne Hill to the editor, March 7, 1890, in *ibid.*, March 13, 1890, 169.

22 *Ibid.*, July 7, 1881, 421.

23 Minutes of the Trustees, II, 491, 502–504, 506–509. On this campaign, with special reference to Lewisburg, see the *Lewisburg Chronicle,* June 2, October 6 and 13, and November 10, 1881. Also see the *Mifflinburg Telegraph,* April 27, October 19, and November 16, 1881, and the Philadelphia *National Baptist,* October 20 and 27, and November 10, 1881, 657, 676–677, 705, 712.

24 Minutes of the Trustees, II, 510–512, 514–516.

25 *Ibid.*, III, 27.

26 An undated clipping (Clippings and Memorabilia, 1876–1892) in the Papers of David Jayne Hill in the Library of the University of Rochester. On November 26, 1881, an extemporaneous address was made at a meeting of the Theta Alpha Society on this subject: "Should the name of the University at L. be changed to Bucknell University?" Theta Alpha, Minutes, November 26, 1881.

27 Another undated clipping (Clippings and Memorabilia, 1876–1892).

28 An undated clipping (but of the year 1882) from the *Pittsburgh Messenger, ibid.*

29 *Ibid.*

30 The program that Hill proposed was accomplished, or at least was in the way of being accomplished, by the end of his administration. Bucknell University, *Catalogue, 1888–89,* 4 and *passim;* edit., "Changes, Made and Needed," *University Mirror,* VIII (November, 1888), 17–18.

31 J. Orin Oliphant, *The Library of Bucknell University* (Lewisburg, Pa., 1962), 103.

32 Bucknell University, *Catalogue, 1886–87,* 39.

33 Minutes of the Trustees, III, 73, 75. See the editorial entitled "United Chapel" in the *University Mirror,* VI (October, 1886), 4.

34 Minutes of the Trustees, III, 83. The amendment changing the name of the University is dated May 21, 1887. Bucknell University, *Charter and Bylaws* (Lewisburg, 1956), 37.

35 *University Mirror,* VI (October, 1886), 8.

36 William C. Bartol, "The Observatory's Equipment," *ibid.,* VI (May, 1887), 100–101.

37 *Ibid.*, VI (July, 1887), 135.

38 Minutes of the Trustees, III, 96.

39 *Ibid.*, III, 99; *University Mirror,* VII (April, 1888), 88. Mr. Bucknell gave the

$50,000 on the seventy-sixth anniversary of his birth. Philadelphia *National Baptist,* April 7, 1889, 216.

[40] Minutes of the Trustees, III, 133–134. These buildings are described in the Catalogue of the University for 1890–91, 8–9.

[41] *Ibid.,* III, 162, 166. The Trustees had begun to make plans for such a building as early as June, 1886. *Ibid.,* III, 85. This building is now the Music and Art Building.

[42] Bucknell University, *Catalogue, 1887–88,* 15.

[43] *Ibid., 1879–80,* 16.

[44] *Ibid., 1887–88,* 15. On the problem of electives in the University of Wisconsin, see Merle Curti and Vernon Carstensen, *The University of Wisconsin: A History, 1848–1925* (Madison, 1949), I, 396–402. For a general account of the triumph of the elective principle in the United States, see R. Freeman Butts, *The College Charts its Course . . .* (New York and London, 1939), 159–250. See also Frederick Rudolph, *The American College and University: A History* (New York, 1962), 287–306.

[45] At their meeting on December 30, 1879, the Trustees approved President Hill's request that the Catalogue of the University for 1879–80 "consist of about 80 pages, including all departments," and that there be printed no fewer than three thousand copies of it. Minutes of the Trustees, II, 461. Theretofore, since 1855, the Female Institute had published a separate catalogue.

[46] University at Lewisburg, *Catalogue, 1879–80,* 21–27; *ibid., 1887–88,* 22–28.

[47] *Ibid., 1887–88,* 16.

[48] Ordinarily, at the beginning of the academic year, the schedule of lectures for the year was agreed upon at a meeting of the faculty. See, for example, Minutes of the Faculty, II, September 19, 1881, 237–238.

[49] Minutes of the Faculty, II, December 8, 1879, 165; Bucknell University, *Catalogue, 1879–80,* 43.

[50] Bucknell University, *Catalogue, 1915–16,* 100–101.

[51] On the organization of American universities after the Civil War, see the excellent materials assembled in Part VII of Richard Hofstadter and Wilson Smith, eds., *American Higher Education: A Documentary History* (Chicago, 1961), II, 593–695.

[52] Bucknell Alumni Association, Minutes, June 22, 1886, 163.

[53] Minutes of the Faculty, II, October 22, 1886, 468. In the Catalogue of the University for 1886–87, 19, appears this statement: "The Faculty have under favorable consideration the recommendation of the Alumni, made at their last annual meeting, in regard to the early establishment of Post Graduate Courses of study." It was repeated in the Catalogue for 1887–88, p. 15, but not in any subsequent Catalogue.

[54] Minutes of the Faculty, II, November 13 and December 18, 1886, 471, 472–474.

[55] Minutes of the Trustees, III, 88. The *Commencement Daily News,* in an editorial in its issue of June 29, 1887, affirmed emphatically that those who completed in the University "a three years' Course in the post-graduate studies would receive the degree of *Doctor of Philosophy*." In November, 1889, the *University Mirror* (IX, 147) asked, probably without expecting an answer, "What has become of the promised graduate courses?" Bucknell was not the only small Baptist collegiate institution that was attacked, late in the nineteenth century, by the "university" virus. During the 1890's, President Daniel B. Purinton tried to make Denison a real university, but his successor, Emory W. Hunt, reversed the tendency, and presently the studies leading to the degree of Doctor of Philosophy were dropped from the Catalogue. G. Wallace Chessman, *Denison: The Story of an Ohio College* (Denison University, *c.* 1957), 247–248.

[56] See, for example, the Catalogue of the University for 1886–87, 47.

[57] University at Lewisburg, *Catalogue, 1879–80,* 69.

[58] Bucknell University, *Catalogue, 1882–83,* 69.

[59] *Ibid., 1884–85,* 68.

[60] *Ibid., 1887–88,* 65.

[61] *College Herald,* I (January, 1871), 4–5. By this time the practice of coeducation was getting a foothold in colleges in northern New England. Bates had been coeducational from its beginning in 1864, and both Colby and the University of Vermont became

coeducational in 1871. Edwin Carey Whittemore, *Colby College, 1820–1925* (Waterville, 1927), 205. As early as February, 1870, a woman had been admitted to the Classical Program in the University of Michigan. Elizabeth M. Farrand, *History of the University of Michigan* (Ann Arbor, 1885), 202.

62 Editorial in the *College Herald,* III (May, 1872), 7; National Baptist Educational Convention, *Proceedings, 1872* (New York, 1872), 29. The writer of the above-cited editorial, commenting on the beginning of coeducation at Cornell, argued that, because the "true sphere of woman" is so far removed from that of man, the education of the two should be "essentially different." Consequently, he affirmed, coeducation is practicable only where the elective system prevails. But his real opposition to coeducation appeared in this sentence: "Disbelieving, as we do, in the introduction of women into public life, it seems unnatural to invest females with a masculinity that robs them of their divinest charms, and unfits them for the duties of the domestic circle." The minutes of the two collegiate literary societies in the University at Lewisburg show that the subject of coeducation was debated on December 9, 1871, and on November 16, 1872, by Alpha Theta, and on January 29, 1870, and on February 24, 1872, by Euepia. On the early history of coeducation at Cornell, see Morris Bishop, *A History of Cornell* (Ithaca, 1962), 143–152.

63 *College Herald,* III (November, 1872), 55; *ibid.,* IV (July, 1873), 20; "College News," *ibid.,* VIII (December, 1877), 123.

64 O. J., "Identical Education and Co-Education of the Sexes," *ibid.,* IV (January, 1874), 50.

65 Report to the Board of Curators, in 1877, of its committee to attend examinations at the Female Institute. Ms. in the Archives of Bucknell University.

66 Minutes of the Faculty, II, December 19, 1879, 166–167.

67 *College Herald,* X (April, 1880), 119; *ibid.,* XI (December, 1880), 155.

68 Philadelphia *National Baptist,* August 18, September 29, October 6, November 3, 1881, *passim.*

69 Minutes of the Trustees, III, 29.

70 *Ibid.,* III, 51.

71 Minutes of the Faculty, II, 320–321. "The joint recitation of the Senior classes of the Seminary and College, in the study of psychology, has proved so much of a success that it has been decided to instruct these classes together for the present in all the branches taught by President Hill." *University Mirror,* III (November, 1883), 23.

72 Minutes of the Trustees, III, 62.

73 Minutes of the Faculty, II, 365–366, 379.

74 Minutes of the Trustees, III, 73.

75 Minutes of the Faculty, II, 365, 388, 409. On the subject of the education of women in the United States, see Rudolph, *op. cit.,* 307–308.

76 *Bucknell Mirror,* XIV (February 10, 1895), 79.

77 Edit., "Co-Education," *Orange and Blue,* October 20, 1902.

78 University at Lewisburg, *Catalogue, 1879–80,* 38.

79 *Ibid.;* Minutes of the Trustees, II, 459.

80 University at Lewisburg, *Catalogue, 1879–80,* 38; *Lewisburg Chronicle,* July 24, 1879.

81 Bucknell University, *Catalogue, 1887–88,* 29; J. Orin Oliphant, *The Library of Bucknell University* (Lewisburg, Pa., 1962), 70–71.

82 *University Mirror,* V (April, 1886), 90; *Lewisburg Chronicle,* December 16, 1886.

83 Minutes of the Trustees, III, 90; Bucknell University, *Catalogue, 1887–88,* 29; Treasurer of Bucknell University, *Report . . . for the Year Ending June 30, 1961,* 28.

84 Oliphant, *op. cit.,* 73–75.

85 *Ibid.,* 76–79.

86 Minutes of the Trustees, III, 73.

87 Oliphant, *op. cit.,* 79–81.

88 *Ibid.,* 81–83.

89 Morris Bishop, *op. cit.,* 240–241; *University Mirror,* VII (July, 1888), 129.

[90] University at Lewisburg, *Catalogue, 1879–80,* 46; *ibid., 1887–88,* 38.
[91] *Memorials of Bucknell University, 1846–1896* (Lewisburg, Pa., 1896), 28, 30.
[92] *Ibid.,* 26.
[93] *University Mirror,* VII (June, 1888), 117.
[94] David Jayne Hill, Autobiography (Confessions of a Grandfather), 547.
[95] William Bucknell to David Jayne Hill, June 20, 1888, in the Papers of David Jayne Hill, Library of the University of Rochester.
[96] Minutes of the Trustees, III, 119.
[97] David Jayne Hill to Martin B. Anderson, June 20 and July 9, 1888, in the Martin B. Anderson Papers, Library of the University of Rochester; David Jayne Hill to Edward Bright, July 9, 1888, in the David Jayne Hill Papers, Library of the University of Rochester.
[98] Minutes of the Trustees, III, 120–123.

CHAPTER SEVEN

[1] The secretaries to the faculty before 1882 can be identified by consulting the Minutes of the Board of Curators, one of the governing bodies of the University from its beginning to its reorganization in 1882. To this Board the faculty, by its secretary, recommended for degrees the approved members of each graduating class. The Minutes of the Curators are in the Archives of Bucknell University. At least a part of the Minutes of the Faculty before 1874–75 were in the possession of Professor James, who was officially requested in September, 1879, to return them to the keeping of the faculty. Minutes of the Faculty, September 29, 1879, 154–155.
[2] Minutes of the Faculty, II, 1–3, 273–274.
[3] Bucknell University, *Catalogue, 1887–88,* 16.
[4] For a full description of Commencement Week in 1874, see O. W. Spratt, ed., *The University at Lewisburg: Report of the Twenty-Fourth Annual Commencement, Lewisburg, Pa., June 19–24, 1874* (Philadelphia, 1874); for a fairly full covering of Commencement Week in 1889, see the several issues of *Commencement News* for that week. For the beginning of the practice of having a Corporation dinner, a dinner which, in the 1850's was given by the Alumni Association, see the report of President Loomis to the Trustees on July 26, 1859, in the Minutes of the Trustees under that date, and a report on Commencement Week in 1858 in the *Lewisburg Chronicle,* July 30, 1858.
[5] *Commencement News,* 2d ed., June 26, 1889. The acting president on this occasion was Professor George G. Groff.
[6] Spratt, ed., *op. cit.,* 25.
[7] University Female Institute, Minutes of Teachers' Meetings, 1885–1903.
[8] *Ibid.,* November 13, 1857; July 3, 1858; December 8, 1862; February 2, 1863; June 19, 1873; September 16, 1889.
[9] *Ibid.,* September 16, 1886, and September 17, 1887; *University Mirror,* VI (October, 1886), 11.
[10] U. F. I., Minutes of Teachers' Meetings, December 23, 1886.
[11] *Ibid.,* September 17, 1888, and September 16, 1889.
[12] *Ibid.,* September 17, 1888.
[13] University at Lewisburg, *Catalogue, 1854–55,* 22; *Lewisburg Chronicle,* March 27, 1857; Bucknell University, *Catalogue, 1885–86,* 79, and *ibid., 1888–89,* 79.
[14] Euepia and Theta Alpha in the College; Philomathean and Calomathean during the 1870's and Hyperion during the 1880's in the Female Institute; Euodia in the Preparatory Department; Hermenian in the Academy, and, from 1888 on, also Adelphia.
[15] By the decade of the 1870's, literary societies nearly everywhere in the country were in a state of decline. Frederick Rudolph, *The American College and University: A History* (New York, 1962), 145–146. One evidence of their decline on the campus of the University at Lewisburg, somewhat later, was their waning interest in their libraries.

In the spring of 1887, the *University Mirror* was recommending that all the collegiate societies deposit their small libraries in the collegiate library. *University Mirror,* VI (April, 1887), 90.

16 As late as the spring of 1874, the practice of holding inter-society debates had not been started in the University. Subsequently, the practice was introduced, and it was being maintained as late as 1889. *College Herald,* V (May, 1874), 4; *Commencement News,* June 26, 1889.

17 Merle Curti and Vernon Carstensen, *The University of Wisconsin: A History, 1848–1925* (Madison, 1949), I, 433–434; *College Herald,* II (May, 1871), 7; *ibid.,* V (May, 1874), 4.

17a *College Herald,* II (May, 1871), 7.

18 Minutes of the Faculty, II, 242, 244.

19 *University Mirror,* I (February, 1882), 6–7. One month later the *Mirror* could announce that the "war" between the literary societies had ended, and that Euepia and Theta Alpha were "again working in the utmost harmony and brotherly love." *Ibid.,* I (March, 1882), 23.

20 U. F. I., *Catalogue, 1854–55,* 15; *College Herald,* I (July, 1870), 3.

21 In his "Sketch of the History of Our University," *College Herald,* I (May, 1870), 2.

22 William C. Bartol, "Looking Backward," *Bucknellian,* April 26, 1928, 7; *College Herald,* I (January, 1871), 9.

23 William C. Bartol, "Baseball in the Sixties," *L'Agenda,* 1911, 196–198; *College Herald,* I (May, 1870), 5.

24 *College Herald,* I (January, 1871), 8; *ibid.,* IV (June, 1873), 15; *Lewisburg Chronicle,* October 11, 1872; *College Herald,* III (November, 1872), 57.

25 *College Herald,* III (January, 1873), 80.

26 *Ibid.,* IV (June, 1873), 15.

27 *Ibid.,* V (June, 1874), 14; *ibid.,* VII (October, 1877), 111.

28 *University Mirror,* I (February, 1882), 7.

29 *Ibid.,* V (April, 1886), 93; *ibid.,* V (May, 1886), 108; *ibid.,* V (June, 1886), 123.

30 *Ibid.,* VI (May, 1887), 107.

31 *Ibid.,* VII (April, 1888), 93.

32 *Ibid.,* VII (June, 1888), 121.

33 *Ibid.,* VIII (May, 1889), 95–96; *Commencement News,* June 26, 1889.

34 *University Mirror,* I (February, 1882), 7.

35 *Mifflinburg Telegraph,* November 28, 1883.

36 *University Mirror,* III (December, 1883), 38–40.

37 *Ibid.,* V (June, 1886), 119.

38 "Foot ball in Bucknell is gaining ground. The team this year is much superior to that of last, owing to a wider experience, greater enthusiasm and more careful practice." *Ibid.,* VIII (October, 1888), 8.

39 Minutes of the Faculty, II, 522, 524.

40 *University Mirror,* VIII (November, 1888), 22; Theta Alpha, Minutes, November 2, 1888.

41 *University Mirror,* VIII (February, 1889), 56–57.

42 *College Herald,* III (April, 1873), 115; *ibid.,* IV (July, 1873), 22.

43 *Ibid.,* IV (June, 1873), 15–16.

44 *Ibid.,* IV (May, 1874), 6.

45 *Ibid.,* VII (October, 1876), 28.

46 *University Mirror,* I (May, 1882), 57; *ibid.,* II (April, 1883), 106.

47 *Ibid.,* III (April, 1884), 105; *ibid.,* VIII (April, 1889), 92.

48 *Ibid.,* VIII (June, 1889), 112. See also William C. Bartol's "History of University Athletics," in William C. Gretzinger and Charles A. Walker, eds., *An Historical Sketch of Bucknell University, Lewisburg, Pa.* (Lewisburg, 1890), 28–30.

49 *College Herald,* II (October, 1871), 9. A year earlier we are told that croquet "has become quite popular with some of the 'boys' during the present term. Whether in-

dulged in for the sake of exercise, or because the participants have 'girlish tendencies' is not quite clear to us." *Ibid.*, I (October, 1870), 4.

50 *Ibid.*, II (July, 1871), 9.

51 *Ibid.*, IV (May, 1873), 7.

52 *University Mirror*, III (February, 1884), 73, 76; *ibid.*, VIII (February and March, 1889), 66, 78.

53 *Ibid.*, IV (May, 1885), 114.

54 *Ibid.*, VI (November, 1886), 23; *ibid.*, VI (July, 1887), 138; *ibid.*, VII (May, 1888), 107, 108; *ibid.*, IX (November, 1889), 147; *L'Agenda*, 1888, 61. "The number of bicycles is rapidly increasing in the University and the organization of a club is now being agitated." *University Mirror*, VI (May, 1888), 106. In 1887 a riding club was formed in the Female Institute, the members of which "greatly enjoyed their exhilarating trips to the neighboring towns." *Ibid.*, VII (December, 1887), 37.

55 *College Herald*, I (October, 1870), 5.

56 *Ibid.*, V (December, 1874), 46; *University Mirror*, II (December, 1882), 41; *Mifflinburg Telegraph*, March 25, 1885; *University Mirror*, V (December, 1885), 39; *ibid.*, V (July, 1886), 135; *Lewisburg Chronicle*, March 8, 1888; *University Mirror*, VII (June, 1888), 120; *ibid.*, VIII (April, 1889), 92; edit., "The University Glee Club," *ibid.*, IX (October, 1889), 130.

57 Minutes of the Trustees, III, 96, 141; *Orange and Blue*, September 28, 1908.

58 *University Mirror*, V (March, 1886), 77.

59 *College Herald*, I (March, 1871), 9; *ibid.*, V (April, 1875), 79. As late as 1869, the Trustees were collecting from each student $3 a year as pew rent, but from 1874 onward for several years the University paid annually to the Baptist Church in Lewisburg $500 for pews for students. Minutes of the Trustees, II, 260, 341, 412. For an account of a revival in the University in 1869, see the Minutes of the Euepia Society for March 6 of that year. Somewhat more than a year later, in a Philadelphia periodical, we find this story: "On Sunday afternoon, April 3d, Rev. R. Lowry baptized three candidates. Two of these were young ladies from the Seminary. The late heavy rains had swollen the river, and the back water made a fine and convenient baptistry in the Seminary grove. The attendance was large and the occasion solemn." Philadelphia *National Baptist*, April 14, 1870, 4.

60 U. F. I., Minutes of the Teachers' Meetings, December 24, 1885, and June 30, 1887; *University Mirror*, V (May, 1886), 109; *ibid.*, VIII (October, 1889), 139.

61 *University Mirror*, VI (October, 1886), 2–3; *ibid.*, VI (June, 1887), 113–114; T. J. Shanks, ed., *A College of Colleges: Led by D. L. Moody . . .* (Chicago and New York, 1887), *passim; L'Agenda*, 1893, 57; F. J. Rawlinson, "Bucknell Volunteer Band," *Bucknell Mirror*, XVIII (April, 1899), 162–164.

62 Minutes of the Trustees, II, 236.

63 *Lewisburg Chronicle*, December 25, 1879.

64 *College Herald*, IV (November, 1873), 38.

65 *Ibid.*, X (January, 1880), 101.

66 *University Mirror*, II (January, 1883), 58.

67 *Ibid.*, VII (January, 1888), 53. For interesting recollections of life in the University during the late 1870's, see William G. Owens, '80, "Those Were the Good Old Days," *Bucknell Alumni Monthly*, XXVI (May, 1942), 5, 10.

68 *University Mirror*, I (June, 1882), 80; *ibid.*, II (October, 1882), 10; quotation from *Grit* in the *Mifflinburg Telegraph*, April 25, 1883.

69 *University Mirror*, II (February, 1883), 13; *ibid.*, V (October, 1885), 9; *ibid.*, V (March, 1886), 79; an observer, "The College Fraternity," *ibid.*, VIII (May, 1889), 98–99, condemning fraternities, and Thomas Quintin, "The College Fraternity," *ibid.*, VIII (June, 1889), 109–110, replying to "an observer."

70 *College Herald*, I (June, 1870), 5. As early as 1851, picnics were being held at Blue Hill. J. Merrill Linn, Diary, July 2, 1851.

71 *College Herald*, II (May, 1871), 9; *ibid.*, III (June, 1872), 20.

72 *Ibid.*, V (May, 1874), 13; *ibid.*, V (July, 1874), 22; *ibid.*, VIII (July, 1877), 101.

[73] *University Mirror,* I (June, 1882), 73.

[74] *College Herald,* VII (October, 1876), 30; *Lewisburg Chronicle,* July 10, 1879; *University Mirror,* V (April, 1886), 90; *ibid.,* VI (April, 1887), 95; *Bucknell Mirror,* XVI (May 10, 1897), 149; *Orange and Blue,* February 21, 1910.

[75] *Lewisburg Chronicle,* October 1, 1885; *University Mirror,* V (October, 1885), 11; *ibid.,* VI (October, 1886), 9.

[76] Minutes of the Faculty, II, 112, 238, 291; *College Herald,* IV (June, 1873), 14.

[77] *College Herald,* II (July, 1871), 6.

[78] *Ibid.,* III (July, 1872), 31; *ibid.,* III (December, 1872), 69; *ibid.,* VIII (March, 1878), 140.

[79] Minutes of the Trustees, II, 456–457; *College Herald,* X (January, 1880), 103; *University Mirror,* I (June, 1882), 71.

[80] *University Mirror,* I (March, 1882), 29–30; Cornelius H. Patton and Walter T. Field, *Eight O'Clock Chapel: A Study of New England College Life in the Eighties* (Boston and New York, 1927), 244.

[81] *University Mirror,* II (November, 1882), 27; *ibid.,* II (December, 1882), 39; *ibid.,* V (October, 1885), 9; *ibid.,* VI (October, 1886), 3–4; *ibid.,* IX (November, 1889), 141–142.

[82] *College Herald,* II (July, 1871), 8; *ibid.,* IX (April, 1879), 63; *University Mirror,* III (April, 1884), 105; *ibid.,* V (January, 1886), 51; *ibid.,* V (March, 1886), 79.

[83] Minutes of the Trustees, August 15, 1854; *Lewisburg Chronicle,* June 30, 1871.

[84] *College Herald,* X (February, 1880), 108; *University Mirror,* X (May, 1891), 379; *ibid.,* X (June, 1891), 384; *ibid.,* X (July, 1891), 403; Minutes of the Trustees, III, 247; Minutes of the Faculty, III, 84.

[85] Elizabeth M. Farrand, *History of the University of Michigan* (Ann Arbor, 1885), 142; Cornelius H. Patton and Walter T. Field, *op. cit.,* 252.

[86] *University Mirror,* I (April, 1882), 40; *ibid.,* III (April, 1884), 106–107; *ibid.,* V (May, 1886), 109.

[87] *Ibid.,* V (June, 1886), 122; *ibid.,* V (July, 1886), 132.

[88] *College Herald,* III (June, 1872), 20; *ibid.,* IV (March, 1874), 69; *ibid.,* VIII (April, 1878), 150.

[89] *University Mirror,* V (December, 1885), 39.

[90] *Ibid.,* V (January, 1886), 51.

[91] *Ibid.,* V (July, 1886), 135.

[92] *Ibid.,* VII (November, 1887), iii of advertising; *ibid.,* VIII (October, 1888), 11; *ibid.,* VIII (April, 1889), 92; Bucknell University, *Catalogue, 1909–1910,* 2; Minutes of the Faculty, III, 272.

[93] Minutes of the Faculty, II, 498; Minutes of the Trustees, III, 112; *University Mirror,* VII (April, 1888), 89.

[94] *University Mirror,* VII (December, 1887), 37.

[95] U. F. I., *Catalogue, 1869–70,* 20; Minutes of Teachers' Meetings, December 19, 1883.

[96] *University Mirror,* VI (November, 1886), 23.

[97] *Commencement News,* 2d ed., June 25 and June 26, 1889.

CHAPTER EIGHT

[1] Bucknell University, Minutes of the Trustees, III, 124–125, 127, 128–129, 130–131. Dr. Harris was elected a trustee in January, 1887. *Ibid.,* 88–89. His letter of formal acceptance of the presidency of Bucknell is dated June 18, 1889. *Ibid.,* 132.

[2] *Bucknell Mirror,* XVI (April 25, 1897), 138; Boston *Watchman,* July 11, 1889. See especially Milton G. Evans, "John Howard Harris at Keystone Academy," in *John Howard Harris: An Appreciation, Bucknell University, 1889–1924* (Bucknell University, *Bulletin,* June, 1924), pages not numbered.

[3] This address was published in the *University Mirror,* VIII (July, 1889), 120–123. Also, bearing the incorrect date of June 27, it was published as a pamphlet in 1889.

[4] See his account of his interview with William Bucknell in 1888. John Howard Harris, *Thirty Years as President of Bucknell* (Privately Printed, 1926), 7–8.

[5] *University Mirror,* VIII (October, 1889), 136.

[6] Minutes of the Trustees, III, June 19, 1894, 199.

[7] Minutes of the Trustees, III, 140, 148–150; *Commencement News,* June 24, 1890; Bucknell University, *Catalogue, 1890–91,* 21.

[8] *Commencement News,* June 23, 1890; Minutes of the Trustees, III, 157, 173; Philadelphia *National Baptist,* June 30, 1892, 401.

[9] Minutes of the Trustees, III, 157, 178.

[10] Bucknell University, *Catalogue, 1890–91,* 3.

[11] Keystone Academy, *Twenty-Second Annual Catalogue, 1890–91,* 4. In the catalogue of this academy for 1893–94, 2, 4, President Harris is listed as a trustee for life and Professor George G. Groff as a lecturer on hygiene.

[12] Article III, Section 6, of the charter, as it was amended in 1882, requires the Trustees to publish annually an abstract of their minutes. *Bucknell University Charter and By-Laws* (Lewisburg, Pa., 1956), 11.

[13] Minutes of the Trustees, III, January 14, 1892, 172; *Lewisburg Chronicle,* February 7, 1889; *University Mirror,* X (November, 1890), 297.

[14] *Mifflinburg Telegraph,* September 16, 1892. In 1891 Gretzinger organized the University Press Bureau, and soon thereafter some of the students of the University were reporting for weekly or daily newspapers. *University Mirror,* XI (November, 1891), 20; *ibid.,* XII (March, 1893), 78.

[15] Registrar's Letter Books, in the Archives of Bucknell University. Minutes of the Trustees, III, 267–268. The annual reports of the Committee of the Trustees on Publication are summarized in the Minutes of the Trustees.

[16] Minutes of the Trustees, III, June 23, 1903, 279–280.

[17] *Quinquennial Catalogue of Bucknell University,* 1900, 16–18; Bucknell University, *Catalogue, 1902–03,* 38, 113, 140. As the students increased in number, the diversity of their interests became greater. Speaking before the Bucknell Alumni Club in Pittsburgh on March 30, 1896, President Harris said that, whereas formerly three-fifths of the students were candidates for the ministry, now only one-fourth of them were looking toward that profession. Nevertheless, he said, the number studying for the ministry had increased. *Bucknell Mirror,* XV (April 10, 1896), 136. The Letter Books of the registrar show, especially between the years 1902 and 1904, that the University employed agents who solicited students. See especially the registrar's letter to M. L. Drum on June 23, 1902, and his letter to President Harris on May 2, 1904.

[18] Minutes of the Trustees, III, 344.

[19] *Ibid.,* III, 413.

[20] Bucknell University, *Catalogue, 1917–18,* 158. "The last Academy classes were held in the school year 1915–16." Professor John W. Rice, A Tale of Two Buildings, 3. A typescript, dated October, 1957, which is preserved in the Archives of Bucknell University.

[21] Minutes of the Trustees, III, 157–158.

[22] Philadelphia *National Baptist,* July 30, 1891.

[23] *University Mirror,* X (June, 1891), 386; *Commencement News,* June 22, 1891.

[24] Minutes of the Trustees, III, 165, 167.

[25] *Ibid.,* III, 169.

[26] American Baptist Education Society, *Fourth Annual Meeting, May 28, 1892* (New York, n. d.), 14.

[27] *University Mirror,* XI (October, 1891), 2, 6, 7; *ibid.,* XI (December, 1891), 31; Philadelphia *National Baptist,* November 19, 1891, 741; *ibid.,* December 24, 1891.

[28] Minutes of the Trustees, III, 177; Philadelphia *National Baptist,* July 7, 1892, 417.

[29] Minutes of the Trustees, III, 181; *University Mirror,* XII (October, 1892), 11; *ibid.* (January, 1893), 49.

[30] Minutes of the Trustees, III, June 23, 1896, 219. As early as December, 1891, some of the students were pleading for a "scientific building" and for a building for the Y.M.C.A. *University Mirror,* XI (December, 1891), 25–26.

[31] Minutes of the Trustees, III, 224. Notwithstanding the priority, the new dormitory for men was erected before the heating plant was constructed. See note 66, *infra.*

[32] *Ibid.,* III, 229–230, 236.

[33] *Orange and Blue,* April 3, 1899.

[34] *Commencement News,* June 20–21, 1899; *ibid.,* June 20, 1900. Bucknell University, *Catalogue, 1900–01,* 7. The clock which later was put on the top of West College was the gift of the Class of 1907. *Commencement News,* June 19, 1907.

[35] Minutes of the Trustees, III, 244–245, 254, 256.

[36] *Ibid.,* 263.

[37] *Ibid.,* 265, 267, 273.

[38] William C. Gretzinger to George H. Hyde, July 5, 1902. Registrar's Letter Books.

[39] Minutes of the Trustees, III, 273.

[40] An address of President Harris before the Philadelphia Club of Bucknell on February 1, 1903, that was reported in the *Orange and Blue,* February 9, 1903. He announced the need of an additional $250,000 for buildings and of an additional $1,000,000 for endowment, and he assured his listeners that Bucknell now had become large enough to appeal to men of wealth.

[41] Minutes of the Trustees, III, 273.

[42] *Orange and Blue,* January 26, 1903. "The Board of Trustees at its meeting in January, 1903, authorized an effort to increase the endowment by one million dollars. It is expected to obtain this sum by gifts and legacies." Bucknell University, *Catalogue, 1904–05,* 4.

[43] John Howard Harris, *op. cit.,* 64–66. On the details of this plan, see also a story entitled "A Policy of Expansion," in the *Orange and Blue,* January 26, 1903.

[44] *Ibid.*

[45] J. Orin Oliphant, *The Library of Bucknell University* (Lewisburg, Pa., 1962), 99–100; Minutes of the Trustees, III, 282.

[46] Minutes of the Trustees, III, 285–286.

[47] *Ibid.,* III, 291–292.

[48] *Commencement News,* June 22, 1904, and June 21, 1905; Oliphant, *op. cit.,* 101; Minutes of the Trustees, III, January 12, 1905, 296.

[49] Bucknell University, *Catalogue, 1906–07,* 10.

[50] Minutes of the Trustees, III, 285–287, 292, 297, 301–302; *Orange and Blue,* January 16, January 23, March 6, September 25, 1905. "The building is a three-story brick building with brownstone trimmings, one hundred and twenty feet long, forty feet wide and will contain eighty-seven rooms." *Commencement News,* June 19, 1905.

[51] Report of President Harris, in the Minutes of the Trustees, III, June 20, 1905, 302.

[52] *Ibid.,* III, 302.

[53] *Ibid.,* III, 307, 311, 313; *Orange and Blue,* June 4, 1906; *Commencement News,* June 19 and 20, 1906.

[54] Minutes of the Trustees, III, 316, 325–326; *Orange and Blue,* September 28, 1908; Minutes of the Trustees, III, 338–339, 340.

[55] *Commencement News* (morning ed.), June 23, 1909; *Orange and Blue,* September 27, 1909; Minutes of the Trustees, III, 363.

[56] Minutes of the Trustees, III, 344.

[57] *Ibid.,* III, 365, 373–374.

[58] *The General Education Board: An Account of its Activities* (New York, 1915), 1–8.

[59] *Ibid.,* 6; Minutes of the Trustees, III, 376–378.

[60] Minutes of the Trustees, III, 393. A few days after the completion of the Fund of 1911, President Harris suggested, and the Trustees approved, a statement for inclusion in the Catalogue of the University, saying that those who give $10,000 to the University shall be designated Founders, and those who give $1,000 or more, but less than $10,000, shall be designated Patrons; and that their names shall be printed in each issue of the Catalogue. This statement appeared for the first time in the Catalogue for 1911–12, p. 3. In the issue for 1963–64, the names of the Founders and Patrons fill more than eight pages.

[61] Minutes of the Trustees, III, 386–387, 393–394, 399–400. On the effort to raise a part of the money in Lewisburg, see the *Orange and Blue,* October 14 and 21, 1912. Bucknell's grant from the General Education Board was one of eight received by as many colleges in Pennsylvania. The largest of these grants, $250,000, was made to Bryn Mawr College. *General Education Board,* 159.

[62] Minutes of the Trustees, III, 401.

[63] *Ibid.*, III, 401–402.

[64] *Commencement News,* June 16, 1914; *ibid.* (morning ed.), June 17, 1914.

[65] This guide was published, in the form of an advertisement, in each issue of the *Commencement News* for 1914.

[66] Bucknell University, *Catalogue, 1900–01,* 10; *Commencement News,* June 17, 1901; Bucknell University, *Catalogue, 1903–1904,* 10; *ibid., 1909–1910,* 10, 11–12. In November, 1901, this building was under roof. *Orange and Blue,* November 19, 1901.

[67] *College Herald,* I (May, 1870), 6; *University Mirror,* V (June, 1886), 122; *ibid.*, VI (October, 1886), 8; *ibid.*, VII (October, 1887), 1; Philadelphia *National Baptist,* December 16, 1886, 788; *Lewisburg Chronicle,* August 8, 1889; John Howard Harris, *op. cit.*, 16; *University Mirror,* IX (November, 1889), 142; *Commencement News,* June 25, 1890.

[68] Minutes of the Trustees, III, June 18, 1912, 382; *ibid.*, III, January 14, 1915, 411.

[69] *Ibid.*, III, 425; *Orange and Blue,* September 27, 1915; Bucknell University, *Catalogue, 1915–16,* 14. The Catalogue for 1919–20, 22, says that two additional residences adjoining the campus have been acquired for the use of women.

[70] Minutes of the Trustees, III, 461.

[71] Philadelphia *National Baptist,* October 12, 1893, 654. See the sketch of General Charles Miller in *L'Agenda,* 1902, 4–5.

[72] Bucknell University, *Catalogue, 1903–04,* 110; Minutes of the Faculty, III, March 20, 1894, 624; Bucknell University, *Catalogue, 1896–97,* 67; *ibid., 1900–01,* 79.

[73] William C. Gretzinger to George T. Street, June 21, 1902, in Registrar's Letter Books; Bucknell University, *Catalogue, 1903–04,* 111; *ibid., 1918–19,* 101.

[74] Minutes of the Trustees, III, 187.

[75] *Ibid.*, III, 282.

[76] Bucknell University, *Catalogue, 1917–18,* 101; Minutes of the Trustees, III, January 10, 1918, 446.

[77] Minutes of the Trustees, III, 316, 377.

[78] *Ibid.*, III, 387.

[79] Oliphant, *op. cit.*, 88–109. In 1893 Mr. Martin was made an instructor in logic and anthropology in the College and was relieved of his work in Latin in the Academy. A year later he was made professor of logic and librarian, and he was requested "to conduct Chapel services in the absence of the President of the University." Minutes of the Trustees, III, 192, 198.

[80] Dr. Harris said that he had "had hopes," after 1914, of undertaking a campaign to raise "one million additional for endowment and two hundred and fifty thousand for the plant." But he learned that the Board of Trustees thought that the time for such an undertaking was not propitious. John Howard Harris, *op. cit.*, 93.

[81] Minutes of the Trustees, III, 432–433.

[82] *Bucknell Alumni Monthly,* III (May 28, 1917), 1; *ibid.*, III (October, 1917), 1.

[83] Minutes of the Trustees, III, 442.

[84] *Ibid.*, III, 446–447, 452, 458.

[85] *Ibid.*, 453.

[86] *Ibid.*, 228, 447, 543.

[87] *Ibid.*, 225–226, 228, 289, 299, 415–416, 417.

[88] This printed report, addressed to the Board of Trustees, is dated June 3, 1918. A copy of it is in the Archives of Bucknell University. As to his reference to the raising of a million and a quarter dollars, see Note 80, *supra.* At the time of his withdrawal from the University in 1924, there was brought out a pamphlet entitled *John Howard Harris: An Appreciation, Bucknell University, 1889–1924* (Bucknell University, *Bul-*

letin, June, 1924). This pamphlet contains more or less perceptive essays by Professors Lewis E. Theiss, Frank E. Rockwood, and Ephraim M. Heim, together with one by Dr. Milton G. Evans, president of the Crozer Theological Seminary.

CHAPTER NINE

1 Bucknell University, *Catalogue, 1899–1900,* 3, 31.

2 *University Mirror,* XI (October, 1891), 1, 5.

3 James H. Rohback, "A Plea for Bucknell," *Commencement News* (afternoon ed.), June 22, 1892.

4 Edit., "A Year's Progress," *Commencement News,* June 18, 1894. "For three years past, Bucknell has prepared students for the second year's work in Medical Schools of the standing of the Universities of Pennsylvania and Michigan. These students have done well, maintaining good positions in their classes." *Bucknell Mirror,* XV (November 25, 1895), 37.

5 Edit., "The Year 1894–95," *Bucknell Mirror,* XIV (June 25, 1895), 153.

6 *Ibid.,* XVIII (December 10, 1898), 58.

7 *Commencement News* (morning ed.), June 20, 1900. For other comments on the progress that Bucknell was making during the 1890's, see the *University Mirror,* XI (February, 1892), 56; *L'Agenda,* 1893, 21–22; Philadelphia *National Baptist,* July 20, 1893, 460; and Kate Goddard, "Growth of College Spirit," *Bucknell Mirror,* XV (January 10, 1896), 63.

8 Bucknell University, *Catalogue, 1889–90,* 19.

9 *Ibid., 1893–94,* 23; *ibid., 1895–96,* 28; *ibid., 1899–1900,* 31–32.

10 *Ibid., 1900–01,* 37.

11 *Ibid., 1899–1900,* 87; *ibid., 1900–01,* 96.

12 *Ibid., 1900–01,* 120–121.

13 Bucknell University, Minutes of the Trustees, June 18, 1901, 261.

14 Bucknell University, Minutes of the Faculty, III, 116. On January 12, 1899, Judge Harold M. McClure had been approved as a stated lecturer on English common law, and in the spring of that year he began lecturing on Blackstone. Minutes of the Faculty, III, March 6, 1899, 67; Minutes of the Trustees, III, 236.

15 Bucknell University, *Catalogue, 1901–02,* 51–52. In April, 1902, the registrar explained that regular students in the College could not elect courses in law before the junior year. "In the third term of the Sophomore year," he said, "there is given a course in Elementary law, preparatory to the larger course." Subsequently, he recommended the program in Jurisprudence as the appropriate one for pre-legal students to pursue. William C. Gretzinger to E. Hulley, April 29, 1902, and to C. H. Tate, December 14, 1904. Registrar's Letter Books, Archives of Bucknell University.

16 Minutes of the Faculty, III, November 24, 1917, 385.

17 Bucknell University, *Catalogue, 1901–02,* 69–71.

18 William C. Gretzinger to Dr. M. L. Emerick, September 3, 1903. Registrar's Letter Books.

19 William C. Gretzinger to N. E. Henry, November 28, 1905. *Ibid.* In February, 1902, the collegiate newspaper had said that the work in the Department of Medicine had been so enlarged as to make it the equivalent of the first two years of work in a medical college, but in June of that year President Harris had reported to the Trustees that he was having difficulty in the matter of affiliating the College with medical schools; but he hoped for eventual success. *Orange and Blue,* February 18, 1902; Minutes of the Trustees, III, 272.

20 As late as the autumn of 1907, however, a dissecting room was being constructed on the third floor of the Chemical Laboratory. "This addition to the crowded laboratory," a writer in the collegiate newspaper remarked, "is extremely necessary and will do away with a great many of the objectionable features that prevailed when the 'fellows with the knife' occupied a room of the general laboratory." *Orange and*

Blue, October 28, 1907. Dr. John W. Rice, now professor of biology, emeritus, says that, after the appearance of Dr. Abraham Flexner's survey of medical education in the United States, the Medical Preparatory Department at Bucknell was abandoned. John W. Rice, *A History of the Teaching of Biology at Bucknell University* (preface dated December, 1952), 3. See Abraham Flexner's *Medical Education in the United States and Canada* (New York, *c.* 1910).

21 Bucknell University, *Catalogue, 1902–03,* 60–61; *University Mirror,* VIII (April, 1889), 83; *Lewisburg Chronicle,* May 16, 1889.

22 Bucknell University, *Catalogue, 1897–98,* 42, 64.

23 *Ibid., 1900–01,* 49.

24 *Ibid., 1902–03,* 60–61.

25 Minutes of the Trustees, III, 289, 415.

26 Bucknell University, *Catalogue, 1916–17,* 58–59.

27 Bucknell University, Minutes of the Faculty, III, 56.

28 Bucknell University, *Catalogue, 1900–01,* 65.

29 This "differentiation" in the degree of Bachelor of Science was highly pleasing to the editor of the collegiate newspaper, who remarked that the University of California had seven of them and that Harvard had eleven. "The diploma in each case," he said, "specifies the line in which the student has specialized. Thus in Bucknell the student who completes the course in Engineering will receive the degree of Bachelor of Science *in Civil Engineering.*" *Orange and Blue,* November 24, 1902.

30 William C. Gretzinger to an unnamed person, March 20, 1902, in Registrar's Letter Books; Minutes of the Trustees, III, 269.

31 *Bucknell Mirror,* XXII (January, 1903), 80; Bucknell University, Minutes of the Faculty, III, 158; Bucknell University, *Catalogue, 1907–08,* 128.

32 *Orange and Blue,* September 25, 1905; Bucknell University, *Catalogue, 1908–09,* 130.

33 Bucknell University, Minutes of the Faculty, III, 272; *Orange and Blue,* November 8, 1909.

34 *Orange and Blue,* November 8, 1909.

35 Bucknell University, *Catalogue, 1913–14,* 100; *ibid., 1914–15,* 101.

36 *Ibid., 1912–13,* 169; *Orange and Blue,* February 10, 1913.

37 Minutes of the Trustees, III, 399, 401.

38 Bucknell University, *Catalogue, 1913–14,* 167–168, 171; *Commencement News* (afternood ed.), June 17, 1914; Bucknell University, *Catalogue, 1916–17,* 175–177.

39 Minutes of the Trustees, III, 438; Bucknell University, *Catalogue, 1919–20,* 102.

40 Bucknell University, *Catalogue, 1899–1900,* 57.

41 Dr. Lemuel Moss had been professor of theology in the University at Lewisburg from 1865 to 1868. *Quinquennial Catalogue of Bucknell University, 1900,* 30.

42 Bucknell University, *Catalogue, 1898–99,* 60.

43 John Howard Harris, *Thirty Years as President of Bucknell* (privately printed, 1926), 36.

44 Bucknell University, *Catalogue, 1903–04,* 48–49.

45 *Ibid., 1916–17,* 25–26.

46 Minutes of the Trustees, III, 296.

47 Bucknell University, *Catalogue, 1904–05,* 165. In a letter to Margaret W. Wagner, dated September 21, 1905, William C. Gretzinger wrote that "Graduates of Bucknell Institute who have taught five years and who have done one year's work in literature can secure the degree of Bachelor of Letters." Registrar's Letter Books.

48 Bucknell University, *Catalogue, 1912–13,* 100.

49 Minutes of the Faculty, III, 134.

50 Bucknell University, *Catalogue, 1908–09,* 57; *ibid., 1915–16,* 23.

51 Minutes of the Faculty, III, 385.

52 Bucknell University, *Catalogue, 1917–18,* 64.

53 Bucknell University, President's Reports, 1915–1918, *passim.* Archives of Bucknell University.

54 Bucknell University, *Catalogue, 1917–18,* 65.

55 Minutes of the Faculty, III, June 4, 1891, 58; Minutes of the Trustees, III, 167.

56 Bucknell University, *Catalogue, 1902–03*, 44; *ibid., 1917–18*, 110. On October 24, 1904, the registrar informed an inquirer that Bucknell no longer granted the master's degree "in course." William C. Gretzinger to J. D. McNab. Registrar's Letter Books.

57 *Commencement News* (morning ed.), June 20, 1894; *Bucknell Mirror*, XIV (October 25, 1894), 13; Minutes of the Faculty, III, 104, 134–135.

58 Minutes of the Faculty, III, June 16, 1902, 129.

59 *Ibid.*, June 15, 1903, 152. On October 24, 1904, William C. Gretzinger wrote to C. W. Williams, saying that two years of advanced work completed in the Crozer Theological Seminary would entitle one to receive a master's degree from Bucknell. Registrar's Letter Books.

60 Bucknell University, *Catalogue, 1909–10*, 57; *ibid., 1918–19*, 26–27.

61 *Ibid., 1906–07*, 57. "The following regulation was adopted: The degree of Civil Engineer, C.E., and that of Electrical Engineer, E.E., are conferred upon graduates of Bucknell College who have completed the corresponding courses, and who have been engaged for not less than three consecutive years in successful professional practice and who have performed prescribed courses of study and presented theses upon subjects pertaining to their branch of engineering." Minutes of the Faculty, III, March 4, 1907, 222.

62 Bucknell University, *Catalogue, 1918–19*, 27.

63 This degree was conferred in 1889. Bucknell University, *Catalogue, 1889–90*, 41.

64 Minutes of the Faculty, III, 114, 144; Minutes of the Trustees, III, 257, 276; Bucknell University, *Catalogue, 1901–02*, 89.

65 *Bucknell Mirror*, XVI (April 25, 1897), 139.

66 *University Mirror*, V (April and June, 1886), 93, 122; *ibid.*, VIII (October, 1888), 7; *ibid.*, VIII (April, 1889), 89; *Lewisburg Chronicle*, September 5, 1889; Minutes of the Trustees, III, 74, 126.

67 Minutes of the Trustees, III, 294, 342, 349; *Orange and Blue*, October 23, 1905, and October 10, 1910.

68 See the lists in the *Quinquennial Catalogue of Bucknell University*, 1900, 31–34.

69 Minutes of the Faculty, III, June 19, 1899, 74.

70 *Ibid.*, III, June 15, 1912, 316; Minutes of the Trustees, III, 383–384.

71 The recipient of this degree was Lewis Edwin Theiss, professor of journalism. Bucknell University, *Catalogue, 1924–25*, 138.

72 John Howard Harris, *op. cit.*, 51.

73 Minutes of the Faculty, III, 373–374.

74 For the schedule of lectures on Mondays during the spring term, 1917, see *ibid.*, 374.

75 Bucknell University, *Catalogue, 1889–90*, 81.

76 *Ibid., 1896–97*, 27; *ibid., 1901–02*, 36. In March, 1902, the registrar wrote that of the students then in Bucknell 151 came from high schools, 122 from academies, and the rest from "other colleges, Normal Schools, [and] Private Schools." William C. Gretzinger to W. A. Wetzel, March 19, 1902. Registrar's Letter Books.

77 Bucknell University, *Catalogue, 1902–03*, 42.

78 Claude M. Fuess, *The College Board: Its First Fifty Years* (New York, 1950), chap. 1.

79 Minutes of the Faculty, III, 123.

80 Bucknell University, *Catalogue, 1906–07*, 53.

81 Bucknell University, *Catalogue, 1918–19*, 102; *ibid., 1889–90*, 42.

82 *Ibid., 1899–1900*, 77, 100, 128.

83 *Ibid., 1918–19*, 102–103.

84 *Ibid.*, 166.

85 *Orange and Blue*, October 26, 1906.

86 *Ibid.*, June 9, 1913.

87 *Ibid.*, October 10, 1899.

88 Anon., "The Evolution of the Class Memorial," *L'Agenda*, 1909, 227–229; edit.,

"Class Memorials," *Commencement News* (morning ed.), June 20, 1906; *ibid.*, June 19, 1907.

89 Bucknell University, *Catalogue, 1963–64,* 70.

90 The *Bucknell Mirror* devoted most of its issue for March, 1899, to the literary societies. One of the articles on the value of such societies was contributed by David Jayne Hill. During the preceding years of the 1890's, the *Mirror* had given considerable attention to the literary societies.

91 *Bucknell Mirror,* XVII (October 10 and 15, 1897) 7, 11, 18; Minutes of the Faculty, III, 8, 26.

92 *Bucknell Mirror,* XV (December 10, 1895), 45. See also the *Commencement News,* June 19, 1901, and the *Orange and Blue,* October 8, 1901.

93 Vol. XIII, 158.

94 *Commencement News,* June 15, 1908.

95 *Orange and Blue,* April 1 and April 22, 1912; *Commencement News* (morning ed.), June 19, 1912; Bucknell University, *Catalogue, 1916–17,* 97–98.

96 Minutes of the Faculty, III, 43–44. For an addition touching both scholarship and deportment made on June 1, 1900, see p. 92. On September 12, 1903, the faculty "authorized" for 1903–04 these fraternities: Phi Kappa Psi, Sigma Chi, Phi Gamma Delta, Sigma Alpha Epsilon, Kappa Sigma, Theta Delta Tau, Hand and Eye, Alpha Kappa Alpha, and Phi Delta Sigma. It also "authorized" two sororities, Pi Beta Phi and Phi Alpha Zeta. The faculty, however, stressed the fact that its approval of these organizations was merely a permission, not a recommendation, to join one of them. Minutes of the Faculty, 159–160.

97 The constitution of the organization formed to publish this newpaper was printed in the *Orange and Blue* for March 23, 1897. The influences which had been uniting the students were discussed by Kate Goddard in the "Growth of College Spirit," *Bucknell Mirror,* XV (January 10, 1896), 63. She emphasized as significant influences the prosperity of the University, the rise of athletics, and the coming of elective studies.

98 George G. Groff, "College Athletics," *Bucknell Mirror,* XIII (January, 1894), 56–59.

99 "President Eliot's Report," *Harvard Graduates' Magazine,* III (March, 1895), 369.

100 "President Eliot's Report for 1899–1900," *ibid.,* IX (March, 1901), 452.

101 *Orange and Blue,* January 28, 1907.

102 Bucknell University, *Catalogue, 1890–91,* 43; *ibid., 1905–06,* 13, 117.

103 *Ibid., 1893–94,* 53; *ibid., 1899–1900,* 70; *ibid., 1910–11,* 91.

104 William C. Gretzinger to J. F. McCabe, April 11, 1906. Registrar's Letter Books.

105 *L'Agenda,* 1912, 192–194, 196–198.

106 *Bucknell Mirror,* XVI (February 25, 1897), 91.

107 *Ibid.,* XV (November 28, 1895), 43; *ibid.,* XV (January 10, 1896), 67.

108 Bucknell University, *Catalogue, 1890–91,* 43.

109 Minutes of the Faculty, III, 40. These two regulations were in the Catalogue as late as 1918–19.

110 Minutes of the Faculty, III, September 24, 1908, 250.

111 On January 21, 1903, the faculty voted that the maximum number of games should be as follows: football, 11; basketball 12 (not more than 5 away from home); baseball, 20, of which not more than 10 could be played away from home and not more than two could be played on any one trip. Minutes of the Faculty, III, 144.

112 *Orange and Blue,* January 28, 1907.

113 Minutes of the Faculty, III, 284, 300–301, 306–307; Minutes of the Trustees, III, 364, 367.

114 Minutes of the Faculty, III, 330.

115 Minutes of the Trustees, III, 383.

116 *Bucknell Mirror,* XVIII (December 10, 1898), 63; *Orange and Blue,* December 18, 1900; *Commencement News,* June 19, 1906.

117 *Orange and Blue,* May 24 and June 14, 1898; Minutes of the Trustees, III, 234, 255.

[118] Edit., "The $5.00 Assessment," *Orange and Blue,* September 25, 1905; *ibid.,* June 11, 1906.
[119] Minutes of the Trustees, III, 304, 367, 374.
[120] *Commencement News,* June 18, 1913, and June 15, 1915.
[121] Minutes of the Trustees, III, June 3, 1918, 452.
[122] *Ibid.,* III, 471.
[123] Vol. IV, 2.
[124] *Commencement News* (morning ed.), June 23, 1897; *ibid;* (morning ed.), June 17, 1914.
[125] John Howard Harris, *op. cit.,* 74.
[126] Bucknell University, *Catalogue, 1907–08,* 208. On the Day of Prayer for 1900, see the *Orange and Blue,* January 23, 1900.
[127] *Commencement News,* June 18, 1912.
[128] *Bucknell Mirror,* XIII (October 10, 1893), 1.
[129] *Orange and Blue,* October 26, 1914.
[130] *Ibid.,* March 17, 1913; *Students' Handbook, 1915–16,* 29.
[131] *Commencement News* (morning ed.), June 17, 1914; *Students' Handbook, 1915–16,* 48; *L'Agenda,* 1918, 173.
[132] *Bucknell Mirror:* XI, 7; XII, 62; XIII, 73; XIV, 27; XV, 126; *L'Agenda,* 1896, 55.
[133] *Orange and Blue,* October 29, 1901; *ibid.,* October 12, 1908; Minutes of the Faculty, III, November 8, 1915, 356; *L'Agenda,* 1918, *passim.*
[134] *Commencement News,* June 21, 1909; *Orange and Blue,* February 19, 1912.
[135] Frill and Frown, a dramatic club for women, was founded on October 13, 1900; Cap and Dagger, a dramatic club for men, was founded on January 18, 1906. *L'Agenda,* 1915, 163.
[136] *Commencement News,* June 18, 1902; Minutes of the Faculty, III, 152.

CHAPTER TEN

[1] *Who Was Who in America* (1943), 607–608; *Commencement News* (morning ed.), June 24, 1919; Bucknell University, Minutes of the Trustees, III, 461–462, 468.
[2] Minutes of the Trustees, III, 466.
[3] Bucknell University, Minutes of the Faculty, III, 404, 408, 414; Bucknell University, *Catalogue, 1919–20,* 28–29.
[4] Bucknell University, *Catalogue, 1919–20,* 30–32, 86–88, and *passim;* Minutes of the Faculty, III, 405, 414; *Bucknell Alumni Monthly,* IV (January, 1920), 1.
[5] Emory W. Hunt, "Annual Report of the President for the Year 1922–23," Bucknell University, *Bulletin* (July, 1923), 10.
[6] "Ten Years of Progress," *Bucknell Alumni Monthly,* VI (January, 1922), 4–5; Bucknell University, *Catalogue, 1922–23,* 144; *ibid., 1924–25,* 165.
[7] Emory W. Hunt, "Annual Report of the President for the Year 1922–23," *loc. cit.,* 6.
[8] *Ibid.,* 7.
[9] Minutes of the Trustees, III, 480.
[10] *Bucknell Alumni Monthly,* IV (March, 1920), 1.
[11] Minutes of the Trustees, III, 486–487; John T. Judd, treasurer of Bucknell University, in the *Bucknell Alumni Monthly,* IV (July, 1920), 2; Emory W. Hunt, "The Present Outlook," *ibid.,* 2.
[12] Bucknell University, Treasurer's Book of Endowments, 1902–1928, 248. Archives of Bucknell University.
[13] Minutes of the Trustees, IV, December 23, 1922, 3–4.
[14] *Ibid.,* 4.
[15] Lewis E. Theiss, ed., *Memorials of Bucknell University, 1919–1931* (n. p., n. d.), 95.
[16] Emory W. Hunt, "Annual Report of the President for the Year 1922–23," *loc. cit.,* 8. See also the *Bucknell Alumni Monthly,* VII (June, 1923), 3.

[17] Treasurer's Book of Endowments, 1902–1928, 271–288; *Bucknell Alumni Monthly,* VIII (March, 1924), 18.

[18] *Bucknell Alumni Monthly,* VIII (October, 1923), 5.

[19] J. R. Wood, "The Endowment Campaign," *Bucknell Alumni Monthly,* IX (March, 1925), 9–10; *ibid.,* X (January, 1926), 1; *ibid.,* XI (January, 1927), 5.

[20] Treasurer's Book of Endowments, 1902–1928, 269.

[21] Minutes of the Trustees, III, 478–479.

[22] *Ibid.,* III, 481; Emory W. Hunt, "Report of the President to the Board of Trustees of Bucknell University, 1919–1929," Bucknell University, *Bulletin* (June, 1929), 2.

[23] Minutes of the Trustees, III, 493; *Bucknell Alumni Monthly,* XIV (October, 1929), 2; Minutes of the Trustees, June 11, 1929, 5; *ibid.,* December 21, 1929, 3; *Bucknell Alumni Monthly,* XV (November, 1930), 4.

[24] Minutes of the Trustees, December 19, 1931, 3; Emory W. Hunt, "Report of the President to the Board of Trustees of Bucknell University, 1919–1929," *loc. cit.,* 6.

[25] Minutes of the Trustees, June 15, 1920, 9; *Memorials of Bucknell University, 1919–1931,* 103–104; Treasurer's Book of Endowments, 1902–1928, 242.

[26] Minutes of the Trustees, December 18, 1920, 9; *Bucknell Alumni Monthly,* VI (October, 1921), 3; Treasurer's Book of Endowments, 1902–1928, 242.

[27] Minutes of the Trustees, June 8, 1923, 1; *Memorials of Bucknell University, 1919–1931,* 97; *Bucknell Alumni Monthly,* IX (November, 1924), 8–9. Interestingly enough, it was in June, 1924, when the University was preparing new athletic fields, that the Trustees voted "that the present athletic field, adjacent to the Tustin Gymnasium, be henceforth designated as Loomis Field, in honor of former President Justin R. Loomis." Minutes of the Trustees, June 17, 1924, 3. See also the *Bucknell Alumni Monthly,* VIII (June, 1924), 10. About fifty years earlier, it will be recalled, President Loomis and his son had made a large contribution toward the improvement of this field.

[28] E. B. Riehl, Diary, October 18, 1924. This diary is in the Archives of Bucknell University.

[29] Treasurer's Book of Endowments, 1902–1928, 310–311; *Bucknell Alumni Monthly,* XII (December, 1927), 3, 8; *ibid.,* XII (January, 1928), 7; *ibid.,* XII (June, 1928), 9–10.

[30] Minutes of the Trustees, June 8, 1926, 2; *ibid.,* June 7, 1927, 1, 4; Treasurer's Book of Endowments, 1902–1928, 311–312; *Bucknell Alumni Monthly,* XII (June, 1928), 6–7; *Memorials of Bucknell University, 1919–1931,* 107–108.

[31] Minutes of the Trustees, December 17, 1927, 2; Treasurer's Book of Endowments, 1902–1928, 309.

[32] *Bucknell Alumni Monthly,* XIII (December, 1928), 3.

[33] Minutes of the Trustees, December 18, 1926, 4.

[34] *Ibid.,* June 7, 1927, 2; *Bucknell Alumni Monthly,* XII (February, 1928), 7; Treasurer's Book of Endowments, 1902–1928, 299–305; *Memorials of Bucknell University, 1919–1931,* 108.

[35] Bucknell University, *Catalogue, 1932–33,* 24.

[36] Minutes of the Trustees, June 7, 1927, 4; *ibid.,* December 17, 1927, 2.

[37] The word "semites" had been used in earlier years to designate the women of the Female Institute, a branch of the University which was familiarly known as the "Seminary."

[38] *Bucknell Alumni Monthly,* XII (February, 1928), 2.

[39] *Ibid.,* XIII (January, 1929), 2; Treasurer's Book of Endowments, 1902–1928, 307, 310.

[40] Treasurer's Book of Endowments, 1902–1928, 242.

[41] *Ibid.,* 313.

[42] Minutes of the Trustees, June 11, 1929, 4.

[43] Emory W. Hunt, "Report of the President to the Board of Trustees of Bucknell University, 1919–1929," *loc. cit.,* 6–7.

[44] Minutes of the Trustees, III, 472.

[45] *Bucknell University Charter and By-Laws* (Bucknell University, 1956), 38–39.

[46] John Howard Harris, Special Report to the Board of Trustees of Bucknell University, June 3, 1918. Archives of Bucknell University.

[47] Minutes of the Trustees, December 19, 1925, 4–5.

[48] *Bucknell Alumni Monthly,* IX (April, 1925), 1.

[49] Minutes of the Faculty, III, 465. See also "Ten Years of Progress," *Bucknell Alumni Monthly,* VI (January, 1922), 4–5.

[50] Emory W. Hunt, "The Ideals of Bucknell," *Bucknell Alumni Monthly,* VI (January, 1922), 3.

[51] Minutes of the Trustees, June 17, 1924, 4, and December 13, 1924, 1. See also on this subject the letter of June 3, 1926, from a special committee of the Board of Trustees, in the Minutes of the Trustees of that date.

[52] *Ibid.,* III, 471, 476; *Memorials of Bucknell University, 1919–1931,* 135.

[53] *Bucknell Alumni Monthly,* VI (October, 1921), 2.

[54] *Ibid.,* XV (November, 1930), 10; *ibid.,* XV (June, 1931), 2.

[55] Emory W. Hunt, "Report of the President to the Board of Trustees of Bucknell University, 1919–1929," *loc. cit.,* 7–8; Minutes of the Trustees, December 19, 1925, 2; *Bucknell Alumni Monthly,* X (January, 1926), 1.

[56] Minutes of the Faculty, December 17, 1927, 2; *Memorials of Bucknell University, 1919–1929,* 112.

[57] Emory W. Hunt, "Report of the President to the Trustees of Bucknell University, 1919–1929," *loc. cit.,* 8; *Memorials of Bucknell University, 1919–1931,* 33–34.

[58] Kendrick Babcock to Emory W. Hunt, May 22, 1922; Adam Leroy Jones to Emory W. Hunt, December 14, 1926, and November 14, 1927; Ella Lonn to Emory W. Hunt, March 17, 1927. From President Hunt's file of letters in the Archives of Bucknell University.

[59] Edit., "Good News," *Bucknell Alumni Monthly,* XV (April, 1931), 2.

[60] Minutes of the Faculty, III, 408; Bucknell University, *Catalogue, 1919–20,* 30–36.

[61] Bucknell University, *Catalogue, 1919–20,* 32–35.

[62] Minutes of the Faculty, III, 414, 417.

[63] *Memorials of Bucknell University, 1919–1931,* 46–47. To say that Greek had a "dominant" place in the curricular offerings of Bucknell in 1919 is to pay scant respect to the truth. As a matter of fact, Greek at Bucknell, well before that year, had fallen on evil days.

[64] Bucknell University, *Catalogue, 1930–31,* 38–39.

[65] The faculty adopted the "scheme" of quality credits on December 16, 1925, as its Minutes of that date show. See also Bucknell University, *Catalogue, 1925–26,* 43.

[66] Bucknell University, *Catalogue, 1930–31,* 37–39.

[67] *Ibid.,* 42–59.

[68] *Ibid., 1920–21,* 47–48. Work in absentia for the master's degree was abolished by vote of the faculty on November 6, 1923. Minutes of the Faculty, IV, 56. See also *Memorials of Bucknell University, 1919–1931,* 92.

[69] Bucknell University, *Catalogue, 1926–27,* 58–59.

[70] *Ibid., 1930–31,* 62–63.

[71] *Ibid., 1926–27,* 151. The program leading to the degree of Bachelor of Science in Home Economics was abolished by vote of the faculty on December 4, 1924. Minutes of the Faculty, IV, 108.

[72] Bucknell University, *Catalogue, 1932–33,* 173. The program leading to this degree was approved by the faculty on June 2, 1928. Minutes of the Faculty, IV, 233–235. See also the *Bucknell Alumni Monthly,* XIII (October, 1928), 2.

[73] Bucknell University, *Catalogue, 1925–26,* 140. This program was established by vote of the faculty on November 6, 1923. Minutes of the Faculty, IV, 56. See also the *Bucknell Alumni Monthly,* VIII (March, 1924), 3.

[74] Romeyn H. Rivenburg, "The Year's Scholastic Progress," *Bucknell Alumni Monthly,* VIII (June, 1924), 11.

[75] This department had been established by vote of the faculty on May 9, 1919. Minutes of the Faculty, III, 401.

[76] Minutes of the Faculty, III, 350. The Trustees approved a summer session on the condition that the University should not incur any responsibility for its maintenance.

Minutes of the Trustees, III, June 15, 1915, 418. See also the *Catalogue, 1915–16,* 103–104. The assertion that the summer session was discontinued in 1917 because of the war (*Bucknell Alumni Monthly,* VIII, February, 1923, 12) is incorrect. The Treasurer's Semi-Annual Report of November 30, 1918, shows that "summer-school" salaries had been paid in 1918. The *Catalogue, 1918–19,* 105, says that a session would be held in the summer of 1919, and the Trustees, as late as June 4, 1919, approved the continuance of the summer session in that year. Minutes of the Trustees, III, 468.

77 *Memorials of Bucknell University, 1919–1931,* 91; Bucknell University, *Catalogue, 1923–24,* 121–122.

78 *Memorials of Bucknell University, 1919–1931,* 90–91; Bucknell University, *Catalogue, 1928–29,* 33, 175–181.

79 On the history of the library during the administration of President Hunt, see J. Orin Oliphant, *The Library of Bucknell University* (Lewisburg, Pa., 1962), 110–128, and the references therein cited.

80 *Memorials of Bucknell University, 1919–1931,* 145–147; *Students' Handbook,* XXX (1926–27), 61–62.

81 Bucknell University, *Catalogue, 1920–21,* 86.

82 *Ibid., 1925–26,* 113.

83 *Ibid., 1930–31,* 153.

84 *Ibid.,* 1921–22, 89. In the Archives of Bucknell University there is a file of the printed annual *Report of Distribution of Student Budget and of Student Organizations of Bucknell University,* beginning with the year 1920–21.

85 Bucknell University, *Catalogue, 1926–27,* 123.

86 Minutes of the Trustees, III, January 23, 1920, 475; *ibid.,* June 17, 1924, 3.

87 Bucknell University, *Catalogue, 1920–21,* 100–101.

88 *Ibid.,* 1929–30, 173–174; *Bucknell Alumni Monthly,* X (December, 1925), 9; *L'Agenda,* 1927, 219. As early as 1926, the Bucknell University Athletic Council was in existence. See its *Constitution and By-Laws* (1926), 3.

89 *L'Agenda,* 1931, 109–111; Bucknell University, *Catalogue, 1930–31,* 159. See the constitution as approved by the faculty in 1919. Minutes of the Faculty, III, October 29, 1919, 408–410.

90 *L'Agenda,* 1933, 178.

91 *Bucknell Alumni Monthly,* XIV (May, 1930), 14.

92 In the Archives of Bucknell University there is a file of correspondence, covering the years 1919 to 1929, that pertains to the efforts of Bucknell during those years to get a chapter of Phi Beta Kappa. President Hunt was a member of this society.

CHAPTER ELEVEN

1 Bucknell University, Minutes of the Trustees, June 11, 1, and December 21, 1929, 4.

2 *Ibid.,* December 20, 1930, 1.

3 *Ibid.,* June 8, 1931, 2; *Bucknell Alumni Monthly,* XV (November, 1931), 3.

4 Homer P. Rainey to Archie M. Palmer, November 18, 1931. President Rainey's File, Archives of Bucknell University.

5 Minutes of the Trustees, June 8, 1931, 2; *Who's Who in America* (1944–45), 1728.

6 Homer P. Rainey, "New Creative Program," *Bucknell Alumni Monthly,* XVIII, (September, 1933), 9. Reprinted from the *New York Times,* July 21, 1933.

7 *Ibid.;* Homer P. Rainey, *The Social Function of the Liberal College: Inaugural Address, . . . November 13, 1931.* A printed copy of this address is in the Archives of Bucknell University.

8 Homer P. Rainey, "New Creative Program," *loc. cit.,* 9–10.

9 *Ibid.,* 10.

10 Bucknell University, Minutes of the Faculty, IV, November 9, 1931, 39; Minutes of the Trustees, December 19, 1931, 1.

[11] *Bucknell Alumni Monthly,* XVI (February, 1932), 7.

[12] *Ibid.,* XVI (April, 1932), 2.

[13] *Ibid.,* 4.

[14] *Ibid.,* XVI (July, 1932), 4. There is a copy of this report in the Archives of Bucknell University. Also, the report is printed in the *Bucknell Alumni Monthly,* XVII (September, 1932), 9–12.

[15] Minutes of the Faculty, IV, September 10, 1932, 66.

[16] *Ibid.,* IV, 69–70, 71–72.

[17] Bucknell University, *Catalogue, 1932–33,* 33.

[18] Minutes of the Faculty, IV, November 30, 1932, 75–76.

[19] *Ibid.,* IV, 74–75.

[20] Homer P. Rainey to Albert Britt, February 9, 1933. President Rainey's File, Archives of Bucknell University.

[21] "President's Page," *Bucknell Alumni Monthly,* XVII (December, 1932), 3.

[22] Minutes of the Faculty, IV, April 6, 1932, 55–56.

[23] *Bucknell Alumni Monthly,* XVI (July, 1932), 3.

[24] Homer P. Rainey, "Building for the Future," *ibid.,* XVII (November, 1932), 3.

[25] Minutes of the Trustees, October 21, 1932, 1. Mr. Larson was strongly recommended to President Rainey in letters written on September 3 and September 9, 1932, by one of the Trustees of Bucknell University, Frank W. Padelford, executive secretary of the Board of Education of the Northern Baptist Convention. These letters, together with a letter of September 9, 1932, from Mr. Larson to President Rainey, are in President Rainey's File, Archives of Bucknell University.

[26] Homer P. Rainey, "Building for the Future," *loc. cit.,* 3.

[27] " 'Old Main' Destroyed by Fire," *Bucknell Alumni Monthly,* XVII, (September, 1932), 1–6.

[28] Homer P. Rainey to the Faculty of Bucknell University, September 15, 1932, 1. There is a mimeographed copy of this statement in the Archives of Bucknell University.

[29] *Ibid.,* 2.

[30] Bucknell University, *Catalogue, 1930–31,* 215; *ibid., 1932–33,* 194.

[31] Romeyn H. Rivenburg, Reports to the Board of Trustees, . . . 1935–1945, pages not numbered. A bound copy of these typewritten reports is in the Archives of Bucknell University.

[32] Minutes of the Trustees, June 6, 1932, 1.

[33] Homer P. Rainey to the Faculty of Bucknell University, September 15, 1932, *loc. cit.*

[34] Earl A. Morton to Homer P. Rainey, November 18, 1932. President Rainey's File, Archives of Bucknell University. See also an editorial on this subject in the *Bucknell Alumni Monthly,* XVII (November, 1932), 2.

[35] Minutes of the Trustees, December 17, 1932, 2. In a letter to "All the Alumni of Bucknell," President Rainey gave the reason for this reduction as follows: "In the last two years we have had a decrease in enrollment of approximately 14 per cent. The income of the University has been decreased accordingly. Financial readjustments have had to be made. Salaries and wages of the entire organization have been reduced and every other possible economy is being made to place the institution on a balanced budget." *Bucknell Alumni Monthly,* XVII (January, 1933), 3.

[36] Minutes of the Faculty, IV, February 8, 1933, 86.

[37] "New Campus Begun," *Bucknell Alumni Monthly,* XVIII (September, 1933), 4–5.

[38] In 1938 it was named in honor of a former chairman of the Board of Trustees and a generous benefactor of Bucknell, Charles P. Vaughan, who had died on March 20, 1936. *Bucknell Alumni Monthly,* XXII (March, 1938), 1.

[39] *Ibid.,* XVIII (March–April, 1934), 2.

[40] J. H. Eisenhauer, "Junior College Opens," *Bucknell Alumni Monthly* (September, 1933), 6.

[41] Frank G. Davis to George R. Faint, May 3, 1940. Bucknell Junior College File, Archives of Bucknell University.

[42] There is a typed copy of this report in the Bucknell Junior College File, *loc. cit.*

[43] Minutes of the Trustees, May 22, 1933, 1.

[44] Homer P. Rainey to the Members of the Faculty, September 16, 1933. A carbon copy of this communication is in a file entitled Surveys of University by Drs. Judd and Haggerty, Archives of Bucknell University.

[45] Romeyn H. Rivenburg to Charles C. Ellis, December 7, 1938. Bucknell Junior College File, *loc. cit.*

[46] Homer P. Rainey to Members of the Faculty, September 16, 1933. In Surveys of the University by Drs. Judd and Haggerty, *loc. cit.*

[47] Minutes of the Faculty, IV, November 27, 1934, 127–133; *ibid.*, December 5, 1934, 134–135; *ibid.*, January 10, 1935, 142–146; *ibid.*, March 13, 1935, 148–149; *ibid.*, June 1, 1935, 157–158.

[48] Romeyn H. Rivenburg, "A Statement from the Dean," *Bucknell Alumni Monthly*, XX (January, 1936), 5–6. On January 29, 1936, the faculty voted to discontinue the comprehensive examination at the close of the sophomore year. Minutes of the Trustees, IV, 179.

[49] Bucknell University, *Catalogue, 1933–34*, 197; *ibid.*, 1934–35, 186; Romeyn H. Rivenburg, Reports to the Board of Trustees, *loc. cit.*

[50] Minutes of the Faculty, IV, November 5, 1934, 125. This committee consisted of Professors Robert L. Matz, Rudolph Peterson, Clarence H. Richardson, William H. Eyster, and Martin L. Drum.

[51] *Ibid.*, IV, December 12, 1934, 138.

[52] A copy of the preliminary report of the Committee of Five is in the file entitled Surveys of the University by Drs. Judd and Haggerty, *loc. cit.*

[53] *Bucknell Alumni Monthly*, XX, October, 1935, 2.

[54] Minutes of the Faculty, IV, November 6, 1935, 168.

[55] *Ibid.*, IV, November 20, 1935, 169–176.

[56] Romeyn H. Rivenburg, "A Statement from the Dean," *loc. cit.*, 6. See also Philip L. Harriman, "Administrative Reorganization at Bucknell: An Experiment in Democratic Faculty Control," *Journal of Higher Education*, VII (April, 1936), 203–206.

[57] *Bucknell Alumni Monthly*, XX (October, 1935), 3.

[58] Minutes of the Trustees, IV, October 5, 1935, 1–3.

[59] *Ibid.*, 4.

[60] *Ibid.*, IV, October 25, 1934, 1.

[61] *Bucknell Alumni Monthly*, XX (November, 1935), 2–3.

[62] Romeyn H. Rivenburg, Report to the Board of Trustees, December 21, 1940, *loc. cit.*

[63] Arnaud C. Marts to Romeyn H. Rivenburg, December 2, 1944, in reply to a letter from Dean Rivenburg dated December 1, 1944. President Marts's Letters and Dean Rivenburg's Correspondence, Archives of Bucknell University.

[64] Arnaud C. Marts to the Faculty, Students, Alumni, and Friends of Bucknell, December 1, 1944, in the *Bucknell Alumnus*, XXIX (December, 1944), 3–4; *ibid.*, XXIX (June, 1945), 3–4.

[65] *Bucknell Alumni Monthly*, XX (November, 1935), 2–3.

[66] *Ibid.*, 2.

[67] Memorandum of Arnaud C. Marts on Daniel C. Roberts, December 19, 1962, in the possession of J. Orin Oliphant. See also Arnaud C. Marts, "The Board of Trustees as the Seed Bed for Capital Gifts to Bucknell's Plant and Endowment," *Bucknell Alumnus*, XXXIV (June, 1950), 19.

[68] Minutes of the Trustees, December 14, 1935, 1–7.

[69] Arnaud C. Marts to Friends of Bucknell, in the *Bucknell Alumni Monthly*, XX (January, 1936), 2.

[70] *Ibid.*, XX (April–May, 1936), 1, 2.

[71] *Ibid.*, XX (July, 1936), inside front cover.

[72] *Ibid.*, XXI (October, 1936), 2, 6.

[73] *Ibid.*, XXI (November, 1936), 2.

[74] *Ibid.*, XXI (February, 1937), 2.

[75] *Ibid.*, XXI (May, 1937), 2.

[76] *Ibid.*, XXI (July, 1937), inside front cover.

[77] *Ibid.*, XXII (December, 1937), 4–5. For a perceptive appraisal of Mr. Roberts, see Arnaud C. Marts, "Daniel C. Roberts," *Bucknell Alumni Monthly*, XXV (October, 1940), 5.

[78] Minutes of the Trustees, April 3, 1937, 4.

[79] *Ibid.*, June 5, 1937, 3.

[80] *Bucknell Alumni Monthly*, XXI (July, 1937), inside front cover.

[81] Minutes of the Executive Committee of the Board of Trustees, July 31, 1937, 1.

[82] *Bucknell Alumni Monthly*, XXII (October, 1937), 2–3.

[83] *Ibid.*, XXII (March, 1938), 3.

[84] *Ibid.*, XXII (July, 1938), 1–4; Minutes of the Trustees, June 11, 1938, 10.

[85] *Bucknell Alumni Monthly*, XXII (July, 1938), 6; Minutes of the Trustees, December 17, 1938, 3.

[86] *Ibid.*, XXIII (November, 1938), 6.

[87] *Ibid.*, 4.

[88] *Ibid.*, XXII (March, 1938), 5; Arnaud C. Marts to Ambrose Saricks, December 16, 1937 (in the possession of J. Orin Oliphant).

[89] Minutes of the Trustees, December 18, 1937, 6.

[90] Copies of both of these letters are in President Marts's File of Letters, Archives of Bucknell University.

[91] On April 12, 1938, Dean Romeyn H. Rivenburg wrote about this affair to William I. King, saying: "I only wish you could have been present at the Lewisburg Baptist Church Thursday morning when Judge Davis announced President Marts' acceptance of the presidency of the University. It was a memorable occasion when Bucknell history of highest importance was made." A carbon copy of this letter is in President Marts's File of Letters, *loc. cit.*

[92] Minutes of the Faculty, IV, April 7, 1938, 234–235.

[93] Minutes of the Trustees, November 13, 1937, 1.

[94] *Ibid.*, June 11, 1938, 9; *Bucknell Alumni Monthly*, XXII (July, 1938), 6; *ibid.*, XXII (November, 1938), 3–4. All told, according to the records of the treasurer of Bucknell University, Mr. Roberts gave $733,575.00 to Bucknell.

[95] George A. Irland, "The New Engineering Building," *Bucknell Alumni Monthly*, XXIV (February, 1940), 2; "President's Page," *ibid.*, XXIV (May, 1940), inside front cover; *Lewisburg Saturday News*, June 13, 1940; Romeyn H. Rivenburg, Report to the Board of Trustees, December 21, 1940, in the Archives of Bucknell University.

[96] Minutes of the Trustees, April 3, 1937, 3; *ibid.*, December 17, 1938, 3.

[97] *Ibid.*, December 16, 1939.

[98] Minutes of the Trustees, June 6, 1936, 3; *ibid.*, December 19, 1936, 1; *ibid.*, June 5, 1937, 3; *ibid.*, December 21, 1940, 1; *ibid.*, December 20, 1941, 1–2.

[99] Statement by President Arnaud C. Marts, July 1, 1937; letter from Arnaud C. Marts to Romeyn H. Rivenburg, November 27, 1942, saying: "The only possible future for the Junior College is for it to become a separate institution. The Junior College is now too hazardous a risk for Bucknell with our small endowment. . . . My aim is definitely a separate college, with its own charter, its own accreditation, and possibly its own name." See also Arnaud C. Marts to William H. Coleman, February 25, 1946. Bucknell Junior College File and Dean Rivenburg's Letters, Archives of Bucknell University.

[100] *Bucknell Alumni Monthly*, XXI (May, 1937), 5; Minutes of the Trustees, June 5, 1937, 2.

[101] *Ibid.*, December 17, 1938, 7; *ibid.*, December 20, 1941, 4.

[102] *Ibid.*, December 19, 1936, 2; *ibid.*, December 18, 1937, 7–8; *ibid.*, June 11, 1938, 2–3.

[103] *Ibid.*, December 17, 1938, 4.

[104] *Ibid.*, December 18, 1937, 4.

[105] Arnaud C. Marts, "Alumni Cooperation with Bucknell's Freshman Admissions Program Is Invited," *Bucknell Alumni Monthly*, XX (December, 1937), 3.

[106] Minutes of the Trustees, December 17, 1938, 6, 10.

[107] Arnaud C. Marts, Memorandum to Trennie E. Eisley, October 26, 1940. Archives of Bucknell University.

[108] Minutes of the Trustees, June 5, 1937, 2.

[109] John T. Judd, "Leroy Stephens, Christian Educator," *Bucknell Alumni Monthly,* VII (December, 1922), 3, 8.

[110] A promotion pamphlet, entitled *Three Hundred Acres Set Apart,* was published by Bucknell University in 1937.

[111] Memorandum to Trennie Eisley, October 26, 1940.

[112] Bucknell University, *Engineering* (October, 1940), 5.

[113] Romeyn H. Rivenburg, Report to the Board of Trustees, December 16, 1939, 4–5.

[114] *Ibid.,* December 19, 1942, 7.

[115] *Bucknell Alumni Monthly,* XXIV (February, 1940), 1.

[116] Minutes of the Trustees, June 8, 1940, 2; Romeyn H. Rivenburg, Report to the Board of Trustees, June 8, 1940, 3.

[117] *Bucknell Alumni Monthly,* XXV (October, 1940), 1; *ibid.,* XXV (May, 1941), 5; Romeyn H. Rivenburg, Report to the Board of Trustees, June 8, 1940, 3.

[118] *Bucknell Alumni Monthly,* XXV (May, 1941), 6.

[119] *Ibid.,* XVIII (September, 1933), 1.

[120] J. Orin Oliphant, *The Library of Bucknell University* (Lewisburg, Pa., 1962), 130–131, and works therein cited.

[121] *Ibid.,* 132–133, 138.

[122] Minutes of the Faculty, IV, January 5 and February 9, 1939, 255, 256; J. Orin Oliphant to Arnaud C. Marts, October 26, 1939, and President Marts's reply thereto (undated), in the personal file of J. Orin Oliphant; Minutes of the Faculty, IV, December 7, 1939, and January 11, 1940, 272–274.

[123] Oliphant, *op. cit.,* 136–138.

[124] Minutes of the Trustees, December 17, 1938, 10.

[125] *Bucknell Alumni Monthly,* XXIII (January, 1939), 2.

[126] *Bibliotheca Bucnellensis,* IV (October, 1939), No. I, 1.

[127] Arnaud C. Marts, *Confidential Statement to the Trustees and a Few Other Friends of Bucknell in Reference to the Library Situation* [1939], printed (but not published) in a limited edition *de luxe.* See 4–5, 8–17, 22.

[128] *Bucknell Alumni Monthly,* XXIV (May, 1940), inside front cover.

[129] Minutes of the Trustees, December 15, 1945, 9.

[130] *Ibid.,* June 5, 1937, 1.

[131] *Ibid.,* June 10, 1939, 6.

[132] Minutes of the Faculty, IV, May 6, 1937, 212; *Bucknell Alumni Monthly,* XXIII (January, 1939), 10.

[133] William H. Eyster and J. Orin Oliphant to Arnaud C. Marts, October 7, 1937; Arnaud C. Marts to William H. Eyster and J. Orin Oliphant, October 8, 1937; William H. Eyster and J. Orin Oliphant to their colleagues, March 2, 1938. Letters in the personal file of J. Orin Oliphant. See also *About Bucknell,* II (April, 1958), 5.

[134] Romeyn H. Rivenburg, Report to the Board of Trustees, June 10, 1939, 3.

[135] Arnaud C. Marts, Memorandum to Trennie E. Eisley, October 26, 1940.

[136] Bucknell University, *Catalogue, 1938–39,* 202; *ibid., 1939–40,* 209; *ibid., 1941–42,* 202.

[137] *Ibid., 1939–40,* 154; *ibid., 1940–41,* 154.

[138] *Ibid., 1939–40,* 154.

[139] *Ibid., 1934–35,* 145; *ibid., 1939–40,* 154.

[140] *Ibid., 1942–43,* 147.

[141] Arnaud C. Marts to Roy G. Bostwick, January 27, 1938. President Marts's File of Letters, Archives of Bucknell University.

[142] *Bucknellian,* May 8, 1933; Philip L. Harriman, "The Student-Faculty Congress," *Bucknell Alumni Monthly,* XXII (December, 1937), 8, 16; *L'Agenda,* 1939, 152.

[143] *Bucknell Alumni Monthly,* XXI (July, 1937), 10; Minutes of the Trustees, June 5, 1937, 5; Romeyn H. Rivenburg's Recommendations to the Committee of the Trustees on Instruction, June 4, 1937, in his Reports to the Board, . . . 1935–1945, *loc. cit.*

[144] *Bucknell Alumni Monthly,* XXI (May, 1937), 3.

[145] Romeyn H. Rivenburg, Report to the Board of Trustees, June 8, 1940. Archives of Bucknell University.

[146] Arnaud C. Marts to Roy G. Bostwick, January 27, 1938, *loc. cit.* Some months earlier President Marts's report to the Trustees on this matter was recorded as follows: "Mr. Marts stated that the University had purchased a tract of land containing about 28 acres of ground at Cowan, to be used as a site for a Lodge to be erected by the Christian Association of the University, a gift of $1,000.00 having been made for that purpose by a friend and it being hoped that additional subscriptions would make it possible to proceed at once with the erection of a Lodge. In the meantime a house already on the property would serve as a center for activities. The site is about seven miles west of the University." Minutes of the Trustees, April 3, 1937, 4–5.

[147] *Bucknell Alumni Monthly,* XXIV (February, 1940), inside front cover.

[148] Arnaud C. Marts to Roy G. Bostwick, January 27, 1938, *loc. cit.*

[149] *Bucknell Alumni Monthly,* XVIII (January–February, 1934), 1, 4.

[150] Arnaud C. Marts, Memorandum to J. Orin Oliphant, December 4, 1962; President Marts's introduction to a bulletin entitled *Physical Education—Recreation—Athletic Week-end, Bucknell University, January 12–14, 1939* (pages not numbered).

[151] *Bucknell Alumni Monthly* (July 1, 1937), 10–11; Romeyn H. Rivenburg to Levering Tyson, president of Muhlenburg College, April 30, 1938, in the file on Athletics, Archives of Bucknell University.

[152] *Bucknell Alumni Monthly,* XXV (October, 1940), 6.

[153] Minutes of the Trustees, June 8, 1940, 3.

[154] *Bucknell Alumni Monthly,* XXIV (October, 1939), 2.

[155] *Ibid.,* XXV (May, 1941), 2; Arnaud C. Marts to Oliver J. Decker, April 10, 1941, in President Marts's File of Letters, Archives of Bucknell University. The faculty approved this action. Minutes of the Faculty, V, April 16, 1941, 7.

CHAPTER TWELVE

[1] On this project Dean Romeyn H. Rivenburg, in December, 1942, wrote as follows: "The Navy has a second group of twenty men on the campus who are taking an intensive ground school course at the college and are taking their flying at the Danville Airport. These men are being housed on the top floor of East College, which was not used for students." Report to the Board of Trustees, December 19, 1942, 7. Archives of Bucknell University.

[2] Bucknell University, Minutes of the Faculty, V, 16–17; Bucknell University, *Catalogue, 1941–42,* 39.

[3] Minutes of the Faculty, V, 18–19.

[4] On this subject in general, see "Bucknell in Wartime," *Bucknell Alumni Monthly,* XXVI (May, 1942), 1 and 11, and Arnaud C. Marts, "A Message from the President," *ibid.,* XXVII (October, 1942), inside front cover.

[5] Romeyn H. Rivenburg, Report to the Board of Trustees, 1942–43, 1.

[6] *Ibid.,* 5–6; *ibid.,* December 18, 1943, *passim;* Minutes of the Trustees, April 22, 1942, 1–2; *ibid.,* December 18, 1943, 6; Ralph E. Page, "600 Navy Men Come to Bucknell," *Bucknell Alumni Monthly,* XXVII (June, 1943), 8–9.

[7] Romeyn H. Rivenburg, Report to the Trustees, June 24, 1944, 6; *ibid.,* December 16, 1944, 5.

[8] *Ibid.,* 1942–43, 1.

[9] *Ibid.,* 2; *ibid.,* June 24, 1944, 1 and 8; Minutes of the Trustees, December 16, 1944, 2.

[10] Minutes of the Trustees, December 16, 1944, 10.

[11] *Ibid.,* May 23, 1942, 4; "Bucknell Continues to Look Ahead," *Bucknell Alumni Monthly,* XXVII (January, 1943), 3 and *passim.* This issue of the *Alumni Monthly* is dedicated to Bucknell's One Hundredth Birthday Gift.

[12] *Bucknell Alumni Monthly,* XXVII (January, 1943), 4–5.

[13] "Bucknell," President Marts also told the alumni, "has been so engrossed in doing

her work that she has not appealed to her children for funds yearly as do most colleges. Now we have a real opportunity to repay in part the great debt we owe her." He assured them that gifts of any amount would be "greatly appreciated," and he urged them to help the Class of 1946 "graduate from a college that has celebrated her One Hundredth Birthday free from debt." *Ibid.*, XXVII (June, 1943), 18.

14 Minutes of the Trustees, June 24, 1944, 9; *ibid.*, December 15, 1945, 6.

15 *Ibid.*, December 20, 1941, 6.

16 "Mr. [Oliver J.] Decker made a Report for the Centennial Committee, in the course of which he stated that since the Annual Meeting of the Board, final arrangements had been made with Dr. Theiss to devote the next four years to writing a History of Bucknell University, and that Dr. Theiss was now engaged on this work." *Ibid.*, December 19, 1942, 4.

17 *Ibid.*, December 16, 1944, 11.

18 *Ibid.*, December 18, 1943, 3.

19 *Ibid.*, June 7, 1947, 9–11; "Wilkes College Receives Charter," *Bucknell Alumnus*, XXXII (September, 1947), 8.

20 "Letter from the President," *Bucknell Alumnus*, XXVIII (May, 1944), inside front cover.

21 *Ibid.*, 20.

22 In his letter of resignation, dated June 24, 1944, President Marts, after reminding the Board of the circumstances under which he assumed leadership at Bucknell, continued as follows: "I am unable to continue to carry these responsibilities indefinitely, and I believe that now is the time, as we approach the re-adjustments which will be made necessary by the termination of the war, to select and install a new President. . . . I urge your prompt action in order that the new President may be given the responsibility for shaping Bucknell's post war policy and program and administration before we find ourselves in the very midst of those post war problems. I shall be glad to serve out my term as a member of the Board of Trustees and I assure you of my fullest interest and co-operation in that relationship." Minutes of the Trustees, June 24, 1944, 8.

23 *Ibid.*, 9.

24 Minutes of the Faculty, V, November 15, 1944, 53; Minutes of the Trustees, December 16, 1945, 1.

25 Minutes of the Trustees, December 16, 1945, 6–7.

26 *Bucknell Alumnus*, XXIX (March, 1945), 2–3.

27 *Inauguration of Herbert Lincoln Spencer as Eighth President of Bucknell, June 23, 1945*. A pamphlet in the Archives of Bucknell University.

28 *Who's Who in America* (1954–55), 2519; *Bucknell Alumnus*, XXIX (March, 1945), 3–4.

29 *Bucknell Alumnus*, XXX (September, 1945), 2.

30 *Inauguration of Herbert Lincoln Spencer, passim.*

31 Minutes of the Trustees, December 15, 1945, 1–2.

32 *Ibid.*, June 29, 1946, 2, 8.

33 *Bucknell Alumnus*, XXX (June, 1946), 2.

34 *Ibid.*, XXVII (January, 1943), 4.

35 "A coed selected from the centennial class, Miss Sara Krone of York, presented the last remaining note to Bucknell's President Herbert L. Spencer, and he in turn burned the note, lighting it from a large birthday candle placed at one end of the gym floor." *Ibid.*, XXX (March, 1946), 4.

36 "Highlights from Centennial Commencement," *ibid.*, XXXI (September, 1946), 8–9, 20–21.

37 "The Centennial Homecoming," *ibid.*, XXXI (December, 1946), 3–4.

38 Bucknell University, *Official Proceedings of the Centennial Commencement, June 27–30, 1946*, 38.

39 *Bucknell Alumnus*, XXXI (December, 1946), 2.

40 "Bucknell's Centennial summer has indeed been a busy one as we prepare for the opening of the fall term on September 19. At that time we shall enroll approximately

2,000 students to set an all-time high for Bucknell's student body." President Herbert L. Spencer, in the *Bucknell Alumnus,* XXXI (September, 1946), 7.

41 *Bucknell Alumnus,* XXXI (December, 1946), 7; Minutes of the Trustees, December 7, 1946, 1. One of the several charts which President Spencer presented to the Trustees at this meeting shows how, during the preceding twenty years, the denominational affiliations of the students at Bucknell had changed. On this subject we learn that "In 1926, enrolment 1037, the Baptists ranked first, when 25.0% of the students were classified as Baptists, while in 1946, enrolment 2043, this denomination ranks fifth with 9.8% of the students classified as Baptists. The Presbyterians now rank first with 18.7% of the students so classified." *Ibid.,* 2.

42 Herbert L. Spencer, "Report from the Campus," *Bucknell Alumnus,* XXXI (March, 1947), 3–4; *Bucknellian,* September 19, 1946, and January 9, 1947; Minutes of the Trustees, December 7, 1946, 2; *ibid.,* December 6, 1947, 7. In June, 1947, the chairman of the Finance Committee of the Trustees reported that "the G.I. housing project had been completed at a cost to the University of $39,704.71," and that "the faculty housing project had been completed at a cost of approximately $180,000 to the University." Minutes of the Trustees, June 7, 1947, 7.

43 Minutes of the Trustees, December 7, 1946, 10; Herbert L. Spencer, "Report from the Campus," *loc. cit.,* 3; Bucknell University, *Catalogue, 1949–50,* 27.

44 *The Second Century, Bulletin of Bucknell University's Development Program,* I (October, 1947), 1.

45 *Ibid.*

46 Minutes of the Trustees, December 7, 1946, 3.

47 *The Second Century,* I (October, 1947), 1.

48 Minutes of the Trustees, June 7, 1941, 6; *ibid.,* December 20, 1941, 5.

49 *Ibid.,* June 24, 1944, 5; *ibid.,* December 16, 1944, 12.

50 *Ibid.,* June 29, 1946, 13.

51 *The Second Century,* I (February, 1948), 1.

52 Minutes of the Trustees, June 5, 1948, 4; *The Second Century,* I (April, 1948), 3; Bucknell Development Council, *Report, June 30, 1953,* 4; Minutes of the Trustees, June 4, 1949, 9. During the campaign to raise money for the new heating plant, the University published an illustrated bulletin entitled *Full Steam Ahead.* The contributions of the alumni to the fund for the new heating plant President Spencer, in December, 1948, praised in these words: "I am delighted with the splendid start you have given the [Alumni] Fund through your Heating Plant contributions. . . . About 2,500 of the University's 11,000 Alumni, by their gifts to the Heating Plant, have been listed as contributors to the Alumni Fund in its first year. They have enabled us to proceed with [the] construction of the Plant and, at the same time, have made the Alumni Fund a very welcome reality." *Bucknell Alumnus,* XXXIII (December, 1948), 3. The contributions of the alumni, however, were not enough to pay for the new plant. On February 15, 1951, Rush H. Kress wrote to Joseph W. Henderson, offering to pay $55,000 of the remaining indebtedness of $165,000 on account of the heating plant when he was assured that $110,000 had been contributed by "the Trustees and their friends" for the payment of such indebtedness. A copy of this letter is appended to the Minutes of the Trustees, June 9, 1951.

53 Bucknell University, *Catalogue, 1946–47,* 249; *ibid., 1948–49,* 263; *ibid., 1949–50,* 280.

54 Dean William H. Coleman, Report to the Board of Trustees, December 2, 1946, 2. File of Reports of the Dean of the College, 1945–49, in the Archives of Bucknell University. See also the Minutes of the Trustees, December 7, 1946, 4.

55 On this subject Dean Coleman reported to the Trustees on June 4, 1949, as follows: "At the request of President Spencer, at its last meeting the Board of Trustees agreed to appropriate $600 annually to finance a series of studies under the general caption of *Bucknell University Studies.* The first volume [*i.e.,* the second number] of the studies is now in the press and is scheduled for June publication. . . . The Editorial Board is comprised of Dr. J. Orin Oliphant, Dr. Hulda Magalhaes, Dr. C. Willard Smith, Dr. F. G. Ballentine, President Herbert L. Spencer, and Dean William H. Coleman, *ex-officio.*" Report to the Board of Trustees, *loc. cit.*

[56] W. H. Coleman, "Curriculum Reorganization at Bucknell," *Bucknell Alumnus,* XXXI (September, 1946), 12.

[57] Minutes of the Faculty, V, May 19, 1947, 87–89.

[58] *Ibid.,* 90; Bucknell University, *Catalogue, 1947–48,* 46. Dean Coleman commented briefly on the new curriculum in his Report to the Board of Trustees, December 6, 1947, 7, *loc. cit.*

[59] *The Second Century,* I (October, 1947), 3; Bucknell University, *Catalogue, 1947–48,* 26.

[60] Bucknell University, *The University Course, September, 1948,* 1. This pamphlet was published as a bulletin of the University. See also a story on this course in *The Second Century,* I (February, 1948), 5.

[61] Bucknell University, *Catalogue, 1947–48,* 148.

[62] Minutes of the Faculty, V, May 17, 1948, 100–102.

[63] *Ibid.,* May 25, 1949, 115–116.

[64] J. Orin Oliphant and John T. Shirley, *The Virginia Lands of Bucknell University* (Lewisburg, Pa., 1956), 23.

[65] *Ibid.,* 25–33; Minutes of the Trustees, June 11, 1955, 8. A statement prepared on April 4, 1962, in the office of the treasurer of the University shows that the "total amount realized from Virginia real estate" was $1,090,338.46.

[66] *Ibid.,* 6.

[67] Oliphant and Shirley, *op. cit.,* 17, 34.

[68] Minutes of the Trustees, December 4, 1948, 1–2.

[69] The analysis here given is of the *Summary* which was made by Booz, Allen & Hamilton and submitted as an integral part of the *General Survey.*

[70] The report of this committee, dated February 25, 1949, fills seven pages. It is appended to the Minutes of the Trustees, March 5, 1949.

[71] Minutes of the Trustees, March 5, 1949, 1–2.

[72] *Ibid.,* June 4, 1949, 9–10. At this meeting "Senator Sordoni reviewed briefly the Board's appreciation of the services rendered by Dr. Spencer during his four years as President of Bucknell, and requested the privilege of having the retiring president's portrait painted and placed in Roberts Hall. The offer was readily accepted with thanks by the Board." *Ibid.,* 11.

[73] *Ibid.,* March 5, 1949, 2.

[74] *Ibid.,* June 4, 1949, 12.

[75] *Ibid.,* August 11, 1949, 1.

[76] *Who's Who in America* (1962–63), 1419.

[77] *Bucknell Alumnus,* XXXIV (September, 1949), 2.

[78] Minutes of the Faculty, V, October 5, 1949, 126.

[79] "President Hildreth has entered the drive for wide giving to the Alumni Fund with the offer of a $1000 check to the credit of that class with ten or more members which first reports contributions from all its members." *Bucknell Alumnus,* XXXIV (March, 1950), 22.

[80] *Ibid.,* XXXIV (December, 1950), 5, 28.

[81] Minutes of the Trustees, March 5, 1949, 2.

[82] Minutes of the Faculty, V, May 7, 1952, 254.

[83] Minutes of the Trustees, December 9, 1950, 9.

[84] A copy of this letter was sent to every member of the faculty.

[85] Minutes of the Trustees, June 4, 1949, 6; Minutes of the Faculty, V, April 15, 1953, 364.

[86] Minutes of the Trustees, December 8, 1951, 5.

[87] Section I of the *Handbook,* 1–12, contains the statement of "Traditions, Principles, and Policies" approved by the Board of Trustees; Sections II and III, 13–36, contain matters pertaining to the administration of the University that were adopted by the faculty but "not passed upon nor approved by the Board of Trustees."

[88] Minutes of the Trustees, December 6, 1952, 8–9.

[89] *Ibid.,* May 9, 1953, 1.

[90] Minutes of the Trustees, December 8, 1951, 7–8; Bucknell University, *Catalogue, 1952–53,* 35.

[91] The minutes of the meeting of the Executive Committee are attached to the Minutes of the Trustees, December 9, 1950.

[92] Minutes of the Trustees, December 9, 1950, 9.

[93] In December, 1951, Dean Coleman reported to the Trustees "the establishment of two Reserve Officer Training Corps units on the campus, involving the addition of a Department of Military Science to the faculty and curricula, and assuring an advantageous position under the current draft deferment policies." Minutes of the Trustees, December 8, 1951, 2.

[94] A carbon copy of this letter is in the file of Mrs. Bertrand's Letters, Archives of Bucknell University.

[95] File of Mrs. Bertrand's Letters.

[96] *Ibid.*

[97] The minutes of this meeting of the Executive Committee are appended to the Minutes of the Trustees, June 10, 1950. See also J. Orin Oliphant, *The Library of Bucknell University* (Lewisburg, Pa., 1962), 145–146.

[98] Minutes of the Trustees, June 10, 1950, 4–5. Carbon copies of President Hildreth's letters to Mrs. Bertrand in 1949 and 1950 are in the file of Mrs. Bertrand's Letters.

[99] *Bucknell Alumnus,* XXXV (September, 1950), 24.

[100] *Ibid.,* XXXV (March, 1951), 23; *ibid.,* XXXVI (September, 1951), 4; *ibid.,* XXXVI (December, 1951), 4; announcement of Dean Coleman to the faculty, September 18, 1951.

[101] *Bucknell Alumnus,* XXXV (March, 1951), 10.

[102] Minutes of the Trustees, June 7 and 8, 1952, 3.

[103] *Bucknell Alumnus,* XXXVI (March, 1952), 7; Bucknell Development Council, *Report, June 30, 1953,* 4–5; Minutes of the Trustees, May 9, 1953, 5.

[104] Minutes of the Trustees, May 9, 1953, 8–9. The text of President Hildreth's letter of resignation is appended to the minutes of this meeting of the Board.

[105] *Ibid.,* June 6 and 7, 1953, 5.

[106] Bucknell Development Council, *Report, June 30, 1953,* 13. In a resolution adopted at their meeting in November, 1953, the Trustees expressed their appreciation of President Hildreth in the following words: "In every way Bucknell made progress during the administration of Horace A. Hildreth. For the faculty there were new and increased opportunities for learning and teaching; for the students there was stimulation and understanding; for the alumni there was further participation in the life of the University; for the Trustees there was confidence and guidance; for the public there was an increased awareness of Bucknell's objectives and attainments." Minutes of the Trustees, November 14, 1953, 7.

[107] Minutes of the Trustees, November 14, 1953, 8.

[108] *Ibid.,* June 6 and 7, 1953, 6.

CHAPTER THIRTEEN

[1] Bucknell University, Minutes of the Trustees, November 14, 1953, 5.

[2] Horace A. Hildreth to Daniel A. Poling, February 9, 1953. File on Men's Dormitory, Archives of Bucknell University.

[3] *Bucknell Alumnus,* XXXVIII (March, 1954), 3.

[4] *Ibid.,* 3–4.

[5] Bucknell University, Minutes of the Faculty, February 10, 1954, 5. "Chairman [Joseph W.] Henderson expressed the Board's thanks to the two Vice-Presidents for their work during the past year, including mention of Dr. Coleman's part in securing the grant of the Olin Foundation, and the Trustees gave them a rising vote of appreciation." Minutes of the Trustees, May 8, 1954, 2.

[6] *Bucknell Alumnus,* XXXIX (September, 1954), 4.

[7] *Ibid.,* XL (September, 1955), 5.

8 "To mark the formal presentation of the building to the University, a two-day program was held on September 27 and 28, 1955, to which representatives of both education and industry were invited." Bucknell University, *Dedication of the F. W. Olin Science Building, Wednesday, September 28, 1955,* 3. In this bulletin on the proceedings at the dedication, the address by Dr. John C. Warner is printed, 8–11. Professor Leonard W. Labaree's address appeared in the *Bucknell Review,* V (December, 1955), 1–18. See also the *Bucknellian,* September 29, 1955, and the *Bucknell Alumnus,* XL (November, 1955), 3–4.

9 *About Bucknell,* III (July, 1959), 1, and (January, 1960), 4. See also Merle M. Odgers to Charles L. Horn, June 2, 1959; John F. Zeller to Ralph Clark, December 15, 1959; and Merle M. Odgers to James O. Wynn, December 9, 1959. File on the Olin Science Building Addition, Archives of Bucknell University. In his letter to Mr. Wynn on December 9, 1959, President Odgers said: "The outstanding improvements in Bucknell's physical plant which have been made possible by the Olin Foundation grants are obvious for any who come to the campus to observe our plant."

10 Minutes of the Trustees, June 24, 1954, 1.

11 *Bucknell Alumnus,* XXXIX (January, 1955), 3.

12 *Ibid.,* XXXIX (September, 1954), 3; *Who's Who in America* (1962–63), 2340–2341.

13 A copy of this memorandum is in the Archives of Bucknell University.

14 Merle M. Odgers to the Trustees, June 11, 1955, 11. Dr. Odgers's File of Reports to the Trustees, in the Archives of Bucknell University.

15 Bucknell University, *Report of the President for the Academic Year 1954–55,* 6; *ibid.,* 1957–58, 7.

16 *Ibid., 1960–1961,* 19.

17 Bucknell University, *Dedication of Coleman Hall, Saturday, January 17, 1959,* 8.

18 Minutes of the Trustees, May 8, 1954, 6.

19 Dr. Horace A. Hildreth, then ambassador of the United States to Pakistan, gave an address at the dedicatory exercises of Swartz Hall. *Bucknell Alumnus,* XL (November, 1955), 4. This building was named in honor of a former chairman of the Board of Trustees whose gift of a tract of land in Virginia had greatly increased the endowment of the University.

20 Minutes of the Trustees, November 13, 1954, 2.

21 *Ibid.,* 1–2.

22 Minutes of the Executive Committee of the Board of Trustees, April 23, 1955, 1.

23 *Report of the President for the Academic Year 1954–1955,* 18.

24 Minutes of the Executive Committee, January 12, 1955, 1; Minutes of the Faculty, April 6, 1955; Merle M. Odgers, Announcement of the Reorganization of the Business Function, Faculty Meeting, April 6, 1955, 3, which is appended to the Minutes of the Faculty of that date.

25 Minutes of the Executive Committee, January 12, 1955, 1.

26 *Ibid.*

27 Note 24, *supra.*

28 *Bucknell Alumnus,* XL (November, 1955), 7; *ibid.,* XL (January, 1956), 3; *Report of the President for the Academic Year 1955–1956,* 36.

29 Minutes of the Trustees, November 13, 1954, 1; Forrest D. Brown, "Lodge to be Built at Cowan," *Bucknell Alumnus,* XXXIX (January, 1955), 6; Minutes of a Joint Meeting of the Executive Committee and the Committee on Development, April 28, 1956, 4; *Bucknell Alumnus,* XLI (September, 1956), 7; Minutes and Business of the Bucknell Christian Association, 1955–56, I (pages not numbered). In this volume there is a circular dated July 2, 1956, signed by Forrest D. Brown and saying that the construction of the lodge started in May and that the building should be completed by the first of September, 1956.

30 *Bucknell Alumnus,* XLI (September, 1956), 7.

31 *Report of the President for the Academic Year 1955–1956,* 36–37.

32 President Odgers, in a brief analysis of and comment on this brochure, said that "The ten-million-dollar plan developed by the Committee on Development means ten years of challenge." *Report of the President for the Academic Year 1955–1956,* 24–25.

[33] *About Bucknell,* I (July, 1957), 1.

[34] *Ibid.*

[35] *Bucknell Alumnus,* XLII (November, 1957), 3; *About Bucknell,* I (October, 1957), 1; Bucknell University, *Dedication of Coleman Hall, Saturday, January 17, 1959,* 3–4.

[36] *Bucknell Alumnus,* XLIII (March, 1959), 5.

[37] John Price Jones, Inc., Survey, Analysis and Plan for Fund-Raising for Bucknell University, September, 1958, i–iii.

[38] Memorandum by President Merle M. Odgers, dated October 23, 1958, and disseminated by mail to members of the University. At the Homecoming on October 25 of that year, President Odgers announced that the forthcoming campaign was intended "to put Bucknell into a higher orbit in American education. We are calling this campaign [he said] the 'Double Development Fund,' because it will help Bucknell to match the gifts of others for both 'brains' and 'bricks.'" *Bucknell Alumnus,* XLIII (November, 1958), 24. Presently the fund was called the Dual Development Fund.

[39] *The Bucknell of Tomorrow,* a brochure of six pages, is one of the most important documents of President Odgers's administration.

[40] *Report of the President for the Academic Year 1957–1958,* 33; *Bucknell Alumnus,* XLIII (January, 1959), 20. See also the fifth page of the brochure cited in Note 41, *infra.*

[41] A statement by Harry G. Schad and Kenneth W. Slifer, general co-chairmen of the Dual Development Fund, that was published in a brochure entitled *Three Generous Gifts Pose Three Challenges to Bucknell,* 1–5.

[42] Minutes of the Trustees, June 6, 1959.

[43] *Bucknell Alumnus,* XLVI (September, 1960), 11; *About Bucknell,* IV (July, 1960), 1.

[44] Minutes of the Trustees, December 3, 1960, 7.

[45] Harry G. Schad to Carlton M. Sherwood, February 8, 1961. File of Harry G. Schad's Letters, Archives of Bucknell University. Actually, the goal had been reached on December 28, 1960, "three days before the target date set for achieving the new goal announced last June." But gifts continued to come in after that date. *About Bucknell,* IV (January, 1961), 1.

[46] Bucknell University, *Dual Development Fund Campaign Report* (undated), 1.

[47] *About Bucknell,* IV (April, 1960), 1. "Just this morning Dr. Odgers told me of a gift of $400,000 from the Dana Foundation—which is contingent upon our accomplishing our goal, among other requirements. . . . It is a tremendous boost at this stage of the campaign, but because of the large allocation of gifts to the endowment we shall have to exceed our campaign goal in order to accomplish the goal for building needs. Offhand, we may have to look at a $2,200,000 figure as the necessary goal, with the new monies allocated to buildings." Harry G. Schad to John T. Shirley, March 9, 1960. File of Harry G. Schad's Letters, Archives of Bucknell University.

[48] Minutes of the Trustees, June 1, 1963, 8; *Bucknell Alumnus,* XLVI (March, 1961), 2–3; Bucknell University, *Dual Development Fund Campaign Report,* back cover.

[49] *About Bucknell,* IV (July, 1960), 1, and (October, 1960) 1.

[50] *Ibid.,* IV (January, 1961), 4; *Report of the President for the Academic Year 1960–1961,* 35–36. Guy Payne, Class of 1909, was made "a member of Bucknell's 25-year club" at the first meeting of the faculty in the autumn of 1959. This membership, President Odgers told Mr. Payne when he presented a service pin to him, was given "in recognition of 50 years of friendship between the University and its closest neighbor, 50 years of service to the University by this neighbor, and 50 years of charity and generosity to the University, the faculty, and the student body." At this meeting of the faculty, the announcement was made that Mr. and Mrs. Payne had given the College Inn to the University. *Bucknell Alumnus,* XLV (November, 1959), 8.

[51] *The Second Century,* I (February, 1948), 1.

[52] *About Bucknell,* V (October, 1961), 1.

[53] *Ibid.,* V. (January, 1962), 1.

[54] *Report of the President for the Academic Year 1960–1961,* 34–35.

[55] Minutes of the Trustees, June 6, 1959, 2.

[56] *Bucknell Alumnus,* XLV (November, 1959), 9; Minutes of the Trustees, June 4, 1960, 3.

[57] Minutes of the Trustees, April 19, 1960; *About Bucknell,* V (January, 1962), 2.

[58] Minutes of the Trustees, December 5, 1959, 2.

[59] The University Bookstore was purchased by Bucknell from the Royal Imprints Company in October, 1948. It then occupied a part of the College Inn. In September, 1951, it was given one-half of the first floor of the Carnegie Building, and in 1959, after a complete renovation of the Carnegie Building, it "took over the entire first floor except for a small portion left for the use of the Placement Bureau." Warren E. Elze to J. Orin Oliphant, November 18, 1963. Also, see "15 Years Ago," in the Lewisburg *Union County Journal,* September 5, 1963.

[60] The Placement Bureau, as now constituted, was authorized by the Trustees in December, 1947. Minutes of the Trustees, December 6, 1947. Ray K. Irwin was appointed director of this bureau. See the *Bucknellian,* September 17, 1948.

[61] "Offices of the Christian Association and Counseling Service were moved from the Carnegie Building to the ground floor of the Botany Building this month." *About Bucknell,* V (January, 1962), 4.

[62] *Bucknell Alumnus,* XLVI (September, 1960), 19.

[63] *Ibid.; About Bucknell,* IV (October, 1960), 1.

[64] *About Bucknell,* V (October, 1961), 4.

[65] *Ibid.,* IV (January, 1961), 1; *ibid.,* IV (April, 1961), 1; Minutes of the Trustees, June 3, 1961, 4; *About Bucknell,* V (October, 1961), 1; "The Restored Library and its Promise," *Bibliotheca Bucnellensis,* n. s., I (1961–62), 2.

[66] Minutes of the Trustees, May 9, 1962, 6; *Report of the President for the Academic Year 1962–1963,* 24; *About Bucknell,* VI (July, 1962), 2.

[67] Minutes of the Executive Committee, May 9, 1962, 6; *Report of the President for the Academic Year 1962–1963,* 31.

[68] Minutes of the Executive Committee, May 9, 1962, 7; Minutes of the Trustees, December 1, 1962, 5; *Bucknell Alumnus,* XLVIII (May, 1963), 11; *Report of the President for the Academic Year 1962–1963,* 30–31.

[69] Minutes of the Trustees, June 3, 1961, 10–11.

[70] *Report of the President for the Academic Year 1961–1962,* 32–33; Minutes of the Trustees, June 2, 1962, 2–3.

[71] *Bucknell Blueprint, 1962–1972,* June, 1962.

[72] *Ibid.,* 6–17, *passim.*

[73] Minutes of the Trustees, June 1, 1963, 9; *About Bucknell,* VII (July, 1963), 1; *ibid.,* VII (October, 1963), 1; *Sunbury Daily Item* (Sunbury, Pa.), October 3, 1963; *Cornerstone Ceremony for the Charles M. and Olive S. Rooke Chapel, Bucknell University, Saturday, November 16, 1963* (program).

[74] *Report of the President for the Academic Year 1960–1961,* 23.

[75] *Ibid., 1962–1963,* 32; *About Bucknell,* VII (July, 1963), 3.

[76] *Report of the President for the Academic Year 1962–1963,* 33; Minutes of the Executive Committee, April 29, 1963. Somewhat earlier, Mr. and Mrs. O. V. W. Hawkins, both Bucknellians, had given to the University, "as a retreat for members of the faculty and professional administrative staff," their three-bedroom lodge (Hawkinsonia) on this tract. *Report of the President for the Academic Year 1959–1960,* 6.

[77] John F. Zeller, "Progress in the Portfolio," *Bucknell Alumnus,* XLVII (May, 1962), 4.

[78] Minutes of the Trustees, December 8, 1956, 1. The records of the treasurer of Bucknell University show that the total gifts of Rush H. Kress to his alma mater amounted to $1,744,756.37.

[79] Memorandum from President Odgers to the Trustees, December 19, 1955, 3–4. A copy of this memorandum is appended to the Minutes of the Faculty, January 4, 1956.

[80] John F. Zeller, "Progress in the Portfolio," *loc. cit.,* 4; Minutes of the Trustees, June 1, 1963, 8.

[81] Minutes of the Trustees, December 7, 1963, 2.

[82] *Report of the President for the Academic Year 1962–1963,* 42.

[83] *Ibid., 1955–1956,* 8.

[84] *Ibid., 1958–1959,* 7. In a report on the finances of the University for this year, the vice-president for business and finance wrote on the subject of inadequate salaries

for members of the faculty as follows: "Further upward adjustments must be made if Bucknell is to keep pace with the best colleges of the Middle Atlantic area. The comprehensive fee of $1750 per student pays over 85% of Bucknell's present costs but it is not sufficient to meet future needs and it is several hundred dollars below the cost at many other institutions of Bucknell's caliber." John F. Zeller, "A Report on Finances," *Bucknell Alumnus,* XLV (January, 1960), 10.

85 *Ibid., 1960–1961,* 8.

86 Harry G. Schad to Merle M. Odgers, February 25, 1958. File of Harry G. Schad's Letters, Archives of Bucknell University.

87 Merle M. Odgers to Harry G. Schad, March 18, 1960. *Ibid.*

88 Merle M. Odgers to the Faculty, September 26, 1957; a statement by President Odgers entitled Bucknell University in Brief, January 5, 1962.

89 *Report of the President for the Academic Year 1962–1963,* 42.

90 Merle M. Odgers to the Faculty, February 27, 1961, 2.

91 Merle M. Odgers to the Faculty, January 9, 1956. A copy of this statement is appended to the Minutes of the Faculty, February 1, 1956.

92 Brief accounts of numerous such grants may be found in successive issues of *About Bucknell,* beginning with the issue for April, 1957.

93 *Report of the President for the Academic Year 1958–1959,* 10.

94 *Ibid., 1962–1963,* 8–9.

95 *Ibid., 1960–1961,* 6–7; *About Bucknell,* IV (January, 1961), 3.

96 *Report of the President for the Academic Year 1962–1963,* 7–8.

97 The material in this paragraph is derived from the annual catalogues of the University for the years mentioned.

98 *Report of the President for the Academic Year 1956–1957,* 8.

99 *Ibid., 1957–1958,* 23.

100 "Bucknell's Class of 1967 comes from 26 states, the District of Columbia, and ten foreign countries." Fitz R. Walling, *Admission to Bucknell University,* October, 1963, 1.

101 This material is derived from an annual brochure, entitled *Admission to Bucknell University,* that the director of admissions has published since December, 1959.

102 Bucknell University, *Regulations, Student Government, Information* (Lewisburg, Pa., 1962), 16–48, *passim.*

103 *Ibid.,* 12–13; *Report of the President for the Academic Year 1962–1963,* 20–21.

104 *About Bucknell,* IV (July, 1961), 1. See also the *Report of the President for the Academic Year 1960–1961,* 16–19.

105 A Report on Bucknell University by an Evaluation Team Appointed by the Commission on Higher Education, Middle States Association of Colleges and Secondary Schools, April 1–4, 1962, 3; *About Bucknell,* VI (July, 1962), 1; *Report of the President for the Academic Year 1961–1962,* 15–16.

106 Minutes of the Executive Committee, May 9, 1962, 4; *Report of the President for the Academic Year 1961–1962,* 13; announcement of President Odgers to the Faculty, May 25, 1962.

107 *Academic Organization of Bucknell University, 1963,* 16.

108 *Report of the President for the Academic Year 1961–1962,* 16; *ibid., 1962–1963,* 38–40.

109 *Ibid., 1962–1963,* 30, 47–48.

110 *Bucknell Alumnus,* XLIX (March, 1964), 10.

CHAPTER FOURTEEN

1 Booz, Allen & Hamilton, Summary of General Survey [of] Bucknell University, December 3, 1948, xix.

2 Bucknell University, Minutes of the Trustees, March 5, 1949, 2. The report of the special committee on the Survey is appended to the minutes of this meeting.

[3] *Ibid.*, June 6–7, 1953, 4.
[4] *Ibid.*, 4–5.
[5] *About Bucknell*, II (April, 1958), 2.
[6] *Ibid.*, IV (October, 1960), 2.
[7] *Bucknell Alumnus*, XXXVIII (June, 1954), 7.
[8] Bucknell University, *Report of the President for the Academic Year 1954–1955*, 26–27.
[9] Bucknell University, Minutes of the Faculty, February 28, 1955, 1.
[10] *Ibid.*, May 4, 1955, 2.
[11] *Ibid.*, October 5, 1955, 2. See also his *Report of the President for the Academic Year 1954–1955*, 28.
[12] Minutes of the Faculty, May 2, 1956, 1–2; *ibid.*, May 16, 1956, 1.
[13] Bucknell University, *Catalogue, 1957–58*, 6.
[14] Minutes of the Executive Committee of the Board of Trustees, December 2, 1955, 1; Minutes of the Trustees, December 3, 1955, 4.
[15] *Report of the President for the Academic Year 1956–57*, 32.
[16] William H. Coleman, "Bucknell Self-Study Gains Momentum," *Bucknell Alumnus*, XLI (January, 1957), 3.
[17] *Report of the President for the Academic Year 1957–1958*, 9.
[18] Karl D. Hartzell, The Bucknell Study: Background Information, *passim.* A copy of this paper, subsequently retyped without change for another purpose and dated February 7, 1962, is in the Archives of Bucknell University.
[19] *Report of the President for the Academic Year 1959–1960*, 31.
[20] Karl D. Hartzell, *op. cit.*, 7 and *passim.*
[21] *Ibid.*
[22] *Report of the President for the Academic Year 1958–1959*, 13; *About Bucknell*, III (July, 1959), 3.
[23] Bucknell University, *Catalogue, 1959–60*, 63, 180.
[24] *Ibid., 1960–61*, 66–67, 151.
[25] *Report of the President for the Academic Year 1961–1962*, 18.
[26] Bucknell University, *Catalogue, 1962–63*, 163; *Report of the President for the Academic Year 1962–1963*, 10. On April 19, 1963, the University held a special academic honors convocation for the purpose of honoring "those students who had distinguished themselves by scholastic achievement." *Ibid.*, 17; *About Bucknell*, VII (April, 1963), 2.
[27] Bucknell University, *Catalogue, 1963–64*, 163.
[28] Karl D. Hartzell, *op. cit.*, 3.
[29] Bucknell University, *Catalogue, 1961–62*, 74–75.
[30] *Ibid.*, 75–76.
[31] Alfred H. Fenton, "A Bucknell Experiment Gets Recognition—and Support," *Bucknell Alumnus*, XXXVIII (September, 1953), 23.
[32] Bucknell University, *Catalogue, 1953–54*, 205–206.
[33] *Ibid., 1957–58*, 180–181.
[34] "Reorganization of the curriculum in business administration, made possible by a grant of $25,000 from the Ford Foundation, is proceeding on schedule, with the introduction of the first new course listed for the spring term. The Ford grant will meet increased costs of instruction and expenses for research and consultation involved in [the] establishment of the new curriculum. Nine new courses in business administration will ultimately be created and a new faculty member will be added to the staff, according to Dr. Russell A. Headley, chairman of the department of economics and business administration." *About Bucknell*, III (January, 1960), 3. A few weeks earlier President Odgers had written about this revision as follows: "A complete revision of the Business Administration program with the aid of the new Ford grant is being planned. The economics principles course is being placed at the sophomore level, and this year American history is being required of all Business Administration majors. We recognize that those who have pursued the engineering and business curricula have had the advantage, as they themselves would freely admit, of studying in a university

which is basically a liberal arts institution." *Report of the President for the Academic Year 1958–1959,* 14.

[35] Bucknell University, *Catalogue, 1960–61,* 118–119.

[36] *Ibid., 1951–52,* 97; *ibid., 1963–64,* 178. In an article addressed to the students of engineering in Bucknell University, in the autumn of 1961, Dean Herbert F. Eckberg said: ". . . our objective has two parts—competence in the profession of engineering, and an understanding of human society. It is for this objective that we are at Bucknell." *Bucknell Engineer,* XIII (November, 1901), 9.

[37] "Upon motion by Dr. [George A.] Irland the recommendation of the Coordinating Committee of Liberal Arts and Engineering regarding the Five Year Program in Liberal Arts and Engineering was accepted without debate and the proposed program was adopted." Bucknell University, Minutes of the Faculty, March 5, 1952, 2.

[38] Bucknell University, *Catalogue, 1953–54,* 99–100.

[39] *Ibid., 1963–64,* 184.

[40] *Report of the President for the Academic Year 1958–1959,* 14.

[41] *Ibid., 1960–1961,* 20–21.

[42] *Ibid., 1961–1962,* 16.

[43] *Ibid., 1962–1963,* 11.

[44] *About Bucknell,* VI (January, 1963), 3.

[45] Bucknell University, *Catalogue, 1963–64,* 180–183.

[46] "Design for Excellence," a typescript dated October 21, 1957, was presented by President Odgers on October 22, 1957, "to the General Advisory Committee meeting with the chairmen of the sub-committees of the Bucknell Study." A copy of this paper was sent to each member of the faculty.

[47] Bucknell University, *Catalogue, 1962–63,* 48.

[48] Report on Graduate-Degree Programs in Bucknell University . . . Submitted by the Faculty to the Middle States Evaluation Team as a Basis for Discussion, April 1–4, 1962. A copy of this report is filed with the reports on the Bucknell Study, Folder 5. Archives of Bucknell University.

[49] *Ibid.,* 32.

[50] Bucknell University, *Catalogue, 1962–63,* 197–200. During this year, the graduate program of the College of Business Administration was revised. "Courses were organized," Dean Russell A. Headley reported, "to give three hours of credit instead of two. The thesis now receives six hours of credit instead of three. The program was arranged to provide the possibility for the student to major in one of three areas: Economics, Accounting, or Business Administration." Quoted in the *Report of the President for the Academic Year 1962–1963,* 11.

[51] Memorandum from Mark C. Ebersole to Members of the Faculty and Administration, January 30, 1961; Memorandum from Karl D. Hartzell to Members of the Faculty and Administration, October 27, 1961.

[52] Merle M. Odgers, Commentary on Evaluation Team's Report, September 26, 1962. There is a copy of this commentary in the Archives of Bucknell University.

[53] A Report on Bucknell University by an Evaluation Team Appointed by the Commission on Higher Education, Middle States Association of Colleges and Secondary Schools, April 1–4, 1962, Introduction, 1. A copy of this report is in the Archives of Bucknell University.

[54] *Bucknell Alumnus,* XXXVI (March, 1952), 12; Bucknell University, *Catalogue, 1953–54,* 61–62.

[55] Bucknell University, *Catalogue, 1962–63,* 79.

[56] *Ibid.,* 79–80.

[57] Bucknell Alumnus, XLI (March, 1957), 13; Lester Kieft and Meldrum B. Winstead, Jr., "Encouraging Science Education," *Bucknell Alumnus,* XLIII (January, 1959), 4–5.

[58] *About Bucknell,* VII (January, 1964), 3.

[59] "Dr. Lester Kieft, professor of chemistry, will direct the eighth Summer Institute in Science and Mathematics for 70 high school teachers and the sixth Summer Institute for H. S. Science Students, with an enrollment of 30 boys. The Institute in

the Engineering Sciences, directed for the fourth year by Charles H. Coder, professor of mechanical engineering, will enroll 40 college teachers of physics and pre-engineering courses." *Ibid.*

60 "The third Summer Language Institute, made possible by a grant from the U.S. Office of Education and directed by Dr. Jeanne M. Chew, associate professor of Spanish, will be open to 50 secondary school teachers of French and Spanish." *Ibid.*

61 *About Bucknell,* II (April, 1958), 1; Bucknell University, *Catalogue, 1959–60,* 151–152.

62 Marguerite Pettet to Merle M. Odgers, November 10, 1959; Merle M. Odgers to Marguerite Pettet, November 11, 1959 (Archives of Bucknell University); Bucknell University, *Bulletin,* "Summer School, 1964," 2–3.

63 *Bucknell Alumnus,* XL (January, 1956), 6–7.

64 *About Bucknell,* III (October, 1959), 4.

65 A copy of this statement is in the papers of the author of this book.

66 Bucknell University, *Catalogue, 1963–64,* 78.

67 Bucknell University, *Bulletin,* "Summer School, 1962," 4–5.

68 Bucknell University, *Catalogue, 1963–64,* 78, 225; *About Bucknell,* VI (January, 1963), 2.

69 Bucknell Institute for Foreign Students, *Tenth Annual Report* (Lewisburg, Pa., 1953), 10. In a foreword to this report, the director of the Institute, Dr. C. Willard Smith, wrote as follows: "During the ten years since 1944, when the Institute was established, 360 such students, representing fifty countries, have come to the Bucknell campus during the summer months. In September of each year they have left Bucknell to continue their work. They have been enrolled in ninety-seven different colleges, universities and special scientific institutes or laboratories in twenty-four of the United States."

70 *Report of the President for the Academic Year 1962–1963,* 25–26.

71 "Extension of Remarks of the Hon. Theodore Francis Green, of Rhode Island, in the Senate of the United States, Tuesday, March 12, 1957," reprinted from the *Congressional Record,* 85th Congress, 1st Session.

72 W. C. Bartol, "Dr. M. Shaw Loo, '64," *Bucknell Alumni Monthly,* XIV (December, 1929), 3, 5.

73 Bucknell University, *Special Convocation . . . Saturday, March the First, Nineteen Hundred Fifty-Eight: Souvenir Program of the Tenth Burma-Bucknell Week-End, February 28, March 1 & 2, 1958; About Bucknell,* II (April, 1958), 4; Forrest D. Brown, "Burma-Bucknell Week-End," *Bucknell Alumnus,* XLII (March, 1958), 3, 11.

74 Bucknell University, *The Sixteenth Burma-Bucknell Weekend, March 13, 14, 15, 1964* (Lewisburg, Pa.), 1–3.

75 *Bucknell Alumnus,* XLIX (September, 1963), 14; *Report of the President for the Academic Year 1962–1963,* 26–27; "The Development of an Undergraduate Engineering Program at Córdoba, Argentina," an address by Herbert F. Eckberg at the annual meeting of the American Society for Engineering Education, University of Maine, June 22–26, 1964.

76 *Report of the President for the Academic Year 1959–1960,* 25–29.

77 *Ibid., 1962–1963,* 25.

Index